Cost Benefit Analysis and the Environment

FURTHER DEVELOPMENTS AND POLICY USE

Giles Atkinson, Nils Axel Braathen, Ben Groom
and Susana Mourato

OECD

University of Edinburgh

This work is published under the responsibility of the Secretary-General of the OECD. The opinions expressed and arguments employed herein do not necessarily reflect the official views of OECD member countries.

This document, as well as any data and any map included herein, are without prejudice to the status of or sovereignty over any territory, to the delimitation of international frontiers and boundaries and to the name of any territory, city or area.

Please cite this publication as:
OECD (2018), *Cost-Benefit Analysis and the Environment: Further Developments and Policy Use*, OECD Publishing, Paris.
http://dx.doi.org/10.1787/9789264085169-en

ISBN 978-92-64-08515-2 (print)
ISBN 978-92-64-08516-9 (PDF)
ISBN 978-92-64-29880-4 (HTML)
ISBN 978-92-64-06238-2 (epub)

The statistical data for Israel are supplied by and under the responsibility of the relevant Israeli authorities. The use of such data by the OECD is without prejudice to the status of the Golan Heights, East Jerusalem and Israeli settlements in the West Bank under the terms of international law.

Footnote by Turkey:

The information in this document with reference to "Cyprus" relates to the southern part of the Island. There is no single authority representing both Turkish and Greek Cypriot people on the Island. Turkey recognises the Turkish Republic of Northern Cyprus (TRNC). Until a lasting and equitable solution is found within the context of United Nations, Turkey shall preserve its position concerning the "Cyprus issue".

Footnote by all the European Union Member States of the OECD and the European Union:

The Republic of Cyprus is recognised by all members of the United Nations with the exception of Turkey. The information in this document relates to the area under the effective control of the Government of the Republic of Cyprus.

Photo credits: Cover © Martin Haake.

Corrigenda to OECD publications may be found on line at: *www.oecd.org/about/publishing/corrigenda.htm*.

© OECD 2018

Preface

Cost-benefit analysis has long been a core tool of public policy. The systematic process of calculating the benefits and costs of policy options and projects is now widely regarded as an essential step in the policy process. It helps decision makers to have a clear picture of how society would fare under a range of policy options for achieving particular goals. This is particularly the case for the development of environmental policy, where cost-benefit analysis is central to the design and implementation of policies in many countries.

The OECD has a long tradition of promoting the use of cost-benefit analysis in environmental policy development. This work has covered a wide range of topics, from the evaluation of environmental damages in monetary terms to the role of discounting to case studies of the application of cost-benefit analysis. The 2006 OECD publication on *Cost-Benefit Analysis and the Environment: Recent Developments* has been a reference publication for more than a decade.

This report, *Cost-Benefit Analysis and the Environment: Further Developments and Policy Use*, provides a timely update on recent developments in the theory and practice of cost-benefit analysis. Many important theoretical developments have taken place over the last decade, not least in relation to the economics of climate change and to the treatment of uncertainty and discounting in policy or project assessments. For example, increasing attention has been devoted to assessing the social costs of carbon (SCC). Since carbon emissions have global impacts that vary across time and space and occur in many different sectors, the calculation of the SCC is complex, requiring inputs from many different disciplines. This book explains the underpinnings of the SCC and reviews the different approaches and uncertainties in its estimation, addressing key questions that will influence the policy relevance of such calculations: What path will emissions take? How will emissions affect temperatures? How will temperature changes cause damages?

The report also updates the technical and practical developments in the key issue of discounting. While the theory of social discounting shows clearly how the social discount rate should be defined, in practice numerous questions arise, especially when considering actions with implications for generations in the far distant future: intergenerational projects and policies. In such contexts, there is strengthening theoretical and empirical support for the use of discount rates that decline with time. But this has important implications for the policy debate around major environmental issues such as climate change, air pollution and water management.

The book presents new information on the current use – or lack of use – of cost-benefit analysis in different *ex ante* and *ex post* contexts. There are large variations in the extent to which cost-benefit analysis is being used in environmental policy development across countries. There are also wide differences in the extent to which various environmental impacts are being taken into account in these analyses, across economic sectors and across analytical contexts. For example, in general, energy sector investments and policy proposals are relatively well covered in cost-benefit analyses. But there is often far narrower coverage of non-climate environmental impacts in those assessments than in assessments of investment projects in, for example, the transport sector.

The political economy dimensions of the use of cost-benefit analysis are also explored in the book. While cost-benefit analysis provides extremely valuable information for decision-makers, it necessarily forms just one part of the complex set of considerations that must be taken into account when dealing with challenging environmental issues. How cost-benefit analysis is used in practice, and the constraints and challenges in this use, is critical to ensuring that decision makers have a full understanding of the "use and abuse" of cost-benefit analysis. Clearly, providing decision makers with the flexibility needed in order to "act politically" or meet other policy objectives is essential. But this will shape the nature of the use of cost-benefit analysis in particular ways. Throughout this, the role of CBA remains one of explaining how a decision should look if an economic approach is adopted.

This book is the result of a strong collaboration between leading academics and the OECD countries, working under the auspices of the OECD's Environment Policy Committee. We stand ready to support countries in the implementation of the practices and tools detailed in this study. I am confident that this work will significantly enrich the understanding of cost-benefit analysis and strengthen its use in both OECD and non-OECD countries in tackling our many shared environmental challenges.

Anthony Cox
Acting Director, OECD Environment Directorate

Acknowledgements

This book is an update of the 2006 book on *Cost-Benefit Analysis and the Environment: Recent Developments* (Pearce et al., 2006). It has been written by Giles Atkinson, Ben Groom and Susana Mourato of London School of Economics (LSE) and Nils Axel Braathen of the OECD Secretariat. It has benefitted from numerous comments and suggestions provided by Delegates to the Working Party on Integrating Environmental and Economic Policies under OECD's Environment Policy Committee.

The original volume in 2006 arose as the product of a discussion between David Pearce and the OECD Secretariat. OECD has a distinguished history of pioneering economic analysis of environmental issues, including cost-benefit analysis and environmental valuation. However, prior to Pearce et al. (2006) there was no publication that brought together some of the recent developments in cost-benefit analysis, and, given its record, OECD seemed the right place to locate that original volume. We hope then that this new volume will prove to be as useful to academics and, just as importantly, practitioners, since cost-benefit analysis continues to be ever more widely practised and used.

The current volume has been substantially revised and rewritten to reflect further developments in cost-benefit analysis and the environment. This includes the addition of a number of new chapters. We are immensely grateful to OECD for the opportunity to revisit the 2006 volume as well as remaining deeply appreciative to Jean-Philippe Barde, formerly of the OECD Environment Directorate, for his crucial role in making that original volume happen. We would like to thank Nathalie Girouard and Shardul Agrawala of the OECD Secretariat for their guidance in the production of this work. We would also like to thank Joe Swierzbinski for his invaluable help with what remains Chapter 10 as well Mark Freeman and Daniel Fujiwara for comments on selected chapters. Thanks are also due to a number of those studying "Economic appraisal and valuation" at LSE for their help in proof-reading, and to Elvira Berrueta-Imaz, Janine Treves, Natasha Cline-Thomas, and Catherine Roch of the OECD Secretariat for their help in preparing the book manuscript. Any remaining errors are the responsibility of the authors, needless to say.

Finally, we remain especially indebted to the late David Pearce. David passed away suddenly prior to the publication of the original volume in 2005. He continues to be missed and remembered fondly by the current authors as an inspirational leader, mentor and towering figure in the field of environmental economics. We are then acutely aware of the debt that we owe to David and the heavy responsibility that we bear in preparing this current volume. We hope very much that David would have approved of our efforts and we humbly dedicate this volume to his memory.

Giles Atkinson, Nils Axel Braathen, Ben Groom and Susana Mourato

Table of contents

Part III

Selected issues in environmental cost-benefit analysis

Part IV

Cost-benefit analysis in practice

Tables

Figures

Follow OECD Publications on:

 http://twitter.com/OECD_Pubs

 http://www.facebook.com/OECDPublications

http://www.linkedin.com/groups/OECD-Publications-4645871

 http://www.youtube.com/oecdilibrary

 http://www.oecd.org/oecddirect/

Abbreviations and acronyms

AF	Attributable factor
ANA	Attribute non-attendance
BAU	Business-as-usual
BCR	Benefit-cost ratio
BT	Benefits transfer
BWS	Best-worst scaling
CAA	Clean Air Act (United States)
CAPM	Capital asset pricing model
CBA	Cost-benefit analysis
CCAPM	Consumption-based capital asset pricing model
CEA	Cost-effectiveness analysis
CEA	Council of economic advisors
CER	Cost-effectiveness ratio
CGE	Computable general equilibrium
CO	Carbon monoxide
CO$_2$	Carbon dioxide
COP	Conference of the Parties
CRA	Comparative risk assessment
CRRA	Constant relative risk aversion
CS	Compensating surplus
CT	Cheap talk
CV	Contingent valuation
CV	Compensating variation
CVM	Contingent valuation methods
DCE	Discrete choice experiments
DDR	Declining discount rates
DEFRA	Department for Environment, Food and Rural Affairs (United Kingdom)
DF	Discount factor
DICE	Dynamic Integrated Climate and Economy model
DiD	Difference-in-difference
DU	Discounted utilitarian social welfare function
EC	European Commission
ECS	Equilibrium climate sensitivity
ED	Expected value of development benefits
EIA	Environmental impact assessment
ELS	Entry Level Stewardship (United Kingdom)
ENPV	Expected net present value
EO	Executive Order

EP	Expected value (i.e. probability weighted) of preservation benefits
ES	Equivalent surplus
ES	Ecosystem services
ESM	Experience sampling method
ETS	Emission trading scheme
EUF	Expected utility framework
EUR	Euro
EV	Equivalent variation
EVRI	Environmental Valuation Reference Inventory
EW	Expected value obtained by waiting
FUND	Framework for Uncertainty, Negotiation and Distribution
GBD	Global burden of disease
GBP	Pound sterling
GDP	Gross domestic product
GHG	Greenhouse gas
GIS	Geographical information systems
GNI	Gross national income
HHA	Health-health analysis
HMT	Her Majesty's Treasury
HPM	Hedonic price method
IA	Impact assessment
IAM	Integrated assessment models
IEG	Independent Evaluation Group (World Bank)
IIA	Independence from irrelevant alternatives
i.i.d.	Independent and identically distributed random variables
IPBES	Intergovernmental Science-Policy Platform on Biodiversity and Ecosystems
IPCC	Intergovernmental Panel on Climate Change
IRR	Internal rate of return
IWG	Interagency Working Group
KNPB	KwaZulu-Natal Parks Board
kWh	Kilowatt-hour
LCA	Life-cycle analysis
LCC	London congestion charge
LHS	Left-hand side
MAUT	Multi-attribute utility theory
MCA	Multi-criteria assessment
MPA	Marine protected areas
NAS	National Academy of Sciences (United States)
NB	Net benefit
NCC	Natural Capital Committee (United Kingdom)
NGO	Non-governmental organisation
NOAA	National Oceanic and Atmospheric Administration (United States)
NO_2	Nitrogen dioxide
NO_X	Nitrogen oxides
NPV	Net present value
NZD	New Zealand dollars
OECD	Organisation for Economic Co-operation and Development

ONS	Office for National Statistics, United Kingdom
OV	Option value
PAC	Public Accounts Committee (United Kingdom)
PAGE	Policy Analysis of Greenhouse gas Emissions
PES	Payments for environmental services
PM	Particulate matter
PM$_{2.5}$	Particulate matter with a diameter below 2.5 microns
PM$_{10}$	Particulate matter with a diameter below 10 microns
PV	Present value
QOV	Quasi-option value
RA	Risk assessment
RBA	Risk-benefit analysis
RHS	Right-hand side
RP	Revealed preference
RP	Risk premium
RPC	Regulatory Policy Committee (United Kingdom)
RPM	Revealed preference methods
RPM	Risk premium multiplier
RR	Relative risk
RRA	Risk-risk analysis
RSB	Regulatory Scrutiny Board (European Union)
RUM	Random utility model
SA	Scenario analysis
SC-CO$_2$	Social cost of carbon dioxide
SCC	Social cost of carbon
SDG	Sustainable development goals
SDR	Social discount rate
SEA	Strategic environmental assessment
SOC	Social opportunity cost of capital
SO$_x$	Sulphur oxides
SP	Stated preference
SPC	Shadow price of capital
SRTP	Social rate of time preference
SWB	Subjective well-being
SWF	Social welfare function
SWF	Sovereign wealth funds
TCM	Travel cost method
TCS	Transitory climate sensitivity
TEEB	The Economics of Ecosystems and Biodiversity
TEV	Total economic value
TSP	Total suspended particulates
TTWA	Travel to work area
TWTP	Total willingness-to-pay
TZS	Tanzanian Shillings
UK-NEA	UK National Ecosystem Assessment
UN	United Nations
UNEP	United Nations Environment Program

USD	Unites States dollars
US EPA	Unites States Environment Protection Agency
VSL	Value-of-a-statistical-life
VSLY (or VOLY)	Value-of-a-statistical-life-year
VT	Value transfer
WTA	Willingness-to-accept
WTP	Willingness-to-pay

Executive summary

Imagine a choice between energy project options which involve investing in a coal-fired power plant or a renewable energy investment, such as in wind turbines. In choosing between these options (or deciding not to invest in either), one analytical tool that decision-makers and practitioners might reach for is cost-benefit analysis (CBA). This might start by understanding what these options provide in terms of benefits (defined as increases in human well-being) and costs (defined as reductions in human well-being). Although this may sound simple enough, some way must be found to aggregate environmental and social benefits and costs across different people (within a given geographical boundary) and finding some means of monetising these, accounting for different points in time. For one of these projects to qualify on cost-benefit grounds, its social benefits must exceed its social costs.

Environmental CBA is the application of CBA to projects or policies that have the deliberate aim of environmental improvement or actions that affect, in some way, the natural environment as an indirect consequence. In the past decade, there has been considerable expansion in the uses of CBA and in its policy and investment applications, yet uptake is not as widespread as it might be despite its ongoing usefulness for environmental policy and investment decision-making.

Key developments

- The contribution of climate economics: The attention devoted to estimates of the social cost of carbon emissions, despite being fraught with difficulties and uncertainties (e.g. in relation to climate sensitivity, future economic growth and emissions paths, and the damages that can be expected as a consequence) is underpinning progress in the fight against climate change. Work in this area has also increased the focus on how to value costs and benefits that occur far into the future, and shown that conventional procedures for establishing the social discount rate become problematic in an intergenerational context.

- The extension of valuation techniques to biodiversity and associated ecosystems: while much of this activity has been concerned with how to value ecosystem services, developments in techniques of non-market valuation remain front and centre. This is a good example of the prominence that non-market valuation continues to enjoy. There is considerable evidence of the use of environmental valuation in global and national ecosystem assessments.

- The extension of subjective well-being approaches and advances in established valuation techniques: subjective well-being valuation has opened up a new frontier for helping to monetise values for environmental impacts of policies and investment projects. Progress has also continued, for example, in approaches based on revealed behaviour in terms of extracting many (non-market) environmental goods and services implicitly traded in

19

markets by better establishing causal inference between the transaction for a market good (e.g. buying a house or accepting a job) and the implicit price of an (non-market) environmental good (e.g. air quality in a neighbourhood or the workplace). The influence of behavioural economics has also been useful in environmental economics, recasting what is known about valuation biases and response anomalies in approaches based on stated behaviour, as has been the rise of online surveys, enabling more extensive applications and further testing of biases and their resolution.

- The continued refinement of health valuation: Growing empirical record has enabled further progress in the realm of health valuation, for example via the use of meta-studies. This has established "reference values" for important categories of health impacts such as mortality risk that can be readily used in practical assessment. Increasing evidence of the global burden of disease, and especially the role of pollution as a determinant of this burden, has added a further urgency to this work.

Key findings

- A growing degree of technical sophistication on various elements of environmental CBA, such as stated preference valuation techniques, treatment of uncertainty and the use of discounting, has increased the statistical rigour and allowed for more robust and refined monetary valuation.

- Survey results point to substantial use of CBA across OECD countries in actual assessments of public policies and investment projects, but considerable further progress remains still to be made.

- Survey results also show that appraisal processes often downplay the role of CBA, and actual decisions are often made in a manner that seems to be inconsistent with CBA.

The policy process is characterised by a complicated set of institutions and it is important to place questions about actual use of CBA in that context. Understanding the political economy of CBA is crucial to understanding how it is actually used and what actions might be plausible to affect this in a positive way.

Interestingly, the sorts of institutional developments that might be proposed as part of this political economy approach are actually happening in the broader reform of regulatory frameworks across many national jurisdictions and supranational groupings of countries. The institutional architecture surrounding how environmental CBA is done (and when it is done) has involved the setting up of public (and often independent) bodies that could facilitate a more prominent role for CBA, for example by adding a further tier of scrutiny by in effect scrutinising or "peer-reviewing" official appraisals. The Regulatory Scrutiny Board of the European Commission is a prominent example of this.

Generally speaking, the role of environmental CBA is to act as the instrument to consider the case for (social) efficiency for decisions within the broader policy process. It is the primary objective of this book to assess recent advances in environmental CBA theory and to illustrate the practical use of CBA in policy formulation and in appraisal of investment projects.

Chapter 1

Overview of main issues

This chapter provides a summary of the key themes of the volume. These are the changing character of the developments at the knowledge frontier, the uptake of environmental CBA in actual policy formulation process and the location of possible limits to CBA. An explanation of the structure of the volume is also provided.

Imagine a choice between energy project options which involve investing in a coal-fired power plant or a renewable energy investment, such as in wind turbines. In choosing between these options (or deciding not to invest in either), one analytical tool that decision-makers and practitioners might reach for is cost-benefit analysis (CBA).

This might start by understanding what these options provide in terms of benefits (defined as increases in human well-being or "utility" to use the economic jargon) and costs (defined as reductions in human well-being). For one of these projects to qualify on cost-benefit grounds, its social benefits must exceed its social costs. The geographical boundary for considering the society which is incurring these costs and enjoying these benefits is usually the nation, but this can readily be extended to wider limits. But before getting to this point some way must be found to aggregate benefits and costs across different people (within the geographical boundary) who are affected by the project. This could involve measuring the physical quantities of inputs to the project and its outputs. Crucially, it will also require finding some means to place a monetary value on these quantities, reflecting what winners and losers from this project would be willing to give up or forego in order to obtain (or avoid) these changes. These monetised costs and benefits also occur at different points in time and aggregating these changes over time involves discounting with these discounted future benefits and costs being known as present values. It is the summation of these present values which is the basis of the cost-benefit test and resulting recommendation for choosing between these competing options.

A practitioner undertaking this economic appraisal will benefit from the long-standing character of this policy formulation and investment project selection tool. This is illustrated in the great many authoritative texts on the theory and practice of cost-benefit analysis as well as official guidelines produced by national and supranational jurisdictions or international organisations. For sure these sources indicate that this appraisal will require further considerations that have similarly long standing. This could include concerns about the way in which costs and benefits are distributed across people (within some geographical boundary) or how to address the uncertainty that will characterise the estimated time profile of these net benefit flows.

Importantly, however, a proper consideration of the economic case for each project option would need to draw on developments in environmental CBA. Environmental CBA is defined here as the application of CBA to projects or policies that have the deliberate aim of environmental improvement or actions that affect, in some way, the natural environment as an indirect consequence. In terms of the example above this is relevant for a number of reasons. The implications of each option for global climate change mitigation will be very different and so practitioners may need to find an estimate of the social cost of carbon. Similarly, the contribution of each option to local air quality will differ considerably and assessing this will necessitate tracing the link between emissions (of pollutants such as particulate matter) at, for example, the coal-based power plant and (changes in) ambient air pollution where people live, and ultimately valuing these (relative) environmental risks to human health. In addition, the impacts of the two options mentioned above on biodiversity could be very different.

This is, of course, just one example. The definition of environmental CBA above indicates that this is relevant to a great many policies and projects (perhaps all such actions, to some degree) as well as a great variety of environmental considerations. As another illustration, a very different project might be one that sought to provide coastal protection against rising sea levels.[1] This might involve options involving traditional built (or produced) defences, such as wave breaks or seawalls or nature-based defences which could involve enhancing and restoring natural ecosystems. An important consideration is that the appraisals should start with interdisciplinary dialogue with natural scientists. For example, the ways in which different configurations of (restored) natural habitats will affect wave attenuation and lead to different levels of the flood protection ecosystem service being provided. Again, valuing this service and the changes in benefits to which it contributes involve considering a variety of impacts on human well-being which have no obvious market price. Moreover, this nature-based flood protection will provide impacts into the relatively distant future, possibly "in perpetuity" if suitably managed. The question of how to value far-off future benefits compared with the same benefits received closer to now is important especially as intergenerational concerns loom large here.

The point here is the need to keep track of developments in environmental CBA as a possibly ubiquitous feature of contemporary economic appraisal. It is the objective of this volume to explore such recent developments (and their context) and evaluate their implications for the practice of CBA. Much of the progress made up to 2006 was the subject of the OECD book *Cost-benefit Analysis and the Environment: Recent Developments* by David Pearce et al. (2006). The starting point for that volume was that there had been a number of generally uncorrelated developments in the theory and practice of CBA that, taken together, altered the way in which many economists would argue CBA should be carried out. Notably, quite a few of those developments came from concerns associated with the use of CBA in the context of policies and projects with significant environmental impacts.

This overarching observation is the starting point for the current volume. However, as might be expected, the character of the developments over the past decade or so – upon which the observation is based – represents both continuity and distinctive difference. The remainder of this introduction provides an overview of some of the main themes explored in detail in subsequent chapters.

One of these themes is the nature of developments at the "knowledge frontier". Continuity here is evident given the prominence that environmental valuation (or non-market valuation) still enjoys. This prominence should not be surprising. Given that a major challenge of environmental CBA is how to evaluate (changes in) unpriced inputs and outputs then it is inevitable that developments in techniques of non-market valuation remain at the front and centre. Nevertheless, such developments have changed in a number of ways. As a result of its long standing (relatively speaking), this sub-field shows welcome maturity through now routine use across a variety of environmental contexts.

One consequence of this maturity, however, is arguably fewer significant contributions which break genuinely new ground. This is a matter of degree, of course. Valuation using subjective well-being approaches (Chapter 7) represents a substantial new development. This is important as it possibly opens up a new frontier within this field. More generally there has been an understandable continuation of ways to demonstrate that these valuation techniques can yield robust monetary values for environmental impacts of policies and investment projects.

In the case, for example, of revealed preference (RP) methods (Chapter 3), this has resulted in growing statistical sophistication particularly in better establishing causal inference between the transaction for a market good (e.g. buying a house or accepting a job) and the implicit price of an (non-market) environmental good (e.g. air quality in a neighbourhood or the workplace). These techniques make use of the fact that many (non-market) environmental goods and services are implicitly traded in markets, which allows then for RP methods to uncover these values in a variety of ways, depending on the good in question and the market in which it is implicitly traded. For example, demand for nature recreation is estimated by looking at the travel costs associated with this activity, with recent developments linking this to geographical information systems to improve accuracy, such as in mapping natural attributes at recreational sites. Another prominent application is hedonic techniques which value environmental goods and services as attributes or characteristics of related purchases, notably residential property or decisions such as whether to take a job for a given wage.

For stated preference methods (Chapters 4 and 5), the huge increase in popularity of behavioural economics and, in turn, its influence in environmental economics has been useful, recasting what is known about valuation biases and response anomalies in the light of these alternative theories of behaviour. Also the rise of on-line surveys, have been important to enabling more extensive applications and further testing of biases and their resolution.

Chapter 4 examines the contingent valuation (CV) method where respondents are asked directly for their willingness-to-pay or (willingness-to-accept) for a hypothetical change in the level of provision of a non-market good. There is now a wealth of experience that can be gleaned from the literature on CV that can guide current thinking about good survey design and robust valuation. The central debate remains validity and reliability, e.g. in discussions about specific problems and biases. Increasingly this is being understood as highly related to research on behavioural economics.

Many types of environmental impacts are multidimensional in character. What this means is that an environmental resource that is affected by a proposed project or policy often will give rise to changes in component attributes, each of which command distinct valuations. One tool that can elicit respondents' distinct valuations of these multiple dimensions – (discrete) choice experiments (DCEs) – is discussed in Chapter 5. Curiously perhaps, it is CV which has drawn most of the heat of the controversy about stated preference methods. But DCEs are likely to share many of the advantages and disadvantages and so the discussion in Chapter 4 of validity and reliability issues is relevant here too. Again, the links to behavioural research are highly relevant, such as on heuristics and filtering rules guiding choice that are "good enough" rather than utility-maximising.

What is also notable is the extension of valuation into different and new policy domains and the more routine application of these methods as part of policy assessments. The exemplar here is the valuation of ecosystem services (Chapter 13) which has emerged fully as an important sub-field, partly as a result of a number of global and national ecosystem assessments. While the evidence-base is broad and – at least for some ecosystem services – deep, reflections on this progress indicate a need for greater understanding of ecological production, especially as it relates to spatial variability and complexities in the way that services are produced. This is a truly interdisciplinary activity, given the need for natural science to inform the stages of this analytical process. This situation is fluid and important areas of research remain; particularly in valuing non-use and cultural services from ecosystems, which relatively speaking has been the subject of less attention to date.

Health valuation is a more long-standing application. Even so, increasing evidence of the global burden of disease, and especially the role of environmental pollution as a determinant of this burden, has added a further urgency to this work. Chapter 15 reviews this context and efforts to quantify the physical and economic burden of air pollution in particular. Considerable strides have been made in recent years in terms of clarifying both the meaning and size of the value of statistical life (VSL). One of the main issues has been how to "transfer" VSLs from one country to another, especially where life expectancy of those people who are the object of policy and investment project proposals differs. In terms of practical guidelines, the empirical record has been important in translating findings in base or reference levels. Studies such as OECD (2012) have been important in distilling this empirical record into something highly usable, providing standard values "per unit" of some adverse health outcome, such as VSL in relation to mortalities, for a reference country or groups of countries, which can be adjusted to be applied to countries outside of this reference group.

More generally such developments enable greater use of environmental valuation in policy formulation and appraisal of investment projects. Distilling this empirical record into something more practical for policy use becomes crucial and recognition of this is evident in valuation databases (such as the Environmental Valuation Reference Inventory, EVRI) and "look-up tables" (lists of average values and ranges for various categories of environmental goods and services). These are likely to be important facilitators of uptake so long as lessons from transfer tests are built into applications (so-called "value transfer" – Chapter 6) and similarly distilled into good guidance on use and limitations. A competent application of transfer methods demands informed judgement and expertise and sometimes, according to more demanding commentators, as advanced technical skills as those required for original research. This is something of a paradox as the point of transfer exercises is to make routine valuation more straightforward and widely used.

The contribution of climate economics provides another illustration of this, given the attention devoted to estimates of the social cost of carbon (SCC) emissions (Chapter 14). While this is fraught with difficulties and uncertainties, e.g. in relation to climate sensitivity, future economic growth and emissions paths, and the damages that can be expected as a consequence, this does not obviate the need for practical estimates, since the price of carbon is very unlikely to be zero. However, it does provide a context for advising careful interpretation in policy use. The problem here is the technical complexity of the analytical issues underlying estimation of the SCC. This has led to an emerging desire for transparency and simpler illustrative approaches although it remains early days to decide on how best to provide this clarity in a robust and credible way.

Thinking about CBA in the context of climate economics has had more general import too, especially in terms of the social discount rate (Chapter 8). Intergenerational issues, such as climate change, have provided a formidable challenge to the conventional discounting approach. Not only do the assumptions underpinning conventional discounting become problematic but also the ethical underpinnings of discounting become extremely important.

As a result, there has been considerable interest in how the parameters of the discount rate for social CBA are determined as well as their ethical and practical content. Perhaps the most obvious manifestation of this interest has been the growing consensus around the idea of a declining social discount rate. This still leaves plenty of remaining debate about what the empirical schedule of these declining rates should be. What is clear, however, is that these developments have ramifications beyond the focus on climate economics.

One aspect of a number of these developments is the growing degree of technical sophistication brought to bear on various elements of environmental CBA. This rigour has advantages such as in the statistical rigour which is commonly now a feature of applications of environmental valuation – monetary valuation is more robust as a result. It also places claims, for example, about the social discount rate on a rigorous foundation of theory. A disadvantage is that it makes a lot of these developments the preserve of the economic specialist. At risk then is policy uptake if developments are perceived to make these matters less accessible to a more general audience.

This is not inevitable, although it may need some deliberate and additional effort to translate specialist work into more general terms, as well as to distil possibly complex analytical findings into more readily usable terms. Examples in this respect include statistical modelling in DCE which is increasingly accessible more broadly via a growth in training opportunities and free statistical software, "look-up" tables and valuation databases which summarise an otherwise bewildering large empirical record and practical schedules of declining discount rates.

Of course, it would be surprising along the way if there were not tensions between innovations at the "knowledge frontier" of environmental CBA, on the one hand, and on actual uptake and use of environmental CBA in real policy formulation on the other. Moreover, the reality is also that a number of frontier developments mostly (but not exclusively) emanating from climate economics and sustainability economics appear to circumscribe the use (and usefulness) of CBA. Put another way, one interpretation of this is the discovery of its possible limits to applying environmental CBA.

There is nothing new in this idea of limits, of course. However, the contemporary details are a change and are typically manifested in scientific concerns about thresholds which might characterise ecological systems, combined with the view that breaching such thresholds could be extremely costly indeed in terms of human well-being, or even the sustainability of human development (Chapter 12). This has substantial implications for CBA. For example, in climate economics, a small but significant prospect of catastrophic climate damage will dominate a cost-benefit assessment. If so, then the policy formulation is less about careful deliberation of (marginal) costs and benefits than it is about working out ways of reducing these "fat-tails" of catastrophic risk.

There is also considerable uncertainty (as opposed to known probability distributions) surrounding what is lost when natural capital is degraded or destroyed, and where critical thresholds are actually located. The presumption might be then that precaution is important, rather than assessing costs and benefits. Nor is ethics divorced from reflections about the role of formally weighing up costs and benefits, as these policy questions are fundamentally problems of intergenerational justice.

All this might add up then to a sense in which environmental CBA has a more limited place in terms of informing social decisions about policy formulation and investment projects. This, in turn, might involve imposing (sustainability) constraints on economic recommendations. Or it might involve conducting CBA on specific options only once the strategic policy decision to act has been made. It even might entail downplaying the role of CBA entirely. For example, in terms of the coastal protection case mentioned towards the outset of this chapter, perhaps the question about sustainability concerns shapes strategic decisions and as a result favours nature-based options. So CBA becomes an issue of choosing between natural flood protection options, rather than comparing these with built infrastructure (such as constructed wave-breaks).

While it is important to recognise these limitations on which such responses might be based, there is a risk of over-reaction too. It is entirely possible to push back the knowledge frontier and to extend the tool where previously it was judged to be problematic or difficult, as numerous past developments in environmental CBA have shown. It is also important to convey whether or not there are substantial (opportunity) costs of those constraints. The role of environmental CBA to act as the instrument to consider the case for (social) efficiency for decisions within the broader policy process remains crucial.

Progress here then is a mixture of pushing back existing frontiers and encountering novel frontiers which may prompt fresh questions about where and how CBA can be applied. It is also important to ask how far the journey has proceeded from developments in environmental CBA to use in the formulation of actual policy and investment projects. For example, proposals for integrating distributional concerns into CBA are long-standing (Chapter 11), although practical applications are less frequent. The suspicion might be that this is not only due to a supply problem (a manifestation of the singular emphasis of cost-benefit practitioners on efficiency), but it is also likely to be an issue about demand: i.e. policy makers have not required this information be provided in the terms of reference for the environmental CBA upon which they rely. It is interesting to ask why this is the case. The problem could lie in traditional responses being seen as controversial or arbitrary (such as distributional weighting of costs and benefits according to the vulnerability or income levels of particular groups of people affected by proposals). However, less ambitious, but nevertheless informative, alternatives exist such as cataloguing how costs and benefits are distributed across people but also how particular environmental goods and bads (such as high or low air quality, unwanted land uses, and so on) are distributed.

More generally, whether (environmental) CBA is used in actual policy formulation and actual investment projects is a question to which a more comprehensive response is needed. Yet this is a question that cost-benefit texts, as good as these are in providing rigorous guidance on how CBA *should* be done in theory and practice, by-and-large, often downplays.[2] There are exceptions and the survey of OECD member country practice in this volume is one example of this sort of systematising of the record on official use of environmental CBA (Chapter 16).

That survey echoes past findings that actual use of environmental CBA is perhaps best summed up by the metaphor of a "glass half-empty or half-full". There are large variations in the extent to which CBA is being carried out, and the extent to which various environmental impacts are being taken into account in these analyses, across economic sectors and across analytical contexts. For example, transport and energy sector investments as well as policy *proposals* are relatively well covered in CBAs, but there is far narrower coverage of non-climate environmental impacts in those assessments. While there is evidence of actual use (sometimes extensive), there are also signs that considerable further progress remains still to be made. Needless to say, the policy process is characterised by a complicated set of institutions and it is important to place questions about actual use in that context. Put another way, understanding the political economy of CBA is crucial to understanding how it is actually used and what actions might be plausible to affect this in a positive way.

Political economy then seeks to explain why the economics of the textbook is rarely embodied in actual decision-making and related to this, policy-formulation processes. But explaining the gap between actual and theoretical design is not to justify the gap. So while it is important to have a far better understanding of the pressures that affect actual decisions, the role of CBA remains one of explaining how a decision should look if an efficiency approach is adopted.

Interestingly, the sorts of institutional developments that might be proposed as part of this political economy standpoint are actually happening with the broader context here being reform to regulatory frameworks across many national jurisdictions and supranational groupings of countries. Notably this change in the institutional architecture surrounding how environmental CBA is done (and when it is done) has involved the setting up of public (and often independent) bodies that could facilitate a more prominent role for CBA, for example by adding a further tier of scrutiny by, in effect, "policing" or "peer-reviewing" official appraisals. The Regulatory Scrutiny Board of the European Commission is a prominent example of this.

The rest of this book is organised as follows.

Chapter 2 sets the scene in more detail by providing an overview of the basic framework for environmental CBA, as well as showing how subsequent chapters represent developments to, and reflections on the usefulness of, that framework.

Thereafter there is a series of Chapters which deal in more detail with developments to methods that practitioners of environmental CBA utilise.

This starts with Chapters 3 to 7 which deals with techniques of environmental valuation, including established approaches based on revealed and stated behaviour (as well as "value transfer" exercises using existing studies, which comprise the empirical record). Subjective well-being valuation approaches, based on experienced behaviour, represent a novel addition to this array of techniques.

The next four Chapters 8 to 11 present a number of "classical" elements of the core of CBA, including uncertainty, discounting and (intra-generational) distribution.

Chapters 12 to 15 look at a handful of highly significant policy areas where developments have had substantial implications for environmental CBA. This includes the notion of sustainability as it relates to how natural capital is affected by policies and projects. Also relevant to this is the valuation of ecosystems, which has been a highly visible area of applied research for more than a decade. Similarly, climate economics has been a fruitful source of new challenges, given the characteristics of the climate change problem. The last of these applications, health valuation, is the longest standing one but that leads to interesting questions about distilling the empirical record there into usable "reference value" for policy purposes.

That question about policy use is continued in the final three Chapters 16 to 18. This includes the results from a survey of OECD countries as to the use and influence of CBA across a range of environment-related policy sectors, such as transport and energy. Subsequent chapters on the political economy of CBA and alternative policy formulation tools offer some further context for understanding such findings.

Notes

1. See, for example, Nayaran et al. (2016) and Barbier (2012).

2. There are notable exceptions, perhaps most significantly including the work of Robert Hahn for the United States as well as David Pearce for United Kingdom and for Europe.

References

Barbier, E.B. (2012), "Progress and challenges in valuing coastal and marine ecosystem services", *Review of Environmental Economics and Policy*, Vol. 6/1, pp. 1-19, *https://doi.org/10.1093/reep/rer017*.

Nayaran, S. et al. (2016), "The effectiveness, costs and coastal protection benefits of natural and nature-based defences", *PLOS One*, Vol. 11/5, *http://dx.doi.org/10.1371/journal.pone.0154735*.

OECD (2012), *Mortality Risk Valuation in Environment, Health and Transport Policies*, OECD Publishing, Paris, *http://dx.doi.org/10.1787/9789264130807-en*.

Chapter 2

Environmental cost-benefit analysis: Foundations, stages and evolving issues

The rationale for and foundations of environmental CBA are well known but nevertheless provide a logical starting point. In summary, these are that: benefits are defined as increases in human well-being (or "utility") and costs are defined as reductions in that well-being; for a project or policy to qualify on cost-benefit grounds, its social benefits must exceed its social costs. The geographical boundary for considering these costs and benefits is usually the nation but this can readily be extended to wider limits. Aggregating benefits across different social groups or nations can involve summing willingness to pay or to accept (WTP, WTA) regardless of the circumstances of the beneficiaries or losers (or it can involve giving higher weights to disadvantaged or low-income groups). Aggregating over time involves discounting where discounted future benefits and costs are known as present values. Much of the rest of this volume can be understood as developments to this standard practice with the emphasis on environmental CBA.

2.1. Introduction: Why use CBA?

The primary aim in this volume is to describe recent developments in CBA, with an emphasis on those developments relevant to the environment as well as illustrate their applications. Those developments, of course, need to be placed within a context of what the foundations of CBA are (i.e. to establish more exactly what it is that these developments add). It is also instructive to rehearse why it is that economists tend to favour CBA (not unanimously, however).

The aim and structure of this chapter is, as a result, threefold with its structure in reverse order to the points made above. That is: why use CBA? (the remainder of this introduction); what is CBA? (Section 2.2); and, what emerges in this volume about developments in CBA pertaining to environmental applications (Section 2.3).

Starting with the question of "why use?", arguments for and against CBA have been well rehearsed elsewhere (for critiques see, for example, Sagoff, 1988 and 2004; Heinzerling and Ackerman, 2004. See also Pearce, 2001 for some of the sources of controversy). Often lost in those critical discussions are the reasons why economists broadly agree on favouring CBA.

The first reason for using CBA is that it provides a model of rationality. Independently of its use of money measures of gain and loss, of which this volume has plenty to say later, CBA forces the decision-maker to look at who the beneficiaries and losers are in both the spatial and temporal dimensions. It avoids what might be called "lexical" thinking, whereby decisions are made on the basis of the impacts on a single goal or single group of people. For example, policies might be decided on the basis of human health alone, rather than on the basis of health and ecosystem effects together. CBA's insistence on all gains and losses of "utility" or "well-being" being counted means that it forces the wider view on decision-makers.[1] In this respect, CBA belongs to a group of approaches to policy analysis which do the same thing. Related to this, while it is often ignored in practice, properly executed CBA should show the costs and benefits accruing to different social groups of beneficiaries and losers. But the point remains, these groups should refer to all, not just a single subset of people.

Second, CBA is clear in its requirement that any policy or project should be seen as one of a series of options. Hence, setting out the alternatives for achieving the chosen goal is a fundamental prerequisite of CBA. Again, this feature is shared by some other policy analysis procedures, but not all. A more distinctive element of CBA, however, is that it has the capacity to determine the *optimal scale* of the policy, following an appraisal of these options. This would be where net benefits are maximised. The ability to do this rests on expressing benefits and costs in the same units (which for convenience is typically money values). In the same vein, CBA offers a rule for deciding if anything at all should be chosen, unlike other approaches which can decide only between alternatives to do something.

Third, CBA is explicit that time needs to be accounted for in a rigorous way. This is done through the process of discounting. This rightly remains controversial, but it is impossible not to discount – or to (in one way or another) decide how impacts in the future, including the very distant future, should be regarded compared to present impacts. Note that the treatment of time in other decision-making guidance is far from clear. But failing to discount means using a discount rate of 0% which means that USD 1 of gain 100 years from now is treated as being of equal value to USD 1 of gain now. Zero is a real number. But it is true that what the "correct" real number is, continues to be debated and that debate is reflected amply in this volume.

Fourth, CBA is explicit that it is individuals' preferences that count. To this extent, CBA is "democratic", but some see this as a weakness rather than a strength since it implies that preferences should count, however badly informed the holders of those preferences might be. They also argue that there are two kinds of preference, those made out of an individual's self-interest and those made when the individual expresses a preference as a citizen. There are clearly pros and cons to the underlying value judgement in CBA, namely that preferences count.

Finally, CBA seeks explicit preferences rather than implicit ones. To this extent, CBA looks directly for what people want, although it does so in a variety of ways as environmental applications make clear. All decisions, however they are made, imply preferences and all decisions imply money values. If a decision to choose Policy X over Policy Y is made, and X costs USD 150 million and Y costs USD 100 million, then it follows that the expected benefits of X must exceed the benefits of Y by at least USD 50 million. The unavoidability of money values was pointed out some time ago by Thomas (1963). It may be that leaving decisions to reveal implicit values is better than seeking those values explicitly. But CBA is clear in favouring the latter.

2.2. Basic stages of a CBA

In this section, the basic stages of a CBA are reviewed. This might be viewed as a CBA of any investment project or policy, although where relevant, issues relating to environmental applications are briefly mentioned too. It is also important to bear in mind that CBA has a long-established (albeit much debated) theory from economics as the foundations of such practical steps. This theory is briefly reviewed in Box 1 below and in Annex 2.A1. Subsequent chapters, however, will explore theory a little further in relation to developments in environmental CBA.

2.2.1. Opening questions

While it may seem obvious, the first and fundamentally most important issue to be addressed in practical CBA is what question is being asked. Typically an analysis begins by considering the set of *options* that are available and so the first question is: *what are the options under consideration?* Hopefully there is some reasonably defined goal, although there are likely to be different ways of reaching any given target. Options can be sifted into feasible and non-feasible ones, and other issues, such as the political factors driving the policy, will also tend to limit the options. An option that is often ignored is *when* to commence the policy (or project). This option should be considered whatever the policy or project in question, but also this can be important in the presence of particular characteristics surrounding the policy decision.

The next question that is likely to arise is: *should action X be undertaken at all?* An action here might refer to *policies* or to *projects* (investments) and usually this question will be asked *ex ante*. That is, determining whether something that has not yet been done should be done. But it could also be asked *ex post*. That is, finding out whether something that has been done (or perhaps is in the process of being done) should have been done. The reason for asking the question *ex ante* is to find out whether what are often significant sums of money should be spent in the public interest. The rationale for asking the same question *ex post* is that, while it cannot reverse expenditure already made, it can (a) cast light on the accuracy of the *ex ante* answer, or (b) cast light on whatever decision rule was used to justify the policy or project. In both cases, the answer *ex post* is designed to assist the process of *learning* about what does and what does not contribute to overall social well-being.

As to whether the answer to this question is "yes" depends on whether the present value of expected (*ex ante*) benefits exceeds expected costs, and "no" if expected costs exceed benefits. Note that all this assumes that CBA is either *the* relevant decision-guiding criterion or is *one* of the relevant criteria. In what follows, it will be assumed that CBA is always relevant. In making this assumption, the relevance of other factors – political, ethical and so on – is also pertinent given that in reality, of course, these factors will often influence decisions. But CBA is there as a check on those decisions, so it is always sensible to carry out a CBA wherever practicable.

2.2.2. Who counts?

The issue of "who counts" in a CBA is known as the issue of "standing". Benefits and costs are summed across individuals in accordance with the aggregation rule which defines "society" as the sum of all individuals. There are no hard and fast rules for defining the boundaries of the sum of individuals. Typically, CBA studies work with national boundaries so that "society" is equated with the sum of all individuals in (i.e. residents of) a nation state. But there will be cases where the boundaries need to be set more widely.

Examples that illustrate this are especially relevant to environmental applications of CBA. Benefits and costs to non-nationals should be included if a) the proposal relates to an international context in which there are legal obligations, such as a formal treaty of some kind (acid rain, climate change and so on), or b) there is some accepted ethical reason for counting benefits and costs to non-nationals. Generally speaking, while there are no hard and fast rules, if the well-being of people in country B matters as much to country A as the well-being of A's own residents, then these should be considered in the CBA regardless of to whom they accrue.

In such cases, a CBA of some proposed action might appear in a two-part form. The first part would show the net benefits *to that country* alone of that action. The second part would show, for example, the same costs but the benefits would be shown as those accruing both to the country in question and all other countries that benefit from the action being evaluated.

2.2.3. Valuing costs and benefits

The basic decision-rule for accepting (or recommending) a project or policy is that its benefits outweigh its costs. This deceptively simple rule presupposes a number of critical steps: not least having a numerical basis for comparing benefits and costs. This is a distinctive feature of CBA (and related economic tools) and involves assigning money values to impacts of a project or policy. In what follows, the main details of this procedure are sketched out. Annex 2.A2 makes this more precise in spelling out the details of these valuation concepts.

A benefit or gain in an individual's well-being (utility or welfare) can be measured by the maximum amount of goods or services – or money income (or wealth) – that he or she would be willing to give up or forego in order to obtain the change. Specifically, this could be written as WTP^G as the *willingness-to-pay* of "gainers" from some proposal (G refers to gainers).

Alternatively, if the change reduces well-being, it could be measured by WTP^L. This means that costs are measured by the willingness to pay to avoid the cost (L refers to losers). This is not the only way of measuring these costs. If the "losers" from the project or policy have legitimate property rights to what they lose, then WTP should be replaced by willingness-to-accept (i.e. WTA^L).

The difference, then, is that losses are measured by WTA and not by WTP. It is observed later that WTA can differ significantly from WTP. Until a few decades ago, the assumption (based on what it is expected in theory) would have been that the difference between these two measures of change in well-being would be very small and so of no practical policy relevance. But empirical estimation of these magnitudes has tended to show that they do vary, sometimes significantly, and with WTA > WTP. If so, the choice of WTA or WTP could matter substantially for CBA (see Chapter 4).

The more familiar form of WTP^G and WTP^L (or WTA) simply speaks of benefits and costs. Clearly, benefits refer to the value of the categories of goods and service that a proposal produces. And these policy (or project) costs, in turn, will consist of a number of components. This might include "compliance costs" – falling on the business sector and on households – and "regulatory costs", where relevant, accruing to government in implementing the policy. These are opportunity costs of committing resources to some current action rather than an alternative. This action may impose damage costs on losers too: for example, this could be the case if there was a negative impact on the provision of some environmental good or service.

Inflation: The values of benefits and costs are (or need to be) in real money terms. What this means is that any effects of inflation (a rise in the general level of prices) are netted out and so values are comparable from year to year. This means that a base year issue arises with the usual procedure being to value all costs and benefits at the prices ruling in the year of the appraisal. But it is perfectly possible to change the year prices to confirm with some other rule, e.g. in order to compare the results of one study with another study.

Relative price changes: A relative price change is different again. What this says is that some benefits and costs attract a higher valuation over time *relative to the general level of prices*. This might be because the benefit or cost in question is simply valued more at higher incomes. To use the terminology, it has a positive income elasticity of willingness-to-pay, such that when incomes (e.g. per capita) increase WTP also increases, with the magnitude of that latter change depending on the boost to income and estimated size of the elasticity. Annex 2.A1 shows in more detail how this is accounted for. This is not the only reason for rising (or falling) relative valuation in a CBA. For example, if a good is becoming scarcer, then its marginal value (relative to other goods) might be relatively higher as its availability dwindles. Typically, for this to happen other characteristics of the good will be important. This could include limitations for substituting it for other goods. However, these characteristics might be particularly important to consider in environmental applications.

2.2.4. Discounting costs and benefits

Costs and benefits will accrue over time and the general rule will be that future costs and benefits are weighted so that a unit of benefit or cost in the future has a lower weight than the same unit of benefit or cost now. This temporal weight is known as the *discount factor* and this is written:

$$DF_t = \frac{1}{(1+r)^t} \qquad\qquad [2.1]$$

where DF_t means the discount factor, or weight in period t, and s is the *discount rate*. As long as projects and policies are being evaluated from society's point of view, s is a *social discount rate*. The rationales for discounting are given in Chapter 8.

In terms of discounting the flow of benefits and costs, this can be written as:

$$\sum_{i,t} (B_{i,t} - C_{i,t}) \cdot (1+r)^{-t} \qquad\qquad [2.2]$$

The issue arises of how far into the future these impacts should be estimated. Yet again, there are no hard and fast rules. In its formative years, when CBA was confined to assessing the worth of investment projects, the rule was that the time horizon – the point beyond which costs and benefits are not estimated – was set by the physical or economic life of the investment. For infrastructure such as roads, ports, water supply and treatment, etc., this was usually set at a minimum of 30 years and a maximum of 50 years. Such rules applied even to longer-lived assets, e.g. housing developments which might last over 100 years. The transition to the CBA of policies has made this rule less compelling because it is unclear how long the effects of policies last. This becomes even more crucial an issue as CBA intrudes upon policy questions which have explicitly long-term goals

2.2.5. Risk and uncertainty

Benefits and costs will not be known with certainty. While conventions vary, it seems fair to distinguish "risk" from "uncertainty" in clarifying what this means and its implications for CBA. A risk context is one where benefits or costs (or both) are not known with certainty, but a probability distribution is known. Sometimes these probability distributions can be very crude. On some occasions they can be sophisticated. A context of uncertainty is different. There is no known probability distribution. End points might be known, i.e. it is known or expected that the value cannot be less than a number, and that it cannot be more than another number. But, in other cases, there may be pure uncertainty in the sense that "anything may happen".

The fact that uncertainty characterises CBA will be nothing new to cost-benefit practitioners. Indeed, various procedures for dealing with risk and uncertainty are long-standing. These vary in terms of justification in theory and analytical practicalities. For risk, this includes expected value or expected utility approaches with corresponding assumptions (respectively) about whether the decision-maker are risk-neutral or risk-adverse.[2,3] If the context is one of *uncertainty*, i.e. the distribution of benefits (costs) is not known, then, at the very least, CBA requires that a *sensitivity analysis* is performed. Sensitivity analysis requires that the CBA is computed using different values of the parameters about which there is uncertainty. Such procedures require some assumption about likely minima and maxima, but do not necessarily make assumptions about the distribution of values between these limits. For example, if a discount rate of 4% is chosen as the central case, then, say, 2 and 6% could also be chosen for a sensitivity analysis. One possible outcome is that the sign of the net benefits will be unaffected by these alternatives, in which case the analysis is said to be "robust" with respect to these assumptions. In other cases, changing assumptions may alter the CBA result. If so, then some judgement has to be made about the reasonableness of the chosen values.

2.2.6. Decision rules

In [2.2] benefits and costs are discounted so that when summed over time the resulting magnitude is known as a *present value* (PV). A present value is simply the sum of all the *discounted* future values. [2.2] might therefore be written very conveniently as:

$$PV(B) - PV(C) > 0 \qquad\qquad\qquad [2.3]$$

The correct criterion for reducing benefits and costs to a unique value is the present value criterion. The correct rule is to adopt any project with positive NPVs and to rank projects by their NPVs. When budget constraints exist, however, the criteria become more complex. Single-period constraints – such as capital shortages – can be dealt with by a benefit-cost ratio (BCR) ranking procedure. That is, rank projects according to their BCR and recommend projects in that queue until the capital constraint binds. In other respects, the benefit-cost ratio has less generally to commend it as a decision rule for choosing projects.

There is broad agreement among economists that the internal rate of return (IRR) should not be used to rank and select mutually exclusive projects. Where a project is the only alternative proposal to the status quo, the issue is whether knowing the IRR provides worthwhile additional information. Views differ in this respect. Some argue that there is little merit in calculating a statistic that is either misleading or subservient to the NPV. Others see a role for the IRR in providing a clear signal as regards the sensitivity of a project's net benefits to the discount rate. Yet, whichever perspective is taken, this does not alter the broad conclusion about the general primacy of the NPV rule.

Box 2.1. **The theory of CBA**

Ultimately, CBA is a practical tool which can be used to assist in actual policy formulation. But it would be remiss not to stress that it has theoretical foundations, which support the aforementioned practical stages. These can be briefly summarised as:

- The preferences of individuals are to be taken as the source of value. To say that an individuals' well-being, welfare or utility is higher in state A than in state B is to say that he/she prefers A to B;

- Preferences are measured by a willingness-to-pay (WTP) for a benefit and a willingness-to-accept compensation (WTA compensation) for a cost.[4]

- It is assumed that individuals' preferences can be aggregated so that social benefit is simply the sum of all individuals' benefits and social cost is the sum of all individuals' costs. Effectively, some degree of cardinalisation of utility is assumed;

- If beneficiaries from a change can hypothetically compensate the losers from a change, and have some net gains left over, then the basic test that benefits exceed costs is met.

This latter foundation is the Kaldor-Hicks compensation test. This loosened the highly restrictive condition known as the "Pareto condition", whereby a policy is "good" if at least some people actually gain and no-one actually loses.[5] Virtually all real-life contexts involve gainers and losers and the Kaldor-Hicks "compensation principle" established the idea of hypothetical compensation as a practical rule for deciding on policies and projects in these real-life contexts. All that is required is that gainers can compensate losers to achieve a "potential" Pareto improvement. The compensation principle establishes the prima facie rule that benefits (gains in human well-being) should exceed costs (losses in human well-being) for policies and projects to be sanctioned. Hence, the decision rule in equation [2.3].

> ### Box 2.1. **The theory of CBA** (cont.)
>
> Underlying all this theory, culminating in the Kaldor-Hicks test, is welfare economics or, more strictly, neoclassical welfare economics. This has always been the subject of significant debate originating from both "inside" and "outside" of the economics profession.[6] The "inside" debate, for example, has focused on a number of anomalies that reliance on the "welfarist" underpinning might give rise to. These incongruities mean that perspectives on the cost-benefit case for policy or project options might be held with less confidence, although the practical import of these complications in the theory remains the subject of debate.[7] One starting point for "outside" debate (although it may reflect views held by many economists too) is the proposition that the "welfarist" perspective is too narrow a way to judge the "value" to individuals and society of policy actions or projects. Section 2.3.4 discusses the implications of this and the way it might circumscribe the use of (rather than remove the need for) CBA.

2.3. Recent developments in environmental CBA: Major themes of this volume

While the basic principles of CBA are long-standing, the challenges entailed in applying these principles are constantly evolving. As Chapter 1 emphasised, it is these developments that are the primary focus of this volume. Subsequent chapters set out then a number of important areas of development in more detail. In this section, some of the major themes which emerge from those chapters are identified. In doing so, signposts are provided as to where in the rest of the volume further details and discussion can be found.

2.3.1. Finding money values

At its heart, CBA involves comparing costs and benefits of a given "change" in a common unit, which conventionally are money values, reflecting how much those affected by a project or policy value these changes. It is fair to say that environmental CBA would have very little to say if it were not for several decades of major advances in the various methods which seek to value environmental impacts. As such Chapters 3 to 7 devote a good deal of attention to this progress.

In terms of precepts, this frequently starts with stating that the net sum of all the relevant WTPs and WTAs for a project outcome or policy change defines the *total economic value* (TEV) of any change in well-being due to a project or policy. TEV can be characterised differently according to the type of economic value arising. It is usual to divide TEV into *use* and *non-use* (or *passive use*) values. Use values relate to actual use of the good in question (e.g. a visit to a national park), planned use (a visit planned in the future) or possible use. Actual and planned uses are fairly obvious concepts, but possible use could also be important since people may be willing to pay to maintain a good in existence in order to preserve the *option* of using it in the future. *Option value* thus becomes a form of use value. Non-use value refers to willingness-to-pay to maintain some good in existence even though there is no actual, planned or possible use.

The types of non-use value could be various, but a convenient classification is in terms of a) existence value, b) altruistic value, and c) bequest value. Existence value refers to the WTP to keep a good in existence in a context where the individual expressing the value has no actual or planned use for his/herself *or for anyone else*. Motivations here could vary and might include having a feeling of concern for the asset itself (e.g. a threatened species) or a "stewardship" motive whereby the "valuer" feels some responsibility for the asset. Altruistic value might arise when the individual is concerned that the good in question should be available to others in the current generation. A bequest value is similar but the concern is that the next and future generations should have the option to make use of the good.

The notion of total economic value (TEV) provides an all-encompassing measure of the *economic value* of any environmental asset. It decomposes into use and non-use (or passive use) values, and further sub-classifications can be provided if needed. TEV does not encompass other kinds of values, such as intrinsic values which are usually defined as values residing "in" the asset and unrelated to human preferences or even human observation. However, apart from the problems of making the notion of intrinsic value operational, it can be argued that some people's willingness-to-pay for the conservation of an asset, independently of any use they make of it, is influenced by their own judgements about intrinsic value. This may show up especially in notions of "rights to existence" but also as a form of altruism.

As a practical matter then, techniques of environmental valuation can be seen as measuring (changes in) TEV either in totality or its component parts. There are other (related) ways in which to trace these practical techniques from the economic concepts. For example, one of the contributions of the attention on ecosystem services over the past two decades is the tracing of the implications on how ecosystem services that are supplied by an underlying ecosystem asset (e.g. forest, wetland, agricultural land) – ultimately provide benefits to people and businesses. This is what Freeman et al. (2013) term: "The economic channel through which wellbeing is affected" (p. 13). These channels are manifold (e.g. Brown et al., 2007; Freeman et al., 2013) but broadly speaking can be summarised in three ways.

First, there are ecosystem services which are used as inputs to economic production. Examples include nutrient cycling and pollination resulting in the accumulation of biomass that is an input to agricultural production. Water regulation and water purification services are inputs to those economic (producing) units which need a supply of clean water as an input, perhaps alongside e.g. other factors of production.

Second, ecosystem services can act as joint inputs to household final consumption. That is, there is use of ecosystem services in combination with (or as a substitute for) expenditure on produced goods and services in providing a "product" for consumption. In such cases, an ecosystem service and the market goods or services are complementary (or substitute) inputs, and because of this expenditure on the latter can provide a guide to the value of the former. Examples include nature services which in combination with travel expenditures are used to produce recreation benefits. An example where an ecosystem service is a substitute for market expenditure is air purification services which can substitute for purchase of a produced good which filters air.

Third, ecosystem services can be inputs which directly contribute to household well-being. That is, there is no existing economic production or household consumption where these services are inputs. These services are consumed directly in generating benefits: that is, directly from nature without any other (produced) inputs. Examples here are by their nature rather abstract, but include those services that are valued for reasons of what is usually termed "non-use" or "'passive-use".

An important use of this way of thinking about ecosystems and benefits is that it maps naturally onto appropriate techniques to value unpriced ecosystem services (Day and Maddison, 2015). Some possibilities are summarised in Table 2.1 for example.

Table 2.1. **Techniques of environmental valuation for ecosystem services – an overview**

Economic channel	Explanation from economic perspective	Examples of ecosystem services	Valuation methods
Economic production	Ecosystem good or service is an input to economic production along with other factors	Waste disposal services Non-renewable and renewable ecosystem goods Water quality	Indirect methods such as production functions
Household production or consumption	Households choose level of ecosystem service via purchase of some market good, which is heterogeneous in various characteristics in which it is comprised (including the ecosystem service)	Amenity value Local air quality, Recreational opportunities Non-use value reflected in purchases and donations	Indirect methods such as hedonic pricing (e.g. in property markets)
	Households choose level of ecosystem service to enjoy via purchase of complementary market good (or substitute market good)	Recreation, Water quality Air quality	Indirect methods such as: travel cost, defensive expenditures
	Households enjoy ecosystem service unrelated to any purchase of market good	"Pure" non-use Equable climate	Direct methods such as contingent valuation, (discrete) choice experiment

Source: See text as well as adapted from Brown et al. (2007) and Day and Maddison (2015).

Another important feature of recent ecosystem valuation is the extent to which it has become an interdisciplinary effort. Valuation, of course, often needs to be preceded by quantifying physical impacts. As such a good understanding of the natural science characterising the (change in) provision of an ecosystem is an asset. This need for interdisciplinarity is not restricted to ecosystem assessment, although it has been prominent there (see, for example, MEA, 2006; TEEB, 2010; UK NEA, 2011). Health valuation is just one of many other examples. In this case, what is required is a physical assessment of the response of human health to, say, changes in exposure to air pollutants such as particulate matter (PM), sulphur oxides (SO_X) and nitrogen oxides (NO_X). These health "end states" – changes in premature mortality, reduced respiratory hospital admissions, reduced "restricted activity days" (days when activity is less than would be the case for normal health), and so on – can be valued using a variety of techniques.

One issue in such applications of CBA – the "correspondence problem", and a major reason why it can be limited in practical use, is that scientific information on ecosystem change does not correspond to indicators that individuals recognise. The correspondence problem is less important in the context of health so long as health end states can be defined in recognisable units, such as days away from work, or extra days with eye irritation, etc. Nevertheless, the key point is that this interdisciplinarity is not a one-way street. Just as the science is often needed for subsequent robust valuation so too must there be dialogue, for example, to ensure that the former is measuring things which are meaningful for the latter.

2.3.2. Who gains, who loses

The whole history of neoclassical welfare economics has focused on the extent to which the notion of economic efficiency underlying the Kaldor-Hicks compensation test can or should be separated out from the issue of who gains and loses – the distributional incidence of costs and benefits. Of course, equity and efficiency issues are hard to separate and various "schools of thought" have emerged as to what that implies for CBA. Some argue that distributional incidence has nothing to do with CBA: CBA should be confined to "maximising the cake" so there is more to share round according to some morally or politically determined rule of distributional allocation. Others argue that notions of equity and fairness are more engrained in the human psyche than notions of efficiency, so that distribution should be considered as a prior moral principle, with efficiency taking second place. Others might agree with the second school but would argue that precisely because efficiency is "downgraded" in social discourse that is all the more reason to elevate it to a higher level of importance in CBA. Put another way, one can always rely on the political process raising the equity issue, but not the efficiency issue.

Approaches to considering equity in CBA can be seen as following all these different pathways and this is discussed in Chapter 11. The initial perspective, for example, takes the view that the cost-benefit practitioner should leave well alone such issues and so standard CBA is enough to make recommendations. The second view suggests a more proactive approach. One version of this takes account of income or wealth differences. For example, if the inhabitants of B are poor and the inhabitants of A are rich, allowance might be made for the likelihood that USD 1 of gain or loss to a poor person will have higher well-being (utility) than USD 1 of gain or loss to a rich person. This gives rise to one fairly popular form of "equity weighting".

The final perspective is arguably more ambivalent about what to do. It might stop short of the equity weighting above. One reason for this might be that it is not altogether clear how to weight the money values of benefits and costs by measures of "social deservingness" in this way. If this muddies the waters of a CBA too much then a key strength of this approach arguably is lost. Other ways could be sought to reflect an important consideration. For example, a tabulation of costs and benefits must not only show the aggregate benefits and costs, following the rules outlined above, but should also show who gains and who loses. The "who" here may be different income groups, ethnic groups, geographically located groups and so on. Other forms of distributional incidence concern how benefits and costs might be allocated to business and consumers.

There is a growing interest in why people hold the preferences they do – their motivation – and perhaps in judging some motivations to be acceptable while others are not. Moral notions may also determine human behaviour and if so then arguably such motivations could be encompassed in the CBA framework. Despite the widespread perception of some critics of CBA, there is nothing in the notion of an individual preference that dictates it must always be based on "self-interest" and "greed".

The consideration of distributional issues is important both for CBA generally but it is especially important for the environment. And it should be noted that such concerns (and moral judgements more broadly) arise in many areas of the environmental CBA. Chapter 14 on climate economics and the role this sub-field has played in advancing understanding in this important area of environmental policy makes clear how ethical issues and judgements are pervasive. This theme is also picked up on in the discussion of discount rates in Chapter 8. Chapter 12 on sustainability and CBA is premised on similar concerns about intergenerational equity, albeit looked at from a somewhat different perspective.

2.3.3. Selecting a discount rate

Discounting is a pervasive issue in economics, and arguably nowhere is this more so than in CBA. Indeed, the choice of the discount rate is one of the most debated issues in CBA. Technically speaking, this is "simply" a case of determining (the rate of change of) the shadow price of a unit of consumption in the future: that is, quantifying how much lower that future consumption is compared with a unit of consumption today. The practice of establishing the price that government should use for social CBA, however, is far from simple and gives rise to long-standing debates. As a practical matter, however, this had led to rather large differences in actual discount rates used across national jurisdictions (as well as organisations including international development agencies), cf. Chapter 16.

Prominent too has been concern about the "tyranny of discounting": that is, large costs and benefits accruing in the distant future are insignificant in PV terms because the (shadow) price associated with them becomes vanishing small. Contributions within the ambit of environmental CBA – particularly, more broadly, in climate economics – have broken new ground on this enduring concern about tyrannical outcomes. As Chapter 8 makes clear, this had helped shake the conceptual foundations of discounting, in part through novel technical insights but also (and importantly) through renewed debates about ethical underpinnings.

A substantial part of this contemporary discussion has coalesced around the notion of declining discount rates: a contrast, therefore, with the constant rates familiar in CBA and which was the basis for the initial introduction to cost-benefit analysis above, a constant discount rate – i.e. r was the same regardless of which year in the project or policy life cycle is looked at. This has been reflected in much investigation on the rationale for declining discount rates. The unifying themes here have been that uncertainty about the future combined with prudence (caution by societal decision-makers in the face of these risks) generates a schedule of discount rates which decline with time. This uncertainty, for example, might be about economic growth (both its rate and variance) or future interest rates.

As economic ideas go, there appears to have been relatively rapid solidifying of support in the academic literature for declining discount rates as well as adoption by a number of national governments (see, for example, Groom and Hepburn, 2017). Nonetheless, as Chapter 8 discusses, there are other ways of conceptualising the discount rate debate in ways that are highly relevant for environmental CBA. This includes re-emerging interest in "dual discounting". What this means is that different discount rates could apply to different classes of commodities. For example, one of these classes might be "environmental" goods. Importantly, if those goods are relatively scarce compared with (other) "consumption" goods and, moreover, if environmental goods have limited substitutability, then they should command a different discount rate. A challenge is to make this operational, and one possible avenue for this (Weikard and Zhu, 2005) is to focus on estimating shadow values for environmental goods which reflect those parameters (growing scarcity and limited substitutability).

2.3.4. Circumscribing CBA: What are the limits?

To what extent does using CBA as a policy formulation tool require that the practitioner or user in effect, subscribes to the "welfarist" theory that typically is evoked to support its application? This is an important question, as for many this underpinning theory is a hard line to swallow. Randall (2014) sets out a number of reasons for discomfort with the theory, which essentially stem from its equating the goodness of an individual life narrowly with the level of preference satisfaction that the individual attains and, in turn, judging what is good for society in terms of the level of preference satisfaction enjoyed by its members.

The point made by Randall is that, as a moral theory to guide decisions, this is incomplete. But his assessment comes with an important corollary in that knowing about changes in welfare is far from irrelevant to making judgements about the merits of policy or project decisions. What this means is that concern about welfare changes becomes one principle – for determining the goodness of actions – and that it exists alongside other moral considerations. These other considerations – which might include (but not be restricted to) intrinsic values as well as the rights and duties of people – act then as potential constraints on welfarist considerations and thus CBA.

On the face of it, it seems hard to disagree with this "plurality" of moral perspectives. Few advocates of CBA argue that this is an exclusive and comprehensive rule, i.e. it is not the only value judgement that is relevant. But once this is admitted, it opens up a debate on when it should be admissible and when it should not. For example, in terms of circumscribing CBA, some might see these constraints "everywhere" and perhaps especially in relation to policy decisions about the environment. Others might see these constraints as at best a special case such that welfarism and CBA "almost always" has primacy. Such divergent standpoints notwithstanding, the "value pluralism" set out in Randall (2014) is at least a basis for subsequent debate about the role of CBA, and for understanding disagreement where it exists. In many ways, this volume can be seen as a contribution to that discussion. On the one hand, it sets out recent developments that are important to consider when CBA can be argued to be relevant to environmental decisions. On the other hand, this volume also reflects on circumstances where constraints seem relevant and as such it considers the practical consequences for how CBA is done.

One prominent example where constraints might bind is in reflecting concern about sustainability (defined in terms of intergenerational equity) in CBA as discussed in Chapter 12. While this might involve how to measure shadow values for (changes in) natural capital, this is very much at the frontier of CBA procedures. Routine valuation may not be possible anytime soon; or perhaps even ever. This might be because analysts believe that individuals are poorly informed about the environment and its importance as a life-support asset. In that case guiding policy with measures of human preference could risk other social goals, even human survival itself.

One reaction to this problem could be to specify sustainability constraints in physical terms. That is, if levels of natural capital needing to be conserved can be established, then this might operate as a constraint on project or policy proposals. CBA then would be required to operate within these constraints. In outcome, this is similar to what would be recommended by those who believe other species have "intrinsic value" which are not amenable to analysis using human preferences (unless humans can be judged to take those rights into account when expressing their own preferences). While some CBA practitioners may be uncomfortable at their hands being tied in this way (Pearce, 1998), arguably this is simply a consequence of the applying the "value plurality" that, for example, is proposed by Randall (2014). That said, there still seems a role for assessing the (opportunity) costs of sustainability constraints, as part of understanding what is sacrificed in observing these limits.

2.3.5. *How is CBA actually done (and how to do better)?*

While the emphasis of CBA is mostly on its role as a normative tool, a growing number of studies have provided a positive analysis of "when" and "why" CBA is relied upon to formulate actual policy decisions (and when it is not). Some of this literature emanates from economists looking at how their tools are actually used (e.g. Hahn and Tetlock, 2008; Groom and Hepburn, 2017). Equally interesting evidence can be found in studies by non-economists (notably political scientists and policy analysts), although typically this looks at impact assessment more generally rather than CBA per se (see, for a review, OECD, 2015 and Adelle et al., 2012). There is also evidence increasingly being gathered on use and quality of CBA by novel regulatory bodies such as the EU Regulatory Scrutiny Board (see Chapter 17).

This work has sought also to understand at what stage in the policy process this assessment actually takes place (e.g. at the beginning, when establishing potential policy options or is it well after the political decision to do something has been made). Reading the evidence to date provides a sobering moment of reflection for those who believe that CBA is always used, is always done well and is always influential in policy formulation.

This suggests the importance of ultimately placing developments in policy appraisal, including CBA, within a realistic understanding of how the policy formulation process actually works. For example, if CBA was "simply" required as a rationalistic tool to enhance evidence-based policy-making then apparent lack of quality (poorly measured impacts and so on) are straightforwardly shortcomings of those actual applications. Chapter 17 highlights the view that usage of CBA draws on a range of other motivations too. This includes communicative usages, political usage as well as more symbolic roles. The significance is that these different usages can be an effective way of understanding why the quality of actual CBA may fall short (from the perspective of using it purely as a rationalistic tool as most CBA textbooks "assume").

From the standpoint of what makes good CBA, none of this excuses the shortcomings that have been documented. The point is that a better understanding of what is happening in actual policy formulation allows a more realistic perspective to be crafted about what to do about this. That is, it is not just a case of making further progress at the CBA knowledge frontier, refining established tools (by improving valuation methods) and improving official CBA guidelines. All of that remains important. After all, to the extent that practical CBA is perceived as lacking a robust basis it is presumably less likely to be used and more likely to be dismissed. Nevertheless, this needs to be complemented by thinking about what changes in policy processes such as further institutional infrastructure are needed (of which guidelines are only part).

There are signs of evolving practice within certain jurisdictions, which may move in this direction. Evaluation of CBA used in EU regional policy, and specifically to guide the disbursement of regional funds to infrastructure projects, has combined strengthening of guidelines along with a focus on understanding the incentives that project beneficiaries have in presenting cost-benefit cases and the limited ability of existing institutional processes for scrutinising evidence to align these incentives to what is socially desirable. Such developments reflect a broader trend toward better understanding of the incentives faced by, and the bounded rationality of, policy actors in the CBA process.

Formal organisations are being established too to provide this examination. Examples here are the European Commission's Regulatory Scrutiny Board and the UK's Regulatory Policy Committee. Often however these developments seem to be driven by different policy agendas, which are beyond the core mission of the CBA textbook: particularly the deregulation or public management agendas. Nevertheless, such institutional developments, in an expanded role, could also be used to reinforce and strengthen uptake and use of (environmental) CBA in the future.

One final comment seems worth making. There is a possible irony at work here between developments at the CBA frontier and what is needed for policy use. A number of recent developments, while diverse, reflect relatively technical and, increasingly, specialised debates. This specialisation has clearly been crucial to proper and sustained progress on unavoidably complex issues. But it arguably risks less chance of actual uptake unless, for example, these lessons can be easily translated in practical terms (and moreover economic capacity-building is present in decision-making venues). Translating these novel developments into practical approaches is crucial: the example for declining discount rates is apt here.

2.4. Conclusions

The foundations of CBA can be summarised as follows:

- Benefits are defined as increases in human well-being (utility).

- Costs are defined as reductions in human well-being.

- For a project or policy to qualify on cost-benefit grounds, its social benefits must exceed its social costs.

- The geographical boundary for considering these costs and benefits is usually the nation but this can readily be extended to wider limits.

- Aggregating benefits across different social groups or nations can involve summing willingness-to-pay or to accept (WTP, WTA) regardless of the circumstances of the beneficiaries or losers, or it can involve giving higher weights to disadvantaged or low-income groups. One rationale for this is that marginal utilities of income will vary, being higher for the low-income groups.

- Aggregating over time involves discounting. The rationale for discounting is given later. Discounted future benefits and costs are known as present values.

This Chapter has also identified some major themes in the recent development of environmental CBA. Subsequent chapters in this volume explore all of these in much more detail.

Notes

1. For example, cost-effectiveness analysis (CEA) and multi-criteria analysis (MCA) impose a discipline in terms of defining goals (working out what it is that the policy should achieve) and differentiating costs from indicators of achievement of the goals (see Chapter 18).

2. Risk-neutrality means that the decision-maker is indifferent between any two probability distributions each with the same mean. Yet two distributions could have very different measures of dispersion and still have the same mean. Risk-neutrality implies that the decision-maker does not care about what may be probabilities that very small returns, or even negative returns, might be made from the policy or project. Reasons for supposing risk-neutrality is not an unreasonable assumption relate to the fact that CBA tends to be confined to government decisions. Governments can "pool" the risks of decisions in a number of ways. If then the context is one where probabilities are known and the decision-maker is *risk-neutral*, then the appropriate rule is to take the *expected value* of benefits and costs. Thus if benefit of B_1 is thought to occur with probability p_1, benefit of B_2 occurs with probability of p_2, and so on, the expected value of benefits is simply $\sum_i p_i . B_i$.

3. Where the context is one of risk (probabilities known) but the decision-maker is *risk-averse*, i.e. he or she attaches a higher weight to, say, negative benefits rather than positive benefits, the expected value rule gives way to an *expected utility* rule. The same process as before takes place but this time the relevant calculation is: $\sum_i p_i . U(B_i)$. The expression shows expected utility and this is most easily thought of as reflecting a set of weights that the decision-maker attaches to the outcomes. More formally, these weights are embedded in a *benefit utility function*. Provided some specific form can be given to this function, it is possible to compute what is called the *certainty equivalent* level of benefit that corresponds to the probabilistic level of benefits. It is this certainty equivalent level that would be entered into the CBA formula.

4. The notions of WTP and WTA can be extended to include WTP to avoid a cost and WTA compensation to forego a benefit.

5. Pigou regarded actual payment as being necessary and the task of the economist was to work out how such payments could be made. As noted, however, CBA has proceeded on the basis of saying that if the polluter could compensate the losers and still have a net profit, then the polluting activity passes a cost-benefit test.

6. All of this, of course, precedes contemporary CBA. The body of modern-day welfare economics which underlies CBA was established by Hicks (1939, 1943), Kaldor (1939) and others in the 1930s and 1940s with the contribution of Pareto (1848-1923) being presented much earlier in his Cours d'Economie Politique in 1896

7. For example, one major strand of criticism relates to what happens to income distribution as a policy or project is implemented. In theory, it could change in such a way that the policy originally sanctioned by the potential compensation principle could also be negated by the same principle – i.e. benefits exceed costs for the policy, but the move back to the original pre-policy state could also be sanctioned by CBA. This is the "Scitovsky paradox" (Scitovsky, 1941). Another problem arising from the fact that policies may change income distributions (and hence relative prices) is the "Boadway paradox" (Boadway, 1974). A possibility is that the policy showing the highest net benefits may not in fact, be the best one to undertake. This led to a search for "escapes" from this type of problem starting with Bergson (1938) and focusing on assuming a "social welfare function" – a rule that declared how aggregate welfare would vary with the set of all individuals' welfare. This, in turn, led to further conundrums (see, for example, Arrow, 1951). One of these is the problem of finding a social welfare function that might be regarded as a socially "consensus" function – there are many possible functions and no practical prospect of deciding which one to use.

References

Adelle, C., A. Jordan and J. Turnpenny (2012), "Proceeding in Parallel or Drifting Apart? A Systematic Review of Policy Appraisal Research Practices", *Environment and Planning C: Government and Policy*, Vol. 30, pp. 401-415, *http://dx.doi.org/10.1068/c11104*.

Arrow, K. (1951), (2nd edition 1963), *Social Choice and Individual Values*, Wiley, New York.

Boadway, R. (1974), "The welfare foundations of cost-benefit analysis", *Economic Journal*, Vol. 84, pp. 926-939.

Brown, T.C., J.C. Bergstrom and J.B. Loomis (2007), "Defining, valuing and providing ecosystem goods and services", *Natural Resources Journal*, Vol. 47, pp. 329-376, *www.fs.fed.us/rm/value/docs/defining_valuing_providing_ecosystem_services.pdf*.

Brown, G. and D.A. Hagen (2010), "Behavioral economics and the environment", *Environmental and Resource Economics*, Vol. 46, pp. 139-146, *http://dx.doi.org/10.1007/s10640-010-9357-6*.

Camerer, C.F., G. Loewenstein and M. Rabin (2011), *Advances in Behavioral Economics*, Princeton University Press, USA.

Day, B. and D. Maddison (2015), *Improving Cost Benefit Analysis Guidance*, Natural Capital Committee, London.

Dunlop, C.A. et al. (2012), "The Many Uses of Regulatory Impact Assessment: A Meta-Analysis of EU and UK Cases", *Regulation and Governance*, Vol. 6, pp. 23-45, *http://dx.doi.org/10.1111/j.1748-5991.2011.01123.x*.

Freeman, A.M. III et al. (2013), *The Measurement of Environmental and Resource Values*, 3rd edition, Resources for the Future, Washington, DC.

Groom, B. and C. Hepburn (2017), "Looking back at social discount rates: The influence of papers, presentations, political preconditions and personalities on policy", *Review of Environmental Economics and Policy*, Vol. 11/2, pp. 336-356, London School of Economics, *http://dx.doi.org/10.1093/reep/rex015*.

Heinzerling, L. and F. Ackerman (2004) *Priceless: On Knowing the Price of Everything and the Value of Nothing*, The New York Press, New York.

Hicks, J.R. (1939), "Foundations of welfare economics", *Economic Journal*, Vol. 49, pp. 696-712.

Hicks, J.R. (1943), "The four consumer's surpluses", *Review of Economic Studies*, Vol. 11, pp. 31-41.

HM Treasury (2018), *The Green Book: Central Government Guidance on Appraisal and Evaluation*, HM Treasury, London, *www.gov.uk/government/uploads/system/uploads/attachment_data/file/220541/green_book_complete.pdf*.

Horowitz, J.K., K.E. McConnell and J.J. Murphy (2008), "Behavioral foundations of environmental economics and valuation", in List, J. and M. Price (eds.), *Handbook on Experimental Economics and the Environment*, Edward Elgar, Northampton, MA.

Kaldor, N. (1939), "Welfare propositions of economics and interpersonal comparisons of utility", *Economic Journal*, Vol. 49, pp. 549-552.

OECD (2015), *Regulatory Policy Outlook, 2015*, OECD Publishing, Paris, *http://dx.doi.org/10.1787/9789264238770-en*.

Pearce, D.W. (2001), "Controversies in economic valuation", in P. McMahon and D. Moran (eds.), *Economic Valuation of Water Resources: Policy and Practice*, Terence Dalton, London.

Pigou, A. (1920), *The Economics of Welfare*, Macmillan, London.

Sagoff, M. (1988), *The Economy of the Earth*, Cambridge University Press, Cambridge.

Sagoff, M. (2004), *Price, Principle and the Environment*, Cambridge University Press, Cambridge.

Scitovsky, T. (1941), "A note on welfare propositions in economics", *Review of Economic Studies*, Vol. 9, pp. 77-88.

Shafir, E. (ed.) (2013), *The Behavioral Foundations of Public Policy*, Princeton University Press, New York.

Shogren, J. and L. Taylor, (2008), "On behavioral-environmental economics", *Review of Environmental Economics and Policy*, Vol. 2, pp. 26-44, *https://doi.org/10.1093/reep/rem027*.

TEEB (2010), *The Economics of Ecosystems and Biodiversity, Mainstreaming the Economics of Nature*, A Synthesis of the Approach, Conclusions and Recommendations of TEEB, Routledge, Oxford, *www.teebweb.org/publication/mainstreaming-the-economics-of-nature-a-synthesis-of-the-approach-conclusions-and-recommendations-of-teeb/*.

UK National Ecosystem Assessment (2011), *The UK National Ecosystem Assessment: Synthesis of the Key Findings*, UNEP-WCMC, Cambridge.

Weikard, H.P. and X. Zhu (2005), "Discounting and environmental quality: When should dual rates be used?", *Economic Modelling*, Vol. 22, pp. 868-878, *http://dx.doi.org/10.1016/j.econmod.2005.06.004*.

ANNEX 2.A1

Numerical example

The table below provides a simple numerical example of the calculation of discounted net benefits. It indicates that what is to be aggregated or summed is the discounted value of benefits and costs, not the absolute values: i.e. the bottom line of Table 2.A1.1.

Table 2.A1.1. **CBA – A simple example**

	Year 1	Year 2	Year 3	Year 4
Benefits (in current prices)	0	80	60	40
Cost (in current prices)	-103	24	24	23
Net benefit (in current prices)	-103	64	44	23
Price index (Year 0 = 1.000)	1.030	1.061	1.093	1.126
Net benefit (in constant year 0 prices)	-100	60.0	40.0	20.0
Discount factor (DF) (Discount rate = 5% and DF for Year 0 = 1.000)	0.952	0.907	0.864	0.823
Discounted net benefits (in constant year 0 prices)	-95.2	54.4	34.6	16.5

The minus signs in the table indicate a cost. These costs as well as benefits are measured in current year prices. So to illustrate the procedure for netting out inflation, the table includes a price index which assumes an inflation rate of 3% per year and regards Year 0 (the year the appraisal is being undertaken in) as the base year. Dividing net benefits in current prices by this index computes benefits and costs at constant prices.

The distinction between inflation and discounting should then be clear: the first step is always to ensure that benefits and costs are expressed in constant prices, and it is these magnitudes that are then discounted. The discount factor is computed from equation [2.2], with an assumed discount rate of 5%. The final row shows the discounted net benefits. When these are summed, it will be found that there are positive net benefits of 105.5 which can be compared with the costs of 95.2, i.e. there is a positive net present value (NPV). The example also illustrates the notion of a "base year", i.e. the year to which future costs and benefits are discounted. In this case there is a year 0 so that costs in year 1 are discounted back to year 0 to obtain the present value of year 1 costs (the first column of numbers). A more usual practice is to set the base year as the one in which the initial costs – usually a capital outlay – occurs. Again, there are no hard and fast rules. Any base year can be chosen, so long as the resulting procedures are consistent.

Rising relative valuations could also be built into this estimation. For the example where relative value is increasing because of rising per capita incomes, this would entail calculating the following in any particular year: $(1 + [e \times g])^t$, where e = the income elasticity of willingness-to-pay, i.e. the percentage change in willingness-to-pay arising from a given percentage change in real per capita income and g = the rate of growth in per capita (real) incomes. Evidence would need to be obtained for the likely size of e. But for sake of illustration, assume that the estimated range for the benefit being provided by this simplified example project is around 0.3 to 0.7. For any year t, then, and taking a mid-estimate of 0.5 for e and a rate of growth of real incomes of, say, 2%, a given benefit in that year needs to be multiplied by: $(1 + [0.5 \times 0.02])^t$. If the year is 3 then this means year 4 benefits would be multiplied by 1.04. If the year is 40, then benefits would be multiplied by 1.49. Including relative price changes can therefore make a potentially significant change to the outcome of a CBA.

ANNEX 2.A2

The welfare interpretation of costs and benefits

Consider an individual in an initial state of well-being U_0 that he achieves with a money income Y_0 and an environmental quality level of E_0:

$$U_0 (Y_0, E_0) \tag{A2.1}$$

Suppose that there is a proposal to improve environmental quality from E_0 to E_1. This improvement would increase the individual's well-being to U_1:

$$U_1 (Y_0, E_1) \tag{A2.2}$$

One needs to know by how much the well-being of this individual is increased by this improvement in environmental quality, i.e. $U_1 - U_0$. Since utility cannot be directly measured, one can seek an indirect measure, namely the maximum amount of income the individual would be willing to pay (WTP) for the change. The individual is hypothesised to be considering two combinations of income and environmental quality that both yield the same level of well-being (U_0): one in which his income is reduced and environmental quality is increased, and a second in which his income is not reduced and environmental quality is not increased, i.e.:

$$U_0 (Y_0 - WTP, E_1) = U_0 (Y_0, E_0) \tag{A2.3}$$

The WTP of an individual is the point at which these two combinations of income and environmental quality yield equal well-being. At that point WTP is defined as the monetary value of the change in well-being, $U_1 - U_0$, resulting from the increase in environmental quality from E_0 to E_1. This WTP is termed the individual's *compensating variation*, and it is measured relative to the initial level of well-being, U_0.

An alternative is to ask how much an individual would be willing to accept (WTA) in terms of additional income to forego the improvement in environmental quality and still have the same level of well-being as if environmental quality had been increased. The individual is then considering the combinations of income and environmental quality that yield an equal level of well-being (U_1):

$$U_1 (Y_0 + WTA, E_0) = U_1 (Y_0, E_1) \tag{A2.4}$$

where WTA is a monetary measure of the value to the individual of the change in well-being ($U_1 - U_0$) resulting from the improvement in environmental quality. This is termed the *equivalent variation*. It is measured relative to the level of well-being after the change, W_1. Here the monetary measure of the value of the change in well-being could be infinite if no amount of money could compensate the individual for not experiencing the environmental improvement.

Analogous measures for policy changes that result in losses in well-being can be derived. In this case, the compensating variation is measured by WTA, and the equivalent variation is measured by WTP. Suppose the move from E_0 to E_1 results in a reduction in the individual's well-being. Then, the compensating variation is the amount of money the individual would be willing to accept as compensation to let the change occur and still leave him or her as well off as before the change:

$$U_0 (Y_0 + WTA, E_1) = U_0 (Y_0, E_0) \qquad\qquad [A2.5]$$

The required compensation could again, in principle, be infinite if there was no way that money could fully substitute for the loss in environmental quality.

The equivalent variation is the amount of money the individual would be willing to pay to avoid the change:

$$U_1 (Y_0 - WTP, E_0) = U_1 (Y_0, E_1)... \qquad\qquad [A2.6]$$

In this case the equivalent variation measure of the value to the individual of the change in well-being resulting from a deterioration in environmental quality from E_0 to E_1 is finite and limited by the individual's income.

Table 2.A2.1 summarises the various measures of welfare gains and losses.

Table 2.A2.1. **Compensating and equivalent variation measures**

	Compensating variation = Amount of Y that can be taken from an individual after a change such that he or she is as well off as they were before the change	Equivalent variation = If a change does not occur, the amount of Y that would have to be given to the individual to make him or her as well off as if the change did take place
Increase in human welfare	$U_0 (Y_0\ WTP, E_1) = U_0 (Y_0, E_0)$	$U_1 (Y_0 + WTA, E_0) = U_1 (Y_0, E_1)$
Decrease in human welfare	$U_0 (Y_0 + WTA, E_1) = U_0 (Y_0, E_0)$	$U_1 (Y_0\ WTP, E_0) = U_1 (Y_0, E_1)$

Until a few decades ago, most economists assumed that the difference between compensating and equivalent variation measures of change in well-being would be very small and of no practical policy relevance. That is, for CBA purposes, it mattered little if WTP or WTA was used in either of the relevant contexts (a gain, and a loss). There are theoretical reasons for supposing that WTP and WTA should be very similar. But empirical estimation of these magnitudes has tended to show that they do vary, sometimes significantly, and with WTA > WTP. Depending on one's view of the evidence that WTA and WTP differ in practice, the choice of WTA or WTP could matter substantially for CBA. Accordingly, this issue is deferred for a fuller discussion in Chapter 4. From the perspective of the current discussion, on CBA, this matters. If losers have a legitimate right to what they lose, then WTA for that impact is the appropriate measure of value.

Methods of environmental valuation

PART I

Chapter 3

Revealed preference methods

Revealed preference (RP) methods refer to a range of valuation techniques which all make use of the fact that many (non-market) environmental goods and services are implicitly traded in markets, which allows then for RP methods to uncover these values in a variety of ways, depending on the good in question and the market in which it is implicitly traded. For example, demand for nature recreation can be estimated by looking at the travel costs associated with this activity, with recent developments linking this to geographical information systems to improve accuracy in mapping natural attributes at recreational sites or distances to those sites. Another prominent application are hedonic price techniques which value environmental goods and services as attributes or characteristics of related purchases, notably of residential property, or are used to evaluate the relationship between wages and the occupational risk of death and injury. Finally, averting behaviour and defensive expenditures approaches occur when individuals take costly actions to avoid exposure to a non-market bad. An important development in RP is the ever-growing sophistication of econometric methods brought to bear, reflecting a broader interest in much of applied economics on crucial matters such as causal inference.

3.1. Introduction

An established theme in the appraisal of public policies is the desirability of quantifying in monetary terms the intangible impacts of these proposals (where relevant and practicable) on the well-being of the public. For example, within the domains of environmental or health policy, it is increasingly recognised that these intangible impacts are likely to comprise a meaningful component of the total benefits of policy interventions. However, many of these impacts are non-market goods (or bads). This means that the value that the public places on these impacts cannot simply be observed with reference to market information, such as price and consumption levels. This has given rise to the proliferation of methods that have sought to uncover, in a variety of ways, the value of non-market goods. Some of the more prominent of these methods have been around for many years. Yet, their increasing use – most notably in environmental policy – has provided an additional impetus both in respect of, on the one hand, ever greater sophistication in application and, on the other hand, scrutiny regarding validity and reliability of these methods. This chapter provides an overview of one of the most popular approaches to value non-market goods: revealed preference methods.

The unifying characteristic of revealed preference methods is the valuation of non-market impacts by observing actual behaviour and, in particular, purchases made in actual markets. The focus is solely on use values. To use the terminology of Russell (2001) these methods seek to quantify the market "footprint" of non-market goods (or bads). There are a number of different approaches that have been proposed to fulfil this objective. Boyle (2003) provides a review of the main three methods, summarised in Table 3.1: i) hedonic pricing; ii) travel cost; and iii) averting or defensive behaviour.

Table 3.1. **Overview of revealed preference methods**

Method	Revealed behaviour	Conceptual framework	Types of application
Hedonic price method	Property purchased; choice of job	Demand for differentiated products	Environmental quality; health and mortality risks
Travel cost method/recreation demand models	Participation in recreation activity at chosen site	Household production; complementary goods	Recreation demand
Averting behaviour/defensive expenditure models	Time costs; purchases to avoid harm	Household production; substitute goods	Health: mortality and morbidity

Source: Adapted from Boyle (2003).

Table 3.1 (column 2) outlines the specific aspects of revealed economic behaviour that each method has sought to examine. This might entail the observation of purchases of durable goods such as property in the case of hedonic pricing, or double-glazed windows in the case of defensive expenditures. In most cases, individual or household behaviour is the main focus. Behaviour in each of these markets is thought to reveal something about the implicit price of a related non-market good (or bad). However, the conceptual framework underpinning each approach is different (Table 1: column 3). For example, the purchase of a property can be conceived of as buying a differentiated good whose price depends on a number of characteristics of the property, including the prevalence and quality of environmental amenities its vicinity. In the case of defensive expenditures, this could entail the purchase of a substitute market good such as double-glazed windows in order to compensate for the existence of a non-market bad such as road traffic noise.

RPMs have been applied in a variety of contexts (Table 3.1, column 4). The strength of these approaches is that they are based on actual decisions made by individuals or households. This is in contrast to stated preference methods (Chapters 4 and 5) which ask people how they would hypothetically value changes in the provision of non-market goods. For some commentators this, in principle, makes the findings of market based studies the more reliable indicator of peoples' preferences. This is because they provide actual data on how much people are willing to pay to secure more of a non-market good or to defend themselves against the harm caused by a non-market bad. Of course, the reality is somewhat more complicated. For example, it is not necessarily straightforward to uncover these values in practice. Superiority – relative to alternative valuation methods – in practice might better be considered on a case-by-case basis.

This chapter provides an overview of the conceptual bases of a range of revealed preference approaches to the valuation of non-market economic impacts. The most important issues underpinning the theory of each approach, and implications for their practical application, are highlighted. In each case, give one or more case study examples are given, to illustrate the way the approach has been used, and how some of the theoretical or empirical issues were tackled. The chapter also reviews the latest methodological developments for each of the techniques. The objective is that these discussions will serve to suggest how applicable each of the approaches might be to the valuation of non-market economic impacts in areas other than those in which they have already been used.

3.2. Hedonic price method

The Hedonic Price Method (HPM) (Rosen, 1974) estimates the value of a non-market good by observing behaviour in the market for a related good. Specifically, the HPM uses a market good via which the non-market good is implicitly traded. The starting point for the HPM is the observation that the price of a large number of market goods is a function of a bundle of characteristics. For instance, the price of a car is likely to reflect its fuel efficiency, safety and reliability; the price of a washing machine might depend on its energy efficiency, reliability and variety of washing programmes. The HPM uses statistical techniques to isolate the implicit "price" of each of these characteristics. There are many possible applications of the HPM (e.g. the market for wine, Gustafson et al., 2011), but two types of markets are of particular interest in non-market valuation: a) property markets; and, b) labour markets.

In terms of the housing market, the HPM uses housing market transactions to infer the implicit value of the house's underlying characteristics. We can describe any particular house by its structural characteristics (e.g. the number and size of rooms, the presence and size of a garden), its location/accessibility (e.g. proximity to schools, shops, roads), neighbourhood characteristics (e.g. crime rate) and the local environment and nearby amenities (e.g. air quality, proximity to green spaces). The price of a house is determined by the particular combination of characteristics it displays, so that properties possessing more and better desirable characteristics command higher prices and those with larger quantities of bad qualities command lower prices, everything else being constant. The HPM is concerned with unbundling the contributions of each significant determinant of house prices in order to identify marginal willingness to pay for each housing characteristic. The method has been used extensively in real estate research (Herath and Maier, 2010).

Rosen (1974) presents the theoretical rationale for this analysis, showing that the utility benefit of marginal changes in one component of the bundle of attributes in a composite good like housing can be monetised by measuring the additional expenditure incurred in equilibrium. For example, we might assume that, in general, people would prefer a quiet residential environment to a noisy one, but since no market exists for the amenity "peace and quiet", we have no direct market evidence on how much this amenity is valued where people live. However, peace and quiet can be traded implicitly in the property market. Individuals can express their preference for a quiet environment by purchasing a house in a quiet area. A measure of the value of peace and quiet is then the premium that is paid for a quieter house compared with a noisier but otherwise identical one. These firm foundations in economic theory and observable market behaviour, rather than on stated preference surveys, make the method desirable from an environmental policy perspective.

The HPM involves collecting large amounts of data on prices and characteristics of properties in an area, and applying statistical techniques to estimate a "hedonic price function". This function is a locus of equilibrium prices for the sample of houses. These prices result from the interaction of buyers and sellers in the property market in question. If the array of housing characteristics in the market is approximately continuous, then we can say that buyers will choose levels of each characteristic so that its implicit price is just equal to buyers' marginal valuation of the characteristic. Then, the slope of the hedonic price function with respect to each characteristic is equal to the implicit price. The appropriate functional form for this regression specification is arguable, but many empirical studies have estimated semi-logarithmic regression models of the form:

$$LnHP_{ijt} = \alpha + x'_{it}\beta_{1i} + n'_{it}\beta_{2i} + s'_{it}\beta_{3i} + f_j + \varepsilon_{it} \qquad [3.1]$$

where the dependent variable ($LnHP_{ijt}$) is the natural logarithm of the sale price for each property transaction i in labour market j in period t. The independent variables might include structural housing characteristics s_{it}, neighbourhood characteristics n_{it}, environmental characteristics x_{it}, unobserved labour market characteristics f_j, and other unobserved components ε_{it}. In recent years, the use of geographical information systems (GIS) and the availability of GIS data on environmental features and neighbourhood characteristics have increased the detail, flexibility and accuracy with which these attributes can be linked to house locations (Kong et al., 2007; Noor et al., 2015).

There is a long tradition of studies using the HPM to estimate the effect of environmental amenities and disamenities on property prices, with the first environmental study, an application to air pollution, dating back to 1967 (Ridker and Henning, 1967). Since then, a very large number of studies have analysed the price impacts of a wide range of environmental amenities such as water quality (Walsh et al., 2011; Leggett and Bockstael 2000; Boyle et al., 1999), air quality (Smith and Huang 1995; Bayer et al., 2009) preserved natural areas (Correll et al., 1978; Lee and Linneman 1998), wetlands (Doss and Taff 1996; Mahan et al., 2000), forests (Garrod and Willis 1992; Tyrvainen and Miettinen 2000; Thorsnes 2002), beaches (Landry and Hindsley 2011), agricultural activities (Le Goffe 2000), nature views (Benson et al., 1998; Paterson and Boyle 2002; Luttik 2000; Morancho 2003), urban trees (Anderson and Cordell 1985; Morales 1980; Morales et al., 1983) and open spaces (Cheshire and Sheppard 1995, 1998; Bolitzer and Netusil 2000; Netusil 2005; McConnell and Walls 2005). These environmental hedonic studies typically focus on a single or a very limited number of environmental attributes, thereby possibly failing to account for the interplay between multiple environmental amenities and housing preferences. A recent study by Gibbons, Mourato and Resende (2014) breaks the mould by simultaneously considering a large number of natural amenities (Box 3.1).

Box 3.1. **The Amenity value of English Nature**

Gibbons, Mourato and Resende (2014) use the HPM to estimate the amenity value associated with proximity to several habitats, designated areas, domestic gardens and other natural amenities in England. Unlike previous studies, that mostly tended to focus on a single environmental good, this analysis measured the value associated with a large number of natural amenities in England, on a national scale. It is important to know if the link usually found between environmental characteristics and house prices remains discernible when conducting the analysis over a much wider geographical area with a greater environmental diversity. Moreover, an analysis at a wider geographical scale potentially permits the investigation of the value of larger scale environmental variables, such as different habitats or ecosystems and different types of protected areas.

The authors analyse a sample of 1 million housing transactions from 1996 to 2008, with information on location at full postcode level. The data set includes sales prices and several internal and local characteristics of the houses. Internal housing characteristics are property type, floor area, floor area-squared, central heating type (none or full, part, by type of fuel), garage (space, single, double, none), tenure, new build, age, age-squared, number of bathrooms (dummies), number of bedrooms (dummies), as well as year and month dummies. The authors use Travel to Work Area (TTWA) fixed effects to control for unobserved labour market variables (such as wages and unemployment rates) and other geographical factors. Including the TTWA dummies in the hedonic function regression, means the model utilises only the variation in environmental amenities and housing prices occurring within each TTWA (i.e. within each labour market) and so takes account of more general differences between TTWAs in their labour and housing market characteristics. Other control variables included: distances to various types of transport infrastructure, distance to schools, distance to the centre of the local labour market (TTWA), land area of the ward, population density and local school quality.

In terms of local environmental characteristics, Gibbons et al. (2014) use nine broad habitat categories, describing the physical land cover in terms of the share of the 1km x 1km square in which the property is located: (1) Marine and coastal margins; (2) Freshwater, wetlands and flood plains; (3) Mountains, moors and heathland; (4) Semi-natural grasslands; (5) Enclosed farmland; (6) Coniferous woodland; (7) Broad-leaved/mixed woodland; (8) Urban; and (9) Inland Bare Ground. An additional six land use share variables are also used, depicting the land use share, in the Census ward in which a house is located, of the following land types: (1) Domestic gardens; (2) Green space; (3) Water; (4) Domestic buildings; (5) Non-domestic buildings and (6) "Other" (incorporating transport infrastructure, paths and other land uses). Finally, five "distance to" variables describing distance to various natural and environmental amenities (in 100s of kilometres), were also included: (1) distance to coastline, (2) distance to rivers, (3) distance to National Parks (England and Wales), (4) distance to National Nature Reserves (England and Scotland), and (5) distance to land owned by the National Trust (the UK's leading independent conservation organisation managing large areas of British countryside, coasts and properties). Additionally, the authors used two variables depicting designation status: the proportion of Green Belt land and of National Park land in the Census ward in which a house is located. The idea is to see whether knowledge that certain habitats are protected from development has a value to homebuyers.

Box 3.1. **The Amenity value of English Nature** (*cont.*)

Gibbons and colleagues use a semi-log hedonic price function specification and the estimates are fairly insensitive to changes in specification and sample. This provides some reassurance that the hedonic price results provide a useful representation of the values attached to proximity to environmental amenities in England.

A summary of key findings for England is presented in Table 3.2. Results reveal that the effects of many environmental characteristics on house prices are highly statistically significant, and are quite large in economic magnitude. Gardens, green space and areas of water within census wards all attract a considerable positive price premium. There is also a strong positive effect from freshwater locations, broadleaved woodland, coniferous woodland and enclosed farmland (with urban land cover as a base). Increasing distance to natural amenities such as rivers, National Parks and National Trust sites is unambiguously associated with a fall in house prices. Each 1km increase in distance to the nearest National Park lowers prices by 0.24% or GBP 465. This implies that being inside a National Park (i.e. at zero distance from it), combined with 100% of the ward as a National Park, implies a huge GBP 33 686 premium relative to the average house in England (which is 46.7 km from a National Park). In turn, Green Belt designation becomes important when looking at major metropolitan areas. The results indicate a WTP of around GBP 7 000 for houses in Green Belt locations, which offer access to cities, coupled with tight restrictions on housing supply.

Overall, the authors conclude that the house market in England reveals substantial amenity value attached to a number of habitats, designations, private gardens and local environmental amenities.

Table 3.2. **Implicit prices for key environmental amenities in England**
GBP, capitalised values

Environmental amenity	% change in house value with:	Implicit price in relation to average 2008 house price	
1 percentage point increase in share of land cover:			
Freshwater, wetlands, floodplains	0.36% increase in house prices	GBP 694	***
Enclosed farmland	0.06% increase in house prices	GBP 115	***
Broadleaved woodland	0.19% increase in house prices	GBP 376	***
Coniferous woodland	0.12% increase in house prices	GBP 232	*
1 percentage point increase in land use share:			
Domestic gardens	1.02% increase in house prices	GBP 1 982	***
Green space	1.04% increase in house prices	GBP 2 031	***
Water	0.97% increase in house prices	GBP 1 897	***
Designation:			
Being in the Green Belt (major metro. areas)	3.25% increase in house prices	GBP 6 967	*
Being in a National Park, relative to mean	17.36% increase in house prices	GBP 33 686	***
1 km increase in distance:			
Distance to rivers	0.93% fall in house prices	GBP 1 811	*
Distance to National Parks	0.24% fall in house prices	GBP 465	***
Distance to National Trust land	0.70 % fall in house prices	GBP 1 344	***

Notes: The stars indicate statistical significance levels *** $p < 0.01$, ** $p < 0.05$, * $p < 0.10$. Being in a National Park calculation is based on zero distance from National Park and having a ward share of 100% National Park. The implicit prices in the Table are capitalised values, i.e. present values, rather than annual willingness-to-pay. Long-run annualised figures can be obtained by multiplying the present values by an appropriate discount rate (e.g. 3.5%).

The effect of disamenities and "bads" has also been investigated via the HPM including road, railway and airport noise (Andersson et al., 2009; Day et al., 2006; Wilhelmsson 2000; Pope 2008a), wind turbines (Gibbons 2015; Hoen et al., 2011), electric power plants (Davis 2011), shale gas exploration (Muehlenbachs et al., 2015; Gibbons et al., 2016) and floods (Beltrán-Hernández, 2016). Finally, the method has also been used to evaluate the effects of environmental policies such as the Clean Air Act (Chay and Greenstone, 2005) and the Superfund programme for the clean-up of hazardous waste sites (McCluskey and Rausser, 2003).

The most common methodological approach in these studies has been to include distance from the property to the environmental amenity or disamenity as an explanatory variable in the model. More recently the use of GIS has improved the ability of hedonic regressions to explain variation in house prices by considering not just proximity but also amount and topography of the environmental amenities, for example by using as an explanatory variable the proportion of an amenity existing within a certain radius of a house.

For the most part, this large body of literature has consistently shown an observable effect of environmental factors on property prices, supporting the assumption that that the choice of a house reflects an implicit choice over the nearby environmental amenities so that the value of marginal changes in proximity to these amenities is reflected in house prices.

The HPM has also been used to estimate the value of avoiding risk of death or injury. It has done this by looking for price differentials between wages in jobs with different exposures to physical risk. That is, different occupations involve different risks (in that, for example, being a firefighter entails, on average, very much higher risks of injury or worse than does a desk-bound occupation). Employers must therefore pay a premium to induce workers to undertake jobs entailing higher risk. This premium provides an estimate of the market value of small changes in injury or mortality risks (Kolstad, 2010). Hedonic methods have thus been applied to labour markets in order to disentangle such risk premia from other determinants of wages (e.g. education etc.). An example of this approach is shown in Box 3.2.

Box 3.2. **HPM and wage compensation for workplace risk**

Marin and Psacharopoulos (1982) undertook one of the first studies of the relationship between wages and occupational risk in the UK. The motivations for the work were twofold. First, the study aimed to test the theory that earnings should be higher in higher risk jobs, taking account of non-competitive factors such as unionisation. Second, the objective was to provide an estimate of the value of changes in mortality risk for use in project and policy appraisal.

The authors used data from the General Household Survey and data on occupational risk to estimate an earnings function – a type of hedonic price function – which included variables such as numbers of years of schooling and work experience ("human capital" variables), occupational risk, the extent of unionisation, and a ranking of occupational desirability. Two risk index series were constructed. The first considered the overall relative risk of dying in each occupational group. This measure would by implication include those risks for which compensation might not be required because they are willingly borne (e.g. publicans), the effect of risks borne in other occupations (e.g. higher mortality rates for above-ground mine workers, reflecting health problems contracted in previous (below-ground) employment), and chronic (e.g. cancer) risks which employees are likely to have difficulty in assessing. The measurement problems resulting from this first index led the authors to prefer a more specific risk variable, relating to the risk of death through an

---

Box 3.2. **HPM and wage compensation for workplace risk** (*cont.*)

accident at work, as a more immediate, less "desirable", and more easily perceived risk measure. Thus, this measure was seen as a more labour market-specific risk compared with the first measure which referred to deaths in general.

Marin and Psacharopoulos also included in their earnings function a variable to consider any interaction effect between occupational risk and the extent of unionisation, with no prior expectation of whether the estimated coefficient should be positive or negative. A positive effect could result if unions had better knowledge of risks than individual workers, and used this in collective wage bargaining. A negative effect could occur for a number of reasons. Collective bargaining could take place at a broader level than the occupations considered by the authors, reducing the sensitivity of that bargaining to measures of occupational risk. Second, unions might bargain directly for the implementation of measures to improve on-the-job safety, making risk less important as a bargaining tool in earnings determination.

The results of the analysis confirmed that higher risks of death were associated with higher earnings in the UK. The relationship with workplace accident mortality was stronger than that with overall occupational mortality, as expected. The union-risk interaction term was found to be negative, suggesting (although not strongly) that unionisation tended to weaken the compensating differential between more and less risky jobs.

The implicit value of mortality risk can be translated into a population-level measure, commonly called the "value of statistical life", by calculating the differential of the earnings function with respect to risk. For all workers in the sample (n = 5 509), the value of statistical life computed to GBP 603 000 or GBP 681 000 in 1975 prices (GBP 3.14 m or GBP 3.54 m in 2001 prices), depending on whether union-risk interaction was included. Due to the nature of the hedonic price function, as a locus of equilibrium prices resulting from the interaction of buyers and sellers, these figures also provide estimates of the cost to firms of reducing workplace risk.

Marin and Psacharopoulos also performed estimations on subsamples of the total sample of workers, to consider whether compensating differentials varied across professional, non-manual and manual workers. Estimations for professionals were less successful, given the very low level of risk (and hence casualties) in the associated occupational groups. The authors suggested that this reflects high values of safety on the part of these workers, and low costs to firms of reducing risks for sedentary workers. Estimations for non-manual and manual workers were more satisfactory, and resulted in values of statistical life of around GBP 2.25m for the former group (reflecting non-manual workers higher average income and higher estimated risk coefficient), and figures for the latter group very close to those estimated for the whole sample (GBP 619 000-GBP 686 000). The non-manual value of statistical life translates into a figure of around GBP 11.7 m in 2001 prices.

3.2.1. Limitations

Not surprisingly there are a number of issues surrounding the practical application of the HPM. Firstly, HPM only measures use values, as reflected in property prices. And it is based on a number of assumptions, namely of property markets that are competitive and in equilibrium, requiring that individuals optimise their house choices based on the prices in various locations. It also assumes free mobility, i.e. that individuals are able to adjust the different levels of each characteristic of interest by moving property, with no transaction costs.

Moreover, the HPM assumes perfect information. In reality, individuals might not have perfect information. In the case of wage-risk premia, this means that workers may not be fully aware of the accident risks they face in the workplace, so that their wage-risk choices do not accurately reflect their true valuation of risk. Estimates of the value of risk obtained from observing these choices will then be biased. In the case of environmental variables, house buyers might not be aware of issues such as land contamination or probability of flooding in which case such elements will not be accurately reflected in house prices. Pope (2008b) investigates information asymmetries about flood risk, where sellers are typically better informed than buyers, making it attractive for sellers to wait for an uninformed buyer to make a bid on the house. After the introduction of a seller disclosure law in North Carolina, requiring sellers to disclose flood risks so that buyers are fully informed, the author estimates a 4% decline in housing prices in flood zones. Notably, before the disclosure law came into force, there appeared to be no impact of flood plain designation on housing prices. Pope's results suggest that asymmetric information between buyers and sellers caused an underestimation of the estimated marginal values for flood plains prior to the disclosure law.

The HPM estimation procedure also faces some well-known econometric problems such as the arbitrary choice of a functional form for the hedonic price function, multicollinearity, heteroscedasticity, defining the spatial and temporal extent of property markets, and omitted variable bias. Moreover, the standard approach in the past literature has involved using cross-sectional data, which poses numerous identification problems, having to rely on controls for the large number of factors that affect house prices, many of which are unobservable.

In terms of multicollinearity, non-market characteristics tend to move in tandem: e.g. properties near to roads have greater noise pollution *and* higher concentrations of air pollutants. This means that it is frequently difficult to "tease out" the independent effect of these two forms of pollution on the price of the property. In many cases, researchers have tended to neglect the issue, omitting a potentially important characteristic from the analysis, and producing biased estimates as a result. See Box 3.3 for an example.

Box 3.3. **HPM and the impact of water quality on residential property values**

Leggett and Bockstael (2000) address the issue of multicollinearity directly in their study of the impact of varying water quality on the value of waterside residential property in Chesapeake Bay, USA. Water pollution in Chesapeake Bay can be produced by sewage treatment works and other installations which could also have a negative impact on visual amenity. The potential for bias thereby stems from the fact that properties closest to these installations could suffer both worse water quality and worse visual amenity, making it difficult to determine the price effect of each.

However, to overcome this potential problem, the authors were able to take advantage of a natural feature of Chesapeake Bay. The Bay has a varied coastline, with many localised inlets and a diverse pollution-flushing regime. As a result, it was possible to find a property located on an inlet which suffered from poor water quality but with no direct line of sight to the associated pollution source, and hence no visual disamenity. Similarly, a property located close to a sewage treatment works would not necessarily suffer from poor water quality if the flushing regime in that particular inlet was benign. The natural features of Chesapeake Bay thereby broke the potentially collinear relationship between visual amenity and water quality, allowing both characteristics to be included in the estimation equation without causing statistical problems.

Box 3.3. **HPM and the impact of water quality on residential property values**
(cont.)

In hedonic property studies, as with most studies of the value of environmental resources, some consideration needs to be given of the appropriate way to measure the environmental variable of interest. For instance, laypeople often respond most readily to the visual appearance of water, tending to attach higher values to water of greater clarity. However, biological water quality – which reflects the ecological potential of a water body – is not necessarily related to water clarity. Further, chemical water quality is more important for determining whether a water body is suitable for swimming or other sports where contact with the water is a possibility. Chemical water quality might not be well understood by members of the public, however.

Leggett and Bockstael used reported faecal coliform levels as their measure of water quality. This indicates that it was in general the recreational value of being located close to Chesapeake Bay which was being estimated in their study. These data were advertised in local newspapers and at information points, and the limit at which beaches would be closed for public health reasons was also clearly stated. The authors also obtained good evidence for believing that existing and prospective Chesapeake residents took an active interest in local water quality, providing further support for the possibility of a positive relationship between property values and water quality.

The authors found that standard locational variables had the expected signs in their estimated hedonic price equation. Increased acreage, reduced commuting distance, and proximity to water all had positive impacts on property prices, compared with the average estimated USD 350 000 per one acre plot. The closer a property was to a pollution source, the lower the price would tend to be. Local faecal coliform levels were also negatively related to property prices. For every unit increase in median annual concentration reported at the nearest measuring station, property value was observed to fall by USD 5 000 (average concentration in the sample was one count per ml, with a range of 0.4-23/ml). This could be used as an estimate of the marginal value of small changes in water quality in the Chesapeake area, and elsewhere.

Leggett and Bockstael emphasise that their results cannot be used to estimate the value of significant changes in water quality (as might occur through the introduction of new environmental standards, for instance). This is because a significant change would constitute a shift in the supply of environmental quality to the Chesapeake Bay housing market, and hence would induce a shift in the hedonic price function, as buyers and sellers renegotiated to obtain new optimal house purchase outcomes. This is an important qualification to the policy use of non-market value estimates obtained via the HPM.

The potential for omitted variables in hedonic modelling has long concerned researchers (Kuminoff et al., 2010). Omitted variable bias occurs as there may be unobservable housing characteristics that matter to households that are correlated with the environmental amenity of interest. This potential misspecification of the hedonic price function could result in biased value estimates. In an influential study, Cropper et al. (1988) showed that, in the presence of omitted variables, simpler functional forms such as linear, log-linear, log-log perform best. As a result, most studies published since then have used these simpler models in order to minimise the potential for omitted variable bias.

Care also needs to be taken to specify the extent of the property market accurately. The extent of the market is defined for any one individual house buyer by that individual's search. If properties are included in the analysis which are outside of the individual's market, hedonic price estimates will be biased. If properties are excluded which are in the market, the resulting estimates will be unbiased but inefficient. Unfortunately, with many different individuals searching for property in a given locality, the resulting house purchase data are likely to be drawn from a large number of overlapping markets. In this case, it has been argued that it is probably better to underestimate the extent of the market under study, rather than overestimate it (Palmquist, 1992).

Finally, the overwhelming majority of the HPM literature estimate only the marginal implicit prices associated with the characteristics of interest, as the typical policy question of interest is whether the current stock on a local non-market good is capitalised in the property market. But this is only the first stage of the HPM. Most studies do not go on to estimate demand functions for the characteristics of interest, i.e. the second stage of the HPM, which would allow the estimation of the value of non-marginal and non-localised changes. This is because estimating demand relationships from hedonic price data is theoretically and analytically challenging and requires extensive information. Day et al. (2006) provide a rare example.

3.2.2. Recent developments

In recent years, research into omitted variable bias and resulting endogeneity problems in hedonic price models has led to many econometric developments. In a review of the effects of omitted variable bias in HPM studies, Kuminoff et al. (2010) find that studies using large cross-sectional data sets have started to include spatial fixed effects in the hedonic price function (e.g. fixed effects for travel to work areas such as in Gibbons et al., 2014, or for school districts) in order to control for spatially clustered omitted variables. And as panel data sets and repeated cross-section data sets became increasingly available, researchers have been able to adopt quasi-experimental methods such as fixed effects, first differences and difference-in-differences to address the problem of omitted variables and accurately identify non-market values (e.g. Horsch and Lewis, 2009; Gibbons, 2015; Gibbons et al., 2016). Some authors have also used repeat sales data to address the issue (e.g. Beltrán-Hernández, 2016). Kuminoff et al. (2010) argue that, when spatial fixed effects are used to control for omitted variables, the seminal result by Cropper et al. (1988) regarding the superiority of simpler hedonic price functional forms no longer holds. Instead, they show that there are large gains in estimation accuracy by moving to more flexible specifications of the hedonic price function (such as the quadratic Box-Cox model) when using quasi-experimental identification, spatial fixed effects, and/or temporal controls for housing market adjustments.

Horsch and Lewis (2009) propose a quasi-random experiment to identify the effects of milfoil, an invasive aquatic species, on property values. Milfoil is spread by the movement of boats and since boaters are more likely to visit nice lakes with desirable (and often unobservable) amenities, the likelihood of a lake being invaded by milfoil is correlated with the error term in an hedonic price function (endogeneity). As a result, standard ordinary least squares (OLS) estimation of cross-sectional hedonic price data is likely to produce positively biased coefficient estimates on variables related to the presence of milfoil. Using time series data, that include data on lakes before and after milfoil invasions, the authors propose a difference-in-differences (DiD) analysis, with lake fixed effects. This estimation strategy allows the identification of the effect of milfoil on property values because the fixed effects control for all observable and unobservable lake amenities that affect property values, while the DiD specification exploits the natural experiment features of the dataset, that contains before-and-after data on milfoil invasions. Results indicate that milfoil invasions reduce average property values by around 8%.

In another recent example, Beltrán-Hernández (2016) uses the difference-in-differences approach to measure the ex-post economic benefits of structural flood defences in England, constructed between 1995 and 2004. The study is based on a large panel data set, with over 12 million property transactions, including sale prices of houses that have been sold multiple times. These data were then merged with GIS data containing the spatial location and main characteristics of a total of 1,666 flood defences constructed in England during the period of analysis. The author uses a repeat-sales model to look at the capitalisation of the flood defence infrastructure between two sales of the same property. The repeat-sales model is akin to a first-differences specification of the DiD model. This specification permits the evaluation of the price effect of flood defence construction, which is not uniform across properties, while controlling for time-invariant characteristics. The results suggest that flood defences result in increases in property prices ranging between 1% and 13%, depending on the level of risk and on the type of property (i.e. GBP 2 000 to GBP 30 000, for a median-priced house in 2014). However, in the case of flats (not affected by floods) and rural properties (where flood defences may result in loss of amenity value), the construction of flood protection infrastructure results in significant negative impacts that range from a price discount of -1% to -9% (-GBP 3 000 to -GBP 10 000).

In order to deal with endogeneity, recent studies have also used an instrumental variable approach. An example is Bayer et al.'s (2009) hedonic price study of air quality. Because air pollution is likely to be correlated with unobserved local characteristics, such as economic activity, that also affect property prices, standard estimates of willingness to pay are likely to be biased downwards. To tackle the issue the authors instrument for local air pollution, using the contribution of distant sources to local air pollution as an instrument. This strategy works because many air pollutants come from distant sources and those distant sources are unlikely to be correlated with local economic activity. Instrumenting for air pollution greatly increases the magnitude of the coefficient on air pollution (in this case particulate matter PM10) concentration in the hedonic price regression.

3.3. Travel cost method

The travel cost method (TCM) is a technique that has been developed to estimate recreational use values of non-market goods, typically outdoor natural areas but applicable to any location used for recreational purposes (Clawson and Knetsch 1969; Bockstael and McConnell 2007; Parsons 2017). For example, natural areas are frequently the focus of recreational trips (e.g. parks, woodland, beaches, rivers, lakes etc.). Such natural areas, for a number of reasons, typically do not command a price in the market and so we need to find an alternative means of appraising their value.

The basis of the TCM is the recognition that individuals produce recreational experiences through the input of a number of factors. Amongst these factors are the recreational area itself, travel to and from the recreational area and, in some cases, staying overnight at a location and so on. Typically, while the recreational area itself is an unpriced good, many of the other factors employed in the generation of the recreational experience do command prices in markets, such as travel costs. Travel costs could therefore be used as a proxy for the value of accessing the site.

Most of the early research using the TCM approach was indeed motivated by estimating the value of visits to recreational sites. In time, the method was adapted to be able to also value quality changes. Indeed, the last 50 years have witnessed a considerable evolution of travel cost method techniques, from simple aggregate demand models to very sophisticated analysis of individual level choices.

Parsons (2003) usefully differentiate between travel cost models that estimate demand for a *single* recreational site and models that estimate demand for *multiple* sites. We will now consider these two categories of models in turn.

3.3.1. Single site models

The single site TCM derives from the observation that travel and the recreational area are (weak) complements such that the value of the recreational area can be measured with reference to values expressed in the market for trips to the recreational area. To estimate the TCM, therefore, we need two pieces of information: a) the number of trips that an individual or household takes to a particular recreational area over a period of time (e.g. a year); and b) how much it costs that individual or household to travel to the recreational area, which acts as a proxy for the price of visiting the site.

The costs of travelling to a recreational area, in turn, include two elements: i) the monetary costs in return fares or petrol expenses, wear and tear and depreciation of the vehicle and so on; and ii) the cost of time spent travelling. Time is a scarce resource to the household. Time spent travelling could be spent in some other activity (e.g. working) that could confer well-being. In other words, the individual or household incurs an *opportunity cost* in allocating time to travel. Put more simply, demand for trips will be greater if it takes less time to travel to the recreational area, independent of the monetary cost of travel.

Of course to implement this procedure we require a value for the (shadow) price of time. One possible value for the price of time to an individual is their wage rate (Cesario, 1976). If individuals can choose the number of hours they spend working then they will choose to work up to the point at which an extra hour spent at work is worth the same to them as an hour spent at leisure. At the margin, therefore, leisure time will be valued at the wage rate. In the real world, individuals can only imperfectly choose the number of hours they work and the equality between the value of time in leisure and the wage rate is unlikely to hold. Empirical work has been undertaken that has revealed that time spent travelling is valued at somewhere between a third and a half of the wage rate and travel cost researchers frequently use one or other of these values as an estimate of the price of time (Czajkowski et al., 2015).

The information used in the TCM is usually collected through surveys carried out at the recreational site. With these data, a demand curve for access to the recreational site can be estimated, which explains the number of visits (i.e. the quantity) as a function of travel costs (i.e. the price) and other relevant explanatory variables. This demand curve is typically downward sloping as the number of trips normally declines the higher the costs of the trip. Higher costs are normally associated with people living further away from the site. The points along the demand curve indicate consumer willingness to pay to visit the site. The non-market value associated with the recreation benefits at the site is estimated as the consumer surplus, i.e. the area under the demand curve between an individual's WTP and their travel cost expenditure.

Initial applications of the TCM used what is known as the *zonal* TCM (Parsons, 2003). Zonal TCM calculated aggregate visit rates (i.e. number of visits from an area divided by the population of that area) and average cost trips from different pre-defined geographical zones surrounding the recreational site of interest. This permitted the estimation of number of visits per capita for each of the zones considered. The approach therefore looked at the average behavior of groups of visitors rather than at individual choices. Because of its lack of consistency with economic theory the use of the zonal model has declined over time.

Today, the most commonly applied variant of the single-site TCM is the *individual* TCM. This approach makes use of individual-level rather than aggregate data, namely, the number of individual visits to a recreational site over a period of time (e.g. a year) and their respective costs. The method has been applied to value a wide range of outdoor recreation pursuits such as forest recreation (Christie et al., 2006), lake visits (Corrigan et al., 2007), recreational fishing (Shrestha et al., 2002), ski centre visits (Steriani and Soutsas, 2005), mountain biking (Chakraborty and Keith, 2000), National Parks (Heberling and Templeton, 2009), deer hunting (Creel and Loomis, 1990) and many more.

In early individual TCM models the number of visits was treated as a continuous variable and OLS regression methods were typically used, leading to biased estimates. In the late 80's researchers started to use instead more appropriate count data models such as Poisson and negative binomial regression models which take into account the nature of the visitation data: i.e. visits are non-negative integers; data is often truncated at zero due to on-site sampling meaning that respondents will have at least one visit; and the visit distribution tends to be typically skewed towards small numbers of trips (Parsons, 2017).

A limitation of the individual TCM is that it does not easily accommodate the presence of substitute recreational sites. In many real-world situations individuals are faced with a wide range of substitute recreational sites: e.g. choice of which beach to go to, which river to go fishing in, which ski resort to visit, or even, choices between different types of sites, say whether to go to a woodland or a national park. In such cases, we require an approach capable of adequately modelling the discrete choice that consumers make between sites rather than an approach that focus on the "continuous" choice of how many trips to make to single site. The next section presents the model typically used in such cases, the Random Utility Model.

3.3.2. Multiple sites models

The standard method applied in the case of multiple sites is the *Random Utility Model* (RUM) (Bockstael et al., 1987). The RUM is a discrete choice modelling technique where, in the presence of multiple recreational sites, individuals are assumed to choose which site to visit based on the site characteristics as well as the costs of travelling to the different substitute sites. Although the RUM is often described as an extension of the TCM it is in fact more akin to a theory of choice rather than a valuation technique and can be applied in any situation in which households' make discrete choices that involve combinations of market goods and environmental goods and services (Maddison and Day, 2015).

In recent years, the popularity of random utility modelling for recreational choice has boomed, in parallel with a decrease in application of more traditional travel cost models. It is now the dominant revealed preference method for recreation demand estimation (Phaneuf and Smith, 2005) and has been applied to a very extensive range of recreational experiences including fishing, swimming, climbing, boating/cannoing/kayaking, hunting, hiking, skiing, and park/forest/river visits, amongst others. For policy and management purposes, the RUM approach is very useful as it allows the estimation of the value of changes in site quality as well as site closures, in multiple sites. Phaneuf and Smith (2005) and Parsons (2017) offer detailed overviews of the evolution of RUM and its applications to recreational demand. Box 3.4 contains an application to the choice of game parks in South Africa (Day, 2002).

Box 3.4. **The recreational value of game reserves in South Africa**

Day (2002) provides a relatively sophisticated application of the multiple site travel cost method to four of South Africa's game parks. These internationally renowned games reserves – Hluhluwe, Umfolozi, Mkuzi and Itala – each cover vast land areas of roughly several hundred square kilometres and are managed by the KwaZulu-Natal Parks Board (KNPB).

The premise for Day's approach is that a visit to any one of these game reserves reflects a choice between four key cost determinants: i) the economic cost of travel to the site; ii) the cost of time while travelling; iii) the cost of accommodation at the site; and, iv) the cost of time whilst on-site. Most travel cost approaches have focused only on costs i) and ii). For many recreational sites this is sufficient. However, Day argues that overnight trips are an important feature of visits to the reserves that he examines in this study. In order to take account of this trip characteristic, Day extends the RUM framework often used in recreational contexts to predict that an individual will choose to make a given visit to a particular site rather its alternatives because the chosen site provides that individual with the most utility (or well-being) from the options available. Such a model is thus ideally suited to explaining a visitor's decision with reference to the qualities of alternative sites (e.g. number and variety of fauna and flora) as well as the different costs of travelling to these sites. Day further extends this framework in order to take account of visitor choice of accommodation and length of stay at the site.

The data used in this study are based upon a (random) sample of 1 000 visitors to the four different reserves. For each of these visitors, this included information on, for example, length of stay, size of party and how much. In total, that the visit cost each household. It is worth noting that this study did not need to use on-site surveys say of visitor total travel costs and demographic/ socioeconomic characteristics. For example, with respect to physical distance travelled, this was calculated by the author with reference to data on visitor addresses combined with a Geographical Information Systems (GIS) model in order to calculate the distance that each visitor travelled "door-to-door". Only visitors living in South Africa were sampled to minimise the problem of multipurpose trips.

An interesting feature of Day's study is the determination of the money value to be assigned to an hour spent travelling relative to an hour spent on-site. Day demonstrates quite reasonably that an hour spent travelling is likely to be valued less highly than an hour spent on-site at the reserve. Furthermore, he argues that the former is likely to be valued more than time in general because there could be a significant disutility associated with time spent travelling. In other words, people enjoy time travelling a lot less than most other uses of time and so this activity has a high opportunity cost. By contrast, the latter is likely to be valued less than time in general because there could be a significant utility associated with time spent on-site. In terms of proportions of the wage rate, Day concludes that his analysis justifies valuing travel time at 150% of the household wage rate while on-site time is valued at 34% of the wage rate. Whereas the latter seems consistent with previous findings in the literature (see discussion above) the former is somewhat higher than conventionally assumed by travel cost practitioners.

Box 3.4. **The recreational value of game reserves in South Africa** (*cont.*)

Day uses assembled data on cost, trip duration and accommodation decision variables as well as other trip characteristics as inputs to a sophisticated statistical analysis of the determinants of the choice to take a given trip to a particular reserve (using a nested logit model). Ultimately, the findings of this detailed analysis can be used to derive policy relevant information on the benefits provided by the reserves. For example, Day calculates the amount of money that would have to be given to affected households in South Africa following the (hypothetical) closure of one of the reserves in order to fully compensate them for the loss of this recreational amenity. Since only South African visitors were considered in the analysis, the estimates, these estimates do not include the welfare costs that would be associated with the loss of visitors from abroad. A summary of these findings is presented in Table 3.3.

Table 3.3. **Per trip values for game reserves of KwaZulu-Natal**

1994/95

Game reserve	Average per trip welfare loss (USD)	Total annual welfare loss (USD)
Hluhluwe	49.7	473 884
Umfolozi	30.5	290 448
Itala	20.4	194 169
Mkuzi	18.7	178 026
Hluhluwe and Umfolozi	105.6	1 006 208

Source: Day (2002).

Why are these data important? Day argues that one response to this question is that the KNPB is finding itself under increasing pressure to justify the substantial public funding that it receives. Demonstrating the monetary value of the recreational benefits provided by the KNPB might be one crucial way in which this body can make its case for public funds. Thus the values in Table 3.3 (column 2) can be thought of as the per trip benefits attributable to the current management regime at each reserve. Alternatively, this is the (yearly) per trip loss of welfare or well-being. In money terms, that occurs if the reserve were to be closed "tomorrow".

Column 3 in Table 3.3 illustrates the total annual welfare losses for each reserve: i.e. the per trip value multiplied by the number of trips which would no longer be taken over a year if the reserve was closed. In effect, this column provides policy-makers with one basis for assessing the dollar magnitude of the (non-market) recreational benefits generated by public expenditure on each reserve. Finally, it is interesting to note that the final row in Table 3.3 indicates that if both Hluhluwe and Umfolozi (i.e. the most highly valued) reserves were to close then the combined welfare loss is greater (than the sum of individual values in column 3, rows 2 and 3). The intuitive explanation for this is that these two parks are in close proximity to each other. Removing one or other would mean that many households would most likely just switch their visits to the remaining reserve. However, if both of these sites were to be no longer available for visits then the loss for households would be disproportionately greater reflecting the absence of remaining substitutes.

Application of the RUM is data intensive and requires data on individuals' choice of site, place of residence, socio-economic and demographic characteristics, frequency of visits to the site of interest and other similar sites, as well as trip cost information. These data can be collected from either an on-site or off-site survey. Data are also required on the characteristics of the different recreation sites under consideration, and their quality.

These can either be collected from objective datasets (e.g. water quality measurements) or be based on subjective perceptions of quality by visitors.

The RUM models the probability of visiting a particular site as a function of the characteristics of the sites in the choice set of possible sites to visit. The estimated model controls for visitors' socio-economic characteristics, travel costs and travel time, and site quality characteristics to estimate the benefit derived from a recreation visit. The value of a change in environmental quality is then estimated by relating the estimated model coefficient for environmental quality to the costs of a visit, as inferred from the travel costs.

3.3.3. Limitations

The TCM has narrow applicability to the estimation of recreational use values and requires the availability of large data sets on recreational activities, including extensive GIS analysis of travel cost data and site characteristics (for RUM studies).

Some of the limitations associated with the single-site TCM model, such as the lack of consideration for substitute sites can be resolved by the use of the RUM variant. But one issue remaining is the problem of multiple purpose trips (Parsons, 2017). Many recreational trips are undertaken for more than one purpose. For example, standard travel cost methods cannot easily be applied to trips undertaken by international tourists since such tourists will usually visit more than one destination. One solution to this problem has been to ask visitors (as part of the on-site survey) to estimate the proportion of the enjoyment they derived from their entire trip that they would assign to visiting the specific recreational area of interest. Total travel costs for the entire trip are multiplied by this amount and this can be used as the basis for assessing travel costs at the recreational site.

Other challenges include the valuation of travel time as often results are very sensitive to the assumptions made. As noted above, TCM researchers need to make assumptions about how visitors would have used their time in other welfare raising activities, if they had not been travelling for recreation. Such assumptions are mostly ad-hoc, typically based on using a fraction of the wage rate, and difficult to validate in empirical studies. Critics of the wage-based value of time approach also note that it makes little sense for people without wages (e.g. students or homemakers), to assume that their marginal utility of time is zero (Czajkowski et al., 2015).

3.3.4. Recent developments

As with the hedonic price method discussed above, many of the innovations in recreational demand modelling have been in the econometric analysis methods used. Discrete choice models in particular have witnessed a literal revolution in recent years, with ever increasing sophistication in estimation. Examples of such developments include new approaches to deal with the incorporation of unobserved heterogeneity (e.g. via mixed logit models and latent class models), instrumental variables, models for handling on-site sampling, and dealing with corner solutions (Phaneuf and Smith, 2005; Parsons, 2017). Moreover, recreation models could also benefit from modern quasi-random experimental designs when evaluating changes in policies and management practices in recreational sites (Phaneuf and Smith, 2017).

In parallel, there has been a move to integrate TCM models with stated preference data (Adamowicz et al., 1994; Englin and Cameron, 1996; Whitehead et al., 2000; Landry and Liu, 2011). The advantage of the combined approach is the ability to measure changes in the quality of recreation sites that have not yet happened. Most of the efforts have concentrated on the single site TCM model, using it in combination with contingent valuation or contingent behavior questions. For example, Corrigan et al. (2007) combined an individual TCM with a contingent behaviour question to estimate the value of improved water quality at Clear Lake in Iowa (USA). In addition to reporting how many visits they took in the past year, households surveyed were also asked how many trips they would have taken if water quality at the lake been improved, as per a contingent scenario described in the survey. The inclusion of a contingent behaviour question allowed the estimation of willingness to pay values for improvements in water quality at the lake. The average value of water quality improvements at Clear Lake was estimated to be around $140 per household per year for a small improvement and $350 per household per year for a large improvement. Analysis of the combined dataset typically involves stacking data from the two different sources and estimating a single model using the two types of observations.

Finally, the treatment of the opportunity cost of travel time in TCM models has become an area of active research in an attempt to overcome the limitations posed by the commonly used wage-based value of time assumptions (Czajkowski et al., 2015). Several authors have used stated preference methods to elicit stated values of time (Álvarez-Farizo, Hanley, and Barberán, 2001; Ovaskainen, Neuvonen, and Pouta, 2012; Czajkowski et al., 2015). Álvarez-Farizo et al. (2001) found a significant variation in leisure time values. Other authors have focused on revealed valuations of travel time. For example, Fezzi, Bateman, and Ferrini (2014) used a natural experiment to identify the value of time, where individuals had a choice of travelling via a toll road, which is faster, or not paying a toll and taking more time to reach the recreation site. Finally, Larson and Lew (2014) proposed a system of joint labour-recreation equations to capture the fact that the demand for time depends on whether individuals can freely substitute recreation for work or whether they have instead fixed work hours.

3.4. Averting behaviour and defensive expenditures method

Methods based on averting behaviour take as their main premise the notion that individuals and households can insulate themselves from a non-market bad by selecting more costly types of behavior (Dickie, 2017). These behaviours might be more costly in terms of the time requirements they imply, or of the restrictions they impose on what the individual would otherwise wish to do. Alternatively, individuals might be able to avoid exposure to non-market bads via the purchase of a market good. These financial outlays are known as defensive expenditures. The value of each of these purchases represents an implicit price for the non-market good or bad in question.

There are numerous instances which provide an illustration of these methods to value non-market goods and bads. Garrod and Willis (1999) offer the example of households installing double-glazed windows to decrease exposure to road traffic noise. Essentially, double-glazing is a market good which, in this example, acts as a substitute for a non-market good (peace and quiet, in the sense of the absence of road traffic noise). If noise levels decrease for other reasons – perhaps as a result of a local authority's implementation of traffic calming measures – then households will spend less on these defensive outlays. Changes in expenditures on this substitute good provide a good measure of households' valuations of traffic calming policies that decrease noise pollution (a bad) and, correspondingly, increase the supply of peace of quiet (a good). Many other examples exist as reviewed in Dickie (2017), the majority of which are applications to the valuation of reduced mortality and morbidity. Provins (2011) reviews recent empirical applications of the defensive expenditures method to value health impacts from water services, particularly focusing on drinking water quality. Box 3.5 summarises a well-known application to bicycle helmets and children safety (Jenkins, Owens and Wiggins, 2001).

Box 3.5. **Purchases of bicycle helmets and the value of children's safety**

There is growing policy interest in actions which reduce health risks to children and addressing how these benefits should be handled within a cost-benefit framework (see Chapter 15). A study by Jenkins, Owens and Wiggins (2001) provides a simple but interesting example of the application of a revealed preference approach – specifically defensive expenditure – to this question. The authors argue that there is no reason why it should simply be assumed that the value of reductions in, say, children's mortality risks can be approximated with reference to values derived in the context of mortality risks faced by adults. On the one hand, children have (on average) greater life years remaining than the typical adult in such studies. Furthermore, it is plausible that society places a premium on the safety of children, especially very young children. On the other hand, children are not currently economically productive nor will they be in the near future. In other words, Jenkins and colleagues argue that there are a number of reasons to believe that the value that society would choose to assign to a given mortality risk faced by a child will diverge (in possibly offsetting ways) from how an adult would value their own risk of death.

The case examined by Jenkins, Owens and Wiggins (2001) is the purchase of safety products that target children. Specifically, the authors look at the US market for bicycle helmets which significantly reduce the wearer's risk of death as a result of head injury. This product, they argue, has a number of desirable properties for indicating the implicit price of a person's safety. For example, the good provides a benefit to the wearer only (unlike other defensive purchases such as smoke alarms which protect all those living within a home). This is useful if what are wanted are values of reducing individual (as opposed to household) risks. In addition, the authors claim that bicycle helmets do not generate diverse joint products to the same extent as other defensive goods (such as air conditioning or double-glazed windows). This is not to say that complications do not exist. For example, a bicycle helmet not only protects its wearer from risk of fatal head injuries: clearly, it reduces the risk of non-fatal injury as well.

The basis of this study's use of the cost of bicycle helmets as a proxy for the value of fatal injury risk reduction is the assumption that a consumer purchases a helmet when his or her value for reducing risk is greater than the (net) cost of the product. Of course, in the case of the purchase of a child's helmet it is typically the parent that is the buyer and hence the decision-maker. In other words, Jenkins and colleagues are concerned with evaluating the revealed preferences of parents for their children's safety. To restate the logic of this approach in this context: a parent purchases a helmet when he or she perceives that the value of reducing risks to his or her child is greater than the (net) cost of the product. The authors use this insight as the basis for estimating the (implied) value of a statistical life for the typical helmet wearing bicycling child. This is defined as the (annualised) cost of the helmet divided by the change in the probability of death due to the purchase of the helmet.

Jenkins et al.'s study estimated that the value of a statistical life for US children aged 5 to 9 years old was roughly USD 2.9 million in 1997. The calculation underpinning this finding is the following. Firstly, it is reckoned that the annualised cost of a helmet is about USD 6.50. Secondly, the authors calculate that wearing helmets when cycling most (but not all) of the time amongst this age group results (nationally) in about 32 fewer deaths. Given

---

Box 3.5. **Purchases of bicycle helmets and the value of children's safety** (*cont.*)

that the 5 to 9 year old bicycle riding population was about 14.3 million in 1997, this gives an annual fatal risk reduction of 0.0000024: i.e. 32/14.3 million (or 1 in 446 875). The value of a statistical life for the typical 5 to 9 year old child of bicycle helmet purchasing parents is calculated as USD 6.50/0.0000024 or USD 2.9 million. Note that this assumes that the only benefit that the good provides is the reduction of fatal head injuries. In practice, wearing a helmet will reduce non-fatal head injury risks as well. The authors deal with this issue by arbitrarily assuming that the desire for reducing a child's risk of a fatal injury accounts for one half of the decision to purchase a helmet: i.e. multiply USD 2.9 million by 0.5 to obtain a more conservative figure for the value of statistical life of USD 1.5 million (GBP 933 000 in 2001 prices).

While the broad logic of this approach is sound, it assumes that helmet-buying parents are extremely well informed about the risks to children of cycling, and are motivated to purchase market goods which provide only apparently minor reductions in risk. It might be argued that, in reality, parents see an annual USD 6.50 as a small price to pay for *any* reduction in risk for their children. On the other hand, GBP 933 000 is not a high value of statistical life in comparison with estimates obtained via other market and non-market methods. This might then serve as a reminder that, through their purchases, parents are revealing a value of a statistical life (of their child) of *at least* this amount, when in practice, their maximum valuation might be a lot higher than this. In other words, the defensive expenditure approach reveals *lower-bound* estimates of the value of the non-market good in question.

Examples of defensive expenditure focus on the purchase of market goods which act as a substitute for a non-market good. However, individuals might change their behaviour in costly but perhaps less obvious ways in order to avoid an adverse impact on their well-being. Freeman et al. (2014) use the example of an individual who spends additional time indoors to avoid exposure to outdoor air pollution. In this case, the allocation of time to avoiding a non-market bad (i.e. the risk of adverse health impacts like asthma attacks, or coughing and sneezing episodes) is typically not observable and the substitute item is itself a non-market good (i.e. time that could have been used more productively). Nevertheless, the avoidance costs of spending time indoors could be evaluated by asking people directly about their time-use. Moreover, time use has a market analogue in the form of wages that would be paid to an individual if the time spent indoors could otherwise be spent working (see discussion of value of time in the travel cost method section above). Box 3.6 presents an example of the application of the method in the face of averting behaviour to reduce the health risks associated with air pollution (Bresnahan, Dickie and Gerking, 1997).

In terms of policy, the fact that individuals can take significant action to minimise their exposure to environmental risks and/or incur in defensive expenditures will have an impact on the measurement accuracy of the physical effect of the environmental risks. Accounting for these behavioural responses is therefore essential to accurately measure the effect of changes in environmental risks and provide information on the economic benefits of pollution control. Ignoring these actions can lead to severely biased estimates, namely an underestimation of the physical damage that would result from increases in environmental risk factors (Neidell, 2009; Dickie, 2017).

Box 3.6. **Averting behaviour and air quality in Los Angeles**

Bresnahan, Dickie and Gerking (1997) examine behaviour and changes in health risks. Specifically, these health risks arise from exposure to concentrations of ground-level ozone with sunlight (ground-level ozone in cities can arise from a combination of certain pollutants, emitted as a result of energy generation and use of motor vehicles). Acute health impairment particularly in response to peak concentrations of ozone has been documented in a number of epidemiological and medical studies. Moreover, the authors note that spending less time outdoors on bad air quality days – e.g. days when ozone concentrations exceed recommended standards – can effectively decrease exposure to pollution for certain at-risk groups. Their study seeks to evaluate the extent of actual defensive expenditure and averting behaviour amongst members of these groups living in the Los Angeles area.

Data were drawn from repeated survey responses of a sample of (non-smoking) Los Angeles residents living in areas with relatively high concentrations of local air pollutants. In addition, the sample contained a high proportion of individuals with compromised respiratory functions. Respondents were asked a range of questions about, for example, their health status, purchase of durable goods that might mitigate indoor exposure to ground-level ozone, their outdoor behaviour in general and on bad air quality days in particular.

The findings of the Bresnahan, Dickie and Gerking (1997) study were that two-thirds of their sample reported changing their behaviour in some meaningful way on days when air quality was poor. For example, 40% of respondents claimed either to re-arrange leisure activities or stay indoors during such days, and 20% of respondents increased their use of home air conditioning units. Furthermore, those respondents who experienced (acute) air pollution-related symptoms tended to spend less time outside on bad air quality days. Finally, The authors found tentative evidence that averting behaviour increases with medical costs that would otherwise be incurred if a respondent became ill.

In summary, bad air quality days appeared in this study to lead to significant changes in behavior (although these findings do not capture permanent decisions to take recreation indoors regardless of air quality on particular days). It is reasonable to speculate that these behavioural changes impose non-trivial economic costs on respondents. For example, these burdens might take the form of the purchase and running of air conditioning with an air purifying unit or the inconvenience imposed by spending time indoors. However, Bresnahan and colleagues do not attempt to put a monetary value on these actions. As Dickie and Gerking (2002) point out, this would not necessarily be a straightforward exercise. For example, and as we have already argued, time spent indoors avoiding exposure to air pollution is not necessarily time wasted. In other words, there is no simple way of valuing a person's time when time which an individual would have spent enjoying outdoor leisure activities is substituted for time spent enjoying indoor leisure activities.

3.4.1. Limitations

A number of complications arise in the practical application of averting behaviour and defensive expenditure approaches to valuing non-market goods. Dickie (2017) argues that the challenges confronting the method are responsible for its more limited impact on practical policy analysis when compared with that of other revealed preference methods discussed in this chapter.

Four problems in particular, are worth noting here. First, defensive expenditures typically represent a partial or lower bound estimate of the value of the impact of the non-market bad on well-being. For example, in the double-glazing case, greater indoor tranquillity may be achieved, but gardens will still be exposed to road traffic noise at the same levels, so double-glazing will not help homeowners to avoid the costs of road traffic noise completely. Moreover, households' willingness-to-pay for tranquillity might exceed what they paid for double glazing.

Second, many averting behaviours or defensive expenditures create joint products. For instance, time spent indoors avoiding air pollution is not otherwise wasted. This time can also be put to other productive uses that have value, such as undertaking household chores, indoor leisure activities or working from home. The double-glazing case also creates joint products – e.g. energy conservation. It is the *net* cost of the expenditure or change in behaviour – that is, the cost after taking account of the value of alternative uses of time, for instance, or energy savings – which is the correct measure of the value of the associated reduction in the non-market bad. However, distinguishing the determinant of behaviour that is of interest, and the costs of the various components, might not be an easy matter in practice.

Third, it is not easy to assign a monetary value to behavioural changes associated with defensive actions. Dickie (2017) cites the example of keeping a child indoors to avoid exposure to outdoor air pollution. The monetary cost of keeping a child indoors rather than outdoors is not easily estimated, particularly as the wage-based value of time approach would not be applicable for children.

Finally, it can be difficult to causally identify the effects of the disamenity and of averting behaviour on the outcome of interest, in the presence of unobserved factors related to both the behaviour and the outcome (Dickie, 2017). Consider again the case of health and the defensive behaviour where children are kept indoors to avoid exposure to outdoor air pollution. Some children will have poorer health and be more susceptible to air pollution, and might therefore be kept indoors more often. When there are unobserved effects (i.e. an omitted variable), such as children's heterogeneous natural resistance to illness, that are related to both the health outcome and the averting behaviour, then the impact of pollution on health and the impact of averting behaviour on health are both badly measured due to endogeneity. The problem of causal identification of the effect of the disamenity, and of the behaviour on the outcome of interest, is one of the key challenges of the averting behaviour approach.

3.4.2. Recent developments

As was the case with other revealed preference methods discussed in this chapter, there have been some significant econometric developments of relevance for the averting behaviour approach. In particular, recent years have witnessed improvements in causal identification strategies. Together with the increasing availability of detailed and comprehensive data sets, namely on health and pollution (e.g. Deschênes and Greenstone, 2011; Ziving et al., 2011), these developments are expected to lead to more accurate estimations and consequently, growing influence of averting behaviour methods in applied policy analysis.

There are many examples of econometric approaches used to tackle the identification challenge. For example, Neidell (2009) investigates the behavioural response to the provision of information about asthma risks associated with exposure to ozone in Southern California. To identify the effect of information provided via smog alerts, a regression discontinuity design is employed, by exploiting the deterministic selection rule used for issuing the alerts.

The author finds that smog alerts significantly reduce daily attendance at two large outdoor facilities: the Los Angeles Zoo and the Griffith Park Observatory. Then, using daily time-series regression models, that include time and area fixed effects, Neidell examines the impact of ozone on asthma hospitalisations. He finds that the estimates of the effect of ozone on hospital admissions of children and the elderly, accounting for the information effects, are significantly larger than estimates where such effects are not considered (by about 160 per cent for children and 40 per cent for the elderly). The author concludes that failure to account for the substantial actions that individuals may take to reduce their exposure to air pollution in the face of information, such as decreasing the amount of time spent outside, will lead to biased estimates of air pollution damages.

Deschênes and Greenstone (2011) estimate the impact of climate change on mortality, and the impact of defensive expenditures against the impacts of climate change. Energy consumption (via air conditioning, used to protect against high temperatures) is utilised as the measure of self-protection. The analysis benefits from a large comprehensive dataset on mortality, energy consumption, weather, and climate change predictions for the whole continental United States. The identification strategy to deal with possible omitted variable bias relies on random yearly local variation in temperature, and the statistical models used include county and state-by-year fixed effects to adjust for differences in unobserved health across the country, due to sorting. The authors find a statistically significant relationship between mortality and daily temperatures, with extremely cold and hot days being associated with elevated mortality rates. But the effect is smaller than what would be predicted based on previous heat waves. Deschênes and Greenstone also find substantial heterogeneity in the behavioural responses to extreme temperatures across the country. They conclude that the weaker than expected mortality-temperature relationship is at least partially due to the self-protection provided by individuals' avertive (cooling) behavior, as reflected in increased energy consumption.

Finally, a number of authors have started to combine averting expenditures/defensive behavior methods with stated preference methods (e.g. Rosado et al., 2006), and/or attitudinal/perception data from survey questions. As an example of the latter, Lanz (2015) investigates averting expenditures to deal with tap water hardness and aesthetic quality in terms of taste and odour. The averting expenditures include water softener devices, bottled water, water filter devices, or adding squash or cordial before drinking water. Via a survey, he finds that 39% of respondents report at least one such behaviour, with mean yearly expenditure around GBP 92 (substantial vis-à-vis a yearly average household bill of GBP 186 for water services). Lanz argues that it is the *perceived* (rather than actual) failure to reach the desired water quality that will determine these averting expenditures: failure to control for perceptions may therefore generate biased estimates. To fix this, he includes information on both objective and perceived water quality (elicited through the survey). Unobserved factors might affect both the averting behaviour and the water quality perception, leading to biased identification of marginal WTP. To control for this possible endogeneity, Lanz models the relationship between objective and subjective water quality in a first stage regression, and then includes instrumented subjective quality as part of the valuation function. Results confirm that perceived water quality is endogenous, and the associated marginal WTP estimates are biased downwards; instrumenting perceived quality with objective quality yields marginal WTP estimates that are approximately two times higher for water hardness and three times higher for aesthetic quality.

3.5. Conclusions

Economists have developed a range of approaches to estimate the economic value of non-market or intangible impacts. Those which we have considered in this chapter share the common feature of using market information and behaviour to infer the economic value of an associated non-market impact.

These approaches have different conceptual bases. Methods based on hedonic pricing utilise the fact that some market goods are in fact bundles of characteristics, some of which are intangible goods (or bads). By trading these market goods, consumers are thereby able to express their values for the intangible goods, and these values can be uncovered through the use of statistical techniques. This process can be hindered, however, by the fact that a market good can have several intangible characteristics, and that these can be collinear. It can also be difficult to measure the intangible characteristics in a meaningful way. Moreover, the potential for omitted variables and consequent misspecification of the hedonic price function is an on-going concern.

Travel cost and random utility methods utilise the fact that market and intangible goods can be complements, to the extent that purchase of market goods and services is required to access an intangible good. Specifically, people have to spend time and money travelling to recreational sites, and these costs reveal something of the value of the recreational experience to those people incurring them. The situation is complicated, however, by the presence of substitute sites, the fact that travel itself can have value, that some of the costs are themselves intangible (e.g. the opportunity costs of time), and that many trips are multipurpose.

Averting behaviour and defensive expenditure approaches are similar to the previous two, but differ to the extent that they refer to individual behaviour to avoid negative intangible impacts. Therefore, people might buy goods such as safety helmets to reduce accident risk, and double-glazing to reduce traffic noise, thereby revealing their valuation of these bads. However, again the situation is complicated by the fact that these market goods might have more benefits than simply that of reducing an intangible bad. Averting behaviour occurs when individuals take costly actions to avoid exposure to a non-market bad (which might, for instance, include additional travel costs to avoid a risky way of getting from A to B). Again, we need to take account of the fact that valuing these alternative actions might not be a straightforward task, for instance, if time which would have been spent doing one thing is instead used to do something else, not only avoiding exposure to the non-market impact in question, but also producing valuable economic outputs. Moreover, it is often difficult to causally identify the effects of the disamenity and of the averting behaviour on the outcome of interest.

This chapter has shown that revealed preference methods are widely used, in a range of environmental policy applications. Recent decades have witnessed substantial developments particularly in the sophistication of the econometric methods used to elicit causal relationships, in the detail, accuracy and comprehensive nature of the available data sets, and in methods being used in combination. Overall, we find that methods where the value of the environmental good or service is inferred through observations from real world market purchases have the potential to play a central role in policy analysis.

References

Adamowicz, W.L., J. Louviere and M. Williams (1994), "Combining Revealed and Stated Preference Methods for Valuing Environmental Amenities", *Journal of Environmental Economics and Management*, Vol. 26, pp. 271-292, *https://doi.org/10.1006/jeem.1994.1017*.

Álvarez-Farizo, B., N. Hanley and R. Barberán (2001), "The Value of Leisure Time: A Contingent Rating Approach", *Journal of Environmental Planning & Management*, Vol. 44/5, pp. 681-699, *http://dx.doi.org/10.1080/09640560120079975*.

Andersson, H., L. Jonsson and M. Ogren (2009), "Property Prices and Exposure to Multiple Noise Sources: Hedonic Regression with Road and Railway Noise", *Environmental and Resource Economics*, Vol. 45/1, pp. 73-89, *http://dx.doi.org/10.1007/s10640-009-9306-4*.

Anderson, L.M. and H.K. Cordell (1985), "Residential property values improve by landscaping with trees", *Southern Journal of Applied Forestry*, Vol. 9, pp. 162-166.

Bayer, P., N. Keohane and C. Timmins (2009), "Migration and hedonic valuation: The case of air quality", *Journal of Environmental Economics & Management*, Vol. 58, pp. 1-14, *https://doi.org/10.1016/j.jeem.2008.08.004*.

Beltrán-Hernández, A. (2016), "Essays on the economic valuation of flood risks", *PhD Thesis*, University of Birmingham.

Benson, E.D. et al. (1998), "Pricing residential amenities: The value of a view", *Journal of Real Estate Economics Finance*, Vol. 16, pp. 55-73, *http://dx.doi.org/10.1023/A:1007785315925*.

Bockstael, N.E. and K. McConnell (2007), *Environmental and Resource Valuation with Revealed Preferences*, Springer, Netherlands, *http://dx.doi.org/10.1007/978-1-4020-5318-4*.

Bockstael, N.E., W.M. Hanemann and C.L. Kling (1987), "Estimating the value of water quality improvements in a recreational demand framework", *Water Resources Research*, Vol. 23, pp. 951-960.

Bolitzer, B. and N.R. Netusil (2000), "The impact of open space on property values in Portland, Oregon", *Journal of Environmental Management*, Vol. 59/3, pp. 185-193, *http://dx.doi.org/10.1006/jema.2000.0351*.

Boyle, K.J. (2003), "Introduction to revealed preference methods", in Champ, P.A., K.J. Boyle and T.C. Brown (eds.) (2003), *A Primer on Nonmarket Valuation*, Kluwer, Dordrecht.

Boyle, K.J., P.J. Poor and L.O. Taylor (1999), "Estimating the demand for protecting freshwater lakes from eutrophication", *American Journal of Agricultural Economics*, Vol. 81/5, pp. 1118-1122, *https://doi.org/10.2307/1244094*.

Bresnahan, B.W., M. Dickie and S. Gerking (1997), "Averting behaviour and urban air pollution", *Land Economics*, Vol. 73/3, pp. 340-357.

Cesario, F.J. (1976), "Value of Time in Recreation Benefit Studies", *Land Economics*, Vol. 52/1, pp. 32-41.

Chakraborty, K. and J.E. Keith (2000), "Estimating the Recreation Demand and Economic Value of Mountain Biking in Moab, Utah: An Application of Count Data Models", *Journal of Environmental Planning & Management*, Vol. 43/4, pp. 461-469, *http://dx.doi.org/10.5367/000000006776387097*.

Chay, K.Y. and M. Greenstone (2005), "Does air quality matter? Evidence from the housing market", *Journal of Political Economy*, Vol. 113, pp. 376-424, *https://doi.org/10.1086/427462*.

Czajkowski, M. et al. (2015), "The Individual Travel Cost Method with Consumer-Specific Values of Travel Time Savings", Faculty of Economic Sciences, *University of Warsaw Working Papers* 12/2015(160), *www.wne.uw.edu.pl/files/6714/2651/1660/WNE_WP160.pdf*.

Cheshire, P.C. and S. Sheppard (1995), "On the Price of Land and the Value of Amenities", *Economica*, Vol. 62, pp. 247-267.

Cheshire, P.C. and S. Sheppard, (1998), "Estimating the demand for housing, land and neighbourhood characteristics", *Oxford Bulletin of Economics and Statistics*, Vol. 60, pp. 357-382, *http://dx.doi.org/10.1111/1468-0084.00104*.

Cheshire, P.C. and S. Sheppard (2002), "The welfare economics of land use planning", *Journal of Urban Economics*, Vol. 52, pp. 242-269, *https://doi.org/10.1016/S0094-1190(02)00003-7*.

Christie M. et al. (2006), *Valuing forest recreation activities*, Report to the UK Forestry Commission. *www.forestry.gov.uk/pdf/vfrfcfinalreportv5.pdf/$file/vfrfcfinalreportv5.pdf*.

Clawson, M. and J.L. Knetsch (1969), *Economics of Outdoor Recreation*, John Hopkins University, Baltimore.

Correll, M.R., J.H. Lillydahl and L.D. Singell (1978), "The Effects of Greenbelts on Residential Property Values: Some Findings on the Political Economy of Open Space", *Land Economics*, Vol. 54, pp. 207-17.

Corrigan, J.R., K.J. Egan, and J.A. Downing (2007), "Aesthetic Values of Lakes and Rivers", in Likens, G.E. (ed.), *Encyclopedia of Inland Waters*, Elsevier, Amsterdam.

Creel, M. and J. B. Loomis (1990), "Theoretical and empirical advantages of truncated count data estimators for analysis of deer hunting in California", *American Journal of Agricultural Economics*, Vol. 72, pp. 434-441.

Cropper, M.L., L.B. Deck and K.E. McConnell (1988), "On the choice of functional form for hedonic price functions", *Review of Economics & Statistics*, Vol. 70, pp. 668-675.

Davis, L.W. (2011), "The effect of power plants on local housing values and rents", *Review of Economics and Statistics*, Vol. 93/4, pp. 1391-1402, *http://dx.doi.org/10.1162/REST_a_00119*.

Day, B. (2002), "Valuing visits to game parks in South Africa," in Pearce, D.W., C. Pearce and P. Palmer (eds.) *Valuing the Environment in Developing Countries: Case Studies*, Edward Elgar, Cheltenham.

Day, B., I. Bateman and I. Lake (2006), "Estimating the demand for peace and quiet using property market data", *CSERGE Working Paper* EDM 06-03, University of East Anglia, *www.econstor.eu/bitstream/10419/80288/1/511176120.pdf*.

Deschênes, O. and M. Greenstone (2011), "Climate Change, Mortality, and Adaptation: Evidence from Annual Fluctuations in Weather in the US", *American Economic Journal: Applied Economics*, Vol. 3/4, pp. 152-185, *http://dx.doi.org/10.1257/app.3.4.152*.

Dickie, M. (2017), "Averting Behavior Methods", in Champ, P.A. K.J. Boyle and T.C. Brown (eds.) *A Primer on Nonmarket Valuation, 2nd Edition*, Kluwer, Dordrecht.

Dickie, M. and S. Gerking (2002), "Willingness to Pay for Reduced Morbidity", *Department of Economics Working Paper* 02-07, University of Central Florida.

Doss, C.R. and S.J. Taff (1996), "The Influence of Wetland Type and Wetland Proximity on Residential Property Values", *Journal of Agricultural and Resource Economics*, Vol. 21/1, pp. 120-29, *https://core.ac.uk/download/pdf/7060414.pdf*.

Earnhart, D. (2001), "Combining revealed and stated preference methods to value environmental amenities at residential locations", *Land Economics*, Vol. 77/1, pp. 12-29.

Englin, J. and T. Cameron (1996), "Augmenting travel cost models with contingent behaviour data", *Environmental & Resource Economics*, Vol. 7/2, pp. 133-147, *http://dx.doi.org/10.1007/BF00699288*.

Fezzi, C., I. J. Bateman and S. Ferrini (2014), "Using revealed preferences to estimate the Value of Travel Time to recreation sites", *Journal of Environmental Economics and Management*, Vol. 67/1, pp. 58-70, *https://doi.org/10.1016/j.jeem.2013.10.003*.

Freeman, A.M. III, J.A. Herriges and C.L. Kling (2014), *The Measurement of Environmental and Resource Values*, 3rd Edition, Resources for the Future, Washington, DC.

Garrod, G.D. and K.G. Willis (1992), "The Environmental Economic Impact of Woodland: A Two State Hedonic Price Model of the Amenity Value of Forestry in Britain", *Applied Economics*, Vol. 24/7, pp. 715-28, *http://dx.doi.org/10.1007/BF00304970*.

Garrod, G.D. and K.G. Willis (1999), *Economic Valuation of the Environment*, Edward Elgar Publishing Ltd., Cheltenham.

Geoghegan, J. (2002), "The value of open spaces in residential land use", *Land Use Policy*, Vol. 19/1, pp. 91-98.

Gibbons, S. (2015), "Gone with the Wind: Valuing the visual impacts of wind turbines through house prices", *Journal of Environmental Economics and Management*, Vol. 72, pp. 177-196, *https://doi.org/10.1016/j.jeem.2015.04.006*.

Gibbons, S. et al. (2016), "Fear of Fracking? The Impact of the Shale Gas Exploration on House Prices in Britain", *SERC Discussion Paper 207*, London School of Economics & Political Science, London, *www.spatialeconomics.ac.uk/textonly/SERC/publications/download/sercdp0207.pdf*.

Gibbons, S., S. Mourato and G. Resende (2014), "The amenity value of English nature: A hedonic price approach", *Environmental and Resource Economics*, Vol. 57, pp. 175-196, *http://dx.doi.org/10.1007/s10640-013-9664-9*.

Gustafson, C.R., T.J. Lybbert and D.A. Sumner (2011), "Consumer Characteristics, Identification, and Hedonic Valuation of Wine Attributes: Exploiting Data from a Field Experiment", Centre for Wine Economics, *RMI-CWE Working Paper* Number 1102, *http://ageconsearch.umn.edu/record/162517/files/cwe1102.pdf*.

Heberling, M. and J. Templeton (2009), "Estimating the economic value of national parks with count data models using on-site, secondary data: The case of the great sand dunes national park and preserve", *Environmental Management*, Vol. 43/4, pp. 619-627, *http://dx.doi.org/10.1007/s00267-008-9149-8*.

Herath, S. and G. Maier (2010), "The hedonic price method in real estate and housing market research. A review of the literature", *SRE – Discussion Papers*, 2010/03, WU Vienna University of Economics and Business, Vienna, *http://epub.wu.ac.at/588/1/sre-disc-2010_03.pdf*.

Hoen, B. et al. (2011), "Wind energy facilities and residential properties: The effect of proximity and view on sales prices", *Journal of Real Estate Research*, Vol. 33/3, pp. 279-316, *http://pages.jh.edu/jrer/papers/pdf/past/vol33n03/01.279_316.pdf*.

Horsch, E.J. and D.J. Lewis (2009), "The Effects of Aquatic Invasive Species on Property Values: Evidence from a Quasi-Experiment", *Land Economics*, Vol. 85/3, pp. 391-409, *http://dx.doi.org/10.3368/le.85.3.391*.

Jenkins, R.R., N. Owens and L.B. Wiggins (2001), "Valuing reduced risks to children: The case of bicycle safety helmets", *Contemporary Economic Policy*, Vol. 19/4, pp. 397-408, *http://dx.doi.org/10.1093/cep/19.4.397*.

Kolstad, C.D. (2010), *Environmental Economics*, 2nd Edition, Oxford University Press, Oxford.

Kong F., H. Yin and N. Nakagoshi (2007), "Using GIS and landscape metrics in the hedonic price modeling of the amenity value of urban green space: A case study in Jinan City, China", *Landscape & Urban Planning*, Vol. 79, pp. 240-252, *http://dx.doi.org/10.1016/j.landurbplan.2006.02.013*.

Kuminoff, N.V., C.F. Parmeter and J.C. Pope (2010), "Which hedonic models can we trust to recover the marginal willingness to pay for environmental amenities?", *Journal of Environmental Economics and Management*, Vol. 60, pp. 145-160, *http://dx.doi.org/10.1016/j.jeem.2010.06.001*.

Landry C. and P. Hindsley (2011), "Valuing beach quality with hedonic property models", *Land Economics*, Vol. 87/1, pp. 92-108, *http://dx.doi.org/10.3368/le.87.1.92*.

Landry, C.E. and H. Liu (2011), "Econometric Models for Joint Estimation of Revealed and Stated Preference Site-Frequency Recreation Demand Models", in Whitehead, J., T. Haab and J.-C. Huang (eds.) (2011) *Preference Data for Environmental Valuation: Combining Revealed and Stated Approaches*, Routledge, London.

Lanz, B. (2015), "Avertive expenditures, endogenous quality perception, and the demand for public goods: An instrumental variable approach", *Research Paper* 36, Graduate Institute Geneva, *http://repec.graduateinstitute.ch/pdfs/ciesrp/CIES_RP_36.pdf*.

Larson, D.M. and D.K. Lew (2014), "The opportunity cost of travel time as a noisy wage fraction", *American Journal of Agricultural Economics*, Vol. 96/2, pp. 420-437, *https://doi.org/10.1093/ajae/aat093*.

Lee, C.M. and P. Linneman (1998), "Dynamics of the Greenbelt Amenity Effect on the land market: The case of Seoul's greenbelt", *Real Estate Economics*, Vol. 26/1, pp. 107-29.

Leggett, C.G. and N.E. Bockstael (2000), "Evidence of the effects of water quality on residential land prices", *Journal of Environmental Economics and Management*, Vol. 39/2, pp. 121-44, *https://doi.org/10.1006/jeem.1999.1096*.

Le Goffe, P. (2000), "Hedonic pricing of agriculture and forestry externalities", *Environmental and Resource Economics*, Vol. 15/4, pp. 397- 401, *http://dx.doi.org/10.1023/A:1008383920586*.

Luttik, J. (2000), "The value of trees, water and open space as reflected by house prices in the Netherlands", *Landscape and Urban Planning*, Vol. 48/3-4, pp. 161-167, *https://doi.org/10.1016/S0169-2046(00)00039-6*.

Neidell, M. (2009), "Information, avoidance behavior, and health: The effect of ozone on asthma hospitalizations", *Journal of Human Resources*, Vol. 44/2, pp. 450-478, *http://dx.doi.org/10.3368/jhr.44.2.450*.

Maddison, D. and B. Day (2015), *Improving Cost-Benefit Analysis Guidance: A Report to the Natural Capital Committee*, London, UK: Natural Capital Committee, *www.gov.uk/government/uploads/system/uploads/attachment_data/file/517027/ncc-research-improving-cost-benefit-guidance-final-report.pdf*.

Mahan, B.L., S. Polasky and R.M. Adams (2000), "Valuing urban wetlands: A property price approach", *Land Economics*, Vol. 76, pp. 100-113.

Marin, A. and G. Psacharopoulos (1982), "The reward for risk in the labor market: Evidence from the United Kingdom and a reconciliation with other studies", *Journal of Political Economy*, Vol. 90/4, pp. 827-853.

McCluskey, J.J. and G.C. Rausser (2003), "Stigmatized asset value: Is it temporary or long-term?", *Review of Economics & Statistics*, Vol. 85, pp. 276-28, *http://dx.doi.org/10.1162/003465303765299800*.

81

McConnell, V. and M. Walls (2005), *The value of open space: Evidence from studies of nonmarket behavior*, Resources for the Future, Washington, DC, *www.rff.org/files/sharepoint/WorkImages/Download/RFF-REPORT-Open%20Spaces.pdf*.

Morales, D.J. (1980), "The contribution of trees to residential property value", *Journal of Arboriculture*, Vol. 7, pp. 109-12.

Morales, D.J., F.R. Micha and R.L. Weber (1983), "Two Methods of Valuating Trees on Residential Sites", *Journal of Arboriculture*, Vol. 9, pp. 21-24.

Morancho, A.B. (2003), "A hedonic valuation of urban green areas", *Landscape and Urban Planning*, Vol. 66/1, pp. 35-41, *http://dx.doi.org/10.1016/S0169-2046(03)00093-8*.

Muehlenbachs, L., E. Spiller and C. Timmins (2015), "The Housing Market Impacts of Shale Gas Development", *American Economic Review*, Vol. 105/12, pp. 3633-3659, *http://dx.doi.org/10.1257/aer.20140079*.

Netusil, N.R. (2005), "The effect of environmental zoning and amenities on property values: Portland, Oregon", *Land Economics*, Vol. 81/2, pp. 227-246, *http://dx.doi.org/10.3368/le.81.2.227*.

Netusil, N.R., S. Chattopadhyay and K.F. Kovacs (2010), "Estimating the demand for tree canopy: A second-stage hedonic price analysis in Portland, Oregon", *Land Economics*, Vol. 86/2, pp. 281-293, *http://dx.doi.org/10.3368/le.86.2.281*.

Noor, N.M., M.Z. Asmawi and A. Abdullah (2015), "Sustainable Urban Regeneration: GIS and Hedonic Pricing Method in determining the value of green space in housing area", *Procedia – Social and Behavioral Sciences*, Vol. 170, pp. 669-679, *https://doi.org/10.1016/j.sbspro.2015.01.069*.

Ovaskainen, V., M. Neuvonen and E. Pouta (2012), "Modelling recreation demand with respondent-reported driving cost and stated cost of travel time: A Finnish case", *Journal of Forest Economics*, Vol. 18/4, pp. 303-317, *https://doi.org/10.1016/j.jfe.2012.06.001*.

Palmquist, R.B. (1992), "Valuing localized externalities", *Journal of Urban Economics*, Vol. 31, pp. 59-68.

Parsons, G.R (2017), "The Travel Cost Model", in Champ, P.A., K.J. Boyle and T.C. Brown (eds.) (2017) *A Primer on Nonmarket Valuation, 2nd Edition*, Kluwer, Dordrecht, *www.springer.com/us/book/9781402014451*.

Paterson, R.W. and K.J. Boyle (2002), "Out of sight, out of mind? Using GIS to incorporate visibility in hedonic property value model", *Land Economics*, Vol. 78/3, pp. 417-425, *http://dx.doi.org/10.2307/3146899*.

Pearson, L.J., C. Tisdell and A.T. Lisle (2002), "The impact of Noosa National Park on surrounding property values: An application of the hedonic price method", *Economic Analysis & Policy*, Vol. 32/2, pp. 155-171, *https://doi.org/10.1016/S0313-5926(02)50023-0*.

Phaneuf, D.J. and V.K. Smith, (2005), "Chapter 15: Recreation demand models", in: Mäler, K. and J. Vincent (eds.) (2005), *Handbook of Environmental Economics*, pp. 671-761, *http://dx.doi.org/10.1016/S1574-0099(05)02015-2*.

Poor, P.J., K.L. Pessagnob and R.W. Paul (2007), "Exploring the hedonic value of ambient water quality: A local watershed-based study", *Ecological Economics*, Vol. 60/4, pp. 797-807, *http://dx.doi.org/10.1016/j.ecolecon.2006.02.013*.

Pope, J.C. (2008a), "Buyer information and the hedonic: The impact of a seller disclosure on the implicit price for airport noise", *Journal of Urban Economics*, Vol. 63/2, pp. 498-516, *http://dx.doi.org/10.1016/j.jue.2007.03.003*.

Pope, J.C. (2008b), "Do seller disclosures affect property values? Buyer information and the hedonic model", *Land Economics*, Vol. 84/4, pp. 551-572, *http://dx.doi.org/10.3368/le.84.4.551*.

Provins, A. (2011), *The Use of Revealed Customer Behaviour in Future Price Limits*, Final Report to Ofwat, Eftec and Cascade Consulting, *www.ofwat.gov.uk/wp-content/uploads/2015/11/rpt_com_201105eftec_casc_reveal.pdf*.

Randall, A. (2014), "Weak sustainability, conservation and precaution", in Atkinson, G. et al. (eds.) *Handbook of Sustainable Development*, Edward Elgar Publishing, Cheltenham.

Ridker, R.B. and J.A. Henning (1967), "The determinants of residential property values with special reference to air pollution", *Review of Economics and Statistics*, Vol. 49/2, pp. 246-257.

Rosado, M. et al. (2006), "Combining averting behavior and contingent valuation data: An application to drinking water treatment in Brazil", *Environment & Development Economics*, Vol. 11/6, pp. 729-746, *https://doi.org/10.1017/S1355770X0600324X*.

Rosen, S. (1974), "Hedonic prices and implicit markets: Product differentiation in pure competition", *Journal of Political Economy*, Vol. 82/1, pp. 34-55.

Russell, C.S. (2001), *Applying Economics to the Environment*, Oxford University Press, Oxford.

Shrestha, R.K., A.F. Seidl and A.S. Moraes (2002), "Value of recreational fishing in the Brazilian Pantanal: A travel cost analysis using count data models", *Ecological Economics*, Vol. 42/1, pp. 289-299, *https://doi.org/10.1016/S0921-8009(02)00106-4*.

Smith, V.K. and J. Huang (1995), "Can markets value air quality? A meta-analysis of hedonic property value models", *Journal of Political Economy* 103, pp. 209-227, *https://doi.org/10.1086/261981*.

Steriani, M.K. and K.P. Soutsas (2005), "Recreation demand model construction through the use of regression analysis with optimal scaling", *New Medit*, Vol. 4, pp. 25-30, *http://newmedit.iamb.it/share/img_new_medit_articoli/116_25steriani.pdf*.

Thorsnes, P. (2002), "The value of a suburban forest preserve: Estimates from sales of vacant residential building lots", *Land Economics*, Vol. 78/3, pp. 426-441, *http://dx.doi.org/10.2307/3146900*.

Tyrvainen, L. and A. Miettinen (2000), "Property prices and urban forest amenities", *Journal of Environmental Economics and Management*, Vol. 39/2, pp. 205-223, *http://dx.doi.org/10.1006/jeem.1999.1097*.

Walsh, P.J., J.W. Milon and D.O. Scrogin (2011), "The spatial extent of water quality benefits in urban housing markets", *Land Economics*, Vol. 87/4, pp. 628-644, *http://dx.doi.org/10.3368/le.87.4.628*.

Whitehead, J.C., T.C. Haab and J.-C. Huang (2000), "Measuring recreation benefits of quality improvements with revealed and stated behavior data", *Resource & Energy Economics*, Vol. 22/4, pp. 339-354, *https://doi.org/10.1016/S0928-7655(00)00023-3*.

Wilhelmsson, M. (2000), "The impact of traffic noise on the values of single-family houses", *Journal of Environmental Planning and Management*, Vol. 43, pp. 799-815, *http://dx.doi.org/10.1080/09640560020001692*.

Yusuf, H.R. et al. (1996), "Leisure-time physical activity among older adults, United States, 1990", *Archives of Internal Medicine*, Vol. 156, pp. 1321-1326, *http://dx.doi.org/10.1001/archinte.1996.00440110093012*.

Zivin, J.G., M. Neidell and W. Schlenker (2011), "Water quality violations and avoidance behavior: Evidence from bottled water consumption", *American Economic Review*, Vol. 101/3, pp. 448-453, *http://dx.doi.org/10.1257/aer.101.3.448*.

PART I

Chapter 4

Contingent valuation method

The contingent valuation (CV) method is a stated preference approach where respondents are asked directly for their willingness to pay (or willingness to accept compensation) for a hypothetical change in the level of provision of a non-market good. CV is applicable to a wide range of situations, including future changes and changes involving non-use values. As this chapter documents, there is now a wealth of experience that can be gleaned from the literature on CV that can guide current thinking about good survey design and robust valuation. This is critical as the central debate remains regarding the method's validity, manifesting itself in discussions about specific problems and biases. Increasingly some of these problems are being investigated in the light of findings from research on behavioural economics. Other significant developments, notably the rise of on-line surveys, have been important in enabling more extensive applications, and further testing of biases and possible bias reduction mechanisms.

4.1. Introduction

The contingent valuation (CV) method is a survey-based stated preference technique that elicits people's intended future behaviour in constructed markets. In a contingent valuation questionnaire, a hypothetical market is described where the good in question can be traded. This contingent market defines the good itself, the institutional context in which it would be provided, and the way it would be financed. Respondents are asked directly for their willingness-to-pay (or willingness-to-accept) for a hypothetical change in the level of provision of the good (Mitchell and Carson, 1989). Respondents are assumed to behave as though they were in a real market.

One of the strengths of stated preference methods lies in their flexibility. Because of its hypothetical nature and non-reliance on existing markets, the contingent valuation method is applicable, in principle, to almost all non-market goods, to past changes and future changes, and is one of the few available methodologies able to capture *all* types of benefits from a non-market good or service, including those unrelated to current or future use, i.e. so-called non-use values.

The CV idea was first introduced by von Ciriacy-Wantrup (1947) and the first application was undertaken by Davis (1963) valuing the benefits attached to outdoor recreation. Over time, CV became the dominant stated preference method, extensively applied to the valuation of a wide range of non-market changes both in developed and developing countries: water quality, outdoor recreation, species preservation, forest protection, air quality, visual amenity, waste management, sanitation improvements, biodiversity, health impacts, natural resource damage, environmental risk reductions, cultural heritage, and new energy technologies, to list but a few. Much of the impetus to this expansion were the conclusions of the special panel appointed by the US National Oceanic and Atmospheric Administration (NOAA) in 1993 (Arrow et al., 1993) following the Exxon Valdez oil spill in Alaska in 1989 (Nelson, 2017). The panel concluded that, subject to a number of best-practice recommendations, CV studies could produce estimates reliable enough to be used in a judicial process of natural resource damage assessment. And despite criticism from some quarters at the time (e.g. Diamond and Hausman, 1994), the number of contingent valuation studies has increased substantially since. In 2011, Carson published an annotated bibliography of contingent valuation studies (published and unpublished): it contained over 7 500 entries from over 130 countries (Carson, 2011). And a search on the Web of Science for publications using the search term "contingent valuation" produced almost 6 000 hits as of January 2017.

It is now almost twenty-five years since the NOAA deliberations and it is no exaggeration to say that a discussion of methodological tests and developments in the field of stated preference methods and contingent valuation in particular, could command several volumes. The intervening years have seen stated preference research being applied routinely in policy. Government-commissioned guidelines now exist for using these methods to inform UK public policy in general (Bateman et al., 2002), and also specific guidance for particular sectors (e.g. Bakhshi et al., 2015, for the UK cultural sector). State-of-the-art guidance on most aspects of non-market (environmental) valuation for the United States has also been published (Champ et al., 2003). The most recent contemporary guidance for stated preference studies can be found in Johnston et al. (2017).

Developments have not been restricted only to the application of these tools in the field of environmental economics. There has also been important cross-fertilisation with, for example, health economics and, more recently, cultural economics, sports economics and other areas of public policy. Moreover, research in stated preference methods has also played a role in advancing the whole field of economics. According to Kerry Smith (2006), "Contingent valuation has prompted the most serious investigation of individual preferences that has ever been undertaken in economics" (p. 46). Notably, the recent rise to prominence of behavioural and experimental economics owes much to the research around investigating anomalies in stated preference methods (Carson and Hanemann, 2005; Carlsson, 2010; Nelson, 2017). Most promisingly, much more is now known about in what circumstances stated preference methods work well – in terms of resulting in valid and reliable findings – and where problems can be expected. Behavioural economics research has shown that some of the anomalies that were first detected in hypothetical markets also occur in real-markets and are an inescapable feature of how people behave and react to incentives and information (rather than resulting from shortcomings specific to CV). Such findings have had an important bearing on progressing best practice in how to design a contingent valuation questionnaire.

However, despite thousands of studies, numerous methodological developments and widespread policy application, contingent valuation remains a source of controversy. Long-time critics, like Jerry Hausman, remain unconvinced about the merits of stated preferences and of CV in particular. In 1994, Diamond and Hausman published a much-cited critique of CVM (Diamond and Hausman, 1994), where doubts were expressed about its validity with a focus on scope insensitivity. More recently, in 2012, Hausman updated his concerns in a blunt set of criticisms, where he contends that CV is a "hopeless" technique, despite all the wealth of experiences and advances in the intermediating years (Hausman, 2012). Hausman remains worried about three well-known potential limitations of CV, namely hypothetical bias, insensitivity to scope and disparity between WTP and WTA. After performing a "selective" review of CV studies he concludes that respondents "invent their answers on the fly" and that "no number is still better than a contingent valuation number". Controversially, Hausman goes on to defend the use of experts for the creation of economic values. Detailed discussion and counterarguments can be found in Kling et al. (2012), Carson (2012) and Haab et al. (2013).

This chapter seeks to distil some of the recent important developments in contingent valuation, and in that light, critically reviews the evidence on its validity. Section 4.2 summarises the conceptual framework. Section 4.3 discusses and evaluates a number of key points that guide good survey design, on the basis that valid and reliable estimates of non-market values are far more likely to emerge from studies which draw on the wealth of experience that can be gleaned from the literature on contingent valuation. Section 4.4 outlines issues related to divergences between mean and median WTP – an issue of particular importance in aggregating the findings from stated preference studies. Section 4.5 discusses the evidence on validity and reliability and critically considers a number of potential problems and biases that have been cited as being amongst the most important challenges facing contingent valuation practitioners. Section 4.6 contains an overview of recent developments, such as the influence of related research on behavioural economics and the rise of on-line surveys. Finally, Section 4.7 offers some concluding remarks and policy guidance.

4.2. Conceptual foundation

The value of a non-market good or service relates to the impact that it has on human welfare, measured in monetary terms. Hicks (1943) proposed four measures of economic value holding utility constant, in contrast to Marshallian consumer surplus which holds income constant. The Hicksian welfare measures comprise compensating variation and compensating surplus which measure gains or losses relative to the initial utility level (i.e. the implied property right is in the status quo); and equivalent variation and equivalent surplus, which measure gains or loses relative to an alternative utility level (i.e. the implied property right is in the new situation) (Mitchell and Carson, 1989). Variation measures are used for price changes, when as a response the individual can vary the quantity of the good or service of interest, while surplus measures are used for situations involving changes in the quantity or quality of goods and services, and where the individual can only buy fixed amounts (Freeman, 1994). A more detailed explanation of the Hicksian welfare measures can be found in Annex 4.A1. Most environmental applications deal with situations involving fixed increases or decreases in the quantity or quality of a non-market good or service. In such contexts, the relevant welfare measures are therefore the Hicksian welfare surplus measures: compensating and equivalent surplus (Freeman, 1994):

- *Compensating surplus* (CS) is the change in income, paid or received, that will leave the individual in his *initial* welfare position *after* a change in provision of the good or service;

- *Equivalent surplus* (ES) is the change in income, paid or received, that will leave the individual in his *subsequent* welfare position *in absence* of a change in provision of the good or service.

Formally, for a welfare improvement, these welfare measures can be derived as follows (Freeman, 1993):

$$u\left(Q^{0}, M^{0}\right) = u\left(Q^{1}, M^{0} - CS\right) \tag{4.1}$$

$$u\left(Q^{0}, M^{0} + ES\right) = u\left(Q^{1}, M^{0}\right) \tag{4.2}$$

where u is the indirect utility function, M is money or income, Q is the non-market good, CS is the compensating surplus, ES is the equivalent surplus, and the 0 and 1 superscripts refer to before and after provision of the non-market good.

Depending on whether the change of interest has a positive or negative effect on welfare, CS and ES can be rephrased in terms of willingness-to-pay (WTP) or willingness-to-accept (WTA). Table 4.1 summarises the four possible measures (Freeman, 1994).

Table 4.1. **Hicksian compensating and equivalent surplus measures of welfare**

	Compensating surplus (CS)	Equivalent surplus (ES)
Welfare gain	(1) WTP to secure the positive change	(2) WTA compensation to forego the positive change
Welfare loss	(3) WTA compensation to put up with the negative change	(4) WTP to avoid the negative change

4.3. Designing a contingent valuation questionnaire

As with other survey techniques, a key element in any CV study is a properly designed questionnaire: i.e. a data-collection instrument that sets out, in a formal way, the questions designed to elicit the desired information (Dillon et al., 1994). Questionnaire design may seem to be a trivial task where all that is required is to put together a number of questions about the subject of interest. But this apparent simplicity lies at the root of many badly designed surveys that elicit biased, inaccurate and useless information, possibly at a great cost. In fact, even very simple questions require proper wording, format, content, placement and organisation if they are to elicit accurate information.[1] Moreover, any draft questionnaire needs to be adequately piloted before it can said to be ready for implementation in the field. In this context, Mitchell and Carson (1989, p. 120) note that:

"*the principal challenge facing the designer of a CV study is to make the scenario sufficiently understandable, plausible and meaningful to respondents so that they can and will give valid and reliable values despite their lack of experience with one or more of the scenario dimensions*".

This section introduces the basics of contingent valuation questionnaire design, the typical aim of which is to elicit individual preferences, in monetary terms, for changes in the quantity or quality of a non-market good or service. The questionnaire intends to uncover individuals' estimates of how much having or avoiding the change in question is worth to them. Expressing preferences in monetary terms means finding out people's maximum willingness-to-pay (WTP) or minimum willingness-to-accept (WTA) for various changes of interest. In other words, a CV questionnaire is a survey instrument that sets out a number of questions to elicit the monetary value of a change in a non-market good. Typically, the change described is hypothetical.

There are three basic parts to most CV survey instruments.

First, it is customary to ask a set of attitudinal and behavioural questions about the good to be valued as a preparation for responding to the valuation question and in order to reveal the most important underlying factors driving respondents' attitudes towards the public good.

Second, the contingent scenario is presented and respondents are asked for their monetary evaluations. The scenario includes a description of the commodity and of the terms under which it is to be hypothetically offered. Information is also provided on the quality and reliability of provision, timing and logistics, and the method of payment. Then respondents are asked questions to determine how much they would value the good if confronted with the opportunity to obtain it under the specified terms and conditions. The elicitation question can be asked in a number of different ways as discussed later in this chapter. Respondents are also reminded of substitute goods and of the need to make compensating adjustments in other types of expenditure to accommodate the additional financial transaction. The design of the contingent scenario and of the value elicitation questions are the core elements of the CV method.

Finally, questions about the socio-economic and demographic characteristics of the respondent are asked in order to ascertain the representativeness of the survey sample relative to the population of interest, to examine the similarity of the groups receiving different versions of the questionnaire and to study how willingness-to-pay varies according to respondents' characteristics.

Econometric techniques are then applied to the survey results to derive the desired welfare measures such as mean or median WTP (and are used to explain what are the most significant determinants of WTP).

In the remainder of this section we focus on the second and core part of a CV questionnaire that comprises three interrelated stages: i) identifying the good to be valued; ii) constructing the hypothetical scenario; and iii) eliciting the monetary values.

4.3.1. What is the policy change being valued?

Before starting to design the questionnaire, researchers must have a very clear idea of what policy change they want to value, i.e. which quality or quantity change(s) is of interest and of what particular non-market good(s) or service(s). This is in essence the formulation of the valuation problem. But as fundamental as this is, formulating the problem to be valued may not be straightforward. First, there may be scientific uncertainty surrounding the physical effects of particular changes. Second, it may be unclear how physical changes affect human well-being. Third, the effects of some changes may be difficult to translate into terms and sentences that can be readily understood by respondents. Fourth, some changes are very complex and multidimensional and cannot be adequately described within the timeframe and the means available to conduct the questionnaire. Fifth, textual descriptions of some changes may provide only a limited picture of the reality (e.g. changes in noise, odour or visual impacts). Table 4.2 presents examples of changes that may be difficult to define.

Table 4.2. **Examples of possible valuation topics and potential problems**

Change to be valued	Problems
Damages caused in a river from increased water abstractions	Scientific uncertainty surrounding the physical changes caused by increased abstractions; Difficulty in describing a wide range of changes in the fauna, flora, visual amenity, water quality and recreational potential, without causing information overload; Difficulty in isolating abstraction impacts in one river from impacts in other rivers; The damages may be different in different stretches of the river and in different periods of the year.
Reduced risk of contracting a disease or infection	Risk and probability changes are not easily understood; Difficulties in conveying the idea of small risk changes; Difficulties in isolating pain and suffering impacts from the cost of medication or of lost wages.
Damages caused by traffic emissions on an historical building	Difficulties in isolating the impact of traffic-related air pollution and other sources of air pollution; Difficulty in explaining the type of damage caused (e.g. soiling of the stone vs. erosion of the stone); Difficulty in conveying the visual impacts of the change if visual aids are not used.
Damages caused by the introduction of a plant pest	Limited scientific information may not permit full identification of the wide range of environmental impacts caused by plant pests; Difficulty in explaining in lay terms the idea of damages to biodiversity and ecosystems; The impacts of a pest may be too complex to explain in the limited time that the questionnaire lasts.

4.3.2. Constructing the hypothetical scenario

As with all surveys, CV surveys are context dependent. That is, the values estimated are contingent on various aspects of the scenario presented and the questions asked. While some elements of the survey are expected to be neutral, others are thought to have a significant influence on respondents' valuation. These include the information provided about the good, the wording and type of the valuation questions, the institutional arrangements and the payment mechanism. Hence, the design of the hypothetical scenario and the payment mechanism is of crucial importance for the elicitation of accurate and reliable responses.

A hypothetical scenario has three essential elements: i) a description of the policy change of interest; ii) a description of the constructed market; and iii) a description of the method of payment.

Description of the policy change of interest

For single-impact policies, the description of the policy change to be valued entails a number of steps. Clearly, there must be a description of the attributes of the good under investigation in a way that is meaningful and understandable to respondents. Some of those issues outlined in Table 4.2 arise in this context, as these force complex and potentially overwhelmingly large amounts of information to be translated into a few meaningful "headline indicators". The description of available substitutes for the good (its degree of local, national or global uniqueness) and of alternative expenditure possibilities may affect respondents' values and should also be part of the scenario description. Lastly, the scenario should include a description of the proposed policy change and of how the attributes of the good of interest will change accordingly.[2] In particular, the *reference* (status quo or baseline level) and *target levels* (state of the world with the proposed change) of each attribute of interest need to be clearly described.

If a multidimensional policy is to be appraised, then this provides extra challenges in terms of questionnaire design. For example, if the specific change being valued is part of a more inclusive policy that comprises a number of other changes occurring simultaneously (e.g. protecting the white tiger when protection of black rhinos, blue whales, giant pandas and mountain gorillas are also on the agenda) then it is fundamental to present the individual change as part of the broader package. This provides respondents with a chance to consider all the possible substitution, complementarity and income effects between the various policy components, which would have been impossible had the policy component been presented in isolation (which would have led to possible embedding effects, where respondents equate the value of "part" of a policy change with how they actually value the "whole" and so an overestimation of the value of the policy component).

One such approach is to follow a top-down procedure, whereby respondents are first asked to value the more inclusive policy and then to partition that total value across its components. There is an obvious limitation to the number of components that can be valued in such a way: as one tries to value an increasing number of policy changes, the description of each becomes necessarily shorter, reducing the accuracy of the scenario, while respondents may also become fatigued or confused. It should be noted that while contingent valuation is in theory applicable to value multidimensional changes, as described above, a more efficient way of dealing with such changes might be to adopt a choice modelling approach (see Chapter 5).

Description of the constructed market

The constructed market refers to the social context in which the hypothetical CV transaction, i.e. the policy change, takes place. A number of elements of the constructed market are important.

The *institution* that is responsible for proving the good or change is of interest. This can be a government, a local council, a non-governmental organisation or NGO, a research institute, industry, a charity and so on. Institutional arrangements will affect WTP as respondents may hold views about particular institutions' level of effectiveness, reliability and trust. *The technical and political feasibility of the change* is a fundamental consideration in the design of the questionnaire. Respondents can only provide meaningful valuations if they believe that the scenario described is feasible.

Conditions for provision of the good include respondents' perceived payment obligation and respondents' expectations about provision. Regarding the former, there are several possibilities: respondents may believe they will have to pay the amounts they state; they may think the amount they have to pay is uncertain (more or less than their stated WTP amount); or they may be told that they will pay a fixed amount, or proportion of the costs of provision. Regarding the latter, the basic question is whether respondents believe or not that provision of the good is conditional on their WTP amount. Both types of information are important as each different combination evokes a different type of strategic behaviour (Mitchell and Carson, 1989). In particular, it is important to provide respondents with incentives to reveal their true valuations, i.e. to design an *incentive compatible* mechanism. This issue is addressed at various points, later in this chapter (see in particular Box 4.2).

The timing of provision – when and for how long the good will be provided – also needs to be explicitly stated. Given individual time preferences, a good provided now will be more valuable than a good provided in 10 years' time. Also, the amount of time over which the good or service will be provided can be of crucial importance. For example, the value of a programme that saves black rhinos for 50 years is only a fraction of the value of the same programme where protection is awarded indefinitely.

Description of the method of payment

A number of aspects of the method of payment should be clearly defined in CV questionnaires. Most fundamentally, the choice of benefit measure is a fundamental step in any CV survey. Box 4.1 notes a further issue regarding the possible existence and elicitation of negative WTP in situations where some respondents could just as conceivably value the status quo.

Box 4.1. **Eliciting negative WTP**

Policy makers often are concerned with choosing between a proposed environmental change – or number of proposed changes – and the status quo. To help in making such a decision, stated preference survey techniques such as the CV method may be employed to gauge the size of the welfare benefits of adopting each one of the proposed changes. In the case of changes in the provision in, for example, rural landscapes opinion could be split with some respondents favouring the change, whilst others wishing to indicate a preference for the status quo. In such cases, CV practitioners could consider in designing a survey to allow respondents to express either a monetary value of their welfare gain or welfare loss for any particular change.

A number of studies have sought to examine this problem of negative WTP, including Clinch and Murphy (2001) and Bohara et al. (2001). One example of the issues that can arise is illustrated in Atkinson et al. (2004). In this CV study of preferences for new designs for the towers (or pylons), which convey high voltage electricity transmission lines, opinion on the new designs was divided. Some respondents favoured a change, whilst others indicated a preference for the status quo. Indeed, for some respondents, a number of the new designs were considered sufficiently unsightly that they felt the landscape would be visually poorer for their installation.

For those respondents preferring a new design to the current design, WTP was elicited using the payment vehicle of a one-off change of the standing charge of their household electricity bill. For those people preferring the current design to some or all of the new tower designs, the procedure was less straightforward. Respondents could be asked for their willingness-to-accept (WTA) a reduced standing charge as compensation for the disamenity of viewing towers of the new design. This reduction, for example, could be explained as reflecting reductions in the maintenance costs of the newer design. Here a particular respondent might prefer one change to the status quo whilst "dispreferring"

> ## Box 4.1. **Eliciting negative WTP** (*cont.*)
>
> another. Yet, within the context of seeking separate values for each of a number of different changes, this would require respondents to believe a scenario in which preferred changes happened to trigger increases in bills but less preferred changes resulted in reductions in bills. Whether respondents would find this credible or not was a question that was considered by the authors.
>
> As an alternative, respondents were asked instead to state which of a number of increasingly arduous tasks they would perform in order to avert the replacement of the current towers with towers of a new design. These tasks are described in the first column in Table 4.3 and involved signing petitions, writing complaint letters or making donations to protest groups. Each intended action can then be given a monetary dimension by relating it to the associated value of time lost (writing letters, signing petitions) or loss of money (donations).
>
> The second column in Table 4.3 describes the results of imputing WTP values to each of the possible actions to avoid replacing the current design where the value in money terms of the time, effort and expense involved in writing a letter of complaint is described by c. A respondent who indicated that he/she would not do anything was assumed to be stating indifference, i.e. a zero WTP to retain the current design. A respondent stating that they would sign a petition but not go as far as writing a letter to their MP was assumed to be indicating that they were not indifferent but would not suffer a sufficient welfare loss to invest the time, effort and expense in writing a letter. Hence, their WTP was larger than zero but less than c. A respondent stating they would write a letter but would not pay GBP 10 to a protest group was indicating that their welfare loss lay in the interval between c (inclusive) and c + GBP 10 (exclusive). Respondents stating they would write a letter and pay GBP 10 to a fighting fund but not pay GBP 30 were indicating that their welfare loss lay in the interval above or equal to c + GBP 10 but below c + GBP 30. For those willing to donate GBP 30, it can be inferred that their maximum WTP is above or equal to c + GBP 30.
>
> #### Table 4.3. **Translating intended actions into WTP estimates**
>
> | Intended action | Assumed WTP to retain the current design |
> | --- | --- |
> | I wouldn't do anything as I don't really care | WTP = 0 |
> | I would sign a petition complaining to my MP and local council | $0 < WTP < c$ |
> | I would sign a petition and independently write to my local council and/or MP and/or electricity company in order to complain. | $c \leq WTP < GBP\ 10 + c$ |
> | As well as signing a petition and writing letters of complaint I would be prepared to donate GBP 10 to a group coordinating protest | $GBP\ 10 + c \leq WTP < GBP\ 30 + c$ |
> | As well as signing a petition and writing letters of complaint I would be prepared to donate GBP 30 to a group coordinating protest | $WTP \geq GBP\ 30 + c$ |
>
> *Note:* c is the value in money terms of the time, effort and expense involved in writing a letter of complaint.
> *Source:* Atkinson et al. (2004).
>
> Given that c is of an unknown magnitude, the assumption was made that it takes an hour to produce and mail such a letter. Put another way, c is the value the household places on one hour of its time. Following some frequently used assumptions concerning the value of non-labour time, c is calculated from the annual after-tax income. Specifically, the value of time is taken as a third of the wage rate, which is approximated as a two-thousandth of the annual after-tax income of the household.

With regards to the payment vehicle – how the provision of the good is to be financed – the basic choice is between voluntary or coercive payments. Coercive payment vehicles include taxes, rates, fees, charges or prices. Voluntary payments are donations and gifts. The payment vehicle forms a substantive part of the overall package under evaluation and is generally believed to be a non-neutral element of the survey. Mechanisms such as income taxes and water rates are clearly non-neutral and it is relatively common to find respondents refusing to answer the valuation question on the grounds that they object in principle to paying higher taxes or water rates, in spite of the fact that the proposed change is welfare enhancing. The use of taxes also raises issues of accountability, trust in the government, knowledge that taxes are generally not hypothecated, excludes non-tax payers from the sample and may not be credible when the scenario is one of WTA, i.e. corresponding to a tax rebate. Voluntary payments on the other hand might encourage free-riding, as respondents have an incentive to overestimate their WTP to secure provision, with a voluntary later decision on whether or not to purchase in the future (see Box 4.2). The use of prices also poses problems as respondents may agree to pay more but simply adjust the quantities consumed so that the total expenditure remains the same.

Box 4.2. **Coercion vs. voluntarism and WTP for a public good**

Carson, Groves and Machina (2007) have analysed extensively the conditions under which CV respondents have incentives to free-ride. They conclude that the provision of a public good by means of voluntary contributions is particularly troublesome as there is a strong incentive to overstate WTP in the survey context (if stated WTP is perceived to unrelated to actual payment). This is because overstating hypothetical WTP increases the chances of provision of the desired public good without having to pay for it. Conversely, respondents may choose to free-ride (state a lower WTP value than they would pay in reality) if stated values were perceived to translate credibly into actual contributions. The implication is that voluntary contribution mechanisms should generally be avoided in CV surveys, as that seems to be the cause of the bias rather than the hypothetical nature of the method. Incentive compatible payment methods should be used to minimise the risk of strategic behaviour.

A study by Champ et al. (2002) has sought to test some of these ideas. The authors examined three types of payment vehicle, which they used to elicit WTP for the creation of an open space in Boulder County, Colorado: (A) voluntary individual contribution to a trust fund; (B) voluntary individual contribution to a trust fund, which would be reimbursed in full if the open space project did not go ahead; and, (C) one-off tax on residents based on the results of a referendum. Assuming that respondent believed their WTP values could form the basis of the charge they would actually face to finance the project, it was hypothesised that theory (as just described) would predict that:

1. WTP (C) $\leq$ WTP(A)

2. WTP(C) $\leq$ WTP(B)

3. WTP(A) $\leq$ WTP(B)

Put another way, the authors reckoned that the relatively coercive form(s) of payment vehicle would be less likely to encourage free-riding than the relatively voluntary form(s). The findings of this study appear to confirm this in part as strong evidence was detected for the first prediction. That is, WTP in form of a tax (C) was significantly smaller than WTP in the form of voluntary contributions (A). While there was less strong evidence (if any) for

---

Box 4.2. **Coercion vs. voluntarism and WTP for a public good** (*cont.*)

the remaining two hypotheses, these findings, nevertheless, provide some support for the conjecture that coercive payment vehicles reduce implicit behaviour that might be interpreted as having some strategic element. However, as the authors note, this is just one desirable criterion of a payment vehicle and, in practice, the credibility of any payment medium will also play a large part in determining its relative merits.

Although there seems to be some consensus that voluntary payment vehicles should generally be avoided due to the insurmountable problem of free-riding, ultimately, the choice of the payment vehicle will depend on the actual good being studied and the context in which it is to be provided. Credibility and acceptability are important considerations here. A simple guideline is to use the vehicle, which is likely to be employed in the real-world decision: i.e. if water rates are the method by which the change in provision will be affected then there should be a presumption in favour of using water rates or charges in the contingent market. A caveat to this guide arises where this causes conflict with certain of the criteria set out above. For example, a study by Georgiou et al. (1998) found considerable resistance to the use of a water rates vehicle in the immediate aftermath of the privatisation of the public water utilities in the UK. As a practical, in such cases, the use of a different payment vehicle (if credible) might well be justified.

Eliciting monetary values

After the presentation of the hypothetical scenario, the provision mechanism and the payment mechanism, respondents are asked questions to determine how much they would value the good if confronted with the opportunity to obtain it, under the specified terms and conditions.

The elicitation question can be asked in a number of different ways. Table 4.4 summarises the principal formats of eliciting values as applied to the case of valuing changes in landscape around Stonehenge in the United Kingdom (Maddison and Mourato, 2002). The examples in the table all relate to the elicitation of WTP but could easily be framed in terms of WTA.

The direct *open-ended* elicitation format is a straightforward way of uncovering values, does not provide respondents with cues about what the value of the change might be, is very informative as maximum WTP can be identified for each respondent and requires relatively straightforward statistical techniques. Hence, there is no anchoring or starting point bias – i.e. respondents are not influenced by the starting values and succeeding bids used. However, due to a number of problems, CV practitioners have progressively abandoned this elicitation format (although there are instances in which open ended elicitation might work well, see Box 4.3). Open-ended questioning leads to large non-response rates, protest answers, zero answers and outliers and generally to unreliable responses (Mitchell and Carson, 1989).[3] This is because it may be very difficult for respondents to come up with their true maximum WTP, "out of the blue", for a change they are unfamiliar with and have never thought about valuing before. Moreover, most daily market transactions involve deciding whether or not to buy goods at given prices, rather than stating maximum WTP values.

The *bidding game* was one of the most widely used technique used in the 1970s and 1980s. In this approach, as in an auction, respondents are faced with several rounds of

Table 4.4. **Examples of common elicitation formats**

Format	Description
Open ended	What is the maximum amount that you would be prepared to pay every year, through a tax increase (or surcharge), to improve the landscape around Stonehenge in the ways I have just described?
Bidding game	Would you pay GBP 5 every year, through a tax increase (or surcharge), to improve the landscape around Stonehenge in the ways I have just described? If Yes: Interviewer keeps increasing the bid until the respondent answers No. Then maximum WTP is elicited. If No: Interviewer keeps decreasing the bid until respondent answers Yes. Then maximum WTP is elicited.
Payment card	Which of the amounts listed below best describes your maximum willingness-to-pay every year, through a tax increase (or surcharge), to improve the landscape around Stonehenge in the ways I have just described? 0 GBP 0.5 GBP 1 GBP 2 GBP 3 GBP 4 GBP 5 GBP 7.5 GBP 10 GBP 14.5 GBP 15 GBP 20 GBP 30 GBP 40 GBP 50 GBP 75 GBP 100 GBP 150 GBP 200 >GBP 200
Single-bounded dichotomous choice	Would you pay GBP 5 every year, through a tax increase (or surcharge), to improve the landscape around Stonehenge in the ways I have just described? (The amount is varied randomly across the sample.)
Double-bounded dichotomous choice	Would you pay GBP 5 every year, through a tax increase (or surcharge), to improve the landscape around Stonehenge in the ways I have just described? (The amount is varied randomly across the sample.) If Yes: And would you pay GBP 10? If No: And would you pay GBP 1?

Source: Pearce et al. (2006).

discrete choice questions, with the final question being an open-ended WTP question. This iterative format was reckoned to facilitate respondents' thought processes and thus encourage them to consider their preferences carefully. A major disadvantage lies in the possibility of anchoring or starting bias. It also leads to large number of outliers, that is unrealistically large bids and to a phenomenon that has been labelled as "yea-saying", that is respondents accepting to pay the specified amounts to avoid the socially embarrassing position of having to say no. Bidding games have mostly been discontinued in contingent valuation practice.

Payment card approaches were developed as improved alternatives to the open-ended and bidding game methods. Presenting respondents with a visual aid containing a large number of monetary amounts facilitates the valuation task, by providing a context to their bids, while avoiding starting point bias at the same time. The number of outliers is also reduced in comparison to the previous methods. Some versions of the payment card show how the values in the card relate to actual household expenditures or taxes (benchmarks). In on-line surveys, payment cards can be presented as sliding scales, where respondents slide the cursor along to select their value (Figure 4.1). Several variants of the payment card method have also been developed to deal with particular empirical issues, such as the presence of uncertainty in valuations. Box 4.3 presents an example of an especially designed

Figure 4.1. **Example of a payment card sliding scale from an on-line survey**

	0	5	10	15	20	25	30	35	40	45	50	55	60	65	70	75
Tax per Gallon (in Cents)																

Source: Arold (2016), The Effect of Newspaper Framing on the Public Support of the Paris Climate Agreement, MSc thesis, Department of Geography & Environment, LSE.

Box 4.3. Tailored open-ended WTA elicitation: Valuing land-use change in the Peruvian Amazon

Mourato and Smith (2002) used a tailored open-ended elicitation mechanism to estimate the compensation required by slash-and-burn farmers in the Peruvian Amazon to switch to more sustainable agroforestry systems. A total of 214 farmers in the Campo Verde district, Peru, were surveyed face-to-face. Simple black and white drawings were used to depict the scenario and the elicitation mechanism (Figure 4.2) as most farmers were illiterate.

Figure 4.2. **Pictorial elicitation mechanism**

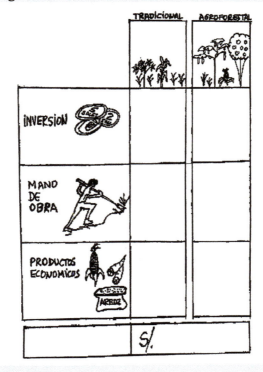

Farmers were presented with a possible project in which utility companies in developed countries, driven by the possibility of emission reduction legislation, were willing to compensate farmers who preserved forest by adopting multistrata agroforestry systems. A fixed annual payment would be made for each hectare of agroforestry. Payments would cease if the area was deforested.

> **Box 4.3. Tailored open-ended WTA elicitation: Valuing land-use change in the Peruvian Amazon** *(cont.)*
>
> With the aid of the drawings in Figure 4.2, farmers were asked about the potential economic impacts of agroforestry in terms of investment, labour, yields, and available products, when compared with the traditional slash-and-burn system. Then, they were asked, in an open-ended procedure, for their minimum annual willingness-to-accept compensation to convert one hectare of primary or secondary forest, destined for slash-and-burn agriculture, to multistrata agroforestry.
>
> Simultaneously, farmers were reminded that they were competing against alternative suppliers of carbon services. Therefore, it was advisable to minimise bids, and there was no guarantee that any bids would be accepted. This mechanism served the dual purpose of increasing the realism of the scenario and minimising the occurrence of over-bidding, which is one of the caveats associated with WTA formats.
>
> The piloting stages of the study had showed that dichotomous choice approaches did not to work well: farmers were a close-knit community, and disclosed the bids received to one another, creating general discontent. Instead, using the especially designed procedure described above, farmers were able to think through the costs and benefits of the different land uses and formulate bids in this way. Given the relatively small sample size, this approach was also more informative.
>
> The mean compensation required for adoption of agroforestry from the CV survey was USD 138. This was found to be very close to the average difference in returns between slash-and-burn and agroforestry in the first two years, from experimental data (USD 144). Hence, the estimated compensations from the open-ended WTA elicitation procedure, embedded in a competitive setting, seem to reflect expected economic losses rather than strategic bidding.

payment card to identify certain and uncertain values. The payment card is nevertheless vulnerable to biases relating to the range of the numbers used in the card and the location of the benchmarks.

Single-bounded dichotomous choice or referendum methods became increasingly popular in the 1990s. This elicitation format is thought to simplify the cognitive task faced by respondents (respondents only have to make a judgement about a given price, in the same way as they decide whether or not to buy a supermarket good at a certain price) while at the same time providing incentives for the truthful revelation of preferences under certain circumstances (that is, it is in the respondent's strategic interest to accept the bid if his WTP is greater or equal than the price asked and to reject otherwise, see Box 4.2 for an explanation of incentive compatibility). This procedure minimises non-response and avoids outliers. The presumed supremacy of the dichotomous choice approach reached its climax in 1993 when it received the endorsement of the NOAA panel (Arrow et al., 1993). However, enthusiasm for closed-ended formats gradually waned as an increasing number of empirical studies revealed that values obtained from dichotomous choice elicitation were significantly and substantially larger than those resulting from comparable open-ended questions. Some degree of yea-saying is also possible. In addition, dichotomous choice formats are relatively inefficient in that less information is available from each respondent (the researcher only knows whether WTP is above or below a certain amount), so that larger samples and stronger statistical assumptions are required. This makes surveys more expensive and their results more sensitive to the statistical assumptions made.

Double-bounded dichotomous choice formats are more efficient than their single-bounded counterpart as more information is elicited about each respondent's WTP. For example, one knows that a person's true value lies between GBP 5 and GBP 10 if she accepted to pay GBP 5 in the first question but rejected GBP 10 in the second. But all the limitations of the single-bounded procedure still apply in this case. An added problem is the possible loss of incentive compatibility due to the fact that the second question may not be viewed by respondents as separate to the choice situation and the added possibility of anchoring and yea-saying biases.

Other developments in elicitation formats include Hanemann and Kanninen's (1999) proposal of a *one and a half bound dichotomous choice* procedure whereby respondents are initially informed that costs of providing the good in question will be between GBP X and GBP Y (X < Y), with the amounts X and Y being varied across the sample. Respondents are then asked whether they are prepared to pay the lower amount GBP X. If the response is negative, no further questions are asked; if the response is positive, then respondents are asked if they would pay GBP Y. Conversely respondents may be presented with the upper amount GBP Y initially and asked about amount GBP X if the former is refused.

The choice of elicitation format is of dramatic importance as different elicitation formats typically produce different estimates. That is, the elicitation format is a non-neutral element of the questionnaire. Carson et al. (2001) summarises a number of stylised facts regarding elicitation formats. These are described in Table 4.5. Considering the pros and cons of each of the approaches above, contributions such as Bateman et al. (2002) and Champ et al. (2003) typically recommend dichotomous choice approaches and, to some extent, payment cards. The latter are more informative about respondents' WTP and cheaper to implement than the latter and are superior to both direct open-ended questions and bidding games. The former may be incentive compatible and facilitates respondents' valuation task.[4] The newer one and a half bounds approach also shows potential. A final consideration is that while it is important to find out which elicitation format is the more valid and reliable, some degree of flexibility and variety in use of formats should be expected, and consideration needs to be given to the empirical circumstances of each application, as suggested by the examples in Boxs 4.3 and 4.4.

Table 4.5. **Elicitation formats – some stylised facts**

Elicitation format	Main problems
Open-ended	Large number of zero responses, few small positive responses
Bidding game	Final estimate shows dependence on starting point used
Payment card	Weak dependence of estimate on amounts used in the card
Single-bounded dichotomous choice	Estimates typically higher than other formats
Double-bounded dichotomous choice	The two responses do not correspond to the same underlying WTP distribution

Source: Carson et al. (2001), "Contingent Valuation: Controversies and Evidence", *Journal of Environmental and Resource Economics*, Vol. 19(2), pp. 173-210.

Whatever the elicitation format adopted, respondents should be reminded of substitute goods and of their budget constraints (and the possible need to make compensating adjustments in other types of expenditure to accommodate the additional financial transaction implied by the survey). The former reminds respondents that the good in question may not be unique and that this has implications upon its value; the latter reminds respondents of their limited incomes and of the need to trade-off money for environmental

Box 4.4. **Value uncertainty in payment cards**

It seems plausible that some individuals may not have precise preferences for changes in the provision of certain non-market goods. Within stated preference studies this might manifest itself in respondent difficulty in expressing single and exact values. If so, then it might be worthwhile to allow respondents to express a range of values within which, for example, their WTP would most likely reside. A few studies have attempted to allow respondents in CV surveys to be able to express this uncertainty. For example, Dubourg et al. (1997) and Hanley and Kriström (2003) both adapt a payment card elicitation format in order to assess the significance of this uncertainty.

The latter study describes a CV survey of WTP for improvements in coastal water quality in two locations in Scotland. A payment card (see Table 4.6) with values ranging from GBP 1 to GBP 125 was presented to those respondents in their sample of the Scottish population around these locations who had indicated that their WTP for the improvement was positive. In order to test whether these particular respondents were uncertain about their exact WTP, the authors posed the valuation question in two ways.

Table 4.6. **Payment card in CV study of improvements in Scottish coastal waters**

GBP per annum	A: I would definitely pay (✓)	B: I would definitely NOT pay (✗)
1	✓	
2	✓	
5	✓	
10	✓	
13	✓	
15	✓	
20	✓	
26	✓	
34	✓	
40		
52		
60		✗
65		✗
70		✗
93		✗
104		✗
125		✗

Source: Adapted from Hanley and Kriström (2003), *What's It Worth? Exploring Value Uncertainty Using Interval Questions in Contingent Valuation*, Department of Economics, University of Glasgow, mimeo.

First, respondents were asked if they would definitely pay the lowest amount on the card (i.e. GBP 1) for improving coastal water quality. If the answer was "yes", then the respondent was asked whether they would definitely pay the second lowest amount on the card (i.e. GBP 2) and so and on and so forth with successively higher amounts being proposed until the respondent said "no" to a particular amount.

Second, in addition to this conventional way of eliciting WTP using a payment card, respondents were then asked to consider whether the highest amount on the payment card (i.e. GBP 125) was too much for them to pay. If "yes" then the respondent was asked whether the second highest amount on the card (i.e. 104) was too much to pay and so on and so forth with successively lower amounts being proposed to the respondent until the respondent

> ### Box 4.4. **Value uncertainty in payment cards** (*cont.*)
>
> stated that they were not sure that a particular amount was too much.An illustration of this process to capture respondent uncertainty is described in Table 4.6. The difference between the ticks and crosses on this payment card indicates how uncertain respondents are about their exact WTP: in this case, the respondent would be prepared to pay GBP 34 for sure, would definitely not pay GBP 60 and is unsure whether he/she would pay amounts ranging between GBP 34 and GBP 60. Understanding more about the source of this uncertainty, that may stem from a number of candidate explanations, and whether it varies depending on the non-market good being valued are clearly important questions for future research of this kind.

improvements. Once the WTP elicitation process is over, debriefing and follow-up questions can help the analyst to understand why respondents were or were not willing to pay for the change presented. These questions are important to identify invalid (e.g. protest) answers: that is, answers that do not reflect people's welfare change from the good considered.

4.4. Mean versus median willingness-to-pay

In using the findings of a cost-benefit analysis (CBA), a decision-maker accepts measures of individuals' preferences, expressed as WTP sums, as valid measures of the welfare consequences of a given change in provision of say some public good. Generally, no account is taken of how ability to pay might constrain those WTP sums (i.e. the present distribution of income is taken as given) and those expressing a higher WTP are considered as simply reflecting their higher preferences for the good. (However, see Chapter 11 for a discussion of ways in which to take account of distribution.) In this system, mean WTP is preferred to median WTP as a more accurate reflection of the variance in preferences across the mass of individuals whose aggregation is considered to represent society's preference.

For a number of environmental and cultural goods, a not uncommon finding is that the distribution of WTP is skewed in that, for example, there are a very small number of respondents bidding very large values and a very large number of respondents bidding very small (or even zero) values. In other words, the problem in such cases is that *mean* WTP gives "excessive" weight to a minority of respondents who have strong and positive preferences. While mean WTP is the theoretically correct measure to use in CBA, median WTP is the better predictor of what the majority of people would actually be willing to pay (when there is a wide distribution of values). From a practical viewpoint, this is extremely important if a decision-maker wishes to capture some portion of the benefits of a project in order say to recover the costs of its implementation. As median WTP reflects what the majority of people would be willing to pay, passing on no more than this amount to individuals should have a correspondingly greater degree of public acceptability than seeking to pass on an amount which is closer to a mean WTP, which might have been overly influenced by a relatively few very large bids.

While CBA describes how micro-level project appraisals are evaluated, it does not provide a model for how major political issues are decided – namely, the election of government. Here, if one simplifies to a simple two-option system (to allow comparison with the "project on" or "project off" scenario of the valuation exercise), the decision is based on a simple majority of the relevant constituency. This system is analogous to the median WTP measure of a CV study. This argument, between the dominance of preference values or a referendum, is an ongoing debate within environmental economics, which has yet to be resolved. In short, both the mean and median measures deserve consideration in contemporary decision-making and the management of environmental goods.

4.5. Validity and reliability

Despite numerous methodological improvements and a widespread application, particularly in the field of environmental economics, the contingent valuation method still raises some controversy (e.g. Hausman, 2012). One of the main areas of concern regards the ability of the method to produce valid and reliable estimates of WTP. It is not straightforward to assess the validity (i.e. the degree to which a study measures the intended quantity, or absence of systematic bias) and reliability (i.e. the degree of replicability of a measurement, or absence of random bias) of the estimates produced by contingent valuation studies for the obvious reason that actual payments are unobservable. Nevertheless it is possible to test indirectly various aspects of validity and reliability.

4.5.1. Validity

Face or content validity tests look at the adequacy, realism and neutrality of the survey instrument as well as at respondents' understanding, perception and reactions to the questionnaire. The former aspects can be checked by having stakeholder meetings at the start of the project, and an advisory board throughout, to advise on various aspects of the policy change and survey design. The latter aspects can be tested in the piloting stages of the questionnaire, which may include focus groups, in-depth interviews and, importantly, field pilots (Bateman et al., 2002). Additionally, the rate of protests provides valuable information on how respondents react to the scenarios and payment mechanisms.

Convergent validity tests compare the estimates derived from a CV study with values for the same or a similar good derived from alternative valuation methods, such as those based on revealed preferences. Carson et al. (1996) conducted a meta-analysis looking at 616 value estimates from 83 studies that used more than one valuation method. The authors concluded that, in general, contingent valuation estimates were very similar and somewhat smaller than revealed preference estimates, with both being highly correlated (with 0.78-0.92 correlation coefficients). As will be discussed in more detail later in this section, a common claim of CV critics is that WTP estimates, obtained through the CV method, represent gross overestimates of respondents' true values (e.g. Cummings et al., 1986). Such findings lend support to the claim that the values estimated by CV studies provide reasonable estimates of the value of environmental goods, as they are very similar to those based on actual revealed behaviour, in spite of the hypothetical nature of the method. The usefulness of convergent validity testing is, however, restricted to quasi-public goods as only estimates of use values can be compared due to the limited scope of revealed preference techniques. Hence, values for pure public goods cannot be analysed in this way.

Perhaps the most common validity test is to check whether CV results conform to the predictions of economic theory. This corresponds to the concept of *theoretical validity* (Bateman et al., 2002). In general, theoretical validity tests examine the influence of a number of demographic, economic, attitudinal and locational variables, thought to be WTP determinants, on some measure of the estimated WTP. The test is normally formulated by regressing estimated WTP on these variables and checking whether the coefficients are significant, with the expected sign and size. These tests are now standard CV practice and most studies report them. A common theoretical validity test is to check whether the percentage of respondents willing to pay a particular price falls as the price they are asked to pay increases (in dichotomous choice elicitation). This is similar to a negative price elasticity of demand for a private good and is generally tested by checking whether the price coefficient is negative and significant. The condition is almost universally observed in CV studies (Carson et al., 1996).

Another common theoretical validity test consists of analysing the relationship between income and WTP. If the environmental good being valued is a normal good, then a positive and significant income coefficient is to be expected.[5] A positive income elasticity of WTP that is significantly less than one is the usual empirical finding in CV studies of environmental goods. The small magnitude of this income elasticity has been the focus of some of the criticism directed at contingent values: since most environmental commodities are generally regarded as luxury goods rather than necessity goods, many authors expected to find larger-than-unity income elasticities of WTP. However, as Flores and Carson (1997) point out, CV studies yield income elasticities of WTP for a fixed quantity, which are different from income elasticities of demand, a measured based on varying quantity. The authors show that a luxury good in the demand sense can have an income elasticity of WTP which is less than zero, between zero and one or greater than one. They also analyse the conditions under which the income elasticity of WTP is likely to be smaller than the corresponding income elasticity of demand.

In a comprehensive overview of 20 years of contingent valuation research in developing countries, Whittington (2010) shows that WTP is typically low in these countries, in absolute terms, as a percentage of income, and also relative to the cost of provision. This finding applies to the wide range of non-market goods and services covered by the review: e.g. improved water infrastructure, sanitation and sewage, household water treatment, ecosystem services and watershed protection, solid waste management, marine turtle conservation, cholera and typhoid vaccines, and preservation of cultural heritage. The result is of course unsurprising in the sense that average ability to pay is very low in developing countries, with many people living at a subsistence level and having very little income to spare. Moreover, Whittington notes that people may have other priorities and pressing needs aside the non-market goods or services being offered. The policy solution will involve subsidies, international assistance, and other forms of sponsorship, or delaying the projects until incomes rise.

Other tests of theoretical validity involve checking whether values are sensitive to the scope of the good or service being valued, and whether WTP and WTA measures of a similar change are similar. The problems of insensitivity to scope (or embedding bias), as well as the disparity between WTP and WTA, are being discussed further below.

Arguably, the most powerful and direct way of checking the validity and accuracy of contingent values is to compare contingent valuation hypothetical values with "true" or "real" values, when these can be discerned in actual behaviour. These *criterion validity* tests analyse the extent to which the hypothetical nature of the CV systematically biases the results, when all other factors are controlled for. This is the most difficult validity test to perform as is not feasible for many types of good. Indeed, many of the criterion validity tests have been conducted in a laboratory setting, using simulated "real money" transactions and most have been undertaken with private goods. Many of these studies point towards a tendency to overstate WTP in hypothetical markets. These results are discussed in more detail below, when hypothetical bias is reviewed.

4.5.2. Bias testing and correction

Key areas of concern for empirical methodologies such as contingent valuation relate to their susceptibility to various biases (see Mitchell and Carson, 1989; Bateman et al., 2002; or Champ et al., 2002, for extensive reviews). Validity can also be interpreted as the absence of systematic bias and validity testing often involves checking for the presence of certain biases. Many such biases are not specific to the CV method but are common to most survey based techniques and are largely attributable to survey design and implementation problems. But generally, the further from reality and the less familiar the scenario is, the harder it will be for respondents to act like they would in a real market setting. Importantly, some of the anomalies detected in contingent markets also happen in actual markets and hence are not so much a problem with the method, but a feature of how people actually behave (Carson and Hanemann, 2005). This is discussed in more detail in Section 4.6.

Amongst the most examined problems are hypothetical bias (umbrella designation for problems arising from the hypothetical nature of the CV market); insensitivity to scope (where the valuation is insensitive to the scope of the good); WTP/WTA disparity (where WTA is much higher than WTP); and framing effects/information bias (when the framing of the question unduly influences the answer). These biases are discussed in more detail next.

Hypothetical bias

Unsurprisingly, given the hypothetical nature of stated preference scenarios, the criticism of CV that has perhaps received the most attention is hypothetical bias (Arrow and Solow, 1993; Champ and Bishop, 2001; Hausman, 2012; Loomis, 2014), where individuals have been found to systematically overstate stated WTP, when compared with actual payments, due to the hypothetical nature of the survey. Foster et al. (1997) conducted a review of the literature in this area covering both field and laboratory experiments. Voluntary payment mechanisms are typically used given the difficulty associated in conducting experiments with taxes. The empirical evidence shows that there is a tendency of hypothetical CV studies to exaggerate actual WTP. Most calibration factors (i.e. ratios of hypothetical to actual WTP) were found to fall in the range of 1.3 to 14. Carson et al. (1997) notes that hypothetical bias is more prevalent when *voluntary payment mechanisms* are used, as respondents have incentives to free-ride. The evidence suggests that there is a strong incentive to overstate WTP in the survey context and to free-ride on actual contributions (a phenomenon known as strategic bias). This is because overstating WTP increases the chances of provision of the desired public good without having to pay for it. In order to explain what accounts for the discrepancy found in their review between real and hypothetical values, Foster et al. (1997) also conducted an experiment comparing data on actual donations, in response to a fund-raising appeal for an endangered bird-species, with CV studies focusing on similar environmental resources. The main finding was that the divergence between the data on real and hypothetical valuations might be due as much to free-riding behaviour – because of the voluntary nature of the payment mechanism – as to the hypothetical nature of the CV approach.

Moreover, hypothetical bias tends to arise most commonly when valuing distant, complex and unfamiliar goods and services, where people may not have well-defined prior preferences and may be unable to establish their preferences within the short duration of a (one-off) survey. It is a problem that might affect particularly some types of non-use values for less known and distant policy changes. Use-related values, and goods and services that people are generally familiar with, are arguably less prone to hypothetical bias. A recent CV survey investigating visitor WTP to access London's Natural History

Museum, via an entry fee, elicited values of just under GBP 7 per visit (Bakhshi et al., 2015). These use values are credible and in line with prices currently charged for paid exhibitions in cultural institutions in the United Kingdom.

A range of counteractive procedures or corrective adjustments have been developed to help minimise hypothetical biases (Loomis, 2014). Many such mechanisms are *ex ante*, preceding the valuation, and involving developments in the design and implementation of CV surveys. First, as noted above, hypothetical bias is associated with the use of voluntary payment mechanisms, as respondents have incentives to free-ride (Carson et al., 1997). The implication for practitioners is to *avoid using voluntary payments* where possible and select instead compulsory payment mechanisms such as taxes, fees or prices (see Box 4.2).

Another development has been the use of *provision point mechanisms* in the contingent scenario, which are designed to reduce free-riding behaviour when using voluntary payment mechanisms as a payment vehicle. In a provision point mechanism, respondents are told that the project will only go ahead if a certain donations threshold is reached (i.e. the provision point). If the total donations collected fail to meet the threshold, then the project does not go ahead and the donations made are refunded to the respondents. As indicated by lab experiments (Bagnoli and McKee, 1991), the mechanism incentivises truth telling, as underbidding might result in the project not going ahead. Poe et al. (2002) found that the provision point design also works in a field contingent valuation study setting, incentivising true revelation of WTP. However, there are also potential caveats with this design. Champ et al. (2002) did not find a difference between a provision point mechanism with money back guarantee and a standard voluntary contribution design, as many respondents did not believe the provision point would be met, and were therefore possibly discouraged from contributing. Similarly, Groothuis and Whitehead (2009) found that those that did not believe the provision point would be met were more likely to reject a dichotomous choice bid amount, as a protest.

Counteractive (i.e. ex ante) treatments are often employed through so-called entreaties in the survey text. Famously, Cummings and Taylor (1999) developed a *cheap talk entreaty* for reducing hypothetical bias, whereby a script describes the bias problem and a plea is made to respondents not to overstate their true willingness-to-pay. The evidence suggests that use of cheap talk reduces, but not completely eliminates, hypothetical bias (e.g. Aadland and Caplan, 2006; Carlsson et al., 2005; Carlsson and Martinsson, 2006; List and Lucking-Reiley, 2000; Lusk, 2003; Murphy et al., 2003).[6] Further details of the cheap talk experimental work are described in Box 4.5.

A recently proposed entreaty is the *oath script*, which typically asks respondents to agree to promise or swear that they will respond to questions or state values honestly. Within environmental economics, the oath script has seen only a small number of applications (e.g. Carlsson et al., 2013; de-Magistris and Pascucci, 2014; Ehmke et al., 2008; Jacquemet et al., 2013; Stevens et al., 2013; Bakhshi et al., 2015). In an investigation of preferences for insect sushi, De-Magistris and Pascucci (2014) found evidence of efficacy of the oath script in lowering WTP estimates, relative to both a cheap talk script and a control group. In a recent study estimating the value of securing the future of two UK cultural institutions, Bakhshi et al. (2015) found that the oath script reduced mean WTP either alone, or in combination with cheap talk. These results suggest that oath scripts are a promising way to address hypothetical bias in contingent valuation surveys.

Some changes are complex and difficult to convey and respondents might be uncertain about how their welfare might be affected. Uncertainty typically occurs for goods and

---

Box 4.5. **Hypothetically speaking: Cheap talk and CVM**

A small but growing number of studies have sought to investigate the impact on hypothetical bias of adapting "cheap talk" (CT) concepts (defined as the costless transmission of information) in CV-like experiments. These studies include the pioneering experiments of Cummings and Taylor (1999) and Brown et al. (2003).

Hypothetical bias is described in these studies as the difference in what individuals say they would pay in a hypothetical setting vis-à-vis what they pay when the payment context is real. CT adds an additional text or script to the (hypothetical) question posed, explaining the problem of hypothetical bias and asking respondents to answer as if the payment context was real. Put another way, the objective of this approach to see if people can be talked out of behaving as if the experiment was hypothetical.

Although there are a number of psychological concerns about the effect that this CT information will have on respondents – will it bias them the other way and/or be too blatant a warning? – the results from these studies have been both interesting and important. For example, Cummings and Taylor (1999) only use one bid level which participants are asked to vote "yes" or "no" to. They find the CT-script to work well in reducing hypothetical bias: that is, bringing stated WTP amounts more in line with actual payments. Brown et al. (2003) vary the bid-level across respondents and still find that CT works well on similar terms.

Most of these studies are based on experiments using (paid) university students; i.e. not based on applications in the field amongst the public. This enables the CT-script to be relatively long. One concern is that the script needs to be much shorter if this method is to be widely applied in the field. However, the impacts of script-shortening on survey success do not appear to be encouraging, neither in experiments (Loomis et al., 1996) nor in the field (Poe et al., 1997).

---

services which are intricate and unfamiliar. Champ and Bishop (2001) tested the use of *certainty questions* (e.g. "how certain are you that you would really pay the amount indicated if asked") in an experiment with real payments. They found that respondents with a higher level of certainty regarding their stated WTP values were more likely to state they would actually pay the amounts when asked to do so. This suggests that the predictive accuracy of results may be increased by, for example, recoding uncertain WTP responses as zero payments (an *ex post* adjustment). Although typically ignored in many valuation studies, identifying certainty in valuation responses appears to play a role in enhancing their validity.

Other important considerations for reducing hypothetical bias include designing the contingent scenario to be credible, neutral and realistic; making sure, where possible, that surveys are perceived as consequential; i.e. respondents should believe that their responses will matter and have an impact; including reminders of budget constraints and substitute goods; and giving respondents time to think (Arrow et al., 1993; Mitchell and Carson, 1989; Bateman et al., 2002; Whittington, 1992; Carson and Groves, 2007; Haab et al., 2013).

Finally, it is important to note that, despite the potential for problems arising due to the hypothetical nature of CV, this is also its greatest strength, as it allows a degree of flexibility, applicability and scope, that other methods do not have, reliant as they are on existing data.

Insensitivity to scope

Insensitivity to scope[7] relates to a lack of sensitivity of respondents' valuations towards changes in the scope of the good or service being valued. More formally, insensitivity to scope occurs when stated values do not vary significant (or more strictly still, proportionally) to the scope of the provided benefit (i.e. broadly, larger benefits should be associated with larger WTP values) (Mitchell and Carson, 1989, Bateman et al., 2002). Compliance of CV estimates with the scope test is one of the most significant controversies in the CV validity debate. The debate can be traced back to two widely cited studies, Kahneman and Knetsch (1992) and Desvousges et al. (1993), who found that individuals' CV responses did not vary significantly with changes in the scope and coverage of the good being valued. Scope tests can be internal, whereby the same sample is asked to value different levels of the good; or these tests can be external, where different, but equivalent, sub-samples are asked to value different levels of the good. Internal tests of scope typically reject the hypothesis that respondents are not sensitive to the amount of the benefit being provided by the hypothetical policy change. The focus of the controversy has been based on the more powerful external scope tests. One important point to note here is that, because of income constraints and sometimes strongly diminishing marginal utility, WTP is not expected to vary linearly with the scope of a change; but it is nevertheless expected to show some variation.

A number of explanations have been advanced for this phenomenon. Kahneman and Knetsch (1992) argued that, because individuals' do not possess strongly articulated preferences for environmental goods, they tend to focus on other facets of the environment, such as the moral satisfaction associated with giving to a good cause. This "warm glow" effect would be independent of the size of the cause. Avoiding the use of donations as a payment vehicle would clearly minimise this possibility, as paying taxes is unlikely to generate a warm glow. Others have argued that embedding is more an artefact of poor survey design: for example, the use of vague descriptions of the good to be valued, or the failure to adequately convey information about the scope of the change (Carson, Flores and Meade, 2001; Smith, 1992). Another suggestion is that, to make valuation and financial decisions easier, people think in terms of a system of expenditure budgets, or "mental accounts", to which they allocate their income (Thaler, 1984). For environmental improvements, if the amount allocated to the "environment account" is quite small, then this might result in an inability to adjust valuations substantially in response to changes in the size and scope of an environmental good. Essentially, embedding might be a result of valuations' being determined by an income constraint which is inflexible and relatively strict compared with assessments of an individual's total (or full) income.

To assess the empirical importance of this phenomenon, Carson (1998) undertook a comprehensive review of the literature on split-sample tests of sensitivity to scope. This showed that, since 1984, 31 studies rejected the insensitivity hypothesis while 4 did not. Another way of looking at this issue involves comparing different studies valuing similar goods. A meta-analysis of valuation of air quality improvements (Smith and Osborne, 1996) also rejected the embedding hypothesis and showed that CV estimates from different studies varied in a systematic and expected way with differences in the characteristics of the good. Hence, it seems that early conclusions about the persistence of insensitivity to scope can partly be attributed to the lack of statistical power in the test used to detect differences in values.

Many practitioners have concluded that insensitivity to scope is normally a product of misspecified scenarios or vague and abstract definitions of the policy change that can lead respondents not to perceive any real difference between impacts of varying scope (Carson and Mitchell, 1995). Well-designed surveys should therefore be capable of overcoming to some extent the potential for scope insensitivity. A clear, detailed and meaningful definition of the scope of the proposed policy change is required. A possible design solution involves the adoption of a *top-down approach*, where respondents are first asked to value the larger good or service, and are subsequently asked to allocate a proportion of that value to the smaller component goods or services. The increase in popularity of online CV surveys makes it arguably easier to communicate information, test understanding and indeed to tailor information to respondents that might be having difficulties understanding the details of what they are being asked to value. Avoiding donations (to avoid warm glows), and giving respondents time to think to carefully read the scenarios and pick up differences in scope, are other suggestions.

Nevertheless, there are instances where describing the scope of policy changes is particularly difficult. A typical example is the presentation of small changes in health risks (e.g. small percentage changes) where insensitivity to scope has consistently been found, despite researchers' efforts to convey the information in simple and "respondent-friendly" ways (see Box 4.6). This is because people have difficulty in computing small numbers, and find it cognitively very problematic to distinguish between what are, in absolute terms, very small variations in scope. This limitation is not exclusive to surveys but is a feature of the way people behave in real markets.

Box 4.6. **Risk insensitivity in stated preference studies**

Past evidence has indicated that respondent WTP, in stated preference surveys, might be insufficiently sensitive to the size of the reduction in risk specified and that this is particularly the case for changes in very small baseline risks (Jones-Lee et al., 1985; Beattie et al., 1998). In a comprehensive review, Hammitt and Graham (1999) concluded that: "Overall, the limited evidence available concerning health-related CV studies is not reassuring with regard to sensitivity of WTP to probability variation." (p40). Interestingly, however, Corso et al. (2000) found that, on the one hand, there was evidence of risk insensitivity when risk reductions were only communicated verbally to respondents but, on the other hand, there was significant evidence of risk sensitivity when risk changes were also communicated visually. This important finding has led many practitioners to adopt visual aids to better depict the concept of risk changes.

This particular visual variant has been used successfully in a study of the preferences of individuals for reductions in mortality risks in Canada and the United States, by Alberini et al. (2004). Respondents were asked – using a dichotomous choice format – for their WTP to reduce this risk over a 10 year period by either 1 in 1 000 or 5 in 1 000: i.e. an external scope test. In order to assist respondents to visualise these small changes, the authors used the type of risk communication mechanism recommended by Corso et al. (2000), which in this case was a 1 000 square grid where red squares represented the prevalence of risks (used alongside other devices to familiarise respondents with the idea of mortality risk). Initial questions to respondents sought to identify those who had grasped these ideas and those who apparently had not. For example, respondents were asked to compare grids for two hypothetical people and to state which of the two had the higher risk of dying. Interestingly, roughly 12% of respondents in both the United States and Canada failed this test in that they (wrongly) chose the person with the lower risk of dying (i.e. fewer red squares on that hypothetical person's grid).

The point of this, and other screening questions that the authors used, was to identify those respondents in the sample who "adequately" comprehended risks – in the sense of readiness to answer subsequent WTP questions – and those who did not. The authors' expectations

---

> ## Box 4.6. **Risk Insensitivity in Stated Preference studies** (cont.)
>
> were that the responses of those in the former group were more likely to satisfy a test of scope (e.g. proportionality of WTP with the size of the change in risk) than those "contaminated" by the responses of those in the latter group. However, while the authors find that restricting the analysis to those who passed risk comprehensive tests leads to significantly different WTP amounts for the 1 in 1 000 and 5 in 1 000 risk reductions, this does not result in the sort of proportionality that many demand of this particular scope test: i.e. is WTP for the 5 in 1 000 risk change (about) 5 times WTP for the 1 in 1 000 risk change?
>
> What seems to make a difference in this study is a subsequent self-assessment question based on how confident a respondent felt they were about their WTP response. The results are summarised in Table 4.7. More confident respondents, on balance, appear to state WTP amounts, which pass the stricter scope test of proportionately. (The ratios of median WTP are not exactly 5 in either the US or Canadian case. However, the important thing here is that the numbers are not statistically different from this value.) The median WTP values based only on those respondents who were not so confident about their WTP answers, by contrast, did not pass this particular scope test. In other words, these findings appear to provide some important clues in the understanding of WTP and risk insensitivity.
>
> #### Table 4.7. **A scope test for mortality risks**
> Median WTP, USD
>
> | Risk reduction | Canada median WTP | | US median WTP | |
> | --- | --- | --- | --- | --- |
> | | More confident | Less confident | More confident | Less confident |
> | 5 in 1 000 | 414 | 268 | 205 | 445 |
> | 1 in 1 000 | 126 | 136 | 23 | 236 |
> | Ratio | 3.3 | 2.0 | 8.9 | 1.9 |
>
> Source: Alberini et al. (2004), "Does the value of statistical life vary with age and health status? Evidence from the US and Canada", Journal of Environmental Economics and Management, Vol. 48, pp. 769-792.

WTP-WTA disparity

As explained in Section 4.2, the Hicksian welfare measures that CV studies are designed to estimate can be elicited via either WTP or WTA questions. In theory, both value measures should be similar,[8] but in practice empirical evidence consistently shows that WTA values can be significantly larger than the corresponding WTP values. Horowitz and McConnell (2002) reviewed 45 usable studies reporting both WTP and WTA and found significant discrepancies between WTP and WTA (Table 4.8). They found that WTA was on average 7 times higher than WTP and that the further away the good being valued was from being an ordinary private good, the higher was the ratio of WTA to WTP. Importantly, Horowitz and McConnell also found that surveys using real goods showed no lower ratios than surveys with hypothetical goods. This suggests that the disparity between WTP and WTA is not peculiar to the hypothetical contexts that characterise stated preference studies;, one of the explanations sometimes advanced for the disparity, but once again an inherent feature of consumers' real behaviour.

This evidence prompted the NOAA guidelines to favour WTP measures of value (Arrow et al., 1993): given that WTP is bounded by income it is less prone to overstatement. However, WTA measures are often the conceptually correct welfare measures to use. Mitchell and Carson (1989) argue that the choice between WTP and WTA formulations depends on the property rights of the respondent in relation to the good being valued: if the

Table 4.8. **WTA/WTP for different types of goods**

Type of good	Ratio	Standard error
Public or non-market	10.4	2.5
Health and safety	10.1	2.3
Private goods	2.9	0.3
Lotteries	2.1	0.2
All goods	7.2	0.9

Source: Horowitz and McConnell (2002), "A review of WTA/WTP studies", Journal of Environmental Economics and Management, Vol. 44, pp. 426-447.

respondent is being asked to give up an entitlement, then the WTA measure is appropriate (Carson, 2000). For example, in the Mourato and Smith (2002) study summarised in Box 4.3, farmers were offered compensation to switch from their preferred land use to an alternative land use, that would not be as profitable for them in the short-term; in this case, it would not make sense to elicit WTP to switch land use.

Several hypotheses have been put forward to explain the disparity between WTP and WTA. Some of the main explanations are discussed in turn. The absence of close substitutes for the valued goods and services will lead to greater disparity between WTP and WTA (Hanemann 1991, 1999). Intuitively, if environmental goods have few substitutes then very high levels of compensation will be required to tolerate a reduction in their quantity. More technically, the ratio of WTA to WTP depends on the ratio of the income effect to the substitution effect.

Another popular explanation for the disparity between WTP and WTA, and the subject of a substantial literature, has developed around the notion of "loss aversion" and "reference dependence" which, if correct, would have major implications for cost-benefit analysis. The basic idea is that the loss of an established property right will require higher compensation than the gain of a new property right. This is because losses are weighted far more heavily than gains, where loss and gain are measured equally in terms of quantities. The point of reference for the loss and gain is an endowment point which is often the bundle of goods, or the amount of a specific good, already owned or possessed, but could be some other point, e.g. an aspiration level. The reference dependency model is owed mainly to Tversky and Kahnemann (1991) and builds on the earlier "prospect theory" work of Kahnemann and Tversky (1979). Many of the seminal works on reference dependency are collected together in Kahnemann and Tversky (2000). The explanation of reference dependency is essentially psychological: advocates of the approach argue that it is an observed feature of many gain or loss contexts, so that theory is essentially being advanced as an explanation of observed behaviour. Further behavioural explanations for observed stated preference anomalies are discussed below. Whether substitution effects alone or an endowment effect alone explains the disparity between WTA and WTP is ultimately an empirical issue. Some authors (e.g. Morrison, 1996; 1997; Knetsch, 1989; Knetsch and Sinden, 1984) have argued that both an endowment effect and a substitution effect explain the disparity. Effectively, loss aversion magnifies the substitution effect by shifting the indifference curve.

A number of other explanations have been proposed. Uncertain respondents tend to state low WTP and high WTA values as a result of their unfamiliarity either with the elicitation procedure or with the good (Bateman et al., 2002). Respondents who are asked to state a compensation to forego their initial property rights, may state very high WTA values as a form of protest (Mitchell and Carson, 1989). The disparity between WTP and

WTA may also, to some extent, be a product of informational constraints and inexperience. For example, List (2003) found that the behaviour of more experienced traders (in a number of different real markets) showed no signs of an endowment effect. And poor design of WTA studies can lead to an overestimation of stated compensation amounts by failing to remind respondents that the welfare measure required is the *minimum* compensation that would produce the same (not higher) well-being level as the change they are asked to forgo (in the case of a well-being-enhancing policy) (Bateman et al., 2002).

Framing bias

The quality of CV responses is crucially dependent on the *information* provided in the contingent scenario, namely on the accuracy and plausibility of the scenarios in order to engage respondents in the revelation of truthful preferences or to incentivise their formation. In recent years, the increased use of online CV surveys has facilitated the presentation of information, expediting the tailoring of information to respondent's needs (and level of understanding), measuring the time spent reading the information (effort), testing understanding, and enabling the use of alternative media, such as images, film or sound. Nevertheless, despite an extensive literature on information effects in CV (e.g. Hoehn and Randall, 2002; Blomquist and Whitehead, 1998; Ajzen, Brown and Rosenthal, 1996; Bergstrom, Stoll and Randall, 1990, 1989; Samples, Dixon and Gowen, 1986) empirical evidence about the "right" amount of information within a survey remains limited.

Another important area concerning the presentation of information relates to whether policy changes are presented in isolation, in sequence, or simultaneously, as part of a group of changes (Carson and Mitchell, 1995; Carson et al., 2001). Single modes of evaluation can elicit different preference rankings and monetary values to joint or multiple modes of evaluation because information is used differently when a point of comparison is available (Hsee and Zhang, 2004). This can result in preference reversals, and inconsistent value rankings depending on the order in which policy changes are evaluated (e.g. Brown 1984; Gregory et al., 1993; Irwin, et al., 1993). Moreover, surveys that focus on a single policy issue run the risk of artificially inflating its importance (also called focussing bias) (Kahneman and Thaler, 2006). This is because, at the time of preference elicitation, people are focusing only on the salient aspects of the policy and this may not reflect how they would actually experience this policy in real life where many other phenomena compete for their attention (Kahneman et al., 2006; Dolan and Kahneman, 2008). Also, people might adapt to certain changes and hence value them differently after some time.

Ultimately, the information presentation in a survey should match how the policy changes are expected to occur in practice, i.e. in isolation, in sequence or simultaneously. To avoid an excessive focus on the policy change being evaluated, stated preference surveys should be careful not to over-emphasise their importance. The changes of interest should be presented within the wider context of people's lives and experiences. For this purpose, it is important to include in the scenario reminders of substitute goods and services, as well as reminders of budget constraints and other possible expenses (Bateman et al., 2002; Arrow and Solow, 1993). If respondents are not reminded about other similar goods they may overestimate their WTP for a specific good or instead state the value they hold for the general type of good (Arrow and Solow, 1993; Loomis et al., 1994). In this respect, information overload concerns might occur because in order to ensure respondents adequately consider substitutes, it is necessary to provide a similar amount of information about substitutes, as the good and service of interest (Rolfe, Bennett and Louviere, 2002).

Moreover, it is beneficial where possible to give respondents extended periods of time to think about the issue, about how much it matters to them, to consider their respective valuations, and to allow an opportunity to discuss it with other relevant people. Whittington et al. (1992) showed that giving respondents the chance to go home and think about the survey for 24 hours had a significant negative impact on WTP values, as respondents were able to reflect on the importance of the issue in the wider context of their lives. With on-line surveys, it can be possible for respondents to interrupt the survey, and continue it at a later time, giving them extra time to think.

4.5.3. Reliability

Reliability is a measure of the stability and reproducibility of a measure. A common test of reliability is to assess the replicability of CV estimates over time (test-retest procedure). McConnell et al. (1997) reviewed the available evidence on temporal reliability tests and found a high correlation between individuals' WTP over time (generally between 0.5 and 0.9), regardless of the nature of the good and the population being surveyed, indicating that the contingent valuation method appears to be a reliable measurement approach. In addition, the original state-of-the-art Alaska Exxon Valdez questionnaire (Carson et al., 1992) was administered to a new sample two years later: the coefficients on the two regression equations predicting WTP were almost identical (Carson et al., 1997).

4.6. Recent developments and frontier issues

4.6.1. Insights from behavioural economics

The last decade has witnessed a huge increase in popularity of behavioural economics (BE) (see Camerer et al., 2011, for an early review as well as the edited volume by Shafir, 2013) and, in turn, of its influences in environmental economics (e.g. Horowitz et al., 2008; Shogren and Taylor, 2008; Brown and Hagen, 2010). Experimental research in this area has repeatedly identified empirical phenomena that are not adequately explained by traditional neo-classical economic analysis. Rabin (2010) talks about three waves in the development of behavioural economics, from the initial focus on the identification of behavioural anomalies, to formalising alternative theoretical conceptualisations in precise models, to fully integrating these alternatives into economic analysis, thereby improving and reshaping economic principles.

With the growth of behavioural economics, some of the known issues of stated preference methods were recast in the light of these alternative theories of behaviour. According to Shogren and Taylor (2004, p. 29) "Behavioural economics has probably had the biggest impact on environmental economics through research on the nonmarket valuation for environmental goods". Of note, two special editions of the journal *Environmental and Resources Economics* (in September 2005 and in June 2010) were dedicated to behavioural economics and the environment and to methods that have been developed to deal with preference anomalies in stated preference valuation studies.

In reality, most stated preference biases had been identified before behavioural economics came into vogue as a way of summarising such findings (Mitchell and Carson, 1989; Carson et al., 2001; Carson and Hanemann, 2005; Kahneman, 1986). For example, what used to be called information effects is now often referred to as framing, priming or focussing anomalies as a result of this general behavioural turn in economics. In fact, the relationship between environmental valuation and behavioural economics is complex and the historical developments of both are deeply intertwined. It is thought that research into perceived anomalies in stated preference studies was a contributing factor in the development and popularity of behavioural economics. Carson and Hanemann (2005, p. 30) noted that: "[t]here is, of course, some irony in that many of the key tenets of what is now often referred to as the behavioural economics revolution were first demonstrated in CV studies and declared anomalies of the method rather than actual economic behavior." As discussed earlier in this chapter, issues like limited cognitive ability to deal with small numbers, or loss aversion are found in actual market behaviour and are not simply an artefact of hypothetical markets, as was initially posited by CV critics. Fifteen years later, Carlsson (2010) also argued that the marriage of behavioural economics with non-market valuation techniques was inspired by anomalies that appeared in applied stated preference studies. And, as Horowitz et al. (2008, p. 4) put it, "Valuation is a form of experimentation and this experimentation has played a large role in learning about preferences and by extension, behavioural economics". More recently, Nelson (2017) argued that it was the oil industry's efforts to discredit CV after the Exxon Valdez disaster that helped to advance a new generation of behavioural economics.

Anomalies in stated preference data often emerge where bounded rationality exists (typically for complex and ill-understood changes) and can take many forms. This includes preferences which are imprecise or are only learned and constructed during the administration of the survey itself (and so likely to remain incomplete). It also includes factors which should be superfluous to determining respondent preferences but might not be in practice (e.g. context, such as current personal mood or immediate environment); or the change being valued commanding greater importance for respondents at the time of the survey when this is not a true reflection of how they would otherwise view its significance (the focussing illusion). A range of issues related to the complexity of valuation tasks may also be viewed in this way, including choice under risk and uncertainty (Sugden, 2005; Swait and Adamowicz, 2001; Horowitz et al., 2008; Shogren and Taylor, 2008; DellaVigna, 2009; Brown and Hagen, 2010; Carlsson, 2010; Gsottbauer and van den Bergh, 2011; Bosworth and Taylor, 2012).

Sugden (2005, p.7) states that when trying to comprehend the anomalies found in even the best designed stated preference studies, "we need to take account of evidence from the widest range of related judgement and decision-making tasks". These include assessing laboratory experiments of psychologists, behavioural economists and economic behaviour observed outside of stated preference studies. Gaining a better understanding from the behavioural economics literature of the source of the problems in stated preferences will make it possible to design better solutions to minimise them, as discussed further below.

Various studies have shown that the *Homo economicus* view of behaviour concerning self-interest consistently deviates from real-life actions of people, in that individuals typically care about reciprocity and equality (Fehr and Gächter, 2000; Camerer et al., 2011). Individuals have been found to punish others who operate in an uncooperative manner, whilst rewarding those who act in the communal interest. Cai et al. (2010) found that respondents in an internet-based hypothetical CV valuation study (measuring WTP for climate change mitigation strategies) exhibited increased WTP values when they believed that the negative effects of climate change would fall disproportionately on the world's poorest people and when larger cost shares were paid by those deemed to shoulder greater responsibility for mitigation. Moreover, the social context in which the valuation takes place also matters, as people care about others and about their approval. Alpizar et al. (2008)

found that contributions to a public good stated in public were 25% greater than contributions stated in private.

The role of emotions on the formation of stated preferences for non-market goods has also been investigated (Peters, 2006). Peters, Slovic, and Gregory (2003) looked at the impact of affect on the disparity between WTP and WTA. They found that buyers with stronger positive feelings about the good were willing to pay more for it, while sellers with stronger negative feelings about no longer having the good were willing to accept a greater minimum payment in exchange for it. Similarly, Araña and León (2008) looked at changes in emotion intensity to predict anchoring effects and WTP. And in a recent paper, Hanley et al. (2016) looked at the role of general incidental emotions (happy, sad and neutral, unrelated to the good being valued) on the valuation of changes in coastal water quality and fish populations in New Zealand. In this study, no statistically significant effects were found of changes in emotional state on WTP.

As discussed above, there is a well-documented difference in derived values between WTP and WTA studies (Horowitz and McConnell, 2002). Knetsch (2010) focused on which of these two elicitation methods to choose, depending on the case in question, highlighting that an understanding of reference states will help to avoid under-valuation of non-market environmental goods. Taking insights from behavioural economics, Bateman et al. (2009) found that by increasing the simplicity of tasks faced by respondents, the difference between WTP and WTA values regarding land use changes was reduced. Horowitz et al. (2008, p. 3) also discussed the divergence of WTP and WTA values in some detail, showing that behavioural knowledge of survey design and context dependence can help to understand the WTP-WTA gap: "making sense of the gaps is an essential component of sustaining the validity of this valuation method".

The results from the meta-analysis of CV studies by Brander and Koetse (2011) highlighted the effect of study design on value estimates and the authors discussed the need to recognise and accommodate this when using CV results (see also OECD, 2012). They found that the methodological design of a CV study had a sizable influence on results and that values derived using payment vehicles such as donations or taxes tended to be significantly lower than other payment scenarios. As with many other studies, the authors found that the use of dichotomous choice or payment card methods produced significantly reduced values compared with open-ended methods. Brown and Hagen (2010) considered that differences in behaviour might be mitigated by using survey devices such as budget constraint reminders and "time-to-think" procedures.

Looking at seven empirical studies, in which WTP value estimates were adjusted with preference uncertainty scores which quantify on a numerical scale how uncertain respondents stated they were about their WTP (e.g. from 0 to 10 where 0 might be wholly uncertain and 10 might be extremely certain) and then compared with conventional (i.e. unadjusted) double-bounded CV WTP estimates, Akter et al. (2008) discussed whether or not respondent uncertainty could be measured accurately. Contrary to the NOAA Panel (Arrow et al., 1993) advice, the empirical evidence explored in this study suggested that incorporating information on uncertainty led to largely inconsistent (and less efficient) welfare estimates. That said, an awareness of respondents' valuation confidence can be helpful in understanding survey results. Conversely, Morrison and Brown (2009) investigated techniques for reducing hypothetical bias, such as certainty scales, cheap talk and dissonance minimisation (where respondents are allowed to express support for a programme without having to pay for it). They found that certainty scales and dissonance minimisation were the most effective in reducing the bias.

Finally, in a seminal paper, Bateman et al. (2008) argued that a key mechanism for anomaly reduction in CV studies lies in providing respondents with opportunities for learning by repetition and experience. The authors tested three alternative conceptualisations of individual preferences: i) *a-priori* well-formed preferences, that are capable of being elicited via a single dichotomous choice question, as recommended by the NOAA guidelines (Arrow et al., 1993); ii) learned or "discovered" preferences through a process of repetition and experience, based on Plott's (1996) "discovered preference hypothesis", where stable and consistent preferences are argued to be not pre-existent, but the product of experience gained through repetition; and iii) internally coherent preferences but strongly influenced by arbitrary anchors, inspired by the work of Ariely et al. (2003).The latter argued that, even when individual choices are internally coherent, they can still be strongly anchored to some arbitrary starting point, and by altering this starting point, values can be arbitrarily manipulated (a type of behaviour coined as "coherent arbitrariness").

In order to test these alternatives, Bateman et al. (2008) develop the so called "learning design contingent valuation" method, which is essentially a double-bound dichotomous choice payment format (Hanemann et al., 1991), applied repeatedly to mutually exclusive goods, to allow for learning and experience in the valuation tasks and for the opportunity to "discover" preferences within the duration of the survey. Their findings support a model in which preferences converge towards standard expectations through a process of repetition and learning, i.e. the discovered preferences hypothesis (Plott, 1996). Knowledge of the operating rules of the contingent market was also found to be a prerequisite for producing reliable and accurate values.

Bateman et al. (2008) results suggest a number of practical empirical fixes for common CV issues. First, it supports the use of double-bounded dichotomous choice formats rather than one-shot single-bounded designs. Double-bounded designs have the added advantage of also permitting a substantial improvement in the statistical results of a given sample relative to that provided by applying a single-bounded format (because it contains more information about respondents' preferences). As a result, double-bounded CV formats have risen in popularity in recent years and have arguably become one of the most prevalent CV designs. Second, it indicates that it is the last response in a series of valuations which should be attended to rather than the first. Third, it supports the use of "practice" questions (such as those described by Plott and Zeiler, 2005), which could then be followed by a single, incentive-compatible, contingent valuation question. Finally, it also highlights the advantage of the increasingly common choice experiment method, discussed in the following chapter, as a means of developing institutional and value learning. The idea of preference learning during repeated choices has also been observed by researchers using choice experiments. Several studies have shown that estimates of both preferences and variance obtained from the initial choices are often out of line with those obtained from subsequent choices (Carlsson et al., 2012; Hess et al., 2012; Czajkowski et al., 2014).

It is hoped that wider adoption of elicitation approaches that provide opportunities for learning might lead to a reduction in issues in stated preference studies which have previously been regarded as insoluble anomalies. Particularly, it appears to be a promising avenue for exploring potentially more accurate estimates of non-use values, where unfamiliar goods and ill-formed preferences are particularly prone to a range of heuristics and framing effects.

4.6.2. Developments in technology and social media

On a more practical note, much progress has been made in the implementation of stated preference surveys. With the development of the internet, the growth in broadband penetration and the popularity of on-line forums, there has been a strong move towards designing and implementing surveys on-line (Lindhjem and Navrud, 2010). There are now many excellent (both proprietary and open-source) software products that can be used to produce high-quality web surveys (e.g. Qualtrics and Survey Monkey). Typically the implementation is carried out via a market research company that has access to an on-line panel of respondents, covering a wide range of demographics, which is paid to complete the surveys. Alternatively, there are also new crowdsourcing resources, such as Amazon's human intelligence task marketplace, Mechanical Turk. Here researchers (the "Requesters") are able to post tasks directly (in this case surveys). Prospective respondents (the "Turkers") then browse the existing tasks and choose to complete them for a monetary incentive set by the researchers.

Online surveys offer many advantages: they are very quick to implement (i.e. it is common to get hundreds of completed surveys back within 24 hours of launching); they are inexpensive (particularly when compared with face-to-face interviews); there is no need to input the data onto a spreadsheet as this is done automatically; the responses are immune to interviewer bias; and respondents are likely to feel more comfortable answering sensitive questions and moving through the survey at their own pace on their own and in familiar surroundings (Bateman et al., 2002; MacKerron et al., 2009). Crucially, these surveys provide a large amount of flexibility in terms of implementation. For example, the questionnaire can be tailored to the respondent, and it is easy to alter the flow of the questions depending on certain responses. Sound and images can be easily presented and it is possible to monitor the time taken on a particular page, or whether extra information was accessed.

Needless to say, there are pitfalls too. Not everyone has access to the internet (although in time this will become less of an issue as broadband reach extends, even to developing countries) and on-line surveys might not be the best option for certain groups such as the very elderly, or illiterate populations (although it is possible to design pictorial surveys to avoid this problem). Moreover, it is not possible to offer clarification if respondents get confused with certain parts of the text or the questions. A sizeable number of studies have investigated the impact of survey mode on stated values (e.g. Dickie et al., 2007; Marta-Pedroso et al., 2007).

Reassuringly, it seems that many reported problems with web-based valuation surveys can potentially be controlled for or avoided altogether. For example, respondents who speed through the survey can easily be detected and, if judged appropriate, discarded from the sample. Questions can be included to check attention and understanding. Learning mechanisms and trial questions can be added if the pilots reveal difficulties, and so on. More positively, some studies suggest that Internet panel surveys have desirable properties along several dimensions of interest (Bell et al., 2011). Importantly, Lindhjem and Navrud (2010) found no significant differences between CV values obtained between Internet and in-person administration. Within this context, these authors envisage a possible mass exodus from in-person interviews, the traditional gold standard in CV survey administration, to the much faster and cost-effective Internet surveys.

4.7. Summary and guidance for policy makers

Although controversial in some quarters, the contingent valuation method has gained increased acceptance amongst many academics and policy makers as a versatile and powerful methodology for estimating the monetary value of non-market impacts of projects and policies. Stated preference methods more generally offer a direct survey approach to estimating consumer preferences and more specifically WTP amounts for changes in provision of (non-market) goods, which are related to respondents' underlying preferences in a consistent manner. Hence, this technique is of particular worth when assessing impacts on public goods, the value of which cannot be uncovered using revealed preference methods. However, it is worth noting that contingent valuation methods are being used even where a revealed preference option is available.

This growing interest has resulted in research in the field of contingent valuation evolving substantially over the past 25 years or so. For example, the favoured choice of elicitation formats for WTP questions in contingent valuation surveys has already passed through a number of distinct stages, as previously discussed in this chapter. This does not mean that homogeneity across studies in the design of stated preference surveys can be expected any time soon. Nor would this particular development necessarily be desirable. The discussion in this chapter has illustrated findings from studies that show how, for example, legitimate priorities to minimise respondent strategic bias by always opting for incentive-compatible payment mechanisms must be balanced against equally justifiable concerns about the credibility of a payment vehicle. The point is that the answer to this problem is likely to vary across different types of project and policy problems.

As with any empirical methodology, there remain concerns about the validity of the findings of contingent valuation studies, particular in what concerns the measurement of non-use values. Much of the research in this field has sought to construct rigorous tests of the robustness of the methodology across a variety of policy contexts and non-market goods and services. CV has been subject to more stringent testing than any other similar methodology – and has become stronger as a result. The analysis of anomalies first detected in CV, led to the realisation that these were not necessarily an artefact of CV but in many cases reflected the way people behaved in reality. Contingent valuation turned out to be fertile ground for the development of behavioural economics.

By and large, the overview provided in the latter part of this chapter has struck an optimistic note about the use of contingent valuation to estimate the value of non-market goods. In this interpretation of recent developments, there is a virtuous circle between translating the lessons from tests of validity and reliability into practical guidance for future survey design. Indeed, many of the criticisms of the technique can be said to be imputable to problems at the survey design and implementation stage (and associated with the way people behave) rather than to some intrinsic methodological flaw. Taken as a whole, the empirical findings largely support the potential validity and reliability of CV estimates.

On the whole, developments in CV research overwhelmingly point to the merits (in terms of validity and reliability) of good quality studies and so point to the need for practitioners to follow, in some way, guidelines for best practice. While the NOAA guidelines continue to be a focal point, there are a number of more recent guidelines (e.g. the very recent Johnston et al., 2017, guidance, Bateman et al., 2002, which is intended to guide official applications of stated preference methods in the United Kingdom and Champ et al., 2003, for the United States), which also provide useful and state-of-art reference points for practitioners.

Notes

1. Clearly, there are general principles for writing valid questions and of questionnaire form and layout as well as guidelines in the context of stated preference research. Guidelines as regards these general issues can be found in a number of sources (see, for example, Tourangeau et al., 2000).

2. Describing the good and the policy change of interest may require a combination of textual information, photographs, drawings, maps, charts and graphs. For example, OECD (2012) presents a meta-analysis of studies of WTP for changes in mortality risks using stated preference methods and concludes that: "There is strong indication that if a visual tool or a specific oral or written explanation was used to explain the risk changes to the respondents in the survey, the estimated VSL [value of statistical life] tends to be lower" (p. 70).

3. Protest answers occur when respondents who are positively affected by a policy nevertheless reveal only a zero value for it, in payment card or open-ended elicitation, or reject any bid in a dichotomous choice setting. Outlying answers refer to unrealistically high values expressed typically in open-ended WTP or WTA questions.

4. It is worth mentioning some adjustments that have to be made in the arguments presented above when WTA is used rather than WTP. First, contrary to what happens when WTP is used, under a WTA format, open-ended elicitation procedures will likely produce higher average values than dichotomous choice procedures. Open-ended elicitation may also yield very large outliers. In this case, dichotomous choice is the conservative approach. Given that WTA measures are not constrained by income, respondents may have a tendency to overbid. Attention may have to be given to mechanisms to counteract this tendency.

5. It should be emphasised that the fact that income or ability to pay influences WTP is not a bias of stated preference methods. On the contrary, it shows that WTP accords to theoretical expectations. Such methods attempt to mimic what would happen in a market if a real market existed for the good or service in question. In a real market, ability to pay influences purchases; hence, one would expect the same to happen in hypothetical markets.

6. Entreaties have many other potential uses. Atkinson et al. (2012) for example use a cheap talk entreaty to reduce protest answers in a CV study eliciting the value of protecting tropical biodiversity amongst distant beneficiaries.

7. Insensitivity to scope is often called the "embedding effect".

8. In an influential article, Willig (1976) argued that the disparity between WTP and WTA must be small as the income effects are small.

References

Aadland, D. and A.J. Caplan (2006), "Cheap talk reconsidered: New evidence from CVM", *Journal of Economic Behavior & Organization*, Vol. 60(4), pp. 562-578.

Azjen, I., T.C. Brown and L.H. Rosenthal (1996), "Information bias in contingent valuation: Effects of personal relevance, Quality of Information, and Motivational Orientation", *Journal of Environmental Economics and Management*, Vol. 30(1), pp. 43-57, http://dx.doi.org/10.1006/jeem.1996.0004.

Akter, S., J. Bennett and S. Akhter (2008), "Preference uncertainty in contingent valuation", *Ecological Economics*, Vol. 67(3), pp. 345-351, http://dx.doi.org/10.1016/j.ecolecon.2008.07.009.

Alberini, A. et al. (2004), "Does the value of statistical life vary with age and health status? Evidence from the US and Canada", *Journal of Environmental Economics and Management*, Vol. 48, pp. 769-792, http://dx.doi.org/10.1016/j.jeem.2003.10.005.

Alpizar, F., F. Carlsson and O. Johansson-Stenman (2008), "Does context matter more for hypothetical than for actual contributions. Evidence from a natural field experiment", *Experimental Economics*, Vol. 11, pp. 299-314, http://dx.doi.org/10.1007/s10683-007-9194-9.

Araña, J.E. and C.J. León, (2008), "Do emotions matter? Coherent preferences under anchoring and emotional effects", *Ecological Economics*, Vol. 66 (4), pp. 700-711, http://dx.doi.org/10.1016/j.ecolecon.2007.11.005.

Ariely, D., G. Loewenstein and D. Prelec (2003), "'Coherent arbitrariness': Stable demand curves without stable preferences", *Quarterly Journal of Economics*, Vol. 118(1), pp. 73-105, https://doi.org/10.1162/00335530360535153.

Arold, B. (2016), *The Effect of Newspaper Framing on the Public Support of the Paris Climate Agreement*, MSc thesis, Department of Geography & Environment, LSE.

Arrow, K. and R. Solow (1993), *Report of the NOAA Panel on Contingent Valuation*, National Oceanic and Atmospheric Administration, Washington, DC, *https://sites.google.com/site/economiayambiente/PanelNOAA.pdf*.

Atkinson, G. et al. (2012), "When to Take No for an Answer? Using Entreaties to Reduce Protest Zeros in Contingent Valuation Surveys", *Environmental and Resource Economics*, Vol. 51 (4), pp. 497-523, *http://dx.doi.org/10.1007/s10640-011-9509-3*.

Atkinson, G. et al. (2004), "'Amenity' or 'Eyesore'? Negative willingness to pay for options to replace electricity transmission towers", *Applied Economic Letters*, Vol. 14(5), pp. 203-208, *http://dx.doi.org/10.1080/13504850410001674803*.

Bagnoli, M. and M. Mckee (1991), "Voluntary Contribution Games: Efficient Private Provision of Public Goods", *Economic Inquiry*, Vol. 29(2), pp. 351-366, *http://dx.doi.org/10.1111/j.1465-7295.1991.tb01276.x*.

Bakhshi, H. et al. (2015), *Measuring Economic Value in Cultural Institutions*, Arts and Humanities Research Council, *www.ahrc.ac.uk/documents/project-reports-and-reviews/measuringeconomicvalue/*.

Bateman, I.J. et al. (2009), "Reducing gain-loss asymmetry: A virtual reality choice experiment valuing land use change", *Journal of Environmental Economics and Management*, Vol. 58, pp. 106-118, *http://dx.doi.org/10.1016/j.jeem.2008.05.003*.

Bateman, I.J. et al. (2008), "Learning design contingent valuation (LDCV): NOAA guidelines, preference learning and coherent arbitrariness", *Journal of Environmental Economics and Management*, Vol. 55, pp. 127-141, *http://dx.doi.org/10.1016/j.jeem.2007.08.003*.

Bateman, I.J. et al. (2002), *Economic Valuation with Stated Preference Techniques: A Manual*, Edward Elgar, Cheltenham, United Kingdom.

Beattie, J. et al. (1998), "On the contingent valuation of safety and the safety of contingent valuation: Part 1 – Caveat investigator", *Journal of Risk and Uncertainty*, Vol. 17, pp. 5-25, *http://dx.doi.org/10.1023/A:1007711416843*.

Bell, J., J. Huber and W. Kip Viscusi (2011), "Survey mode effects on valuation of environmental goods", *International Journal of Environmental Research on Public Health*, Vol. 8(4), pp. 1222-1243, *http://dx.doi.org/10.3390/ijerph8041222*.

Bergstrom, J.C., J.R. Stoll and A. Randall, (1989), "Information effects in contingent markets", *American Journal of Agricultural Economics*, Vol. 71(3), pp. 685-691.

Bergstrom, J.C., J.R. Stoll and A. Randall (1990), "The impact of information on environmental commodity valuation decisions", *American Journal of Agricultural Economics*, Vol. 72(3), pp. 614-621.

Blomquist, G.C. and J.C. Whitehead (1998), "Resource quality information and validity of willingness to pay in contingent valuation", *Resource and Energy Economics*, Vol. 20(2), pp. 179-196, *https://doi.org/10.1016/S0928-7655(97)00035-3*.

Bosworth, R. and L.O. Taylor (2012), "Hypothetical bias in choice experiments: Is cheap talk effective at eliminating bias on the intensive and extensive margins of choice?", *B.E. Journal of Economic Analysis and Policy*, Vol. 12, pp. 1, *http://dx.doi.org/10.1515/1935-1682.3278*.

Brander, L.M. and M.J. Koetse (2011), "The value of urban open space: Meta-analyses of contingent valuation and hedonic pricing results", *Journal of Environmental Management*, Vol. 92(10), pp. 2763-2773, *http://dx.doi.org/10.1016/j.jenvman.2011.06.019*.

Brown, T.C. (1984), "The concept of value in resource allocation", *Land Economics*, Vol. 60, pp. 231-246.

Brown, T.C., I. Ajzen and D. Hrubes (2003), "Further tests of entreaties to avoid hypothetical bias in referendum contingent valuation", *Journal of Environmental Economics and Management*, Vol. 46(2), pp. 353-361, *http://dx.doi.org/10.1016/S0095-0696(02)00041-4*.

Brown, G. and D.A. Hagen (2010), "Behavioral economics and the environment", *Environmental and Resource Economics*, Vol. 46, pp. 139-146, *http://dx.doi.org/10.1007/s10640-010-9357-6*.

Cai, B., T.A. Cameron and G.R. Gerdes (2008), "Distributional preferences and the incidence of costs and benefits in climate change policy", *Environmental and Resource Economics*, Vol. 46, pp. 429-458, *http://dx.doi.org/10.1007/s10640-010-9348-7*.

Camerer, C.F., G. Loewenstein and M. Rabin (2011), *Advances in Behavioral Economics*, Princeton University Press, USA.

Carlsson, F. (2010), "Design of Stated Preference Surveys: Is There More to Learn from Behavioral Economics?", *Environmental and Resource Economics*, Vol. 46, pp. 167-177, *http://dx.doi.org/10.1007/s10640-010-9359-4*.

Carlsson, F., P. Frykblom and C. Lagerkvist (2005), "Using cheap talk as a test of validity in choice experiments", *Economics Letters*, Vol. 89(2), pp. 147-152, *http://dx.doi.org/10.1016/j.econlet.2005.03.010*.

Carlsson, F. et al. (2013), "The truth, the whole truth, and nothing but the truth – A multiple country test of an oath script", *Journal of Economic Behaviour and Organisation*, Vol. 89, pp. 105-121, *http://dx.doi.org/10.1016/j.jebo.2013.02.003*.

Carlsson, F. and P. Martinsson (2006), "Do experience and cheap talk influence willingness to pay in an open-ended contingent valuation survey?" *Working Papers in Economics* 109, Department of Economics School of Business, Economics and Law, Göteborg University. *https://gupea.ub.gu.se/bitstream/2077/2732/1/gunwpe0190.pdf*.

Carlsson, F., M.R. Mørbak and S.B. Olsen (2012), "The first time is the hardest: A test of ordering effects in choice experiments", *Journal of Choice Modelling*, Vol. 5(2), pp. 19-37, *http://dx.doi.org/10.1016/S1755-5345(13)70051-4*.

Carson, R.T. (1998), "Contingent Valuation Surveys and Tests of Insensitivity to Scope", in Kopp, R., W. Pommerhene and N. Schwartz, (eds.), *Determining the Value of Non-Marketed Goods: Economic, Psychological and Policy Relevant Aspects of Contingent Valuation Methods*, Kluwer, Boston.

Carson, R.T. (2000), "Contingent Valuation: A User's Guide", *Environment Science and Technology*, Vol. 34, pp. 1413-1418, *http://dx.doi.org/10.1021/es990728j*.

Carson, R.T. (2011), *Contingent Valuation: A Comprehensive Bibliography and History*, Edward Elgar, Cheltenham.

Carson, R.T. (2012), "Contingent Valuation: A Practical Alternative When Prices Aren't Available", *Journal of Economic Perspectives*, Vol. 26(4), pp. 27-42, *http://dx.doi.org/10.1257/jep.26.4.27*.

Carson, R.T. et al. (1996), "Contingent valuation and revealed preference methodologies: Comparing estimates for quasi-public goods", *Land Economics*, Vol. 72, pp. 80-99.

Carson, R.T., N.E. Flores and N.F. Meade (2001), "Contingent Valuation: Controversies and Evidence", *Environmental and Resource Economics*, Vol. 19(2), pp. 173-210, *http://dx.doi.org/10.1023/A:1011128332243*.

Carson, R.T., T. Groves and M.J. Machina (1997), "Stated preference questions: Context and optimal response", in *National Science Foundation Preference Elicitation Symposium*, University of California, Berkeley.

Carson, R.T. and T. Groves (2007), "Incentive and Informational Properties of Preference Questions", *Environmental and Resource Economics*, Vol. 37(1), pp. 181-210, *http://dx.doi.org/10.1007/s10640-007-9124-5*.

Carson, R. and W.M. Hanemann (2005), "Contingent Valuation", in Mäler, K.-G. and J.R. Vincent (eds.), *Handbook of Environmental Economics*, Elsevier, Amsterdam.

Carson, R.T. and J.J. Louviere (2011), "A common nomenclature for stated preference elicitation approaches", *Environmental and Resource Economics*, Vol. 49(4), pp. 539-559, *http://dx.doi.org/10.1007/s10640-010-9450-x*.

Carson, R.T. and R.C. Mitchell (1995), "Sequencing and nesting in contingent valuation surveys", *Journal of Environmental Economics and Management*, Vol. 28(2), pp. 155-173, *http://dx.doi.org/10.1006/jeem.1995.1011*.

Carson, R.T. et al. (1992), *A Contingent Valuation Study of Lost Passive Use Values Resulting from the Exxon Valdez Oil Spill*, Report to the Attorney General of the State of Alaska, prepared by Natural Resource Damage Assessment, Inc, La Jolla, CA, *www.evostc.state.ak.us/Universal/Documents/Publications/Economic/Econ_Passive.pdf*.

Champ, P.A. and R.C. Bishop (2001), "Donation payment mechanisms and contingent valuation: An empirical study of hypothetical bias", *Environmental and Resource Economics*, Vol. 19(4), pp. 383-402, *http://dx.doi.org/10.1023/A:1011604818385*.

Champ, P. A. et al. (2002), "Contingent valuation and incentives", *Land Economics*, Vol. 78(4), pp. 591-604, *www.fs.fed.us/rm/value/docs/contingent_valuation_incentives.pdf*.

Champ, P.A., K.J. Boyle and T.C. Brown (eds.) (2003), *A Primer on Nonmarket Valuation*, Kluwer Academic Publishers, Dordrecht.

Corso, P.S., J.K. Hammitt and J.D. Graham (2001), "Valuing mortality-risk reduction: Using visual aids to improve the validity of contingent valuation", *Journal of Risk and Uncertainty*, Vol. 23, pp. 165-84, *http://dx.doi.org/10.1023/A:1011184119153*.

Cummings, R.G., D.S. Brookshire and W.D. Schulze (eds.) (1986), *Valuing Environmental Goods: An Assessment of the Contingent Valuation Method*, Rowman and Allanhed, Totowa, New Jersey.

Cummings, R.G. and L.O. Taylor (1999), "Unbiased value estimates for environmental goods: A cheap talk design for the contingent valuation method", *American Economic Review*, Vol. 89(3), pp. 649-665, *http://dx.doi.org/10.1257/aer.89.3.649.*

Czajkowski, M., M. Giergiczny and W. Greene (2014), "Learning and fatigue effects revisited. The impact of accounting for unobservable preference and scale heterogeneity", *Land Economics*, Vol. 90(2), pp. 324-351, *http://dx.doi.org/10.3368/le.90.2.324.*

Davis, R. (1963), "Recreation Planning as an Economic Problem", *Natural Resources Journal*, Vol. 3, pp. 239-249.

DellaVigna, S. (2009), "Psychology and economics: Evidence from the field", *Journal of Economic Literature*, Vol. 47, pp. 315-372, *http://dx.doi.org/10.1257/jel.47.2.315.*

de-Magistris, T. and S. Pascucci (2014), "The effect of the solemn oath script in hypothetical choice experiment survey: A pilot study", *Economic Letters*, Vol. 123, pp. 252-255, *http://dx.doi.org/10.1016/j.econlet.2014.02.016.*

Desvousges, W. et al. (1993), "Measuring Natural Resource Damages with Contingent Valuation: Tests of Validity and Reliability", in Hausman, J. (ed.) *Contingent Valuation: A Critical Assessment*, North-Holland, Amsterdam.

Diamond, P.A. and J.A. Hausman (1994), "Contingent Valuation: Is Some Number Better Than No Number?", *Journal of Economic Perspectives*, Vol. 8, pp. 45-64.

Dickie, M., S. Gerking and W.L. Goffe (2007), "Valuation of non-market goods using computer-assisted surveys: A comparison of data quality from internet and Rdd samples", presentation at European Association of Environmental and Resource Economists, Thessaloniki, Greece, *http://cook.rfe.org/Survey_Comparison_3.pdf.*

Dillon, W.R., T.J. Madden and N.H. Firtle (1994), *Marketing Research in a Marketing Environment*, 3rd Edition, Irwin, Boston

Dolan, P. and D. Kahneman (2008), "Interpretations of utility and their implications for the valuation of health", *The Economic Journal*, Vol. 118(525), pp. 215-234, *http://dx.doi.org/10.1111/j.1468-0297. 2007.02110.x.*

Dubourg, W.R., M.W. Jones-Lee and G. Loomes (1997), "Imprecise preferences and survey design in contingent valuation", *Economica*, Vol. 64, pp. 681-702, *http://dx.doi.org/10.1111/1468-0335.00106.*

Ehmke, M.D., J.L. Lusk and J.A. List (2008), "Is Hypothetical Bias a Universal Phenomenon? A Multinational Investigation", *Land Economics*, Vol. 84, pp. 489-500, *http://dx.doi.org/10.3368/le.84.3.489.*

Fehr, E. and S. Gächter (2000), "Fairness and retaliation: The economics of reciprocity", *Journal of Economic Perspectives*, Vol. 14(3), pp. 159-181, *http://dx.doi.org/10.1257/jep.14.3.159.*

Flores, N. and R. Carson (1997), "The relationship between income elasticities of demand and willingness to pay", *Journal of Environmental Economics and Management*, Vol. 33, pp. 287-295, *http://dx.doi.org/10.1006/jeem.1997.0998.*

Foster, V., I. Bateman and D. Harley (1997), "A non-experimental comparison of real and hypothetical willingness to pay", *Journal of Agricultural Economics*, Vol. 48(2), pp. 123-138, *http://dx.doi.org/10.1111/j.1477-9552.1997.tb01140.x.*

Freeman III, A.M. (1994), *The Measurement of Environmental and Resource Values: Theory and Methods*, Resources for the Future, Washington, DC.

Georgiou, S. et al. (1998), "Determinants of individuals' willingness to pay for perceived reductions in environmental health risks: A case study of bathing water quality", *Environment and Planning A*, Vol. 30, pp. 577-594, *http://dx.doi.org/10.1068/a300577.*

Gsottbauer, E. and J.C. van den Bergh (2011), "Environmental policy theory given bounded rationality and other-regarding preferences", *Environmental and Resource Economics*, Vol. 49: 263-304, *http://dx.doi.org/10.1007/s10640-010-9433-y.*

Gregory, R., S. Lichtenstein and P.Slovic (1993), "Valuing environmental resources: A constructive approach", *Journal of Risk and Uncertainty*, Vol. 7(2), pp. 177-197, *http://dx.doi.org/10.1007/BF01065813.*

Groothuis, P.A. and J.C. Whitehead (2009), "The Provision Point Mechanism and Scenario Rejection in Contingent Valuation", *Agricultural and Resource Economics Review*, Vol. 38(2), pp. 271-280, *http://dx.doi.org/10.1017/S1068280500003257.*

Haab T.C. et al. (2013), "From Hopeless to Curious? Thoughts on Hausman's 'Dubious to Hopeless' Critique of Contingent Valuation", *Applied Economic Perspectives and Policy*, Vol. 35(4), pp. 593-612, *https://doi.org/10.1093/aepp/ppt029.*

Hammitt, J. and J. Graham (1999), "Willingness to pay for health protection: Inadequate sensitivity to probability?", *Journal of Risk and Uncertainty*, Vol. 18, pp. 33-62, https://doi.org/10.1023/A:1007760327375.

Hanemann, M. (1991), "Willingness to pay and willingness to accept: How much can they differ?", *American Economic Review*, Vol. 81, pp. 635-647, https://doi.org/10.1257/000282803321455430.

Hanemann, M. (1999), "The economic theory of WTP and WTA", in, Bateman, I. and K. Willis (eds). *Valuing Environmental Preferences: Theory and Practice of the Contingent Valuation Method in the US, EU and Developing Countries*, Oxford University Press, Oxford.

Hanemann, W.M. and B. Kanninen, (1999), "The Statistical Analysis of Discrete-Response CV Data", in Bateman, I.J. and K.G. Willis (eds.) *Valuing Environmental Preferences: Theory and Practice of the Contingent Valuation Method in the US, EU, and Developing Countries*, Oxford University Press, Oxford.

Hanemann, M., J. Loomis and B. Kanninen (1991), "Statistical efficiency of double-bounded dichotomous choice contingent valuation", *American Journal of Agricultural Economics*, Vol. 73(4), pp. 1255-1263, https://doi.org/10.2307/1242453.

Hanley, N., C. Boyce, M. Czajkowski, S. Tucker, C. Noussair and M. Townsend (2016), "Sad or happy? The effects of emotions on stated preferences for environmental goods", *Environmental and Resource Economics*, https://doi.org/10.1007/s10640-016-0048-9.

Hanley, N. and B. Kriström (2003), *What's It Worth? Exploring Value Uncertainty Using Interval Questions in Contingent Valuation*, Department of Economics, University of Glasgow, mimeo, www.gla.ac.uk/media/media_22253_en.pdf.

Hausman, J. (2012), "Contingent Valuation: From Dubious to Hopeless", *Journal of Economic Perspectives*, Vol. 26(4), pp. 43-56, https://doi.org/10.1257/jep.26.4.43.

Hess, S., D.A. Hensher and A. Daly (2012), "Not bored yet – Revisiting respondent fatigue in stated choice experiments", *Transportation Research Part A*, Vol. 46, pp. 626-644, http://dx.doi.org/10.1016/j.tra.2011.11.008.

Hicks, J.R. (1943), "The four consumer's surpluses", *Review of Economic Studies*, Vol. 11, pp. 31-41, http://dx.doi.org/10.2307/2967517.

Hoehn, J.P. and A. Randall (2002), "The effect of resource quality information on resource injury perceptions and contingent values", *Resource and Energy Economics*, Vol. 24(1-2), pp. 13-31, http://dx.doi.org/10.1016/S0928-7655(01)00051-3.

Horowitz, J. and K. McConnell (2002), "A review of WTA/WTP studies", *Journal of Environmental Economics and Management*, Vol. 44, pp. 426-447, http://dx.doi.org/10.1006/jeem.2001.1215.

Horowitz, J.K., K.E. McConnell and J.J. Murphy (2008), "Behavioral foundations of environmental economics and valuation", in List, J. and M. Price (eds.), *Handbook on Experimental Economics and the Environment*, Edward Elgar, Northampton, MA.

Hsee, C.K. and J. Zhang, (2004), "Distinction Bias: Misprediction and Mischoice Due to Joint Evaluation", *Journal of Perspectives in Social Psychology*, Vol. 86, pp. 680-695, http://dx.doi.org/10.1037/0022-3514.86.5.680.

Irwin, J.R. et al. (1993), "Preference reversals and the measurement of environmental values", *Journal of Risk and Uncertainty*, Vol. 6(1), pp. 5-18, http://dx.doi.org/10.1007/BF01065347.

Jacquemet, N. et al. (2013), "Preference elicitation under oath", *Journal of Environmental Economics and Management*, Vol. 65, pp. 110-132, http://dx.doi.org/10.1016/j.jeem.2012.05.004.

Johnston, R.J. et al. (2017), "Contemporary guidance for stated preference studies", *Journal of the Association of Environmental and Resource Economists*, Vol. 4, pp. 319-405, https://doi.org/10.1086/691697.

Jones-Lee, M.W., M. Hammerton and P.R. Phillips (1985), "The value of safety: Results from a national sample survey", *Economic Journal*, Vol. 95, pp. 49-72, http://dx.doi.org/10.2307/2233468.

Kahneman, D. (1986), "Comments", in Cummings, R., D. Brookshire and W. Schulze (eds.), *Valuing Environmental Goods: An Assessment of the Contingent Valuation Method*, Rowman and Allenheld, Totowa, NJ.

Kahneman, D. and J.L. Knetsch (1992), "Valuing public goods: The purchase of moral satisfaction", *Journal of Environmental Economics and Management*, Vol. 22(1), pp. 57-70, http://dx.doi.org/10.1016/0095-0696(92)90019-S.

Kahneman, D. et al. (2006), "Would you be happier if you were richer? A focusing illusion", *Science*, Vol. 312(5782), pp. 1908-1910, http://dx.doi.org/10.1126/science.1129688.

Kahneman, D. and R.H. Thaler (2006), "Anomalies: Utility maximization and experienced utility", *Journal of Economic Perspectives*, Vol. 20(1), pp. 221-234, http://dx.doi.org/10.1257/089533006776526076.

Kahneman, D. and A. Tversky (1979), "Prospect Theory: An Analysis of Decision under Risk", *Econometrica*, Vol. 47, pp. 263-291, *http://dx.doi.org/10.2307/1914185*.

Kahnemann, D. and A. Tversky (eds.) (2000), *Choice, Values and Frames*, Cambridge University Press, Cambridge.

Kling, C.L., D.J. Phaneuf and J. Zhao (2012), "From Exxon to BP: Has Some Number Become Better Than No Number?", *Journal of Economic Perspectives*, Vol. 26(4), pp. 3-26, *http://dx.doi.org/10.1257/jep.26.4.3*.

Knetsch, J. (1989), "The endowment effect and evidence of non-reversible indifference curves", *American Economic Review*, Vol. LXXIX, pp. 1277-84.

Knetsch, J. (2010), "Values of gains and losses: Reference states and choice of measure", *Environmental and Resource Economics*, Vol. 46(2), pp. 179-188, *http://dx.doi.org/10.1007/s10640-010-9355-8*.

Knetsch, J. and J. Sinden (1984), "Willingness to pay and compensation demanded: Experimental evidence of an unexpected disparity in measures of value", *Quarterly Journal of Economics*, Vol. XCIX, pp. 507-21, *http://dx.doi.org/10.2307/1885962*.

Lindhjem, H. and S. Navrud (2010), "Can cheap panel-based internet surveys substitute costly in-person interviews in CV surveys?", Department of Economics and Resource Management, Norwegian University of Life Sciences, *http://citeseerx.ist.psu.edu/viewdoc/download?doi=10.1.1.969.3518&rep=rep1&type=pdf*.

List, J.A. (2003), "Does market experience eliminate market anomalies?", *Quarterly Journal of Economics*, Vol. 118, pp. 41-72, *https://doi.org/10 1162/00335530360535144*.

List, J.A. and D. Lucking-Reiley (2000) "Demand reduction in multiunit auctions: Evidence from a sportscard field experiment", *American Economic Review*, Vol. 90(4), pp. 961-972, *http://dx.doi.org/10.1257/aer.90.4.961*.

Loomis, J. (2014), "Strategies for overcoming hypothetical bias in stated preference surveys", *Journal of Agricultural and Resource Economics*, Vol. 39/1, pp. 34-46.

Loomis, J.B., T. Lucero and G. Peterson (1996), "Improving validity experiments of contingent valuation methods: Results of efforts to reduce the disparity of hypothetical and actual willingness to pay", *Land Economics*, Vol. 72(4), pp. 450-61.

Loomis, J., A. Gonzalez-Caban and R. Gregory (1994), "Do reminders of substitutes and budget constraints influence contingent valuation estimates?", *Land Economics*, Vol. 70, pp. 499-506.

Lusk, J.L. (2003), "Effects of cheap talk on consumer willingness-to-pay for golden rice", *American Journal of Agricultural Economics*, Vol. 85(4), pp. 840-856, *https://doi.org/10.1111/1467-8276.00492*.

MacKerron, G. et al. (2009), "Willingness to Pay for Carbon Offset Certification and Co-Benefits Among (High-)Flying Young Adults in the UK", *Energy Policy*, Vol. 37, pp. 1372-1381, *http://eprints.lse.ac.uk/44829/*.

Maddison, D. and S. Mourato (2002), "Valuing different road options for Stonehenge", in S. Navrud and R. Ready (eds.) *Valuing Cultural Heritage*, Edward Elgar, Cheltenham.

Marta-Pedroso, C., H. Freitas and T. Domingos (2007), "Testing for the survey mode effect on contingent valuation data quality: A case study of web based versus in-person interviews", *Ecological Economics*, Vol. 62, pp. 388-398, *http://dx.doi.org/10.1016/j.ecolecon.2007.02.005*.

McConnell, K., I.E. Strand and S. Valdes (1997), "Testing temporal reliability and carry-over effect: The role of correlated responses in test-retest reliability studies", *Environmental and Resource Economics*, Vol. 12, pp. 357-374, *http://dx.doi.org/10.1023/A:1008264922331*.

Mitchell, R.C. and R.T. Carson (1989), *Using Surveys to Value Public Goods: The Contingent Valuation Method*, Resources for the Future, Washington, DC.

Morrison, G. (1996), "Willingness to pay and willingness to accept: Some evidence of an endowment effect", *Discussion Paper 9646*, Department of Economics, Southampton University.

Morrison, G. (1997), "Willingness to pay and willingness to accept: Have the differences been resolved?", *American Economic Review*, Vol. 87/1, pp. 236-240.

Morrison, M. and T.C. Brown, (2009), "Testing the effectiveness of certainty scales, cheap talk, and dissonance-minimization in reducing hypothetical bias in contingent valuation studies", *Environmental and Resource Economics*, Vol. 44/3, pp. 307-326, *http://dx.doi.org/10.1007/s10640-009-9287-3*.

Mourato, S. and J. Smith (2002), "Can carbon trading reduce deforestation by slash-and-burn farmers? Evidence from the Peruvian Amazon", in Pearce, D., C. Pearce and C. Palmer (eds.) (2002), *Valuing the Environment in Developing Countries: Case Studies*, Edward Elgar, Cheltenham, UK.

Murphy, J.J., T. Stevens and D. Weatherhead (2003), "An empirical study of hypothetical bias in voluntary contribution contingent valuation: Does cheap talk matter?", *Working Paper*, University of Massachusetts, Amherst.

Nelson, S.H. (2017) Containing Environmentalism: Risk, Rationality, and Value in the Wake of the Exxon Valdez, *Capitalism Nature Socialism*, Vol. 28(1), pp. 118-136.

OECD (2012), *Mortality Risk Valuation in Environment, Health and Transport Policies*, OECD Publishing, Paris, *http://dx.doi.org/10.1787/9789264130807-en*.

Peters, E. (2006), "The functions of affect in the construction of preferences", in Lichtenstein, S. and P. Slovic (eds.) (2006) *The Construction of Preferences*, Cambridge University Press, New York.

Peters, E., P. Slovic and R. Gregory (2003) "The role of affect in the WTA/WTP disparity", *Journal of Behavioral Decision Making*, Vol. 16 (4), pp. 309-330, *http://dx.doi.org/10.1002/bdm.448*.

Plott, C.R. (1996), "Rational individual behavior in markets and social choice processes: The discovered preference hypothesis", in K. Arrow et al. (eds.) *Rational Foundations of Economic Behavior*, Macmillan, London and St. Martin's, New York.

Plott, C.R. and K. Zeiler (2005), "The willingness to pay-willingness to accept gap, the 'endowment effect', subject misconceptions, and experimental procedures for eliciting valuations", *American Economic Review*, Vol. 95(3), pp. 530-545, *http://dx.doi.org/10.1257/0002828054201387*.

Poe, G.L. et al. (2002), "Provision Point Mechanisms and Field Validity Tests of Contingent Valuation", *Environmental and Resource Economics*, Vol. 23, pp. 105-131, *http://dx.doi.org/10.1023/A:1020242907259*.

Poe, G., M. Welsh and P. Champ (1997), "Measuring the difference in mean willingness to pay when dichotomous choice valuation responses are not independent", *Land Economics*, Vol. 73(2), pp. 255-267.

Rabin, M. (2010), "Behavioral Economics", Lecture to the American Economic Association (AEA) Continuing Education Program in Behavioral Economics, Atlanta, January 5-7, available on-line at: *https://scholar.harvard.edu/files/laibson/files/atlantapostmatthew.pdf*.

Rolfe, J., J. Bennett and J. Louviere (2002), "Stated values and reminders of substitute goods: Testing for framing effects with choice modelling", *Australian Journal of Agricultural and Resource Economics*, Vol. 46(1), pp. 1-20, *http://dx.doi.org/10.1111/1467-8489.00164*.

Samples, K.C., J.A. Dixon and M.M. Gowen (1986), "Information disclosure and endangered species valuation", *Land Economics*, Vol. 62, pp. 306-312.

Shogren, J. and L. Taylor (2008), "On behavioral-environmental economics", *Review of Environmental Economics and Policy*, Vol. 2(1), pp. 26-44, *https://doi.org/10.1093/reep/rem027*.

Smith, V.K. (1992), "Arbitrary values, good causes, and premature verdicts", *Journal of Environmental Economics and Management*, Vol. 22, pp. 71-89, *http://dx.doi.org/10.1016/0095-0696(92)90020-W*.

Smith, V.K. (2006), "Fifty years of contingent valuation", in A. Alberini, and J.R., Kahn, (eds.) (2006), *Handbook on Contingent Valuation*, Edward Elgar, Cheltenham.

Smith, V.K. and L. Osborne, (1996), "Do Contingent Valuation Estimates Pass a Scope Test? A Meta-Analysis", *Journal of Environmental Economics and Management*, Vol. 31, pp. 287-301, *http://dx.doi.org/10.1006/jeem.1996.0045*.

Stevens, T.H., M. Tabatabaei and D. Lass (2013), "Oaths and hypothetical bias", *Journal of Environmental Management*, Vol. 127, pp. 135-141, *http://dx.doi.org/10.1016/j.jenvman.2013.04.038*.

Sugden, R. (2005), "Anomalies and stated preference techniques: A framework for a discussion of coping strategies", *Environmental and Resource Economics*, Vol. 32, pp. 1-12, *http://dx.doi.org/10.1007/s10640-005-6025-3*.

Swait, J. and W. Adamowicz (2001), "Choice environment, market complexity, and consumer behavior: A theoretical and empirical approach for incorporating decision complexity into models of consumer choice", *Organizational behavior and human decision processes*, Vol. 86 (2), pp. 141-167, *http://dx.doi.org/10.1006/obhd.2000.2941*.

Thaler, R. (1984), "Towards a Positive Theory of Consumer Choice", *Journal of Economic Behaviour and Organisation*, Vol. 1, pp. 29-60, *www.eief.it/butler/files/2009/11/thaler80.pdf*.

Tversky, A. and D. Kahneman, (1991), "Loss aversion in riskless choice: A reference-dependent model", *Quarterly Journal of Economics*, Vol. 106(4), pp. 1039-1061, *https://doi.org/10.2307/2937956*.

von Ciriacy-Wantrup, S. (1947), "Capital returns from soil-conservation practices", *Journal of Farm Economics*, Vol. 29, pp. 1181-1196.

Whittington, D. (2010), "What have we learned from 20 years of stated preference research in less-developed countries?", *Annual Review of Resource Economics*, Vol. 2, pp. 209-236, *http://dx.doi.org/10.1146/annurev.resource.012809.103908*.

Whittington, D. et al. (1992), "Giving respondents time to think in contingent valuation studies: A developing country application", *Journal of Environmental Economics and Management*, Vol. 22, pp. 205-225, *http://dx.doi.org/10.1016/0095-0696(92)90029-V*.

Willig, R. (1976), "Consumers' surplus without apology", *American Economic Review*, Vol. 66 (4), pp. 589-597, *www.jstor.org/stable/1806699*.

ANNEX 4.A1

Hicks's measures of consumer's surplus for a price change

Compensating variation (CV)

Consider a price *decrease*. The individual is better off with the price decrease than without it. CV is then the maximum sum that could be taken away from the individual such that he is indifferent between the post-change (new) situation and the pre-change (original) situation. The reference point is the *original* level of welfare.

Consider a price *increase*. The individual is worse off with the price increase than without it. CV is then the compensation required by the individual to make him indifferent between the new and old situations. The reference point is again the *original* level of welfare.

The CV measures relate to a context in which the change in question takes place. In this case they relate to the situation in which the price falls. CV in the context of a price fall thus measures the individual's *maximum willingness to pay* rather than relinquish the price reduction. In the context of a price rise, CV is the *minimum amount the individual is willing to accept* by way of compensation to tolerate the higher price. Note that the implicit assumption about property rights with CV is that the individual is entitled to the pre-change situation.

Equivalent variation (EV)

Consider a price *decrease*. The individual is better off with the price decrease than without it. EV measures the sum of money that would have to be given to the individual in the original situation to make him as well off as he would be in the new situation. The reference point is the level of welfare in the *new* situation.

Consider a price *increase*. EV is now the individual's willingness to pay to avoid the price increase, i.e. to avoid the decrease in welfare that would arise in the post-change situation. The reference point is the level of welfare in the *new* situation.

The EV measures relate to a context in which *the price change does not take place*. EV for a price fall is the *minimum willingness to accept* to forego the price fall. EV for a price rise is the *maximum willingness to pay* to avoid the price rise. Note that the implicit assumption about property rights with EV is that the individual is entitled to the post change situation.

Compensating surplus (CS)

The compensating surplus, CS, and equivalent surplus (ES) measures relate to contexts in which the individual is constrained to consume either the new quantity of X (CS) or the old quantity of X (ES) arising from the price change. CS is then defined as the sum that would make the individual indifferent between the original situation and a situation in which he is constrained to buy the quantity of X that results from the price change. If the context is a price *decrease*, then CS is a measure of the *willingness to pay* to secure that decrease. If the context is one of a price *increase*, then CS is a measure of the *willingness to accept* compensation for the price increase.

Equivalent surplus (ES)

ES is similarly quantity-constrained and is defined as the sum that would make the individual indifferent between the new situation (with the price change) and the old situation if the individual is constrained to buy the quantity of X in the original situation. If the context is a price *decrease*, then ES is a measure of the *willingness to accept* compensation to forego the benefit of the price decrease. If the context is one of a price *increase*, then ES is a measure of the *willingness to pay* to avoid the increase.

The concepts can be shown diagrammatically, as in Figure A4.1 which shows the situation for a price fall. The following relationships hold for equivalent price changes:

- CV price fall = –EV price rise.
- EV price fall = –CV price rise.
- EV = CV if the income elasticity of demand for X is zero.
- EV > CV for a price decrease if the income elasticity of demand is positive.
- EV < CV for a price increase if the income elasticity of demand is positive.
- The higher the income elasticity of demand for X, the greater the disparity between CV and EV.

Note that Figure A4.1 shows the four measures of surplus for a price fall. The same notions will apply to a price rise, giving eight measures in all.

Figure A4.1. **Hicks's four consumer's surpluses for a price fall**

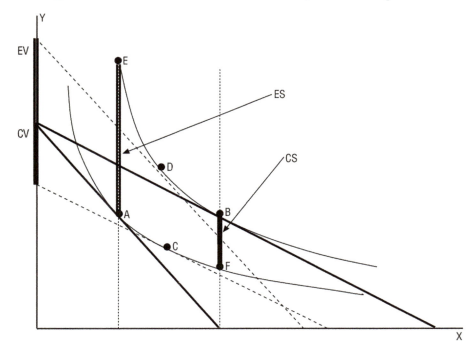

PART I

Chapter 5

Discrete choice experiments

Many types of environmental impacts are multidimensional in character. What this means is that an environmental resource that is affected by a proposed project or policy often will give rise to changes in component attributes each of which command distinct valuations. One tool that can elicit respondents' distinct valuations of these multiple dimensions, and account for trade-offs between them, are (discrete) choice experiments (DCEs). DCEs share strengths and weaknesses with contingent valuation but also have some distinctive characteristics that may differentially affect its performance and accuracy. A number of developments, on the face of it, appear to work against one another. The selection of the experimental design, i.e. the combination of attributes and levels to be presented to respondents in the choice sets, is a key stage and the tendency has been to opt for increasingly complex designs, to improve response efficiency. Yet this creates inevitable cognitive difficulty for respondents, associated with making multiple complex choices between bundles, with many attributes and levels. There is a limit to how much information respondents can meaningfully handle while making a decision, possibly leading to error and imprecision, depending on whether fatigue or learning dominate respondent reactions. The links to behavioural research are again highly relevant such as on heuristics, and filtering rules guiding choices that are "good enough" rather than utility-maximising. The growing sophistication of statistical modelling of responses is another notable characteristic of this work and has enabled far better account for considerations such as preference heterogeneity. While the domain of specialists, this modelling is increasingly accessible more broadly via a growth in training opportunities and free statistical software.

5.1. Introduction

Discrete choice experiments (DCEs) are a multi-attribute stated preference technique initially developed by Louviere and Hensher (1982) and Louviere and Woodworth (1983) in the context of transport and market research literatures (e.g. Green and Srinivasan, 1978; Henscher, 1994). Since then, DCEs have become increasingly popular in environmental valuation (Adamowicz et al., 1998; Louviere, Hensher and Swait, 2000; Hanley, Mourato and Wright, 2001; Bennett and Blamey, 2001; Hensher, Rose and Greene, 2015; Adamowicz, 2004; Kanninen, 2007; Hoyos, 2010). They are part of the choice modelling (or conjoint analysis) approach, which also includes contingent ranking, contingent rating and paired comparisons (Bateman et al., 2002; Hanley, Mourato and Wright, 2001). DCEs are, however, the only choice modelling approach which definitively meets the requirements of welfare theory (Bateman et al., 2002). A recent review shows that, in the last decade, DCEs are becoming more popular than its sister stated preference technique, contingent valuation (Chapter 4), both in terms of number of publications and of citations (Mahieu et al., 2014).

The DCE method is derived from Lancaster's (1966) characteristics of value theory which states that any good may be described by a bundle of characteristics and the levels that these may take. Underpinned by the random utility framework, it relies on the application of statistical design theory to construct choice cards, describing particular policy options, in which respondents are required to choose their preferred option amongst a series of mutually exclusive alternatives (typically 2 or 3) which are differentiated in terms of their attributes and levels. By varying the levels the attributes take across the options and by including a monetary attribute it is possible to estimate the total value of a change in a good or service as well as the value of its component attributes. These values are not stated directly but instead are indirectly recovered from people's choices. Moreover, non-monetary trade-offs between attributes can also be calculated. A baseline or opt-out alternative must be included to make the economic choice more realistic; this avoids the problem of respondents being forced to choose options when they may not prefer this. As contingent valuation, choice modelling can also measure all forms of value including non-use values.

While some of the arguments for claims that choice modelling approaches can overcome problems with the dominant contingent valuation approach are still, at this time, a matter of speculation (Hanley, Mourato and Wright, 2001), perhaps the most convincing case for the former is based on cases where changes to be valued are multidimensional, that is, entailing changes in a number of attributes of interest, and the trade-offs between the attributes are important. Contingent valuation, typically, would be used to uncover the value of the total change in a multi-dimensional good. However, if policy-makers require measures of the change in each of the dimensions or attributes of the good then some variant of choice modelling might be considered.

This chapter is organised as follows. Section 5.2 reviews the conceptual foundations of choice experiments. In Section 5.3 the stages of the DCE approach are presented and illustrated via examples. Section 5.4 discusses the advantages and disadvantages of DCEs, when compared with contingent valuation. A selection of recent developments is discussed in Section 5.5. Section 5.6 concludes.

5.2. Conceptual foundation

The DCE approach was initially developed by Louviere and Hensher (1982) and Louviere and Woodworth (1983). Choice experiments share a common theoretical framework with dichotomous-choice contingent valuation in the Random Utility Model (Luce, 1959; McFadden, 1973), as well as a common basis of empirical analysis in limited dependent variable econometrics (Greene, 2008). According to this framework, the indirect utility function for each respondent i (U) can be decomposed into two parts: a deterministic element (V), which is typically specified as a linear index of the attributes (X) of the j different alternatives in the choice set, and a stochastic element (e), which represents unobservable influences on individual choice. This is shown in equation [5.1]:

$$U_{ij} = V_{ij}(X_{ij}) + e_{ij} = bX_{ij} + e_{ij} \qquad [5.1]$$

Thus, the probability that any particular respondent prefers option g in the choice set to any alternative option h, can be expressed as the probability that the utility associated with option g exceeds that associated with all other options, as stated in equation [5.2]:

$$P[(U_{ig} > U_{ih}) \forall h \neq g] = P[(V_{ig} - V_{ih}) > (e_{ih} - e_{ig})] \qquad [5.2]$$

In order to derive an explicit expression for this probability, it is necessary to know the distribution of the error terms (e_{ij}). A typical assumption is that they are independently and identically distributed with an extreme-value (Weibull) distribution:

$$P(e_{ij} \leq t) = F(t) = \exp(-\exp(-t)) \qquad [5.3]$$

The above distribution of the error term implies that the probability of any particular alternative g being chosen as the most preferred can be expressed in terms of the logistic distribution (McFadden, 1973) stated in equation [5.4]. This specification is known as the *conditional logit model*:

$$P(U_{ig} > U_{ih}, \forall h \neq g) = \frac{\exp(\mu V_{ig})}{\sum_j \exp(\mu V_{ij})} \qquad [5.4]$$

where μ is a scale parameter, inversely proportional to the standard deviation of the error distribution. This parameter cannot be separately identified and is therefore typically assumed to be one. An important implication of this specification is that selections from the choice set must obey the Independence from Irrelevant Alternatives (IIA) property (or Luce's Choice Axiom; Luce, 1959), which states that the relative probabilities of two options being selected are unaffected by the introduction or removal of other alternatives. This property follows from the independence of the Weibull error terms across the different options contained in the choice set.

This model can be estimated by conventional maximum likelihood procedures, with the respective log-likelihood functions stated in equation [5.5] below, where y_{ij} is an indicator variable which takes a value of one if respondent j chose option i and zero otherwise.

$$\log L = \sum_{i=1}^{N} \sum_{j=1}^{J} y_{ij} \log[\frac{\exp(V_{ij})}{\sum_{j=1}^{J} \exp(V_{ij})}] \qquad [5.5]$$

Socio-economic variables can be included along with choice set attributes in the X terms in equation [5.1], but since they are constant across choice occasions for any given individual (e.g. income is the same when the first choice is made as the second), they can only be entered as interaction terms, i.e. interacted with choice specific attributes.

This standard practice of giving respondents a series of choice set cards is not however without its problems. Typically, analysts treat the response to each choice set as a separate data point. In other words, responses for each of the choice sets presented to each respondent are regarded as completely independent observations. This is most probably incorrect, since it is likely that there will be some correlation between the error terms of each group of sets considered by the same individual. The data thus is effectively a panel with n "time periods" corresponding to the n choice sets faced by each individual. Hence, standard models over-estimate the amount of information contained in the dataset. There are procedures to deal with this problem. In some cases an *ex post* correction can be made by multiplying the standard errors attached to the coefficients for each attribute by the square root of the number of questions administered to each respondent. Other types of model used to estimate DCE data – such the random parameters logit model – automatically correct for this bias within the estimation procedure.

Once the parameter estimates have been obtained, a monetary compensating surplus welfare measure that conforms to demand theory can be derived for each attribute using the formula given by [5.6] (Hanemann, 1984; Parsons and Kealy, 1992) where V^0 represents the utility of the initial state and V^1 represents the utility of the alternative state. The coefficient b_c gives the marginal utility of income and is the coefficient of the cost attribute.

$$Monetary\ value = \frac{ln\left\{\dfrac{\sum_i exp\left(V_i^1\right)}{\sum_i exp\left(V_i^0\right)}\right\}}{b_c} \qquad [5.6]$$

It is straightforward to show that, for the linear utility index specified in [5.1], the above formulae can be simplified to the ratio of coefficients given in equation [5.7] where b_x is the coefficient of any of the (non-monetary) attributes and b_c is the coefficient of the cost attribute. These ratios are often known as implicit prices.

$$Monetary\ value = \left|\frac{b_x}{b_c}\right| \qquad [5.7]$$

Choice experiments are therefore consistent with utility maximisation and demand theory, at least when a status quo option is included in the choice set.

Notice however that specifying standard errors for the implicit price ratios is more complex. Although the asymptotic distribution of the maximum likelihood estimator for the parameters b is known, the asymptotic distribution of the maximum likelihood estimator of the welfare measure is not, since it is a non-linear function of the parameter vector. One way of obtaining confidence intervals for this measure is by means of the procedure developed by Krinsky and Robb (1986). This technique simulates the asymptotic distribution of the coefficients by taking repeated random draws from the multivariate normal distribution defined by the coefficient estimates and their associated covariance matrix. These are used to generate an empirical distribution for the welfare measure and the associated confidence intervals can then be computed.

Finally, DCE data can be used to estimate the welfare values associated with different combinations of attributes and levels (Bennett and Blamey, 2001). Using the implicit prices estimated for the various attributes allows the researcher to calculate the economic value of particular policy options (defined as specific packages of attributes and levels) in relation to the status quo. Multiple compensating surplus estimates can be derived depending on the levels of the attributes that are selected.

If a violation of the IIA hypothesis is observed, then more complex statistical models are necessary that relax some of the assumptions used. These include the multinomial probit (Hausman and Wise, 1978), the nested logit (McFadden, 1981), the mixed logit or random parameters logit model (Train, 1998), and the latent class model (Boxall and Adamowicz, 2002). IIA can be tested using a procedure suggested by Hausman and McFadden (1984). This basically involves constructing a likelihood ratio test around different versions of the model where choice alternatives are excluded. If IIA holds, then the model estimated on all choices should be the same as that estimated for a sub-set of alternatives (see Foster and Mourato, 2002, for an example).

5.3. Stages of a discrete choice experiment

As described in Section 5.2, the conceptual framework for DCEs assumes that consumers' or respondents' utilities for a good can be decomposed into utilities or well-being derived from the composing characteristics of the good as well as a stochastic element. Respondents are presented with a series of alternatives, differing in terms of attributes and levels, and asked to choose their most preferred. A baseline alternative, corresponding to the status quo or "do nothing" situation, is usually included in each choice set. The inclusion of a baseline or do-nothing option is an important element of the DCE approach; respondents are not forced into choosing alternatives they see as worse than what they currently have and so it permits the analysts to interpret results in standard (welfare) economic terms.

A typical DCE exercise is characterised by a number of key stages (Hanley, Mourato and Wright, 2001; Bennett and Blamey, 2001; Bateman et al., 2002; Hoyos, 2010). These are described in Table 5.1.

Table 5.1. **Stages of a discrete choice experiment**

Stage	Description
Selection of the good/service/ policy to be valued	A multi-attribute policy, good or service is selected to be valued.
Selection of attributes	Identification of the relevant attributes of the good/ service/ policy. Literature reviews and focus groups are used to select attributes that are relevant to people while expert consultations help to identify the attributes that will be impacted by the policy. A monetary cost is typically one of the attributes to allow the estimation of WTP or WTA.
Assignment of levels	The attribute levels should be feasible, realistic, non-linearly spaced, and span the range of respondents' preference maps. Focus groups, pilot surveys, literature reviews and consultations with experts are instrumental in selecting appropriate attribute levels. A baseline "status quo" level is usually included.
Choice of experimental design	Statistical design theory is used to combine the levels of the attributes into a number of alternative scenarios or profiles to be presented to respondents. Complete factorial designs consist of all possible combinations of attributes and levels and allow the estimation of the full effects of the attributes upon choices: that includes the effects of each of the individual attributes presented (main effects) and the extent to which behaviour is connected with variations in the combination of different attributes offered (interactions). These designs often originate an impractically large number of combinations to be evaluated: for example, 27 options would be generated by a full factorial design of 3 attributes with 3 levels each. Fractional factorial designs, where only a subset of combinations is selected, are able to reduce the number of scenario combinations presented with a concomitant loss in estimating power (i.e. some or all of the interactions will not be detected). For example, the 27 options can be reduced to 9 using a fractional factorial. These designs are available through specialised software.
Construction of choice sets	The profiles identified by the experimental design are then grouped into choice sets to be presented to respondents. Profiles can be presented in pairs or in larger groups typically triplets. For example, the 9 options identified by the fractional factorial design can be grouped into three sets of 4-way comparisons.
Measurement of preferences	Individual preferences can be uncovered by asking respondents to choose their most preferred option amongst the sets of options they are presented with.
Value estimation	Econometric analysis (e.g. via conditional logit, nested logit, random parameters logit, or latent class models) is used to estimate implicit prices for each attribute as well as welfare values for combinations of attributes.

5.3.1. Example: Measuring preferences for nuclear energy scenarios in Italy

We will illustrate how DCEs work through an example, a recent study of preferences for nuclear energy options in Italy (see Contu, Strazzera and Mourato, 2016, for full details). The planned re-introduction of nuclear energy in Italy was abandoned in the aftermath of the Fukushima nuclear accident, following a referendum that revealed widespread public opposition. But a new "revolutionary" nuclear energy technology, i.e. the fourth generation technology, currently under research and development, is expected to address many of the problems of the current technology, namely minimising the probability of catastrophic accidents as well as the amount of nuclear waste produced. Since nuclear energy remains a key technology in terms of allowing countries to meet their greenhouse gas (GHG) emission reduction targets, it is important to ascertain social acceptance of a new safer nuclear technology.

DCEs were chosen over contingent valuation for the valuation of preferences for nuclear energy. As noted above, DCEs are particularly well suited to value changes that are multidimensional (with scenarios being presented as bundles of attributes) and where trade-offs between the various dimensions are of interest. Nuclear energy scenarios have multiple dimensions that are important to people, some negative and some positive, such as perceived risk of an accident as well as environmental benefits. Second, values are inferred implicitly from the stated choices, avoiding the need for respondents to directly place a monetary value on scenario changes. This latter characteristic has led to suggestions that DCE formats may be less prone to protest responses than contingent valuation as attention is not solely focused on the monetary attribute but on all the scenario attributes (Hanley et al., 2001). This is particularly relevant when dealing with nuclear energy-related scenarios that may be particularly prone to protest votes, given the notoriously strong views held towards nuclear energy by many people.

The choice experiment scenario asked respondents to imagine they had a chance to choose between a series of options regarding the construction of 4th generation nuclear power plants in Italy. The attributes chosen were: GHG emissions reductions (when compared with current emissions, without nuclear technology); nuclear waste reduction (a benefit of the 4th generation nuclear technology when compared with current technology); distance of city of residence from the nuclear power plant (due to safety concerns, living far away from a nuclear power plant is perceived as a benefit); public investments (nuclear power installations are often accompanied by investments in the local area, such as new hospitals and land recovery measures); and electricity bill reductions, per household, per year. The monetary attribute (i.e. bill reductions) is therefore expressed as a monetary compensation. Table 5.2 depicts the attributes and their levels.

Table 5.2. **Attributes and levels of the choice experiment**

Attributes	Levels
Distance from the nuclear plant	20, 50, 100, 200 km from city of residence
Nuclear waste reduction	30%, 20%, 10%, no reduction
Atmospheric emission reduction	20%, 10%, no reduction
Electricity bill reduction	30%, 20%, 10%, no reduction
Public investments	Construction of hospitals, land recovery measures, no investments

Respondents were presented with a series of choice sets and asked to choose their most preferred scenario in each case. Each choice set consisted of a pair of nuclear energy scenarios, containing the five attributes and levels described in Table 2, and a "none" option so that respondents could decide to opt out and choose neither of the two nuclear energy options. Given the five attributes and their levels, with two options per choice task, the total number of possible choice scenarios is 576 (4 distance levels * 4 waste reduction levels * 3 emission reduction levels * 4 bill reduction levels * 3 public investment levels). To reduce the number of choice tasks to present to respondents a main effects orthogonal design was used leading to a total of 64 choice pairs, which were then organised into 8 blocks of 8 choice sets each. For clarity purposes, after piloting, the public investment attribute was presented as two separate attributes: construction of new hospitals (yes or no), and land recovery measures (yes or no). Figure 5.1 depicts an example of a choice set used in the survey.

Figure 5.1. **Example of a choice set**

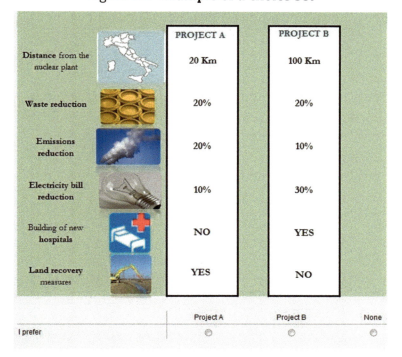

Discrete choice experiments are consistent with utility maximisation and demand theory, at least when a status quo or opt out option is included in the choice set, as in this case. If a status quo/opt out alternative is not included in the choice set, respondents are effectively being "forced" to choose one of the policy alternatives presented, which they may not desire at all. If, for some respondents, the most preferred option is the current baseline situation (in this case with no nuclear energy), then any model based on a design in which the baseline is not present will yield inaccurate estimates of consumer welfare.

The survey was programmed in Qualtrics and implemented on-line in 2014 on a panel of 1 200 Italian respondents, representative in gender, age and region. Unsurprisingly, the nuclear energy scenarios divided respondents: some 23% of the sample chose none of the nuclear energy scenarios in every single choice set; while a similar proportion always selected one of the nuclear scenarios in every choice instance.

The choice experiment data was analysed employing a conditional logit model, a random parameters model with error components and a latent class model (see Section 5.2). Here we present the results from the conditional logit model. The analysis assumes that the deterministic component of the utility or well-being function V_{ij} (of the ith respondent for the j different alternatives in the choice set) depends simply (and linearly) on the attributes of the choices presented as follows:

$$V_{ij} = \beta_1 ASC + \beta_2 Distance_{200} + \beta_3 Distance_{100} + \beta_4 Distance_{50} + \beta_5 Waste_{30} + \beta_6 Waste_{20} +$$
$$\beta_7 Waste_{10} + \beta_8 Emissions + \beta_9 Hospitals + \beta_{10} Land + \beta_{11} Bill \qquad [5.8]$$

where βi are the model coefficients, and the remaining variables are the choice experiment attributes as described in Table 5.2. The ASC is an alternative specific constant capturing the variation in choices that is not explained by the attributes. Here it represents the "none" option in each choice set. A positive coefficient β_1 will indicate that individuals are more likely to choose none of the nuclear energy scenarios, thereby providing a measure of overall opposition towards nuclear energy. Because of non-linearities, some of the attributes are coded as dummy variables: Distancex (distance of city of residence from the nuclear power plant, dummies for 50, 100 and 200 km, baseline 20 km), Wastex (nuclear waste reduction, dummies for 10, 20 and 30% reduction, baseline "no reduction") and the public investments Hospitals and Land (construction of hospitals, and land recovery measures respectively, baseline "no investment" in each case). The final two attributes are Emissions (representing atmospheric emission reductions, in 10% intervals) and Bill (representing electricity bill reductions per household, per year, in EUR, obtained by applying the bill reduction percentages to the average of the sampled respondents' annual electricity bill.

Using the conditional logit model to estimate equation [5.8], the coefficient levels were found to be: $\beta_1 = 1.60$; $\beta_2 = 0.72$; $\beta_3 = 0.579$; $\beta_4 = 0.431$; $\beta_5 = 0.726$; $\beta_6 = 0.606$; $\beta_7 = 0.367$; $\beta_8 = 0.274$; $\beta_9 = 0.326$; $\beta_{10} = 0.516$; $\beta_{11} = 0.00213$. The coefficients on these attributes are all positive as having more of any of these particular things increases utility or well-being, i.e. being located further away from a nuclear power plant, reducing nuclear waste, reducing emissions, investing in new hospitals and land recovery measures, and reducing electricity bills. Moreover, the effect of distance to the nuclear site is non-linear: the magnitude of the coefficients increases with distance.

From these findings the analyst can obtain monetary value estimates by dividing the coefficient of each non-monetary attribute (e.g. β_2, the coefficient of Distance 200 km) by the coefficient of the monetary attribute (i.e. β_{11}), as per equations [5.6] and [5.7] above. These values represent willingness to accept compensations, in terms of electricity bill reductions, for a utility-decreasing level of a given attribute (for example, a nuclear power plant situated closer to home); or, alternatively, the willingness to pay (in terms of foregone compensation) for a utility-enhancing level of an attribute (for example, a nuclear power plant situated further away from home, or a reduction in emissions). In this case, as all the attributes are framed in terms of benefits, the valuations can be interpreted as WTP estimates (i.e. foregone compensations). The implicit prices of each attribute are therefore:

$$WTP_{ASC\ no\ nuclear} = \beta_1 / \beta_{11} = 1.60 / 0.00213 = EUR\ 751$$
$$WTP_{Distance\ 200km} = \beta_2 / \beta_{11} = 0.72 / 0.00213 = EUR\ 338$$
$$WTP_{Distance\ 100km} = \beta_3 / \beta_{11} = 0.579 / 0.00213 = EUR\ 272$$
$$WTP_{Distance\ 50km} = \beta_4 / \beta_{11} = 0.431 / 0.00213 = EUR\ 202$$
$$WTP_{Waste\ 30\%} = \beta_5 / \beta_{11} = 0.726 / 0.00213 = EUR\ 341$$
$$WTP_{Waste\ 20\%} = \beta_6 / \beta_{11} = 0.606 / 0.00213 = EUR\ 285$$
$$WTP_{Waste\ 10\%} = \beta_7 / \beta_{11} = 0.367 / 0.00213 = EUR\ 172$$
$$WTP_{Emissions} = \beta_8 / \beta_{11} = 0.274 / 0.00213 = EUR\ 129$$

$$\text{WTP}_{\text{Hospitals}} \quad = \beta_9 \, / \, \beta_{11} = 0.326 \, / \, 0.00213 = \text{ EUR } 153$$
$$\text{WTP}_{\text{Land recovery}} \quad = \beta_{10} \, / \, \beta_{11} = 0.516 \, / \, 0.00213 = \text{ EUR } 242$$

On average, the results show that Italian households are willing to forgo a compensation of EUR 338 per year for a nuclear plant situated 200 km away (vis-à-vis a baseline of 20 km away); this reduces to EUR 202 for a distance of just 50 km. In addition, waste reduction is valued up to EUR 341 (for a 30% reduction), more than land recovery measures (EUR 242) and hospitals (EUR 153). Finally, emission reductions are found to be highly valued at EUR 129 for a 10% reduction. Of note, the ASC representing the status quo, with no nuclear energy, is positive and very highly valued (EUR 751), indicating a broad preference for scenarios not involving nuclear energy.

In 2004, Adamowicz (2004) envisaged a move away from focusing on values for environmental goods to focusing instead on choice behaviour. This prediction seems to have come to fruition: today, DCEs appear to be more popular than CV (Mahieu et al., 2014). Applications abound in transport, health, marketing, agriculture and also environment, both in developed and developing countries. An example of an application in a developing country can be found in Box 5.1.

Box 5.1. **Fishers preferences for marine PES schemes in Tanzania**

Tanzanian marine fisheries have suffered a significant decline in biodiversity and productivity in the past three decades. As population and fisher numbers continue to increase, these coastal resources come under increasing pressure. Marine management has generally favoured regulatory solutions such as the establishment of marine protected areas (MPAs), involving total prohibitions on fishing. But MPAs can be inefficient and ineffectual, posing further unrealistic burdens on local low-income fishing communities. PES have the potential to complement existing marine management instruments through the provision of short-term incentives to put up with fishing restrictions – whether they be a spatial or gear restriction – in the form of compensation for loss of catch.

Barr and Mourato (2014) used DCEs to investigate how compensating fishers in Tanzania to adopt restrictions in fishing in a local marine park – through closed areas and gear modifications –, induces participation in a marine PES scheme. Table 3 describes the attributes and levels of the DCE: size of the no-fishing area within the marine park (against a baseline of no spatial restrictions), size of permitted net meshing (where 3mm mesh size was the legal minimum: the wider the meshing the more fish can escape), and monetary compensation. The piloting stages showed a high degree of variation in management attribute preferences. Certain attribute levels (such as a tighter mesh size) were considered highly beneficial to some fishers to the point that they would be willing to pay for it. As such the final monetary attribute included a negative compensation, which is equivalent to a willingness to pay amount.

Table 5.3. **Attributes and attribute levels in choice model experiment**

PSE scheme attribute	Description	Attribute level
Size of no-take area	Areas as % of current fishing area in which fishing will no longer be permitted and declared MPA.	0, 10, 25, 50
Size of permitted net meshing	Net mesh size in inches that fishers are permitted to use within fishing grounds. Mesh size is measured as size when mesh pulled in each corner.	1, 3, 6
Payment	Weekly payment in Tanzanian Shillings (TZS) made under the PSE scheme.	-1 000, 5 000, 10 000, 20 000

Box 5.1. **Fishers preferences for marine PES schemes in Tanzania** (*cont.*)

Given that almost 30% of fishers had no formal education and most of the remaining had only some primary level education, the DCE attributes and levels were depicted visually, using simple black and white drawings (Figure 5.2). Eighteen experimentally designed management scenarios were produced and organised into choice sets. The first two scenario cards were picked at random by the enumerator, without replacement, from a bag containing all 18 scenarios. The status quo baseline scenario was then added, creating a choice set triplet. Each respondent was presented with six of these randomly-generated choice set triplets (Figure 5.2).

Figure 5.2. **Tanzanian fishers' choice set example**

Attributes	Management Option 1	Management Option 2	Status Quo
Closure % closed of current fishing grounds	10	50	0
Net mesh size in "	6 	1 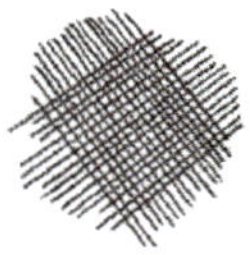	3 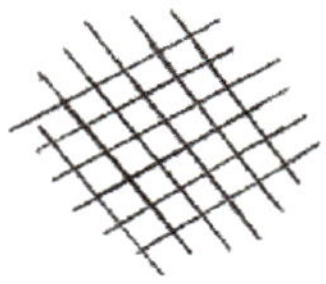
Payment	10,000	5,000	0

Face-to-face interviews were conducted in 2010 with 317 fishers from six coastal villages located in southern Tanzania. The choice data were analysed using a nested logit model. Results show that moving away from the status quo was seen as a significant loss, with fishers requiring an average compensation of USD 12.7 per week (average fishing income in the villages ranged from USD 4.8 to USD 1.3 per day). This was unsurprising given that the status quo was found to be the preferred choice in just over half of the choice sets, with 30% of fishers (96) choosing the status quo in all six choices, revealing aversion to change.

Other results revealed that additional mesh restrictions represented a high utility cost to fishers: weekly compensation amounts of almost USD 10 per fisher were required to move from 3 in. to 6 in. minimum size; while closure of an additional 10% of seascape to fishing activities would require only a compensation of USD 1.60 per week. Fishers appear to equate a 20% closure of fishing grounds as similar in utility loss to that of a 1 in. increase in allowable mesh size. Aggregating the relevant combinations of implicit prices reveals the economic values associated with the various possible PES marine management scenarios, in contrast to the current situation (Table 5.4).

All PES programmes were associated with a high utility loss for fishers, reflecting their aversion to change. The scenario with the lowest restrictions (a closure of just 10% of fishing grounds and maintenance of the current mesh size of 3 in.) reduced fisher utility by

Box 5.1. **Fishers preferences for marine PES schemes in Tanzania** *(cont.)*

Table 5.4. **Economic welfare values under differing management options**

USD per week

Mesh size in inches	Size of closure (% closure of current fishing grounds)			
	0	10	25	50
1	-11.499	-13.082	-15.457	-19.414
3	-	-14.304	-16.678	-20.635
6	-22.072	-23.655	-26.029	-29.987

USD 14.3 per week (calculated as USD 12.7 to move away from the status quo plus USD 1.60 to put up with the reduction of fishing grounds). As expected, the greatest utility loss was associated with those management options with the greatest restrictions.

Overall, Barr and Mourato (2014) results show an aversion to change and relatively low predicted rates of PES adoption. Approximately only half of the fishers would be willing to sign up for a PES scheme with the lowest restriction of a 10% fishing grounds closure and no change in mesh size. This indicates that the marine PES scheme costs may be high: creating an enabling environment where changes are not met with apprehension and hostility could be as important as investing into conditional in-kind compensation mechanisms.

5.4. Relative strengths and weaknesses of discrete choice experiments

Given that DCEs are a stated preference method, and in effect a generalisation of discrete choice CV, they share many of its advantages and disadvantages. Similar to CV, choice experiments are based on hypothetical scenarios and non-consequential choices with the caveats that this may imply (see Chapter 4). Also like CV, DCEs are very flexible, and are able to measure future changes as well as non-use values. But DCEs have some distinctive characteristics that may differentially affect its performance and accuracy. This section reviews some of the key advantages and disadvantages of DCEs relative to contingent valuation.

5.4.1. Strengths

DCE approaches possess a number of advantages relative to the standard contingent valuation technique (Hanley, Mourato and Wright, 2001; Mahieu et al., 2014). Principal among the attractions of DCEs are claimed to be the following:

1. DCEs are particularly suited to deal with situations where changes are multi-dimensional, and trade-offs between the dimensions are of particular interest, because of their natural ability to separately identify the value of individual attributes of a good or programme, typically supplied in combination with one another. Whilst in principle CV can also be applied to estimate the value of the attributes of a programme, for example by including a series of CV scenarios in a questionnaire or by conducting a series of CV studies, it is a more costly and cumbersome alternative. Hence DCEs do a better job than CV in measuring the marginal value of changes in various characteristics of say environmental programmes, as well as providing a deeper understanding of the trade-offs between them. This is often a more useful focus from a management/policy perspective than focussing on either the overall gain or loss of the good, or on a single discrete change in its attributes. For example,

a water company wanting to identify potential areas for investment may need to assess which of the many services they provide are most valued by their customers, and compare those values (i.e. benefits) with the costs of provision. The services provided have multiple dimensions: drinking water quality (e.g. taste and smell of water, hardness of water, water colour, and possible need for boil water notices), reliability of supply (e.g. water pressure, supply interruptions, water leakage, and internal water flooding) and environmental impacts (river water quality, river levels and flow, and possible need for hosepipe bans). Hence, DCEs provide an ideal framework to assess such values.

2. The focus on attributes might increase the potential for generalisation of results making DCEs more appropriate from a value transfer viewpoint (Rolfe, 2006; Rolfe and Windle, 2008). Morrison et al. (1998) provided encouraging early evidence on the use of DCEs in value transfer, highlighting advantages such as allowing for differences in environmental improvements between sites as well as differences in socio-economic characteristics between respondent populations. More recently, Rolf, Windle and Bennett (2015) discuss several reasons why DCEs might lend themselves more easily to value transfer. These reasons relate mostly to the richness and detail of the value estimate output that is produced by DCEs, in terms of multiple attributes and levels. This richness of data is especially relevant when performing benefits transfer using a value transfer function (see Chapter 6 for a discussion of value transfer approaches). The welfare values estimated in DCE studies are a function of both site characteristics and respondent characteristics in the original study site. This same function can then be used for value transfer to a different policy site, using the levels associated with the new site and population's characteristics, as long as these levels are within the range used in the original study (Rolf, Windle and Bennett, 2015).

3. Insensitivity to the scope of the change is one of the key challengers for CVM (see Chapter 4). In contrast, the simultaneous presentation of the whole and the parts in DCE forces some internal consistency in respondents' choices. DCEs therefore provide a natural internal (within subjects) scope test due to the elicitation of multiple responses per individual. The internal test is however weaker than an external (between subjects) split-sample scope test in as much as the answers given by any particular individual are not independent from each other and thus sensitivity to scope is to some extent forced. In one of the few existing formal tests of sensitivity to scope in both CV and DCEs, Foster and Mourato (2003) undertook separate CV studies of two nested public goods both of which were explicitly incorporated in a parallel DCE survey. The authors found that, while there was evidence that both CV and DCE produced results which exhibited sensitivity to scope, the evidence for the DCE method was much stronger than that for CV. This result conforms with prior expectations as the scope test used for the CV method was an external test and consequently more demanding than the internal test provided by the DCE method.

4. DCEs are more informative than discrete choice CV studies as respondents get multiple chances to express their preference for a valued good over a range of payment amounts: for example, if respondents are given 8 choice pairs and a "do nothing" option, they may respond to as many as 17 bid prices, including zero. In fact, DCEs can be seen as a generalisation of discrete choice contingent valuation concerning a sequence of discrete choice valuation questions where there are two or more goods involved (Hanley, Mourato and Wright, 2001). When valuing multi-attribute programmes, DCE studies can potentially reduce the expense of valuation studies, because of their natural ability to

value programme attributes in one single questionnaire and because they are more informative than discrete choice CV surveys.

5. Choice experiments generally avoid an explicit elicitation of respondents' willingness to pay (or willingness to accept) by relying instead on choices amongst a series of alternative packages of characteristics from where willingness to pay can be indirectly inferred. As such, DCEs may minimise some of the response difficulties found in CVM such as protest bids, strategic behaviour, or yeah saying (Hanley, Mourato and Wright, 2001). But this point, while intuitive, is speculative and has yet to be demonstrated. In a recent review of DCE studies, Rakotonarivo et al. (2016) find rates of protest ranging from 2% to 58% in developed countries, but since there were no comparative studies performed using CV we cannot say whether CV would have performed any worse.

5.4.2. Weaknesses

Experience with DCEs in environmental contexts and more widely in the fields of transport, marketing and health also highlight a number of potential problems:

1. Arguably, the main disadvantage of DCE approaches lies in the cognitive difficulty associated with multiple complex choices between bundles with many attributes and levels. While the drive for statistical efficiency is improved by asking a large number of difficult trade-off questions, respondents fare better (i.e. response efficiency) when confronted with a smaller number of easier trade-offs (Johnson et al., 2013). Both experimental economists and psychologists have found ample evidence that there is a limit to how much information respondents can meaningfully handle while making a decision. One common finding is that the choice complexity can lead to greater random errors or at least imprecision in responses (see Box 5.2). More generally, since respondents are typically presented with large number of choice sets there is scope for both learning and fatigue effects and an important issue is which – on average – will predominate and when. Handling repeated answers per respondent also poses statistical problems and the correlation between responses in such cases needs to be taken into account and properly modelled (Adamowicz, Louviere and Swait, 1998).

This implies that, whilst the researcher might want to include many attributes and levels, unless very large samples are collected, respondents will be faced with daunting choice tasks. The consequence is that, in presence of complex choices, respondents may use heuristics or rules of thumb to simplify the decision task. These filtering rules lead to options being chosen that are good enough although not necessarily the best, avoiding the need to solve the underlying utility-maximisation problem (i.e. a satisficing approach rather than a maximising one). Heuristics often associated with difficult choice tasks include maximin and maximax strategies and lexicographic orderings (Tversky, 1972; Foster and Mourato, 2002). Hence, it is important to incorporate consistency tests into DCEs studies in order to detect the range of problems discussed above (see, for example, Box 5.2). Section 5 below discusses some recent developments in this area.

2. It is more difficult for DCE approaches to derive values for a sequence of elements implemented by policy or project, when compared with a contingent valuation alternative. Hence, valuing the sequential provision of goods in multi-attribute programmes is probably better undertaken by contingent valuation (Hanley, Mourato and Wright, 2001).

3. In order to estimate the total value of a public programme or a good from a DCEs, as distinct from a change in one of its attributes, it is necessary to assume that the value of

Box 5.2. **Testing cognitive burden**

Contingent ranking is a variant of choice modelling whereby respondents are required to rank a set of alternative options (Hanley, Mourato and Wright, 2001; Bateman et al., 2002), rather than simply choosing their most preferred option as in DCEs. Similarly to DCEs, each alternative is characterised by a number of attributes, offered at different levels, and a status quo option is normally included in the choice set to ensure welfare consistent results. However, the ranking task imposes a significant cognitive burden on the survey population, a burden which escalates with the number of attributes used and the number of alternatives presented to each individual. This raises questions as to whether respondents are genuinely able to provide meaningful answers to such questions. A study by Foster and Mourato (2002) looks at three different aspects of logical consistency within the context of a contingent ranking experiment: dominance, rank consistency, and transitivity of rank order. Each of these concepts are defined below before we proceed to outline the findings of this study:

Dominance: One alternative is said to dominate a second when it is at least as good as the second in terms of every attribute. If Option A dominates Option B, then it would clearly be inconsistent for any respondent to rank Option B more highly than Option A. Dominant pairs are sometimes excluded from choice modelling designs on the grounds that they do not provide any additional information about preferences. However, their deliberate inclusion can be used as a test of the coherence of the responses of those being surveyed.

Rank consistency: Where respondents are given a sequence of ranking sets, it also becomes possible to test for rank-consistency across questions. This can be done by designing the experiment so that common pairs of options appear in successive ranking sets. For example, a respondent might be asked to rank Options A, B, C, D in the first question and Options A, B, E, F in the second question. Rank-consistency requires that a respondent who prefers Option B over Option A in the first question, continues to do so in the second question.

Transitivity: Transitivity of rank order requires that a respondent who has expressed a preference for Option A over B in a first question, and for Option B over C elsewhere, should not thereafter express a preference for Option C over A in any other question. There are clearly parallels here with the transitivity axiom underlying neo-classical consumer theory.

The data set which forms the basis of the tests outlined in Foster and Mourato (2002) is a contingent ranking survey of the social costs of pesticide use in bread production in the United Kingdom. Three product attributes were considered in the survey, each of them offered at three different levels: the price of bread, together with measures of the human health – annual cases of illness as a result of field exposure to pesticides – and the environmental impacts of pesticides – number of farmland bird species in a state of long-term decline as a result of pesticide use. An example choice card for this study is illustrated in Table 5.5.

Table 5.5. **Sample Contingent Ranking Question from Pesticide Survey**

	Process A	Process B	Process C	Process D
Price of bread	GBP 0.60 per loaf	GBP 0.85 per loaf	GBP 0.85 per loaf	GBP 1.15 per loaf
Health effects on general public	100 cases of ill health per year	40 cases of ill health per year	40 cases of ill health per year	60 cases of ill health per year
Effects on farmland birds	9 bird species in decline	2 bird species in decline	5 bird species in decline	2 bird species in decline
Ranking				

Notes: Process A: current technology for wheat cultivation; Processes B-D: alternative environmentally friendly options for wheat cultivation.

Box 5.2. **Testing cognitive burden** *(cont.)*

The basic results of the authors' tests for logical consistency are presented in Table 5.6. Each respondent was classified in one of three categories: i) "no failure" means that these respondents always passed a particular test; ii) "occasional failures" refers to those respondents who passed on some occasions but not on others; while, iii) "systematic failures" refers to those respondents who failed a test on every occasion that the test was presented.

Table 5.6. **Comparison of test failures**

	No failures	Occasional failures	Systematic failures
Dominance	83%	13%	4%
Rank consistency	67%	32%	1%
Transitivity	87%	13%	0%
ALL	54%	41%	5%

Note: The overall percentage of occasional failures reported in the final row of the table is net of all individuals who systematically failed any one of the tests.

The results show that on a test-by-test basis, the vast majority of respondents register passes. More than 80% pass dominance and transitivity tests on every occasion, while two thirds pass the rank-consistency test. Of those who fail, the vast majority only fail occasionally. The highest failure rate is for the rank-consistency test, which is failed by 32% of the sample, while only 13% of the sample fails each of the other two tests. Systematic failures are comparatively rare, with none at all in the case of transitivity.

When the results of the tests are pooled, Table 5 indicates that only 5% of the sample makes systematic failures. The overall "no failure" sample accounts for 54% of the total. The fact that this is substantially smaller than the "no failure" sample for each individual test indicates that different respondents are failing different tests rather than a small group of respondents failing all of the tests. Yet, this finding also indicates a relatively high rate of occasional failures among respondents with nearly half of the sample failing at least one of the tests some of the time.

Results such as these could have important implications for the contingent ranking method and choice modelling more generally. The fact that a substantial proportion of respondents evidently find difficulty in providing coherent responses to contingent ranking problems raises some concerns about the methodology, when the ultimate research goal is to estimate coefficient values with which to derive valid and reliable WTP amounts. On the other hand, most errors seem to be occasional, and arguably their frequency should diminish in the simpler setting of a DCE, where only the most preferred alternative (rather than full tanks) need to be identified.

the whole is equal to the sum of the parts (see Box 5.1). This raises two potential problems. First, there may be additional attributes of the good not included in the design, which generate utility (in practice, these effects can be captured in other ways). Second, the value of the "whole" may not be simply additive in this way. Elsewhere in economics, objections have been raised about the assumption that the value of the whole is indeed equal to the sum of its parts. This has sometimes been referred to as "package effects" in the grey literature (e.g. eftec and ICS Consulting, 2013). Package effects in DCEs are more likely to be a significant issue when marginal WTP values for changes in attributes are applied to policies involving large and multiple simultaneous changes in attributes, i.e. where substitution effects may be expected.

In order to test whether this is a valid objection in the case of DCEs, values of a full programme or good obtained from DCEs could be compared with values obtained for the same resource using some other method such as contingent valuation, under similar circumstances. In the transport field, research for London Underground and London Buses among others has shown clear evidence that values of whole bundles of improvements are valued less than the sum of the component values, all measured using DCEs (SDG, 1999, 2000). As noted above, Foster and Mourato (2003) found that the estimates from a choice experiment on the total value of charitable services in the UK were significantly larger than results obtained from a parallel contingent valuation survey. They concluded that summing up the individual components of the choice set might seriously overestimate the value of the whole set.

4. A common observation in DCEs is a disproportionate number of respondents choosing the status quo, the baseline, or the opt-out alternative (e.g. Ben Akiva et al., 1991; Meyerhoff and Liebe, 2009). This could reflect status quo bias, i.e. a bias towards the current or baseline situation (Samuelson and Zeckhauser, 1988) that may arise for a number of reasons: inertia, biased perceptions, limited cognitive ability, uncertainty, distrust in institutions, doubts about the effectiveness of the programme proposed, or task complexity (Meyerhoff and Liebe, 2009). A small number of studies authors have experimented with different presentations of the status quo option in DCEs to examine its effects on choice behaviour (Banzhaf, Johnson and Mathews, 2001; Kontoleon and Yabe, 2004).

5. As is the case with all stated preference techniques, welfare estimates obtained with DCEs are sensitive to study design. For example, the choice of attributes, the levels chosen to represent them, and the way in which choices are relayed to respondents (e.g. use of photographs vs. text descriptions, choices vs. ranks) are not neutral and may impact on the values of estimates of consumers' surplus and marginal utilities.

5.5. Recent developments and frontier issues

As stated preference techniques reach maturity, breakthrough developments become less likely. Choice modelling methods have been no exception. Most of the developments in the last decade have been small improvements in statistical design, econometric analysis and in survey implementation methods (with the advent of on-line surveying as discussed in Chapter 4). But there have also been improvements in our understanding of the way individual choices are formulated in sequential choice contexts, as well as developments of new choice model variants. This section provides a brief overview of some of the key developments in understanding respondent behaviour in choice experiment contexts.

5.5.1. Experimental design methods

The selection of the experimental design, i.e. the combination of attributes and levels to be presented to respondents in the choice sets, is a key stage in the development of DCEs, when using fractional factorial designs (Section 2). Recent years have witnessed many developments in experimental design methods (De Bekker-Grob et al., 2012; Johnson et al., 2013). Orthogonal designs (where attributes are statistically independent from one another and the levels appear an equal number of times) are widely used and available from design catalogues, on-line tables of orthogonal arrays, or more commonly from statistical programmes such as SPSS (SPSS, 2008), SPEED (Bradley, 1991), or SAS (Kuhfeld, 2010).

More recently statistically efficient designs (aiming to minimise the standard errors of the parameter estimates for a given sample size) have been developed and are being increasingly used. Amongst these, designs using the D-efficiency criterion are the most common (available in the SAS software). New advanced design software packages designed specifically for DCEs have also been developed in recent years. Specifically, the increasingly popular Ngene (Choice Metrics, 2014) is able to generate designs for a wide range of DCE models, can use Bayesian priors and accommodate specifications with constraints and interaction effects. Finally, as in CV (Chapter 4), web-based surveys have become the most popular way to administer DCEs (Mahieu et al., 2014) and this development has in turn facilitated the implementation of advanced experimental designs.

5.5.2. Understanding response efficiency

The overall precision of parameter estimates in DCE models depends not only on the statistical efficiency of the experimental design discussed in 5.1 but also on response efficiency, i.e. the measurement error that results from respondents' mistakes and non-optimal choice behaviour (Johnson et al., 2013).

As noted above, it is well known that, in a choice experiment setting, respondents might adopt different processing strategies or heuristics to simplify the choice task (Heiner et al., 1983; Payne et al., 1993). Such aids to the mental thought involved in making a decision in a choice experiment might be a conscious judgement made by the respondent. For example, individuals might rationally choose to make choices considering only a subset of the information provided (De Palma et al., 1994). Alternatively, individuals could resort to heuristics (perhaps sub-consciously) due to limited cognitive capabilities or information overload (Simon, 1955; Miller, 1955; Lowenstein and Lerner, 2003).

In line with this, accumulating evidence has been associating different complexity of choice tasks to variations in error variance (Mazzotta and Opaluch, 1995; Dellaert et al., 1999; Swait and Adamowicz, 2001; DeShazo and Fermo, 2002; Arentze et al., 2003; Cassuade et al., 2005; Islam et al., 2007; Bech et al., 2011; Carlsson et al., 2012; Czajkowski et al., 2014; Mayerhoff et al., 2014), suggesting the importance of simultaneously taking into account statistical and respondent efficiency. In other words, respondents could experience fatigue when the choice experiment is complex and/or fail to engage; similarly, the first choice sets might be used by respondents to learn the choice task and employ one, or more, decision rules.

The level of complexity of a choice experiment is defined at the experimental design stage, when the combinations that will be presented to the respondents are determined. On this note, Louviere et al. (2008) provide evidence of a negative relationship between the number of attributes and levels and choice consistency. Concerns regarding respondent efficiency have led to the common practice of dividing the total number of choice sets into smaller blocks so as to reduce the number of choice tasks presented to each respondent (as well as more economical designs to determine the number of these choice sets, such as fractional factorial designs). The blocking procedure can be applied to either a full factorial or to a fractional factorial. The growing attention being given to more flexible and efficient design of DCEs might also help in reducing respondent cognitive burden (see, for example, Severin, 2001; Sándor and Franses, 2009; Danthurebandara et al., 2011).

5.5.3. Non-fully compensatory choice behaviour

It has been widely acknowledged that individuals might present a preference structure which is not as well-behaved as the standard discrete choice models would impose. The standard interpretation of the way in which respondents choose their preferred options in DCEs is that they do so by considering (and trading off) all of the attributes comprising that choice. However, a number of studies have found evidence of departures from this fully compensatory behavior, where respondents may not make such trade-offs and instead make decisions which are non-compensatory, with relatively less preferred attributes never being able to compensate for an attribute that is favoured more. Or perhaps respondents make these trade-offs only partially, making decisions which are semi-compensatory, i.e. it would take a really large amount of some less preferred attribute to compensate for losses in an attribute that respondents favour more. As a result, a wide range of non-compensatory and semi-compensatory decision strategies has been put forward in the literature, to aid the analysis of respondent choices. This has implications in terms of the econometric models employed at the estimation phase as well as at the experimental design phase.

Since the work of Hensher et al. (2005), many studies have been focusing on modelling attribute non-attendance. *Attribute non-attendance* (ANA) refers to a situation where respondents consider only a subset of the attributes presented in each choice task (i.e. they do not fully trade-off between all the attributes present in the task before them). It has been shown that taking ANA into account might lead to significantly different monetary valuations and/or parameters' estimates (Hensher, 2006; Hensher and Rose, 2009; Hess and Hensher, 2010; Hole, 2011; Scarpa et al., 2009; Scarpa et al., 2010; Campbell et al., 2011; Puckett and Hensher, 2008; Puckett and Hensher, 2009; Lagarde, 2013).

Attribute non-attendance is usually identified either by directly asking respondents to state whether and which of the attributes they have not considered or, alternatively, inferring this information by means of an appropriate econometric model. *Stated* ANA was firstly introduced by Hensher et al. (2005); however, it has been questioned as the information obtained poses concerns in terms of its reliability (Campbell and Lorimer, 2009; Carlsson et al., 2010; Hess and Hensher, 2010; Hess et al., 2012; Hess et al., 2013; Kaye-Blake et al., 2009; Kragt, 2013), with some authors putting forward the opposite argument (Hole et al., 2013). As it seems unsatisfactory to crudely discriminate between fully attending and non-fully attending respondents, authors have suggested gathering a more thorough and nuanced information on attribute attendance (Alemu et al., 2013; Colombo et al., 2013; Scarpa et al., 2013). In turn, the *inferred* ANA literature has proposed that it may be more appropriate to reduce the magnitude of a parameter when there are indications of non-attendance for the corresponding attribute, rather than setting its magnitude equal to zero altogether (Balcombe et al., 2011; Cameron and DeShazo, 2010; Kehlbecher et al., 2013).

Outside of the debate concerning *stated* ANA versus *inferred* ANA, other streams of research have been exploring alternative avenues. One example is the concept of *stated attribute importance*, where respondents are asked to rank the choice experiment attributes in order of importance for their choices (see, for example, Balcombe et al., 2014). Some of this research has also considered the way in which behavioural science might inform how respondent choices are understood. For example, the typical assumption is that a respondent processes choice situations according to a Random Utility Model, where the respondent chooses combinations of attributes within a choice set according to which option provides him or her with the highest utility. However, a respondent's choice might plausibly reflect other decision procedures such as a Random Regret Model, in which a respondent chooses a preferred option in order to minimise his or her chances of experiencing regret about that choice (Boeri et al., 2012; Chorus et al., 2008, 2014).

Further possibilities exist. Respondents may exhibit lexicographic preferences, where their choice is made according to a strict order based on choosing the option which contains the highest value of a favoured attribute while ignoring other attributes (Sælensminde, 2001; Scott, 2002; Rosenberger et al., 2003; Gelso and Peterson, 2005; Campbell et al., 2006; Lancsar and Louviere, 2006; Hess et al., 2010); while others may use criteria such as Elimination by Aspect (Cantillo and Ortúzar, 2005; Swait, 2001) or reference points (Hess et al., 2012). Finally, the same individual may on some occasions behave according to a full compensatory model, and on other occasions adopt a simplifying strategy (Araña et al., 2008; Leong and Hensher, 2012).

Whether respondents adopt a single or a mixture of decision-making rules depends on the specific case study. What is relevant for the practitioner is that, if heterogeneity in the decision rules used by respondents is present, it should be detected and taken into account when analysing choices in a statistical model. Failure to do so may lead to biased coefficient estimates and, crucially from a policy perspective, monetary valuations. Research is needed so as to identify a set of decision rules which are deemed to best represent the heterogeneity of decision processes whilst still allowing for preference heterogeneity (Hess et al., 2012; Araña et al., 2008; Boeri et al., 2012). Finally, future research still needs to investigate how to interpret or estimate monetary valuations from respondents who exhibit this decisional diversity.

5.5.4. Econometric modelling

Although a sizeable number of studies continues to use the basic conditional logit model (Louviere and Lancsar, 2009), recent reviews of the DCE literature suggest a shift towards more flexible econometric models, that relax some of the restrictive assumptions of the standard model (see Section 2). As noted earlier, researchers have increasingly adopted models such as the nested logit, mixed logit or latent class, that relax the IIA assumption, and importantly better account for preference heterogeneity. In their review of DCE applications in the health field, De Bekker-Grobb et al. (2012) find a small increase in application of these models in the period 2001-2008, when compared with the previous decade. Mahieu et al. (2014) find that the use of more flexible econometric models is more common in environmental research than in health or agricultural research.

The use of advanced econometric models is expected to continue to grow fueled by a number of factors: increased availability of specialist DCE textbooks (e.g. Hensher, Rose and Greene, 2015; Train, 2009); proliferation of DCE courses (e.g. Advanced Choice Modelling Course run by the Centre for Choice Modelling at the University of Leeds; Discrete Choice Analysis course run both at MIT and École Polytechnique Fédérale de Lausanne; Stated Preference Methods: State of the Art Modelling course at the Swedish University of Agricultural Sciences); specialist DCE conferences (e.g. the International Choice Modelling Conference series: *www.stata.com*).

5.5.5. Best-worst scaling models

Recently, there has been some interest in the use of Best-Worst Scaling (BWS), an alternative choice-based method that involves less cognitive burden than DCEs. BWS was initially developed by Finn and Louviere (1992), with Marley and Louviere (2005) offering formal proof of its measurement properties. In the BWS approach respondents are presented with a set of three or more items, and asked to choose the two extreme items on an underlying latent scale of interest: best/worst or most/least important, or whatever extremes are appropriate to the study. Respondents are presented with several of these sets, one at a time, and in each case are asked to choose the two extreme items (e.g. the best and the worst) within the set. Experimental design is used to come up with the sets.

Unlike DCEs, in a BWS exercise, respondents are presented with a single scenario at a time, and asked to indicate the best and the worst attribute of that scenario. The aim is to elicit the relative weight or importance that respondents allocate to the various items contained in a set (e.g. attributes of a policy). The focus of the BWS is therefore on preferences for individual attributes rather than scenarios, which sometimes is a useful policy question. However, unless combined with a DCE (e.g. Scarpa et al., 2011), it is not possible to derive monetary values through BWS. BWS is also subject to a number of biases such as position bias (Campbell and Erden, 2015).

Potoglu et al. (2011) formally compared BWS with a DCE for the same good: social care related quality of life. Figure 5.3 illustrates what the BWS choice set looked like, while Figure 5.4 contains an example of two choice sets used in the parallel DCE. The authors found that both techniques revealed a similar pattern in preferences.

Figure 5.3. **Example of a Best-Worst Scaling set**

Which of these nine points would rate as being the best and which as being the worst?

Best (mark "X")	Aspect of life	Worst (mark "X")
	I can get all the food and drink I need	
	I have poor personal hygiene so I don't feel at all clean or presentable	
	My home is as clean and comfortable as I want	
	Sometimes I don't feel safe enough	
	Sometimes I feel lonely but have some contact with people I like	
	I spend my time as I want doing things I value or enjoy	
	I have adequate control over my daily life	
	The way I'm helped undermines the way I think and feel about myself	
	And I am living in my own home	

Source: Potoglu et al. (2011).

The number of applications of BSW has grown in recent years particularly in the field of health (e.g. Flynn et al., 2007). There are also emerging examples in the food, agricultural and environmental literatures (see Campbell and Erdem, 2015, for an overview).

Figure 5.4. **Example of discrete choice experiment sets**

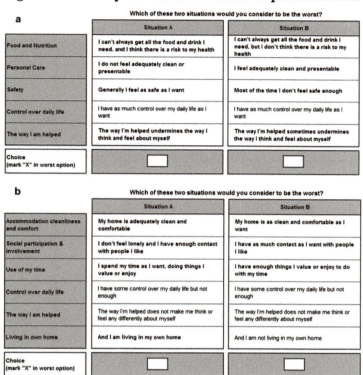

Source: Potoglu et al. (2011).

5.6. Conclusions

Many types of environmental impacts are multidimensional in character. What this means is that an environmental asset that is affected by a proposed project or policy often will give rise to changes in component attributes each of which command distinct valuations. This is not unlike the conceptual premise underlying the hedonic approach, a revealed preference method discussed in Chapter 3, where the value of particular goods such as properties can be thought of comprising consumers' valuations of bundles of characteristics, which can be "teased out" using appropriate statistical analysis. In contrast, however, the suite of stated preference methods known as discrete choice experiments discussed in this chapter must estimate respondents' valuations of the multiple dimensions of environmental goods, when the good's total value is not itself observable because no market for it exists. Indeed, it is this information about the (marginal) value of each dimension that is subsequently used to estimate the total value of the change in provision of the environmental good.

While there are a number of different approaches under the choice modelling umbrella, it is arguably the choice experiment variant that has become the dominant approach with regard to applications to environmental goods. In a choice experiment, respondents are asked to choose their most preferred from a choice set of at least two options one of which is the status quo or current situation. This DCE approach can be interpreted in standard welfare economic terms, an obvious strength where consistency with the theory of cost-benefit analysis is a desirable criterion.

Given that DCEs are a stated preference method, they share many of the advantages and disadvantages of the contingent valuation method. Much of the discussion in

Chapter 4 about, for example, validity and reliability issues in the context of CVM studies is likely to apply in the context of DCEs. Like CV, choice experiments are based on hypothetical scenarios. Similarly, DCEs are very flexible, and are able to measure future changes as well as non-use values. But, as discussed in this chapter, DCEs also have some distinctive characteristics that may differentially affect its performance and accuracy.

The application of DCE approaches to valuing multidimensional environmental problems has been growing steadily in recent years. DCEs are now routinely discussed alongside the arguably better-known contingent valuation method in state-of-the-art manuals regarding the design, analysis and use of stated preference studies. And in recent years, DCEs appear to have overtaken CV in terms of number of applications and citations (Mahieu et al., 2014) in the fields of environment, agriculture and health. Several factors discussed in this chapter explain the popularity of DCEs. DCE's are efficient in that they extract extensive information from survey respondents. Their statistical design, implementation and econometric analysis have been facilitated by the development of specialist statistical software and the technology for web surveys, which enables a user-friendly presentation of choice sets to respondents and expedites implementation and analysis considerably. New specialist textbooks, courses, conferences and even a journal (the *Journal of Choice Modelling*) have helped popularise the method across several disciplines.

Overall, the evidence discussed here seems to point to the superiority of DCEs when valuing complex multidimensional changes. That is, if the focus is on valuing individual components of a policy, and the trade-offs between them are important, then DCEs are possibly the method of choice. Moreover, DCEs are also advantageous when direct elicitation of values might be problematic. But if, instead, we are interested in estimating the total value of a policy then CV would arguably be the preferred method. The choice of method is ultimately case specific, i.e. DCEs should be used when the circumstances demand. As such, whether the two methods should be seen as always competing against one another – in the sense of which is the superior method – is debatable. Both approaches are likely to have their role in cost-benefit appraisals and a useful contribution of any future research would be to aid understanding of when one approach should be used rather than the other. Like CVM, DCEs are very much an important part of the cost benefit analyst's portfolio of valuation techniques.

References

Adamowicz, W. (2004), "What's it worth? An examination of historical trends and future directions in environmental valuation", *Australian Journal of Agricultural and Resource Economics*, Vol. 48, pp. 419-443, http://dx.doi.org/10.1111/j.1467-8489.2004.00258.x.

Adamowicz, W., J. Louviere and J. Swait (1998), "Introduction to Attribute-Based Stated Choice Methods", *Final Report*, NOAA, Washington, DC.

Adamowicz, W. et al. (1998), "Stated Preference Approaches for Measuring Passive Use Values: Choice Experiments and Contingent Valuation", *American Journal of Agricultural Economics*, Vol. 80(1), pp. 64-75, https://doi.org/10.2307/3180269.

Alemu, M.H. et al. (2013), "Attending to the reasons for attribute non-attendance in choice experiments", *Environmental and Resource Economics*, Vol. 54, pp. 333-359, http://dx.doi.org/10.1007/s10640-012-9597-8.

Araña, J.E., C.J. Leon and M.W. Hanemann (2008), "Emotions and decision rules in discrete choice experiments for valuing health care programmes for the elderly", *Journal of Health Economics*, Vol. 27, pp. 753-769, http://dx.doi.org/10.1016/j.jhealeco.2007.10.003.

Arentze, T. et al. (2003), "Transport stated choice responses: Effects of task complexity, presentation format and literacy", *Transportation Research Part E*, Vol. 39, pp. 229-244, http://dx.doi.org/10.1016/S1366-5545(02)00047-9.

Balcombe, K. et al. (2014), "Using attribute rankings within discrete choice experiments: An application to valuing bread attributes", *Journal of Agricultural Economics*, Vol. 0(2), pp. 446-462, *http://dx.doi.org/10.1111/1477-9552.12051*.

Balcombe, K.G., M. Burton and D. Rigby (2011), "Skew and attribute non-attendance within Bayesian mixed logit model", *Journal of Environmental Economics and Management*, Vol. 62(3), pp. 446-461, *https://doi.org/10.1016/j.jeem.2011.04.004*.

Banzhaf, M.R., F.R. Johnson and K.E. Mathews (2001), "Opt-Out Alternatives and Anglers' Stated Preferences", in Bennett J. and R. Blamey (eds.) (2001), *The Choice Modelling Approach to Environmental Valuation*, Edward Elgar Publishing Company, Cheltenham, *www.e-elgar.com/shop/the-choice-modelling-approach-to-environmental-valuation*.

Barr, R. and S. Mourato (2014), "Investigating Fishers' Preferences for the Design of Marine Payments for Environmental Services Schemes", *Ecological Economics*, Vol. 108, pp. 91-103, *http://dx.doi.org/10.1016/j.ecolecon.2014.09.006*.

Bateman, I.J. et al. (2002), *Economic valuation with stated preference techniques: A manual*, Edward Elgar, Cheltenham, *www.e-elgar.com/shop/economic-valuation-with-stated-preference-techniques?___website=uk_warehouse*.

Bateman, I.J. et al. (2009), "Reducing gain-loss asymmetry: A virtual reality choice experiment valuing land use change", *Journal of Environmental Economics and Management*, Vol. 58, pp. 106-118, *http://dx.doi.org/10.1016/j.jeem.2008.05.003*.

Bech, M., T. Kjaer and J. Lauridsen (2011), "Does the number of choice sets matter? Results from a web survey applying a discrete choice experiment", *Health Economics*, Vol. 20, pp. 273-286, *http://dx.doi.org/10.1002/hec.1587*.

Ben-Akiva, M., T. Morikawa and F. Shiroishi (1991), "Analysis of the Reliability of Preference Ranking Data", *Journal of Business Research*, Vol. 23, pp. 253-268.

Bennett, J. and R. Blamey (2001), *The choice modelling approach to environmental valuation*, Edward Elgar, Cheltenham, *www.e-elgar.com/shop/the-choice-modelling-approach-to-environmental-valuation*.

Bierlaire, M. (2003), "BIOGEME: A free package for the estimation of discrete choice models", *Proceedings of the 3rd Swiss Transportation Research Conference*, Ascona, Switzerland.

Boeri, M. et al. (2012), "Site choices in recreational demand: A matter of utility maximization or regret minimization?", *Journal of Environmental Economics and Policy*, Vol. 1, pp. 32-47, *http://dx.doi.org/10.1080/21606544.2011.640844*.

Boxall, P. and W.L. Adamowicz (2002), "Understanding heterogeneous preferences in random utility models: A latent class approach", *Environmental and Resource Economics*, Vol. 23, pp. 421-446, *http://dx.doi.org/10.1023/A:1021351721619*.

Bradley, M. (1991), *User's manual for Speed version 2.1*, Hague Consulting Group, Hague.

Cameron, T.A. and J.R. de DeShazo (2010), "Differential attention to attributes in utility-theoretic choice models", *Journal of Choice Modelling*, Vol. 3(3), pp. 73-115, *www.sciencedirect.com/science/journal/17555345/3*.

Campbell, D., C.D. Aravena and W.G. Hutchinson (2011), "Cheap and expensive alternatives in stated choice experiments: Are they equally considered by respondents?", *Applied Economics Letters*, Vol. 18, pp. 743-747, *http://dx.doi.org/10.1080/13504851.2010.498341*.

Campbell, D. and S. Erdem (2015), "Position Bias In Best-Worst Scaling Surveys: A Case Study on Trust in Institutions", *American Journal of Agricultural Economics*, Vol. 97(2), pp. 526-545, *https://doi.org/10.1093/ajae/aau112*.

Campbell, D., W.G. Hutchinson and R. Scarpa (2006), "Lexicographic preferences in discrete choice experiments: Consequences on individual-specific willingness to pay estimates", *Nota di lavoro* 128.2006, Fondazione Eni Enrico Mattei, Milano, *http://ageconsearch.umn.edu/bitstream/12224/1/wp060128.pdf*.

Campbell, D. and V.S. Lorimer (2009), *Accommodating attribute processing strategies in stated choice analysis: Do respondents do what they say they do?*, 17th Annual Conference of the European Association of Environmental and Resource Economics, Amsterdam, *www.webmeets.com/files/papers/EAERE/2009/558/Campbell_Lorimer_EAERE2009.pdf*.

Cantillo, V. and J. de D. Ortuzar (2005), "Implication of thresholds in discrete choice modelling", *Transport Reviews*, Vol. 26(6), pp. 667-691, *http://dx.doi.org/10.1080/01441640500487275*.

Carlsson, F. (2010), "Design of stated preference surveys: Is there more to learn from behavioral economics?", *Environmental and Resource Economics*, Vol. 46, pp. 167-177, *http://dx.doi.org/10.1007/s10640-010-9359-4*.

Carlsson, F., M.R. Mørbak and S.B. Olsen (2012), "The first time is the hardest: A test of ordering effects in choice experiments", *Journal of Choice Modelling*, Vol. 5(2), pp. 19-37, *https://doi.org/10.1016/S1755-5345(13)70051-4*.

Cassuade, S. et al. (2005), "Assessing the influence of design dimension on stated choice experiment estimates", *Transportation Research Part B*, Vol. 39, pp. 621-640, *http://dx.doi.org/10.1016/j.trb.2004.07.006*.

ChoiceMetrics (2014), *Ngene 1.1.2.: User Manual and Reference Guide. The Cutting Edge in Experimental Design*, ChoiceMetrics Pty Ltd.

Chorus, C.G., T.A. Arentze and H.J.P. Timmermans (2008), "A random regret-minimization model of travel choice", *Transportation Research Part B Methodology*, Vol. 42, pp. 1-18, *http://dx.doi.org/10.1016/j.trb.2007.05.004*.

Chorus, C.G., S. van Cranenburgh and T. Dekker (2014), "Random regret minimization for consumer choice modeling: Assessment of empirical evidence", *Journal of Business Research*, Vol. 67(11), pp. 2428-2436, *https://doi.org/10.1016/j.jbusres.2014.02.010*.

Colombo, S., M. Christie and N. Hanley (2013), "What are the consequences of ignoring attributes in choice experiments? Implications for ecosystem service valuation", *Ecological Economics*, Vol. 96, pp. 25-35, *https://doi.org/10.1016/j.ecolecon.2013.08.016*.

Contu, D., E. Strazzera and S. Mourato (2016), "Modeling individual preferences for energy sources: the case of IV generation nuclear energy in Italy", *Ecological Economics*, Vol. 127, pp. 37-58, *http://dx.doi.org/10.1016/j.ecolecon.2016.03.008*.

Czajkowski, M., M. Giergiczny and W. Greene (2014), "Learning and fatigue effects revisited. The impact of accounting for unobservable preference and scale heterogeneity", *Land Economics*, Vol. 90(2), pp. 324-351, *http://dx.doi.org/10.3368/le.90.2.324*.

Danthurebandara, V.M., J. Yu and M. Vanderbroek (2011), "Effect of choice complexity on design efficiency in conjoint choice experiments", *Journal of Statistical Planning and Inference*, Vol. 141, pp. 2276-2286, *http://dx.doi.org/10.1016/j.jspi.2011.01.008*.

De Bekker-Grob, E.W., M. Ryan and K. Gerard (2012), "Discrete choice experiments in health economics: A review of the literature", *Health Economics*, Vol. 21, pp. 145-172, *http://dx.doi.org/10.1002/hec.1697*.

Dellaert, B.G.C., J.D. Brazell and J. Louviere (1999), "The effect of attribute variation on consumer choice consistency", *Marketing Letters*, Vol. 10(2), pp. 139-147, *http://dx.doi.org/10.1023/A:1008088930464*.

De Palma, A., G. Myers and Y. Papeorgiou (1994), "Rational choice under imperfect ability to choose", *American Economic Review*, Vol. 84, pp. 419-440.

DeShazo, J.R. and G. Fermo (2002), "Designing choice sets for stated preference methods: The effects of complexity on choice consistency", *Journal of Environmental Economics and Management*, Vol. 44, pp. 123-143, *http://dx.doi.org/10.1006/jeem.2001.1199*.

Eftec and ICS Consulting (2013), *South Staffs Water PR14 Stated Preference Study: Final Report*, Economics for the Environment Consultancy, London, *www.south-staffs-water.co.uk/media/1163/final_report_ssw_pr14_wtp_study.pdf*.

Finn, A. and J.J. Louviere (1992), "Determining the appropriate response to evidence of public concern: The case of food safety", *Journal of Public Policy and Marketing*, Vol. 11, pp. 12-25.

Flynn, T.N. et al. (2007), "Best-worst scaling: What it can do for health care research and how to do it", *Journal of Health Economics*, Vol. 26, pp. 171-189, *http://dx.doi.org/10.1016/j.jhealeco.2006.04.002*.

Foster, V. and S. Mourato (2002), "Testing for consistency in contingent ranking experiments", *Journal of Environmental Economics and Management*, Vol. 44, pp. 309-328, *https://doi.org/10.1006/jeem.2001.1203*.

Foster, V. and S. Mourato (2003), "Elicitation format and sensitivity to scope", *Environmental and Resource Economics*, Vol. 24, pp. 141-160, *http://dx.doi.org/10.1006/jeem.2001.1203*.

Gelso, B.R. and J.M. Peterson (2005), "The influence of ethical attitudes on the demand for environmental recreation: Incorporating lexicographic preferences", *Ecological Economics*, Vol. 53(1), pp. 35-45, *http://dx.doi.org/10.1016/j.ecolecon.2004.01.021*.

Green, P. and V. Srinivasan (1978), "Conjoint analysis in consumer research: Issues and outlook", *Journal of Consumer Research*, Vol. 5, pp. 103-123.

Greene, W.H. (2008), *Econometric Analysis*, 6th Edition, Macmillan, New York.

Greene, W.H. (2016), NLogit 6 (software), Econometric Software, Inc.

Hanemann, W.M. (1984), "Discrete/continuous models of consumer demand", *Econometrica*, Vol. 52, pp. 541-561.

Hanley, N., S. Mourato and R. Wright (2001), "Choice modelling approaches: A superior alternative for environmental Valuation?", *Journal of Economic Surveys*, Vol. 15, pp. 435-462, *http://dx.doi.org/10.1111/1467-6419.00145*.

Hausman, J. (ed.) (1993), *Contingent Valuation: A Critical Assessment*, North Holland, Amsterdam.

Hausman, J. (2012), "Contingent valuation: From dubious to hopeless", *Journal of Economic Perspectives*, Vol. 26, pp. 43-56, *http://dx.doi.org/10.1257/jep.26.4.43*.

Hausman, J. and D. Wise (1978), "A conditional Probit model for qualitative choice: discrete decisions recognising interdependence and heterogeneous preferences", *Econometrica*, Vol. 42, pp. 403-426.

Hausman, J. and D. McFadden (1984), "Specification tests for the multinomial Logit model", *Econometrica*, Vol. 52, pp. 1219-1240.

Heiner, R. (1983), "The origin of predictive behaviour", *American Economic Review*, Vol. 73, pp. 560-595.

Hensher, D.A., J.M. Rose and W.H. Greene (2015), *Applied Choice Analysis*, 2nd edition, Cambridge University Press, New York.

Hensher, D.A., J.M. Rose and W.H. Greene (2005), "The implication on willingness to pay of respondents ignoring specific attributes", *Transportation*, Vol. 32, pp. 203-222, *http://dx.doi.org/10.1007/s11116-004-7613-8*.

Hensher, D.A. (2006), "How do respondent process stated choice experiments? Attribute consideration under varying information load", *Journal of Applied Econometrics*, Vol. 21, pp. 861-878, *http://dx.doi.org/10.1002/jae.877*.

Hensher, D.A. and J.M. Rose (2009), 'Simplifying choice through attribute preservation or non-attendance: Implication for willingness to pay", *Transportation Research E*, Vol. 45(4), pp. 583-590, *http://dx.doi.org/10.1016/j.tre.2008.12.001*.

Hensher, D.A. (1994), "Stated preference analysis of travel choices: the state of practice," *Transportation*, Vol. 21, pp. 107-133.

Hess, S. and D.A. Hensher (2010), "Using conditioning on observed choices to retrieve individual-specific attribute processing strategies", *Transport Research Part B*, Vol. 44, pp. 781-790, *http://dx.doi.org/10.1016/j.trb.2009.12.001*.

Hess, S., D. Hensher and A.J. Daly (2012), "Not bored yet: Revisiting fatigue in stated choice experiments", *Transportation Research Part A*, Vol. 46(3), pp. 626-644, *http://dx.doi.org/10.1016/j.tra.2011.11.008*.

Hess, S., J.M. Rose and J. Polak (2010), "Non-trading, lexicographic and inconsistent behaviour in stated choice data", *Transportation Research Part D*, Vol. 15, pp. 405-417, *http://dx.doi.org/10.1016/j.trd.2010.04.008*.

Hess, S. et al. (2013), "It's not that I don't care, I just don't care very much: Confounding between attribute non-attendance and taste heterogeneity", *Transportation*, Vol. 40(3), pp. 583-607, *http://dx.doi.org/10.1007/s11116-012-9438-1*.

Hole, A.R. (2011), "A discrete choice model with endogenous attribute attendance", *Economics Letters*, Vol. 110, pp. 203-205, *http://dx.doi.org/10.1016/j.econlet.2010.11.033*.

Hole, A.R., J.R. Kolstad and D. Gyrd-Hansen (2013), "Inferred vs. stated attribute non-attendance in choice experiments: A study of doctors' prescription behaviour", *Journal of Economic Behavior & Organization*, Vol. 96, pp. 21-31, *http://dx.doi.org/10.1016/j.jebo.2013.09.009*.

Hoyos, D. (2010), "The state of the art of environmental valuation with discrete choice experiments", *Ecological Economics*, Vol. 69, pp. 1595-1603, *http://dx.doi.org/10.1016/j.ecolecon.2010.04.011*.

Islam, T., J.J. Louviere and P.F. Burke (2007), "Modelling the effects of including/excluding attributes in choice experiments on systematic and random components", *International Journal of Research in Marketing*, Vol. 24, pp. 289-300, *http://dx.doi.org/10.1016/j.ijresmar.2007.04.002*.

Johnson, F.R. et al. (2013), "Constructing Experimental Designs for Discrete-Choice Experiments: Report of the ISPOR Conjoint Analysis Experimental Design Good Research Practices Task Force," *Value in Health*, Vol. 16, pp. 3-13, *http://dx.doi.org/10.1016/j.jval.2012.08.2223*.

Kahneman, D. and J. Knetsch (1992), "Valuing public goods: the purchase of moral satisfaction", *Journal of Environmental Economics and Management*, Vol. 22, pp. 57-70.

Kanninen, B.J. (ed.) (2007), *Valuing Environmental Amenities Using Stated Choice Studies*, Springer, Dordrecht.

Kaye-Blake, W.H., W.L. Abell and E. Zellman (2009), "Respondents' ignoring of attributes information in a choice modelling survey", *Australian Journal of Agricultural and Resource Economics*, Vol. 53(4), pp. , *http://dx.doi.org/547-564. 10.1111/j.1467-8489.2009.00467.x*.

Kehlbacher, A., K. Balcombe and R. Bennet (2013), "Stated attribute non-attendance in successive choice experiments", *Journal of Agricultural Economics*, Vol. 64(3), pp. 693-706, *http://dx.doi.org/10.1111/1477-9552.12021*.

Kontoleon, A. and M. Yabe (2004), "Assessing the Impacts of Alternative 'Opt-out' Formats in Choice Experiment Studies", *Journal of Agricultural Policy Research*, Vol. 5, pp. 1-32.

Kragt, M.E. (2013), "Stated and inferred attribute non-attendance models: A comparison with environmental choice experiments", *Journal of Agricultural Economics*, Vol. 64(3), pp. 719-736, *http://dx.doi.org/10.1111/1477-9552.12032*.

Krinsky, I. and A. Robb (1986), "On approximating the statistical properties of elasticities", *Review of Economics and Statistics*, Vol. 68, pp. 715-719.

Kuhfeld, W.F. (2010), *Marketing research methods in SAS*, SAS Institute Inc Cary. *https://support.sas.com/techsup/technote/mr2010.pdf*.

Lancaster, K. (1966), "A new approach to consumer theory", *Journal of Political Economy*, Vol. 74, pp. 132-157, *https://doi.org/10.1086/259131*.

Lagarde, M. (2013), "Investigating attribute non-attendance and its consequences in choice experiments with latent class models", *Health Economics*, Vol. 22, pp. 554-567.

Lancsar, E. and J. Louviere (2006), "Deleting 'irrational' responses from discrete choice experiments: A case of investigating or imposing preferences?", *Health Economics*, Vol. 15(8), pp. 797-811, *http://dx.doi.org/10.1002/hec.2824*.

Leong, W. and D.A. Hensher (2012), "Embedding heuristics into choice models: An exploratory analysis", *Journal of Choice Modelling*, Vol. 5(3), pp. 131-144, *http://dx.doi.org/10.1016/j.jocm.2013.03.001*.

Loewenstein, G and J.S. Lerner (2003), "The role of affect in decision making", in Davidson, R.J., K.R. Scherer and H.H. Goldsmith (eds.) (2003), *Handbook of Affective Sciences*, Oxford University Press, Oxford.

Louviere, J.J. and D.A. Hensher (1982), "On the design and analysis of simulated choice or allocation experiments in travel choice modelling", *Transportation Research Record*, Vol. 890, pp. 11-17.

Louviere, J.J. et al. (2008), "Designing discrete choice experiments: Do optimal designs come at a price?", *Journal of Consumer Research*, Vol. 35, pp. 360-375, *http://dx.doi.org/10.1086/586913%20*.

Louviere, J.J., D.A. Hensher and J.Swait (2000), *Stated choice methods: Analysis and applications*, Cambridge University Press, Cambridge.

Louviere, J.J. and E. Lancsar (2009), "Choice experiments in health: The good, the bad, and the ugly and toward a brighter future", *Health Economics, Policy, and Law*, Vol. 4, pp. 527-546, *http://dx.doi.org/10.1017/S1744133109990193*.

Louviere, J.J. and G. Woodworth (1983), "Design and analysis of simulated consumer choice or allocation experiments: An approach based on aggregate data", *Journal of Marketing Research*, Vol. 20, pp. 350-367.

Luce, R.D. (1959), *Individual Choice Behavior: A Theoretical Analysis*, John Wiley & Sons, New York.

Mahieu, P.-A. et al. (2014), "Is choice experiment becoming more popular than contingent valuation? A systematic review in agriculture, environment and health", *FAERE Working Paper 2014.12*, *http://faere.fr/pub/WorkingPapers/Mahieu_Andersson_Beaumais_Crastes_Wolff_FAERE_WP2014.12.pdf*.

Marley, A.A.J. and J.J. Louviere (2005), "Some Probabilistic Models of Best, Worst, and Best-Worst Choices", *Journal of Mathematical Psychology*, Vol. 49(6), pp. 464-480, *http://dx.doi.org/10.1016/j.jmp.2005.05.003*.

Mazzotta, M.J. and J.J. Opaluch (1995), "Decision making when choices are complex: A test of Heiner's hypothesis", *Land Economics*, Vol. 71(4), pp. 500-515.

McFadden, D. (1973), "Conditional Logit analysis of qualitative choice behaviour", in Zarembka, P. (ed.) *Frontiers in Econometrics*, Academic Press, New York.

McFadden, D. (1981), "Econometric models of probabilistic choice", in Manski, C. and D. McFadden, (eds.) (1981), *Structural Analysis of Discrete Data with Econometric Applications*, MIT Press, Cambridge.

Meyerhoff, J. and U. Liebe (2009), "Status Quo Effect in Choice Experiments: Empirical Evidence on Attitudes and Choice Task Complexity", *Land Economics*, Vol. 85(3), pp. 515-528.

Meyerhoff, J., M. Oehlmann and P. Weller (2014), "The influence of design dimension on stated choice. An example from environmental valuation using a design of design approach", *Environmental and Resource Economics*, Vol. 61(3), pp. 385-407, *http://dx.doi.org/10.1007/s10640-014-9797-5%20*.

Miller, G.A. (1955), "The magical number seven, plus or minus two. Some limits on our capacity of processing information", *Psychological Review*, Vol. 101(2), pp. 343-352.

Morrison, M. et al. (1998), "Choice Modelling and Tests of Benefit Transfer", *Choice Modelling Research Report 8*, University College, University of New South Wales, Canberra.

Munro, A. and N. Hanley (1999), "Information, uncertainty and contingent valuation", in Bateman, I.J. and K.G. Willis (eds.) (1999), *Contingent Valuation of Environmental Preferences: Assessing Theory and Practice in the USA, Europe, and Developing Countries*, Oxford University Press, Oxford.

Parsons, G.R. and M.J. Kealy (1992), "Randomly drawn opportunity sets in a random utility model of lake recreation", *Land Economics*, Vol. 68(1), pp. 93-106.

Payne, J.W., J.R. Bettman and E.L. Johnson (1993), *The Adaptive Decision Maker*, Cambridge University Press, Cambridge.

Potoglou, D. et al. (2011), "Best-worst scaling vs. discrete choice experiments: An empirical comparison using social care data", *Social Science & Medicine*, Vol. 72, pp. 1717-1727, *http://dx.doi.org/10.1016/j.socscimed.2011.03.027*.

Puckett, S.M. and D.A. Hensher (2008), "The role of attribute processing strategies in estimating the preferences of road freight stakeholders under variable road user charges", *Transportation Research E*, Vol. 44(3), pp. 379-395, *http://dx.doi.org/10.1016/j.tre.2007.01.002*.

Puckett, S.M. and D.A. Hensher (2009), "Revealing the extent of process heterogeneity in choice analysis. An empirical assessment", *Transportation Research Part A: Policy and Practice*, Vol. 43(2), pp., *http://dx.doi.org/117-126.%2010.1016/j.tra.2008.07.003*.

Rakotonarivo, O.S., M. Schaafsma and N. Hockley (2016), "A systematic review of the reliability and validity of discrete choice experiments in valuing non-market environmental goods", *Journal of Environmental Management*, Vol. 183, pp. 98-109, *http://dx.doi.org/10.1016/j.jenvman.2016.08.032*.

Rolfe, J. (2006), "Theoretical issues in using choice modelling data for benefit transfer", in Rolfe, J. and J. Bennett, (eds.) (2006), *Choice Modelling and the Transfer of Environmental Values*, Edward Elgar, Cheltenham.

Rolfe, J. and J. Windle, (2008), "Testing for differences in benefit transfer values between state and regional frameworks", *Australian Journal of Agricultural and Resource Economics*, Vol. 52, pp. 149-168, *http://dx.doi.org/10.1111/j.1467-8489.2008.00405.x*.

Rolfe, J., J. Windle and J. Bennett (2015), "Benefit Transfer: Insights from Choice Experiments", in Johnson, R.J. et al. (eds.) (2015), *Benefit Transfer of Environmental and Resource Values: A Guide for Researchers and Practitioners*, Springer, Dordrecht.

Rosenberger, R.S. et al. (2003), "Measuring dispositions for lexicographic preferences of environmental goods: Integrating economics, psychology and ethics", *Ecological Economics*, Vol. 44, pp. 63-76.

Sælensminde, K. (2001), "Inconsistent choices in stated choice data: Use of the logit scaling approach to handle resulting variance increases", *Transportation*, Vol. 28, pp. 269-296.

Samuelson, W. and R. Zeckhauser (1988), "Status Quo Bias in Decision Making", *Journal of Risk and Uncertainty*, Vol. 1, pp. 7-59.

Sándor, Z. and H. Franses (2009), "Consumer price evaluations through choice experiments", *Journal of Applied Econometrics*, Vol. 24, pp. 517-535, *http://dx.doi.org/10.1002/jae.1061*.

Scarpa, R. et al. (2011), "Exploring Scale Effects of Best/Worst Rank Ordered Choice Data to Estimate Benefits of Tourism in Alpine Grazing Commons", *American Journal of Agricultural Economics*, Vol. 93(3), pp. 813-28, *http://dx.doi.org/10.1093/ajae/aaq174*.

Scarpa, R., M. Thiene and D.A. Hensher (2010), "Monitoring choice task attribute attendance in non-market valuation of multiple park management services: Does it matter?", *Land Economics*, Vol. 86(4), pp. 817-839, *http://dx.doi.org/10.3368/le.86.4.817*.

Scarpa, R. et al. (2013), "Inferred and stated attribute non-attendance in food choice experiments", *American Journal of Agricultural Economics*, Vol. 95(1), pp. 165-180, *http://dx.doi.org/10.1093/ajae/aas073*.

Scott, A. (2002), "Identifying and analysing dominant preferences in discrete choice experiments: An application in health care", *Journal of Economic Psychology*, Vol. 23(3), pp. 383-398.

Steer Davies Gleave (SDG) (1999), *Bus Station Passenger Preferences*, Report for London Transport Buses, London Transport, London.

Steer Davies Gleave (SDG) (2000), *London Underground Customer Priorities Research*, Report for London Undergound, London Underground, London.

Severin, V. (2001), *Comparing Statistical and Respondent Efficiency in Choice Experiments*, Ph.D. Dissertation, Faculty of Economics and Business, the University of Sydney.

Simon, H.A. (1955), "A behavioral model of rational choice", *Quarterly Journal of Economics*, Vol. 69, pp. 99-118.

SPSS (2008), *Computer software*, SPSS Inc Chicago.

Swait, J. and W. Adamowicz (2001), "Choice environment. Market complexity, and consumer behavior: A theoretical and empirical approach for incorporating decision complexity into models of consumer choice", *Organizational behavior and human decision processes*, Vol. 86 (2), pp. 141-167, *http://dx.doi.org/10.1006/obhd.2000.2941*.

Swait, J. (2001), "A non-compensatory choice model incorporating attribute cutoffs", *Transportation Research B*, Vol. 35(10), pp. 903-928.

Train, K.E. (1998), "Recreation demand models with taste differences across people", *Land Economics*, Vol. 74(2), pp. 230-239.

Train, K.E. (2009), *Discrete Choice Methods with Simulation*, 2nd Edition, Cambridge University Press, Cambridge.

Tversky, A. (1972), "Elimination by aspects: A theory of choice", *Psychological Review*, Vol. 79, pp. 281-299.

Viton, P.A. (2015), *Discrete Choice Logit Models with R*, Ohio State University, Colombus, *http://facweb.knowlton.ohio-state.edu/pviton/courses2/crp5700/5700-mlogit.pdf*.

PART I

Chapter 6

Value transfer

Value transfers are the bedrock of practical policy analysis in that only infrequently are policy analysts afforded the luxury of designing and implementing original studies. Thus, in such instances, analysts must fall back on the information that can be gleaned from past studies in order to estimate monetary values for some current policy or project proposal. Whether this is a defensible short-cut is the object of value transfer tests, which provide important guidance about situations in which value transfer can be carried out confidently and when practitioners should proceed with more caution. The general lesson is that there are possibly significant trade-offs between simplicity and accuracy of the resulting transfer. Thus, a competent application of transfer methods demands informed judgement and expertise and sometimes, according to more demanding commentators, as advanced technical skills as those required for original research. This is something of a paradox then for surely the point of transfer exercises is to make routine valuation more straightforward and widely used. Another development which may help in this respect is valuation databases (such as EVRI) and "look-up tables" (lists of average values and ranges for various categories of environmental goods and services). These are important facilitators of valuation uptake in policy formulation, although in turn these do require good guidance on practice and use.

6.1. Introduction

Advances in methods to value environmental goods and services (and non-market commodities, more generally) have been a striking feature of modern cost-benefit analysis (CBA). Just as prominent has been the growing use of these methods to help inform policy and investment project choices across an increasing number of countries. Taking full advantage of this apparent willingness amongst decision-makers to employ the fruits of these advances in this practical way depends, in turn, on a number of further considerations.

An example is the need for a crucial ingredient: plenty of original valuation studies which can be applied to these nascent policy and project questions. However, these ingredients are costly and, as a result, may be in short supply. If so, then practitioners may have to be more enterprising in meeting the policy world's demand for CBA. One example of this initiative is a greater reliance on value (or, more narrowly, benefits) transfer: that is, taking a unit value of a non-market good estimated in an original or primary study and using this estimate – perhaps after some adjustment – to value benefits or costs that arise when a new policy (or investment project) is implemented.

Value transfer is now the subject of a large literature. The reason is obvious. If value transfer were a valid procedure, then the need for costly and time-consuming original (or "primary") studies of non-market values would be vastly reduced. In other words, the valuation process can make do with fewer ingredients. To stretch this culinary metaphor further, however, a number of other considerations have to borne in mind. The original ingredients need to be of sufficiently good quality for the resulting dish to be palatable and there needs to be a recipe guiding use of these ingredients. For these reasons, Rolfe et al. (2015) describe value transfer as "… superficially attractive …" (p. 4).

It is this, the validity of value transfer – rather than the abundance of good quality studies – that is the primary focus of much of this Chapter. At the risk of caricature, endeavour in value transfer often reflects two possibly opposing traditions. The first reflects a quest to make valuation as accessible as conceivable. An aspect of this, for example, is "look-up" values: standard values for (non-market) impacts routinely valued in the appraisal of policies or investment projects. The second starts with concern that poorly done value transfer may result in policy selection mistakes and a key ingredient in understanding this is tests of when the value transfer works and when it does not. Perhaps ironically, both traditions are understandable. There will surely be an issue about uptake if valuation is the preserve of the highly trained and specialised experts allowing value transfer but requiring it to be ever more sophisticated in its application. Equally, the cause of applying cost-benefit thinking to policy and investment is not helped by valuation estimates which are not sufficiently robust so as to be easily challenged.

This is because the validity and reliability of value transfers remains open to scrutiny, and – as various tests in the literature show – can give rise to inaccuracy of varying degrees of magnitude. Of course, conclusions about the accuracy of value transfers must be contain some degree of pragmatism. Put another way, some inaccuracy is almost inevitable and the finding that transfers are invalid might be based on criteria, which are too strict. As a practical issue, it could be that some greater degree of inaccuracy "does not matter", although there is a legitimate debate to be had about what this really means.

Clearly then there is a balance to strike and practical considerations should not translate into an "anything goes" approach. The scrutiny of value transfer to date has also been important in showing how it seems to work better in some contexts and situations than in others. The reasons for this are becoming clearer as the empirical record grows along with the quality of the tests conducted. As a result, such findings can help to guide the use of value transfer by indicating when it can be relied upon and when more caution must be applied. This should allow better value transfer to be done as a result. An example here is the issue of spatial variability. For ecosystem services, location matters and transfers which do not account for this could be highly misleading. However, if these spatial considerations can be accommodated, then value transfer can be a useful and possibly powerful means of evaluating new policies and investment projects.

The holy grail of value transfer is a comprehensive database of studies or specific non-market values or, which can be taken "off the shelf" and applied to new policies and projects as needed. A number of examples of these databases now exist, with perhaps the EVRI inventory[1] being the most prominent as well as the most longstanding. The establishment of "reference values" and "look-up" tables used by, for example, national government while not common is also a notable development. A critical question is whether these (welcome) developments are accompanied by sufficient guidance about how to transfer values in a valid and reliable way.

The remainder of this Chapter is organised as follows. Section 6.2 provides a definition of value transfer and then goes on to outline the steps that a value transfer approach typically might take. It also looks at ways in which values (to be transferred) might be adjusted to "fit better" the characteristics (of the good and the affected population) that accompany a new policy. A brief review of what is known about how robust these transfers are is then offered in Section 6.3. Section 6.4 describes how one lesson of those tests has been used to guide better use of value transfer for the case of spatial variability. Section 6.5 discusses efforts to develop comprehensive databases of values for use in future transfers. Section 6.6 offers concluding remarks on issues such as best practice in the light of the preceding discussion.

6.2. Value transfer: Basic concepts and methods

6.2.1. Defining value transfer

Value or benefit transfer (VT or BT) concepts have been advanced in a number of articles over the past 25 years or so. Early developments include the pioneering contributions in the 1992 issue of *Water Resources Research* (Vol. 28, No. 3), which was dedicated specifically to BT. A definition of BT offered in that volume was: "…the transfer of existing estimates of non-market values to a new study which is different from the study for which the values were originally estimated" (Boyle and Bergstrom, 1992). Since then the number and quality of VT and BT studies have increased significantly. Another milestone was Desvousges, Johnson and Banzhaf (1998), one of the first major published studies of the validity of BT. That volume distinguished two basic definitions of BT, which still largely apply now.

The first definition is a *broader* concept based on the use of existing information designed for one specific context (original context) to address policy questions in another context (transfer context). These types of transfer studies are not limited to cost-benefit analysis (CBA) and related applications. They occur whenever analysts draw on past studies to predict effects of policies in another context. Put this way, value transfer – in some shape or form – is far more pervasive to policy analysis than many perhaps would fully realise.

The second definition is a *narrower* concept based on the use of values of a good estimated in one site (the "study site") as a proxy for values of the (same) good in another site (the "policy site"). This is the type of VT most commonly used in CBA and thus it is this more specific definition that is the basis of this Chapter.

The application of this latter type of value transfer covers a remarkably wide range of goods. For example, the provision of a non-market good at a policy site might refer to a river at a particular geographical location (where study sites relate to rivers at different locations). However, relevant impacts at a site might also entail some change in a human health state change. A policy-site also might be a wholly different country to that where the study was originally conducted. That is, perhaps values are being transferred from countries, which are data-rich (i.e. the minority) to countries where there is a paucity of such information (i.e. the majority).

6.2.2. Transfer methods

An important point is that value transfer is not necessarily a passive or straightforward choice for analysts. Once value transfer has been selected as the assessment method (itself a choice requiring some reflection), then judgement and insight is required for all of the basic steps entailed in undertaking a VT exercise. For example, information needs to be obtained on baseline environmental quality and changes as well as relevant socio-economic data. In addition, original studies for transfer need to be identified. Published and unpublished (e.g. so-called "grey") literature might be sought in this regard. It may be, however, that a database of past studies exists in which case consulting this source would seem an appropriate starting point. Later on, this Chapter describes efforts to construct databases of environmental valuation studies (see Section 6.5).

In general rule a transfer can be no more reliable than the original estimates upon which it is based. Given a lack of good quality original studies for many types of non-market values and the fact that even good studies typically have not been designed specifically for transfer applications, care must be taken here. Clearly, the analyst needs to have some criteria for judging the quality of studies if no "official" (or other) guidance exists.

Perhaps the most crucial stage is where existing estimates or models are selected and estimated effects are obtained for the policy site (e.g. per household benefits). This is the point at which the actual transfer occurs and implies choosing a particular transfer approach (see below). In addition, the population at the relevant policy site must be determined. Aggregation is achieved by multiplying per household values by population, the choice of which itself requires careful consideration.

One example of the problems of deciding the population over which to aggregate was the use of VT in the United Kingdom to guide decisions about withholding abstraction licences to water companies on the basis of alleviating low flow problems in English waterways. One of these decisions was overturned on the basis of a judicial review, which determined that those households previously ascribed non-use value for one river (the Kennet) by a factor of 75.[2] This is a now rather dated example, but at the time many viewed it this decision as a serious blow to CBA (or at least its use in environmental decision-making in the United Kingdom) (Pearce, 1998). With hindsight, those fears have proven to be overblown; however, such episodes should not be forgotten as a cautionary tale relevant for today.

There are at least three different types of adjustment of increasing sophistication for the analyst to choose from. These options are reviewed in what follows.

Unadjusted (or Naïve) value transfer

The procedure here is to "borrow" an estimate of WTP in context S (the study site) and apply it to context P (the policy site). The estimate is usually left unadjusted:

$$WTP_S = WTP_P.$$

A variety of unit values may be transferred; the most typical being mean or median measures. Mean values are readily compatible with CBA studies as they allow simple transformation to aggregate benefit estimates: e.g. multiply mean – average – WTP by the relevant affected population to calculate aggregate benefits.

The virtue of this approach is clearly its simplicity and the ease with which it can be applied once suitable original studies have been identified. Of course, the flipside of this relative straightforwardness is that it fails to capture important differences between the characteristics of an original study site (or sites) and a new policy site. If these differences are significant determinants of WTP, then this transfer approach – which is sometimes more prescriptively known as a naïve transfer – will fail to reflect likely divergences in WTP at the study and policy sites.

Determinants of WTP that might differ between study and policy sites include:

- The socio-economic and demographic characteristics of the relevant populations. This might include income, educational attainment and age.

- The physical characteristics of the study and policy sites. This might include the environmental services that the good provides such as, in the case of a river, opportunities for recreation in general and angling in particular.

- The proposed change in provision between the sites of the good to be valued. For example, the value of water quality improvements from studies involving small improvements may not apply to a policy involving a large change in quantity or quality (e.g. WTP and quantity may not have a straightforward linear relationship).

- Differences in the "market" conditions applying to the sites. For example, variation in the availability of substitutes in the case of recreational resources such as rivers. Two otherwise identical rivers might be characterised by different levels of alternative recreational opportunities. Other things being equal (by assumption in this case), mean WTP to prevent a lowering of water quality at a river where there are few substitutes should be greater than WTP for avoiding the same quality loss at a river where there is an abundance of substitutes. The reason for this the former is a more scarce recreational resource than the latter.

- Temporal changes. There may be changes in valuations over time, perhaps because of increasing incomes and/or decreasing availability of clean rivers.

As a general rule, there is little evidence that the conditions for accepting unadjusted value transfer hold in practice. Effectively, those conditions amount to saying that the various conditions listed above all do not hold, i.e. "sites" are effectively "identical" in all these characteristics (or that characteristics are not significant determinants of WTP, a conclusion which sits at odds with economic theory).

Value transfer with adjustment

A widely used formula for adjusted transfer is:

$$WTP_P = WTP_S \, (Y_P/Y_S)^e,$$

where Y is income per capita, WTP is willingness-to-pay, and e is the income elasticity of WTP.[3] This latter term is an estimate of how the WTP for the (non-market) good in question varies with changes in income). According to this expression, if e is assumed to be equal to one, then the ratio of WTP at sites S and P is equivalent to the ratio of per capita incomes at the two sites (i.e. $WTP_P/WTP_S = Y_P/Y_S$). In this example, values are simply adjusted upwards for projects affecting people with higher than average incomes and downwards for projects that affect people with lower than average incomes. As an example, Hamilton et al. (2014), based in turn on OECD (2014), transfer WTP for various health states (particularly mortality risks) using the ratio of incomes between two areas (and various assumptions about the income elasticity of WTP) in order to estimate the health burden of $PM_{2.5}$ which is co-produced by industrial processes along with carbon dioxide.

In the above commonly used adjustment, the only feature that is changed between the two sites is income per capita. The rationale for this is perhaps this is the most important factor determining in changes in WTP, as meta-studies such as OECD (2014) appear to find. Of course, to the extent that say income is not the sole determinant of WTP, then even this improvement may well fall short of approximating actual WTP at the study site. However, it is also possible to make a similar adjustment for, say, changes in age structure between the two sites, changes in population density, and so on. Making multiple changes of these kind amounts to transferring benefit functions and this last transfer approach is considered below.

Value function transfer

A more sophisticated approach is to transfer the *benefit* or *value function* from S and apply it to P. Thus, if it is known that WTP at the study site is a function of a range of physical features of the site and its use as well as the socio-economic (and demographic) characteristics of the population at the site, then this information itself can be used as part of the transfer. For example, if $WTP_S = f(A, B, C, Y)$ where A, B, C are additional and significant factors affecting WTP (in addition to Y) at site S, then WTP_P can be estimated using the coefficients from this equation, but using the values of A, B, C, Y at site P: i.e.

$$WTP_S = f(A, B, C, Y)$$
$$WTP_S = a_0 + a_1 A + a_2 B + a_3 C + a_4 Y,$$

where the terms a_i refer to the coefficients which quantify the change in WTP as a result of a (marginal) change in that variable. For example, assume that WTP (simply) depends on the income, age and educational attainment of the population at the study site and that the analysts undertaking that study estimated the following relationship between WTP and these (explanatory) variables:

$$WTP_S = 3 + 0.5 Y_S - 0.3 \, AGE_S + 2.2 \, EDUC_S$$

That is, WTP_S increases with income and educational attainment but decreases with age as described. In this transfer approach, the entire benefit function would be transferred as follows:

$$\Rightarrow WTP_P = 3 + 0.5 Y_P - 0.3 \, AGE_P + 2.2 \, EDUC_P$$

As an example of the implications of this approach, if the population at the policy site is generally much older than that at the study site, then WTP_P – other things being equal – will be lower than WTP_S.

A still more ambitious approach is that of meta-analysis (e.g. Bateman et al., 2000). This is a statistical analysis of summary results of a (typically) large group of studies. The aim is to explain why different studies result in different mean (or median) estimates of WTP. At its simplest, a meta-analysis might take an average of existing estimates of WTP, provided the dispersion about the average is not found to be substantial, and use that average in policy site studies. Alternatively, average values might be weighted by the dispersion about the mean; the wider the dispersion, the lower the weight that an estimate would receive.

The results from past studies can also be analysed in such a way that variations in WTP found can be explained. This should enable better transfer of values since the analyst can learn about what WTP systematically depends on. In the meta-analysis case, whole functions are transferred rather than average values, but the functions do not come from a single study, but from collections of studies. As an illustration, assume that the following function is estimated using past valuation studies of wetland provision in a particular country:

$WTP = a_1 + a_2$ TYPE OF SITE $+ a_3$ SIZE OF CHANGE $+ a_4$ VISITORS $+ a_5$ NON-USERS $+ a_6$ INCOME $+ a_7$ ELICITATION FORMAT $+ a_8$ YEAR

This illustrative meta-analysis attempts to explain WTP with reference not only to the features of the wetland study sites (type, size of change in provision in the wetland as well as distinguishing between visitors and non-users) and socio-economic characteristics (income) but also process variables relating to the methods used in original studies (elicitation format in stated preference studies and so on) and the year in which the study was undertaken. Application of meta-analysis to the field of non-market valuation has expanded rapidly in recent years. Studies have taken place in respect of urban pollution, recreation, the ecological functions of wetlands, values of statistical life, noise and congestion.

Many commentators have concluded that, at least in theory, the more sophisticated the approach is the better, in terms of accuracy of the transfer. The rationale for this conclusion presumably being that there is little to commend VT if it is inaccurate and misleading. However, many have understandably also combined this aspiration for accuracy with some pragmatism about dismissing simplistic approaches altogether. On this view there is little to commend VT if it cannot be routinely applied. This latter point means that the appeal of VT is likely to be diminished if it is always and everywhere the preserve of the highly trained specialist. Meta studies such as OECD (2014) make clearer the situations in which simple approaches are justified and when they are not. However, tensions still exist as illustrated by the growing presence of sophisticated meta-functions for transferring values on the one hand and avowedly practical "look-up tables" (e.g. lists of average WTP values, and ranges, for ecosystem services) and valuation databases on the other.

6.3. How robust is value transfer?

Determining when value transfer is a robust procedure is clearly a crucial element in relying on it more and more for CBA. The responds to this challenge in VT studies broadly speaking has been two-fold. First, a growing number of studies has sought to ascertain the likely size of transfer errors and, importantly, understand when and where these errors are most likely to occur (as well be large). Second, actual practice has used these insights to improve transfers. The current section reviews the former development, while one illustration of the latter is explained in the section that follows.

A growing number of studies that have sought to test the validity of the value transfer. The basic idea underlying these validation tests is to carry out an original study at the policy site as well. The proposed value to be transferred can then be compared with the value that was obtained from the primary study. The overall merits of the transfer are clearly indicated by whether or not the transferred value and the primary estimate are similar judged on the basis of some (statistical or other) criterion or criteria.

The most prominent way of assessing this is with reference to *convergent validity*. That is, to what extent is there agreement or errors (a divergence or convergence) between WTP estimated at the study site and policy site? To measure how large this magnitude is – arising from a value transfer – each site in a VT test is, in turn, treated as the "target" or policy site of a transfer. That is, each is treated as the site for which a value estimate is needed. The transferred estimate is then compared with the own-study estimate for the target site, and the transfer error can be calculated as follows:

$$\text{Transfer error} = \frac{(\text{Transferred estimate} - \text{Own-study estimate})}{\text{Own-study estimate}} \times 100$$

Brouwer et al. (2015) note that a virtue of discrete choice experiments (DCE) (see Chapter 5) is their valuation of marginal changes in individual attributes which comprise a policy change. In principle then this provides a solid basis for subsequent value transfers, especially where these attributes vary considerably between policy site and study site(s). To test this, these authors look at the transferability of values across countries. Specifically, the study covers Greece, Italy, Spain and Australia and uses a choice experiment (DCE). The focus is that all these countries are drought prone and the tests conducted look at the transferability of non-market values for water conservation. This refers to water as a good which, in turn, results in benefits enjoyed by domestic use of water by households as well as contributing to household well-being by enhancing ecosystems. The DCE attributes were: ecological status related to water flow; the probability of outdoor water use restrictions for households; and cost to a household in the form of its water bill.

A number of transfer approaches were conducted. This included transfers from single country to another single country (e.g. transferring values from Greece to Australia) as well as transfers of mean values from a pooled group of countries to a single country (e.g. transferring values from a pool consisting of Greece, Italy and Spain to Australia). Different statistical models to estimating attribute values were also used with an emphasis on using different models which could account for varying socioeconomic characteristics across these countries as well as preference heterogeneity in a relatively sophisticated way (i.e. a mixed logit model). As often seems to be the case with these tests, the results are both reassuring for pragmatists and disturbing for purists. The degree of transfer error is reduced considerably when pooling country data and adjusting for socioeconomic differences between policy and study site(s). However, unobserved preference heterogeneity is important too and that, by its very nature, cannot be so "easily" controlled for.

Kaul et al. (2013) provides a test of transfer errors using a relatively comprehensive meta-study of more than 30 past studies, comprising in total more than 1 000 estimates of transfer error (although mostly drawn from the United States and Europe). As a result their paper provides influential findings on what critical empirical insights can be gleaned given this stock of past studies. A number of findings emerge. The possible ranges of error are extremely large indeed. That is, for a typical study, the error can vary from just a few% to an order of magnitude of that amount (and sometimes even more). Controlling for extreme outliers, however, (which reduces the sample to 925 VT tests), the average transfer error is about 40%.

A number of further identifiable things also appear to contribute to differences in errors. More sophisticated approaches (based on benefit function transfers) outperformed simpler approaches (based on largely unadjusted value transfers) in terms of reducing the likely error range, although pooling estimates also helps reduce error. Geographical proximity between policy and study sites reduces transfer error. In addition, transfer errors are smaller for policies involving changes in environmental quantities than for those involving changes in environmental quality.

These findings are important in that, as the authors suggest, they help provide guidance as to when practitioners should be more cautious about using VT. This does not necessarily mean that VT should be avoided. It may be the only analytical option for valuing policy or project changes, after all. However, what may be appropriate is greater care and use of sensitivity analysis, and so on. Evaluating policy changes when environmental quality is the issue is a case in point.

In making sense of these findings, it still remains important to ask how much transfer error policy makers (or analysts) should be willing to expose themselves to in order to inform better policy advice. One interpretation is that whether these (and other) margins of error should be considered "large" or "too large" might depend on the use of the results. For some project and policy applications, it is probably acceptable for errors of the magnitude suggested in Figure 6.1. Indeed, Ready et al. (2004) argue that, as a practical matter, relative to other sources of uncertainty in a policy analysis, the scale of error that they find is probably acceptable. Any uncertainty of the final results can be dealt with through sensitivity analysis.

Figure 6.1. Continuum of decision settings and the required accuracy of a value transfer

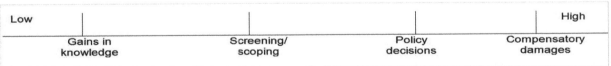

Source: Brookshire (1992).

There is a legitimate discussion to be had regarding how much accuracy is required. An early but valuable contribution to frame this thinking is Brookshire (1992). Figure 6.1 indicates that if the objective of a value transfer study is to gain more knowledge about some value at a policy site or provide an initial assessment of the value of policy options (i.e. scoping/screening), then it may be that a relatively low level of accuracy is acceptable. Once the analyst moves towards undertaking a transfer study to inform an actual policy decision or natural resource damage assessment compensation litigation, then a greater degree of accuracy is arguably desirable. In such cases, presumably, either compelling evidence for the validity of value transfer needs to exist or an original valuation study may be warranted.

6.4. Value transfer and spatial variability[4]

Tests of the validity of VT as well as meta-studies of those tests (such as Kaul et al., 2013) make clear that geographical similarity tends to reduce possible errors. In other words, transfers where this condition of "similarity" does not hold needs to be done with extra care. Critically, spatial variability needs to be considered when performing a value transfer. Some of the issues can be illustrated with regards to standard values on per hectare ecosystem services provided by broad habitat types (such as uplands, urban green space, and so on). The possible problems are several in naïvely estimating total value as the product of this representative unit value and (say the change of) total ecosystem area of a particular type.

One example is Barbier et al. (2008), which focuses on the possibly non-linear relationship between ecosystem extent and the functions and so services that it provides. Using the example of Thailand's mangroves in attenuating wave damage from more commonly experienced storm events, spatial heterogeneity arises because proximity (of mangroves) to shorelines is a critical determinant of the degree to which this function is provided: that is, it diminishes the further the ecosystem is (inland) from the shore. Taking explicit account of this heterogeneity is needed as a more defensible basis for aggregation. This is also required for more accurate policy analysis. Put another way, what Barbier et al., show is the (estimated) marginal value of mangrove area in their study area in Thailand is declining. Clearly, taking account of such non-linearity is important for more robust transfers.

One of the largest ecosystem service value transfer exercises conducted to date involved the core of the economic analysis underpinning the UK National Ecosystem Assessment (UK-NEA, 2011). Value functions were estimated for multiple ecosystem services, including the provisioning value of agricultural food production, the regulating services of the environment as a store for greenhouse gases (GHGs) and the so-called cultural services of both rural and urban nature recreation. The approach taken followed Bateman et al. (2011), with value functions simplified to focus upon the main determinants of value, so as to provide a degree of generality to subsequent general. The functions were also constructed in a unified way linking each to the others. As an illustration, if provisioning values are increased as a result of agricultural intensification, this intensification also might translate into an increase in GHG emissions and deterioration of rural recreation opportunities.

Figure 6.2 illustrates findings from the UK-NEA analysis of rural recreation benefits arising from a change of land use from conventional farming towards multipurpose, open-access, woodland (see also Bateman et al., 2003). The distribution obtained by transferring a recreational value function across the entirety of Wales reflects various factors, including the distribution of population and the availability and quality of the road network. Such spatially disaggregated outputs allow decision makers to target resources in a more efficient manner. These advantages were quickly realised by UK policy makers and the lessons of the UK NEA were explicitly incorporated in the UK Natural Environment White Paper (Defra, 2011), published in the aftermath of the NEA report.

As an example of these transfer exercise outputs, Bateman et al. (2011) estimate that, in the United Kingdom, ecosystem services help contribute to 3 billion outdoor recreational visits annually with the social value of the output created by these trips likely to be more than GBP 10 billion. Importantly, location (of these sites) matters a great deal and not surprisingly, the aggregate picture is only part of the story. A specific and moderate sized nature recreation site, for example, might generate values of between GBP 1 000 and GBP 65 000 per annum depending solely on where it is located. A critical determinant of this range is perhaps not

Figure 6.2. **Recreational values arising from a change in land use**
From farming to multi-purpose open access woodland in Wales.

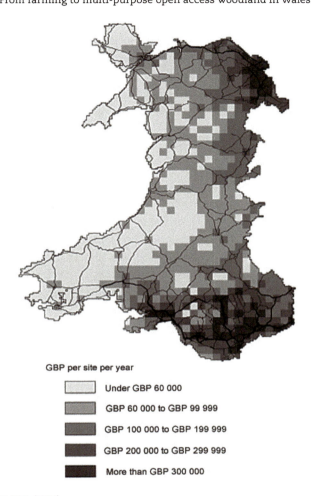

GBP per site per year

Under GBP 60 000

GBP 60 000 to GBP 99 999

GBP 100 000 to GBP 199 999

GBP 200 000 to GBP 299 999

More than GBP 300 000

Source: Adapted from UK-NEA (2011).

surprisingly proximity to significant conurbations. Put another way, woodlands in the "wrong" place (i.e. relatively far from potential visiting populations) are unlikely to give rise to such high social values (other things being equal), an insight of particular importance if policy makers are contemplating new investments in these nature sites.

6.5. Value transfer databases and guidelines

Without a readily accessible stock of value studies any VT exercise may be hampered by the daunting task of collecting past studies. Even this assumes that there is an abundance of original studies in the first place waiting to be collated in this way. This assumption may be optimistic. Surveys of VT studies and practice, such as Johnston and Rosenberger (2010) and Johnston et al. (2015), typically make important points about problems here. This includes the geographical skew in studies (e.g. mostly from North America and Western Europe). It also includes observations about the nature of research endeavour in the space of environmental valuation, which typically prizes academic novelty (i.e. generating new knowledge) over generating more empirically replicable but high quality data. This is one example of where progress at the CBA frontier may not serving policy needs as effectively it might. While Johnston and Rosenberger (2010) rightly reprove the research community for this bias, the question as to whether policy makers have sufficiently incentivised researcher direction also seems important. Loomis (2015) notes emerging evidence of exceptions to this trend in damage assessment of oil spills along US coastlines.

It has been long claimed that it is necessary to establish databases of valuation studies which is accessible for the researcher who intends to conduct benefit transfer. Indeed, one practical example of this is long-established. International collaboration between Environment Canada, the US EPA and the UK Ministry with environmental responsibilities (DEFRA) has resulted in the development of a substantial library of benefit estimates: the EVRI system.

Value transfer databases and manuals, in general, are a welcome development in the literature, as those analysts who have spent time searching for values no doubt would testify. There are caveats of course. There is still the need for expert judgement and analysis in selecting and adjusting values. In principle, the database provides information on the likely quality of the studies, although how this evaluation might work in practice is less clear at this point in time. That the analyst's job is made much easier and more defensible as the findings of previous valuation studies are systematically distilled and organised, this is a welcome addition to the VT "tool-kit".

A variant of the VT database are look-up values: "official" non-market values for benefit categories that practitioners charged with the task of appraising policies and investment projects, on behalf of decision-makers, should use when the need arises. An example of this for Germany (specifically, the German Federal Environment Agency) is Schwermer et al. (2014). This contains a range of unit values some of which are illustrated in Table 6.1 for air pollutants.

Table 6.1. **German Federal Environment Agency "Look-up" values**

a) Costs of air pollution by total and damage category, EUR per tonne, 2010 values

	Health	Biodiversity loss	Crop damage	Material damage	Total
PM$_{2.5}$	55 400				55 400
NO$_x$	12 600	2 200	500	100	15 400

b) Costs of PM$_{2.5}$ by emission source and location, EUR per tonne, 2010 values

	Industry	Power station	Road transport
Urban	56 000	30 600	364 100
Rural	55 400	30 600	122 800

Source: Adapted from Schwermer et al. (2014).

While its relative ease of calculation means that the approach can be widely practised, many analysts might balk at the potential over-simplicity, without accompanying guidance on how VT should be done in a robust way. So much depends on how the data are being used as well as resulting summary values are based on an abundance of good quality evidence. While there are some variation in the table depending on emission source and whether emissions occur in urban and rural areas (especially for road transport), to the extent that values such as those in Table 6.1 simply are being "pulled off-the-shelf" and applied unadjusted then the questions that arise are what degree of accuracy is being sacrificed. The general lesson is that benefit transfer database approaches are to be welcomed but it would be worthwhile allying these efforts to the establishment of widely agreed and authoritative protocols as to what is best practice with regards to using catalogued values. Schwermer et al. (2012), in a separate but accompanying document, provides information here, making the point for example that unit values such as those in the table, provide the basis to "... only permit a rough calculation of possible damage due to air pollutant emissions" (p. 22).

One conclusion of Rolfe et al. (2015) is the absence of such guidelines more generally, or at least the absence of general agreement on this. However, one example for the United Kingdom is eftec (2009), which provides the basis for conducting VT in official CBA. That is, it augments Defra guidance on valuing ecosystem services, which is in turn is an extension of the CBA guidelines published by HM Treasury (i.e. the so-called Green Book, HM Treasury, 2018). This advice sets out eight steps in all for conducting a VT for policy or investment project appraisal. Some of these steps involve general points about environmental CBA: for example, define the policy change, define the affected population at the outset of the analysis. Other steps are more specific to the VT task and involve asking a series of questions about the quality of primary studies to be used for the transfer as well as about the differences that might exist between study and policy sites. The emphasis is on practical demonstration on how these differences might be taken into account when conducting the transfer and how the sensitivity of findings might be tested.

6.6. Concluding remarks

Transfer studies are the bedrock of practical policy analysis in that only infrequently are policy analysts afforded the luxury of designing and implementing original studies. Thus, in such instances, analysts must fall back on the information that can be gleaned from past studies. Almost inevitably, VT introduces subjectivity and greater uncertainty into appraisals in that analysts must make a number of *additional* assumptions and judgements to those contained in original studies. Of course, this comment should be kept in context as the same could be said of almost any modelling exercise. The key question is whether the added subjectivity and uncertainty surrounding the transfer is acceptable and whether the transfer is still informative.

The discussion in this Chapter suggests that despite the central role played in public decision-making, transfer studies need to avoid employing simplistic methods for interpreting, summarising and integrating available information. The reason for this is the danger that there are likely to be significant trade-offs between simplicity and accuracy of the resulting transfer. Thus, a competent application of transfer methods demands informed judgement and expertise and sometimes, according to more demanding commentators, as advanced technical skills as those required for original research. Yet, the simplicity versus accuracy dilemma may only be part of the story given that a number of influential studies have cast doubt on whether more sophisticated approaches always yield more precise transfer values. Even so, it is unlikely – as well as undesirable – that reliable transfer exercises will ever be a purely mechanical procedure. Indeed, some experience shows that treating this process in this way can have risky implications for the wider regard in which cost-benefit approaches are held.

Certain conditions probably have to be met for a valid benefit transfer to take place. Surprisingly perhaps there are fewer generally accepted protocols in this regard (although see eftec, 2009 as one example here). However, there are a number of widely cited pieces of the puzzle with regards to what might constitute best practice in benefit transfer.

The studies included in the analysis must themselves be sound. Initial but crucial steps of any transfer are very much a matter of carefully scrutinising the accuracy and quality of the original studies. This in itself requires considerable judgement although the consolidation of information in the developing EVRI database, along with any assessment of the quality of each study within the system, makes this particular task less problematic. There is a need for parallel efforts to establish (official) protocols for best practice in value transfer as regards the "correct" procedures for, say, selecting and adjusting study site values. It is only in this way can the value of databases be fully and sensibly realised.

In conducting a value transfer, the study and policy sites must be similar in terms of affected population and population characteristics. If not then differences in population, and their implications for WTP values, need to be taken into account. Just as importantly, the change in the provision of the good being valued at the two sites also should be similar. This particular consideration raises many issues including that of whether the context in which a good is being provided is an important determinant of WTP. At some level, dissimilarity is the norm (e.g. the unique ecosystem habitats or the spatial pattern of substitutes around a site are unique). However, it is the degree to which this dissimilarity affects values which is the crucial point.

Tests of benefit transfer essentially have attempted to evaluate whether apparently similar goods can actually be characterised as such in reality. One reading of the results of these tests is that the validity and accuracy of benefit transfer can be questioned. Another interpretation is that those tests themselves provide important guidance about in what situations value transfer can be carried out confidently and when practitioners should proceed with more caution and scrutiny.

Notes

1. See *www.evri.ca/en/splashify-splash*.

2. From 7.5 million people to just 100 000.

3. This is the approach applied in e.g. OECD (2014) and in Roy and Braathen (2017).

4. This section is adapted from Atkinson et al. (2012).

References

Atkinson, G., I.J. Bateman and S. Mourato (2012), "Recent advances in the valuation of ecosystem services and biodiversity", *Oxford Review of Economic Policy*, Vol. 28/1, pp. 22-47, *https://doi.org/10.1093/oxrep/grs007*.

Barbier, E.B. et al. (2008) "Coastal ecosystem-based management with nonlinear ecological functions and Values", *Science*, Vol. 319, pp. 321-323, *https://doi.org/10.1126/science.1150349*.

Bateman, I.J. et al. (2011a), "Economic analysis for ecosystems assessments", *Environmental and Resource Economics*, Vol. 48, pp. 177-218, *https://doi.org/10.1007/s10640-010-9418-x*.

Bateman, I.J. et al. (2011b), "Economic values from ecosystems", in *The UK National Ecosystem Assessment Technical Report*, UK National Ecosystem Assessment, UNEP-WCMC, Cambridge, also available from *http://uknea.unep-wcmc.org/*.

Bateman, I.J. et al. (2011c), "Making benefit transfers work: Deriving and testing principles for value transfers for similar and dissimilar sites using a case study of the non-market benefits of water quality improvements across Europe", *Environmental and Resource Economics*, Vol. 50/3, pp. 356-387, *https://doi.org/10.1007/s10640-011-9476-8*.

Bateman, I.J. et al. (2000), *Benefits Transfer in Theory and Practice: A Review and Some New Studies*, Centre for Social and Economic Research on the Global Environment (CSERGE) and School of Environmental Sciences, University of East Anglia, Norwich.

Boyle, K.J. and J.C. Bergstrom (1992), "Benefits transfer studies: Myths, pragmatism and idealism", *Water Resources Research*, Vol. 28/3, pp. 657-663.

Brookshire, D.S. (1992), "Issues regarding benefits transfer", *Paper* presented at the Association of Environmental and Resource Economists Workshop, Utah, June 1992.

Brouwer, R. et al. (2015), "Improving value transfer through socio-economic adjustments in a multi-country Choice Experiment of Water Conservation Alternatives", *Australian Journal of Agricultural and Resource Economics*, Vol. 59, pp. 458-478, *https://doi.org/10.1111/1467-8489.12099*.

Defra (Department for Environment, Food and Rural Affairs) (2011), *The Natural Choice: Securing the Value of Nature*, Cm 8082, The Stationery Office, London, *www.gov.uk/government/uploads/system/uploads/attachment_data/file/228842/8082.pdf*.

Desvousges, W., F.R. Johnson H.S. and Banzaf (1998), *Environmental Policy Analysis with Limited Information: Principles and Applications of the Transfer Method*, Cheltenham: Edward Elgar.

Eftec (2009), *Valuing Environmental Impacts: Practical Guidelines for the Use of Value Transfer in Policy and Project Appraisal*, report for Defra, eftec Ltd., London, *www.gov.uk/government/uploads/system/uploads/attachment_data/file/182376/vt-guidelines.pdf*.

Hamilton, K. et al. (2014), *Multiple Benefits from Climate Mitigation: Assessing the Evidence*, report for New Climate Economy.

HM Treasury (2018), *The Green Book: Central Government Guidance on Appraisal and Evaluation*, HM Treasury, London, *www.gov.uk/government/uploads/system/uploads/attachment_data/file/220541/green_book_complete.pdf*.

Johnston, R. and R. Rosenberger (2010), "Methods, trends and controversies in contemporary benefit Transfer", *Journal of Economic Surveys*, Vol. 24/3, pp. 479-510, *https://doi.org/10.1111/j.1467-6419.2009.00592.x*.

Johnston, R. et al. (eds.) (2015), *Benefit Transfer of Environmental and Resource Values: A Guide for Researchers and Practitioners*, Springer, Dortrecht.

Kaul, S. et al. (2013) "What can we learn from benefit transfer errors? Evidence from 20 years of research on convergent validity", *Journal of Environmental Economics and Management*, Vol. 66, pp. 90-104, *http://dx.doi.org/10.1016/j.jeem.2013.03.001*.

Loomis, J. (2015), "The Use of Benefit Transfer in the US", in Johnston, R. et al. (eds.) *Benefit Transfer of Environmental and Resource Values: A Guide for Researchers and Practitioners*, Springer, Dortrecht.

OECD (2014), *The Cost of Air Pollution: Health Impacts of Road Transport*, OECD Publishing, *http://dx.doi.org/10.1787/9789264210448-en*.

Ready, R. et al. (2004), "Benefit transfer in Europe: How reliable are transfers between countries?", *Environmental and Resource Economics*, Vol. 29, pp. 67-82, *https://doi.org/10.1023/B:EARE.0000035441.37039.8a*.

Rolfe, J. et al. (2015), "Introduction: Benefit Transfer of Environmental and Resource Values", in Johnston, R. et al. (eds.) *Benefit Transfer of Environmental and Resource Values: A Guide for Researchers and Practitioners*, Springer, Dortrecht.

Rosenberger, R.S. and J.B. Loomis (2003), "Benefits transfer", in Champ, P.A., K.J. Boyle and T.C. Brown (eds.), *A Primer on Nonmarket Valuation*, Kluwer Academic Publishers, Dordrecht.

Roy, R. and N. Braathen (2017), "The Rising Cost of Ambient Air Pollution thus far in the 21st Century: Results from the BRIICS and the OECD Countries", *OECD Environment Working Papers*, No. 124, OECD Publishing, Paris, *http://dx.doi.org/10.1787/d1b2b844-en*.

Schwermer et al. (2014), *Economic Valuation Methods: Annex B to "Economic Valuation of Environmental Damage – Methodological Convention 2.0 for Estimates of Environmental Costs*, Unwelt Bundesamt/German Federal Environment Agency, Dessau.

Schwermer, S. et al. (2012), *Economic Valuation Methods: Annex A to "Economic Valuation of Environmental Damage – Methodological Convention 2.0 for Estimates of Environmental Costs*, Unwelt Bundesamt/German Federal Environment Agency, Dessau.

UK-NEA (UK National Ecosystem Assessment) (2011), *The UK National Ecosystem Assessment: Technical Report*. UNEP-WCMC, Cambridge, UK.

PART I

Chapter 7

Subjective well-being valuation

Subjective well-being (SWB) valuation is a newly developed method that differs from other non-market valuation methods as values are based on how non-market goods impact on self-reported measures of well-being such as life satisfaction. In other words, the values are based on experienced utility rather than decision utility. Much less is known about the limitations and biases of this nascent SWB valuation approach than RP and SP methods that have a much longer history of research and applications in economics. But overall, the SWB approach offers a promising new way of valuing non-market goods, and as future research and applications unfold time will tell if this promise holds.

7.1. Subjective well-being

The last decade has witnessed an exponential growth in research on subjective well-being, also referred to as happiness (MacKerron 2012; Mackie and Smith, 2015), and, to a lesser extent, on subjective well-being valuation (Welsch and Kuhling, 2009; Ferreira and Moro, 2010). In parallel, using subjective well-being measures to appraise policies, inform policy design and monitor progress has become increasingly popular in the public policy sphere (Fujiwara and Campbell, 2011; Dolan et al., 2011; OECD, 2013; Tinkler, 2015; Fujiwara and Dolan, 2016).

Subjective well-being (SWB) refers to self-reported measures of personal well-being, usually collected via surveys. Based on Diener (2005), the OECD (2013) offers a broad definition of SWB, encompassing both evaluative and experienced elements: "good mental states, including all of the various evaluations, positive and negative, that people make of their lives, and the affective reactions of people to their experiences". Expanding on this definition, there are three key dimensions of SWB:

- *Evaluative subjective well-being (or life satisfaction).* This dimension is a self-evaluation of one's life according to some positive criterion (Kahneman et al., 1999). It can be measured on an aggregate level as a single-item (e.g. life as a whole; this is captured in for example Cantril's Ladder, where the top rung represents the best possible life and the bottom rung represents the worst possible life [OECD, 2013]) or instead split into distinct life domains in a multiple-item scale (e.g. Cummings, 1996, proposed seven domains of life satisfaction: material well-being, health, productivity, intimacy, safety, community, and emotional well-being). For example: "All things considered, how satisfied are you with your life as a whole?" with responses being measured on numeric scales, such as, for example, 0 to 10. Typically, this is measured over long periods of time – for example once per year in annual surveys.

- *Eudaimonic subjective well-being.* This dimension refers to the process of achieving a flourishing and worthwhile life where one's true potential is realised (Waterman, 1993; Ryan & Deci, 2001). It relates to intrinsic aspirations, self-realisation, personal growth, and sense of purpose and meaning in life, in other words, to what people perceive is important in life. It attempts to capture Aristotelian theories of well-being within a self-reported approach. For example: "Overall, to what extent do you feel that the things you do in your life are worthwhile?" or "Does your life have meaning and purpose?" As with evaluative well-being, eudaimonic well-being tends to get measured periodically in annual surveys.

- *Momentary subjective well-being (or affect).* This dimension measures feelings, affect or mood at a particular point in time (MacKerron and Mourato, 2013). It is highly influenced by recent events or news and can change quickly. It encompasses both positive emotions (e.g. happiness, joy and contentment) as well as negative ones (e.g. anxiety, anger, worry) (Tinkler, 2015). Traditionally, momentary measures of SWB have been elicited using the Positive and Negative Affect Schedule (PANAS, Watson et al., 1988), a widely-used psychometric scale to measure mood. However, there is evidence to suggest that positive and negative affect are not mutually exclusive and can be experienced at the same time. Alternatively, simple single-day measures, eliciting feelings on the day, or on the day before, are also commonly used. For example: "How happy are you right now?", or "How anxious were you yesterday?'" Perhaps the most comprehensive way to measure affect is by taking numerous responses from people over a day and tracking this over a period of time, such as a week, month or year. This is known as the Experience Sampling Method (ESM) and has been facilitated by the use of mobile technologies.

These dimensions of SWB are conceptually distinct but interrelated. Momentary SWB is a real-time assessment of a person's feelings at a point in time, while life satisfaction provides a similar evaluation but over a longer period of time, involving a recollection of multiple events and emotions. Sense of purpose (eudaimonic well-being) can be measured in relation to either a momentary situation or a life evaluation, but is more commonly estimated in relation to the latter. By way of analogy, evaluative and eudaimonic well-being provide snapshots of people's lives akin to something like a photography whilst momentary well-being is like an ongoing video recording of life. Correlations between the three measures have been found to be significant but small: for example, 0.13 between life satisfaction and eudaimonic well-being, 0.23 between life satisfaction and positive affect, 0.14 between eudaimonia and positive affect, and -0.39 between positive and negative affect (OECD, 2013). The various measures therefore seem to capture different underlying phenomena.

The influential Stiglitz Commission (Stiglitz et al., 2009) argued that all three measures of SWB are useful for policy, as a way of assessing society's progress, and should therefore be regularly and separately measured, via large-scale surveys undertaken by official statistical offices. In line with this recommendation, in 2010, as part of the UK Government National Well-being Programme, the UK Office for National Statistics started collecting data on all three key dimensions of personal SWB (Box 7.1). In the same year, the HM Treasury published supplementary Green Book guidance on using the subjective well-being for valuing non-market goods in cost-benefit analysis (Fujiwara and Campbell, 2011). In 2013, the OECD published a set of extensive and detailed guidelines on how to measure subjective well-being (OECD, 2013), with the aim of encouraging national statistical offices to start collecting SWB information. By 2015, 32 out of 34 OECD countries had started to collect SWB measures (Mackie and Smith, 2015). In the USA, the National Academy of Sciences published a report that reviewed SWB applications in the United States and provided guidance for future measurement efforts in official government surveys (Stone and Mackie, 2013). At about the same time, SWB questions started to be included in the American Time Use Survey (Stone and Mackie, 2013). But despite this progress in developing official measures, non-official sources of SWB data remain the most commonly used for international analysis. Collection of SWB measures by national statistical offices worldwide is very recent and still lacks international consistency. The largest and most widely used international SWB data sets, providing information on a number of aspects of SWB, are Gallup's World Poll (covering 160 countries) and World Values Survey (covering almost 100 countries), as well as the European Social Survey and the Eurobarometer covering European countries. SWB data has also been collected in several waves of the annual Latin America Barometer survey (Latinobarómetro), covering 18 countries in the region.

Meanwhile, in the academic arena, research interest and publications in subjective well-being (or more commonly referred to as happiness) have enjoyed extraordinary growth, particularly from 2000 onwards (Box 7.2). That year coincided also with the foundation of the *Journal of Happiness Studies*. But, even excluding publications in this journal, the growth in

SWB-related publications has been remarkable. Moreover, SWB articles started to be published in some of the most prestigious journals in economics such as the *Journal of Economic Literature*, the *Journal of Economic Perspectives, the Economic Journal,* and the *Journal of Political Economy* (MacKerron, 2011).

Finally, it should be noted that *subjective* well-being is not synonymous with the broader concept of well-being but can be interpreted as a subset of it (Mackie and Smith, 2015; Milner-Gulland et al., 2014). When measuring overall well-being, there are many other important variables. The OECD (2011) *How's life? Measuring well-being* report presents a widely accepted empirical framework for measuring these multiple aspects of well-being, considering both objective and subjective aspects, under the headings of material conditions (e.g. income, jobs, housing) and quality of life (e.g. health, education, social capital, environmental quality, security and SWB). This is similar to an earlier well-being framework developed by Gough and McGregor (2007) that encompassed three conditions: meeting objective needs, freedom to pursue goals, and quality of life (including SWB). Agarwala et al. (2015) reviews a number of additional empirical frameworks to measure overall well-being.

Along similar lines, in the academic literature, SWB has been described as one of three possible accounts of well-being (Parfit, 1984; Dolan et al., 2011):

- *Objective* lists refer to the fulfilment of basic material, psychological and social human needs and rights. Typically these are identified "exogenously"; that is, proposed by experts or the logical extension of a theory of, or body of ideas about, well-being. Sen's (1999) capability approach is an example of this account and expresses well-being as ultimately determined by the capability of people to enjoy opportunities afforded by freedom from e.g. political oppression, malnutrition and illiteracy;

- *Preference satisfaction* is the well-being account associated with neo-classical economic theory. It is based on the premise that we can infer well-being (or its close relative, utility) from people's preferences and choices (Parfit, 1984). As such, the preference satisfaction account is widely used and is behind economic appraisal techniques, such as cost-benefit analysis;

- *Mental states* correspond to people's self-reports about their own well-being and is therefore what was called subjective well-being above, including life satisfaction, affect and eudaimonic well-being. It is popular not just in social sciences such as psychology but also, increasingly, in economics.

The links between these various accounts of well-being are not easy to map out as they ultimately refer to different constructs. Peasgood (2008) measured the three types of well-being for the same population and noted that, for some people, there were large differences between the various accounts. In terms of SWB and preference satisfaction, the two accounts that are of the most interest here, SWB is often described as an "experienced utility" measure, which is related to how people feel about their life and circumstances, in contrast with the traditional, preference-based concept of "decision" or "expected utility, which is based on what people want (Kahneman et al., 1997; Kahneman and Sugden, 2005). MacKerron (2011) argues, however, that the differences between the two approaches are deeper than simply being prospective and retrospective versions of the same equivalent metric. In many instances, the two conceptualisations may coincide, when the things people want are also the ones that make them happy, but this is not always the case. For Kimball and Willis (2006) utility reflects people's choices, while happiness is how the feel about their choices. In their perspective, SWB can be seen as an argument of the utility function, that can be traded-off against other dimensions of utility. For a review of the similarities and differences between the subjective well-being and the preference satisfaction approach, see MacKerron (2011).

Box 7.1. **Subjective well-being questions used by the UK Office for National Statistics**

In April 2011, the UK Office for National Statistics (ONS) introduced four new subjective well-being questions to its Annual Population Survey, the United Kingdom's largest household survey. The questions cover the three core elements of SWB and use a 0-10 scale:

Life satisfaction: Overall, how satisfied are you with your life nowadays?

Eudaimonic well-being: Overall, to what extent do you feel the things you do in your life are worthwhile?

Affect: Overall, how happy did you feel yesterday? (positive)

Overall, how anxious did you feel yesterday? (negative)

Tinkler (2015) reports on the results of these SWB measures by age:

Figure 7.1. **Average subjective well-being in the United Kingdom**
By age group (2012-13)

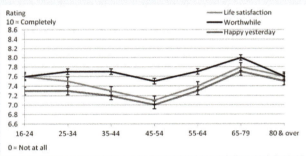

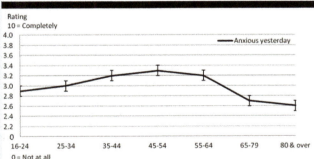

Source: Annual Population Survey (ONS).

The results illustrate the well-documented U-shaped relationship between SWB and age: SWB is found to be higher amongst the younger and older segments of the population and is at its lowest amongst 45-54 year olds, which are also those with the highest levels of anxiety. Interestingly, eudaimonic well-being (sense of purpose) is higher than the other two measures, for all ages, and the dip in the middle years is less pronounced. In all cases, SWB starts declining again beyond 79 years, despite diminishing levels of anxiety.

> ### Box 7.2. **The growth of subjective well-being (happiness) studies**
>
> Using publications in the Web of Science, Kullenberg and Nelhans (2015) analysed the number of papers published from 1960 to 2013, using the terms "happiness", "subjective well-being", "life satisfaction" or "positive affect". Figure 7.2 depicts the results.
>
> #### Figure 7.2. **Published articles in absolute numbers**
> Search term results, (left y-axis), compared with Web of Science total per year (right y-axis)
>
>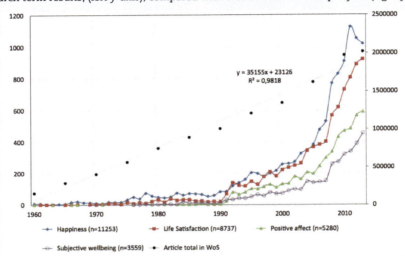
>
> *Source:* Kullenberg and Nelhans (2015).

The graph shows SWB (or happiness) to be a rapidly growing field of research, when compared with the linear growth in all Web of Science studies: some 36 % of all articles were published very recently, between 2010 and 2013. While studies using the broad "happiness" terminology and "life satisfaction" are the most common, there has been a significant increase, in more recent years, in research on "positive affect" and "subjective well-being". Studies in the field come from a range of scientific disciplines, including biology, neuroscience, medicine, psychiatry, psychology, sociology and economics.

Kullenberg and Nelhans (2015) conclude that SWB or happiness studies have gained a high enough publication frequency to be recognised as an autonomous field of research, in its own right, producing meaningful patterns and regularities.

7.2. Subjective well-being and the environment

Most existing research has focused on the measurement and determinants of the life satisfaction (LS) measure of SWB. In comprehensive reviews of the literature, Dolan et al. (2008) and MacKerron (2011) find that unemployment, commuting, ill health, divorce/separation and widowhood can all be shown to negatively affect LS; while income, marriage, trust, friendships, group membership, democracy and belief in God are positive influences. There is overwhelming evidence of the existence of a U-shaped relationship with age with younger and older respondents being happiest; while the effect of having children is mixed.

A number of studies have looked at the relationship between LS and environmental variables. This includes for example studies on noise (van Praag and Baarsma, 2005;

Weinhold, 2013; Lawton and Fujiwara, 2015), climate (Rehdanz and Maddison 2005; Frijters and van Praag, 1998), air pollution (e.g. MacKerron and Mourato, 2009; Brereton et al., 2008; Ferreira and Moro, 2010; Rehdanz and Maddison, 2008; Welsch, 2002, 2006, 2007; Levinson, 2009; Luechinger, 2009), species diversity (Rehdanz, 2007), drought (Caroll et al., 2009) natural capital (Engelbrecht, 2009; Vemuri and Costanza, 2006), connectedness with nature (Skianis, 2012), nature views (Kaplan, 2001), and green spaces (Mourato et al., 2010). The signs of the estimated relationships are mostly in the expected direction with pollution, noise and extreme climates having a detrimental effect on LS, and green spaces, nature views, connectedness with nature and species diversity having a positive effect.

In contrast, substantially less in known about eudaimonic well-being (Skianis, 2012; OECD, 2013). Of the three SWB conceptualisations, eudaimonia is by far the less studied and more work is needed to assess its validity and reliability. Despite the lack of research, inclusion of a stronger eudaimonic dimension in research and policy making is thought to be important and beneficial. Many public policies and individual behaviours are arguably aimed at enhancing opportunities for people to flourish, to be fulfilled and to achieve a sense of meaning and purpose in life, rather than pursuing pleasure per se. Eudaimonia therefore covers an important element of subjective well-being that is not covered by the other conceptualisations. A good example relates to having children which is found to have a negligible or mildly negative correlation with LS, as well as a low level of positive affect, but which is associated with a much higher sense of meaning and purpose in life (Mackie and Smith, 2015).

A notable exception to the scarcity of evidence on eudaimonia is the work of Skianis (2012). Using a specially designed survey instrument applied to almost 4 200 secondary school students in Greece and the United Kingdom, he performed a structured comparison of LS measures and eudaimonic well-being, with particular focus on estimating the relationship with the natural environment. He found some common determinants of both SWB dimensions: health, self-esteem and reading for school are common positive determinants; while involvement with electronic media appears to be detrimental to both. Interestingly, exposure to nature is a significant determinant of pupils' well-being, increasing not only life satisfaction, but also offering opportunities for personal growth and expressiveness. Additionally, students with stronger awareness of global problems such as climate change and species extinction, and deep respect for nature's unique value (moralistic values) exhibit higher levels of eudaimonia; while students benefitting from a green neighbourhood, proximity to an area of outstanding natural beauty, and less local environmental problems appear to have higher life satisfaction. Skianis concludes that focusing solely on LS provides an incomplete picture of the links between SWB and affiliation to nature.

Momentary subjective well-being (affect) has been more commonly evaluated in the psychology literature. The gold standard for the measurement of affect is the Experience Sampling Method (ESM), which collects assessments of activities and emotions at several points in a day in real time. Traditionally, the ESM involved respondents carrying cumbersome electronic devices to record their emotions and thus had low applicability and response rates. But in recent years, fuelled by technological developments that facilitate the collection of instant SWB data via mobile smartphone devices and apps, there has been an incipient but growing body of research on momentary subjective well-being (for reviews see MacKerron, 2011; Stone and Mackie, 2013; OECD, 2013). Alternatively, data can be gathered via the reconstruction of emotions from experiences recorded earlier in the day (Day Reconstruction Method – DRM). Responses from ESM and DRM have been found to be closely correlated. Momentary SWB is typically correlated with a similar set of covariates as LS, although the relative importance of some variables is different (Boarini et al., 2012). There is, however, very scant evidence on the relationship between affect and the natural environment. A notable exception is MacKerron and Mourato (2013)'s novel iphone-based ESM study presented in Box 7.3.

Box 7.3. **Mappiness: Analysing momentary happiness in space and time**

In 2010, MacKerron and Mourato (2013) developed a novel iPhone app, called Mappiness, to investigate links between momentary SWB and environmental factors, in space and time. The app collects geo-located information on activities and company, as well as instant subjective well-being measurements, in real-time, with unprecedented power and precision: the accuracy of the outdoor location is within 100 m in over 90% of cases.

Study participants in this state-of-the-art ESM study use their own mobile devices (iPhones). They are beeped at random moments during the day, and asked to report on their subjective well-being and immediate context: companionship, activity and location. The app collects longitudinal data, which enables all time-invariant confounding factors at the individual level to be controlled for. The combination of GPS (satellite) geo-location and real-time SWB measures is a novel addition. Although the study is limited to iPhone users, it has nevertheless the largest sample ever achieved by an ESM study: the MacKerron and Mourato (2013) article is based on more than 500 000 responses from over 18 000 respondents across the United Kingdom. The study is on-going with so far, over 66 500 participants from various countries.

The results show that momentary well-being is significantly higher in natural environments. On average, respondents were found to be happiest outdoors. High energy pursuits, such as sports, running and exercise, were associated with a 6% increase in happiness, while more contemplative activities, such as nature watching, were linked with a 3% increase in happiness. When outdoors, higher happiness levels were associated with higher temperatures; unsurprisingly rain and wind were linked to lower happiness. Habitats such as marine and coastal margins, mountains, moorlands and heaths, and coniferous woodlands were found to be linked with significantly higher happiness levels than urban habitats. As an example, the predicted happiness of a person who is outdoors, birdwatching, with friends, in heathland, on a hot and sunny Sunday early afternoon is approximately 26 scale points (on a 0-100 scale) higher than that of someone who is commuting, on his own, in a city, in a vehicle, on a cold, grey, early weekday morning.

A particular strength of SWB evaluation measures is that it does not require respondents to be aware or understand the causal pathway by which a particular change might affect their well-being, focusing simply on the outcomes (OECD, 2013). And being based on experienced utility, it does not require respondents to immerse themselves in hypothetical situations and predict how they would behave or feel, and so it might provide more accurate insights into how people adapt to, and experience, real life circumstances (Fujiwara and Dolan, 2014). This is related to the phenomenon of hedonic adaptation or habituation, where people adapt or partially adapt to changes in their life, so that impacts on SWB are only transient (Mackie and Smith, 2015). People are typically unable to accurately predict their levels of adaptation ex-ante using preference-based methods. Moreover, SWB data is now extensively available, in large data sets, making it a cost-effective evaluation (Fujiwara and Campbell, 2011).

Amongst the key limitations of the approach is the fact that a large number of SWB analyses have used observational cross-sectional data and therefore capture only correlations rather than causal links (due to possible omitted variable bias and sample selection bias). Reverse causality might also occur, where a reciprocal relationship exists between SWB and the variable of interest (e.g. outdoor activity could increase LS, but also be more likely to be pursued by happier people). Better measures could use panel data or an experimental setting where treatments are randomly assigned, to capture causal relationships (Fujiwara and Campbell, 2011). Hedonic adaptation, mentioned above, can also be a concern in some circumstances. Specifically, the potential to habituate to bad circumstances and the moral hazard associated with the "happy slave" phenomenon, has been an obstacle to the use of SWB in development work (MacKerron, 2011). Additionally, there are also numerous possible biases associated with the measurement technique and scales used to capture SWB, problems associated with accurately recollecting past events and emotions, survey context effects, response scale effects, as well as broader conceptual problems associated with the validity of making cardinal assessments of well-being, and interpersonal comparisons, as is the case with this approach. For a detailed analysis of the validity and reliability of SWB assessments, see OECD (2013), Mackie and Smith (2015), Stone and Mackie (2013), Fujiwara and Campbell (2011), Fujiwara and Dolan (2016), or MacKerron (2011).

7.3. Subjective well-being valuation

Subjective well-being data provides a new and alternative way to value non-market changes. That is, one can estimate monetary welfare measures based on people's self-reported well-being. This has become known as the Subjective Well-being Valuation approach (Frey et al., 2004a; Frey et al., 2009; Welsch, 2009; Fujiwara and Dolan, 2016; HM Treasury, 2018). Given a change in the determinant of interest, say environmental quality, the approach works by calculating the change in income that would produce a SWB impact of equivalent size.

This new method of monetary valuation could potentially be a useful complement to revealed and stated preference methods, as it does not require assumptions about rationality regarding people's preferences and choices, is not subject to the same types of biases affecting some of those techniques (for example, hypothetical bias), and does not require individuals to be conscious of the levels or effects of the parameters being valued (Welsch and Kuhling, 2009).

One of the key assumptions required in order to use SWB data for non-market valuation is that SWB is a direct measure of individual welfare. Hence, by observing SWB one can estimate direct monetary measures of welfare change associated with a non-market change using a direct utility (as measured by SWB) function, as long as income is one of the determinants included. With few exceptions (e.g. Powdthavee and Van den Berg, 2011), researchers have mostly used only one of the three subjective well-being dimensions described above, i.e. life satisfaction, for monetary valuation.

Following Fujiwara and Campbell (2011), consider the following direct SWB function:

$$SWB(Q, M, X) \tag{7.1}$$

where Q is the non-market good (e.g. air quality), M is income and X represents other determinants of SWB. The value associated with a welfare-increasing change in the provision of the non-market good from 0 to 1 is estimated as:

$$SWB(Q^0, M^0, X^0) = SWB(Q^1, M^1 - CS, X) \tag{7.2}$$

where CS is the Hicksian compensating surplus measure of welfare associated with the change. Empirically, the SWB function can be estimated as:

$$SWB_i = \alpha + \beta_M M_i + \beta_Q Q_i + \beta_X X_i + \varepsilon_i \tag{7.3}$$

where α is a constant, β_M, β_Q and β_X are the coefficients associated with the determinants of SWB, ε is the error term and the i represents the individual. Equation [7.3] can also be estimated using experimental data from randomised trials or field experiments, but here the focus is on observational data. In this respect, the SWB function can be estimated with either cross-sectional data or panel data, using a range of multivariate statistical methods. Some authors treat the SWB data as being cardinal, while others relax this assumption and use statistical models to analyse the ordered data. A critical assumption is that there is a causal link between the two variables of interest (Q_i and M_i) and SWB (Dolan et al., 2008; Fujiwara and Dolan, 2016); that is β_Q and β_M are unbiased estimates.

Measures of welfare change can then be uncovered from the marginal rates of substitution between the non-market good and income, specifically using the ratio of the non-market good and the income coefficients from model [7.3]:

$$CS = \beta_Q / \beta_M \tag{7.4}$$

Equation [7.4] can be interpreted as the amount of money that would be required to keep SWB constant in absence of the non-market good (for goods that provide positive well-being). The income term is typically modelled in log form, $\ln(M_i)$, in order to account for the diminishing marginal utility of income. In this case, the welfare value measure is calculated as (where M^0 is the status quo level of income for the individual, usually assumed to be the sample average level of income):

$$CS = M^0 - exp^{\left[\ln(M^0) - \frac{\beta_Q}{\beta_M}\right]} \tag{7.5}$$

The SWB valuation method was first proposed by Ferrer-i-Carbonell and Van Praag (2002) in an application to the valuation of health. Since then the SWV method has been used most frequently in the valuation of environmental changes to do, for example, with air quality, noise, climate change or droughts (van Praag and Baarsma, 2005; Carroll et al., 2009; MacKerron and Mourato, 2009; Rehdanz and Maddison, 2008; Welsch, 2002, 2006, 2007). For a review of environmental valuation applications, see Welsch and Kuhling (2009) and Ferreira and Moro (2010). But interest in the application of SWV is growing in other areas as well: for example, employment (Clark and Oswald, 2002); terrorist attacks (Frey et al., 2004a); health (Ferrer-i-Carbonell and Van Praag, 2002; Groot and van den Brink, 2006); macroeconomic events (Blanchflower and Oswald, 2004); corruption (Welsch, 2008); crime (Cohen, 2008);

social relationships (Powdthavee, 2008); adult learning (Dolan and Fujiwara, 2012); housing quality (Fujiwara, 2014); and cultural activities and events (Fujiwara, 2013a; Fujiwara et al., 2014) and heritage sites (Bakhshi et al., 2015). In the UK, new tools such as the Social Value Bank (*http://socialvaluebank.org*), have also been developed to facilitate the measuring of social impact using SWB valuation methods based on large scale existing national SWB survey data (Trotter et al., 2014). Created in 2014, the Social Value Bank uses SWB valuation to value over 70 different social outcomes (e.g. employment, health, financial comfort, access to the internet, relief from depression, keeping fit, membership of a social group, gardening, good neighbourhood, homelessness, etc.).

Early attempts at valuation using the SWB approach have been widely criticised for originating values that were unrealistically large. For example, MacKerron and Mourato (2009) found that a small 1% increase in NO_2 levels was equivalent to a 5.3% drop in income; Frey et al. (2007) found that the value of reducing terrorist activity in Northern Ireland to the same level as in the Republic of Ireland was equivalent to 41% of personal income; Clark and Oswald (2002) estimated the value of employment to be an implausibly high GBP 276 000 per year to an individual, in addition to their wage income; Frey and Stutzer (2005) estimated that Paris residents valued reducing terrorism levels to the level experienced elsewhere in France at 14% of their income; and Powdthavee (2008) found that an increase in the level of interactions with friends and relatives from "less than once a month" to "most days" was worth GBP 85 000 a year.

The overestimation problem could be due to a number of reasons such as unrepresentative samples, and the influence of extreme outliers in the data. But the key problem is thought to be in the estimation of Q_i and M_i. An upward bias in the coefficient on Q_i and/or a downward bias in the coefficient on M_i would lead to a high value, but a lot of focus has been aimed at the difficulty of estimating the marginal utility of income. The income coefficient can be downward biased for a wide range of reasons: endogeneity, measurement error and because many of the channels through which income affects subjective well-being are controlled for in equation [7.3]. This results in an over-estimation of welfare values, as the income coefficient appears in the denominator of the valuation equation ratio (see equation [7.4]). This issue is discussed in more detail in the following section.

7.3.1. Advantages and limitations of the SWB valuation approach

Subjective well-being valuation has a number of limitations but also several advantages when compared with traditional preference-based non-market valuation approaches. Here the most important pros and cons are discussed.

Limitations

Income coefficient underestimation. As noted above, perhaps the largest problem associated with using the SWB valuation method is the inability of SWB models to *accurately estimate the income coefficient*, which has been found to be substantially biased downward, because of measurement error, endogeneity, reverse causality and parametric restrictions (Fujiwara and Campbell, 2011). Undervaluation of the income coefficient leads, in turn to an overestimation of welfare values (see equation [7.4]). In an early attempt at comparing preference-based contingent valuation and subjective well-being valuation, Dolan and Metcalfe (2008) found large differences between the two methods with the SWB valuation approach producing significantly larger values (GBP 19 000 vs GBP 245), on a study of the value of an urban regeneration project.

It is typical to assume that statistical models of the determinants of SWB identify causal relationships; that is, for example, the finding that income is a significant explanatory variable in a SWB regression is taken as evidence that income increases well-being. However, in many studies, the associations estimated between the explanatory regressors and the well-being variable cannot be interpreted as causal effects. This is because SWB may itself determine some of the explanatory variables (reverse causality). For example, there is some evidence to suggest that happier people may be healthier, earn more money and be more likely to get married (Fujiwara and Campbell, 2011). Moreover, there may be omitted variables in the model that affect both the dependent and the independent variables. In order to be able to make causal inferences from SWB models, more sophisticated statistical or other research design methods are needed.

Non-use value estimation.   It is not clear how to use the SWB valuation approach to measure *non-use values*. As such the approach, as things stand, does not offer any obvious advantages in what is arguably the most difficult area in non-market valuation. It is of course conceptually feasible that one could use subjective well-being to capture non-use values if, for example, finding out about an oil spill reduced people's SWB. If it were possible to identify behaviours or experiences that reflect non-use values, one could try to measure the subjective well-being associated with these behaviours and in turn, calculate monetary value equivalents. Examples of such behaviours include donations to good causes that one is not likely to benefit from directly. But clearly, where related financial behaviours exist one does not need SWB valuation as one can simply observe the behaviours (e.g. the level if donations). And in most policy-relevant cases, there are no observable behaviours for non-use values.

Valuing future policies and marginal changes.   Because SWB is based on experienced utility, it also poses limitations when attempting to estimate the *impact of future policy changes*. Valuing future changes would have to rely on observing similar changes that have already occurred at some point in the past.

Moreover, SWB is arguably better suited to measure large changes that clearly impact on subjective well-being, than *marginal changes*, whose impact might be impossible to detect due to the bounded nature of the SWB scales (e.g. 0-10) (Fujiwara and Campbell, 2011). Researchers have experimented with wider scales, say from 0 to 100, but this raises the issue of whether respondents can accurately pinpoint their level of SWB in such detailed scales.

Selecting between the various SWB dimensions.   While stated and revealed preference methods typically use money as a measuring unit, there is more than one subjective well-being measure that can be used (life satisfaction, eudaimonic well-being and momentary well-being) and it is *not clear which measure should be used for which purpose* (Dolan et al., 2011; Powdthavee and Van Den Berg, 2011). Different types of SWB will have different determinants. For example, life satisfaction is more strongly correlated with income than momentary happiness, that might be more correlated with the type of activity being undertaken or the company one is with at the time. It is conceivable that some policies may affect one type of well-being but not another, and hence a decision needs to be made as to what measure of well-being is relevant to what type of policy.

Moreover, it may be impossible to fully separate out the three key dimensions of well-being identified above: Seligman (2011) finds that mood determines around 70% of the life satisfaction reported on average, with less than 30% being determined by how well people judge their life to be going.

Measurement issues. Finally, SWB metrics also have their own *measurement challenges* as noted above. For example, measures such as life satisfaction involve a retrospective judgement of one's life and it is well known that people have imperfect recollection of past experiences (Kahneman and Krueger, 2006). The SWB scores may also be influenced by arbitrary contextual factors like the weather or the performance of football teams on the day of the interview (Schwarz and Strack, 1999). SWB responses may also be influenced by the order in which they appear in a survey. The commonly used single-item measures of SWB (e.g. to measure overall life satisfaction) are opaque and do not allow the researcher to investigate if and how the various dimensions of life were accounted for and aggregated by respondents.

To compound the problems, narrow scales (e.g. 1-5) may not be broad enough to be able to reflect all that is important to our lives (Loewenstein and Ubel, 2008). Moreover, evidence shows that people adapt relatively quickly to change, both positive and negative (e.g. unemployment, disability, pay rise, marriage) in what was called the phenomenon of "hedonic adaptation". Therefore, changes in policy may not be reflected in the level of SWB (Loewenstein and Ubel, 2008). But as already noted above, this could also be seen as a positive feature of the SWB approach (more on this point below).

Advantages

Despite these issues, the SWB valuation approach offers solutions to many of the problems faced in preference-based valuation methods and also offers new avenues for valuation research.

Values based on actual experience. The SWB valuation approach is based on actual rather than hypothetical experiences, which is an attractive feature for policy makers. This means that it is possible to assess how policy outcomes actually impact on people's lives in the lived experience. Whilst preference-based approaches rely on how people predict they are going to feel about a non-market outcome, SWB values are based on real experience capturing issues such as adaptation in real life situations. This is advantageous as numerous studies have shown that people are often unable to predict how an outcome will really impact on their lives, especially in complex policy areas such as the environment (Loewenstein and Adler, 1995; Read and van Leeuwen, 1998; Wilson and Gilbert, 2003). This leads to interesting policy implications: for example, Fujiwara and Dolan (2014) show that SWB data may provide a better representation of how people are affected by health conditions than stated preference methods that are used as part of measuring Quality Adjusted Life Years (QALYs). Relatedly, the SWB approach can potentially capture the effect of changes that people may either not be consciously aware of, or fail to attribute to particular causes or policies.

Rationality assumptions. Whilst preference-based valuation methods rely on a strict set of rationality assumptions (such as completeness and transitivity) in order to be assured that preference is measuring welfare, since the SWB approach directly measures welfare these types of assumptions are not necessary. All that is required is that people can accurately state their level of well-being (Stutzer and Frey, 2010; van den Berg and Ferrer-i-Carbonell, 2007).

Difficult-to-value outcomes. The SWB approach might be useful to estimate values for non-market changes that may be particularly difficult to be directly valued with willingness to pay approaches, such as health and those involving community benefits, spiritual benefits, equality and distributional issues and so on. Relatedly, the SWB approach is better suited to valuing non-marginal non-market changes. Use of stated preference methods is usually restricted to measuring small changes such as the risk of a significant outcome happening rather than the whole outcome itself. This is due mainly to problems associated with asking people their willingness to pay for hypothetical life-changing events in a survey. Since in the SWB valuation approach people are not asked to state their willingness to pay, large events and significant changes from the status quo can be valued: for example, drought (Carroll et al., 2009), rather than the risk of drought.

Survey biases. Whilst, as discussed above, the context and environment can bias or affect SWB responses, this is also true of stated preference methods. Problems such as strategic bias and hypothetical bias are eliminated and the SWB approach is probably less sensitive to contextual influences such as priming effects, because willingness to pay is not elicited (Fujiwara and Campbell, 2011; Stutzer and Frey, 2010). Importantly, SWB valuation also eliminates "focussing illusion" issues (Schkade and Kahneman, 1998), since respondents *typically* are not asked about the value of a particular policy change the "importance" of which then dominates their thinking during the survey process, but that value is instead inferred *ex post* from the econometric analysis.

Cost-effectiveness. Where the SWB valuation approach can be employed using national pre-administered data sets it represents a highly cost and resource effective method for valuing non-market changes because the data already exist on which to perform the analysis and do not need to be collected through primary data collection. In this respect, the SWB valuation approach is similar to revealed preference methods which can also be conducted without primary data collection.

7.3.2. New developments

Improved ways of modelling income

In the last few years the methodology for SWB valuation has evolved and some promising solutions involving instrumental variables for the income variable (e.g. Luechinger, 2009; Fujiwara, 2013b) have been developed, to account for the problems of selection bias, reverse causality and measurement error that produced biased estimates of the causal effect of income on life satisfaction.

More accurate estimation of the effect of income on SWB using instrumental variables could lead to larger income coefficients and, in turn, to more realistic welfare values estimated using SWB valuation. A promising development is the three-stage SWB valuation procedure proposed by Fujiwara (2013b), using lottery wins (an exogenous income windfall) as an instrument for income: i) in the first stage, a SWB model is estimated; ii) in the second stage, a separate income regression model is estimated using data on lottery wins as an instrumental variable (Gardner and Oswald, 2007) in a two-stage least squares model framework to derive a robust causal estimate of the impact of income on SWB; iii) and in the final stage the results from the two models are used to derive unbiased monetary values. Other suggested ways to improve the estimation of income effects involve including relative income in the SWB equation, as well as controlling for other factors that are related to income, such as hours of work and commuting time (Fujiwara and Campbell, 2011).

In a more recent comparison study, Fujiwara and Dolan (2012) found that estimates of the value of an adult learning course that improved life satisfaction, estimated using both contingent valuation and SWB valuation approaches, were similar (GBP 947 and GBP 754, respectively) and also alike to the real market price of similar courses. To control for problem of endogeneity of the income variable, the authors used an instrumental variable model, where income was instrumented by whether a person has a mortgage and whether their spouse is employed. But such attempts at comparing SWB valuation and stated preference valuation are rare, and still mostly in the grey literature. More research work is needed to establish the degree of comparability between both approaches and the conditions under which SWB valuation might be a suitable method to use.

Of course, the values obtained using the SWB approach do not have to necessarily coincide to those obtained using the traditional preference-based valuation approaches. As explained above, both valuations are derived from a different theoretical measure of well-being: preference-based methods are based on decision utility, used in purchasing decisions, i.e. what people would be prepared to pay for an improvement; while subjective well-being valuation is based on experienced utility, i.e. people's actual experiences. For example, Fujiwara (2014) shows that while "lack of space" is often cited as a key factor behind the decision to move house, it does not however, seem to affect life satisfaction, i.e. the actual life experience of living in a particular house. People's preferences and experiences can diverge, and consequently so can values based on preference and experiences, and it is to a certain extent an empirical matter which is most relevant for a particular policy.

Anchoring vignettes

A potentially promising way in which SWB valuation could be used to measure non-use values is through a so-called "anchoring vignette" study (King et al., 2004; MacKerron, 2012). In such studies, respondents are presented with a hypothetical event, pertaining to themselves or a third person, and asked questions about how this event might affect SWB. In the case of non-use values, this could involve a short scenario describing a hypothetical individual donating money to a non-use policy, say the conservation of the rare Iberian lynx. The respondent is then asked to imagine what impact this policy might have on the SWB (e.g. life satisfaction) of the hypothetical individual. While this approach presents a potential way of dealing with non-use values, it also brings the SWB approach into the realms of hypothetical scenarios and so risks facing the same sorts of problems as stated preference methods.

Anchoring vignettes are increasingly being used in well-being and health research, although it has yet to be applied to the measurement of non-use values. For example, Kapteyn et al. (2011) compared self-reported satisfaction with incomes in the Netherlands and the USA and used vignettes to anchor the effect of cultural differences in responses. More recently, Bakhshi et al. (2015) adopted the vignette approach to determine and value the effect of visiting a large museum in London, the National History Museum, on life satisfaction (i.e. a use value). The approach adopted was a *first-person vignette,* where the hypothetical scenario referred to the individual or respondent themselves (rather than a third person). Specifically, respondents were asked to imagine a situation where they were able to visit the museum more frequently and were asked what their level of life satisfaction would be, holding all other factors in their lives constant. The visit frequency was varied randomly across the sample. The vignette study was used to derive estimates of the impact of museum visits on life satisfaction and, given the estimated impact of income on life satisfaction (estimated separately, using a standard LS regression), the value of these visits. The value of a visit was estimated to be GBP 40, using this approach.

The vignette-based SWB approach study therefore offers another way of possibly deriving values for events or changes, based on life satisfaction impacts. It tentatively suggests a way to estimate non-use values using SWB data. Moreover, the vignette approach could also be used to measure the effect of future events or changes, i.e. respondents could be presented with a scenario which reflected some future change. As noted above, this is not dissimilar from the valuation scenario in a stated preference survey which describes some policy change of interest.

Hybrid SWB-contingent valuation approach

A persistent problem in contingent valuation (CV) studies is that estimates of WTA (willingness-to-accept) typically far exceed that of WTP (willingness-to-pay), which violates the underlying theory of economic preference satisfaction (Hausman, 2012). In a recent study estimating the value of cultural institutions in the United Kingdom, Bakhshi et al. (2015) proposed a novel hybrid SWB-CV valuation approach. The hybrid contingent/well-being valuation approach takes the hypothetical setting of stated preference methods and combines it with the underlying theory of SWB, offering an alternative approach to valuing public goods when compensatory measures (i.e. WTA) are of interest. Specifically, Bakhshi and colleagues asked respondents directly how much monetary compensation they would require if they were not able to visit a cultural institution for one year due to a hypothetical closure, such that their life satisfaction would remain unaffected. Crucially, compensation was only offered to those who previously indicated that their life satisfaction would decrease if the institution were temporarily closed. The study finds that the hybrid SWB-CV willingness to accept approach, based on life satisfaction and combining elements of both methods, delivers plausible values, where WTA values were similar to WTP values for entry to the cultural institutions. See Box 7.4 for further details.

Box 7.4. Hybrid SWB-CV approach

Bakhshi et al. (2015) elicit the value of avoiding the closure of a cultural institution for one year using a hybrid SWB-CV approach, via a one-off cash compensation. The study addresses the well-known WTP-WTA disparity (Horowitz and McConnell, 2002; Shogren et al., 1994) by assessing whether constraining the WTA scenario by setting it explicitly in the context of changes in life satisfaction produces reasonable WTA values relative to an equivalent WTP measure. The hypothesised mechanism for this is that respondents are asked explicitly to think about the WTA question within the framework of economic theory, i.e. they are compensated directly for changes in their welfare, in this case life satisfaction. Importantly, compensation is only offered for those that say their life satisfaction would be negatively affected in the first place, from the institutional closure.

Willingness-to-accept compensation questions are sometimes used in CV, but – despite the Bateman et al. (2002) example – typically respondents are not asked for compensation in terms of well-being or life satisfaction impacts, but simply asked for compensation for the change of interest. Elements of the hybrid approach are also similar in some respects to the work by Lau et al. (2013), who asked survey participants in the United Kingdom and

---

Box 7.4. **Hybrid SWB-CV approach** (*cont.*)

Hong Kong, China their WTP to re-create the experience of feeling [a certain type of mood] for one hour. The moods included happiness, love, fear, sadness and so on (where for negative moods, respondents were asked WTP to avoid the mood). Respondents were asked to equate a specific feeling of well-being to a monetary figure.

Two case studies were used by Bakhshi and colleagues: a study of London's Natural History Museum, and a study of Tate Liverpool, each involving the hypothetical closure of each institution for one year. The authors define this mostly as a use value and an option value, as closure would prevent access and future access to the institution but not, say, on-going research and conservation. The question used in the National History Museum survey was the following:

For this next question, please imagine that the Natural History Museum had to close to the public for one year for vital maintenance work. No one would be able to visit any parts of the Museum during this period. Other museums would remain open as usual. Now don't worry, there are no plans for the museum to close! But we would like you to think about what your life would be like if it did close for one year. How would the closure affect your level of life satisfaction?

- *The closure would have very little effect on my life satisfaction*
- *The closure would reduce my life satisfaction*
- *The closure would increase my life satisfaction*

If the respondent selected option 2 then they were asked the following question:

Now imagine the following situation. Suppose that in order to compensate you for not being able to visit the Natural History Museum during one year, you were given a cash compensation. How much money would you have to receive, as a one-off payment, to give you the same life satisfaction that you have now (not better nor worse, but just the same) during this period until the Museum re-opened? Think about this for a moment please.

WTA values were elicited using a payment card with values ranging from GBP 0 to GBP 150.

The hybrid contingent-well-being valuation approach was found to provide plausible values per visit of GBP 6.89 and GBP 7.13 for the Natural History Museum and the Tate Liverpool, respectively. These figures were comparable to equivalent WTP values.

Although WTP has now become the preferred monetary elicitation method in the CV literature, it is acknowledged that there are times when WTA is warranted, for example when property rights are such that respondents believe they have some intrinsic right to the good or service in question (culture is arguably a good example of such a case). In such cases, the hybrid approach grounded also in the theory of SWV can potentially deliver plausible WTA values.

7.3.3. Concluding thoughts

Subjective well-being valuation is a newly developed method that differs from other non-market valuation methods as values are based on how non-market goods impact on self-reported measures of well-being such as life satisfaction. In other words, the values are based on experienced rather than decision utility. Much less is known about the limitations and biases of this nascent SWB valuation approach than revealed and stated preference methods that have a much longer history of research and applications in economics. But overall, the SWB approach offers a promising new way of valuing non-market goods. Future research and applications will tell if this promise holds.

References

Adler, M. (2012), *Well-Being and Fair Distribution: Beyond Cost-Benefit Analysis*, Oxford University Press, Oxford.

Agarwala, M. et al. (2015), "Assessing the relationship between human well-being and ecosystem services: A review of frameworks", *Conservation and Society*, Vol. 12(4), pp. 437-449, *http://dx.doi.org/ 10.4103/0972-4923.155592*.

Araña, J.E., C.J. Leon and M.W. Hanemann (2008), "Emotions and decision rules in discrete choice experiments for valuing health care programmes for the elderly", *Journal of Health Economics*, Vol. 27, pp. 753-769, *http://dx.doi.org/10.1016/j.jhealeco.2007.10.003*.

Bakhshi, H. et al. (2015), *Measuring Economic Value in Cultural Institutions*, Arts and Humanities Research Council, *www.ahrc.ac.uk/documents/project-reports-and-reviews/measuringeconomicvalue/*.

Bateman, I.J. et al. (2011), *Chapter 22: Economic Values From Ecosystems, National Ecosystem Assessment*, Final report to United Nations Environment Programme (UNEP)/World Conservation Monitoring Centre (WCMC), *www.lse.ac.uk/GranthamInstitute/wp-content/uploads/2014/04/economic-values-ecosystems.pdf*.

Bateman, I.J. et al. (2008), "Learning design contingent valuation (LDCV): NOAA guidelines, preference learning and coherent arbitrariness", *Journal of Environmental Economics and Management*, Vol. 55, pp. 127-141, *http://dx.doi.org/10.1016/j.jeem.2007.08.003*.

Bateman, I.J. et al. (2002), *Economic valuation with stated preference techniques: A manual*, Edward Elgar, Cheltenham, *www.e-elgar.com/shop/economic-valuation-with-stated-preference-techniques?___website= uk_warehouse*.

Bateman, I.J. et al. (2011), "Economic analysis for ecosystem service assessments", *Environmental and Resource Economics*, Vol. 48, pp. 177-218, *http://dx.doi.org/10.1007/s10640-010-9418-x*.

Blanchflower, D.G. and A.J. Oswald (2004), "Well-being over time in Britain and the USA", *Journal of Public Economics*, Vol. 88, pp. 1359-1386, *http://dx.doi.org/10.1016/S0047-2727(02)00168-8*.

Boarini, R. et al. (2012), "What Makes for a Better Life? The Determinants of Subjective Well-Being in OECD Countries – Evidence from the Gallup World Poll", *OECD Statistics Working Papers*, No. 2012/03, OECD Publishing, Paris, *http://dx.doi.org/10.1787/5k9b9ltjm937-en*.

Brereton, F., J.P. Clinch and S. Ferreira (2008), "Happiness, geography and the environment", *Ecological Economics* 65(2): pp. 386-396.

Carroll, N., P. Frijters and M. Shields (2009), "Quantifying the costs of drought: New evidence from life satisfaction data", *Journal of Population Economics*, Vol. 22, pp. 445-461, *http://dx.doi.org/10.1007/ s00148-007-0174-3*.

Clark, A.E. and A.J. Oswald (2002), "A simple statistical method for measuring how life events affect happiness", *International Journal of Epidemiology*, Vol. 31, pp. 1139-1144, *https://doi.org/10.1093/ije/ 31.6.1139*.

Clark, A.E. and A.J. Oswald (1996), "Satisfaction and comparison income", *Journal of Public Economics*, Vol. 61, pp. 359-381.

Cohen, M.A. (2008), "The effect of crime on life satisfaction", *Journal of Legal Studies*, Vol. 37, 37, Issue S2, pp. S325-S353.

Diener, E. (2005), "Guidelines for national indicators of subjective well-being and ill-being", *Journal of Happiness Studies*, Vol. 7, pp. 397-404, *http://dx.doi.org/10.1007/s10902-006-9000-y*.

Dolan, P., R. Layard and R. Metcalfe (2011), "Measuring subjective well-being for public policy: recommendations on measures", *Special Paper* No. 23, Centre for Economic Performance, London School of Economics and Political Science, London, *http://cep.lse.ac.uk/pubs/download/special/ cepsp23.pdf*.

Dolan, P. and R. Metcalfe (2008), "Comparing willingness to pay and subjective well-being in the context of non-market goods", *Discussion paper* No. 890, Centre for Economic Performance, London School of Economics, London, *http://cep.lse.ac.uk/pubs/download/dp0890.pdf*.

Dolan, P., T. Peasgood and M. White (2008), "Do we really know what makes us happy? A review of the economic literature on the factors associated with subjective well-being", *Journal of Economic Psychology*, Vol. 29, pp. 94-122, *http://dx.doi.org/10.1016/j.joep.2007.09.001*.

Engelbrecht, E.-J. (2009), "Natural capital, subjective well-being, and the new welfare economics of sustainability: Some evidence from cross-country regressions", *Ecological Economics*, Vol. 69(2), pp. 380-388, *http://dx.doi.org/10.1016/j.ecolecon.2009.08.011*.

Ferreira, S., A. Akay, F. Brereton, J. Cunado, P. Martinsson, M. Moro and T.F. Ningal (2013), "Life Satisfaction and Air Quality in Europe", *Ecological Economics*, Vol. 88, pp. 1-10, *http://dx.doi.org/10.1016/j.ecolecon.2012.12.027*.

Ferreira, S. and M. Moro (2010), "On the use of subjective well-being data for environmental valuation", *Environmental and Resource Economics*, Vol. 46(3), pp. 249-273, *http://dx.doi.org/10.1007/s10640-009-9339-8*.

Ferrer-i-Carbonell, A. and B. van Praag (2002), "The subjective costs of health losses due to chronic diseases. An alternative model for monetary appraisal", *Health Economics*, Vol. 11, pp. 709-722, *http://dx.doi.org/10.1002/hec.696*.

Fleurbaey, M. and D. Blanchet (2013), *Beyond GDP: Measuring Welfare and Assessing Sustainability*, Oxford University Press, Oxford.

Fleurbaey, M. et al. (2013), "Equivalent income and fair evaluation of health care", *Health Economics*, Vol. 22, pp. 711-729, *http://dx.doi.org/10.1002/hec.2859*.

Frey, B.S., S. Luechinger and A. Stutzer (2004a), "Valuing public goods: The life satisfaction approach", *Institute for Empirical Research in Economics University of Zurich Working Paper Series 184*, *www.econ.uzh.ch/static/wp_iew/iewwp184.pdf*.

Frey, B.S., S. Luechinger and A. Stutzar (2004b), "Calculating tragedy: Assessing the costs of terrorism", *CESIFO Working Paper No. 1341*, *www.cesifo.de/pls/guestci/download/CESifo%20Working%20Papers%202004/CESifo%20Working%20Papers%20November%202004/cesifo1_wp1341.pdf*.

Frey, B.S., S. Luechinger and A. Stutzar (2009), "The life satisfaction approach to environmental valuation", *Discussion Paper No. 4478*, Institute for the Study of Labor, Bonn, *http://ftp.iza.org/dp4478.pdf*.

Frijters, P. and B.M.S. van Praag (1998), "The effects of climate on welfare and well-being in Russia", *Climatic Change*, Vol. 39, pp. 61-81.

Fujiwara, D. (2013a), "Museums and Happiness", *Happy Museum Research Paper*, *http://happymuseumproject.org/happy-museums-are-good-for-you-report-publication/museums-and-happiness/*.

Fujiwara, D. (2013b), "A general method for valuing non-market goods using well-being data: three-stage well-being valuation", *CEP Discussion Paper No 1233*, Centre for Economic Performance, London, *http://eprints.lse.ac.uk/51577/1/dp1233.pdf*.

Fujiwara, D. (2014), *The social impact of housing providers*, HACT, Legal & General, Plus Dane Group, London.

Fujiwara, D. and D. Campbell, (2011), *Valuation Techniques for Cost Benefit Analysis: Stated Preference, Revealed Preference and Subjective Well-Being Approaches*, HM Treasury, London, *www.gov.uk/government/uploads/system/uploads/attachment_data/file/209107/greenbook_valuationtechniques.pdf*.

Fujiwara, D. and P. Dolan (2012), "Valuing Adult Learning: Comparing Well-being Valuation to Contingent Valuation", *BIS Research Paper 85*, UK Department for Business, Innovation and Skills, London, *www.gov.uk/government/uploads/system/uploads/attachment_data/file/34598/12-1127-valuing-adult-learning-comparing-well-being-to-contingent.pdf*.

Fujiwara, D. and P. Dolan (2014), "Valuing mental health. How a subjective wellbeing approach can show just how much it matters", UK Council for Psychotherapy, *https://docs.wixstatic.com/ugd/9ccf1d_b3cfc47c5b2043ec92b32f558d15d97f.pdf*.

Fujiwara, D. and P. Dolan (2016), "Happiness-Based Policy Analysis", Chapter 10 in Adler, M.D. and M. Fleurbaey (eds.) (2016) *The Oxford Handbook of Well-Being and Public Policy*, Oxford University Press.

Fujiwara, D., L. Kudrna and P. Dolan (2014), "Quantifying and valuing the well-being impacts of culture and sport", *Department for Culture Media and Sport Research Paper*, Department for Culture Media and Sport, London, *www.gov.uk/government/uploads/system/uploads/attachment_data/file/304899/Quantifying_and_valuing_the_well-being_impacts_of_sport_and_culture.pdf*.

Fujiwara, D., R. Lawton and S. Mourato (2015), *The health and well-being benefits of public libraries*, Report for the Arts Council England, Arts Council England, London, *www.artscouncil.org.uk/sites/default/files/download-file/The%20health%2Cand%20well-being%20benefits%20of%20public%20libraries.pdf*.

Gardner, J. and A.J. Oswald (2007), "Money and mental well-being: A longitudinal study of medium-sized lottery wins", *Journal of Health Economics*, Vol. 26, pp. 49-60, *http://dx.doi.org/10.1016/j.jhealeco.2006.08.004*.

Gough, I. and J.A. McGregor (eds.) (2007), *Well-being in Developing Countries: From Theory to Research*, Cambridge University Press, Cambridge.

Groot, W. and H.M. van den Brink, (2006), "The compensating income variation of cardiovascular disease", *Health Economics Letters*, Vol. 15, pp. 1143-1148, *http://dx.doi.org/10.1002/hec.1116*.

HM Treasury (2018), *The Green Book: Central Government Guidance on Appraisal and Evaluation*, HM Treasury, London, *www.gov.uk/government/uploads/system/uploads/attachment_data/file/220541/green_book_complete.pdf*.

Lawton, R. and D. Fujiwara (2015), "Living with aircraft noise: Airport proximity, aviation noise and subjective wellbeing in England", *Transportation Research Part D: Transport and Environment* 42: pp. 104-118.

Levinson, A. (2009), "Valuing public goods using happiness data: The case of air quality", *NBER Working Paper No. 15156*, National Bureau of Economic Research, Cambridge, MA, *www.nber.org/papers/w15156*.

Loewenstein, G. and D. Adler (1995), "A bias in the prediction of tastes", *The Economic Journal*, 105(431), pp. 929-937.

Luechinger, S. (2009), "Valuing air quality using the life satisfaction approach", *Economic Journal*, Vol. 119(536), pp. 482-515.

Kahneman, D. (1986), "Comments", in Cummings, R., D. Brookshire, and W. Schulze (eds.), (1986) *Valuing Environmental Goods: An Assessment of the Contingent Valuation Method*, Rowman and Allenheld, Totowa.

Kahneman, D. and A.B. Krueger (2006), "Developments in the measurement of subjective well-being", *Journal of Economic Perspectives*, Vol. 20, pp. 3-24, *http://dx.doi.org/10.1257/089533006776526030*.

Kahneman, D., P.P. Wakker and R. Sarin (1997), "Back to Bentham? Explorations of experienced utility", *Quarterly Journal of Economics*, Vol. 112, pp. 375-405.

Kahneman, D. and R. Sugden (2005), "Experienced Utility as a standard of policy evaluation", *Environmental and Resource Economics*, Vol. 32, pp. 161-181, *http://dx.doi.org/10.1007/s10640-005-6032-4*.

Kahneman, D., E. Dienerand and N. Schwarz (1999), *Well-being: The foundation of hedonic psychology*, Russell Sage Foundation, New York.

Kaplan, R. (2001), "The Nature of the View from Home: Psychological Benefits", *Environment and Behavior*, Vol. 33(4), pp. 507-542.

Kapteyn, A. et al. (2011), "Anchoring vignettes and response consistency", *SSRN Scholarly Paper No. ID 1799563*, Social Science Research Network, Rochester, *www.rand.org/content/dam/rand/pubs/working_papers/2011/RAND_WR840.pdf*.

Kimball, M. and R. Willis (2006), "Happiness and Utility", paper presented at the Macroeconomics and Individual Decision Making (Behavioural Macroeconomics) Conference, 4 November 2016, Yale University, *www.econ.yale.edu/ shiller/behmacro/2006-11/kimball-willis.pdf*.

King, G. et al. (2004), "Enhancing the validity and cross-cultural comparability of measurement in survey research", *The American Political Science Review*, Vol. 98(1), pp. 191-207, *https://doi.org/10.1017/S000305540400108X*.

Kullenberg, C. and G. Nelhans (2015), "The happiness turn? Mapping the emergence of "happiness studies" using cited references", *Scientometrics*, Vol. 103(2), pp. 615-630, *http://dx.doi.org/10.1007/s11192-015-1536-3*.

Lau, H.P.B., M.P. White and S. Schnall (2013), "Quantifying the Value of Emotions Using a Willingness to Pay Approach", *Journal of Happiness Studies*, Vol. 14, pp. 1543-1561, *http://dx.doi.org/10.1007/s10902-012-9394-7*.

Loewenstein, G. and P.A. Ubel (2008), "Hedonic adaptation and the role of decision and experience utility in public policy", *Journal of Public Economics*, Special Issue: Happiness and Public Economics, Vol. 92, pp. 1795-1810, *http://dx.doi.org/10.1016/j.jpubeco.2007.12.011*.

Loewenstein, G. and J.S. Lerner (2003), "The role of affect in decision making", in Davidson, R.J., K.R. Scherer and H.H. Goldsmith (eds.) (2003), *Handbook of Affective Sciences*, Oxford University Press, Oxford.

MacKerron, G. (2012), "Happiness economics from 35 000 feet", *Journal of Economic Surveys*, Vol. 26(4), pp. 705-735, *http://dx.doi.org/10.1111/j.1467-6419.2010.00672.x*.

MacKerron, G. and S. Mourato (2009), "Life satisfaction and air quality in London", *Ecological Economics*, Vol. 68, pp. 1441-1453, *http://dx.doi.org/10.1016/j.ecolecon.2008.10.004*.

MacKerron, G. and S. Mourato (2013), "Happiness is greater in natural environments", *Global Environmental Change*, Vol. 23(5), pp. 992-1000, *http://dx.doi.org/10.1016/j.gloenvcha.2013.03.010*.

Mackie, C. and C. Smith, (2015), "Conceptualizing subjective well-being and its many dimensions – implications for data collection in official statistics and for policy relevance", *Statistics in Transition*, Vol. 16(3), pp. 335-372.

Milner-Gulland, E.J. et al. (2014), "Accounting for the impact of conservation on human well-being", *Conservation Biology*, Vol. 28(5), pp. 1160-1166, *http://dx.doi.org/10.1111/cobi.12277*.

Mitchell, R.C. and R.T. Carson (1989), *Using Surveys to Value Public Goods: The Contingent Valuation Method*, Resources for the Future, Washington, DC.

Mourato, S. et al. (2010), *Economic Analysis of Cultural Services*, Background Report to the UK NEA Economic Analysis Report, UNEP-WCMC, Cambridge, *http://uknea.unep-wcmc.org/LinkClick.aspx? fileticket=xAcO6D5eOUI%3D&tabid=82*.

NEA (UK National Ecosystem Assessment), (2011), *National Ecosystem Assessment Technical Report*, UK National Ecosystem Assessment, UNEP-WCMC, Cambridge, *http://uknea.unep-wcmc.org/Resources/ tabid/82/Default.aspx*.

OECD (2013), *OECD Guidelines on Measuring Subjective Well-being*, OECD Publishing, Paris, *http://dx.doi.org/ 10.1787/9789264191655-en*.

OECD (2011), *How's life? Measuring well-being*, OECD Publishing, Paris, *http://dx.doi.org/10.1787/ 9789264121164-en*.

Peasgood, T. (2008), Measuring Well-Being for Public Policy, *PhD thesis*, Imperial College London, London.

Plott, C.R. (1996), "Rational individual behavior in markets and social choice processes: The discovered preference hypothesis", in Arrow, K. et al. (eds.) (1996), *Rational Foundations of Economic Behavior*, Macmillan, London.

Powdthavee, N. (2008), "Putting a price tag on friends, relatives, and neighbours: Using surveys of life satisfaction to value social relationships", *Journal of Socio-Economics*, Vol. 37, pp. 1459-1480, *https:// doi.org/10.1016/j.socec.2007.04.004*.

Powdthavee, N. and B. van den Berg (2011), "Putting different price tags on the same health condition: Re-evaluating the well-being valuation approach", *Journal of Health Economics*, Vol. 30 (5), pp. 1032-1043, *https://doi.org/10.1016/j.jhealeco.2011.06.001*.

Pretty, J. et al. (2011), *Chapter 23: Health Values from Ecosystems*, National Ecosystem Assessment. Final Report to United Nations Environment Programme (UNEP)/World Conservation Monitoring Centre (WCMC), *www.cbd.int/financial/values/unitedkingdom-health.pdf*.

Read, D. and B. van Leeuwen (1998), "Predicting hunger: The effects of appetite and delay on choice". *Organizational Behavior and Human Decision Processes*, 76(2), pp. 189-205.

Rehdanz, K. (2007), "Species diversity and human well-being: A spatial econometric approach," *Working paper FNU-151*, Hamburg University and Centre for Marine and Atmospheric Science, Hamburg, *www.fnu.zmaw.de/fileadmin/fnu-files/publication/working-papers/FNU151.pdf*.

Rehdanz, K. and D. Maddison (2005), "Climate and happiness", *Ecological Economics*, Vol. 52, pp. 111-125, *http://dx.doi.org/10.1016/j.ecolecon.2004.06.015*.

Rehdanz, K. and D. Maddison (2008), "Local environmental quality and life-satisfaction in Germany", *Ecological Economics* 64: pp. 787-797.

Ryan, R.M. and L.E. Deci (2001), "On happiness and human potentials: A review of research on hedonic and eudaimonic well-being", in Fiske, S. (ed.), *Annual Review of Psychology*, 52, Annual Reviews Inc., Palo Alto, *https://doi.org/10.1146/annurev.psych.52.1.141*.

Schkade, D.A. and D. Kahneman (1998), "Does living in California make people happy? A focusing illusion in judgments of life satisfaction", *Psychological Science*, Vol. 9, pp. 340-346.

Seligman, M. (2011), *Flourish: A new understanding of happiness and well-being and how to achieve them*, Nicholas Brealey Publishing, London.

Skianis, V. (2012), *The influence of nature on secondary school students' subjective well-being in England and Greece*, PhD Thesis, London School of Economics and Political Science, London, *http:// etheses.lse.ac.uk/753/1/Scalvini_Muslims_embrace_value.pdf*.

Stone, A. and C. Mackie (eds.) (2013), *Measuring Happiness, Suffering, and Other Dimensions of Experience*, National Academy of Sciences, Washington, DC, *www.nap.edu/read/18548/chapter/1*.

Stutzer, A., and B.S. Frey (2010), "Recent Advances in the Economics of Individual Subjective Well-Being", *IZA Discussion Paper* 4850.

Tinkler, L. (2015), "The Office for National Statistics experience of collecting and measuring subjective well-being", *Statistics in Transition*, Vol. 16(3), pp. 373-396.

Trotter, L., J. Vine, M. Leach and D. Fujiwara (2014), "Measuring the Social Impact of Community Investment: A Guide to using the Wellbeing Valuation Approach", HACT.

van den Berg, B. and A. Ferrer-i-Carbonell (2007), "Monetary Valuation of Informal Care: The Well-Being Valuation Method", *Health Economics* 16: pp. 1227-44.

van Praag, B.M.S. and B.E. Baarsma (2005), "Using happiness surveys to value intangibles: The case of airport noise", *Economic Journal*, Vol. 115, pp. 224-246, *http://dx.doi.org/10.1111/j.1468-0297.2004.00967.x.*

Vemuri, W.A. and R. Constanza (2006), "The role of human, social, built, and natural capital in explaining life satisfaction at the country level: Toward a National Well-being Index (NWI)", *Ecological Economics*, Vol. 58 (1), pp. 119-133, *http://dx.doi.org/10.1016/j.ecolecon.2005.02.008.*

Waterman, A.S. (1993), "Two conceptions of happiness: Contrasts of personal expressiveness (eudaimonia), and hedonic enjoyment", *Journal of Personality and Social Psychology*, Vol. 64(4), pp. 678-691.

Watson, D., L.A. Clark and A. Tellegen (1988), "Development and validation of brief measures of positive and negative affect: The PANAS scales", *Journal of Psychology*, Vol. 54(6), pp. 1063-1070.

Weinhold, D. (2013), "The Happiness Reducing Costs of Noise Pollution", *Journal of Regional Science*, Vol. 53(2), pp. 292-303, *http://dx.doi.org/10.1111/jors.12001.*

Welsch, H. (2009), "Implications of happiness research for environmental economics", *Ecological Economics*, Vol. 68, pp. 2735-2742, *http://dx.doi.org/10.1016/j.ecolecon.2009.06.003.*

Welsch, H. (2008), "The welfare costs of corruption", *Applied Economics*, Vol. 40, pp. 1839-1849, *http://dx.doi.org/10.1080/00036840600905225.*

Welsch, H. (2007), "Environmental welfare analysis: A life satisfaction approach", *Ecological Economics*, Vol. 62, pp. 544-551, *http://dx.doi.org/10.1016/j.ecolecon.2006.07.017.*

Welsch, H. (2006), "Environment and happiness: Valuation of air pollution using life satisfaction data", *Ecological Economics*, Vol. 58, pp. 801-813, *http://dx.doi.org/10.1016/j.ecolecon.2005.09.006.*

Welsch, H. (2002), "Preferences over prosperity and pollution: Environmental valuation based on happiness surveys", *Kyklos*, Vol. 55, pp. 473-494, *http://dx.doi.org/10.1111/1467-6435.00198.*

Welsch, H. and J. Kuhling (2009), "Using happiness data for environmental valuation: Issues and applications", *Journal of Economic Surveys*, Vol. 23(2), pp. 385-406, *http://dx.doi.org/10.1111/j.1467-6419.2008.00566.x.*

Wilson, T.D. and D.T. Gilber (2003), "Affective forecasting", *Advances in Experimental Social Psychology*, 35, pp. 345-411.

PART II

Core elements
of cost-benefit analysis

PART II

Chapter 8

Discounting

Discounting is both a critical and pervasive issue in CBA, and this is nowhere more so than in environmental applications. On the one hand, this is a technical matter arising from the standard assumption in CBA that the social or shadow price of a unit of consumption in the future is lower than the price of a unit of consumption today. The discount rate simply measures the rate of change of the shadow price. This simplicity is, of course, a matter of extent. While the theory of social discounting shows clearly how the social discount rate should be defined, in practice numerous questions arise especially when considering actions with implications for generations in the far distant future: intergenerational projects and policies. Not only do the assumptions underpinning conventional discounting become problematic but also the ethical underpinnings of discounting become extremely important and influential. As a result, the chapter discusses how the parameters of the discount rate for social CBA are determined as well as their ethical and practical content. This involves a discussion of the problems introduced to the conventional discounting approach by intergenerational projects such as climate change and the strengthening of theoretical and empirical support for schedule of discount rates that decline with time.

8.1. Introduction

Martin Weitzman referred to discounting as one of the most "critical problems in all of economics" (Weitzman, 2001, p. 261). It is a pervasive issue in many economic analyses, particularly in cost-benefit analysis (CBA) and Cost Effectiveness Analysis (CEA). The sensitivity of CBA and CEA to the social discount rate it particularly pronounced when considering public policy or investments with long-lived costs and benefits, such as energy investments (e.g. nuclear power), investments in public health (e.g. eradication of disease), and mitigation of climate change and other long-lived environmental benefits or infrastructure. In this chapter the arguments and social discounting are described in theoretical and empirical terms, and the way in which international practice has interpreted these arguments is described.

In order to place all goods and services in a common metric or numeraire, CBA uses market or *shadow* prices. In this way the social value of apples, oranges, clean air etc., can be compared in terms of Euros or Dollars of consumption. When costs and benefits occur over time, CBA must also place these costs and benefits in a common *temporal* metric to account for changes in the social (real inflation-adjusted) value of the numeraire at future dates. The typical approach is to convert all costs and benefits into present day values, that is, calculate the *present value* of costs and benefits. The process of calculating the present value reflects the idea that there is a price associated with the date at which benefits and costs occur. Typically in CBA it is assumed that the *shadow* price of a unit of consumption in the future is lower than the price of a unit of consumption today. So when one adds up the net benefits of a particular project over time, future costs and benefits receive less weight (lower price) than present ones. The *social discount rate* (SDR) measures the (negative) rate of change over time of the shadow price of the numeraire. A positive discount rate means the shadow price is declining with the time horizon.

This chapter outlines the arguments for using a positive discount rate. There are pure welfare arguments associated with how society values welfare at different points in time, and there are opportunity cost arguments, reflecting the fact that there are alternative projects that a government could invest in. Given that the SDR relates to a price, asset pricing theory can also inform the appropriate price of a claim on a cost or benefit at some future point in time. There remains disagreement among academics and practitioners as to which approach should be taken to social discounting in any given circumstance, and in practice a variety of approaches have been taken by Governments around the world. Among the two main sources of disagreement is whether a normative/prescriptive or a positive/descriptive approach should be taken to the evaluation of public investment and regulations.

The normative approach focusses on the trajectory of social welfare as measured by discounted social welfare (utility) while largely ignoring the trajectory of the rate of return to capital on the opportunity cost side. This approach focusses on the question of the price that *ought* to be placed on future costs and benefits. The positive approach focusses on the trajectory of observable rates of return as its source of information for the SDR. The methodology is positive/descriptive since it focusses on the inter-temporal trade-offs that take place in the economy currently, and selects an SDR for public policy analysis from the rates of return that are observable in the economy. In doing so, the positive approach ignores the trajectory of social welfare.

In the medium term context of many public investments (10-30 years), the arguments surrounding the SDR only make a minor a practical difference to the outcome of CBA. It is when CBA is undertaken over longer time horizons that different positions on the SDR have a material consequence on the type of project that will pass a NPV test. Marginal projects in the realm of energy, climate change mitigation, biodiversity conservation and public health have time horizons of hundreds of years, and consequences for as yet unborn generations. Many argue that in such contexts, the positive approach is constrained by the time horizon of observable assets, which is limited to the 40-50 year duration of government bonds. In such cases the normative arguments for the SDR have become much more prevalent. Ultimately, different governments take different approaches even in the medium term, with the UK government and the EU guidelines on CBA focussing on the normative welfare arguments, whereas the US, Norwegian and Dutch governments, for instance, take a clear positive perspective and embed their SDRs in observable market rates of return. Yet when it comes to project appraisal for long-time horizons, for *intergenerational* projects, many governments now recognise that the standard discounting arguments may need to be augmented, or alternative approaches to appraisal should be considered.

Another important issue that relates to social discounting is risk. This chapter first outlines the theory of social discounting in a risk-free context in which interest rates and growth rates of consumption are certain and projects have sure benefits and costs. This defines a risk-free social discount rate: the rate applicable to risk free projects in a risk free world. The analysis is then extended to deal with risk. First, the impact on the risk free rate associated with the uncertain consumption in the future is described. Second, the implication for the SDR of project risk is described, and the need for risk premium for risky projects outlined. Again, in practice governments differ in their treatment of risk in CBA, with some using a risk-free rate, others adding a risk premium.

When considering the policies, projects and investments with implications for generations in the far distant future i.e. intergenerational projects, conventional discounting leads to a situation in which large costs and benefits that accrue in the distant future become insignificant in PV terms, because the shadow price associated with that time horizon is very small indeed. As this chapter outlines, there are some good theoretical reasons for this apparently myopic outcome. However, not only do the assumptions underpinning conventional discounting theory become problematic when such long time horizons are considered, but also the ethical underpinnings of discounting become extremely more influential. Exactly this kind of ethical debate has taken place in recent years in relation to climate change policy, and it is equally applicable to other important long-term policy questions, e.g. biodiversity conservation and nuclear power. The theoretical arguments for time varying discount rates are outlined, explaining in particular the theoretical arguments for declining risk-free discount rates. Many governments now deploy declining discount rates in their guidance on the basis of these arguments, and the later sections of this chapter discuss the empirical side of operationalising these theories.

Once the discount rate is known, then CBA or CEA of different investments or policies can be undertaken by calculating the present value (PV) and comparing it to the status quo (no other project), or to other potential public investments. A simple numerical example is provided to explain this calculation (See Box 8.1).

Box 8.1. **Discounting and the net present value criterion**

Imagine a consumer can always earn a rate of return r per period on funds invested in the bank. This means that an investment of EUR 1 in period 0 will earn EUR $1*(1+r)$ one period in the future. Any alternative investment can now be compared to this baseline by calculating the present value (PV). The baseline rate of return, r, becomes the opportunity cost of investing in another project. Given this, one can calculate the relative "price" associated with returns in period 1 rather than in period 0, or the *discount factor* (DF), using r as the *discount rate* as follows:

$$DF = \frac{1}{(1+r)}$$

More generally, the discount factor for a benefit (or cost) accruing at any time t periods in the future is:

$$DF_t = \frac{1}{(1+r)^t}$$

The discount factor makes it possible to evaluate the desirability of other investments by stating their returns in today's terms taking into account what could have been earned in the bank. Suppose another investment opportunity provides a return **B** at time period 1 for a EUR 1 investment at time 0. One can compare this to the returns with the bank by comparing the benefits at time 1. Since they both cost EUR1 the project is preferred if:

$$\underset{\text{Project payoff}}{B} > \underset{\text{Bank payoff}}{(1+r)}$$

But this is an equivalent criterion to:

$$\frac{B}{(1+r)} > 1$$

Where the LHS is simply the present value of B and the RHS is the present value of the returns from the bank. So the evaluation criterion becomes:

$$PV_{Project} = \frac{B}{(1+r)} > 1 = PV_{Bank}$$

The PV of returns from investment in the bank is EUR 1 (= EUR $1*(1+r)/(1+r)$). So, comparing present values means that the alternative investment yields higher profits than funds invested in the bank if the following criterion holds:

$$PV_{Project} > 1$$

More generally, the net present value (NPV) is the present value of benefits minus the present value of costs. Since the project cost EUR 1, the NPV of the project is given by:

$$NPV_B = PV_B - 1$$

NPV is therefore another criterion with which to evaluate investments. If NPV > 0 then the project is worthwhile since the present value of cash is higher, otherwise, the returns from the bank are higher. More generally, with benefits and costs at time t given by B_t and C_t respectively, the NPV for any project can be calculated as follows:

$$NPV = \sum_{t=0}^{T} \frac{B_t - C_t}{(1+r)^t}$$

The question for CBA is, what is the appropriate social discount rate for calculating the NPV of public projects?

This chapter brings all of these issues together. In order to clarify the welfare/consumption side arguments and the opportunity cost arguments for social discounting, and how they are related to one another, the chapter begins with an introduction to the neoclassical theory of discounting and the Ramsey Rule. This discussion illustrates the welfare significance of the various candidates for the social discount rate (SDR): the social opportunity cost of capital (SOC) and the social rate of time preference (SRTP), as well as hybrid methods. The chapter discusses which rates of return can be used to inform each approach. It also explains what the parameters of the SRTP mean, how they are determined and their ethical content. The chapter then progresses to the issues of inter-generational equity associated with discounting the far distant future. Some of the issues that arise are technical problems, but there are ethical issues at stake too.

The chapter concludes with some examples of international practice and some advice on the issues that have to be borne in mind when deciding on a discounting policy such as when the SOC method should be preferred to the SRTP approach, how to deal with long-term issues, and how to deal with growth and project based risk. The chapter serves as a short summary of the exploding literature in social discounting that followed the Stern Review on the economics of climate change (Stern, 2007).

8.2. Discounting theory

In order to illustrate the welfare arguments for social discounting in CBA, and how the opportunity cost arguments relate to social welfare, this section explains the Ramsey Rule. What this makes clear is the relationship between a positive NPV (see Box 8.1) and an increase in social welfare: if the NPV calculated using the social discount rate is positive, then social welfare is increased. The relationship between the Ramsey Rule and the consumption based asset price theory is also explained.

8.2.1. The Ramsey Rule

A conventional analysis of the social discount rate begins by embedding the evaluation of projects in the context of a well-defined measure of inter-temporal social welfare. The standard approach uses the discounted utilitarian social welfare function (DU). The DU approach is a representative agent model in which the well-being of society is measured by the utility of a representative person's utility function: $U(_c)$. This was the approach taken by Ramsey (1928) in his seminal analysis of the optimal savings rate. The objective in the Ramsey model is to choose savings and consumption to maximise the discounted sum of utility over an infinite time horizon:

$$\max\nolimits_{c_t} \sum_{t=0}^{\infty} \frac{U(c_t)}{(1+\delta)^t} \tag{8.1}$$

given a return to savings/investment equal to the marginal product of capital: $f_k(k) = r$, and where δ is the *utility discount rate*.[1] In CBA, the social discount rate is given by the answer to the question: at what rate should society be compensated in the future for giving up a unit of consumption today such that overall well-being is preserved. The answer is given by the optimality condition known as the Ramsey Rule:

$$r = \delta + \eta g \tag{8.2}$$

The right hand side is the welfare-preserving rate of return to consumption, often known as the *social rate of time preference* (SRTP). This consists of the utility discount rate, δ, the elasticity of marginal utility, η, and the growth rate of per-capita consumption, g. The left hand side is the social rate of return to capital, r, available in the economy. This reflects the opportunity cost arguments for discounting.

Why is [8.2] informative about the social discount rate? If a project funded by a unit of consumption today has a rate of return in the future higher than the SRTP, then it will increase inter-temporal welfare as measured by [8.1], since the SRTP is the rate that just compensates for the unit of consumption foregone. If a project funded by displacing investment has a higher rate of return than the forgone investments, which have a rate of return r, then it too will increase [8.1]. Along the optimal path, or if markets are perfect, these rates will be the same. For this reason either r or SRTP are valid candidates for the *social discount rate*, SDR. When undertaking CBA in this economy, projects whose consumption valued costs and benefits have a positive (negative) net present value when discounted using the SRTP or r will increase (decrease) social welfare. The Annex has a proof of this statement.

There is no uncertainty in the model so far. The rate of growth in consumption and rate of return to capital are known. Furthermore, the proof in the Annex assumes that the benefits and costs of the project are certain: there is no project risk. Therefore, the Ramsey Rule in [8.2] is generally only appropriate for risk-free projects: the SRTP and r are risk-free rates.

The Ramsey Rule can also be understood in terms of asset pricing theory. The RHS relates to the asset price to a claim on a risk-free consumption valued benefit with a maturity t in the future. The Annex shows the fundamental equation of asset prices and shows how one obtains the RHS of the Ramsey Rule in this context.

The Ramsey Rule is an optimality condition, which also holds in a perfectly competitive, perfect-foresight, decentralised economy. The RHS defines the welfare arguments for social discounting, the LHS relates to the opportunity cost arguments. When the economy is not on the optimal path, or is not perfectly competitive, e.g. distorted by taxation, questions arise as to which side of the Ramsey Rule should inform the SDR. This question is the source of disagreement between those who argue for a normative or prescriptive approach and those who argue for a positive or descriptive approach to the SDR. The former approach involves calibrating the social welfare function and the parameters of the RHS of [8.2]. The latter would search for an appropriate rate of return – a risk-free rate in this case – in the market place.

Related to this debate are the well-known asset-pricing puzzles: the risk-free rate puzzle and the equity-premium puzzle. The risk-free rate puzzle is the observation that if a consumption-based asset pricing model, like the RHS of the Ramsey Rule in [8.2], is calibrated using standard parameters, it over-estimates the observed risk-free rates. The equity-premium puzzle[2] relates to a similar problem in the context of risky assets: the standard model under-estimates the equity premium and hence the rates of return to risky assets. These puzzles are discussed in more detail later in the chapter, but they illustrate the differences that can arise between simple normative models like the DU model, and the observed rates of return that define the positive approach.

The normative and positive approaches as now discussed in detail in the risk-free context, before looking at these broader issues.

8.2.2. A normative approach to the SDR: calibrating the social rate of time preference (SRTP)

The normative approach to the SDR focusses directly on the welfare and consumption side of the Ramsey equation in [8.2], rather than production side. The normative approach answers the question: how *ought* we to discount future societal costs and benefits? The RHS of [8.2], $\delta + \eta g$, is known as the social rate of time preference (SRTP) and reflects the consumption-side motivation for discounting. It indicates the rate at which consumption tomorrow would have to increase to keep social welfare constant given a unit reduction in consumption today, given that the economy is growing at a rate g. Two approaches exist to estimating the SRTP. The *normative* approach calibrates the parameters on the RHS of [8.2]. The *positive* approach uses post-tax returns to saving to reflect the way in which individuals trade-off consumption and saving over time.

The parameters of the Ramsey rule essentially define the form of the welfare function in [8.1]. The following sections will now describe the conceptual meaning of the parameters of the SRTP in more detail, before remarks on how to evaluate them numerically are being presented:

8.2.3. The utility discount rate, δ

This parameter component has typically reflected two distinct concepts:

- *Pure time preference*: A preference for units of social welfare today rather than tomorrow. For social CBA it should reflect society's pure time preference, rather than that of individuals. However, when considering long-term projects, this parameter has an important ethical interpretation and reflects a judgement on intergenerational equity (Beckerman and Hepburn, 2007).

- *Life chances*: It is often argued that another reason to discount future welfare or utility arises because of uncertainty. At an individual level, this would reflect the risk of death. However, for society the appropriate risk to incorporate is the risk of catastrophe eliminating a society. Dasgupta and Heal (1979) stated that positive utility discount rate can be justified because there is a positive probability that society will not exist in the future. Different interpretations have led to different ways of measuring this component.

8.2.4. The elasticity of marginal utility, η

This term also has numerous interpretations depending on the context. In general, it describes the nature of the relationship between consumption, c_t, and welfare/utility in the function, $U(c_t)$. In fact, it is a measure of the curvature of the utility function. Diminishing marginal utility is the typical assumption, which implies $\eta > 0$. In practice η is treated as if it is a fixed parameter, and yet in principal the elasticity could vary with the level of consumption.[3] The elasticity of marginal utility can be interpreted in the following different ways:

- *Consumption smoothing*: The extent to which an individual wishes to smooth consumption over time, i.e. avoid large fluctuations in consumption. Larger values of η indicate a stronger desire for stable consumption.

- *Inter- and intra-generational inequality aversion*: η is often understood to be a measure of both *inter-* and *intra-*generational inequality aversion, that is, the strength of preferences for more equal distributions of income. For instance, if $\eta = 1$, this means that the marginal utility of an additional unit of consumption is twice as much for a person with only a half of the income. With $\eta = 2$, marginal utility is 4 times higher, and for $\eta = X$, 2^X time higher for the person with half the income. So higher values of η reflect greater aversion to income inequality and place higher values on income accruing to the poor.

- *Relative risk aversion*: When consumption or project risks are present, η also measures risk aversion. A high value of η indicates a strong aversion to risk.

Taken together, the SRTP embodies two reasons why one may wish to discount risk-free projects:

Utility discounting, δ: if one values future utilities less for reasons of impatience or hazard: $\delta > 0$;

The wealth effect, ηg: The weight one places on the future depends on what state one will find oneself (or future generations) in the future. If society is richer in the future, $g > 0$, and has a preference for consumption smoothing, or is averse to the income inequality that growth introduces, $\eta > 0$, then less value will be placed on increments to consumption in the future, hence future benefits and costs are discounted. Society values projects that have payoffs in the future less if the future is richer and there is diminishing marginal utility.

8.2.5. The social opportunity cost of capital, r

The left hand side of the Ramsey equation broadly reflects the production possibilities in the economy, rather than the consumption possibilities reflected by the SRTP. The term r in [8.2] is the equilibrium social marginal productivity of capital in the economy. This is another candidate for the SDR since it reflects the social opportunity cost of capital (SOC), that is, the alternative rate of return that a government could obtain by investing public funds elsewhere in the economy, or, the cost of financing a public project from the capital markets. The SOC is a natural yardstick against which the use of public funds should be measured. Many countries use the SOC approach for social discounting (See Table 8.4). One complication is that the SOC will depend upon the precise source of funding for the project.

In the deterministic framework that has been presented here, the LHS of the Ramsey Rule as stated in equation [8.2] refers to a *risk-free* rate of return to capital, henceforth, r_f. In theory, in a competitive economy, the risk-free rate of return to capital will equate to the risk-free market interest rate. For this reason, observed rates of return on (relatively) risk-free assets are seen as an appropriate source of information for the social discount rate. As discussed in later sections, the typical asset used to inform the SDR is the return to government bonds as the SDR. These are seen as relatively riskless and of sufficient maturity for use in discounting public projects. They also reflect the cost of government borrowing.[4] For instance, the Norwegian and Dutch governments use the return on relatively risk free assets such as bonds to inform their SDR, albeit with a risk premium added to account for project risks (See Table 8.4).

The SOC is sometimes estimated using some pre-tax rate of return to business, or the post-tax rate of return to consumer saving or foreign finance, or some weighted average of these rates depending on the expected source of funds (Spackman 2017, p. 12). The argument for the former is that funding for government projects crowds out the private sector, and so the opportunity cost to the economy should be represented by some aggregate return in the private sector. This raises several issues concerning the riskiness of these returns which are discussed below. Finally, the SOC is sometimes estimated by looking at the rates of return to public capital (Harberger and Jenkins 2015).

8.2.6. Discounting in the second-best (risk-free) world

Only when markets are perfectly competitive and function perfectly both within and between time periods and for all inputs and outputs, will the decentralised economy of utility maximising agents and profit maximising firms equate the rate of return to capital, r, and the SRTP, as in the Ramsey rule (2). Under these circumstances all rates coincide, the source of funding is of no consequence and either r or SRTP are in theory valid SDRs. When this assumption fails, which is most of the time, due to externalities and distortionary taxes for instance, then a decision must be made concerning which of these discount rates should be employed for CBA and CEA of public projects. Box 8.2 provides an example of the issue from Lind (1982b). Several solutions to this have been proposed in these circumstances.

One solution is to use a *weighted average of the SRTP and SOC (r)*, where the weights reflect the relative proportions in which investible funds are drawn from consumption and private capital respectively (See Box 8.2 for an example). Arguments of this type have been used in the US guidelines (OMB 1992) and are discussed in Harberger and Jenkins (2015). These recommendations take the view that the SRTP can be reflected by the post-tax returns to consumer saving and that the SOC is given by the pre-tax return in the private sector.

A related approach is to use the *shadow price of capital (SPC)* following e.g. Bradford (1975) or Cline (1992). The SPC approach takes into account the opportunity costs associated with public investment by calculating the *price* (conversion factor) of public investment/capital in terms of consumption and then converting all investment costs (in, e.g., Euros) into units (Euros) of consumption using this price. The NPV of the project is then calculated using the SRTP to discount the adjusted costs and project benefits (See Box 8.2 for an example). The SPC is the present value of consumption displaced by a unit (e.g. 1 Euro) of public investment. A rough approximation of the SPC can be given by r/SRTP. The logic (as shown in Box 8.2) is that each unit of public investment displaces r Euros of consumption each year for the life of the project. The present value of this stream of consumption is approximately r/SRTP for long-horizons.[5] This means that a rule of thumb is that the SPC will raise (lower) the cost of public investment when expressed in units of consumption when $r >$ (<) SRTP.

Using the methodology discussed in Box 8.2, estimates of the SPC range from 1.2 (Bradford, 1979) to 2 (Cline, 1992), meaning that a unit of capital is worth anything between 1.2 and 2 units of consumption. As Harrison (2010, p99-100) notes, the weighted average approach and the SPC approach are identical for the two period time horizon, but typically diverge for longer time horizons. The precise conditions under which the two approaches coincide are discussed at length in Sjaastad and Wisecarver (1977, p. 523).

With a similar principle in mind, i.e. properly evaluating the cost of public investment, an alternative approach is to look at the *marginal cost of taxation* by calculating the deadweight welfare losses from consumer and producer surplus. Using this approach, estimates of 1.3-1.1 are typically obtained. Again these factors would be used to multiply the costs of public investment which would then be discounted using the SRTP. This adjustment is also applicable, using SOC, when projects are financed by taxation rather than the capital markets (see e.g. Spackman, 2017, p. 5-6). Incorporating the SPC into the appraisal of public policy and investment will raise the return required to pass a NPV test if the SOC is greater than the SRTP, and vice versa. Adding the marginal cost of taxation would have similar consequences.

Finally, there are some circumstances in which the SOC approach is not relevant. The first concerns CEA. With CEA or "Choice of Technique" a comparison of the implication for consumption of different solutions to a given problem is required. The opportunity cost of funds will typically not determine the preferred technique (Feldstein, 1970; Spackman, 2017).

Spackman (2017) summarises many of these arguments. In practice, discounting costs and benefits using the SOC, or converting costs into units of consumption using the SPC then discounting using the SRTP, will in general lead to similar public investment advice.

Yet most governments do not use the SPC approach, neither do they make any other adjustments to public investment costs to reflect funding issues such as the cost of increased taxation. The reasons for this absence are essentially twofold: i) Complexity or arbitrariness: the calculation of the SPC introduces a layer of debatable assumptions, and the implication that the SPC will vary from one project to another (e.g. time-horizon of displaced private capital, proportion of project benefits consumed versus reinvested); ii) Impact: the impact of such adjustments is minor in most policy contexts. Yet it remains important to understand the funding implications of CBA and their implications for social discounting and valuation of costs and benefits.

8.2.7. Summary

As the final section shows, some governments use an observed rate of return to capital as the SDR, others use the SRTP approach either in a normative sense by calibrating the Ramsey Rule or in a positive sense by using the post-tax rate of return to saving as a risk-free rate of return as a proxy for the SRTP (See Table 8.4). There are theoretical arguments for using the SPC approach, and yet government guidelines for social CBA typically over-look these arguments. In practice, the theoretical guidance falls foul of its informational requirements and practicalities of policy implementation. Often institutional differences concerning public finance will determine which of these approaches is taken (Groom and Hepburn, 2017; Spackman, 2017). The use of rates of return in the private sector, however, raises the issue of risk, and how this should be incorporated in the discount rate.

8.3. Discounting and risk

So far social discounting has been discussed in a risk-free context, assuming sure pay-offs from projects, no background risk associated with growth or interest rates, and certainly no-correlation of systematic, macro-economic risk with the project benefits. However, each of these aspects are important for project appraisal.

8.3.1. Growth risk and the risk-free rate: Theoretical arguments

The SRTP in [8.2] contains a wealth effect, which is one reason why society might want discount the future. This captures the idea that the discount rate is dependent upon the prediction of the future well-being of society. But what if the growth rate of consumption is uncertain? What does the wealth effect look like in these circumstances, and how should the discount rate be modified to reflect this?

When the project benefits are sure/risk-free and the only source of uncertainty is consumption growth, the typical approach is to use expected utility as the measure of welfare. In this case [8.1] becomes:

$$W = \Sigma_{t=0}^{T} \frac{E\left[U(\tilde{c}_t)\right]}{(1+\delta)^t} \qquad [8.3]$$

Gollier (2012) shows that the impact on the SRTP will depend on the diffusion process of growth over time. The basic result was first shown by Mankiw (1980) in the context in which growth follows a Brownian motion process: the growth of consumption is independently identically distributed (i.i.d.) normal with mean μ and variance σ_c^2, and utility is iso-elastic.[6] In words, this means that growth tomorrow is entirely independent of growth today. In this case the SRTP becomes:

$$SRTP = \delta + \eta\bar{g} - 0.5\eta(\eta+1)\sigma_c^2 \qquad [8.4]$$

Box 8.2. **Private rate of return (r) and SRTP in the presence of taxation**

Lind (1982) provides the following example of the impact of corporation and income taxes on the relationship between r and the after-tax rate of return to capital, which is used as a proxy for the SRTP in the Ramsey Rule. Imagine that corporation (or profit) tax is 50% and income tax paid on dividends is at 25%. Suppose also that the post tax SRTP is 6%; that is, this is the after tax rate of return that shareholders require to invest. Given the tax regime, what is the private rate of return on capital that is required to provide this minimal rate of return to shareholders?

In order to receive 6% after income tax of 25% the rate must be 8%. In order to have 8% return after a 50% corporation tax, a gross private rate of rate of return of 16% is required. Hence, the presence of this tax regime generates a divergence between the rate of return on private investment and the SRTP: 16% vs 6%. So, what is the SDR in this case?

Weighted average approach: Where a public project displaces both consumption and private investment, some economists have suggested that a weighted average of r and SRTP should be used. For instance, if r = 16% and SRTP = 6%, and the proportion of funds coming from consumption and private sector investment is 0.8 and 0.2 respectively, then the appropriate SDR should be:

8% = 0.8*6%+0.2*16%

This is a somewhat ad hoc approach that assumes all benefits are consumed rather than invested. Alternative formulae can be used which relax this assumption. Harberger and Jenkins (2015) have a comprehensive discussion of this method.

Shadow price of capital: Cline (1992) provides the following rational for the calculation of the SPC. Suppose a EUR 1 investment in the capital markets provides an annuity benefit B measured in units of consumption in each of N years, which is solely consumed.[7] The SPC is then given by:

$$SPC = \Sigma_{t=0}^{N} B(1+SRTP)^{-t} \qquad [a]$$

The SPC is equal to the present value of the annuity stream of consumption generated from a unit investment. Suppose that this investment has an internal rate of return equal to r, the private rate of return on capital, that is:

$$-1 + \Sigma_{t=0}^{N} B(1+r)^{-t} = 0 \qquad [b]$$

Rearranging (b) to obtain a formula for B and inserting into (a) yields the following formula:

$$SPC = \frac{r}{SRTP} \cdot \frac{1-(1+SRTP)^{-N}}{1-(1+r)^{-N}} \qquad [c]$$

Inserting the values from before: r = 16%, SRTP = 6%, and assuming a time horizon of 15 years, one obtains a value of SPC = 1.742. The SPC depends on the time horizon of the project, as well as the disparity between r and SRTP. As the time horizon considered increases, the estimate of SPC approaches r/SRTP, which in this example is 2.67. Cline finds support for values of SPC between 1.5 and 2, compared to 0.98-1.12 for Bradford (1975). Cline's estimates imply that a unit of capital is worth up to 2 units of consumption.

Cline's approach has some advantages over the approach found in Lind (1982b, p. 40), which cannot constrain the SPC to be non-negative or less than infinite for reasonable parameter values. Cline (1992, Annex 6), argues that Lind and Bradford are guilty of double counting the returns from reinvestment.

Source: Cline (1992, Annex 6A), Pearce and Ulph (1999).

In the context of risky growth, the Ramsey rule is extended and reduced by the term $-0.5\eta(\eta+1)\sigma_c^2$. This reflects the fact that although under uncertainty growth could be higher or lower in the future, it is the low growth scenarios that have the main influence. In the face of growth uncertainty, a prudent planner will save more for the future to protect against the possible low growth scenarios. This has the effect of raising the value of additional risk-free consumption in the future, hence lowering the risk-free discount rate. The extension to the Ramsey Rule reflects *prudence* in the face of uncertainty. The reduction of the SDR is higher the larger are volatility of growth, σ_c^2, and the larger are volatility of growth, sigma, and the elasticity of marginal utility, eta.[8]

The theoretical impact of this prudence effect is very small when calibrated to developed country data because the volatility of growth is very small. In developing countries, which have much higher volatility of growth, the prudence term could well be important. Gollier (2012, Ch 4) has a discussion. However, are independent and momentary growth shocks realistic? What if shocks to growth have a persistent component? When growth shocks are persistent, the SRTP varies with the time horizon. The details of time-varying discount rates are discussed below.

The risk-free rate puzzle: An empirical puzzle known as the risk-free rate puzzle exists in relation to the prudence effect and the Ramsey Rule in general. The puzzle stems from the fact that usual calibrations of the theoretical Ramsey Rule in [8.4] predict a risk-free rate that is much higher than that observed in the real world among relatively riskless assets. The puzzle highlights two issues. First, the normative approach may differ from the positive approach. Second, if the standard consumption side approach is to be treated as a positive model that predicts market outcomes, it needs to be augmented.

One way in which this puzzle has been partially solved is by including catastrophic or "jump-risks", such as the prospect of major depressions, into the uncertainty surrounding growth. Barro (2006) shows that such risks increase the prudence term significantly and may explain consistently low risk-free rates. But perhaps a more immediate aspect of risk for CBA is the presence of project specific risk. Gollier (2012, p. 75-76) provides a simple example of this point. Supposing that the percentage reduction in GDP is given by the parameter λ, and this shock (e.g. a depression due to a financial crash) occurs with a probability p. Together with the other assumptions made in this section, the risk free SDR now becomes:

$$SRTP_{\lambda} = \delta - \ln\left[p(1-\lambda)^{-\eta} + (1-p)\exp\left(-\eta\bar{g} + 0.5\eta^2\sigma_c^2\right)\right] \qquad [8.5]$$

which is less than [8.4]. The potential for an economic depression, although unlikely, increases the precautionary motive for saving and lowers the risk-free SDR. This is one of the more intuitive solutions to the risk-free puzzle, and has implications for social discounting.[9]

8.3.2. Project risk

In a number of countries, France, Norway and the Netherlands included, the discount rate is adjusted to account for project risks. There are two basic forms of project risk, one of which is important from the perspective of the SDR, another which is not.

Unsystematic risk is the risk associated with over or under-estimating the costs and benefits of the project. In any given project elements will turn out to be more or less expensive than expected for unforeseen technical or other reasons. These risks are diversifiable across the portfolio of public projects and the theory of asset pricing shows that this kind of risk ought not to affect the price of an asset, and hence the appropriate discount rate.[10] The second type of risk is *systematic risk*, which describes a situation where risky costs and benefits are correlated to returns available in the macro-economy. Systematic risk cannot be diversified across different projects due to the macro scale of the riskiness. Where the project's net benefits are correlated with uncertainty to the wider macro economy, asset pricing theory shows that the discount rate should be augmented by a risk premium which reflects the project specific risk profile of systematic risk, not the diversifiable risk (See Annex 8.A2).

The implications for social discounting of project-based systematic risk are as follows. The asset pricing formula of Annex 8.2A shows that the RHS of the Ramsey risk free rate can be extended to accommodate systematic risks. Indeed, this is an example of the *consumption-based capital asset pricing model* (CCAPM) approach to asset pricing. The CCAPM considers the riskiness of projects and their correlation with returns to societal wealth, where the returns to societal wealth are measured by consumption. In this context, if a project is pro-cyclical, i.e. its benefits are positively correlated with aggregate consumption, then the high payoffs from this project occur in good (high consumption) states of the macro economy. In such states, these payoffs are worth less in welfare terms since marginal utility is lower. Similarly, low payoffs happen in the bad (poor) states when marginal utility is high. Society will want a higher rate of return from such projects in order to bear these extra risks.

Alternatively, some projects might be anti-cyclical, and have high payoffs in bad states of the world, and low payoffs in the good states of the world. Such projects serve an insurance function, and reduce risk in the macro-economy. From a welfare perspective society might be willing to pay for insurance by accepting a lower return from projects like this. In either case, there is a *systematic risk premium* associated with the project, $\pi(\beta)$.

As shown in Annex 8.A2, with the assumptions made in this section regarding utility and growth, coupled with the assumption that the project net benefits and consumption growth follow a bivariate normal distribution, incorporating project risk into the appraisal of projects leads to a simple extension to the RHS of the Ramsey Formula for risky project i:

$$SRTP_i = \delta + \eta\mu_c - 0.5\eta^2\sigma_c^2 + \pi\left(\beta_i\right)$$
$$= \delta + \eta\mu_c - 0.5\eta^2\sigma_c^2 + \eta\beta_i\sigma_c^2$$

[8.6]

where the first three terms are the risk free rate in equation [8.4], and the fourth term is the systematic risk premium $\pi\left(\beta_i\right) = \eta\beta_i\sigma_c^2$.[11] The parameter β_i is the consumption "beta" which measures the correlation between the net benefits of project i and systematic risk associated with consumption growth. E.g. if $\beta = 1$, then a 1% increase in consumption growth will be expected to lead to a 1% growth in the project net benefits. If $\beta > 1$ then the project benefits are expected to increase by more than 1% when consumption grows by 1%, hence introducing proportionally more systematic risk than exists in the economy. If $\beta < 0$, the project reduces risk and has the insurance properties described above.

The consumption CAPM approach social discounting can be thought of as a normative approach since it focusses on the implications of project risk from the welfare perspective of a representative agent who is fully invested in the macro-economy. The CCAPM requires the estimation of normative parameters for this purpose.

However, many models used in finance use market based proxies for marginal utility and in the context of social discounting can be considered *positive* approaches to the SDR. A common example which has been influential in social discounting, is the *capital asset pricing model* (CAPM). The CAPM pricing formula prices-in the risk associated with an asset by adding a risk premium to the risk-free rate of return in a manner similar CCAPM. The CAPM asset return formula is

$$r_i = r_f + \beta_{i,W}\left(r_m - r_f\right)$$ [8.7]

where r_f is the risk free rate of return, r_m is the rate of return on the market/wealth portfolio and $\beta_{i,W}$ is the project "beta" which reflects the correlation between the asset i and the market portfolio. The risk premium for this project is given by the market premium $\left(r_m - r_f\right)$ multiplied by the project beta, $\beta_{i,W}$. The risk-premium will be positive when $\beta_{i,W}$ is positive. The logic of this pricing formula is similar to the CCAPM except the covariance is with a market portfolio of assets rather than consumption. This formula for the SDR is project specific, but can be calculated by looking at suitable market returns and calculating the associated project betas.

The equity premium puzzle: Analogous to the risk-free rate puzzle, the CCAPM model calibrated using standard parameter values, based on normative perspectives or actual behaviour, leads to a much smaller equity premium (systematic risk premium) than is observed in real life among risky assets. With a $\beta = 1$, $\sigma_c = 3.6\%$ (volatility of GDPpc in the US) and $\eta = 2$, the systematic risk premium that should be added to the risk free rate is 0.26%. The observed risk premium as calculated as the difference between the return on equities and bonds has on average been much higher in the US between 1970 and 2006, at around 5% (Gollier 2012, p188). Once again, the normative approach leads to very different recommendations for risk free and risky projects compared to the positive approach.

The French CBA guidelines recommend project specific SDRs based on the CCAPM approach. The Dutch government recommends a flat 3% risk premium for all projects based more on the CAPM approach. The Norwegian government follows a CAPM approach with a constant risk premium. The UK does not take project risk into account in the discount rate other than a general 1% addition to pure time preference that represents some kind of generalised catastrophic risk, rather than project specific risk. The main difficulty with incorporating risk into the discount rate is calculating the project specific betas. This partly explains why it is either not applied across all governments, and when it is applied it is done so as a standard risk adjustment, as in the Netherlands. Table 8.5 has more examples.

Yet in France an array of different project specific betas have been calculated. The Gollier Report (Gollier 2011), which led to a risky SDR being recommended in the French guidelines on CBA (Quinet 2013), provides a table of the available estimates of sector specific betas. Table 8.1 shows that most public projects are pro-cyclical and warrant a positive project beta.

Table 8.1. **Sector level betas**

Sector	Estimated consumption Beta
Agriculture, Silviculture and Fisheries	0.85
Industry	2.09
Automobile Industry	4.98
Manufacture of Mechanical Equipment	3.00
Intermediate Industries	2.76
Energy	0.85
Construction	1,45
Transport	1.60
Administrative Services	-0.09
Education	0.11
Health	-0.24
Financial Services	0.15
Financial Intermediation	0.49
Assurance	-0.36

Source: Adapted from Gollier (2011, p. 226-227).

8.4. Declining discount rates

When long time horizons are considered, the theory of social discounting needs to be more precise because long-term CBA becomes ever more sensitive to the choice of SDR. Two issues turn out to be important. First, the persistent uncertainty surrounding some of the primitives of the discount rate, such as growth or the interest rate, need to be modelled more carefully. Second, when intergenerational projects are being evaluated, ethical issues arise.

In this section the issue of declining discount rates (DDRs) is discussed as an example of when more careful consideration of uncertainty can affect the appropriate SDR. This strand of the literature stems from more careful consideration of the term structure of discount rates. The past decade has seen an explosion of research into the term structure of the social discount rate and the applicability of DDRs to CBA. Some arguments stem from the consumption side, and extensions to the Ramsey rule. Others have focussed on uncertainty in the the return to capital and the interest rate.

8.4.1. Persistent growth risks and DDRs

Equation [8.4] presented the Mankiw (1980) result that when growth is i.i.d. normal (as defined above) the SRTP is reduced by a precautionary term: uncertainty in growth reduces the risk-free discount rate, where risk-free here means that one is considering projects with sure returns. But what happens in the more realistic case in which growth shocks persist, and today's growth is highly correlated to tomorrow's? It turns out that persistence of this type makes the prudence term increase with the time horizon considered. The persistence in growth can take many forms, here one such case is considered.

Suppose that growth is still i.i.d normal with mean μ and variance σ_c^2 but there is uncertainty about the mean and variance of growth. In practice what this means is that one is unsure of the regime that one will find oneself in in the future. It could be a high-growth regime, or a low-growth regime, and the volatility around this mean may be uncertain also. Gollier (2008) describes this case in detail. Consider the case when just the mean parameter is uncertain and dependent on some parameter, θ, which represents some uncertain technological or other state of the world upon which the growth regime is dependent. In this case, the extension to the Ramsey rule becomes:

$$\text{SRTP} = \delta - \frac{1}{t} \ln E_\theta \left[\exp \left[-\eta t \left(\mu(\theta) - 0.5\sigma_c^2 \right) \right] \right] \qquad [8.8]$$

It is easy to show that the second term on the right hand side is increasing with the time horizon t.[12] In essence, uncertainty over the parameters of the growth distribution introduces further uncertainty which increases with the time horizon. Once again, this has a precautionary savings effect on the prudent social planner, which manifests itself in a declining discount rate. Interestingly, this rationale for DDRs was one of the arguments used to motivate the French government's recommendation to use DDRs (Lebegue, 2005).

There are several other characterisations of growth uncertainty that lead to the same result. In short, provided that growth shocks are persistent over time, so that high growth is more likely to follow high growth, and vice versa, and provided the representative agent is *prudent*, then the outcome is DDRs. Gollier's work, documented in Gollier (2012a), is a powerful set of arguments.

8.4.2. Uncertain interest rates

A popular argument for DDRs comes from two contributions by Martin Weitzman which focus on interest rate uncertainty. Compared to the theoretical basis of the consumption-side arguments above, Weitzman (1998, 2001) are much more stylised and ad hoc. Their power lies in the simplicity of the algebraic arguments, making them easy to explain numerically, if not intuitively. Weitzman (1998) can be thought of as follows. Suppose that one has a project that costs EUR 1 today and provides EUR B_t at time t in the future. Suppose that the interest rate, r, that is used to calculate the present value of the project is uncertain. Weitzman proposes an expected net present value (ENPV) criterion to evaluate the project's desirability:

$$ENPV = -1 + E\exp(-\tilde{r}t)B_t \qquad [8.9]$$

The project should be approved if ENPV is greater than zero. The decision criterion can be re-framed in terms of the *certainty-equivalent discount rate*, that is, the certain discount rate that if applied over the time horizon t would yield the same ENPV. The certainty equivalent discount rate, $r_{CE}(t)$, can be defined as follows:

$$\exp(-r_{CE}(t)t) = E\exp(-\tilde{r}t)$$
$$\Rightarrow \qquad [8.10]$$
$$r_{CE}(t) = -\frac{1}{t}\ln(E\exp(-\tilde{r}t))$$

Due to the fact that the exponential function is convex, and more so with larger t, it can be shown that the certainty-equivalent decreases with time. In fact, Weitzman (1998) shows that $r_{CE}(0) = E[\tilde{r}]$ and $\lim_{t\to\infty} r_{CE}(t) = r_{min}$; that is, the certainty-equivalent discount rate should decline from its expected value to the lowest imaginable realisation of the return to capital. The essential insight here is that with the ENPV approach, one calculates the expected discount *factor* rather than the expected discount *rate*. The certainty-equivalent discount rate is a DDR. Table 8.2 has a simple numerical example for 10 equally likely interest rate scenarios.

Table 8.2. **Numerical example of Weitzman's declining certainty-equivalent discount rate**

Interest rate scenarios	Discount factors in period t				
	10	50	100	200	500
1%	0.91	0.61	0.37	0.14	0.01
2%	0.82	0.37	0.14	0.02	0.00
3%	0.74	0.23	0.05	0.00	0.00
4%	0.68	0.14	0.02	0.00	0.00
5%	0.61	0.09	0.01	0.00	0.00
6%	0.56	0.05	0.00	0.00	0.00
7%	0.51	0.03	0.00	0.00	0.00
8%	0.46	0.02	0.00	0.00	0.00
9%	0.42	0.01	0.00	0.00	0.00
10%	0.39	0.01	0.00	0.00	0.00
Certainty-equivalent discount factor	0.61	0.16	0.06	0.02	0.00
Certainty-equivalent discount rate	4.73%	2.54%	1.61%	1.16%	1.01%

Source: Adapted from Pearce et al. (2003).

The question is what is the welfare interpretation of the ENPV criterion? While it seems like an intuitive criterion, it is not clear that a project that passes this criterion will contribute to any well-defined notion of social welfare. It turns out that there are some situations in which the ENPV criterion, in which r is the risk-free rate of return, has such a theoretical basis. But the informational assumptions and the requirements are quite stringent.

Recent work by Freeman and Groom (2015, 2016) discusses the ENPV criterion in detail. Gollier (2016) highlights in detail the limitations of the ENPV approach and shows that those who use the ENPV approach are likely to be "short-termist" in the sense that the term structure does not decline sufficiently quickly compared to the theoretically sound equivalent. Given all its inadequacies, it is surprising that it has been so influential at the policy level. Objections have not gained too much traction, perhaps because practitioners thought that it is better to be approximately right, than precisely wrong on the issue of DDRs (Groom and Hepburn, 2017).

8.4.3. Ethical issues

The debate between positive and normative approaches to social discounting becomes particularly important when considering inter-generational projects. In such cases the public policy decision affects future unborn generations and the current generation is in the position of custodian of future well-being. One potential problem with the positive approach to social discounting is that there are no obvious assets with sufficient maturity that can be used to price costs and benefits that accrue in the distant future, say 200-300 years hence (Gollier 2012, ch3). Furthermore, any market rate observed today reflects the preferences and behaviours of people today who are most likely not thinking about future generations when they make those decisions (e.g. Beckerman and Hepburn, 2007). While some empirical work does exist on very long-term asset prices (see Giglio et al., 2015) it is not clear that these assets (housing) are relevant to alternative projects in health, transport and climate change mitigation due to their risk characteristics.

The debate in recent years was exemplified in the discussions between Stern (2007) on the one hand and Nordhaus (2007) on the other in the context of climate change and Discounted Utilitarianism (DU). Stern took the view that the DU welfare function should not contain a positive utility discount rate ($\delta = 0$), and that views on intergenerational equity should guide the way in which future welfare should be evaluated. The utility discount rate should only be positive for reasons of catastrophic risk which was estimated to be 0.1%. Nordhaus preferred to calibrate the parameters of the DU social welfare via the Ramsey Rule based on an observable market rate of return on equities. The central discount rate in the Stern Review was 1.4% ($\delta = 0.1\%, \eta = 1, g = 1.3\%$), whereas Nordhaus' calibration of social welfare anchored on the 4-5% witnessed in the equities market in recent history in the United States. Not surprisingly, the Stern Review recommended far more stringent action on climate change than Nordhaus' gradual approach.

Nordhaus used a standard opportunity cost argument: using a low discount rate to analyse climate change mitigation investment means that one is disadvantaging future generations by investing in low return projects now. Better to ensure that investment increases wealth and makes the future better off, than reducing the test discount rate and allowing low return projects (Nordhaus, 2007).[13] Others argue that following such a strategy, and putting off investment in climate change mitigation can subject future generations to catastrophic risks, which would see dramatic reductions in their welfare. This type of risk is unlikely to be captured by current rates of return and standard positive discounting procedures (Weitzman, 2009). Chapter 13 goes into more depth on the specific issues associated with climate change and catastrophic risk. The normative vs. positive debate on inter-temporal welfare analysis and social discounting continues (Drupp et al., 2017).

8.5. Dual discounting

In recent years the issue of dual discounting has resurfaced, that is, applying different discount rates to different classes of commodities. The clearest analytical discussion of dual discounting can be found in Weikard and Zhu (2005), where two classes of goods are considered: consumption goods and "environmental" goods.

Suppose that instantaneous utility depends on consumption C and a stock of environmental goods, E. Intertemporal social welfare is then given by:

$$W = \Sigma_{t=0}^{T} \frac{U(C_t, E_t)}{(1+\delta)^t} \tag{8.11}$$

where δ is the utility discount rate (which here does not differ between environmental and consumption goods). Now there is an SRTP for each of these arguments of the utility function. These are:[14]

$$\rho_C(t) = \delta + \eta_{CC}g_C + \eta_{EC}g_E \tag{8.12}$$

$$\rho_E(t) = \delta + \eta_{EE}g_E + \eta_{CE}g_C \tag{8.13}$$

where $\eta_{ij} = -x_i \dfrac{U_{ij}}{U_i}$ for all i and j and is the elasticity of marginal utility in each case. These should be compared to the standard single good framework of Ramsey in which the social discount rate for consumption goods is simply $\rho = \delta + \eta g$. This is the typical framework for the analysis of dual (meaning separate) discounting of environmental benefits and costs on the one hand, and consumption goods on the other. The practice here is clearly different to the standard approach. But how can this be implemented?

Baumgartner et al. (2014) follows the previous theoretical literature (e.g. Hoel and Sterner, 2007) and assume a constant elasticity of substitution utility function:

$$U(C,E) = \frac{1}{(1-\eta)} \left[(1-\gamma)C^{1-\frac{1}{\sigma}} + \gamma E^{1-\frac{1}{\sigma}} \right]^{\frac{(1-\eta)\sigma}{\sigma-1}} \tag{8.14}$$

where σ is the elasticity of substitution between E and C. With this additional structure, the difference between consumption and environmental discount is reduced to:

$$\rho_C - \rho_E = \frac{1}{\sigma}(g_C - g_E) \tag{8.15}$$

which is a matter of estimating three parameters: the growth rate of consumption, g_C, the growth rate of environmental stocks, g_E, and the elasticity of substitution, σ. So in principle, the application of dual discounting is possible, and Baumgartner et al. (2014) illustrate how this might be done.

However, adjusting the discount rate can be a tricky business at the best of times. Fortunately, Weikard and Zhu (2005) showed the difference between the consumption and environmental discount rates has an alternative and practically identical interpretation: it reflects the change in the relative shadow prices for the environment.[15] In practice then, this dual discounting approach could be implemented by making sure that the shadow prices for the environment change according to [8.15] relative to consumption. Accounting for differences in relative prices is a standard piece of guidance in cost-benefit analysis, and so this seems like a more likely approach to be taken up (see e.g. HM Treasury, 2003). Indeed, the Dutch Government is currently investigating this possibility.

What dual discounting highlights in relation to the environment, is the importance of accounting for scarcity of environmental goods when undertaking CBA. This depends on their growth but more importantly on the elasticity of substitution with consumption. If environmental goods are perfectly substitutable with consumption then $\sigma = \infty$, and relative prices are unimportant. If the environment is critical to utility, and not substitutable at all, $\sigma = 0$, and the relative scarcity of environmental resources is paramount to CBA. These are realistic cases, although the middle cases are also likely. It will depend on the resource. Sterner and Persson (2008) make these points in relation to climate change.

8.6. Empirics of the SDR

In this section the empirical estimates of the SDR and its components are discussed. The next section discusses the empirics associated with defining an empirical schedule of DDRs.

8.6.1. Estimating the social rate of time preference

In order to estimate the standard SDR in (1), estimates of three parameters are needed: δ, η and g. The methods used to do this naturally depend on the interpretation of the parameter.

For *the utility discount rate*, δ, several interpretations were described above, and each interpretation provides a potential method for estimation. One way to approach the issue is to disentangle two components of δ: the pure rate of time preference or pure impatience, φ, and some element of hazard, such as life chances or catastrophes, L.

1. *Pure impatience, φ*: The pure desire to have utility sooner, sometimes described as "myopia", rather than later can be estimated by looking at aggregate or individual savings behaviour and estimating an equation based on [8.2]. In the past (some of these applications are quite old) this lead to estimates of around 0.3% to 0.5%. The highest values for this parameter are estimated by Nordhaus (1993). Interestingly, experimental evidence often leads to very high levels of impatience. Some studies record estimates of between 10 and 30% (Warner and Pleeter, 2001; Harrison et al., 2002). Such evidence is typically not regarded as useful for social discount rates.

2. *Life chances, L*: estimation of the hazard that one may not be around to enjoy the benefits of government investment usually focusses on life chances. For example, Ulph and Pearce (1999) estimated life chances as the average probability of death for an average individual. The formula they used for this purpose was:

$$\text{Change in Life Chances}\ =\ \frac{\text{Total Deaths in UK}}{\text{Total Population in UK}} = \frac{0.6466mm}{57.56m}$$

where "mm" refers to mortalities per million. This figure should be interpreted as the risk of death that the average individual faces each year. This lead to an estimate of 1.3%, but in general this type of approach yields estimates ranging from 1% to 1.3% (Kula, 1987; Scott, 1989).

3. *Risk of extinction or catastrophe, L*: Many have argued that when considering the appropriate discount rate for evaluating social projects, the SDR, it is inappropriate to use individual life chances. More appropriate, particularly for intergenerational projects is the risk of the extinction of *society* as a whole. Several estimates exist for this alarming concept. Estimates vary between 0.1% and 1.5%, depending on the method of estimation (see Box 8.3). Newbery (1992) for instance, estimates the "perceived risk of the end of mankind in 100 years" as 1%. This is the value that the UK Treasury uses for L.

Methods i) – iii) above are all *positive* methods in that they generally use revealed preference or observed outcomes as their empirical basis. Often a more *normative* or *prescriptive* stance is taken towards the pure rate of time preference, particularly when projects have intergenerational consequences. Normative approaches address the question of what one ought to do, positive approaches look at observed behaviour. In the intergenerational case, some argue that the normative and ethical case is more important for social discounting than observed market behaviour. In recent years, differences of opinion emerged on this matter between Stern and Nordhaus after the Stern Review. Stern believed for ethical reasons that $\delta = 0$ and the well-being of all generations should count equally in the evaluation of social welfare. Nordhaus believed that δ should be imputed from market behaviour so that the discount rate should reflect the returns available in the market, which is a rough measure of how people actually make inter-temporal trade-offs. The latter approach led to $\delta = 3\%$, which places a lot less weight on future utilities. Nordhaus' approach leads to radically less stringent recommendations for action on climate change than the Stern Review (Stern, 2007).

So opinions differ on the matter of the pure rate of time preference, and the general motives for discounting future generations' utilities. A recent of survey of experts (as judged by their publications on the matter) by Drupp et al. (2017) casts more light on this issue. Table 8.3 shows that on the matter of δ the pure rate of time preference, the experts mean (median, mode) was 1% (0.5%, 0%). These responses reflect a variety of different approaches to estimating δ for long-term (> 100 years) projects.

Box 8.3. Estimates of the utility discount rate, η

Source	Estimate	Theoretical Basis
Scott (1977)	1.5%	Myopia: 0.5%, destruction of society: 1%
Kula (1987)	1.2%	Average annual survival probability in UK 1900-1975
Scott (1989)	1.3%	Myopia: 0.3%, risk of total destruction of society: 1%
Newbery (1992)	1%	Risk of end of mankind in next 100 years
Nordhaus (1993)	2-3%	Calibration of DICE model to actual data on savings etc.
Evans (2004)	1-1.5%	Catastrophic risks: 1% for EU, 1.5 for non-EU countries
Stern Review (2006)	0.1%	Probability of extinction of the human race per year, based on likelihood of catastrophe in next 100 years

Source: Adapted from ADB (2007).

The *elasticity of marginal utility of consumption*, η, also has a number of different interpretations. As described above, this parameter can reflect several features of societal preferences: i) Consumption smoothing; ii) Intertemporal or intratemporal inequality aversion; iii) Societal risk aversion. Since this parameter captures many dimensions of behaviour, there are numerous empirical strategies that can be employed to estimate it. Box 8.4 has a summary of the estimates from the literature. Not only is the underlying rationale important, but so is the source of data for estimation. The following examples contain estimates from both *revealed* and *stated* preferences.

1. *Consumption smoothing*: Many of the estimates of this parameter use econometric techniques applied to individual or aggregate (revealed) data on savings and consumption behaviour

over time. The estimates range between values of 1 and 10 and depend upon the behavioural assumptions underpinning the econometric models, as well as the country in question. Stern (1977) and Pearce and Ulph (1999) review these estimates. For the United Kingdom, Groom and Maddison (2017) estimate the elasticity of intertemporal substitution, which is the inverse of η, and find that $\eta = 1.5$.

2. *Inter- and intra-generational inequality aversion*: Inequality aversion has been estimated using both revealed and stated preference methods. When students are asked, estimates of inequality aversion vary from 0.2 to 0.8. *Revealed social values* can be imputed under some assumptions from the extent of redistribution from progressive taxation systems. Evans (2005) suggests values between 1 and 2 for EU countries, while Atkinson and Brandolini (2007) suggest lower values. Groom and Maddison (2017) find that whether looked at over time or in the cross section, $\eta = 1.5$. Tol (2008) looks at the values of international inequality aversion implied by transfers between developed and developing countries and finds very low levels of inequality aversion.

3. *Risk aversion*: Estimates of η which capture risk aversion have a wider range in general. These estimates are obtained from revealed behaviour in markets for insurance, or from stated preference surveys in which individuals are asked for their preferences over a set of gambles. Indeed Gollier (2006) reviews some of the evidence and suggests that values lie in the range of 2-4. This reflects individual risks, and it is arguable whether these values are directly relevant to social decisions.

8.6.2. The social opportunity cost of capital: which rates?

There is also a debate as to which rates of return should be used if one thinks that *the social opportunity cost of capital (r) is the correct SDR?* The typical source of information for the risk-free rate would be government bonds. In fact, these assets are not entirely risk free since, compared to risk-free short term Treasury Bills for instance, bonds contain inflation risk. The use of treasury bills is not recommended however due to their short maturity. Most governments use the returns on government bonds as their (relatively) risk free SDR.

Dimson et al. (2017) have collated historical interest rate data and find that over the period 1900-2016 the global average real interest rate for relatively risk-free assets was approximately 0.8% and -0.5% for bills since 2000. For bonds the rates were 1.8% and 4.8% respectively. Each country will have its own appropriate rate of return.

It has long been argued that argued that the government can pool risks across many different projects, hence the appropriate SDR is a risk-free rate (Lind, 1982). The usual theoretical justification for this is the Arrow-Lind theorem (Arrow and Lind, 1972), which some interpret as meaning that public investment is inherently less risky than private investment. However, as shown by Baumstark and Gollier (2015), this is not necessarily the implication of the *Arrow-Lind theorem*, and in fact ignoring the risks associated with public investment may lead to the government taking on too many risky projects. When project risk is a significant factor, Baumstark and Gollier (2015) argue that the appropriate discount rate should reflect the returns available from a project with a similar risk profile, as discussed in the context of the CCAPM above.

The US government, for instance, proposes a SDR of 7% based on the observed rates of return to equities, for projects which are expected to draw upon or displace private business capital. The motivation for this discount rate stems from the source of funding rather than issues of risk. Yet such rates reflect a premium for bearing risk. This leads to the question of whether SDRs that embody risky returns are appropriate for the evaluation of public projects. This speaks to the broader question of how to deal with project specific risks in social discounting discussed above.

Box 8.4. **Estimates of η**

Source	Estimate	Theoretical Basis
Stated Preference		
Barsky et al. (1995)	4.0	Risk aversion of middle aged people in the US
Amiel et al. (1999)	0.2-0.8	Inequality aversion of US students
Gollier (2006)	2 – 4	Risk aversion in gambling
Individual Revealed Preference		
Kula (1989)	1.89	US data, constant elasticity of demand
Blundell (1993)	1.06-1.37	UK data: Aggregate and micro (QUAIDS) models
Gollier (2006)	2 – 4	Risk preference revealed in insurance markets
Social Revealed Preference		
Atkinson and Brandolini (2007)	< 1	Public decision making on redistribution and taxation
Evans (2005)	1.25-1.45	20 OECD countries' tax schedules
Tol (2008)	-0.1 – 0.9	Redistribution of OECD countries to developing countries via

Source: ADB (2007), Dietz et al. (2008), Pearce and Ulph (1999).

Table 8.3. **Estimates of the elasticity of marginal utility**

Methodology	η	Standard error
Inequality Aversion (Equal sacrifice, Weighted)	1.515	0.047
Inequality Aversion (Equal sacrifice, Historical)	1.573	0.481
Inter-temporal substitution (Euler equation)	1.584	0.205
Elasticity of Marginal Utility (Additive preferences, Rotterdam model)	3.566	2.188
Elasticity of Marginal Utility (Additive preferences, CEM)	2.011	1.337
Risk Aversion (Demand for insurance)	2.187	0.242
Subjective well-being (Happiness data)	1.320	0.168
Pooled estimate (Fixed Effects)	1.528	
Pooled estimate (Random Effects)	1.591	
Parameter homogeneity	Chi-sq(6) = 10.10 (p = 0.121)	

Source: Groom and Maddison (2017).

Table 8.4. **Survey results for intergenerational discounting**

Variable	Mean	StdDev	Median	Mode	Min	Max	N
Real growth rate per capita (g)	1.70	0.91	1.60	2.00	-2.00	5.00	181
Rate of societal pure time preference (δ)	1.10	1.47	0.50	0.00	0.00	8.00	180
Elasticity of marginal utility of consumption (η)	1.35	0.85	1.00	1.00	0.00	5.00	173
Real risk free interest rate (r)	2.38	1.32	2.00	2.00	0.00	6.00	176
Social Discount Rate (SDR)	2.27	1.62	2.00	2.00	0.00	10.00	181
SDR lower bound	1.12	1.37	1.00	0.00	-3.00	8.00	182
SDR upper bound	4.14	2.80	3.50	3.00	0.00	20.00	183
Social Rate of Time Preference (SRTP)	3.48	3.52	3.00	4.00	-2.00	26.00	172

Note: The SRTP is imputed from the individual determinants: the rate of societal pure time preference, and an interaction term of the real growth rate of per-capita consumption and the elasticity of marginal utility of consumption. See Drupp et al. (2017) for details. This equates to the RHS of equation [8.2].

8.7. The empirics of declining discount rates

8.7.1. Consumption side DDRs

In principle, when using the consumption-side approach to DDRs, such as those described by Gollier (2012a), there are two empirical steps that are required:

1. Empirical estimation of the long-term growth process

2. Estimation of the parameters of the theoretical term structure

In practice, only one of these steps is undertaken. The typical approach is to decide on a particular model of diffusion: e.g. the i.i.d. normal growth discussed above, or parameter uncertainty model in Section 8.3., and then obtain estimates of its underlying parameters: e.g. mean growth, μ, and volatility, σ_c^2. In some cases empirical models of diffusion are estimated and the SDR is calibrated this way. Groom and Maddison (2017) estimate a diffusion model with persistence for the UK economy, and construct a term structure for the United Kingdom in this way. But to date, a serious attempt to compare models of growth by some measures of goodness of fit is lacking in this area, and so the rigour with which the theory is being implemented falls short of that of the theory itself.

8.7.2. Production side DDRs

Where interest rate uncertainty is concerned, a great deal more empirical work has been undertaken in order to calibrate the schedule of DDRs coming from the theoretical structure of Weitzman (1998). Two sources of data that have been used for this purpose are expert opinions (Weitzman, 2001) and historical interest rates (Newell and Pizer, 2003; Groom et al., 2007; Hepburn et al., 2008; Freeman et al., 2015).

In determining which empirical approach is best between the production- and consumption-side approaches, the empirical rigour of those methods using historical interest rate data needs to be balanced against the theoretical rigour of the consumption-side approaches, which as yet have fallen short empirically.

8.8. Social discounting in practice

As the previous theoretical and empirical discussions have made clear, there are many decisions to be made when it comes to choosing the SDR. One approach is to take an opportunity cost perspective. This leads to a discussion about the appropriate rates of return that should inform the SDR. The alternative is to take a consumption side approach, which leads to a discussion about the nature of the social welfare function, the estimation of its parameters, and the empirics of consumption growth. Governments around the world have made different decisions in this regard and in this section we summarise the various approaches that have been employed.

Table 8.5 summarises some of the approaches recently taken in OECD countries on social discounting. Since 2003, many policy changes and reviews have taken place in the United Kingdom, United States, France, Norway and the Netherlands. Other countries have followed suit in some cases, like Denmark and Germany. These changes have happened in concert with an ever expanding literature on social discounting which has accompanied the focus of public policy on very long-term projects, such as nuclear power, biodiversity conservation, public health, transport and, in particular climate change and the social cost of carbon (See Chapter 13). Furthermore, at the time of writing, the World Bank is reviewing its guidance on social discounting for is assistance programmes.

Table 8.5. **Discounting guidance in several OECD countries**

Country	Risk-free discount rate (%)	Rationale	Risk premium (%)	Overall discount rate (%) (short to medium term)	Long-term discount rate
United Kingdom	3.5%	Simple Ramsey Rule, SRTP. Growth risk not incorporated, project risk is minor	0%, although 3.5% contains 1% for "catastrophic risk"	For all projects and regulatory analysis: 3.5%	The forward rate (%) for time horizon in years (H) is respectively: H = (0-30, 31-75, 76-125, 126-200, 201-300, 301+), SDR = (3.5%, 3%, 2.5%, 2%, 1.5%, 1%)
United States	For CBA: 3%, with sensitivity up to 7%	3% = consumption rate of interest, risk-free. (SOC/SRTP) 7% = average corporate returns (SOC)	7% is a risky rate of return, but no project specific risk premia,	Depending on source of funding, projects and regulatory analysis: 3 7%	OMB (2003) recommends lower rate for 'intergenerational' projects, for USEPA (2010) recommends 2.5%.
United States	For CEA: 2%	SRTP	None	2%	No guidance on long-term CEA
France	2.5%	Quinet (2013), Risk free rate of return. (note, Lebegue (2005), Ramsey Rule)	β * 2%, 2% comes from the estimated risk of "deep recession", see Barro (2006).	For risky projects: 2.5%+ β * 2%	Risk free rate: declining to 1.5% after 2070 time horizon. Risky premium: 2% for β = 1 rising to 3.5% after 2070 time horizon.
Norway	2%	CAPM approach, risk-free return to government bonds.	1%: systematic risk premium of 1%, aggregate β = 1, fixed for all projects	Risky projects and regulatory analysis: 3%	Risk free rate declining to 1% after 100 years.
Netherlands	0%	CAPM, opportunity cost approach.	3% systematic risk premium, fixed for all projects.	All projects and regulatory analysis: 3%	Accepts DDRs, but with real interest rates < 0% opted for fixed risk free rate of 0%, and fixed systematic risk premium.

8.9. Conclusions

The social discount rate is central to the appraisal of public policy and public investment using CBA and CEA. During the 60s and 70s, when CBA and CEA were first being introduced to government appraisal, there was much debate about the merits of using the Social Opportunity Cost (SOC) of capital or the Social Rate of Time Preference (SRTP) to inform the Social Discount Rate (SDR). The variety of different approaches to discounting in practice today reflect, in part, different conclusions drawn by different governments on which is the most appropriate (see Table 8.5). Each has its difficulties.

With regard to the SOC, it is not always easy to find the appropriate rate that reflects the cost of government funds. With externalities and poorly functioning capital markets, it is not clear that an observable market rate reflects the welfare trade-offs that society faces when making inter-temporal decisions. The pre-tax business rate, as used in the US in some cases, may not the appropriate opportunity cost for social CBA, particularly as it embodies risks faced by the private sector which may not be relevant to the public sector. Others argue that the cost of borrowing is the appropriate rate of return to inform the SDR, which would recommend the rate of return on government bonds as the SDR. Yet when all of these rates differ, and the sources of funding for a given investment of regulation are diverse, care is required in selecting the appropriate SDR.

With regard to the SRTP, the normative approach embeds the SDR directly in the social welfare function and reflects the welfare aspects of inter-temporal trade-offs. The merit of this approach is that the NPVs that provide a direct statement of whether a public policy and pubic investment increases social welfare, which is the objective of public appraisal. The downside is that the SRTP has to be calibrated in some way, typically following the

Ramsey Rule, and this parameterisation is regarded by some as somewhat arbitrary in some circles. Neither does the use of the SRTP take account of the opportunity cost of government funds or the cost of raising public funds.

The SRTP approach focusses on the consumption side and ignores the production side, which the SOC approach does the opposite. Using the Shadow Price of Capital approach (SPC) is advisable when using the SRTP, so that the opportunity cost of public capital can be reflected in the NPV calculation. This rarely happens in practice due to onerous informational requirements, and the lack of a generally accepted approximation, although Cline (1992, Annex 6A) does offer a way forward.

Recent advances in discounting have focussed on the evaluation of extremely long-horizon projects, such as climate change mitigation and nuclear power. This upsurge in interest has stemmed from the need to analyse intergenerational projects, and the sensitivity of these analyses to the selection of the discount rate. The fact is that large costs on future generations may appear insignificant in a cost-benefit analysis. Similarly, actions now that will benefit future generations for a long-time may not be undertaken in light of a cost-benefit analysis. While there are good reasons for discounting the future, these outcomes are often seen as being unfair to future generations.

The social cost of carbon for instance, which is one of the most important policy parameters for the public appraisal of carbon mitigation projects, is highly sensitive to the discount rate with which it is evaluated. Estimates of the SCC appear in current US evaluations of fuel efficiency regulations, and are incorporated in the CBA of transport projects in many OECD countries (OECD, 2015).

The use of declining discount rates to evaluate public projects is now commonplace in several OECD countries: United Kingdom, France, Norway and Denmark, and has strong theoretical and empirical support when considering risk-free discount rates.

For projects that have an important environmental component, the use of DDRs may or may not be a positive development with regard to conservation. It certainly means that the long-run is more important in standard CBA and CEA. More important from this perspective is the concept of dual discounting which places more emphasis on environmental costs and benefits when environmental quality is becoming scarce. While the theory is not new, the applications are becoming more frequent. The Netherlands has specific guidance on discounting environmental quality changes. However, rather than adjusting the discount rate for environmental quality, the guidance typically focusses on ensuring that changing relative prices for are properly accounted for. Such guidance can also be found more generally in UK Treasury Green Book.

Finally, there is the question of project-risk and whether this should be reflected in the SDR. This time old debate is yet to be generally resolved. The French guidance recommends the use of a systematic, project specific risk premium in the discount rate. The UK Green Book guidance considers project risk to be an issue of relatively insignificant importance. These are the issues that governments need to decide for themselves, being mindful that governments may take on too much risk if they fail to evaluate risk somewhere in their appraisal of projects.

There have been many developments in the world of social discounting in recent years. Groom and Hepburn (2017) chart the changes in 4 OECD countries over the past 20 years, and emphasise the role not just of the technical economic advances, but also the political economy of the times.

In summary, this chapter shows that the following factors are pertinent when choosing the SDR:

First, for non-intergenerational projects of medium time horizons up to 50 years or so:

a) What type of evaluation is taking place? I) CBA of public investment; ii) CBA of regulatory change; or, iii) CEA of Choice of Technique Analysis?

b) The way in which the project is funded is important: i) capital markets; ii) general taxation; iii) foreign loans; iv) user fees; or, v) a mixture of these options.

c) The SDR can be informed by the social opportunity cost of capital (SOC), risk-free rate of return or social rate of time preference (SRTP)? There are strong arguments for using the SRTP for CEA, SOC when private capital will be displaced and risk-free rates when government borrowing funds the project.

d) Theoretically, the cost of public funds should be taken into account via estimates of: i) Weighted SOC/risk-free SRTP approach; ii) Shadow price of capital (SPC) approach; or, iii) Deadweight loss of raising funds via taxation.

e) The SDR can reflect project risk and the uncertainty in growth. A consumption CAPM approach would add a consumption risk premium to the SDR to reflect project risk, alternatively certainty equivalent net benefits could be estimated and discounted using a risk free SDR (risk-free interest rate or SRTP).

f) Dual discounting/relative price effects for environmental scarcity: The government of the Netherlands are currently investigating this approach.

When discounting for long-term intergenerational projects:

a) The SDR for risk-free projects should decline with the time horizon due to uncertainty in the discount rate itself or due to uncertainty in secular consumption growth.

b) The SDR for risky projects: what is the likely term structure of the systematic risk premium for long-term projects? Theoretical work exists (Gollier, 2012; 2016) showing that the same forces that argue for a declining discount rate for risk free rate lead to argument for risk premiums that increase with the time horizon for pro-cyclical projects. Such arguments are included in the French guidelines on CBA.

c) To what extent should ethical consideration inform the SDR and is the SDR a sufficient device for evaluating very long-run projects? The latest UK Green Book will propose to truncate the calculation of the NPV at 120 years, and invoke a separate decision-making approach for evaluating the long-run, such as looking at the distribution of costs and benefits in the long-run.

These are the main issues that should be considered when thinking about social discounting for public policy appraisal.

Notes

1. $f(k)$ is a neoclassical production function which assumes that per capita output/income, y, is a function of per-capita capital stocks, $y = f(k)$, where $f_k(k) = \dfrac{\partial f(k)}{\partial k} > 0$ and there is diminishing returns to capital: $f_{kk}(k) = \dfrac{\partial^2 f(k)}{(\partial k)^2} < 0$

2. The SRTP is sometimes referred to as the Consumption Rate of Interest.

3. Note that the elasticity of marginal utility is defined as: $\eta(c_t) = -c_t u''(c_t) / u'(c_t)$, which is constant when $u(c_t) = (1-\eta)^{-1} c_t^{1-\eta}$, known as iso-elastic utility.

4. Some argue that this rate is a good proxy for the SRTP since it reflects the savings rate available to individuals. Others argue that the risk-free rate is a candidate for the SDR since it reflects the cost of public borrowing (Spackman, 2017; CEA, 2017).

5. This assumes: i) the internal rate of return of stream of consumption the project is zero: $\Sigma_t^N B(1+r)^{-t} - 1 = 0$, which for long time horizons means that $B / r \approx 1$; hence, ii) $B \approx r$ so one can use r Euros rather than B Euros for the approximation of the SPC.

6. Intuitively, i.i.d. normal this means that the growth in any given year is a random number, and each year a new random growth level is drawn. If these draws are i.i.n.d. then each draw comes from the same (normal) probability distribution and is uncorrelated with the previous year's random growth. More formally, if: $c_t = c_0 \exp\left(\Sigma_{\tau=0}^t x_\tau\right)$, where x_τ is annual growth and: $x_\tau \sim N\left(\mu, \sigma_c^2\right)$. If in addition: $U(c_t) = (1-\eta)^{-1} c_t^{1-\eta}$ and $\bar{g} = t^{-1} E\left[(c_t - c_0)/c_0\right]$, which is annualised expected growth, then one obtains [8.4].

7. The weighted average approach and the SPC approach can accommodate situations when benefits are consumed or reinvested. See Cline (1992, Annex 6A).

8. This result only occurs if societal preferences reflect *prudence* in the formal sense. Iso-elastic utility (utility with constant elasticity of marginal utility with respect to consumption: $U(c_t) = (1-\eta)^{-1} c_t^{1-\eta}$) ensure this, but any set of preferences for which $U'''(c_t) > 0$ has this property.

9. For more on the asset price puzzles see Mehra and Prescott (1985) and Weil (1989).

10. Chapter 9 on Uncertainty has more detail.

11. The simplifying assumption here is that project returns and consumption are bivariate normal with correlation coefficient ρ_i. In this context $\beta_i = \rho_i \sigma_B / \sigma_c$, which defines the covariance of project returns and consumption, divided by the volatility of consumption.

12. Defining the certainty equivalent M_t of $\mu(\tilde{\theta}) - 0.5\eta\sigma_c^2$ as follows that $\exp(-t\eta M_t) = E_\theta\left[\exp\left(-\eta t\left(\mu(\tilde{\theta}) - 0.5\eta\sigma_c^2\right)\right)\right]$ it can be seen that M_t is decreasing in t since the exponential function becomes more concave in t. Therefore, the SDR is declining with the time horizon since it can be written as: $SRTP_t = \delta + \eta M_t$. See Gollier (2008).

13. For similar arguments see also Harrison (2010).

14. For each of these, the social discount factor with which to "price" changes in the quantities of each of the arguments, consumption and environment, from the perspective of today (t = 0) is given by:

$$P_i(t,0) = \frac{U_i(C_t, E_t)}{U_i(C_0, E_0)} \exp(-\delta t) \quad \text{for} \quad i = C, E$$

The social discount rate in each case is simply the rate of change of this shadow price which leads to (9) and (10). See Traeger (2010).

15. The shadow price of the environment is the marginal rate of substitution: $p = \frac{U_E}{U_C}$. It is easy to show that the rate of p change of this over time leads to (12) in the CES case, and more generally the difference between (10) and (11) (Weikard and Zhu, 2005)

References

Arrow, K.J. (2013), "Determining Benefits and Costs for Future Generations", *Science*, Vol. 341, Issue 6144, pp. 349-350, http://dx.doi.org/10.1126/science.1235665.

Arrow, K.J. and R.C. Lind (1970), "Uncertainty and the Evaluation of Public Investment Decisions", *American Economic Review*, Vol. 60(3), pp. 364-378.

Arrow, K.J. et al. (2014), "Should Governments Use a Declining Discount Rate in Project Analysis?", *Review of Environmental Economics and Policy*, Vol. 8, pp. 145-163, *https://doi.org/10.1093/reep/reu008*.

Atkinson, G. et al. (2009), "Siblings, Not Triplets: Social Preferences for Risk, Inequality and Time in Discounting Climate Change", *Economics Discussion Papers*, No. 2009-14, Kiel Institute for the World Economy, *www.economics-ejournal.org/economics/discussionpapers/2009-14*.

Barro, R.J. (2006), "Rare Disasters and Asset Markets in the Twentieth century", *The Quarterly Journal of Economics*, Vol. 121 (3), pp. 823-866, *https://doi.org/10.1162/qjec.121.3.823*.

Barro, R.J. (2009), "Rare Disasters, Asset Prices, and Welfare Costs", *American Economic Review*, Vol. 99(1), pp. 243-64, *http://dx.doi.org/10.1257/aer.99.1.243*.

Baumstark, L. and C. Gollier (2013), *The relevance and the limits of the Arrow-Lind Theorem*, Mimeo, Toulouse University, *http://idei.fr/sites/default/files/medias/doc/by/gollier/Arrow-Gollier.pdf*.

Beckerman, W. and C. Hepburn (2007), "Ethics of the Discount Rate and the Stern Review", *World Economics*, Vol. 8(1), pp. 187-210, *http://qed.econ.queensu.ca/pub/faculty/garvie/econ443/debate/beckerman%20and%20hepburn.pdf*.

Blundell, R. (1988), "Consumer Behaviour: Theory and Empirical Evidence – A Survey", *The Economic Journal*, Vol. 98, pp. 16-65.

Bradford, D.A. (1975), "Constraints on government investment opportunities and the choice of discount rate", *American Economic Review*, Vol. 65(5), pp. 887-889.

Cline, W. R. (1992), *The Economics of Global Warming*, Institute for International Economics, Washington, DC.

Council of Economic Advisers (CEA) (2017), *Discounting for Public Policy: Theory and Recent Evidence on the Merits of Updating the Discount Rate*, Council of Economic Advisers, Washington, DC, *https://obamawhitehouse.archives.gov/sites/default/files/page/files/201701_cea_discounting_issue_brief.pdf*.

Cropper, M.L. et al. (2014), "Declining Discount Rates", *American Economic Review: Papers and Proceedings*, Vol. 104(5), pp. 538-43, *http://dx.doi.org/10.1257/aer.104.5.538*.

Dasgupta, P. (2005), "Three Conceptions of Intergenerational Justice", in Lillehammer, H. and D.H. Mellor (eds.), *Ramsey's Legacy*, Clarendon Press, Oxford.

Dasgupta, P. (2008), "Discounting climate change", *Journal of Risk and Uncertainty*, Vol. 37, pp.141-169, *http://dx.doi.org/10.1007/s11166-008-9049-6*.

Dimson, E., P. Marsh and M. Staunton (2011), "Equity Premia Around the World", *SSRN Working Paper*, available at: *http://ssrn.com/abstract=1940165*.

Drupp, M. et al. (2017), "Discounting Disentangled: An Expert Survey on the Components of the Long Term Social Discount Rate", forthcoming in the *American Economic Journal: Policy*. Working paper version: Drupp, M. et al. (2015). Grantham Research Institute on Climate Change and the Environment *Working Paper No. 172*, *www.lse.ac.uk/GranthamInstitute/wp-content/uploads/2015/06/Working-Paper-172-Drupp-et-al.pdf*.

Emmerling, J., B. Groom and T. Wettingfeld (2016), *Discounting and Intra-generational equity: Who should we be discounting?*, mimeo, London School of Economics.

Evans, D.J. and H. Sezer (2002), "A Time Preference Measure of the Social Discount Rate for the UK", *Applied Economics*, Vol. 34, pp. 1925-1934, *http://dx.doi.org/10.1080/00036840210128753*.

Feldstein, M.S. (1970), "Choice of technique in the public sector: A simplification", *The Economic Journal*, Vol. 80, pp. 985-990.

Feldstein, M.S. (1973), "The Inadequacy of Weighted Discount Rates", for a then forthcoming volume of essays in honour of Richard A. Musgrave, reproduced in Layard, R. (1972) (ed.) *Cost-benefit analysis*, Penguin Modern Economics Readings.

Freeman, M.C. (2016), *Long-term corporate and social discount rates for infrastructure and environmental project valuation*, mimeo, Loughborough University, April.

Freeman, M.C. and B. Groom (2015), "Positively Gamma Discounting: Combining the Opinions of Experts on the Social Discount Rate", *The Economic Journal*, Vol. 125, Issue 585, pp. 1015-1024, *http://dx.doi.org/10.1111/ecoj.12129*.

Freeman, M.C. et al. (2015), "Declining Discount Rates and the Fisher Effect: Inflated Past, Discounted Future", *Journal of Environmental Economics and Management*, Vol. 73, pp. 32-49, *http://dx.doi.org/10.1016/j.jeem.2015.06.003*.

Freeman, M.C. and B. Groom (2016), "How certain are we about the certainty equivalent long-run social discount rate?", *Journal of Environmental Economics and Management*, Vol. 79, pp. 152-168, *http://dx.doi.org/10.1016/j.jeem.2016.06.004*.

Giglio, S., M. Maggiori and J. Stroebel (2015), "Very Long-Run Discount Rates", *Quarterly Journal of Economics*, Vol. 130(1), pp. 1-53, *https://doi.org/10.1093/qje/qju036*.

Gollier, C. (2002a), "Discounting an uncertain future", *Journal of Public Economics*, Vol. 85, 149-166, *https://doi.org/10.1016/S0047-2727(01)00079-2*.

Gollier, C. (2002b), "Time horizon and the discount rate", *Journal of Economic Theory*, Vol. 107, 463-473, *http://dx.doi.org/10.1006/jeth.2001.2952*.

Gollier, C. (2008), "Discounting with fat-tailed economic growth", *Journal of Risk and Uncertainty*, Vol. 37, pp. 171-186, *http://dx.doi.org/10.1007/s11166-008-9050-0*.

Gollier, C. (2011), *Le calcul du risque dans les investissements publics*, Centre d'Analyse Stratégique, Rapports & Documents n°36, La Documentation Française, *http://archives.strategie.gouv.fr/cas/system/files/rapport_36_diffusion.pdf*.

Gollier, C. (2012a), *Pricing the Planet's Future: The economics of discounting in an uncertain world*, Princeton Press, *http://press.princeton.edu/titles/9894.html*.

Gollier, C. (2012b), "Term Structures of Discount Rates for Risky Projects", *IDEI working paper*, University of Toulouse, *http://idei.fr/sites/default/files/medias/doc/by/gollier/term_structure_v4.pdf*.

Gollier, C. and J. Hammitt (2014), "The long-run discounting controversy", *Annuual Review of Resource Economics*, Vol. 6, pp. 273-95, *www.annualreviews.org/doi/pdf/10.1146/annurev-resource-100913-012516*.

Groom, B. and C. Hepburn (2017), "Looking back at social discount rates: The influence of papers, presentations and personalities on policy", *Review of Environmental Economics and Policy*. Volume 11, Issue 2, pp. 336-356, *https://doi.org/10.1093/reep/rex015*.

Groom, B. and D.J. Maddison (2013), "Four New Estimates of the Elasticity of Marginal Utility for the UK", forthcoming in *Environment and Resource Economics*. Working paper version: "Non-identical Quadruplets: Four New Estimates of the Elasticity of Marginal Utility for the UK", *Centre for Climate Change Economics and Policy Working Paper* No. 121, Grantham Research Institute on Climate Change and the Environment, London, *www.lse.ac.uk/GranthamInstitute/publication/non-identical-quadruplets-four-new-estimates-of-the-elasticity-of-marginal-utility-for-the-uk-working-paper-121/*.

Groom, B. et al. (2007), "Declining Discount Rates: How much does model selection affect the certainty equivalent discount rate?", *Journal of Applied Econometrics*, Vol. 22(3), pp. 641-656, *http://dx.doi.org/10.1002/jae.937*.

Harberger, A.C. and G.P. Jenkins (2015), "Musings on the Social Discount Rate", *Journal of Benefit Cost Analysis*, Vol. 6(1), pp. 6-32, *https://doi.org/10.1017/bca.2015.2*.

Harrison, M. (2010), "Valuing the Future: The Social Discount Rate in Cost benefit Analysis", *Visiting Researcher Paper*, Australian Productivity Commission, Canberra, *www.pc.gov.au/research/supporting/cost-benefit-discount/cost-benefit-discount.pdf*.

Heal, G. and A. Millner (2014), "Agreeing to disagree on climate policy", *Proceedings of the National Academies of Science*, Vol. 111(10), pp. 3695-3698, *http://dx.doi.org/10.1073/pnas.1315987111*.

Hepburn, C. and B. Groom (2007), "Gamma Discounting and Expected Net Future Value", *Journal of Environmental Economics and Management*, Vol. 53(1), pp. 99-109, *http://dx.doi.org/10.1016/j.jeem.2006.03.005*.

Hepburn, C. et al. (2009), "Social discounting under uncertainty: A cross-country comparison", *Journal of Environmental Economics and Management*, Vol. 57(2), pp. 140-150, *http://dx.doi.org/10.1016/j.jeem.2008.04.004*.

Lebegue, D. (2005), *Revision du taux d'actualisation des investissements publics*, Rapport du groupe de experts, Commisariat Generale de Plan, Paris, *www.documentation.eaufrance.fr/entrepotsOAI/OIEAU/44/223176/223176_doc.pdf*.

Lowe, J. (2008), *Intergenerational wealth transfers and social discounting: Supplementary Green Book guidance*, Office of Public Sector Information, HM Treasury, London, *www.gov.uk/government/uploads/system/uploads/attachment_data/file/193938/Green_Book_supplementary_guidance_intergenerational_wealth_transfers_and_social_discounting.pdf*.

Mehra, R and E.C. Prescott (1985), "The Equity Premium: A puzzle", *Journal of Monetary Economics*, Vol. 15, pp. 145-161.

Millner, A. and G. Heal (2014), "Resolving Intertemporal Conflicts: Economics vs Politics", *NBER Working Paper* No. 20705, National Bureau of Economic Research, Washington, DC, *www.nber.org/papers/w20705*.

Ministry of Finance (2012), "Cost Benefit Analysis", *Official Norwegian Reports*, NOU 2012:16, Ministry of Finance, Norway, *www.regjeringen.no/contentassets/5fce956d51364811b8547eebdbcde52c/en-gb/pdfs/nou201220120016000en_pdfs.pdf*.

Newbery, D. (1992), "Long-Term Discount Rates for the Forest Enterprise", Paper commissioned by The Department of Forestry, Forestry Commission, Edinburgh.

Newell, R.G. and W.A. Pizer (2003), "Discounting the distant future: How much do uncertain rates increase valuations?, *Journal of Environmental Economics and Management*, Vol. 46, pp. 52-71, *http://dx.doi.org/10.1016/S0095-0696(02)00031-1*.

Nordhaus, W.D. (2007), "A Review of the Stern Review on the Economics of Climate Change", *Journal of Economic Literature*, Vol. 45(3), pp. 686-702, *http://dx.doi.org/10.1257/jel.45.3.686*.

OMB (Office of Management and Budget) (1992, 2015), *Circular A-94: Guidelines and Discount Rates for Benefit-Cost Analysis of Federal Programs: Appendix C updated November 2015*, *www.wbdg.org/FFC/FED/OMB/OMB-Circular-A94.pdf* .

OMB (2016) *Cost-Effectiveness, Lease-Purchase, Internal Government Investment, and Asset Sales Analysis*, Not since 20 January 2017 readily available, but previously at *www.whitehouse.gov/sites/default/files/omb/memoranda/2016/m-16-05_0.pdf*.

OECD/ITF (2015), *Adapting Transport Policy to Climate Change: Carbon Valuation, Risk and Uncertainty*, OECD Publishing, Paris, *http://dx.doi.org/10.1787/9789282107928-en*.

ONS (2013), *Middle Income Households, 1977-2011/12*, *http://web.ons.gov.uk/ons/rel/household-income/middle-income-households/index.html*.

Pearce, D. and D. Ulph (1995), "A Social Discount Rate for the United Kingdom", *CSERGE Working Paper* GEC 95-01, Centre for Social and Economic Research on the Global Environment, University of East Anglia, Norwich, UK.

Pearce, D. and D. Ulph (1999), "A Social Discount Rate for the United Kingdom", in Pearce, D. (ed.) *Environmental Economics: Essays in Ecological Economics and Sustainable Development*, Edward Elgar Publishing, Cheltenham.

Pearce, D. et al. (2003), "Valuing the Future: Recent Advances in Social Discounting", *World Economics*, 4(2), pp. 121-141, *www.world-economics-journal.com/Pages/Download.aspx?AID=141*.

Quinet, E. (2013), *L'evaluation socio-economique en periode de transition*, Rapport du groupe de travail preside par Emile Quinet, Tome I, Rapport final, Juin. Commissariat general a la strategie et a la prospective, Paris, *www.strategie.gouv.fr/sites/strategie.gouv.fr/files/archives/CGSP_Evaluation_socioeconomique_17092013.pdf*.

Scott, M. (1977), "The Test Rate of Discount and Changes in Base Level Income in the United Kingdom", *The Economic Journal*, Vol. 87 (346), pp. 219-41.

Sjaastad, L. and D. Wisecarver (1977), "The Social Cost of Public Finance", *Journal of Political Economy*, Vol. 85(3), pp. 513-547.

Spackman, M. (2017), "Social Discounting: The SOC/STP divide", Grantham Research Institute on Cliamte Change and the Environment, *Working Paper* 182, Grantham Research Institute on Climate Change and the Environment, London, *www.lse.ac.uk/GranthamInstitute/wp-content/uploads/2017/02/Working-paper-182-Spackman-Feb2017.pdf*.

Stern, N. (1977), "Welfare Weights and the Elasticity of the Marginal Valuation of Income", in Artis, M. and A.R. Nobay (eds.) *Studies in Modern Economic Analysis*. Basil Blackwell, Oxford.

Stern, N. (2007), *The Stern Review on the Economics of Climate Change*, Cambridge University Press, Cambridge, *www.cambridge.org/catalogue/catalogue.asp?isbn=9780521700801*.

Stern, N. (2008), "The economics of climate change", *American Economic Review*, Vol. 98(2), pp. 1-37, *http://dx.doi.org/10.1257/aer.98.2.1*.

Tol, R.J.T. (2010), "International inequality aversion and the social cost of carbon", *Climate Change Economics*, Vol. 1, pp. 21-32, *https://doi.org/10.1142/S2010007810000029*.

Vissing-Jørgensen, A. and P. Attanasio Orazio (2003), "Stock-Market Participation, Intertemporal Substitution, and Risk-Aversion", *American Economic Review*, Vol. 93, pp. 383-391, *http://dx.doi.org/10.1257/000282803321947399*.

Weil, P. (1989), "The Equity Premium Puzzle and the Risk Free Rate Puzzle", *Journal of Monetary Economics*, Vol. 24, pp. 401-421, *https://doi.org/10.1016/0304-3932(89)90028-7*.

Weitzman, M.L. (1998), "Why the far-distant future should be discounted at its lowest possible rate", *Journal of Environmental Economics and Management*, Vol. 36(3), pp. 201-208, *https://doi.org/10.1006/jeem.1998.1052*.

Weitzman, M.L. (2001), "Gamma discounting", *American Economic Review*, Vol. 91(1), pp. 260-271, *http://dx.doi.org/10.1257/aer.91.1.260*.

Werkgroep discontovoet (2015), *Rapport Werkgroep Discontovoet*, downloadable from *www.rijksoverheid.nl/documenten/rapporten/2015/11/13/rapport-werkgroep-discontovoet-2015-bijlage. Includes a seven-page English Summary.*

ANNEX 8.A1

Positive NPV using SDR increases social welfare

Suppose social welfare is given by Equation [8.1] for two periods:

$$W = U(C_0) + \exp(-\delta)U(C_1)$$

Suppose that a project costs 1 unit of consumption today for sure, but provides sure benefits in consumption ε at time t in the future. That is, there is no project risk. Given that the changes are small, the overall change in welfare from such a project is given by:

$$\Delta W = -U'(C_0) + \exp(-\delta t)U'(C_t)\varepsilon$$

The internal rate of return of the project is given by r_p, so that $\varepsilon = \exp(r_p t)$. If this return just offsets the welfare cost of the project (1 unit of consumption) then:

$$-U'(C_0) + \exp(-\delta t)U'(C_t)\exp(r_p t) = 0$$

$$\Rightarrow$$

$$\exp(r_p t) = \frac{U'(C_0)}{U'(C_t)}\exp(\delta t)$$

$$\Rightarrow$$

$$r_p = \delta - \frac{1}{t}\ln\left[\frac{U'(C_t)}{U'(C_0)}\right]$$

If utility has a constant elasticity of marginal utility: $U'(C) = C^{-\eta}$, then:

$$r_p = \delta - \frac{1}{t}\ln\left[\left(\frac{C_t}{C_0}\right)^{-\eta}\right] = \delta - \frac{1}{t}\ln\left[(\exp(gt))^{-\eta}\right]$$

$$= \delta + \eta g$$

So the rate of return that a project must have to just compensate for a marginal investment at time zero is given by $r_p = \delta + \eta g$, where g is the (continuously compounded) growth rate of consumption. Any project that beats this rate of return will increase social welfare W. Hence, $\delta + \eta g$ is the social discount rate. At the optimal defined by [8.2] this will be equal to the return to capital, r.

ANNEX 8.A2

Fundamental equation of asset pricing and the Ramsey Rule[1]

In the basic consumption based model of asset pricing under uncertainty, the individual consumer's utility is defined over current and future utility: $U(C_0, C_t)$. Typically intertemporal utility is represented by the additive, time-separable form: $U(C_0, C_t) = U(C_0) + \beta^t U(C_t)$, where $\gamma^t = \exp(-\delta t)$, and δ is the utility discount rate. When the future is uncertain, the expected utility model gives:

$$U(C_0, C_t) = U(C_0) + \gamma^t E[U(C_t)]$$

An investor decides how much to consume today, and how much to save for the future of an asset i which has maturity t and an uncertain payoff x_{it}, which has a price today (t = 0) of $p_i(0,t)$. The first order condition for this consumption-saving problem is given by:

$$\Delta U = -U'(C_0)p_i(0,t) + \gamma^t E_0[U'(C_t)x_{it}] = 0$$

Rearranging yields and expression for the asset price:

$$p_i(0,t) = E_0[m_{0,t}x_{it}] \qquad [8.A2.1]$$

where $m_{0,t}$ is the stochastic discount factor which reflects the value of expected marginal utility at time t relative today (t = 0):

$$m_{0,t} = \beta^t \frac{U'(C_t)}{U'(C_0)}$$

Noting that $E[XY] = E[X]E[Y] + \text{cov}(X,Y)$, [8.A2.1] can be re-written as:

$$p_i(0,t) = \frac{E_0[x_{it}]}{r_t^f} + \frac{\text{cov}(\gamma^t U'(C_t), x_t)}{U'(C_0)} \qquad [8.A2.2]$$

where r_t^f is the risk-free rate of return defined by: $\exp(-r_t^f t) = \gamma^t \dfrac{E[U'(C_t)]}{U(C_0)}$ so that:

$$r_t^f = \delta - \frac{1}{t} \ln \frac{E[U'(C_t)]}{U(C_0)} \qquad [8.A2.3]$$

Equation [8.A2.2] has two terms: 1) the asset price for a risk-free asset; 2) an adjustment for a risky asset. Equation [8.A2.3] is the expression for the risk free rate of return. The correspondence of [8.3] with the expression for the Ramsey Rule in Annex 8.A1 is clear. The consumer is thought of as a representative agent in that case.

The risk adjustment in [8.A2.2] reflects the covariance of the asset returns with the stochastic discount factor. [8.A2.2] can be re-written in terms of rates of return by normalising the asset price to 1 and treating the expected payoff $E[x_t]$ as the expected annualised return on asset i, r_i. This yields the following expression for the annualised rate of return:

$$r_i = r^f - \frac{\text{cov}\left(\gamma U'(C_t), r_i\right)}{U'(C_{t-1})}$$

[8.A2.4]

As Gollier (2012, p. 190-193) shows, if utility is iso-elastic: $U(C) = (1 - \eta)^{-1} C^{1-\eta}$, growth is a Brownian motion (as in section 8.3.1), and r_i and $\ln C_t$ are jointly normally distributed with a correlation parameter ρ, then [8.A2.4] becomes:

$$r_i = \delta + \eta \mu_c - 0.5 \eta^2 \sigma_c^2 + \gamma \beta \sigma_c^2 = r^f + \pi(\beta)$$

[8.A2.5]

where $\pi(\beta) = \rho \beta \sigma_c^2$ is the consumption risk premium, and the project "beta" is given by:

$$\beta = \frac{\rho \sigma_r}{\sigma_c} = \frac{\text{cov}\left(\ln x_t / x_{t-1}, \ln C_t / C_{t-1}\right)}{\sigma_c^2}$$

[8.A2.6]

The numerator of the project beta captures the correlation of the growth of the payoffs of the asset, x_t, with the growth rate of consumption. It is this covariance that determines the risk adjustment. If the covariance is positive, then the asset pays off when consumption is high and marginal utility is low. Such assets require a positive risk premium to account for this correlation. The opposite is true for insurance type assets for which the correlation is negative, and which pay out when consumption is low.

Note

1. This Annex follows Gollier (2012, p. 190) and Cochrane (2005, p. 3-17).

PART II

Chapter 9

Uncertainty

Methods of dealing with uncertainty – specifically probabilistic risks – in CBA have typically focused on expected utility theory which provides a strong theoretical basis for deviating from the simple use of expected values in a deterministic framework, towards estimating welfare corrections for use in CBA. However, estimating the resulting certainty equivalent values requires assumptions about the nature of society's utility function, and some demanding estimates of the probability distributions of the risky quantities associated with any given project. Even so, practitioners are increasingly prepared to use these methods, given emerging evidence about the errors associated with simpler approaches. That said, more ad hoc ways of addressing this such as sensitivity analysis and Monte Carlo simulations have their place, and the chapter shows how a nuclear power project appraisal might utilise and interpret a Monte Carlo analyses. Nor should a focus on formal economics ignore the fact that there are many other principles that could be applied in CBA to make decisions in the face of uncertainty, such as "safety first" and "precaution".

Footnote by Turkey:

The information in this document with reference to "Cyprus" relates to the southern part of the Island. There is no single authority representing both Turkish and Greek Cypriot people on the Island. Turkey recognises the Turkish Republic of Northern Cyprus (TRNC). Until a lasting and equitable solution is found within the context of United Nations, Turkey shall preserve its position concerning the "Cyprus issue".

Footnote by all the European Union Member States of the OECD and the European Union:

The Republic of Cyprus is recognised by all members of the United Nations with the exception of Turkey. The information in this document relates to the area under the effective control of the Government of the Republic of Cyprus.

9.1. Introduction

So far it has been implicitly assumed that the costs and benefits of projects are known with certainty. The reality is that estimates of costs and benefits are often very uncertain and subject to random variation over time. The uncertainty can stem from several sources. Technical issues are a chief source of uncertainty. For instance, the precise geological conditions that will arise in the process of implementing large infrastructure projects, like hydro-power schemes or nuclear power stations, are not known with certainty beforehand. In addition to a wide range of project-specific technical matters, the prices of goods and services are also subject to variation over time, and are also therefore uncertain.

Uncertainty matters from the perspective of CBA because the welfare effects of two projects which have identical paths of *expected* costs and benefits (i.e. the average costs and benefits) will have very different welfare effects if a project has uncertain costs and benefits and the other does not. Typically people behave as if they are averse to uncertain situations. Evidence for this comes from the large and ubiquitous demand for insurance, and a burgeoning collection of experimental results and other results (e.g. Holt and Laury, 2002; Andreoni and Sprenger, 2012; Harrison et al., 2002; Groom and Maddison, 2017). For this reason there are strong arguments for aversion to uncertainty to be reflected at the societal level in the appraisal of public projects. Other things equal this would lead to projects with lower levels of uncertainty to be selected. Put another way, projects with more reliable and certain outcomes would be preferred from a welfare perspective.

Beyond the uncertainty in the costs and benefits there is also uncertainty in the macro economy, so-called systematic uncertainty in the level of growth. As discussed in more depth in the discounting chapter, the presence of project-related uncertainty and systematic uncertainty also changes the welfare consequences of public projects if these risks are correlated with one another. If a project has high pay-offs during boom times, the same benefit is valued less in welfare terms than if it occurred during a recession and essentially acted as an insurance policy. The magnitude of the penalty that should be applied to projects with payoffs that are positively correlated with growth depends on the project itself, the societal preferences, and the extent to which a government can spread risks in society.

Economists tend to think about decisions under uncertainty from the perspective of expected utility theory. Doing so leads to some elegant theoretical expressions for welfare changes under uncertainty. However, some of the information needed to operationalise these measures is difficult or expensive to obtain, and the methods are open to debate. For this reason, practitioners of CBA have a number of other methods in their toolkit. These include sensitivity analysis, Monte Carlo simulations, and so forth. These methods are not especially based in the welfare theory that economists are used to, but they do provide a practical way of thinking about the effect of uncertainty, and the sensitivity of the NPV calculation to particular assumptions within project appraisal.

This chapter will start with the theory behind welfare analysis of risky projects. This will entail a brief discussion of the Arrow-Lind theorem (Arrow and Lind, 1970). The chapter will explain the use of certainty equivalence, risk premiums and the willingness-to-pay to reduce or eliminate risks, such as flooding. Indeed, an example of flood risk is presented to show how to use the valuation methods under risk. The chapter then discusses more ad hoc methods of dealing with uncertainty: sensitivity analysis and Monte Carlo simulations. The example of nuclear power is used to illustrate how these methods work. In order to proceed, a more precise definition of uncertainty is needed.

9.2. Risk and uncertainty: Some definitions

If costs or benefits are uncertain it means that *ex ante*, before the project is implemented, they could take on many different possible values. Prior to flipping a coin, the outcome could be heads or tails, for instance. Prior to excavating the foundations of a nuclear power station, the geology could be very favourable, or less so. A key distinction here is between risk and uncertainty. In the case of flipping a coin, one can be pretty sure that the probability of heads or tails is close to 0.5. When it is possible to assign probabilities to the possible events, and indeed know the full range of possibilities, then this is usually referred to as a *risky* situation. When this information is not available, as it might be in relation to the geology example, or in defining the likelihood of a technological failure, this is defined as *uncertainty*. Clearly from an analytical perspective it is easier to deal with risky situations than uncertain ones since one can calculate summary statistics from the distribution of possibilities: expected values, variance, etc., by these definitions.

The remainder of this chapter deals with risk rather than uncertainty, and it is assumed that possible outcomes have some probability distribution associated with them, like the 0.5 chance of getting heads or tails. All the possible outcomes are known, and there are no unknown unknowns. Indeed, the numerical examples make use of such information to undertake some welfare analysis. Importantly though, the terms uncertainty and risk are used interchangeably from hereon.

9.3. Welfare under uncertainty

In a deterministic world, CBA would evaluate the social desirability of a project in terms of the standard Utilitarian Social Welfare Function (SWF) as discussed in Chapter 2:

$$W_0 = \int_0^\infty U(c_t) \exp(-\delta t) dt \qquad [9.1]$$

and project evaluation tests whether or not a given project, and the changes it implies for the current level of consumption across time, c_t, increases this measure of inter-temporal welfare. When consumption is uncertain, and the net benefits of the project are uncertain, society must take a position on how the welfare measure should take into account uncertainty.

The standard approach in economics is to use an expected utility function:

$$V_0 = \int_0^\infty E\big[U(\tilde{c}_t)\big] \exp(-\delta t) dt \qquad [9.2]$$

where consumption is now a random variable, $\tilde{c}_t$, and at time t, the current (non-discounted) value of expected utility is:

$$E\big[U(\tilde{c}_t)\big] = \int_{c_{min}}^{c_{max}} U(c_t) f(c_t) dc_t$$

where $f(c_t)$ is the probability density function of consumption and c_{max} to c_{min} are the maximum and minimum values of $\tilde{c}_t$. For instance, in the discrete case, if there were two possible outcomes for consumption, c_{t1} and c_{t2}, with respective probabilities p_1 and p_2, then $f(c_{t1}) = p_1$ and $f(c_{t2}) = p_2$ and expected consumption at time t would be:

$$E(\tilde{c}_t) = p_1 c_{t1} + p_2 c_{t2}$$

while expected utility at time t would be:

$$E\left[U(\tilde{c}_t)\right] = p_1 U(c_{t1}) + p_2 U(c_{t2})$$

The fact that the range of outcomes for $\tilde{c}_t$ and the probabilities associated with them are defined means that strictly one is in the realm of risk rather than uncertainty as defined above.

The change in the way welfare is evaluated under uncertainty, using expected utility, means that using expected values of consumption in the deterministic framework of (1) is no longer sufficient for measuring changes in well-being. Defining expected consumption as $\bar{c} = E[\tilde{c}_t]$, it follows that if $U(.)$ is non-linear then:

$$U(\bar{c}_t) \neq EU(\tilde{c}_t).$$

Using a deterministic SWF and expected values (the LHS of the above equation) provides the wrong measure of well-being compared to the expected utility framework (the RHS). In fact, if the utility function reflects the preferences of a risk-averse agent, then it is the case that:

$$U(\bar{c}_t) > EU(\tilde{c}_t) \tag{9.3}$$

This would be the case if the utility function is concave in c_t. So using the expected values of uncertain consumption overestimates the value of a risky level of consumption when agents are averse to risk. The reason is obvious. Using expected values as if they are certain ignores the risk associated with them. If agents are risk-averse, one would expect a welfare measure that accounts for risk to be lower. As is shown in the following section, using expected values for project net benefits, which is a common short-cut taken in the appraisal of risky projects in some quarters, will also prove to be an inadequate method for evaluating the welfare contribution of a risky project. The standard measures of the welfare value of uncertain projects show this clearly and provide a means of either a) estimating corrections to incorporate the effect of risk; or, b) show the welfare value of reducing or removing risks altogether.

9.4. Certainty equivalence and risk premiums: Definitions

One way in which one can use the deterministic framework in [9.1] to evaluate well-being and account for risk aversion is to calculate the certainty equivalent value of the uncertain variable. From [9.3] it is clear that a risk-averse expected utility maximiser would be willing to accept some value of consumption with certainty that is lower than the expected value $\bar{c}$. The certain value of consumption that equates both sides of [9.3] is known as the *certainty equivalent*, c_E. It is defined as follows:

$$U(c_E) = EU(\tilde{c}_t). \tag{9.4}$$

For a risk-averse agent, the certainty equivalent is less than the expected consumption: $c_E < \bar{c}$. This leads to another concept useful for CBA, the *risk premium*, RP. RP measures the amount by which the certainty equivalent consumption is less than expected consumption, and is defined as:

$$U(\bar{c} - RP) = EU(\tilde{c}_t) \Leftrightarrow \bar{c} - c_E = RP. \tag{9.5}$$

A simple expression for the risk premium can be derived for small risks. Annex 9.A1 shows that the risk premium can be approximated by:

$$RP(\eta) \approx \frac{1}{2}\eta\sigma_c^2 \tag{9.6}$$

where $\eta = -\dfrac{U''(c)}{U'(c)} c$ is the elasticity of marginal utility, also known as the Coefficient of Relative Risk Aversion, which measures the curvature of the utility function, and σ_c^2 is the variance of consumption. The risk premium measures the willingness-to-pay to receive the expected value of c with certainty, rather than face the risk.

Risk premiums can be estimated in a number of ways. One way would be to estimate each element of [9.6] individually. This pragmatic approach requires an assumption about the specific form of the utility function, as well as knowledge of the variance parameters (see Kind et al., 2016, for an example of this pragmatic approach). The risk premium could also be estimated via suitably designed experiments as the willingness-to-pay to have the expected value of the lottery, rather than the lottery itself. A related measure of risk aversion is the willingness-to-pay to reduce risk. This can be estimated using revealed or stated preferences when the payoffs and changes in risk can be observed.

So, in principle, one way in which to capture the uncertainty in CBA is to use certainty equivalent values in the standard deterministic framework. These values can be estimated in a number of ways.

Up until now, the analysis has been in terms of aggregate consumption. The following section introduces the project net benefits into the analysis, with and without project risks. The concepts of certainty equivalence and risk premiums are used to show how project-specific risks can be incorporated into project appraisal.

9.5. Certainty equivalence: Application in CBA

One way in which to embed the welfare costs of the uncertainty associated with the net benefits of a project is to calculate the certainty equivalent of these net benefits. When the net benefits are compared to the baseline level of income, the certainty equivalent then captures two aspects of uncertainty: i) the uncertainty in the net benefits themselves (due to, say, uncertainty in the amount of a good or service that will be delivered); and, ii) uncertainty in the background level of income/consumption at the time the net benefits accrue. Once calculated the certainty equivalent values can be treated "as if" they are certain. They can then be discounted in the normal way to calculate the Net Present Value using a risk-free discount rate. The certainty equivalent is now defined and an example in project appraisal is developed.

Suppose that a project provides an uncertain net benefit in cash terms of NB. Suppose also that the background level of income, Y, is also uncertain. I.e., it is not known how rich society will be when the net benefits arrive. The current value of additional welfare at a particular point in time with the project is given by its expected utility:

$$E\big[U(Y+NB)\big]$$

and expected utility without the project is given by:

$$E\big[U(Y)\big]$$

The welfare change associated with this project is given by the difference between the two:

$$\Delta W = E\big[U(Y+NB)\big] - E\big[U(Y)\big] \tag{9.7}$$

The Annex shows that by means of Taylor series approximations, the change in welfare for a small value of NB, measured in terms of units of consumption/income, is given by:[1]

$$\Delta W^{*} = \mu_{NB} - \frac{1}{2\bar{Y}}\eta\sigma_{NB}^{2} - \frac{1}{\bar{Y}}\eta\sigma_{Y,NB}$$

[9.8]

where $\eta = -\frac{U''(\bar{Y})}{U'(\bar{Y})}\bar{Y}$, and $\bar{Y} = E[\bar{Y}]$. In the context of a public project, Y can be thought of as national income (or sometimes the portfolio of public projects). Equation [9.8] shows that the welfare change in terms of consumption is basically equivalent to the summation of 3 terms: 1) the expected value of the change in net benefits, μ_{NB}; 2) A risk premium associated with the pure variance of the project net benefit, σ_{NB}^{2}; and, 3) a risk premium reflecting the covariance of the net benefit with national income, Y: $\sigma_{Y,NB}$. As discussed below, in the context of evaluating public projects, the latter two components can be thought of as *diversifiable* and *non-diversifiable* sources of risk. In essence, [9.8] is the certainty equivalent value of the uncertain net benefit, NB, measured in units of consumption. It is the *sure* change in net benefits that would give the same welfare change as the uncertain NB of the project. If it is greater than zero, then the project is worthwhile.[2]

In principle, equation [9.8] provides a means of correcting the expected values of net benefits for the fact that society is risk-averse and the project is risky. In contrast to the definitions above, though, in equations [9.4]-[9.6], the certainty equivalent here contains a risk premium with two components. The first is:

$$RP_{NB} = \frac{1}{2\bar{Y}}\eta\sigma_{NB}^{2}$$

[9.9]

which measures the willingness-to-pay to avoid the variation in the net benefits alone. For a risk-averse agent this will be positive. The second component of the risk premium is:

$$RP_{Y,NB} = \frac{1}{\bar{Y}}\eta\sigma_{Y,NB}.$$

[9.10]

This component reflects the fact that the net benefits may be correlated with the uncertain background national income. This is important because if a project is positively correlated with national income: it has high payoffs when one is rich and low (possibly negative) payoffs when one is poor, then the project clearly contributes to the overall risk that society faces. Projects that add to overall risk should be penalised when society is risk-averse. Inversely, a project's net benefits might be negatively correlated with income. In this case, the project has high net benefits when income is low, and low payoffs when income is high. Such a project reduces risk in society. Such projects should be rewarded in a risk-averse society since they essentially act as insurance policies.

So $RP_{Y,NB}$ represents either the cost of additional risks that a project entails when its net benefits are positively correlated with income ($RP_{Y,NB}>0$), or the benefit of the reduced risks that a project provides if its net benefits are negatively correlated with income ($RP_{Y,NB} < 0$).

Put together these two risk premiums show that using the expected values of the net benefits as a means of dealing with uncertainty could lead to misleading project appraisals because it would ignore the preferences for risk reduction of various types. Expected net benefits should be corrected to account for these two sources of uncertainty in CBA. All that is needed is an estimate of the relevant parameters for these two risk premia. In order to make practical progress here, there are several routes one could take. How to proceed depends on the data that is available. The next section considers how in principle these terms could be estimated. The following section explains how relevant these elements of risk are to public policy decision.

9.5.1. Certainty equivalent net benefits: Estimation and implementation

In order to estimate [9.8] one could take a direct approach, by first estimating the risks that are involved for a particular net benefit, and for income, and then estimating the preference parameter η. Specifically this requires estimates of the variance of the net benefits, σ^2_{NB}, the variance of background income, σ^2_Y, and the covariance of NB and Y, $\sigma_{Y,NB}$. Estimation of the joint probability distribution of Y and NB is needed, from which one can obtain the marginal distribution of Y and NB to estimate the preference parameters. The exposition so far has focussed on risk aversion, i.e. the preferences associated with the variance or spread of outcomes. In principle society will have preferences such as downside risk aversion (aversion to skewness), and aversion to kurtosis (See e.g. Groom et al., 2008). This chapter solely focusses on risk aversion: aversion to spread.

Typically, and mainly for analytical convenience, it is assumed in applied theory and in empirical applications that society has iso-elastic preferences: $U(Y) = (1-\eta)^{-1} Y^{(1-\eta)}$, which is a constant relative risk aversion (CRRA) utility function where the coefficient of relative risk aversion is given by the constant: $\eta = -\dfrac{U''(Y)}{U'(Y)} Y$. Many empirical estimates of this parameter exist, obtained in different contexts. While in the contexts of private decisions individuals behave as if they have values of risk aversion of often as high as $\eta > 10$, experimental studies tend to show that on average agents are risk-averse with $\eta \approx 1$ (e.g. Holt and Laury, 2002; Harrison and Rutstrom, 2009). Groom and Maddison (2017) analyse aggregate risk aversion in insurance markets in the United Kingdom. Such studies have the ubiquity that is probably more relevant to CBA than individual experimental studies. Their estimates show that $\eta \approx 1.5$. Once a parameter is estimated, and the risk characteristics of a project are known, then it is possible to calculate the certainty equivalent values of the net benefits for CBA. Before a numerical example is provided some criticism of certainty equivalence is discussed.

In practice the calculation of the welfare change of an intervention in (8) could proceed as follows. Suppose, rather than looking at the impact to the economy as a whole, the case of an individual farmer who wishes to invest in flood defences is considered. The defences have a net payoff of GBP 350 in the event of a flood, due to avoided damages, and a cost of GBP 100 in the event that no flood occurs. In the background, the farmer's income is GBP 4 000 in the event of a flood, and GBP 5 000 when there is no flood. The flood occurs with a probability of 0.2. These payoffs and their expected values and variances are presented in Table 9.1.[3]

Table 9.1. **The state-dependent project payoffs and incomes**

	Flood	No flood	Expected value	Variances
Income	4 000	5 000	4 800	160 000
Project Payoff	350	-100	-10	32 400
Income + Payoff	4 350	4 900	4 790	48 400
			Covariance	-72 000

Source: Elaboration of Dinwiddy and Teal (1996).

The payoffs of this project have a negative covariance with the income levels. The project therefore has insurance properties since it has a high payoff in the bad times (low income) and a low payoff in the good times (high income). The final state-dependent income has a lower variance in the presence of the project than in the absence

(48 400 compared to 160 000). As such the risk premiums in [9.8] will be of the opposite sign to one another. Table 9.2 shows this to be the case and that the insurance effect of the project can dominate. The first risk premium is negative as expected, but the second risk premium is strongly positive. The welfare value of this project can be much higher than the expected value of the project, which is negative (-10).

Table 9.2. **The welfare change and risk premiums of the flood defence project**

Risk aversion (CRRA: η)	Welfare change (GBP) Equation [9.8]	Risk premium 1 (GBP) Equation [9.9]	Risk premium 2 (GBP) Equation [9.10]	% of Expected Value of Project (E[Z])	
				Risk premium 1	Risk premium 2
0.5	-4.2	-1.7	7.5	16.9%	75.0%
0.6	-3.0	-2.0	9.0	20.3%	90.0%
0.7	-1.9	-2.4	10.5	23.6%	105.0%
0.8	-0.7	-2.7	12.0	27.0%	120.0%
0.9	0.5	-3.0	13.5	30.4%	135.0%
1	1.6	-3.4	15.0	33.8%	150.0%
1.1	2.8	-3.7	16.5	37.1%	165.0%
1.2	4.0	-4.1	18.0	40.5%	180.0%
1.3	5.1	-4.4	19.5	43.9%	195.0%
1.4	6.3	-4.7	21.0	47.3%	210.0%
1.5	7.4	-5.1	22.5	50.6%	225.0%

The importance of the correction for risk increases with the level of risk aversion. Table 9.2 shows that in this case, as risk aversion (η) increases, the risk premium that reflects the insurance properties of the project, equation [9.10] starts to dominate. As the risk aversion parameter η increases beyond $\eta = 0.8$, the welfare impact of the project becomes positive as a result. This illustrates the importance of dealing carefully with project risk and the need to understand the level of risk aversion when evalutating projects under uncertainty.

While in principle these welfare effects are important when considering the well-being of an individual farmer, as is the case here, other considerations are required when public projects are considered in the round at the aggregate level. Concepts of risk sharing and risk pooling become important in this case. In some cases it can be argued that the elements of risk discussed above are irrelevant for public policy appraisal. Irrespective of that, what the previous analysis clearly states is that, when project net benefits are uncertain, at a minimum expected values should be calculated and used for the appraisal of projects. Issues of risk pooling and risk sharing are discussed below.

Before discussing these issues in more depth, a different dimension of project appraisal under risk is addressed: the value of *eliminating* risk. The following section discusses this in the context of removing flood risk.

9.5.2. Willingness-to-pay to eliminate flood risk

The previous example undertook a valuation of an investment with risky payoffs which were correlated with the background income. In the example above, the correlation with background income was negative and the welfare change associated with the project was typically larger than the (negative) expected value. Similar methods could have been applied to the evaluation of a project that is positively correlated with background income, and therefore increases risks in the economy.

Yet, many public projects aim to eliminate the risk entirely, and so have large, non-marginal effects on expected well-being. Flood defences are a good example. In such cases, what may be required is a measure of the welfare benefits of the complete elimination of the risks, rather than a correction for the riskiness of costs and benefits discussed above.

Kind et al. (2016) set out clearly the procedures for undertaking a CBA of the removal of the risk of flooding while taking into account risk aversion using the tools described above. This example illustrates how all the concepts described so far can be used. It also illustrates the potential mistakes that can be made by using expected values of uncertain variables rather than explicitly evaluating the welfare effects of risk.

Suppose society is confronted by a risk of flooding, which would cause a loss of goods and services. Table 9.3 shows the details of the example. In the absence of flooding, households do not suffer any damages and enjoy a consumption level of 100. In the event of the flood, they incur losses of 90 and consume only 10. Flooding happens with a probability $p = 0.2$. The expected consumption is 82, and so the expected damage is 18 (100-82). Assume that utility is iso-elastic with a value of $\eta = 1.2$.

Table 9.3. **Flood risk example: Payoff matrix, expected values and certainty equivalents**

	Payoff	Probabilities	Damages		Utility	
Flood	10.0	0.2	90.0		0.84	
No flood	100.0	0.8	0.0		2.01	
					Expected Utility	1.78
Welfare measures	Expected payoff	82	Expected damages	18	Certainty Equivalent	57.5
					Risk premium	24.5

Table 9.3 provides enough information to evaluate the willingness-to-pay, and hence benefits of, eliminating the flood risk by building flood defences. First, notice that the certainty equivalent is calculated as follows:[4]

$$U(Y_E) = EU(\tilde{Y})$$

$$\Rightarrow Y_E = U^{-1}\left[EU(\tilde{Y})\right] = (1-\eta)\left[p(10)^{1-\eta} + (1-p)(100)^{1-\eta} + 4\right]^{\frac{1}{1-\eta}}$$

$$= 57.5$$

The risk premium is therefore:

$$RP = \bar{Y} - Y_E$$

$$\Rightarrow 82 - 57.5 = 24.5$$

The large positive risk premium shows that there is a large willingness-to-pay for removing the risk associated with the flood. Yet, since removing the entire risk would also remove the expected damages, the value of the removing expected damages should also be added to the risk premium to obtain the total welfare gain. Total willingness-to-pay (TWTP) to eliminate the risk of flooding is therefore given by:

$$
\begin{aligned}
TWTP &= \text{Expected Damages} + \text{Risk Premium} \\
&= 18 \quad\quad\quad\quad\quad + 24.5 \\
&= 42.5
\end{aligned}
$$

In essence, even with quite modest risk aversion ($\eta = 1.2$) focussing only on the expected benefits of flood defences would capture only some of the welfare benefits of the project. Kind et al. (2016) explain that a good summary measure of the error involved in only looking at expected values is given by what they call the "Risk premium multiplier" (RPM). In this numerical example the ratio is 2.3 (= 42.5/18). This is a measure of how much one needs to multiply up expected damages in order to obtain the appropriate welfare measure for a risk elimination project. The measure is defined as follows when utility is iso-elastic (see Annex for derivation):

$$RPM = \frac{1 - \left[1 + p\left\{(1-z)^{1-\eta} - 1\right\}\right]^{\frac{1}{1-\eta}}}{p.x.z} \qquad [9.11]$$

where p is the probability of a flood, and z is the proportion of consumption that is lost due to the flood: in this case $z = 90/100 = 0.9$. Figure 9.1 shows how this error varies with risk aversion and with the risks faced by society (the proportion of income lost in a flood). Figure 9.1 shows that ignoring risk aversion in the welfare analysis will underestimate the welfare gains from risk reduction, especially when the risks (potential damage) and risk aversion are high.

Figure 9.1. **Risk premium multiplier**

As a function of proportion of: Left panel: income lost in flood; Right panel: Relative risk aversion

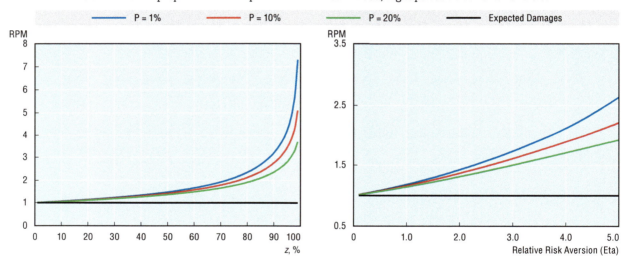

9.6. Risk in the public sector: The Arrow-Lind theorem

Returning to equation [9.8] above, which is reproduced here for convenience:

$$\Delta W^* = \mu_{NB} - \frac{1}{2\overline{Y}}\eta\sigma_{NB}^2 - \frac{1}{\overline{Y}}\eta\sigma_{Y,NB}$$

this section discusses the relevance of the two risk premia to public policy appraisal (the second and third terms on the RHS of [9.8]). The first risk premium relates to the variance of the project itself, and the second risk premium relates to the correlation of project risk with, in the public policy case, *national* income, Y. Two arguments are typically used to make the case that each risk premium is not relevant to the appraisal of public projects.

First, as hinted at above, the first risk premium represents risks which are *diversifiable* across the entire portfolio of projects that a government has. That is, the effect of such risks cancels out across the many projects implemented such that in the aggregate such risks are unimportant. Second, the Arrow-Lind theorem (Arrow and Lind, 1971) states that since the aggregate risk is shared across many individuals in society, at the aggregate level these risks become vanishingly small.

The basic idea can be seen in relation to the example of flood defences seen in Tables 9.1 and 9.2.[5] If the risk associated with the project alone were shared between two parties, so that in the bad times the losses were GBP 50 and in the good times the gains were GBP 175, then the variance of this risk is quartered. The risk reduces by a power of 2 for each increase in the number of people sharing the risk, until it disappears for all practical purposes, so the argument goes.

The second risk premium concerns the correlation of the project net benefits with, in the public policy case, the national income or the macro-economy. Rather than being diversifiable, such risks are referred to as non-diversifiable or *systematic* risks. Historically, it has been argued that this element of risk is likely to be small given the small size of many projects in relation to the macro-economy as a whole. For this reason, this term is frequently ignored. The UK Treasury's "Green Book" takes this position on systematic risk for instance. Yet many countries do take systematic risks into account.

The Arrow-Lind theorem has been hugely influential in the realm of CBA and is the motivation. Yet the Arrow-Lind theorem has always been called into question because of some of the assumptions required for public sector risk sharing. Some argue that it is unrealistic to assume that the diversifiable risks of particular projects will be shared in the way Arrow and Lind (1970) suggest. Furthermore, Baumstark and Gollier (2014) argue that the assumption that benefits of private and public investments are independent of one another is also unrealistic. In short, such arguments imply that both the risk premiums in [9.8] should still be considered in CBA. Ignoring them would lead to poor public project selection and potentially the government taking on a portfolio of projects which are add to macroeconomic risk: e.g. in transport and energy.

9.7. Sensitivity analysis

If there is some uncertainty about the value of some of the key parameters in CBA, then a sensitivity analysis can be used to gain an understanding of how sensitive the NPV of a particular project is, or some particular cost and benefit is, to changes in that parameter. The approach is somewhat arbitrary and ad hoc, and does not have any welfare significance of the kind demonstrated in the previous sections, but practitioners can obtain some idea of the importance of some assumptions in calculating the baseline NPV.

The following discussion uses nuclear power generation as an example of a project where there are uncertainties in the flow of costs and benefits over time, particularly *decommissioning costs*. Furthermore, due to the long time-horizons associated with nuclear power generation and decommission, such projects are likely to be sensitive to the choice of the *discount rate*.

A sensitivity analysis in relation to these two parameters identifies two important concepts in sensitivity analysis: *switching values* and *switching ratios*. The former is value of the parameters at which the NPV changes sign; the latter shows the proportional change in the parameter required from the baseline for the NPV to change sign. The following example undertakes what is known as a *gross sensitivity analysis*, which looks at the sensitivity of the NPV.

9.7.1. Nuclear power: Sensitivity to the discount rate and decommissioning costs

Figure 9.2 shows the cash flows estimated for a nuclear power plant. These values should be considered purely illustrative since the estimates come from the early 2000s. Their source is the UK Cabinet Office's Performance and Innovation Unit Energy Report from 2002 (PIU 2002).[6] The Figure shows that there is a long period of around 6 years of investment costs, followed by a 40 year period of production during which the net benefits are positive. This is followed by a lengthy period of decommissioning costs. Overall, the time horizon for this CBA is a period of around 120 years.

Figure 9.2. **The cash flows of a nuclear power plant**

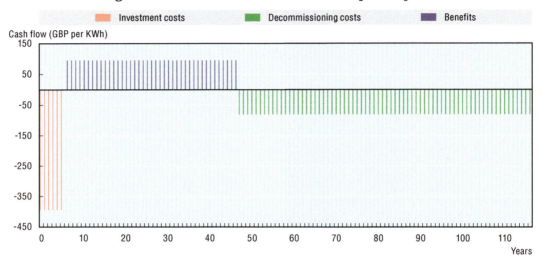

Source: Pearce et al., 2003; PIU, 2002.

Figure 9.3 shows the sensitivity analysis associated with the nuclear power plant. The sensitivity analysis tell us that the NPV is highly sensitive to the discount rate, but in unexpected ways. At 0% the NPV is negative, meaning that the raw sum of the cash flows is negative, mainly due to the duration of the decommissioning costs in the future. As a larger discount rate is applied, the NPV increases, however, as the present value of these decommissioning costs is discounted at ever higher rates. The switching value is at 2.25% above which NPV is positive. This positive relationship between the discount rate and the NPV stems from the fact that the net benefits of the nuclear power project change sign twice. Beyond some value, an increasing discount rate starts to reduce the NPV, as it would in a standard investment project with now tail-end costs. As the future benefits are discounted more and more eventually, at 5.25%, the NPV changes sign once more. The sensitivity analysis has revealed aspects of the project that the analyst might not have known before. First, that there are two switching points for the discount rate, and second that there is only a narrow range of discount rates for which NPV > 0.

As for the switching ratio, there are two of these also. The UK government uses 3.5% as its basic discount rate, so the lower switching ratio is 0.64 (2.25%/3.5%), and the upper is 1.5 (5.25%/3.5%). These are quite close to 1, indicating that the project is very sensitive to the discount rate.

A similar analysis can be done for the decommissioning costs, the present value of which is crucial for the NPV. Figure 9.4 undertakes a gross sensitivity analysis in relation to decommissioning costs which has a monotonic relationship, and a single switching point.

Figure 9.3. **Sensitivity analysis: Discount rate**

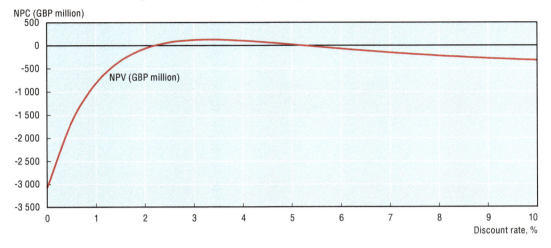

Figure 9.4. **Sensitivity analysis: Decommissioning costs**

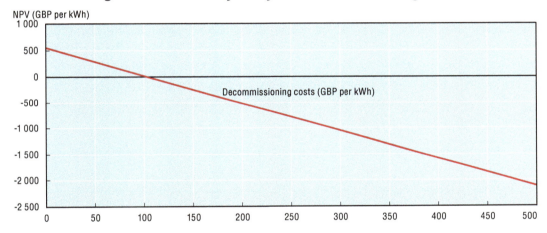

More complicated sensitivity analyses are possible, and better measures of the sensitivity can also be calculated. For instance, one could subject the project to a *stress test* in which NPV is tested against the worst and best case outcomes for singular variables or for all variables together.

Sensitivity analysis provides useful information on the robustness of the NPV to various assumptions concerning variables that are deemed to be uncertain (prices, costs, time horizons for construction, etc.). However, the changes in the variables are rather ad hoc and down to the analyst. For instance, one would have no idea from the previous analysis of the likelihood of the discount rate being between 2.25% and 5.25%, nor of the decommissioning costs being lower than GBP 100 per kWh. A better approach might be to characterise the likelihood of variables taking on particular values, and obtain a picture of the likelihood of the variables approaching the switching values. Monte Carlo analysis provides a means of doing this.[7]

9.8. Monte Carlo Analysis

Monte Carlo analysis uses estimates of the probability distributions of costs and benefits, and other parameters used in CBA, to undertake a probabilistic analysis of the likely NPV to emerge from a particular project. The probability distributions of, say, costs or the discount rate, provide information on the likelihood of different scenarios emerging, e.g. high decommissioning costs, and use this information to build up a probability distribution for NPV. The steps to Monte Carlo analysis are as follows:

1. Estimate the probability distributions for the parameters of interest. Where parameters are likely to be correlated, the joint probability distributions are estimated;

2. Take a random draw of the parameters of interest of sample size n;

3. Estimate the NPV n times using the parameters drawn;

4. Calculate the mean NPV across the n estimates and store the value;

5. Repeat m times until one can plot the probability distribution of mean NPV conditional on the uncertain parameters with sample size n, with m repetitions;

6. Evaluate the likelihood of a positive or negative NPV.

The difficulty in Monte Carlo analysis is accurately reflecting the probability density functions associated with the parameters of interest. One can look at historical data, expert opinion or experimental evidence when looking at preference parameters, like risk aversion. Typically the analysis is undertaken using the deterministic representation of welfare, rather than the expected utility approach. But this is not always the case, and it is also possible to include the preference parameters, such as risk aversion, into the Monte Carlo analysis. This is the approach taken in many integrated assessment models (e.g. Stern, 2007).

To illustrate the technique, the nuclear power example above is continued, with a focus on the two variables that NPV is evidently sensitive to in this case: the discount rate and the decommissioning costs.

9.8.1. Nuclear power: Monte Carlo simulation of discount rates and decommissioning costs

To undertake the Monte Carlo analysis, the joint probability distribution for the discount rate and decommissioning costs is defined according to Table 9.4. While the numbers for decommissioning costs are centred on the values presented in Figure 9.2, the standard deviations associated with them are just illustrative. One could imagine obtaining a distribution of these costs from expert opinions. Such opinions would reflect the nature of the project and expectations of technological change in the future. The discount rate, however, is centred around the 3.5% used by the UK Treasury, and the standard deviation is obtained from the range of expert opinions on the SDR found in Drupp et al. (2017). One could just as easily use historical interest rate data to estimate these parameters if the policy was to use interest rates for social discounting, as in the United States (Groom and Hepburn, 2017). The STATA code for the Monte Carlo simulation can be found in Annex 3. The data are available upon request.

Table 9.4. **Parameter values for Monte Carlo simulation**

	Discount rate (%)	Decommissioning costs (GBP per kWh)
Mean	3.5	80
Standard deviation	2.5	50
Correlation coefficient	+/0.7	
Sample size	1 000	
Repetitions	1 000	

Finally, two simulations which differ in the correlation between discount rates and decommissioning costs are represented. In the first simulation the variables are assumed to be positively correlated, in the second they are assumed to be negatively correlated. Again, there is no clear source of information on this matter, so the simulations simply illustrate the implications of positive or negative correlations between the two random parameters. The sample size n, and the number of repetitions is chosen to be 1 000. Figures 9.5 and 9.6 show the simulated distributions of the mean NPV.

Figure 9.5. **NPV with negatively correlated discount rate and decommissioning costs (r = -0.7)**

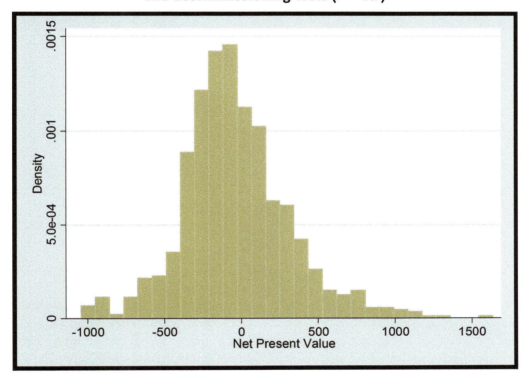

Figure 9.5 shows the distribution of NPV in Simulation 1 which assumes a negative correlation between the discount rate and the decommissioning costs.[8] Here the NPV values are centred below zero. The mean value of the mean NPV is approx. GBP-200 and the median is approx. – GBP150. So, in more than 50% of the simulations, the mean NPV is negative. This shows that there is considerable uncertainty around a mean value of zero. This does not look like a convincing project.

Figure 9.6 shows the results of Simulation 2 where a positive correlation between the discount rate and decommissioning costs is assumed. With a positive correlation, high values of the discount rate are coupled with high values of the decommissioning costs, and vice versa. This tends to lengthen the tail of the distribution of NPV, so that there are is a positive probability of some very bad outcomes: large and negative NPVs. The mean and median values are not tremendously different to in Simulation 1, but the long left skewed distribution is a warning to a risk-averse planner.

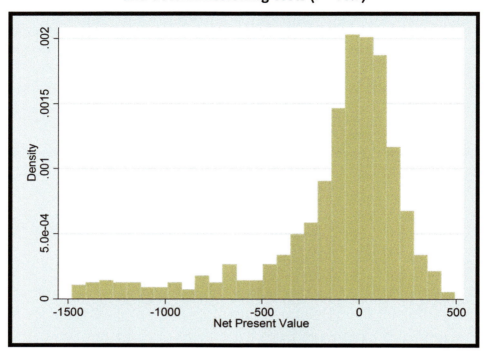

Figure 9.6. **NPV with positively correlated discount rate and decommissioning costs (r = +0.7)**

9.9. Optimism bias

Work by Flyvbjerg (2009) showed the empirical regularity with which public projects would end up being more expensive than anticipated in the original project document. The HM Treasury "Green Book" (HMT 2003, Ch7, p. 85) devotes an entire section of its chapter on Uncertainty to this topic. Optimism bias is often thought to be the chief feature of uncertainty, and the chief fear of policy makers: that the benefits of the project turn out to be lower than expected, or the costs higher. That this happens systematically in project appraisal is the motivation for labelling this type of uncertainty a "bias".

Optimism bias mainly affects the cost side, but can also affect the benefit side of project appraisal. Capital costs are often poorly defined or sometimes overlooked in the planning phase. The duration of works is also frequently underestimated.

The fear of optimism bias has led to all sorts of proposed solutions, some more crude than others (HMT, 2003, p. 85-87):

- Collection of the best evidence on net benefits;
- Performance management systems:
- Competent project managers;
- Break large projects into more manageable smaller projects;
- A premium on the discount rate to reflect optimism bias.

These methods are discussed in HMT (2003). Using the discount rate to control for the optimism bias is not generally to be recommended. Discounting in this way would treat all project net benefits in the same way, ignoring the fact that optimism bias varies from one project to another.

9.10. Conclusions

This chapter has provided an introduction to methods of dealing with uncertainty in CBA. The focus has been on expected utility theory which provides a strong theoretical basis for deviating from the simple use of expected values in a deterministic framework, towards estimating welfare corrections for use in CBA. The use of certainty equivalent net benefits is routinely recommended by economists for the analysis of the public projects. Several practical examples have been explained which show how these welfare adjustments can be made. However, certainty equivalent values require some heroic assumptions about the nature of society's utility function, and some demanding estimates of the probability distributions of the risky quantities associated with any given project.

More commonplace, although more ad hoc, are methods which investigate how the NPV of a project is affected by changes in some crucial parameters. Sensitivity analysis provides an indication of how sensitive NPV can be to some parameters. Monte Carlo analysis can be used to evaluate sensitivity of NPV to multiple parameters based on the likelihood that particular parameter combinations arise. While slightly less ad hoc, Monte Carlo simulations are demanding when it comes to estimating the probability distributions associated with some of the parameters that determine NPV. Examples from a nuclear power project have illustrated how one can use and interpret Monte Carlo analyses.

Of course, the focus on formal welfare economics and expected utility theory should not ignore the fact that there are many other principles that could be applied in CBA to make decisions in the face of uncertainty. "Safety first" approaches and the precautionary principle represent such alternative approaches. Even then, economic analysis can help in defining what is meant by these principles, and the trade-offs involved. In relation to the precautionary principle, the next chapter shows that this principle can be interpreted within an option value framework.

Notes

1. Note, a second-order Taylor series expansion has been used here. Higher order expansions could be used if preferences for higher-order moments of the distribution are thought to be important. Groom et al. (2008) show the theory and provide an application to agriculture.

2. Another way of saying this is to note the correspondence of ΔW^* with the definition of the certainty equivalent of NB:

$$E\left[U\left(Y+NB\right)\right]-E\left[U\left(Y\right)\right]=E\left[U\left(Y+\Delta W^*\right)\right]-E\left[U\left(Y\right)\right]$$
$$\Rightarrow$$
$$E\left[U\left(Y+NB\right)\right]=E\left[U\left(Y+\Delta W^*\right)\right]$$

3. This example is an elaboration of the example shown in Chapter 13 of Dinwiddy and Teal (1996).

4. Utility is rescaled by adding 4 units of utility in the following numerical example.

5. The example comes from Dinwiddy and Teal, 1996, p. 230.

6. In fact, for illustrative purposes, in the numerical example GBP 1 000 per kWh has been added to the NPV in each case so that the NPV is positive for some range of the sensitivity analysis. The raw PIU (2002) data do not support a positive NPV.

7. Staehr (2006) provides a general source of further details on sensitivity analysis.

8. The distribution of the parameters is shown in Annex 9.A3.

References

Andreoni, J. and C. Sprenger (2012), "Estimating time preferences from convex budgets", *American Economic Review*, Vol. 102/7, pp. 3333-3356, *http://dx.doi.org/10.1257/aer.102.7.3333*.

Dinwiddy, C. and F. Teal (1996), *Principles of Cost Benefit Analysis for Developing Countries*, Cambridge University Press, Cambridge.

Drupp, M. et al. (2017), "Discounting Disentangled: An Expert Survey on the Components of the Long Term Social Discount Rate", Forthcoming in the *American Economic Journal: Policy*. Working paper version: Drupp, M. et al. (2015), Grantham Research Institute on Climate Change and the Environment *Working Paper No. 172*, *www.lse.ac.uk/GranthamInstitute/wp-content/uploads/2015/06/Working-Paper-172-Drupp-et-al.pdf*.

Stehr, K. (2006), "Risk and uncertainty in cost benefit analysis", *Toolbox paper*, Environmental Assessment Institute, Copenhagen, *www.ttu.ee/public/k/karsten-staehr/2006_Staehr_-_Risk_and_uncertainty_in_cost_benefit_analysis.pdf*.

Flyvbjerg, B. (2009), "Survival of the unfittest: Why the worst infrastructure gets built – and what we can do about it", *Oxford Review of Economic Policy*, Vol. 25/3, pp. 344-367, *http://dx.doi.org/10.1093/oxrep/grp024*.

Groom, B. and D.J. Maddison (2017), "Four New Estimates of the Elasticity of Marginal Utility for the UK, forthcoming in *Environmental and Resource Economics*. Working paper version: Groom and Maddison (2013). "Non-identical Quadruplets: Four New Estimates of the Elasticity of Marginal Utility for the UK", *Centre for Climate Change Economics and Policy Working Paper* No. 141, Centre for Climate Change Economics and Policy, *www.lse.ac.uk/GranthamInstitute/publication/non-identical-quadruplets-four-new-estimates-of-the-elasticity-of-marginal-utility-for-the-uk-working-paper-121/*.

Groom, B. et al. (2008), "The story of the moment: Risk averse Cypriot farmers respond to drought management", *Applied Economics*, Vol. 40, pp. 315-326, *http://dx.doi.org/10.1080/00036840600592916*.

Groom, B. and C. Hepburn (2017), "Looking back at social discount rates: The influence of papers, presentations and personalities on policy", *Review of Environmental Economics and Policy*, Vol. 11, pp. 336-356, *https://doi.org/10.1093/reep/rex015*.

Harrison, G.W. et al. (2005), "Eliciting risk and time preferences using field experiments: Some methodological issues", in Carpenter, J.P., G.W. Harrison and J.A. List (eds.), *Field Experiments in Economics*, Elsevier, Amsterdam.

Harrison, G.W. et al. (2002), "Estimating individual discount rates in Denmark: A field experiment", *American Economic Review*, Vol. 92/5, pp. 1606-17, *http://dx.doi.org/10.1257/000282802762024674*.

HM Treasury (2003), *The Green Book: Appraisal and Evaluation in Central Government*, HM Treasury, London, *www.gov.uk/government/uploads/system/uploads/attachment_data/file/220541/green_book_complete.pdf*.

Holt, C.A. and S.K. Laury (2002), "Risk aversion and incentive effects", *American Economic Review*, Vol. 92/5, pp. 1644-55, *http://dx.doi.org/10.1257/000282802762024700*.

Kind, J. et al. (2016), Accounting for risk aversion, incoe distribution and social welfare in cost-benefit analysis for flood risk management, *WIREs Climate Change*, e446, *http://dx.doi.org/10.1002/wcc.446*.

Pearce, D. et al. (2003), "Valuing the future: Recent advances in social discounting", *World Economics*, Vol. 4/2, pp. 121-141, *www.world-economics-journal.com/Pages/Download.aspx?AID=141*.

PIU (2002), *The Energy Review*, Cabinet Office, Performance and Innovation Unit, London, *www.gci.org.uk/Documents/TheEnergyReview.pdf*.

Stern, N. (2007), *The Stern Review on the Economics of Climate Change*, Cambridge University Press, Cambridge.

ANNEX 9.A1

Risk premiums

The welfare change:

$$\Delta W = E\big[U(Y + NB)\big] - E\big[U(Y)\big]$$

can be re-written as a Taylor series:

$$\Delta W = U'(E[Y])E[NB] + \frac{1}{2}U''(E[Y])VAR(NB) + U''(E[Y])VAR(Y, NB)$$

This can be converted into units of consumption, in which NB and Y are measured, by dividing through by the marginal utility U'(Y) to give:

$$\Delta W^* = E[NB] + \frac{1}{2}\frac{U''(E[Y])}{U'(E[Y])}VAR(NB) + \frac{U''(E[Y])}{U'(E[Y])}VAR(Y, NB) \qquad [9.A1.1]$$

which is equivalent to equation [9.8] in the text. See Dinwiddy and Teal (1996) for further details of this (Annex to Chapter 14).

ANNEX 9.A2

The risk premium multiplier

The risk premium multiplier (RPM) is derived from the ratio of Total Willingness-to-Pay (TWTP) to Expected Damages. TWTP is given by the difference between income in the absence of a flood and the certainty equivalent $TWTP = M - C_E$, so the ratio to expected damages is:

$$\frac{TWTP}{ED} = \frac{M - C_E}{pD} \qquad\qquad [9.A2.1]$$

The certainty equivalent in the case of iso-elastic preferences is given by:

$$C_E = \left[p(M - D)^{1-\eta} + (1-p)(M)^{1-\eta} \right]^{\frac{1}{1-\eta}}$$

Dividing by M gives;

$$\frac{C_E}{M} = \left[p\left(\frac{M-D}{M}\right)^{1-\eta} + (1-p)\left(\frac{M}{M}\right)^{1-\eta} \right]^{\frac{1}{1-\eta}}$$

$$= \left[1 + p\left((1-z)^{1-\eta} - 1\right) \right]^{\frac{1}{1-\eta}}$$

where $z = D/M$. Expected damages per unit of income is given by $E[D] = pD$, and per unit of total income it is there for $E[D] / M = p.z$. Having divided the numerator and the denominator of [9.A2.1] by M, the RPM can be re-written as in the text:

$$RPM = \frac{TWTP}{ED} = \frac{\left[1 + p\left((1-z)^{1-\eta} - 1\right) \right]^{\frac{1}{1-\eta}}}{p.z} \qquad\qquad [9.A2.2]$$

ANNEX 9.A3

Monte carlo simulation: STATA code and distribution

```
************************************************************************************************

*Start the simulation by assuming iterations and sample size of 1000*¹

************************************************************************************************

forvalues j=1(1)1000 {
```

generate random sample j of 1000 for the discount rate and decommissioning costs

cap drop Discount ***discount factor***

cap drop Decomm ***discount rate***

assume discount factor has a mean parameter of -3.5, and sd of 2

decommissioning costs have mean parameter of 4.5 and sd of 0.7

assume jointly normally distributed with correlation coefficient -0.7,

mkbilogn Discount Decomm, r(-.7) m1(-3.5) s1(2) m2(4.5) s2(.7)

generate discount <u>RATE</u>

cap drop DRate

gen DRate=-ln(Discount)/100

*Simulate Cost benefit analysis using parameters for discount rate and decomm costs**

forvalues i =1(1)1000 {

tempvar DR NB DC DC2 PV

cap drop DC2

gen DC2 =0

local DC= -Decomm in `i'

DC costs kick in after 46 years

replace DC2=`DC' if _n>46

cap drop NB

use netcash flow data from dataset on costs and benefits: Time horizon 1-118 years

gen NB=netcash if _n<118

Replace decommissioning costs with those from the random sample drawn above

replace NB=DC2 if _n>46&_n<118

Use random sample of the discount rates to calculate the preent value

local DR5 = DRate in `i'

replace DFactor=1/((1+`DR5')^yearnumber)

Calculate the PV of NB for each case i for each time period

cap drop PV1

gen PV1 = NB*DFactor if _n<118

sum PV1 if _n<118

Calculate the net present value over time horizon and record

replace NPVsim=r(sum)+1000 in `i'

repeat this 1000 times for each sample j of parameters

}

Take the mean of the i=1000 NPVs and record the PV

sum NPVsim if NPVsim!=0, d

replace PVmean = r(mean) in `j

repeat process 1000 times

}

Figure 9.A3.1. **Distribution of decommissioning costs**

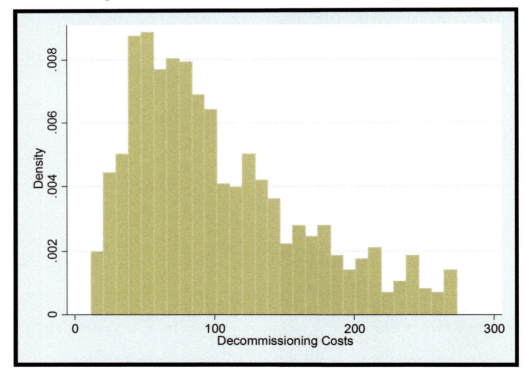

Figure 9.A3.2. **Distribution of the discount rate**

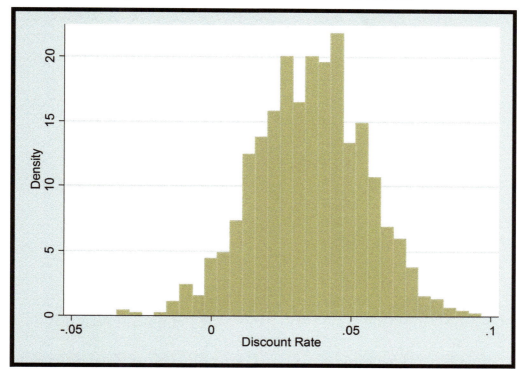

Note

1. Cost and benefit data available on request.

PART II

Chapter 10

Quasi-option value

Another aspect of uncertainty is quasi-option value (QOV) where the notion of precaution is made more formal. Again the starting point here is that costs and benefits are almost never known with certainty. But the insight in QOV is that uncertainty can be reduced in some situations by gathering information. Any decision made now which commits resources or generates costs that cannot subsequently recovered or reversed is an irreversible decision. In this context of both uncertainty and irreversibility it may pay to delay making a decision to commit resources. The value of the information gained from that delay is the QOV. This chapter explains how QOV arises, what it adds to the approaches outlined in Chapter 9 and addresses some of the terminological issues that have arisen in the literature. The concept of QOV can make a significant difference to decision-making especially as it serves as a reminder that such decisions should be based on maximum feasible information about the costs and benefits involved, and that includes "knowing that we do not (currently) know". If this ignorance cannot be resolved then there is nothing to be gained by delay. But if further information can resolve it, then delay can improve the quality of the decision. How large is this gain is an empirical question.

10.1. Some terminology

Intuitively, most people would argue that a decision that involves the irreversible loss of an asset should be made more cautiously than one where the asset is lost but can be recreated if it is later judged that there has been a mistake. The argument seems especially relevant when there is uncertainty about the future benefits of the asset. Environmental assets are good examples of assets about which we have only limited information: for example, many millions of species have not been screened for their full information, no-one is sure what exists in the canopy of rain forests, or in coral reefs. In such contexts, the CBA rules do not seem quite appropriate: benefits are uncertain, their loss may be irreversible and the scale of the loss could be substantial. CBA appears to ignore the combination of uncertainty and irreversibility. There may also be irreversibility on the cost side. We can imagine an investment decision that requires us to commit resources to the investment such that, if conditions change, there is little or nothing to be done to reverse the investment costs. This will be the case, for example, with "dedicated" investment expenditures – expenditures on capital equipment which has only one specific use and which cannot be readily converted to other uses. In the natural resources literature, the example of fishing fleet investments is often cited. So, both benefit streams and investment or policy costs may be irreversible.

In fact the CBA decision rule can be reformulated to take account of the combination of uncertainty and irreversibility, so long as there is also a third element present – the opportunity for learning more, i.e. gathering new information.[1] This involves the notion of *quasi-option value* (QOV), which was introduced and developed by Arrow and Fisher (1974) and Henry (1974). QOV is the value of information gained by delaying a decision to commit to some irreversible action. Confusingly, in the financial and investment literature, a related concept is called *option value*, or *real option value* (Dixit and Pindyck, 1994). Traeger (2014) shows formally that these two concepts – QOV and "real" OV – are distinct but relate to one another in a demonstrable way.[2]

It is important also to distinguish both these concepts from yet another notion of OV in the environmental economics literature. This latter concept is the difference between *option price* and the *expected value of consumer's surplus*. Option price is the maximum willingness to pay for something in a risky world in which one does not know for sure what the outcomes will be. Option price is an *ex ante* concept, i.e. a willingness to pay know for a future state of affairs which is uncertain. This option price can differ from the expected value of the consumer surplus, and the difference is known as option value. Note that option price and option value arises in contexts where individuals are risk-averse. As we shall see, QOV arises in contexts of both risk aversion and risk neutrality. In general:

$$OP = E(CS) + OV$$

Technically, OV can be positive or negative. In other words, using E(CS), which is what CBA does in practice, could introduce an error in CBA estimates. The problem is that OV cannot be estimated without some knowledge of the underlying structure of preferences of the individuals in question (their *utility functions*). In practice, it is unclear that the error is significant, i.e. making assumptions about the nature of preference structures, the evidence suggests that no major errors are introduced by using E(CS) alone.

This notion of OV is not considered any further here. It may be important in some contexts, but the focus is on the QOV = real OV concept since this is more likely to affect the way CBA is conducted.

To summarise:

1. OV in environmental economics tends to refer to the difference between option price and the expected value of consumer's surplus

2. QOV in environmental economics refers to the value of information secured by delaying a decision where outcomes are uncertain, where one or more benefits (or costs) is uncertain, and where there is an opportunity to learn by delay.

3. OV or real OV in the financial literature refers to the value of information secured by delaying uncertain and irreversible investments, although in somewhat different ways.

10.2. A model of QOV[3]

Most expositions of the QOV concept are intricate and involved. Here we attempt to understand the basics.

Consider a forested area which can either be preserved or converted to, say, agriculture. Call the conversion process "development". Let the current period be 0 and the future period be 1, i.e. for simplicity, there are just two periods. It is immediately obvious that if the forest is converted now, period 0, it cannot be preserved in period 0 or in the future period 1. But if the forest is preserved now it still leaves open the choice of converting or preserved in period 1. Suppose that the agricultural development benefits are known with certainty, but the preservation benefits are not known with certainty. This seems fairly realistic – we can be fairly sure what the forest land will produce by way of crops but we still do not know much about the nature and value of ecological services from forests. By converting now, certain benefits of D_0 and D_1 are secured (D_0 and D_1 can be thought of as present values). By preserving now, there is a conservation value of V_0, plus an uncertain conservation value of V_1 in period 1. Keeping the analysis simple, let these uncertain values in period 1 be V_{high} and V_{low}. V_{high} might correspond to some very valuable genetic information in the forest. V_{low} would arise if that information turns out to be very much less valuable. Let the probabilities of V_{high} and V_{low} be p and $(1-p)$ respectively. The expected value (i.e. probability weighted) of preservation benefits (EP) in both periods, arising from the decision to conserve now, is therefore:

$$EP = V_0 + pV_{high} + (1-p)V_{low} \qquad [10.1]$$

A moment's reflection shows that if the forest is converted in 0 the expected value of development benefits will be the same as the certain value of the development benefits:

$$ED = D_0 + D_1 \qquad [10.2]$$

If the decision to preserve or develop has to be taken now, then a simple comparison of [10.1] and [10.2] will suffice. Thus, the forest would be developed if:

$$ED > EP, or, [D_0 + D_1] > [V_0 + pV_{high} + (1-p)V_{low}] \qquad [10.3]$$

This is how most cost-benefit studies would proceed: the expected value of the development (which, in this case, is certain) would be compared with the expected value of preservation. The relevance of QOV is that it changes the cost-benefit rule by allowing for postponing a decision. While political factors may dictate an immediate decision, it is often possible to postpone decisions, i.e. to wait before making the final choice of preservation or development. To see the possible choices, it helps to construct a *decision tree* such as the one shown in Figure 10.1.[4] A decision tree shows each stage of the decision process assuming certain events occur and certain choices are made. In Figure 10.1 the "trunk" of the tree is connected to various "branches" via *decision nodes* (marked as a square) and *probabilistic occurrences* (marked by circles). The analysis begins with a decision node which is either to decide now ('commit') or wait. The decision to commit involves either developing now or preserving now and forever. If the choice is to develop, then the outcome is clearly net benefits of $ED = D_0 + D_1$. If the choice is to preserve then the expected value of benefits is $EP = V_0 + pV_{high} + (1 - p)V_{low}$. In other words, committing now is formally equivalent to the comparison of the two expected values, which we noted was how cost-benefit analysis normally proceeds.

Figure 10.1. **A decision tree**

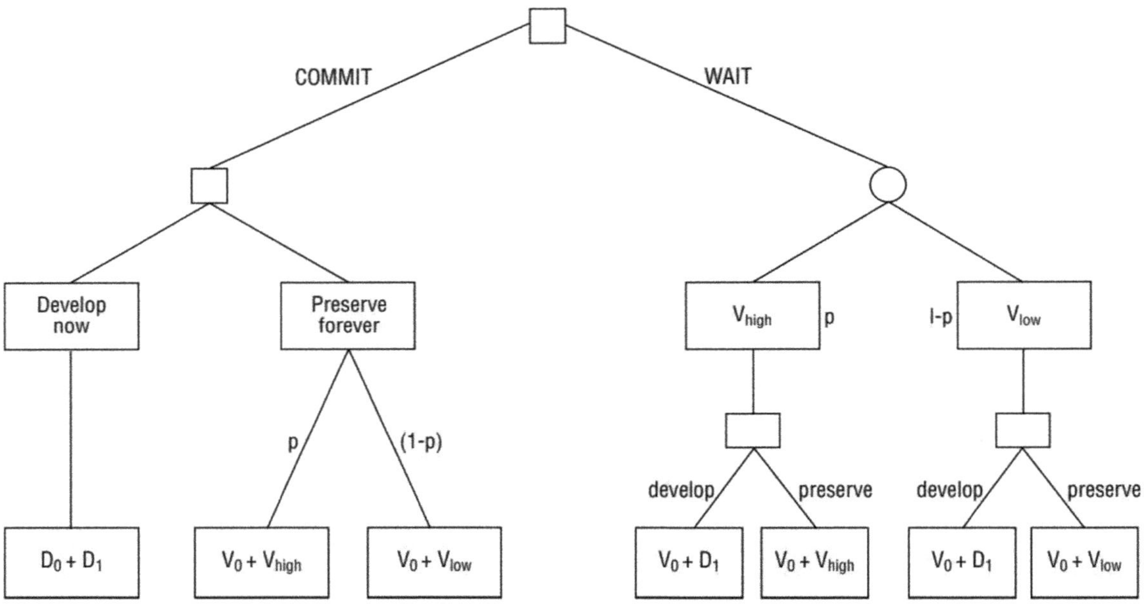

Now consider the decision to wait. This involves moving down the right hand side of Figure 10.1. Waiting means that the decision to develop or preserve is postponed until period 1. Benefits of V_0 this occur in period 0. What happens next depends on whether "high" or "low" preservation benefits occur. Under either scenario, the decision is whether to preserve or develop in period 1. Hence there are 2 x 2 possibilities: if the high preservation benefits occur, developing in 1 will produce a sequence of $V_0 + D_1$ and preserving will produce sequence $V_0 + V_{high}$; if the low preservation benefits occur, the two sequences will be $V_0 + D_1$ and $V_0 + V_{low}$. Notice that we have ruled out the option of development in 0 and preservation in 1. This is because development is regarded as being *irreversible*: once it occurs, it cannot be reversed. This is a useful way of thinking about many problems, but, in practice, there are many gradations of irreversibility. The destruction of a primary forest through agricultural conversion does not, for example, necessarily rule out the recreation of a secondary forest which may well look just like the lost primary forest, although with different ecological features. And one day, the *Jurassic Park* scenario of recreating extinct species may be realisable.

To see which option is best – from the point of view of expected values – it is convenient to attach some hypothetical numbers to the probabilities and outcomes in Figure 10.1. This avoids "getting lost" in the elaborate equations that otherwise emerge.

Let: $V_0 = 20, V_{high} = 300, V_{low} = 40, p = 0.4, (1 - p) = 0.6, D_0 = 60, D_1 = 120$.

Compare waiting and committing. Waiting entails

[a] $V_0 + D_1 = 20 + 120 = 140$, or

[b] $V_0 + V_{high} = 20 + 300 = 320$, or

[c] $V_0 + V_{low} = 20 + 40 = 60$

Committing entails

[d] $D_0 + D_1 = 60 + 120 = 180$, or

[e] $V_0 + V_{high} = 20 + 300 = 320$

[f] $V_0 + V_{low} = 20 + 40 = 60$

Note that outcomes [e] and [f] are the same as outcome [b] and [c].

Which is the best decision? The analysis needed to answer this question is in two stages. Ultimately, the optimal choice requires a comparison of the expected values obtained by committing to immediate development (ED), the expected value obtained by immediately committing to preservation for all time (EP), and the expected value obtained by waiting (EW). However, to calculate EW we must first consider the optimal course of action after we decide to wait. What is the best decision after deciding to wait? It depends on whether V_{high} or V_{low} occurs. If V_{high} occurs, the decision should be *wait and preserve* because 320 > 140, but if V_{low} occurs the decision should be *wait and develop* because this decision produces 140 compared to 60 from wait and preserve. But how do we know if high or low preservation values will emerge? The point about waiting is that it gives us the chance to *find out* which of the two preservation values will occur. Put another way, waiting (postponing) generates *information* and this information can greatly improve the efficiency of decision-making: it reduces the uncertainty of the benefits of preservation. QOV links these important features of decision-making in many environmental contexts:

a) uncertainty

b) irreversibility

c) waiting and learning.

Notice throughout that the decision rule is still based on expected values.

It is often argued that decisions about global warming control should be postponed because the science of global warming is advancing rapidly. Postponing decisions could prevent the irreversible commitment of resources to controlling global warming, resources that could be used perhaps to more social benefit elsewhere. Control decisions could be made later when information has improved. In fact the global warming context is more complex than this. While decisions are postponed, and if warming is a proven fact, then warming increases and any damage associated with it increases. Hence it is necessary to build into the decision tree the likelihood that the waiting option will increase damage if warming turns out to be a genuine phenomenon. There are two irreversibilities here –

unrecoverable costs of action, and irreversible warming. The decision theory approach appears capable of making allowance for this aspect of the decision. The other feature of global warming is that we have very little idea of the probabilities of the outcomes. For example, catastrophic events may be uncertain in their scale, the probability of their occurrence and the time when they might occur. Hence decision making may have to take place in the context of "pure uncertainty", uncertainty associated with no known probabilities. Even here, waiting may enable better information about those probabilities to be revealed, so the QOV framework remains relevant if this is the case.[5] Overall, it should be easy to see that QOV approaches improve the decision-making procedure compared to the simplistic comparison of expected values of costs and benefits in the "no waiting" – i.e. commitment – case. How far such approaches encompass the full range of problems embraced by uncertainty and irreversibility remains open to question, however.

It is possible now to write an expression for the expected value of waiting (EW). This is:

$$EW = V_0 + pV_{high} + (1-p)D_1 \qquad [10.4]$$

To understand this expression, inspect Figure 10.1 again. EW is the value of waiting in period 0 and then choosing the best option in period 1. Waiting clearly secures V_0 in period 0. The numerical example tells us that $V_{high} > D_1 > V_{low}$. V_1 is random – it can be "high" or "low" – and is the value of preservation in period 1. If high preservation values occur we opt for preservation because $D_1 < V_{high}$. If "low" preservation values occur, we develop anyway since $D_1 > V_{low}$. is the weighted average of the high preservation value and the development value: $pV_{high} + (1-p)D_1$ which, when added to V_0 in period 0 gives the expected value of waiting shown in [10.4].

In terms of the numerical values in the hypothetical example, we have:

$$EW = 20 + 0.4(320) + 0.6(140) = 232$$

The value for EW(232) is higher than the value for

$$EP = V_0 + pV_{high} + (1-p)V_{low} = 20 + 0.4(320) + 0.6(40) = 172.$$

Hence, in this example, EW > EP. In fact, it is always better to wait than to commit to preservation forever, so long as $D_1 > V_{low}$. This is because by waiting one can always secure the value of EP since waiting involves preservation in period 0 and this leaves open the option of preserving in period 1. Thus waiting allows a flexible choice: preserve in period 0 and preserve in period 1, and preserve in period 0 and develop in period 1.

The previous argument establishes that, under the conditions stipulated, it is better to wait than commit forever to preservation. What of waiting versus outright development? This requires that we compare EW with ED. We know that $EW = 232$ and $ED = D_0 + D_1 = 180$, so the expected value of waiting exceeds the expected value of outright development.

There are now two "rules" by which development and preservation can be compared. The first emerges from the previous analysis, the second from the conventional cost-benefit approach. Immediate development is justified if either ED > EW or ED > EP. As long as EW > EP, the former rule will be harder for an advocate of development to meet. *Thus, allowing for waiting makes the irreversible development option more difficult to achieve* (recall that "conventional" CBA would simply compare ED and EP).

The final stages of the analysis permit us to identify the meaning of QOV more precisely. First, we rewrite EW as:

$$EW = V_0 + EV_1 + E\max(D_1 - V_1, 0) = EP + E\max[D_1 - V_1, 0] \qquad [10.5]$$

The proof of this is shown in the Annex to this chapter. The term $E\max(D_1 - V_1, 0)$ is to read as follows: it is the expected value of the maximum of $D_1 - V_1$ and 0 as seen from the standpoint of period 0. So, if $D_1 - V_1$ exceeds zero, the expected value of this is entered into equation [10.5] (recall that we do not know V_1 when in period 0, so it is random. We do know it when we move to period 1).

The condition for developing the land immediately was that $ED > EW$ and we observed that this was a stricter condition than simply comparing the two expected values of development and preservation, as would be the case in the conventional cost-benefit case. We can rewrite the condition $ED > EW$ in terms of the expression for EW in [10.5], so that development immediately is only justified if:

$$(D_1 + D_2) > EP + E\max(D_1 - V_1, 0) \tag{10.6}$$

In slightly different form, this is the equation derived in Arrow and Fisher (1994).

Since a lot of derivation has been presented, it is well to summarise the basic finding:

1. "Conventional" cost-benefit analysis would follow a rule that, for development to be justified, $ED > EP$;

2. The "options" approach requires a stricter rule, namely that $ED > EW$

3. EW and EP differ by an amount $E\max(D_1 - V_1, 0)$

4. So EP *understates* the "true" value of preservation by the amount $E\max(D_1 - V_1, 0)$

How should QOV be interpreted? In some analyses QOV would be identified with the last expression above – i.e. $E\max(D_1 - V_1, 0)$. But it is more precise to think of QOV as the increase in expected value of benefits from waiting. The expression for this would be:

$$QOV = EW - \max(ED, EP) \tag{10.7}$$

That is, QOV is the difference between the expected value of waiting and whichever is the larger of ED and EP. Equation [10.5] implies that if $ED < EP$ then QOV and $E\max(D_1 - V_1, 0)$ are the same. But if, as in the example above, $ED > EP$ then QOV is *less* than $E\max(D_1 - V_1, 0)$.

10.3. How large is QOV?

In some ways, asking about the "size" of QOV is not very sensible. What matters is whether consideration of waiting and learning will change the nature of the decision made to commit resources to some policy or project. If that process results in a changed decision relative to the "baseline" of making decisions as if delay was not an option, then QOV may be large relative to the resources committed to the decision. It is in this sense that the financial literature argues that what we have called QOV, and what in that literature is known as the value of an option[6], can be large (Dixit and Pindyck, 1995). In the financial literature, investing irreversibly "kills" the option because the decision cannot be reversed and the option of waiting for new information is also forgone. As a result:

This lost option value is an opportunity cost that must be included as part of the cost of the investment (Dixit and Pindyck, 1994, p. 6).

Finding examples of estimated QOV in environmental economics applications is far harder. Box 10.1 outlines one study of forest conversion. Wesseler (2000) has suggested that QOV has a positive value in the context of postponing the introduction of genetically modified farm crops in Europe.

The discussion should be sufficient to underline an important feature of QOV: *it is not a component of total economic value (TEV)*. Rather, it is a reminder that decisions should be

---

Box 10.1. **The empirics of quasi option value**

It is not hard to envisage a range of environmental and resource concerns in which "quasi option value" (QOV) is both relevant and potentially significant. A natural question to ask then is the extent to which QOV can be demonstrated to be empirically important. A handful of studies have sought to answer this practical question. One early example was Bulte et al. (2002) for tropical forests in Costa Rica. Their empirical estimate of QOV illustrates that uncertainty about forest values justifies more forest conservation than in the case where values are known with certainty. Nevertheless, the authors also find that QOV turns out to be considerably less empirically important for the forest conservation/agricultural conversion decision than sorting out more conventional valuation issues, such as valuing global externalities and making judgements about the rising relative valuation of ever more scarce forestland.

Unfortunately, there seems to be a lack of evidence to consider further whether this is a general finding or not (although it is consistent with an even earlier result in Albers et al., 1996). Other studies have sought to throw light on the empirical significance of QOV (or related concepts) by looking how this influences people's willingness to pay (WTP) for environmental improvements both in theory and by testing this in practice. For example, Zhao and Kling (2009) examine the conceptual consequences of acknowledging that real world policy settings are often dynamic in the sense that there is potential to delay a decision (e.g. a policy to deliver an environmental improvement) and learn about the future. The point is that this opportunity for learning is a tangible characteristic of the decision of how much a person would be willing to pay. Specifically, enjoying the improvement now provides people with a benefit sooner rather than later but it also entails what Zhao and Kling denote as a "commitment cost": i.e. a parallel concept to QOV in this WTP application of the theory. Put another way, people sacrifice the ability to learn about whether the policy change is worthwhile to them or not. The practical consequence of this is a prediction about WTP. For example, in a stated preference survey, asking people for their WTP to receive this environmental improvement sooner rather than later – and where there is uncertainty and the potential for learning – the amount elicited implicitly will reflect a "discount" reflecting the respondent's valuation of the "commitment cost". Put another way, total WTP for this policy change will be lower than in the case where there is no scope for learning; the reason being that in the context of learning there is a lost opportunity that the respondent, in effect, is being asked to give up.

Teasing out this component of WTP is a useful means of assessing the extent to which QOV is important to people in different policy settings. Corrigan et al. (2008) use contingent valuation (or CV, see Chapter 4) to do just this for the case of local water quality improvements in Clear Lake, Iowa in the USA. What this application did is examine the (implied) compensation that respondents require in order to consume the environmental good now, rather than delay this decision for a further year in order to learn more about the consumption value of specified improvements at Clear Lake. In other words, this was a test of whether people were willing to pay less to enact water quality improvements now given that it involves sacrificing this learning opportunity. Notwithstanding a rather small sample (N=158), the results of this study indicate that the "commitment cost" is more than 75% of total (average) WTP for options to improve water quality at Clear Lake.

Strazzera et al. (2010), in a similar vein, use a discrete choice experiment (DCE, see Chapter 5) to assess the value that respondents, drawn from residents of an urban area on the island of Sardinia in Italy, place on improvements to a nearby coastal wetland. Where respondents were told that there exist opportunities for further learning about the "scientific" and "cultural" value of the wetland, they appear to place a significant premium on such options in the choice sets with which they were confronted. That is, WTP is higher for those wetland improvement options which take a cautious approach and seek to avoid irreversible consequences of acting "now" without further information about the consequences of this.

---

made rationally. Despite this, QOV often does appear in the literature as if it is a component of TEV. This is not correct. Freeman et al. (2013) sums it up well:

> Quasi-option value is not a component of the values individuals attach to resource changes. Even if individuals' utility functions were known, quasi-option value could not

be estimated separately and added into a benefit-cost equation. Quasi-option value is a benefit of adopting better decision-making procedures. Its magnitude can only be revealed by comparing two strategies where one of the strategies involves optimal sequential decision making to take advantage of information obtained by delaying irreversible resource commitments. The decision maker who knows how to use an optimal sequential decision making strategy has no reason to calculate quasi-option value. The calculation would be redundant because the best decision is already known. (pp. 250-1).

10.4. Conclusions

The notion of quasi option value was introduced in the environmental economics literature some three decades ago. In parallel, financial economists developed the notion of "option value". Somewhat confusingly, environmental economists also developed a concept of option value that was unlinked to either QOV or the OV of the financial literature. In the end, QOV was recognised as being the same as the financial literature's OV.

QOV is not a separate category of economic value. Rather it is the difference between the net benefits of making an optimal decision and one that is not optimal because it ignores the gains that may be made by delaying a decision and learning during the period of delay. Usually, QOV arises in the context of irreversibility. But it can only emerge if there is uncertainty which can be resolved by learning. If the potential to learn is not there, QOV cannot arise.

Can QOV make a significant difference to decision-making? Potentially, yes. It is there to remind us that decisions should be made on the basis of maximum feasible information about the costs and benefits involved, and that includes "knowing that we do not know". If this ignorance cannot be resolved then nothing is to be gained by delay. But if information can resolve it, then delay can improve the quality of the decision. How large the gain is from this process is essentially an empirical question since QOV is the difference in the net benefits of an optimal decision and a less than optimal one. The financial literature suggests that this difference can be large relative to the scale of resources being committed to a decision. Further study is needed in the environmental context to see if similar results hold. Examples to date are limited.

Notes

1. Which is the more important of these features is open to debate. Some have argued that it is uncertainty and the opportunity for learning that matter most and that irreversibility is a limited consequence. Nonetheless, the literature has generally proceeded on the basis of there being irreversibility in either the commitment of resources or some of the benefits forgone.

2. Specifically, Traeger (2014) notes that QOV represents the value of learning if a project is postponed and that "real" OV is the net value from postponing a project when there is learning, with slightly different implications for going about changing the standard net present value rule in CBA.

3. This section has been adapted from material kindly supplied by Dr. Joseph Swierzbinski of the Department of Economics, University College London and largely comprises a simplification of the original article by Arrow and Fisher (1974).

4. Decision trees are one of the basic constructs of *decision analysis* (e.g. see Merkhofer, 1987).

5. Dixit and Pindyck (1994, pp. 395-6) advocated the use of their "real options" approach to global warming policy evaluation. For an application, see Ulph and Ulph (1997).

6. There are also analogies with financial call options in the financial literature – see Dixit and Pindyck (1994).

References

Arrow, K. and A. Fisher (1974), "Environmental preservation, uncertainty and irreversibility", *Quarterly Journal of Economics*, Vol. 88, pp. 312-319, *https://doi.org/10.2307/1883074*.

Bulte, E., M. Joenje and H. Jansen (2000), "Is there too much or too little forest in the Atlantic Zone of Costa Rica?" *Canadian Journal of Forest Research*, Vol. 30, pp. 495-506.

Bulte, E. et al. (2002), "Forest conservation in Costa Rica when nonuse benefits are uncertain and rising", *American Journal of Agricultural Economics*, Vol. 84 (1), pp. 150-160, *https://doi.org/10.1111/1467-8276.00249*.

Corrigan, J.R., C.L. Kling and J. Zhao (2008), "Willingness to pay and the cost of commitment: An empirical specification and test", *Environmental and Resource Economics*, Vol. 40, pp. 285-298, *https://doi.org/10.1007/s10640-007-9153-0*.

Dixit, A. and R. Pindyck (1994), *Investment Under Uncertainty*, Princeton University Press, Princeton.

Dixit, A. and R. Pindyck (1995), "The options approach to capital investment", *Harvard Business Review*, May-June, pp.105-155, *https://hbr.org/1995/05/the-options-approach-to-capital-investment*.

Freeman, A.M. III. et al. (2003), *The Measurement of Environmental and Resource Values*, 3rd edition, Resources for the Future, Washington, DC.

Henry, C. (1974), "Investment decision under uncertainty: The irreversibility effect", *American Economic Review*, Vol. 64 (6), pp. 1006-12, *www.jstor.org/stable/1815248*.

Merkhofer, M. (1987), *Decision Science and Social Risk Management: A Comparative Evaulation of Cost Benefit Analysis, Decision Analysis and Other Formal Decision-aiding Approaches*, D. Reidel, Boston.

Strazzera, E., E. Cherchi and S. Ferrini (2010), "Assessment of regeneration projects in urban areas of environmental interest: A stated choice approach to estimate use and quasi-option values", *Environment and Planning A*, Vol. 42, pp. 452-468, *https://doi.org/10.1068/a4213*.

Traeger, C.P. (2014), "On option values in environmental and resource economics", *Resource and Energy Economics*, Vol. 37, pp. 242-252, *http://dx.doi.org/10.1016/j.reseneeco.2014.03.001*.

Ulph, A. and D. Ulph (1997), "Global warming, irreversibility and learning", *Economic Journal*, Vol. 197, pp. 646-650, *http://dx.doi.org/10.1111/j.1468-0297.1997.tb00031.x*.

Wesseler, J. (2000), "Temporal uncertainty and irreversibility: A theoretical framework for the decision to approve the release of transgenic crops", in W. Lesser (ed.). *Transitions in Agbiotech: Economics of Strategy and Policy*, Food Marketing Policy Centre, Connecticut.

Zhao, J. and C. Kling (2009), "Welfare measures when agents can learn: a unifying theory", *Economic Journal*, Vol. 119(540), pp. 1560-1585, *http://dx.doi.org/10.1111/j.1468-0297.2009.02272.x*.

ANNEX 10.A1

Deriving the expected value of waiting

Equation [10.5] in the text was written as

$$EW = V_0 + EV_1 + E\max(D_1 - V_1, 0) = EP + E\max[D_1 - V_1, 0] \qquad [10.A1.1]$$

This is derived from the first expression for EW (equation [10.4] in the text) as follows:

$$EW = V_0 + pV_{high} + (1-p)D_1 \qquad [10.A1.2]$$

Add $(1-p)V_{low}$ and then subtract it from [10.A1.2] to give

$$EW = V_0 + pV_{high} + (1-p)V_{low} + (1-p)(D_1 - V_{low}) \qquad [10.A1.3]$$

or

$$EW = EP + (1-p)(D_1 - V_{low}) \qquad [10.A1.4]$$

High preservation benefits occur in period 1 with a probability of p, so the maximum of $D_1 - V_1$ and 0 is 0 since the development value in period 1 is below the high preservation value. Low preservation benefits in period 1 occur with a probability (1-p) and the maximum of $D_1 - V_1$ and 0 is then $D_1 - V_{low}$ since the development value exceeds the low preservation value. Hence:

$$E\max(D_1 - V_1, 0) = (1-p)(D_1 - V_{low}) + p.0 = (1-p)(D_1 - V_{low}, 0) \qquad [10.A1.5]$$

Hence [A10.4] can be written:

$$EW = EP + E\max(D_1 - V_1, 0) \qquad [10.A1.6]$$

which is equation [10.5] in the main text.

PART II

Chapter 11

Distribution and cost-benefit analysis

Conventional CBA for the most part continues to regard (intra-generational) distributional or equity concerns as having little or no place in making its recommendations about policy formulation or investment projects. Identifying this oversight is one thing, responding to it is more controversial especially where this involves weighting costs and benefits according to equity criteria. But this usefully might just involve simply identifying the costs and benefits of individuals and groups on the basis of differences in the characteristic of interest. Perhaps this sounds unambitious but given the starting position (where this seldom happens), more routine cataloguing of this type surely would be useful. Moreover, this could involve not only cataloguing how costs and benefits are distributed across people but also how particular environmental goods and bads (such as air quality, unwanted land uses and so on) are distributed. One catalyst almost certainly could be demand from policy makers. That is, the observation that too much practical CBA neglects distributional concerns may not just be a supply problem (a single-minded focus of cost-benefit practitioners on efficiency), it is also likely to be an issue about demand: perhaps, for example, policy makers perhaps have not required this information in the terms of reference guiding that practical work. Taking this further might involve weighting costs and benefits and scrutinising proposals on the basis of a distributional cost-benefit test. While a long-standing analytical option, there is no easy answer to the equally long-standing question about what value these weights should take. Nevertheless, exploring this question has led to some interesting empirical insights about inequality aversion generally and for specific goods and bads (such as health risks).

11.1. Introduction

Practical cost-benefit analysis (CBA) is concerned (primarily) with efficiency in allocation of economic resources. That is, it recommends actions with benefits greater than costs, where these monetary net benefits reflect the willingness to pay (or accept) that affected people have for various impacts of the proposal. Of course, actual decisions will not solely be based on efficiency. For example, project or policy selection and design may give rise to questions about the "rightness" of a given action or the social desirability of a particular distribution of benefits and costs.

Economic appraisal is not silent on those issues. There exists long-standing and elaborate guidance on incorporating some of these distributional concerns in CBA. How far this advice is actually heeded is another matter, however. For example, in some OECD member states, including estimates of the distribution in CBA across transport investments, energy investments, new policy assessments as well as *ex post* assessments, is done compulsorily but in other members it is less frequent (see Chapter 16). This does not mean that distributional effects are ignored altogether where CBA is done. More likely these are dealt with in other ways, explicitly or otherwise.

A specific example is the economic appraisal that preceded the introduction of the London Congestion Charge (LCC). Under original proposals for the LCC, from February 2003, motorists would pay a uniform charge to enter the congestion charge zone around central London during (weekday) designated peak hours. Certain groups were to be exempted or to face a lower charge, depending on whether they were residents or worked in particular occupations. The charge revenues collected were to be reinvested in London's bus services. Each of these provisions had a distributional rationale, but plausibly entailed some sacrifice in efficiency as, for example, those groups enjoying exemptions from the charge would still treat road-use as being "free" at the point of access.

Presumably London's decision makers reasoned that this sacrifice was worth it if it allayed at least some of the public's concerns about the distributional impacts of the LCC. However, the point here is that, insofar as CBA was concerned, these distributional considerations were (it appears) a "fait accompli'. In other words, the official CBA of this scheme carried out on behalf of the Greater London Authority (GLA) – the body responsible for administering the LCC – was conducted on an option which already had these distributional decisions built into it. One response might be to consider this the natural order of things. That is, distributional concerns were dealt with elsewhere in the impact assessment process, leaving CBA to deal with what is its core activity. However, if practical CBA were better able to reflect concerns about distribution then it too would have an obviously clearer contribution to such earlier deliberations about options.

This is the question considered in this chapter. That is, how distributional implications of projects and policies reasonably can be accommodated within environmental cost-benefit appraisals. This, in turn, reflects an assertion, not necessarily shared by all cost-benefit practitioners, for appraisals to be more sensitive to concerns about distributional justice or equity. (See also Chapters 8 and 12 for a discussion of equity between generations in the context of CBA.) The emphasis is on how this might be done in practice. However, there is also a need for principles and theory to inform this pragmatic approach. And while the onus is on practitioners to advance this agenda, so too is there an onus on decision-makers to require this information; that is, it is about demand as well as supply.

11.2. Equity and CBA

Projects and policies with environmental impacts inevitably have distributional consequences. Indeed, for a great many environmental policies this is the point in that these interventions work by favouring (relative to the status quo) victims of pollution at the expense of polluters. Typically, the economic justification for these interventions is couched in terms of their efficiency (in the sense of giving rise to higher overall economic gains for society). However, this application of the polluter pays principle (e.g. OECD, 1975) owes as much to the perceived desirable distributional consequences of assigning property rights to the victims of pollution or natural capital damage.

Clearly, the relationship between polluter and victim is only one dimension of difference between people affected by project or policy proposals. Polluters might be households or economic producers (such as firms[1]), rich and poor, young and old, as well as vulnerable (in some other way) or otherwise. What is to be distributed between these people or institutions is also of considerable importance given that it can help to define differences in which are thought to be relevant. This could include well-being generally as well as its particular component parts, although it might instead refer to some other set of concepts such as "functionings" and "capabilities" (Kriström, 2005, Decancq et al., 2014).

In the context of economic appraisal, a starting point for this concern presumably is how the *net* benefits are distributed between those affected by a proposed action. A simple illustration is as follows. Assume there are just two individuals in society, this time denoted by R and P, affected by a project and that the net benefit to each individual (R and P) of some environmentally improving project is:

- Individual R: +EUR 200
- Individual P: -EUR 100

The total net benefit of the project is EUR 100; therefore, the project is worthwhile in the sense that it increases economic efficiency. These gains, however, are unevenly distributed. The question is whether this matters.

Much of practical CBA arguably takes the view that this outcome does not matter; that is, Kaldor-Hicks criterion can be invoked. As long as winners can *potentially* compensate the losers then all is well. That is, it makes sense to select proposals so as to maximise the size of economic pie that our society here can enjoy. If, for some reason, there were distributional concerns then policy makers could worry separately about how this pie is divided, using alternative redistributive policy instruments at their disposal. Perhaps, however, it is thought that – in the round – net losers of such a project will be net winners for efficient projects implemented elsewhere. In this case, worrying too much about one decision – in isolation – is a mistake. Alternatively, perhaps distribution is considered to be optimal (in terms of its implications for social welfare). In this case, there is nothing to be gained by shuffling economic resources from one person to another to achieve a better distribution (one that achieves more in terms of social welfare).

The case for arguing that such differences do matter might begin by considering the possible problems with these aforementioned perspectives. In practice, however, efficiency and equity might not be as straightforwardly separated as this standard approach implies. If, for example, compensation is not really feasible to sort out through other policy instruments then project selection (or design) arguably, and within reason, should not be ruled out as a way of addressing society's distributional goals. Whether gains and losses ultimately do even out is another matter (Persky, 2001) – although presumably, an interim conclusion is that the case for believing in such a coincidence act is doubtful, while not impossible. If distribution is not optimal – e.g. maybe there are political or administrative obstacles to introducing the requisite measures – there is a further rationale for worrying about distributional impacts.

Even so, it is not altogether clear exactly to do to reflect distributional concern in an economic appraisal. While the above example is simplicity itself, the possible answers to this can get complicated very quickly. For example, what if individual P – the net loser – is poor relative to the net beneficiary of this project? In other words, the project worsens an already unequal distribution of income or wealth. Presumably, this might temper an otherwise positive interpretation of the net worth of the project. But what if also P is also a polluter and R is vulnerable and its gains reflect how he or she benefits from the environmental improvement. How might this alter again judgements about the proposal, and more importantly, what can a cost-benefit practitioner do about it?

11.3. Analysing the distributional impacts of projects within a cost-benefit framework

Various proposals exist about how to bring the distributional consequences of projects and policies within the ambit of cost-benefit appraisals. One suggestion, which is followed in this chapter, is to view these proposals as a hierarchy necessitating ever more explicit judgement, on the part of the cost-benefit analyst, about the social desirability of possible distributional outcomes. At the heart of any such judgement lies a standpoint or appeal to evidence about how society ought to distribute well-being, income, wealth or some more specific good such as environmental quality.

Kriström (2005) has shown how these proposals can be thought of as a hierarchy of options. These include: 1) identifying and cataloguing how project-related costs and benefits are distributed, in physical units but perhaps also in monetary terms; 2) calculating *implicit* distributional weights: e.g. if a project generates net aggregate losses but net gains are enjoyed by a group that society is particularly worried about, what weight would need to be assigned to these gains such that the project was deemed to have a positive social value?; and lastly, 3) re-calculating the project's net benefit based on assigning *explicit* distributional weights to the benefits received and costs incurred by different societal groups.

Important to all these stages is the consideration of distributional consequences alongside (or within) standard appraisal procedures. In doing so, information can also be provided about the balance (or implied trade-off) between maximising the overall benefits of an intervention and directing interventions towards certain groups. Activities supported in the lower (initial) reaches of this hierarchy are less contentious in that these do not attempt to alter the main recommendation of a CBA. Rather what is done is augment that rule with further information, in effect, provided as an adjunct to a CBA. Towards the top of this hierarchy, however, the decision-rule itself is altered.

11.3.1. Identifying distributional impacts

CBA is frequently criticised as being pre-occupied with a project's or policy's "bottom-line" in the form of its net social benefits. Assuming, for the moment, that this criticism is justified, it is problematic for a variety of reasons, including that it abstracts from information that policy makers worry about: namely, how policy impacts are distributed. This disaggregated information might be valuable for a number of counts. There may be pragmatic reasons for knowing which groups win and which groups lose from implementing the project. Perhaps it is the case the project's losers are in a position to affect the project's success or failure (in the sense of net benefits being realised). But there are also analytical frameworks that are both relevant to a social decision and can be usefully illustrated using such information. This might be the established theory underpinning CBA, based on social welfare functions describing how (changes in) consumption translates in social well-being. But it may be a distinct tradition drawing on other disciplinary or policy perspectives as well perhaps taking as its inspiration the idea of "value plurality" discussed in Chapter 2.

For example, the environmental justice movement in the United States has argued that unwanted or hazardous land-uses (such as waste disposal and transfer facilities) are unfairly or inequitably distributed: i.e. located predominately in areas, which are relatively highly populated by low-income groups or particular ethnic groups. The environmental justice perspective has been broadened to a number of other environmental burdens both within and across countries (e.g. urban air pollution, lack of access to green space and vulnerability to climate change) (see, for example, Walker, 2012). This does have relevance for economic appraisal, based as it is on rationing economic resources to those projects and policies where willingness to pay is highest, whereas the contribution of environmental justice has been to emphasise how benefits and burdens are distributed amongst different socioeconomic or ethnic groups and whether the processes that have led to this distribution can be judged to be fair.

This suggests that, at a minimum, one useful element of a CBA would be the provision of detailed information about distributional impacts. Put this way, there is no requirement that the cost-benefit analyst makes a judgement about the empirical evidence as regards how to weight the impacts enjoyed or suffered by different groups. It requires only that these be documented to the extent that the data and other resources permit. How these distributional consequences might translate into an assessment of the social value of the project can be left to the political process. Of course, it would be naïve to assume that value judgements are wholly eliminated. For example, a decision must be made at some point, about which societal groups are to be described. However, as later sections will illustrate, there is less need for tricky judgements relative to other analytical options in the hierarchy of distributional CBA.

There may be practical difficulties in identifying "winners" and "losers" and their incomes and/or some other aspect of their relative position in society in sufficient detail. Of course, without this basic building block, the more ambitious analysis of distributional concerns (described below) cannot be contemplated either. This problem is likely to be a matter of degree and it is just as likely that many cost-benefit appraisals do not generate these data simply because they are not compelled to do so rather than because of the unfeasibility of the task. It is interesting that much of modern benefit assessment in the form of stated preference methods such as the contingent valuation method (Chapter 3) already may contain a wealth of data about the distribution of non-market impacts (Kriström, 2003).

That is, these studies typically elicit a wealth of information about respondent's demographic and socio-economic characteristics as well as detailed data about, for example, uses and experiences of an environmental good under consideration. Such data could provide valuable insights into how certain project impacts are distributed.

Although not necessarily incorporated within economic appraisals, empirical evidence exists about the way in which a growing number of environmental outcomes (but particularly, air quality) are distributed amongst different societal groups. Studies by Pearce et al. (2011) and Ribeiro et al. (2015) provide similar types of analysis for respectively New Zealand and Portugal. In a similar vein, a study by Defra (2006) for the UK, looked at how a range of air pollutants are distributed including PM_{10}, NO_2, SO_2 and (ground-level) O_3. A measure of multiple deprivation (including income, health and housing) was the object of interest, in that study, in terms of characterising the socioeconomic status of those affected by differential air quality.

A number of interesting findings and nuances emerge from the subsequent mapping of air quality levels and this deprivation index. Exposure to lower ambient air quality is influenced by proximity to urban areas and roads in particular. And, in general, the concerns of those who assert that worse environmental outcomes are associated with higher levels of deprivation appear to be confirmed, especially for PM_{10}. However, in some cases, the resulting socioeconomic distributional outcome is one where those most exposed are those who are the least and the most disadvantaged (i.e. respectively those households in the bottom decile and the top decile of the deprivation index). In other words, geographical detail appears to be important with different areas of the country experiencing a somewhat different relationship between exposure to air pollution and deprivation. Presumably, this has implications for thinking through the distributional consequences of proposed policy interventions.

Day and Maddison (2015) suggest that cost-benefit practitioners could usefully respond to these environmental justice concerns. For example, they note the potential for using evidence about the way in which (air) pollution burdens are distributed by (household) income. These could be summarised in a Gini-coefficient, perhaps calculated for a policy proposal (and compared with the status quo). Examples of this work can be found in the water resource literature (via the so-called "Water Gini"; see, for example, Wang et al., 2012; Seekel et al., 2011). Clearly, however, there are multiple dimensions to inequality and, to be meaningful, such summaries of distribution also need to explicitly account for this (e.g. by age, vulnerability, and so on).

Another manifestation of distributional concern is in judgements about the affordability of policies for households. Practical examples here include the use of CBA in the implementation of environmental Directives amongst relatively new (and lower-income) entrants to the European Union (e.g. European Commission, 2008). This is often codified in (seemingly arbitrary) rules of thumb about when the proportion of income that households pay becomes unaffordable for a particular good (such as water supply or waste collection). Such concerns, however, may conflict with other considerations, such as the polluter pays principle or (where it is considered appropriate) full cost recovery for projects such as waste management. So while affordability is clearly a concern, there is a risk created if this is addressed by widening any gap between project revenues and project costs through setting tariffs too low.

Potential also exists, of course, for greater attention to the distributional impacts in other standard non-market valuation methods of the type discussed in earlier Chapters (see 3-7).

Loomis (2011) illustrates this potential with reference to two empirical studies of non-market values from the United States. Specifically, the author discusses the results from a CV study of willingness to pay (WTP) to low flow alleviation in a river in Colorado in the United States from a distributional perspective. This leads to some interesting (and additional) insights. Benefits do not necessarily vary much with income levels of respondents. But while project selection is not being driven by a "bias" towards the disproportionately high WTP of those with high-income, on the cost side there is concern dependent, of course, on how the improvement is financed. Clearly this is important information for the implementing authority to know.

A further example that Loomis discusses is a hedonic price study in an area of Los Angeles again in the United States. Specifically, the policy measures looked at what are the effects on property values of actions that would decrease the risks of forest fires. This policy, it appears, is skewed towards benefiting the asset values of homes owned by higher income households as well as particular ethnic groups (i.e. predominately White and Hispanic neighbourhoods). Again the issue here is how to use this information on how benefits are distributed to frame policy discussion about how proposals should be financed. Perhaps the most important take-home message from both of these examples is that distributional insights could be garnered from the growing empirical record about environmental valuation. That this potential remains largely unrealised is a missed opportunity.

In a very different context, a relatively well-established finding is that *particular* groups appear to be vulnerable to the loss of ecosystem services. Specifically, a number of studies have highlighted the dependence (of at least some portion) of the rural poor in the developing world on services provided by nature. Ten Brink et al. (2011) term this the "GDP of the poor" although its antecedents can be traced to previous empirical studies of livelihoods including Jodha (1986) and Vedeld et al. (2004). These studies have been important in making plainer the contribution of ecosystems to the economic well-being of such communities, something which is typically only partially reflected in official statistics, if at all.

11.3.2. Implicit distributional weights

Should cost-benefit appraisals limit the analysis of distributional issues to carefully identifying and cataloguing how costs and benefits are distributed? Broadly speaking there are two further options. Both are premised on thinking about how distributional information might be used by policy makers but in a way that is comparable with the standard net benefit rule. This entails revising the CBA recommendation on the basis of the adjusted or distributionally weighted net benefit.

One long-standing way of being explicit about such distributional judgements in CBA is by writing the earlier simple two-person cost-benefit problem as follows: $NB = a_R NB_R + a_P NB_P$, where a weight (a_i) is assigned to each of the parties" costs and benefits. An important feature of conventional CBA becomes apparent. It assumes that $a_1 = a_2 = 1$; that is, weights of unity are assigned to the net benefits of individuals regardless of who it is that receives a unit of benefit or suffers a unit of cost.

What do these weights represent? Essentially, a_i, can be interpreted as providing a numerical description about the preferences of society regarding distributional outcomes. This might be based on an introspective reflection on how say changes in consumption translate into higher levels of well-being for individuals given how affluent they are prior to this change. It might be based on a (related or distinct) standpoint regarding equity for society. (See the Annex to this Chapter for a simple elaboration of this, within the cost-benefit framework.)

The distributional net benefit criterion is that a project should go ahead if the sum of distributional weighted net benefits is at least as great as zero. Not surprisingly, much of the controversy about distributional weighting surrounds debates about the relative merits of using projects in this way as well as the problems entailed in surmising what society's distributional goals are. It is not difficult to imagine that there might exist some trepidation about launching into distributional analysis of this sort, given these difficulties and debates.

A convenient way around this controversy – at least as an interim stage – is to ask instead what set of weights would be required to "tip the balance" between recommending that the project go-ahead (i.e. positive total NB) or not go-ahead (i.e. negative total NB) (Gramlich, 1990; Kriström and Kanninen, 1993)? i.e. $0 = NB = NB_R + a_p NB_p \Rightarrow a_P* = \dfrac{NB_R}{NB_P}$. Hence, this is an implicit distributional test, as it does not require that weights (a_i) be imputed directly. Rather it asks, for $a_R = 1$ and setting NB=0, how large would the implicit weight a_P* need to be to affect the decision about the social worth of the project? For the simple example above, the answer is "2": i.e. $a_P* = \dfrac{NB_R}{NB_P} = \dfrac{200}{100}$.

Once this "tipping point" is known, what can be done with this information? Perhaps most importantly, it could be asked whether assigning this weight (or these weights) is justified, perhaps in the sense of whether or not it is commensurate with society's preferences or what is known about political acceptability. The answer could depend, in this simple example, on the relative income difference between the two individuals as well as the distance that each is from recognised thresholds, such as poverty levels or average income. The catch is that this question arguably cannot be answered properly unless one has recourse to reliable and direct estimates of a_P. Yet, the point of this implicit weighting approach is to allow the cost-benefit analyst to avoid these potentially deep waters. Nevertheless, implicit weights at least can be compared with the range of estimates in the literature, which is discussed in Section 11.3.3 below.

Gramlich (1990) notes a further use of the data previously discussed. Project selection or design is only one of many redistributive mechanisms available to governments. Moreover, critics of distributional CBA, such as Harberger, have argued that it must be asked whether these alternative measures are generally a less socially wasteful means of addressing distributional concerns. For example, this would certainly be true if, say, some fiscal mechanism could costlessly redistribute e.g. income. In such instances, it would always be desirable to shelve inefficient but equitable projects and address distributional disparities using this other redistribution mechanism. Needless to say, any redistributive scheme is inefficient to a greater or lesser extent.[2] However, this emphasis on "extent" is important. One issue then is to compare, as a means of addressing distributional concerns, project selection or design with (practical) alternatives, such as direct ways of transferring incomes across individuals (perhaps via the tax system) or other public programmes, which explicitly focus on, say, raising low incomes.

Assuming that there is information about how inefficient various practical and alternative redistributive mechanisms are, then this sets an upper bound on how much inefficiency is permissible in choosing and designing projects on the basis on distributional criteria. Formally, this entails a comparison of the terms a_P* and $1/(1-c)$. The coefficient, c, is an indicator of how inefficient alternative redistributive mechanisms are (i.e. what proportion of total resources is lost in the "act" of redistribution) and its value will lie between 0 and 1. In the example above, the project should go ahead as long as it is the case that $c \leq 0.5$. In this way, distributional concerns are allowed to influence project choice subject to this being the most cost-effective means of addressing some distributional goal.

11.3.3. Explicit distributional weights

The previous broad analytical option departs from simply asking what values distributional weights would *need to take*. A rather more prescriptive approach would be to impute explicit weights, perhaps based on the findings of past studies. For example, one approach is based on a judgement about the importance of income to those who gain or lose from the project. The assumption of diminishing marginal utility of income implies that the utility value of a unit change in a poor individual's income is greater than the utility value of the same unit change in income of a rich person. Other things being equal, this implies that a dollar or euro of benefit received by the latter receive less weight by the same change for the former reflecting this difference in its relative contribution to social welfare.

One possible weight, following this rationale, is: $a_i = (\overline{Y} / Y_i)^{\eta}$ where: $\overline{Y}$ is average or mean income per capita; Y_i is income of the ith individual (or group); and η is the elasticity of the marginal utility of income or society's valuation of an increment to that individual's income. (The derivation of this weight is illustrated in the Annex to this chapter.) Clearly, whereas data on the two former parameters are (in principle) easily measurable, it is information about η which is crucial. Intuitively, this elasticity is said to reflect society's degree of inequality aversion. A logical starting point then for determining its likely magnitude is to ask the question as to how much inequality "society" is willing to tolerate?

In principle, e could range from 0 to ∞, although, fortunately for analysts, the literature as discussed below suggests that the plausible range is considerably narrower than this. Note that conventional or "unweighted" CBA is equivalent to assuming $\eta = 0$ (as this would result in $a_i = 1$). At the other extreme, as the degree of inequality aversion becomes ever larger ($\eta \to \infty$), the cost-benefit test amounts to always "ruling-out" any project that adversely affects the very worse off. (Conversely, it will always "rule-in" a project that positively affects the very worse off.) And while the simplest assumption, in terms of ease of computation, is to set $\eta = 1$ (and thus compare each individual's income relative to the mean) ultimately it must be asked whether or not this seems to imply stronger societal preferences towards income equality than observed evidence suggests.

Table 11.1 uses the earlier example in section 11.2 to illustrate how the CBA recommendation for this distributional outcome alters depending on what value is taken by e. To this example, the assumption is added that the ratio of the income of our wealthier individual R to our poorer individual P is equal to 3: i.e. $Y_R = 3Y_P$ (e.g. such that perhaps the former is EUR 90 000 and the latter is EUR 30 000). Note that, in general, the effect of assuming values of e which are greater than 0, is to shrink the positive net benefits of individual R and to boost the negative net benefits of individual P. The magnitude of e determines how large this relative adjustment is going to be. Thus, for $\eta = 0.5$ the project still has a small but positive NB. However, for $\eta = 1$, the sum of distributional weighted NB is negative. It is also apparent from the table that larger values of η very quickly result in relatively extreme weights to be placed on the losses suffered by the individual with income below the mean.

Table 11.1. **Distributional weights and CBA – illustrative example**

Degree of inequality aversion:	Net benefits: Individual R	Net benefits: Individual P	Total net benefits
0	200	-100	100
0.5	163	-141	22
1	133	-200	-67
2	89	-400	-311

To reiterate, distributional weights reflect a judgement about the value to be placed on each dollar or euro received by or taken away from each individual or group. A variety of data might be sought in order to justify this judgement. Typically, it is argued that this judgement should be made on the basis on the revealed behaviour of (democratic and accountable) governments with regard to, say, redistributive policies. That is, by examining public policies where distributional issues are a predominant concern, something can be learned about the relative weights to be placed on the costs and benefits of different societal groups. A usual reference point is the income tax system where it is argued that the different marginal tax rates that people, with different incomes, face tells the analyst something useful about society's preferences towards the social value of that income. A prominent variant of this notion is based on equal *absolute* sacrifice and argues that tax system operates by imposing an equal burden in terms of utility losses on all income classes relative to some utility function (Young, 1994; although see, for example, Gramlich, 1990, for a discussion of the problems of using information about marginal tax rates in this way).

Some empirical debate has centred specifically on the magnitude of *e*. Comprehensive reviews of this literature can be found in Pearce and Ulph (1999) and Cowell and Gardiner (1999). While the latter survey concludes that "a reasonable range seems to be 0.5 ... to 4" (p. 33), Pearce and Ulph (1999) argue for a much narrower range in the region of 0.8. On this basis, Pearce (2003) argues that values of η in the range of 0.5 to 1.2 are defensible in the cost-benefit appraisal of climate change policy. Chapter 8 reviews more recent evidence which concludes that the value of η based on variety of analytical strategies and data might be higher. The point is there that this accommodates a range of possible values, and even for the simple example in Table 11.1 less clear implications of a CBA based upon this.

Estimating inequality aversion

Studies of people's preferences for income inequality do appear to indicate that, on average, they prefer distributions which are more equal such that, for example, they find that less income overall is tolerable so long as it is more equally distributed. One implication of this is that policy or project interventions which result in negative net benefits – i.e. less overall consumption – could be preferred if that action results in a better distribution of the consumption that is left. This is the essence of distributional weighted CBA, with the magnitude of inequality aversion, for example, setting the parameters for what is an acceptable trade-off between equity and efficiency. Clearly, there is an interesting question of exactly how much net loss that people will tolerate: i.e. what are the weights that should be used. There is also an interesting question about what weights should apply for risks to non-income outcomes of policy or project interventions.

A study by Cropper et al. (2016), using a stated preference survey, does exactly this for health risks: specifically cancer (and other possibly serious) risks arising from exposure to air pollution. Respondents were asked to consider – and choose between – two scenarios each involving risks faced by two regions of equal population size (within a country) each facing distinct health risks. In one scenario, these health risks are (highly) unequal between these two regions. In another scenario, these risks were equally distributed.

This is described in Table 11.2. What the choice indicates is a respondent's willingness to trade-off how the risk is distributed and the total risk. That is, option B shares the burden equally but entails a population risk of 14/1000 as opposed to option A where the overall risk is 10/1000. Asking multiple respondents to make a series of these choices allows preferences, and the magnitudes of trade-offs that people are prepared to make, to be teased out.

Table 11.2. **Example choice card from Cropper et al. (2016)**

	Choice A	Choice B
Region Y	1/1 000 mortality risk	7/1 000 mortality risk
Region Z	9/1 000 mortality risk	7/1 000 mortality risk
Preferred option?		

The results in Cropper et al. (2016) indicate that most respondents have a preference for greater equality in the way that health risks are distributed. That is, respondents appear to be prepared to tolerate a policy action that increases health risks so long as those risks are shared equally. Specifically, a key finding is that the average respondent is prepared to tolerate more than a 20% increase in total cancer cases that the population faces if everyone is confronted with the same (elevated) risk.

This actually understates the extent of this preference as it excludes those respondents for whom no equitable options were off the table. That is, for these respondents, no matter how high the overall cancer risk rate in the total population, they also chose an option which allocated this risk equally over options which had much lower (but unequally distributed) risks. As such they appear to have lexicographic or very strong preferences for health equality. In total, they accounted for around 30% of the sample. The result of including the preferences of this large group is to push the tolerable increase in total cancer cases up to 50% if these are equally distributed.

How do these trade-offs compare with those found in (analogous) studies of inequalities in income (or attitudes to risk more generally)? Cropper et al., include two further tests. One is a "leaky bucket experiment" whereby respondents are asked to choose between scenarios which involve (different sized) a USD 1 000 reduction in the incomes of the top 40% of income earners while simultaneously increasing the income of those in the bottom 40%. The size of the leak is indicated by how much less the latter is than the former: $0 < X \leq 0$. An option, for example, might involve reducing top earners' income by USD 1 000 but raising the bottom earners' incomes by USD 900 (in which case $X = 100$). Another option might only raise bottom earners' incomes by USD 500 or USD 250 and so on. Again, respondents' choices here can be used to infer preferences about income equality. These results appear to indicate that respondents are willing to sacrifice between 2 and 5% of average (mean) income to secure equality. As such, this study finds evidence that respondents seem to have stronger preferences for health equality than income equality.

Put another way, there is no reason to think that the weights to be used for changes in health risks are the same as those which might be used for changes in income more generally, at least as far as these U.S. respondents are concerned. Of course, determining appropriate weights is also a matter of social judgement rather than just the aggregation of these sort of individual responses. However, presumably such data will have a role in making that determination. Complications abound presumably, many projects involve health inequality and income inequality. For example, there seems to be some evidence that those particularly at risk from poor health as a result of exposure to air pollution are those with low socioeconomic status.

Dietz and Atkinson (2010) also use a stated preference study to look at the *different* distributional preferences of people towards policies which reduce air pollution. Respondents, from different areas of London in the United Kingdom, were asked to choose between options for a policy that differed in terms of conventional outcomes, such as its ambition i.e. how much London's air quality would be reduced and its cost. In addition, some options included provisions for assisting those households with less income with the costs of paying for the policy (through taxation) and whether those who were most responsible for air pollution in London (e.g. motorists) should bear more of the burden of paying for policies which address this.

The results of that study suggest that respondents see a trade-off between distributional outcomes and costs: that is, on average, they are willing to pay more for policies which achieve a given improvement in air quality in a more equitable manner. For example, respondents were willing to pay GBP 153 more for a policy which led to a dramatic improvement in London's air quality (relative to a policy leading to a modest improvement). If, however, this policy was targeted on those most responsible for the problem, these respondents would pay 64% more. If this policy additionally assisted those who were least able to pay, respondents were willing to pay 25% more.

The study by Dietz and Atkinson (2010) also surveyed a further sample of respondents about their distributional preferences for U.K. climate policy, thereby providing a test of how such preferences differ across environmental policy context. The "premium" on constructing a policy that is targeted on polluters is almost identical to that for the local air pollution context (65% compared with 63% above). However, respondents appear to care somewhat more for assisting those on lower incomes in the climate policy context (a "premium" of 43% compared with 25% as above).

11.4. Distributional CBA and climate change

A re-emergence of interest in distributional cost-benefit analysis (CBA) has been particularly prominent in the literature on the economics of climate change damage (see Chapter 14). This has involved a re-evaluation of the way in which the burdens of climate change damage are likely to be distributed between countries, which can be characterised as either rich or poor and vulnerable. As a result, equity weighting is now an established part of efforts to understand the social cost of carbon (SCC). Moreover, it appears that these procedures have influenced guidance on official (i.e. domestic government) positions on what the SCC should be for appraising climate change policy, although does not appear to be a universally held view.

As an illustration, $D_W = \sum_{i=1}^{N} a_i D_i$, where D is the value of global damage from climate change, D_i is the damage suffered by country i and a_i is the weight assigned to this damage in country i. The convention would be for these weights to be calculated as $a_i = \left(Y_W / Y_i\right)^{\eta}$, where Y_W and Y_i is income (or consumption) per capita in the world and in country i respectively and η is a income (or consumption) inequality aversion parameter. Intuitively, if poorer countries suffer disproportionately from climate change damage, then this weighting should result in a higher social cost of carbon. The reality, however, is a little more complicated. A paper by Anthoff et al. (2009) explains why. One reason is that higher values of ε imply a higher discount rate: i.e. $r = \rho + \eta g$, where r is the discount rate, ρ is the pure rate of time preference and g is the growth of per capita consumption. Not surprisingly, this technical issue has important practical ramifications.

Another important issue is highlighted by Anthoff and Tol (2010). Conventional weighting procedures are just one option. There are many others. At one extreme, a country may decide that people abroad have no standing. In terms of the implications for the SCC, this would mean that impacts elsewhere in other countries (i.e. climate change damage abroad) are not considered, when deciding on the SCC to use in appraising its climate policy. Of course, this is a rather extreme position but it provides at least a lower bound for further discussion. Once these impacts elsewhere are considered, there are a range of possible principles which could guide estimation of the SCC (some of which involve equity weighting).

From the perspective of a particular country, SCC can be expressed as follows:

$$SCC = \sum_t D(1+r_t)^{-t} + \omega \sum_i a_i \sum_t D_i \left(1+r_{t,i}\right)^{-t}$$

The first term on the right hand side is the (discounted) value of damage, for the home country. The second term expresses concern for damage caused in other all countries. This latter term includes two weighting procedures. The first is ω and reflects whether or not any consideration at all is given to this damage occurring elsewhere. This can take a value of 0 or 1 (or somewhere in between, if consideration is a matter of extent). The second is an equity weight, which can take a value between (and including) 0 and 1.

Table 11.3 indicates a number of guiding principles (proposed by Anthoff and Tol) which the government within a country might use for estimating the SCC (and each will involve particular specifications of the above expression). The interpretation of each is indicated as well the implications for consideration of the well-being of people in other countries, whether (and what) equity weight to use, as well as the discount rate used to evaluate future damages in other countries. For values of a = 1, this means that damages abroad receive no greater (lesser) weight if a foreign country (f) is poorer (richer), in terms of income (or consumption) per capita (Y), than the home country (h).

Table 11.3. **Distribution and the social cost of carbon – Principles and practice**

SCC Principle	Interpretation	Weight attached to the well-being of citizens aboard	Equity weight	Discount rate
Co-operation	A country behaves as a global decision-maker would: i.e. adopts the SCC that would maximise global welfare	Yes: ω = 1	a = 1	$r = \rho + \eta g_f$
Equity weighting	Equity weighting that the global decision-maker would adopt on the basis on differences of income (or consumption) per capita between countries	Yes: ω = 1	$a = \left(Y_w / Y_f\right)^\eta$	$r = \rho + \eta g_f$
Sovereignty	A country does not consider impacts elsewhere: damage to people abroad has "no standing"	No: ω = 0	–	–
Altruism	A country considers impacts elsewhere to the extent that its citizens care about those abroad	Yes: depending on extent of altruism – i.e. 0 ≤ ω ≤ 1	$a = \left(Y_h / Y_f\right)^\eta$	$r = \rho + \varepsilon g_f$
Compensation	A country considers it has a duty or requirement to compensate (nominally) damages it causes beyond its borders. Compensation refers to how this damage is valued by those in the victim countries	Yes: ω = 1	a = 1	$r = \rho + \eta g_h$
Good neighbour	A country considers impacts elsewhere and cares about those abroad as it would do citizens in its domestic borders	Yes: ω = 1	$a = \left(Y_h / Y_f\right)^\eta$	$r = \rho + \eta g_f$

Source: Adapted from Anthoff and Tol (2011).

Table 11.3 also reports some of the findings for the United States in Anthoff and Tol (2010), assuming a rate of time preference of 1%. These are estimates of the dollar value of the social cost of tonne of carbon which a decision-maker in the United States might estimate, and use in CBA, as an analytical consequence of a particular distributional principle being adopted at the outset of an exercise to establish the SCC. The magnitudes of the results have important ramifications: that is, they provide an indication of the relative aggressiveness of emissions reduction. That is, higher values of SCC will imply more active climate mitigation policy in the home country.

Turning first to the initial column of results, for the case where an U.S. decision-maker simply adopts the SCC that maximises (unweighted) global well-being, this is equal to USD 16/tC. Equity weighting nearly doubles the magnitude of the SCC for the case where $\eta = 1$. Estimating SCC according to the sovereignty principle results in a value which is not much greater than zero (i.e. a few cents per tonne of carbon). Clearly being a "good neighbour" implies by far the highest SCC. It shares similarities with the altruism case with the exception of assuming that $\omega = 1$ (rather than 0.1). Turning now to the sensitivity analysis for values of η equal to 0.5 and 1.5, perhaps paradoxically assuming higher (lower) levels of concern for inequality decreases (increases) the value of the equity weighted SCC in the case where $\eta = 1$. The main reason for this is that ε also influences the discount rate (see Table 11.4).

Table 11.4. **Estimates of the social cost of carbon for the United States**

USD 1995, Time preference rate of 1%

	Assumed value of		
	1	0.5	1.5
Co-operation	16	56	5
Equity weighting	28	72	13
Sovereignty	~0	1	~0
Altruism	13	5	13
Compensation	34	34	14
Good neighbour	125	41	123

Source: Adapted from Anthoff and Tol (2010).

11.5. Concluding remarks

Conventional CBA for the most part continues to regard distributional or equity concerns as having little or no place in making recommendations about project selection and design. While this approach strikes some critics as an oddity, it would be a mistake to conclude that this downgrades the usefulness of CBA. Even if efficiency is only one piece of the puzzle in understanding the social worth of a project, it remains extremely important. Moreover, there are cogent reasons why cost-benefit analysts often take this approach to the appraisal of the costs and benefits of projects and policies. That is, it is not merely unmindful neglect (at least, not always). However, as has been noted in this chapter, each of the reasons supporting this assertion in favour of conventional CBA is contestable. This suggests greater scope for scrutinising the distributional consequences of projects within the cost-benefit framework.

Whatever the particular interpretation that is adopted, incorporating distributional concern implies initially identifying and then possibly weighting the costs and benefits of individuals and groups on the basis of differences in the characteristic of interest. A hierarchy (e.g. Kriström, 2005) is a useful way to understand the demands that a variety of proposals place on the cost-benefit analyst. First, there is the relatively straightforward but possibly arduous task of assembling organising raw (i.e. unadjusted) data on the distribution of project costs and benefits. Second, these data could then be used to ask what weight or distributional adjustment would need to placed on the net benefits (net costs) of a societal group of interest for a given project proposal to pass (fail) a distributional cost-benefit test. Third, explicit weights reflecting judgement about society's preferences towards distributional concerns can be assigned and net benefits re-estimated on this basis.

A crucial question then is where should cost-benefit analysts locate themselves upon this hierarchy? Given that cost-benefit appraisals are sometimes criticised for ignoring distributional consequences altogether then the apparently simplest option of cataloguing how costs and benefits are distributed could offer valuable and additional insights. This suggests that, at a minimum, cost-benefit appraisals arguably should routinely provide these data. Whether more ambitious proposals should be adopted is a matter of deliberating about whether: (a) the gains in terms of being able to scrutinise the (weighted) net benefits of projects in the light of societal concerns about both efficiency and equity outweighs; (b) the losses arising from the need for informed guesswork in interpreting the empirical evidence with regards to the treatment of the latter.

On the one hand, empirical evidence about the "correct" magnitudes of distributional weights can be usefully employed in distributional CBA. On the other hand, even apparently small changes in assumptions about the size of distributional weights – indicated by the range of values in available empirical studies – can have significant implications for recommendations about a project's social worth. This finding should not be a surprise for it primarily reflects the complexity involved in trying to disentangle society's distributional preferences. As a practical matter, the danger is whether the most ambitious proposals for distributional CBA generate more heat than light.

Environmental CBA can play an important part here, notably through valuation practitioners paying greater attention to distributional concerns (e.g. of WTP or environmental impacts in physical terms). What might hasten that response? One catalyst almost certainly could be demand from policy makers. The suspicion must be that this is not only due to a supply problem (a manifestation of the singular emphasis of cost-benefit practitioners on efficiency), but it is also likely to be an issue about demand: i.e. policy makers have not required this information be provided in the terms of reference guiding that work. Addressing that element could have an important role to play.

Notes

1. Although these firms are in turn owned by households.

2. Explanations of why this is the case typically have used Arthur Okun's analogy of the leaky bucket used to equalise the water volumes in two receptacles. Assuming that the distribution of water between the two receptacles is unequal in the first instance, the transfer, via a leaky bucket, inevitably leads to an overall loss of water in pursuit of the goal of a more equal distribution. This is the essence of society's problem: how much efficiency should be traded-off for more equity? For example, in the case of taxation of incomes, the leaky bucket represents incentives affecting the work-leisure choice. That is, ever higher marginal tax rates discourage high-income earners from working more and thereby decreases, in some degree, the total amount of income that society has available to redistribute.

References

Anthoff, D. and R. Tol (2010), "On international equity weights and national decision making on climate change", *Journal of Environmental Economics and Management*, Vol. 60/1, pp. 14-20, *http://dx.doi.org/10.1016/j.jeem.2010.04.002*.

Anthoff, D., C. Hepburn and R. Tol (2009), "Equity weighting and the marginal damage costs of climate change", *Ecological Economics*, Vol. 68/3, pp. 836-849, *http://dx.doi.org/10.1016/j.ecolecon.2008.06.017*.

Cowell, F. and K. Gardiner (1999), *Welfare Weights. Report to the Office of Fair Trading*, Office of Fair Trading, London.

Cropper, M., A. Krupnick and W. Raich (2016) "Preferences for Equality in Environmental Outcomes", Resources for the Future, Washington, DC, *www.rff.org/files/document/file/RFF-DP-16-36.pdf*.

Day, B. and D. Maddison (2015), *Improving Cost-Benefit Analysis Guidance*, Report to the Natural Capital Committee (NCC), NCC, London, *http://nebula.wsimg.com/ad8539d7216f5e6589bbe625c9750fff?Access KeyId=68F83A8E994328D64D3D&disposition=0&alloworigin=1*.

Decancq, K., M. Fleurbaey and M. Schokkaert (2014), "Income, inequality and wellbeing", CORE Discussion Paper No. 2014/18. University of Antwerp, *https://cdn.uclouvain.be/public/Exports%20red dot/core/documents/coredp2014_18web.pdf*.

Defra (2006), *Air Quality and Social Deprivation in the UK: An environmental inequalities analysis*, Final Report to Department of Environment, Food and Rural Affairs, Defra, London, *https://uk-air.defra.gov.uk/assets/documents/reports/cat09/0701110944_AQinequalitiesFNL_AEAT_0506.pdf*.

Dietz, S. and G. Atkinson (2010), "The equity-efficiency trade-off in environmental policy: Evidence from stated preferences", *Land Economics*, Vol. 86/3, pp. 423-443, *http://dx.doi.org/10.3368/le.86.3.423*.

Gramlich, E.M. (1990), *A Guide to Benefit-Cost Analysis*, 2nd Edition, Prospect Heights, Waveland Press, Illinois.

Jodha, N.S. (1986), "Common Property Resources and the Rural Poor in Dry Regions of India", *Economic and Political Weekly*, Vol. 21/27, pp. 1169-1181, *www.jstor.org/stable/4375858*.

Kriström, B. (2005), "Framework for assessing the distribution of financial effects of environmental policies", in Serret, Y. and N. Johnstone (eds.) *The Distribution of Benefits and Costs of Environmental Policies*, Edward Elgar, Cheltenham, *www.oecd.org/env/tools-evaluation/thedistributionaleffectsofenvironmental policy.htm*.

Kanninen, B.J. and B. Kriström (1993), *Welfare Benefit Estimation and Income Distribution*, Beijer Discussion Paper Series No. 20, Beijer Institute of Ecological Economics, Stockholm.

Loomis, J. (2011), "Incorporating distributional issues into benefit-cost analysis: How, why and two empirical examples using non-market valuation", *Journal of Benefit-Cost Analysis*, Vol. 2/1, Article 5, *https://doi.org/10.2202/2152-2812.1044*.

OECD (1975), *The Polluter Pays Principle: Definition, Analysis and Implementation*, Organisation for Economic Co-operation and Development, Paris, *http://dx.doi.org/10.1787/9789264044845-en*.

Pearce, D.W. (2003), "The social costs of carbon and its policy implications", *Oxford Review of Economic Policy*, Vol. 16/3, pp. 362-384, *https://doi.org/10.1093/oxrep/19.3.362*.

Pearce, D.W. and D. Ulph (1999), "A social discount rate for the United Kingdom", in Pearce, D.W. (ed.), *Economics and Environment: Essays on Ecological Economics and Sustainable Development*, Edward Elgar, Cheltenham.

Pearce, J. et al. (2011), "Environmental justice and health: A study of multiple deprivation and geographical inequalities in New Zealand", *Social Science and Medicine*, Vol. 73, pp. 410-420, *http://dx.doi.org/10.1016/j.socscimed.2011.05.039*.

Persky, J. (2001), "Cost-benefit analysis and the classical creed", *Journal of Economic Perspectives*, Vol. 15/4, pp. 199-210, *http://dx.doi.org/10.1257/jep.15.4.199*.

Riberio, A.I., M. de Pina and R. Mitchell (2015), "Development of a measure of multiple physical deprivation. After United Kingdom and New Zealand, Portugal", *European Journal of Public Health*, Vol. 25/4, pp. 610-617, *https://doi.org/10.1093/eurpub/cku242*.

ten Brink, P. (ed.) (2011), *The Economics of Ecosystems and Biodiversity in National and International Policy Making*, Earthscan, London.

Vedeld, P. et al. (2004), "Counting on the environment: Forest incomes and the rural poor", *Environmental Economics Series* No. 98, The World Bank, Washington, DC, *http://documents.worldbank.org/curated/en/825651468778804896/Counting-on-the-environment-forest-incomes-and-the-rural-poor*.

ANNEX 11.A1

A marginal utility of income weighting procedure

Let utility be related to income, i.e. $U = U(Y)$, such that the marginal utility of income function has a constant elasticity. The marginal utility of income function for individual i can then be written:

$$U_i' = \frac{dU}{dY_i} = aY_i^{-e}$$

where $-e$ is now the elasticity of the function. For the average income $\bar{Y}$ we shall therefore have

$$U_{\bar{Y}}' = a\bar{Y}^{-e}$$

and the relative weight for the ith individual would then be

$$\frac{U_{\bar{Y}}'}{U_i'} = \frac{a\bar{Y}^{-e}}{aY^{-e}} = \left(\frac{\bar{Y}}{Y_i}\right)^{-e}$$

Selected issues
in environmental
cost-benefit analysis

PART III

Chapter 12

Sustainability and natural capital

The notion of "sustainable development" has permeated significant parts of policy discourse about the environment. This reflects a number of (related) concerns including the development path that the broader economy is on and specifically the way in which (changes in) natural wealth affects this path. It is important that CBA speaks to those concerns especially as policy and investment projects have the potential to shift a development path (perhaps because of non-marginal actions or the cumulative effect of smaller decisions). There are a few implications of this but one of the most prominent (as well as far-reaching) is to circumscribe CBA by having it live within sustainability constraints, perhaps based on ecological criteria. This places greater emphasis on a single appraisal within the context of a portfolio of policies or projects. That is, the constraint is that this portfolio, on balance, maintains the ecological status quo with practical applications of this approach including biodiversity offsetting. This raises important issues. On the one hand, there is a benefit to avoiding untoward and irreversible damage to (possibly) critical resources. On the other hand, there are opportunity costs to applying the shadow projects approach that need still to be considered.

12.1. Introduction

How far does current CBA practice impart information about the sustainability of policies or projects being evaluated? Clearly, any answer to this question is, in large part, dependent on defining what is meant by the term itself: "sustainability". For example, it might refer narrowly to the internal sustainability of the project itself perhaps because of financing risks and budget constraints. Alternatively, it might refer much more broadly to a whole range of external factors – economic, social or environmental – which could be influenced by an investment project or policy decision. An illustration of the possible breadth of such factors is the 2015 UN Sustainable Development Goals: 17 high-level development objectives with more than 160 sub-objectives.

This breadth could be viewed as implying the need for a multi-criteria approach (see Ch. 18). In some transport applications, for example, the sustainability challenge for appraisal has been interpreted in this way. In this chapter, however, a more specific conceptualisation of sustainability is adopted; one that is drawn from economics albeit with broader interdisciplinary implications (see, for example, Arrow et al., 2012; CGDD, 2015; Hamilton and Atkinson, 2006; Helm, 2015). Its distinguishing features are sustainability as a term articulating concern about future generations (i.e. intergenerational equity) and, as a way of addressing this concern, a focus on what is happening to wealth (e.g. future well-being prospects and assets in an economy, particularly natural capital) as a result of proposals for investment projects and policies.

What then is distinctive about this "sustainability economics" in informing economic appraisal? At the very least, it draws together a number of compelling critiques of CBA. One is scepticism of the Kaldor-Hicks criterion combined with the remedial prescription that interventions which harm certain groups (e.g. future generations) should be accompanied by *actual* compensation. A further concern is that the "marginal" or "incrementalist" approach of much of practical CBA does not consider the sustainability of the broader "system" (Helm, 2015). This might refer to prospects along the development path of an economic system. Such considerations have been a feature of climate economics too (Chapter 14). The emphasis in "sustainability economics", however, is on the way in which a development path is influenced by the culmination of (policy- and project-induced) changes in a whole range of natural systems, characterised commonly as "natural capital".

Dealing with these concerns still leads to a number of distinct possible paths. Indeed, one response might be that there is little wrong with the way with which CBA is conducted and that existing knowledge is evolving in ways that cover a number of the challenges set out by those concerned about sustainability. This is not an indefensible position. A lot of CBA certainly does deal with relevant challenges: environmental valuation, discount rate selection, and decision-making under (future) uncertainty are all relevant examples of this.

For example, given that a lot of the concern about sustainable development is based on judgements about distributional outcomes this reinforces a need to report how costs and benefits are distributed over time. This call is not new (e.g. IPCC, 1996) but has been recently reiterated in Day and Maddison (2015) (see Chapter 10). There is a need to improve the reach and accuracy of methods – including techniques of environmental valuation – for measuring (changes in) natural capital, rather than simply measuring flows of current services. Reconciling CBA with sustainability concerns may also force explicit thinking about how much of nature should be put beyond straightforward cost-benefit thinking, and thus what this implies for how CBA is conducted.

12.2. What is sustainability?

While the question as to "what is sustainability or 'sustainable development'?" is often posed as one that cannot be answered – or at least is a question which has many, perhaps contradictory, answers – this is little help in terms of clarifying how practitioners might better integrate sustainability thinking into CBA. So if, for example, it is defined extremely broadly (i.e. covering "all" aspects of the development process and multidimensional outcomes) as in many existing national sustainable development strategies or the United Nations' SDGs – then potentially the challenge is huge. That is, it is arguable that CBA cannot possibly cover the breadth implied by these high-level frameworks. In such cases, a logical reaction might be to incorporate these concerns in appraisal by using additional assessment tools in making a decision (see Chapter 18).

If instead sustainable development is conceptualised less broadly – perhaps in terms of an economic definition of non-declining (per capita) human well-being over time and, in turn, in terms of how wealth or assets in an economy are managed to achieve that end – then the challenge becomes more tractable, or at least implications can be understood more clearly. This economic approach to sustainability does not have all the answers. However, it provides a useful starting point for understanding a coherent core of the challenge, posed by the sustainability debate. In this way, extensions to that understanding can then be considered.

On this view, future (development) prospects depend on the wealth that an economy has. Projects and policies represent one way in which these prospects are affected. The impact might be large or small but the projects and policies being appraised in a CBA can be interpreted as shifting the development path of an economy over time (e.g. Arrow et al., 2003). These interventions often do this explicitly, perhaps by investing in assets in the economy. Prominent examples traditionally would include physical infrastructure projects in the transport or communications sectors, investment in the public education sector or influencing the health of the nation by spending on better water treatment and sanitation services. However, the impact may also be implicit by creating (potentially) investable resources because an intervention generates net benefits and so entails better prospects for future consumption or well-being.

How projects and policies affects the natural or physical environment is a further, but related, consideration. This natural wealth matters for development because it is itself a determinant of future well-being by providing flows of goods and services that ultimately provide people with benefits that they value. For this reason, this is increasingly referred to under the broad heading: natural capital. What then is "natural capital"? While useful as an umbrella term, a more specific definition is needed as ever to be of use to cost-benefit practitioners. The UK Natural Capital Committee, for example, defines natural capital as: "… the elements of nature that produce value to people (directly and indirectly), such as the stock of forests, rivers, land, minerals and oceans, as well as the natural processes and functions that underpin their operation" (NCC, 2013, pX). What links this diverse and large range of naturally occurring resources is that these are *stocks*. Further properties of these stocks are also relevant to distinguish too, not least because these might imply different recommendations for consideration in a CBA (or social decision-making, more generally).

First, some of these assets are non-renewable. These stocks are fixed in physical extent (although there might be uncertainty about what this extent is), are non-living resources and so are exhaustible. Sub-soil assets, such as conventional oil and gas, are typical examples. Second, some of these assets are renewable. These are living resources or resources which regenerate (perhaps because of natural growth or some other underlying natural regenerative process). A forest or a fishery are well-known examples for CBA practitioners. Ecological or ecosystem assets are a further category that has gained increasing attention in policy debates (see below). These renewal properties lead to further questions about resource management. That is, renewable resources can be sustained at some level even if used, in contrast to non-renewable resources.

What then does this imply, if anything, for cost-benefit practitioners? Of particular interest perhaps are those implications when the investment project or policy being appraised will result in the loss of natural capital. For example, for non-renewable natural capital (such as a mining project or depletion policy) there is a corresponding question about what supplementary actions (if any) must accompany this activity in order to compensate for this loss of asset value. If the asset loss involves some renewable resource – as in the case of land-use change which results in degraded or destroyed ecosystems – then sustainability might imply asking whether this loss can be compensated by building up other assets generally, or whether it requires specific offsetting investment in the renewable asset itself.

12.3. CBA and "weak sustainability"

Building this picture of the challenge that concern about sustainability poses for economic appraisal might start with taking stock of what conventional CBA currently does. In this spirit, Stavins et al. (2003) reflect on what the cost-benefit criterion, and compensation tests, signals and how this might be interpreted in the light of concerns about intergenerational equity. This starts then with the basic Kaldor-Hicks criterion: choose proposals with (maximum) positive net present value, such that winners *potentially* can compensate losers and still remain better off than without the project or policy change. Where "winners" are those in the current generation and "losers" are future generations, the argument goes that at least this signals potentially available economic resources to address concerns about intergenerational equity arising from these interventions.

While in one sense all this does is restate that standard cost-benefit perspective, it usefully draws a link between efficiency and equity over time and between generations. It prompts, for example, immediate questions about not only whether there are mechanisms to straightforwardly facilitate compensation between generations and whether potential compensation really does settle unease about intergenerational equity. One study then that takes this a bit further is an earlier contribution by Farrow (1998) who argues that this compensation – in these sort of cases – should be *actual* rather than potential. This starts by asking explicitly whether a proposal imposes net losses on a particular group: i.e. future generations? If so, compensation actually offered to that particular group, must be at least as great as these net losses. Linking this to what might be happening to natural capital as a result of current decisions, this compensation must be at least as great as any loss in asset value that the proposal causes. The idea here then is that such losses in asset value decrease well-being by diminishing future consumption possibilities. One way of, at least, maintaining these possibilities is by investing in other assets to offset these current losses.

Such ideas are as the genesis for a practical recommendation in, for example, Day and Maddison (2015). They lead with the point that CBA provides useful information about positive net benefits of proposed actions that signal potentially investable economic resources. If a proposal also results in costs which amount to losses in asset values (perhaps because natural capital is depleted or degraded) then the corresponding gains can be used to invest to offset this and, as such, keep capital constant. As for whether this investment is forthcoming in reality, this is a decision in the hands of decision-makers of course. But if decision-makers believe in using CBA to inform policy choices along with a commitment to broader sustainable development then an economic appraisal at least signals the economic resources made to realise this latter obligation.

For practical purposes, this suggests two bits of policy-relevant information should be co-joined. The first is the standard one from a cost-benefit perspective: recommend projects or policies which pass a standard cost-benefit test. The second is to check whether the totality of assets in the economy is at least being held constant. This latter element could be assessed by looking at an indicator of how these assets are changing. As discussed below, such a metric is increasingly referred to as adjusted net – or "genuine" – saving. What this indicates is the extent to which net assets are being accumulated in the economy and, importantly, this includes changes in natural capital. Whether "genuine saving" is positive or otherwise possibly provides this information about the broader sustainability of economies within which CBA is being conducted on specific decisions.

This practical link between changes in total wealth and sustainability was first explored by Pearce and Atkinson (1993). Subsequent growth theoretic literature, including Hamilton and Clemens (1999), Dasgupta and Mäler (2000) and Asheim and Weitzman (2001), has elaborated the theoretical foundations for this approach to measuring sustainability. The basic insight is contained, however, in Hartwick (1977) which showed that future consumption can be sustained when exhaustible resources are extracted if other investments offset the value of resource depletion. By definition, an investment in a mine that enables the extraction of a valuable but finite deposit of some natural resource is financing an unsustainable activity. That is, mining can continue only up to point that the resource is exhausted (either physically or economically). The broader implication for sustainability is another matter. Much depends on whether or not the proceeds from mining the resource are invested in an alternative (productive) asset. If the proceeds of mining are ploughed back into new and productive projects then development can be sustained.

Formally, Hartwick (1977) showed that important earlier insights about this problem (such as Solow, 1974) imply a savings rule where some portion of the revenues (specifically, resource rents) from the depletion of an exhaustible resource is invested in alternative assets. These alternatives are usually thought of as produced assets, but it could also be human capital. In this way, development – defined as the constancy of a consumption path – can be sustained in perpetuity despite the dependency on a finite (exhaustible) natural asset. The way to ensure this is to keep total net savings across all types of capital – or "genuine saving", to use the term coined by Hamilton (1994) for this concept – at or above zero. Solow (1986), in turn, showed how following this guidance implies a constant capital rule. This has become the bedrock of modern thinking about sustainability economics.

A general form of this "Hartwick rule" is a more recent development but has an important property: it is consistent with a possible consumption path which is increasing. Hence, this can accommodate a policy regime where economic growth is the objective rather than just the constancy of economic development along a path. Hamilton and Hartwick (2006) identify a relationship between (the change in) consumption and net saving. This generalised Hartwick rule posits that positive genuine saving can lead to growth in consumption along the development path. A key condition of this is that genuine saving does not grow faster than the interest rate (i.e. the returned on produced capital). Hamilton and Withagen (2007) explore the implications of this a bit further, showing that a constant positive genuine saving rate (the share of saving in national income) implies consumption can increase without bound.

Thus, to the extent that a project entails the (net) accumulation of produced assets or human assets then, other things being equal, it contributes to sustainability. In other words, discussion about sustainable development in the context of CBA needs to consider these desirable wealth-increasing properties of many projects and policies. Of course, to the extent that such actions give rise to environmental liabilities or deplete resource stocks then this loss of natural assets decreases sustainability, other things being equal. However, as previously discussed, the net effect is signalled by aggregate indicators such as genuine saving or the change in per capita net wealth.

A practical example of this sort of thinking is discussed in Box 12.1. This illustrates the use of wealth funds to manage the proceeds of non-renewable resource depletion (such as oil and gas). While the literature on "genuine saving" as one element of how policy can realise concern for future generations, less attention has been given to the productivity of investments. Clearly, this latter issue falls squarely within the domain of CBA. Not only can projects, selected by cost-benefit appraisals, increase net wealth but also can further contribute to sustaining development by ensuring that savings are put to the most productive use.

Box 12.1. **North Sea oil and sovereign wealth funds**

Exhaustible resources and the revenues they generate present two broad problems for macroeconomic management: gross production and tax revenues tend to be large and highly volatile, and the stream of revenues is finite, ending when the resource deposit ceases to be economic. Large flows of resource tax revenues lead to the distinct risk that fiscal policy will be pro-cyclical and hence a source of macroeconomic instability. And the finite nature of the resource revenue stream raises important questions about the sustainability of the macro economy – will well-being fall as the resource is exhausted?

A number of countries are turning to sovereign wealth funds (SWFs) as a way of handling these risks and opportunities including notably Norway which established its fund in the 1990s. Hamilton and Ley (2011) list 12 countries or jurisdictions where resource funds and/or fiscal rules for resource revenues have been implemented. The United Kingdom is an exception here having decided in the late 1970s not to establish a SWF and subsequently never (it appears) revisiting the issue. But given that North Sea revenues reached 9.9% of fiscal revenues and 3.7% of GDP in 1984, with revenues exceeding 1% of GDP from 1979 to 1987, it is fair to ask what are the costs and benefits of that decision.

To explore the likely sacrifice from the establishment of a (hypothetical) sovereign wealth fund in 1975, Atkinson and Hamilton (2016) carry out an *ex post* cost-benefit analysis of an SWF as a public investment. Resource revenues transferred to the fund become costs from the Treasury viewpoint, while fund payouts to the Treasury are benefits. For simplicity

---

Box 12.1. **North Sea oil and sovereign wealth funds** (cont.)

they assume that the petroleum resource was depleted by 2010. Costs of investing in the SWF cease at this point. The fund, however, is assumed to continue paying out an amount equal to its 2010 value (the real return on the portfolio) in perpetuity. Table 12.1 shows the present value of costs and benefits of investing in the SWF, normalised per capita, for different time horizons and discount rate assumptions.

Table 12.1. **Costs and benefits of establishing a sovereign wealth fund**

	Fund established 1975		Fund established 1990	
	Total resource revenue (cost)	SWF returns (benefit)	Total resource revenue (cost)	SWF returns (benefit)
Fixed 3.5% discount rate				
Present value	2 897	3 182	1 251	1 394
Levelised costs and benefits	145	159	88	98
Ratio of benefits to costs	1.10		1.11	
Declining 3.5% discount rate				
Present value	3 000	5 068	1 251	2 510
Levelised costs and benefits	143	240	88	176
Ratio of benefits to costs	1.69		2.00	

Source and notes: Atkinson and Hamilton (2016). The discount rates are derived from *Green Book 2003*. Levelised costs and benefits are calculated over 1975-2010 or 1990-2010 as appropriate.

To isolate the effects of the oil price bubble and other economic circumstances in the early 1980s, the calculations simulate costs and benefits for two assumptions about the year that investment in the fund commenced, 1975 or 1990. Starting in 1975 yields a larger present value of benefits from the fund, but it also yields a high present value of costs because these costs (payments into the fund) are front-end loaded. This front-end loading is much diminished for the fund simulated to commence in 1990.

The first discount rate assumed, fixed 3.5%, is equal to the *Green Book 2003* social discount rate for projects where costs and benefits span 30 years or less. The second discounting scenario uses a discount rate of 3.5% that declines beyond 30 years. This is the *Green Book 2003* social discount rate assumption for assessing policies affecting the long term – which is precisely what a SWF is designed to do.

As shown in Table 12.1, the present value of benefits from the SWF exceeds costs by 10% to 69% for a fund starting in 1975. For a fund starting in 1990, the corresponding figures are 11% and 100%. In terms of net annual benefits (levelised benefits minus levelised costs), these vary from GBP 14 to 10 per capita for the fixed discount rate, and GBP 97 to 88 for the declining discount rate – in each case, the 1990 scenario yields the lower net benefit figures. The fixed discount rate results are more sensitive to the choice of discount rate, with a discount rate of 3.92% (the assumed constant real rate of return of the SWF) yielding 0 net benefits for either start year. This is an artifact of the synthetic nominal SWF return that the authors use to simulate fund returns (which is, in turn, based on average real returns on a globally weighted mix of holdings of equities and bonds).

Establishing a SWF would not have been without sacrifice. However, this *ex post* analysis suggests that if a SWF had been established per Green Book 2003 standards, the net benefits per capita would be positive and moderately large for the assumption of declining discount rates. Importantly, it also potentially generates a sustained source of income from using a finite resource

An interesting development is extensions to settings including renewable natural capital. This leads to at least two important and overarching questions. First, this requires advances in environmental valuation both conceptually and empirically. Secondly, nor are such extensions without controversy. The economic approach to sustainability elaborated above is often labelled under the heading of "weak sustainability". This is a descriptive label used to distinguish this approach from stronger approaches which emphasise far more of a special place for conserving natural capital in thinking about intergenerational concerns. As such, this label is prescriptive too distinguishing it from approaches which are perhaps a lot less permissive in guiding how cost-benefit practitioners respond to the challenge of sustainability. Both these issues about natural capital valuation and "strong sustainability" are considered below.

12.4. Valuing natural capital

A lot of the existing terminology in environmental valuation has focused on valuing *flows*: that is, some flow of a benefit arising perhaps from the consumption of a good or service. Of course, policy interventions such as investments in ecosystem protection (or enhancement) typically will boost the flow of these services over time, thereby introducing a dynamic element into any economic analysis. Moreover, when these same ecosystems are perturbed by some change (be it a shift in land use or a degradation in state) the effect on well-being similarly will have an intertemporal dimension (e.g. Mäler, 2008; Dasgupta, 2009). Put this way, what one needs to think about is the underlying ecosystem asset and, in particular, the changes in asset value that occur as a result of human interventions (be these positive or negative, deliberate or otherwise).

Thus, these flows of services can be viewed as the flows of "production" that are supplied by underlying assets or "natural capital" (e.g. forestland, wetland and so on). Recalling the discussion in the previous section, what needs to be assessed here is the potential change in the *future* prospects given what is happening to this natural capital now. In doing so, this might throw light on whether natural capital use and economic development paths more generally are sustainable or not.

There remains a strong connection to CBA principles in this work. One example is those contributions which seek to assess economic sustainability when there is land-use change such as deforestation as loss of other natural habitats such as mangroves. The basic unit here – following Hamilton and Atkinson (2006) and Barbier (2009) and earlier contributions, particularly Hartwick (1992) – is land. That is, land under a particular use has a distinct asset value. When land-use is changed – as happens when forestland is cleared – this can be viewed from the perspective of CBA; that is, is the change net beneficial? Additionally, there is a corresponding implication for how wealth is changing in the economy that should be accounted for.

In the case of deforestation, decrease in the value of forestland leads also an increase in the value of agricultural land assets. Put another way, what has happened here is a change in composition of the broader portfolio of land assets. For example, if one ecosystem service provided by woodland is climate regulation (via carbon sequestration and storage services), increasing the amount of woodland will increase the provision of these services. But there is likely also to be some loss in the climate regulation services provided by agricultural land and, ideally, these services that are lost also need to be recorded somewhere. Forestland is also an asset providing multiple benefits and it is important that as many of these are accounted for as possible. There are further measurement issues. Clearly, other services that change as a result of the land-use switch need to be accounted for. The broader balance sheet, for example, will reflect the loss in agricultural output and so on. There are also presumably conversion costs associated with changing land use and those investment costs should also be accounted for.

A major element to incorporating better measures of (changing) natural capital into CBA is an extension of valuation to this domain. Progress on environmental valuation – and particularly in the realm of ecosystem (service) valuation – offers some encouragement here. But important debates remain about this progress. And regardless of whether one views the glass as half-full or half-empty in interpreting those debates, addressing this valuation challenge remains work-in-progress. For example, it is clear that a great many development projects have an impact on biodiversity; i.e. by changing land-use and natural habitats. However, it is far from clear that even state-of-the-art appraisal can provide an adequate assessment of the value of this loss. As such the suspicion might be that natural capital valuation might be painting a sufficiently full picture about what happens when investment projects and policies affect natural assets such as ecosystems (and underlying assets such as biodiversity). Judgements about the ability of practitioners to rise to that challenge may require a more circumspect role for CBA in this regard (see next section).

Where valuation is possible, the problem seems analytically more straightforward at least on the face of it. That is, the value of natural capital can be viewed as equal to the capitalised value of flows of future services. Of course, for many categories of (renewable) natural capital such as ecosystems, the prices of the resulting flow of services are not observed and so neither are the prices of ecosystem assets. However, as a number of chapters in this volume illustrate, considerable progress in environmental valuation at least allows an ever more complete response to this challenge (see also Chapter 13). As Box 12.2 illustrate, some practitioners have sought to distil this growing evidence base into truly ambitious estimates of the aggregate value of changing natural capital.

Box 12.2. **The value of aggregate natural capital**

The recent emphasis on large-scale ecosystem assessments – such as the OECD Environmental Outlooks (e.g. OECD, 2012), TEEB and the UK NEA – indicates some interest in searching for clues about the overall scale – in economic terms – of what has been lost (and what is likely to be lost in the future) as a result of the continued destruction of the natural world. While this is not a substitute for more detailed policy analysis, knowledge about these trends might be important for framing policy thinking. In addition, such information might throw light on whether ecosystem and biodiversity decline is a development problem as, for example, Stern (2007) demonstrated in the case of climate change.

There are, however, clear signs of growing interest in this question. An example of this is the linkages being made between (recent and on-going) ecosystem assessments and efforts to understand the way in which changes in natural wealth influence the sustainability of development through greening of national accounts (see, for example, World Bank, 2010; Arrow et al., 2011). The on-going World Bank led consortium "WAVES" project (Global Partnership for Wealth Accounting for the Value of Ecosystem Services) represents a practical application of this work to a number of proposed countries. This has clear relevance to the question at the heart of the economic approach to sustainability: i.e. is enough being saved for the future?

Box 12.2. **The value of aggregate natural capital** (*cont.*)

Some studies have sought to explore these issues but do so by calculating losses in natural assets likely to occur according to possible policy scenarios (and hence in principle ask a more defensible question than that about the totality of the current service flow). Hussain et al. (2012) estimates the losses arising from recent past and projected future loss of the world's aquatic ecosystems (specifically wetlands, mangrove and coral reefs). The present value of this loss over the period 2000 to 2050 (using a discount rate of 4%) is reckoned in excess of USD 2 trillion (in 2007 USD) (with two-thirds of this accounted for by wetlands). The annualised value of this total change is just under USD 100 billion (that is, the value of the loss of these ecosystem assets each year is estimated to be of this magnitude) which, e.g. in 2007, was just 0.2% of global gross income. Chiabai et al. (2011) conclude not entirely dissimilarly for the case of the loss of global forests over the same time period.

Needless to say, such global estimates of ecosystem loss require some heroic assumptions and generalisations (with the same being true of efforts elsewhere to value the global impacts of climate change). Indeed, for some critics, a search for a global value is a flawed project because of this. However, taking these findings at face value it appears that knowing the global magnitude of ecosystem losses might not add significantly to empirical discussion. So while it is entirely possible that these analyses are missing something possibly both large and critically important, a tentative conclusion is that the pragmatic demand for more highly aggregated indicators of trends and concerns about validity both point away from an emphasis on global trends.

Greater practical significance, however, is to be found at the regional or country level. In the case of forests, for Brazil, estimated losses in natural wealth are found by Chiabai et al. (2011) to be substantial (as a percentage of the country's gross national income or GNI). Hussain et al. (2012) find that for aquatic ecosystems, for the South Asia region and for Indonesia, however, these annual losses in natural wealth were respectively 1.7% and 4.0% of GNI (in 2007).

These are magnitudes worth knowing more about. This would necessitate still close scrutiny about the robustness of such estimates. The basic problem of accounting for the value of ecosystems can be put simply. It entails identifying a price or (unit) value and a quantity of (some change in) the provision of e.g. ecosystem service (Boyd and Banzhof, 2007). An immediate challenge, however, lies in identifying the likely limits on how the available empirical record on ecosystem "prices" and "quantities" can be pulled and stretched over the assorted ecosystem areas needed to make robust aggregate generalisations. The issue of spatial variability is central here. This includes properly accounting for variation in the supply characteristics – the type and extent of functions – of ecosystems as well as demand characteristics – of the human population that consumes services that these functions give rise to. All this requires relatively sophisticated mapping and is demanding in information terms. However, it might be that at this national level (or sub-national levels) that these issues become a little more tractable (see, for example, Kaveira et al., 2011).

Of course, much of what is currently termed "ecosystem services" already may be reflected in the national accounts. This is a point made in World Bank (2010). Examples of this might include the natural pollination services that (in effect) are capitalised in the value of agricultural land or the recreational opportunities that are (implicitly and in part) provided by natural areas. On this view, ecosystems support market activity in a number of important (but indirect) ways and the accounting challenge is to correctly re-attribute the service value to the (ecosystem) asset which gave rise to it (Nordhaus, 2006).

> ### Box 12.2. **The value of aggregate natural capital** (*cont.*)
>
> To the extent that ecosystem services are missing entirely from the accounts then clearly these will be neglected in any accounting approach that only looks at re-attribution.[1] For example, many types of cultural services might fall out of the reckoning in this way. However, as a starting point, an emphasis on identifying what is already (somewhere) in the accounts has merit. In particular, given the traditional opposition by the national accountants to non-market valuation in relation to the accounts (Hecht, 2008; de Haan and van de Ven, 2007), this starting point has a strategic benefit.
>
> 1. Vanoli (2015) proposes an approach that integrates a measurement of the deterioration of ecosystems in the national accounts.

The challenge for natural capital valuation is not confined to progress in techniques to measure environmental values. Recommendations about discount rates are important too in capitalising current services in the appraisal of impacts which – given the potential longevity of renewable natural capital – arise in the distant future. So debates about the size of the discount rate – and the term structure of the resulting discount factors – are important here too if the future consequences of current actions are not simply assumed away by the "tyranny of discounting" (see Chapter 8).

Valuing natural capital, however, is likely to involve more than simply capitalising flows of current services. As shown in Fenichel and Abbott (2014), accounting for the value of an ecosystem asset (or renewable natural capital more broadly) requires estimation of a range of parameters, of which the value of the flow of ecosystem services is just one ingredient. First, when the asset is renewable (or regenerates), the ongoing resource productivity must be considered in discounting the (future) value of the asset. Second, there is a capital or holding gain, which Irwin et al. (2016) term as a "scarcity effect" arising from holding the last or marginal unit of the asset.

That is, asset price, $p = \dfrac{V + \dot{p}}{r - \dot{s}}$, where V is the value of the marginal unit (current) service flow from the asset and r is the discount rate. One additional term, in the denominator, is $\dot{s}$, which refers to (net) resource productivity and is used therefore to calculate an effective discount rate. A further term, in the numerator, $\dot{p}$ refers to the "scarcity effect" of holding the last unit of the asset. This suggests then (depending on the magnitudes of $\dot{s}$ and $\dot{p}$) that the simple approach – i.e. capitalisation of current services – is missing something important. As such this has potentially important implications for accounting for natural capital asset values, as well as degradation or enhancement of these assets.

Fenichel et al. (2016) apply this conceptual framework to the challenge of valuing groundwater as an asset in rural Kansas in the USA, over the period 1996 to 2005. The stock of groundwater – the amount of water held in an aquifer of a given size – is defined here as the product of the thickness of the saturated zone (most comprised of rock) and an estimate of its yield. During their study period, the authors find that groundwater was being depleted, in physical terms, at a rate of 0.4% per year. However, this underestimates the corresponding annual change in the economic value of this stock. The reason for this is that as the stock declines, its marginal value increases because of a "scarcity effect". As an illustration of this the authors show that when groundwater is scarce the monetary value of a marginal unit – defined in terms of its value to agriculture – is roughly twice as high as when groundwater is abundant (i.e. around when it is about ten times as plentiful in physical terms). Accounting properly for the economic depreciation of groundwater in Kansas must consider this schedule of prices associated with different degrees of abundance. Fenichel et al. show that this matters empirically: the economic value of the loss in groundwater stocks is 6.5% per year over the study period.

Another type of issue is what to do when environmental valuation of a stock needs to take into account values which are held by people far into the future. Clearly, one cannot possibly know exactly what future preferences will be – that is, what future people will value – beyond those things one can feel confident will continue to be required for survival or basic functioning. The usual practical response to this uncertainty is to assume that future people have the same preferences as those living in the present but to uplift these values to take into account the likely effects of changing (i.e. growing) per capita income. Less common is taking account of the likely path of natural assets. That is, if it is thought that a natural asset will be more scarce in the future, then it is plausible that the (marginal) value that will be placed on future losses of services from this asset will be higher (than now).

A further (but related) question is what happens to such values when the underlying asset is difficult to replace. In the example above from Fenichel et al. (2015), one explanation for the scarcity effect estimate for groundwater is the characteristics of resources, which tends to be localised with limited substitutability. Gerlagh and van der Zwann (2002) consider the general case where these substitution possibilities are a function of the asset stock itself. That is, when a resource such as an ecosystem is relatively abundant, losses in that asset "do not matter" in the sense that this source of well-being could be easily replaced with something else and people essentially would be no worse off. However, after some threshold, substitution possibilities diminish rapidly. In other words, continued loss of the natural asset – beyond this critical point – increasingly cannot be compensated and, on the contrary, increases the prospect of ever higher and higher adverse impacts on future well-being as the resource continues to be depleted.[1] The implications of limited substitutability can be complex. Traeger (2011) shows that this affects the magnitude and term structure of the social discount rate (see Chapter 8). But the basic point remains that a lack of substitution possibilities should translate into a correspondingly higher (marginal) value to assign when natural capital is destroyed or degraded.

These critical issues about substitutability are also explored in contributions by Hoel and Sterner (2007) and Sterner and Persson (2008). Both of these papers show how the value (or shadow price) of a scarce environmental amenity might increase over time. A key parameter here reflects the ease (or difficulty) with which particular natural assets can be replaced: i.e. the "elasticity of substitution". The higher the value of this elasticity (reflecting the greater difficulties of replacing a natural asset with another type of wealth), the faster is the increase of the asset price of an environmental amenity as the natural asset (giving rise to that amenity) becomes more and more scarce.

Using these insights for practical analysis requires that a number of assumptions must be made: most notably, about the elasticity of substitution. Even so, there could be substantial problems such as evaluating future prospects using "sustainability prices" – that is, prices which are consistent with realising a sustainable path (which is a different point to the matter of correcting prices for current market, and other, failures). The point here is that there might be some sustainability problem that appraisal at the project level or aggregate level, for that matter, will not pick up. In principle, a conventional CBA might be able to address these issues. However, in practice this might be fraught with difficulties and may necessitate a rather different treatment of these same concerns within an economic appraisal.

12.5. CBA and (strong) sustainability

This issue of limited (or a lack of) substitutability between natural capital and other assets has important implications for rules for the sustainability of development as well as how CBA might be conducted or interpreted. Part of the challenge is the analysis of what happens when complex assets, such as renewable natural capital, change as a result of policy interventions. One example of this is the concept of "ecological resilience" that might characterise ecological capital (Mäler et al., 2009; Mäler, 2008): the ability of an ecosystem to withstand stresses and shocks (and to continue to provide services).[2] Walker et al. (2010) looks at the value of this resilience to agriculture in South-East Australia of maintaining a saline free water table (mainly through farmers cutting down trees to expand agriculture). Here agricultural expansion represents a driver depleting the stock of non-salinated soils (measured as the depth of soils for which saline intrusion is not a problem). As this depletion driver is increased so the stock of ecological resilience falls. The depleting process itself may generate benefits (here agricultural produce) and so there is a trade-off to be assessed between the benefits of depletion and the fact that losses of resilience may need to be reversed if stocks fall below some threshold level. Breaching the threshold, however, leads to likely irreversible losses in agricultural productivity (because of salinated soils) so this resilience has a distinct value which should incorporated in economic appraisal of actions which move this system towards or away from threshold.

Another problem arises from non-linearity. A cost-benefit analysis that fails to account for thresholds, for example, might recommend the conversion of part of an ecosystem, or other for more direct human use. But the assumption might still be that conversion of this part of the ecosystem would not affect the remaining services provided by the rest of the ecosystem. Non-linearity means that this assumption could be suspect. The real difficulty here arises from interdependencies between the various services provided by the ecosystem. In terms of valuation this means that the economic value of any one service may depend on its relationship to the other services. Valuation concerns *changes* in the ecosystem, and this is itself dependent on how everything changes, not just the service that the practitioner might want to focus on.

This is, incidentally, another reason why estimating "total" value is not feasible – as one, say, decreases the ecosystem dramatically, everything will change. The critical point here though is the ecological area is a "system". Ecosystems have interactive processes, a variable potential to adapt to exogenous change, and the relevant changes are often non-linear (Arrow et al., 2000). If so, then from a policy perspective it should be managed as such and, in turn, this might shape how CBA is used to inform decisions over management options. Importantly, it is not clear that "bottom up" (marginal) approaches whereby each type of service is valued separately and then the values are added to get some idea of the total value of the ecosystem, are capturing the "whole" value of the ecosystem. Put another way, the value of the system as a whole may be more than the value of the sum of its parts. The bottom-up valuation procedure could therefore be misleading. A small economic value for one service might suggest it could be dispensed with, yet its removal could reverberate on the other services through complex changes within the ecosystem.

One further problem is that there is both uncertainty about the nature of the services themselves and, even more so, about their interactions. While many agree that natural capital such as ecosystem assets are characterised by thresholds, there is less certainty about what these thresholds are, especially for the practical purpose of taking account of these in policy formulation tools such as CBA. So the example above for the case of saline-free agricultural land in South East Australia is an exception rather than the rule of what is known empirically. Similarly, while non-linearities may mean that the consequences of losing even modest amounts of ecosystem could be large (as threshold are approached or breached or where there are interactions with other parts of the system).

So converting a natural system may therefore produce unanticipated and adverse effects, which could be irreversible. Efforts at valuation of such changes in a CBA remain important. But it is important to recognise that these are unlikely to provide much information about the scale of "tolerable" change. Moreover, if decisions are made and they turn out to be extremely costly, little can be done to reverse them. Losses of natural capital assets can combine several features: a potential large "scale" effect; irreversibility; and, uncertainty. The argument is that these "strong sustainability" characteristics combine to justify a presumption that natural capital (and its components) should be conserved. The implication is that this view necessitates also a rather different approach to using CBA to make investment and policy decisions.

12.6. Cost-benefit analysis and precaution

Economists have long known that this combination argues strongly for a "precautionary" approach to making decisions (e.g. Dasgupta, 1982). Chapters 9 and 10 observed that there are two ways in which to conduct CBA. The first approach – the one that is most commonly used – operates either in a world of low uncertainty or in a context of uncertainty where the appropriate decision might be made in terms of expected values. The second takes more account of uncertainty and also takes explicit account of irreversibility, either because funds committed cannot be "uncommitted" or because other effects of the policy cannot be reversed (or both). This was described as the "real options" approach to CBA.

On the real options approach, considerable attention would be paid to the opportunities for learning, and thus reducing uncertainty, by delaying irreversible decisions. It seems clear that the many aspects of the issue of natural capital (particularly ecosystem change) fits the real options approach: there is uncertainty, irreversibility and a major chance to learn through scientific progress in understanding better what natural assets do and how they behave. It is in this sense that real options gives rigorous content to a notion like "the precautionary principle". Note that, on this interpretation of the precautionary principle, there would be far more caution about losing ecosystems, but benefits and costs would still be traded off.

Another contender for a precautionary approach would be the "safe minimum standard" (SMS) (Ciriacy-Wantrup, 1968; Bishop, 1978 and Randall, 2014). On this approach, natural capital conversion or loss would not be countenanced unless the opportunity costs – i.e. the value of the forgone "development" – were intolerably high. What the SMS approach does is to reverse the onus of proof, away from assuming that development is justified unless the costs to the environment are shown to be very high, to a presumption that conservation of natural capital is the right option unless its opportunity costs are very high. But determining what is meant by "intolerable costs" is not easy. The level of "tolerance" might be determined by the political process, by reference to some notional benchmark – perhaps a percentage of GNP, or by a more extreme indicator – e.g. the forgone development causes severe hardship or poverty.

The principle of precaution – for the reasons outlined in the previous section and perhaps operating via ethical reasoning and/or a decision-making framework such as the SMS – suggests, in turn, a strong sustainability principle. It argues that no further degradation or loss of natural capital should be tolerated. Incorporating information about scientific thresholds is then one way in which these sustainability constraints can be envisaged. Uncertainty about the location of these thresholds may present a challenge, however. There also remains debate about whether this refers to natural capital in general (assuming some basis for aggregation) or particular classes of natural asset which are critical according to strong sustainability criteria. The tendency, however, is that the latter has been the focus particularly ecosystems such as broad habitat types. The practical implications for CBA are still several. In a very extreme form, this might argue that no existing ecosystem should be degraded. In less extreme form it could argue that any loss has to be offset by the creation of a like asset.

12.6.1. Circumscribing CBA: the example of "biodiversity offsetting"

A number of contributions, beginning with Barbier et al. (1990), have sought to model concern about strong sustainability as a constraint for the purposes of CBA for the reasons outlined earlier in this chapter. While these are largely conceptual contributions, there is also growing practical interest in the application of, for example, resource compensation in assessing real world examples of damage particularly to ecosystems (although the applicability need not be limited to this). The basic approach taken, in theory and in practice, is to recognise that strong sustainability is a concept that is most relevant to the management of a portfolio of projects. That is, for example, imposing a constraint on project selection that each individual project does not damage an ecosystem is arguably too stringent (in the sense that very few projects would presumably yield net benefits yet not damage ecosystems at all).

More flexible proposals for selecting projects and choosing policy options subject to a (strong) sustainability constraint usually advocate that the "net effect" on the ecosystems of projects or policies in a portfolio should be, at least, zero. Leaving aside, for the moment, the issue of what it is precisely that projects should (on balance) seek to conserve, the broad principles of the approaches, for example, in Barbier et al. (1990) and later in Pires (1998) for subjecting a cost-benefit test to a (strong) sustainability constraint.

A practical example of this investment constraint almost dates back the beginnings of those conceptual ideas. This starts from the premise that limits to valuation mean that certain components of natural capital (notably "biodiversity", but not limited to this) need to incorporated within CBA as (sustainability) constraints (see, for example, Quinet et al., 2013, for a discussion of practical issues in valuing biodiversity in official CBA in France). More recent attention has focused on the form these constraints should take with, for example, an emphasis on thresholds and (safe) limits. This, in turn, requires knowledge or judgement about such thresholds across different natural assets. Another example is global climate change. Economic thinking (and CBA as part of that) has been used to help the frame discussion about what should be the appropriate level of ambition in global climate policy (see, for example, Stern, 2007; Weitzman, 2007). However, these political debates about global climate targets arguably have been based to a far greater extent on judgements about what degree of warming can be "tolerated" without physical thresholds being breached (e.g. Rockström et al., 2009; Steffen et al., 2015).

A notable practical development is the implementation of this idea in real-life settings under the guise of "biodiversity offsetting". Common to this earlier literature, which viewed the principle of sustainability as applying to the portfolio of projects, under offsetting proposals, biodiversity – in the round – must be maintained (or enhanced) by requiring that to the extent that any one project degrades or destroys an ecosystem or damages biodiversity, this must be "covered off" by improvements or additions to ecosystems or biodiversity elsewhere: i.e. so-called shadow or compensating projects. Typically, however, the context here is one where adverse impacts are supposed to be prevented or at least minimised at the original site. It is the residual damage that is subject to offsetting via a compensating investment elsewhere (see, for example, Chevassus-au-Louis et al., 2009).

While resource compensation preserves some trade-offs between costs and benefits it plainly circumscribes cost-benefit thinking in a substantial way. Roach and Wade (2006) provide an empirical investigation of this resource compensation or "equivalency" in the context of habitats. And as mentioned, the practical counterpart is policy instruments which variously go by the names of "mitigation banking", "habitat banking", resource equivalency (REMEDE, 2008) or "biodiversity offsets". A commitment to scaling up these schemes can be found variously in the Aichi targets (as part of the UN Convention on Biodiversity), EU Biodiversity Strategy to 2020 and the UK Natural Environment White Paper (Defra, 2011). BBOP (2012) defines the latter as: "… measurable conservation outcomes resulting from actions designed to compensate for significant residual adverse biodiversity impacts arising from project development after appropriate prevention and mitigation measures have been taken." (p. 12).

Moreover, it asserts the goal of these interventions as "… to achieve no net loss and preferably a net gain … with respect to species composition, habitat structure, ecosystem function and people's use and cultural value associated biodiversity" (BBOP, 2012, p. 13). This is a challenging array of attributes to offset. Not surprisingly, practical examples of biodiversity offset schemes have fallen short of this ambition, often relying instead on relatively simple metrics on habitat extent and quality. This has led to debates about whether compensation is genuinely "like-for-like" (and how this might be better guaranteed) as well as other issues such as governance and additionality or leakage (see, for example, Bull et al., 2013; Gardner et al., 2013; POST, 2011). A discussion of these issues, including good practice insights, is provided in OECD (2016).

What biodiversity offsetting does is to place CBA within a strategic constraint. That is, once the constraint is known then the rules for appraising the costs and benefits are relatively simple, at least in principle: CBA must work within this institution with the decision-rule being to maximise net benefits subject to observing the constraint. Needless to say, a number of questions might be posed. For example, are such constraints a special case or rather more general strategic considerations? How are these constraints to be determined?

Turning to the latter question first, given the characteristics of strong sustainability, guidance from the natural sciences, on how much of nature should be conserved, must be focal to this. Presumably social considerations play their part too, not least in crafting this technical advice to what is judged to be politically possible. How far this economic thinking, and especially judging costs and benefits, should be used for determining the strategic constraint is also important to reflect upon. Consideration of costs and benefits cannot have primacy – the point of the strong sustainability constraint is that there are clear limitations to this. However, neither can those considerations be irrelevant. Guiding principles such as the safe minimum standards potentially seek to perform this balancing act.

Another way of understanding these debates, however, is to acknowledge that these reflect different "belief systems" thought to be focal to policy problems. Put this way, CBA represents one belief system; based on an assumption of the importance of being explicit about the implications of policy choices for the way in which economic resources are used and, in particular, the trade-offs that this involves. Alternate belief systems might reject these trade-offs, perhaps by prioritising protecting nature arrived at through particular ethical perspectives. Rather than reject CBA altogether the "sustainability constraint" approach becomes a useful way of viewing the implications of these different beliefs. Not least it facilitates some explicit understanding of the costs of observing constraints (as well as the benefits).

Biodiversity offsetting is a specific constraint, albeit one which applied properly, and consistently, is possibly far-reaching. So too for carbon offsetting. But clearly, strong sustainability is a wider set of concerns about nature, and natural capital, more generally. A reasonable question is whether such constraints are special cases, or something more pervasive, and what the character of these constraints should be. Certainly the spirit of the strong sustainability approach indicates a more ubiquitous role for setting strategic constraints. Chevassus-au-Louis et al. (2009), for example, suggest a distinction between natural capital which has "intrinsic" value and natural capital which does not as a basis for this. In turn, this necessitates practical deliberations on what characteristics might allow particular resources to be categorised as one or the other.

Where constraints are recommended, what these constraints should look like is another matter. One extreme would be a set of (piecemeal) constraints for specific natural assets (e.g. biodiversity, carbon, urban air quality and so on). Another extreme would be to define natural capital in the aggregate (e.g. Helm, 2015). This would permit far more flexibility but inevitably raises questions about whether parts of the natural asset portfolio are substitutable or not. It also requires an index of natural capital, which in principle would be reflect these trade-offs.

Finally, given that strong sustainability constraints – such as those entailed in biodiversity offsetting – necessitate *actual* compensation, ensuring that these corresponding investments do not themselves fail arises as a subsequent challenge. While this is a question that can only really be answered through an *ex post* evaluation, there are a number of *ex ante* considerations that might help mitigate against the failure of offsetting projects. For example, CGDD (2015) identifies a number of such factors relating to technical matters of project planning and execution as well as the institutional arrangements that govern these compensating actions. This proceeds by categorising the risks of offsetting projects such as whether these restore sufficient biophysical quantities (defined against specified metrics, such that the adequacy of these chosen metrics is also relevant). Additionally, the location of what is restored – in the compensating project – relative to what is lost by the initial (natural capital depleting) project might also be relevant: that is, for example, does the former have connectivity with other (related) ecosystems?

What the preceding points suggest is that some sort of structured planning is needed in meeting this need to impose sustainability constraints on policy and project decisions. In other words, institutional arrangements are critical. CGDD (2015) note that paying attention to governance might also anticipate risks of failure of compensating projects by addressing other risks as well. This includes managing project uncertainty generally as well as scrutinising whether management plans and economic resources for long-term ecosystem management are themselves sustainable. In turn, this suggests checking that budgets and contingency funds are adequate and that subsequent management is devolved to appropriate bodies.

12.7. Concluding remarks

The notion of "sustainable development" has permeated significant parts of policy and public discourse about the environment. While there remains debate about it means for development to be sustainable, there is now a coherent body of academic work that has sought to understand what a sustainable development path might look like, how this path can be achieved and how progress towards it might be measured. While it is hardly surprising that these efforts have not generated a consensus, there has been considerable progress in understanding where agreement and disagreement is and why this arises. Perhaps the pre-eminent example of the arrival of sustainability to the policy agenda is the UN Sustainable Development Goals or SDGs.

Much of this work considers the pursuit of sustainable development to be an aggregate or macroeconomic goal. By-and-large cost benefit analysts have not sought actively to engage with this broader debate except insofar as it relates to factors affecting a project's forecast net benefit or rate of return. However, it should be noted that recent developments discussed elsewhere in this volume – most notably on valuing environmental impacts and discounting costs and benefits – are relevant to this issue. In this chapter, we have discussed a number of additional speculations about how cost-benefit appraisals can be extended to take account of recent concerns about sustainable development.

According to one perspective there is an obvious role for appraising projects in the light of these concerns. This notion of strong sustainability starts from the assertion that certain natural assets are so important or critical (for future, and perhaps current, generations) so as to warrant protection at current or above some other target level. If individual preferences cannot be counted on to fully reflect this importance, there is a paternal role for decision-makers in providing this protection. Some have sought to characterise this according to ecological criteria while others have drawn on political precedents or it is seen as dependent on weighting decision-making heavily in favour of precaution. This raises important issues. On the one hand, there is a benefit to avoiding untoward and irreversible damage to (possibly) critical resources. On the other hand, there are opportunity costs to applying the shadow projects approach that need still to be considered.

With regards to the relevance of this approach to cost-benefit appraisals, a handful of contributions have suggested that sustainability is applicable to the management of a *portfolio* of projects. This has resulted in the idea of a shadow or compensating project. For example, this could be interpreted as meaning that projects that cause environmental damage are "covered off" by projects that result in environmental improvements. The overall consequence is that projects in the portfolio, on balance, maintain the environmental status quo. Practical applications of this approach arguably include biodiversity offsetting.

There are further ways of viewing the problem of sustainable development. Whether these alternatives – usually characterised under the heading "weak sustainability" – are complementary or rivals has been a subject of debate. This debate would largely dissolve if it could be determined which assets were critical. As this latter issue is itself a considerable source of uncertainty, as discussed above, the debate continues. However, the so-called "weak" approach to sustainable development is useful for a number of reasons. While it has primarily be viewed as a guide to constructing green national accounts (i.e. better measures of income, saving and wealth), the focus on assets and asset management has a counterpart in thinking about project appraisal. For example, this might emphasise the need for assess stocks of assets before the project intervention and what they are likely to be after the intervention.

Notes

1. Gerlagh and van der Zwann (2002) look at the case where individuals have a very strong preference for natural assets rather than non-substitutability per se. This is very similar to the notion of a lexicographic preference that has been the subject of a mini-literature in stated preference studies. The implications of this assumption, however, are that liquidating a natural asset beyond some threshold plausibly lowers the maximum level that future well-being can take.

2. This approach can also accommodate a crucial concern about the nature of ecosystem assets: namely, that these resources are subject to threshold effects where services are subject to (possibly) greater risks of abrupt and extreme changes once a critical level of the asset has been breached.

References

Asheim, G.B. and M.L. Weitzman (2001), "Does NNP Growth Indicate Welfare Improvement", *Economics Letters*, Vol. 73, pp. 233-239.

Arrow, K.J. et al. (2010), "Sustainability and the Measurement of Wealth", *www.econ.cam.ac.uk/faculty/dasgupta/10/Sust-and-Meas-Wealth-19Oct10.pdf*.

Barbier, E.B. (2011), *Capitalizing on Nature*, Cambridge University Press, Cambridge, *www.cambridge.org/catalogue/catalogue.asp?isbn=0521189276*.

Barbier, E.B. (2009), "Ecosystems as Natural Assets", *Foundations and Trends in Microeconomics*, 4(8), pp. 611-681, *http://dx.doi.org/10.1561/0700000031*.

Barbier, E., A. Markandya and D.W. Pearce (1990), "Environmental sustainability and cost-benefit analysis", *Environment and Planning A*, Vol. 22, pp. 1259-1266, *https://doi.org/10.1068/a221259*.

Boyd, J. and S. Banzhaf (2007), "What are ecosystem services? The need for standardized environmental accounting units", *Ecological Economics*, Vol. 63(2-3), pp. 616-626, *http://dx.doi.org/10.1016/j.ecolecon.2007.01.002*.

Chevassus-au-Louis, B. et al. (2009) *An Economic Approach to Biodiversity and Ecosystem Services: Contribution To Public Decision-Making*, Center for Strategic Analysis, Report and Documents Collection, Paris.

CGDD (Department of the Commissioner General for Sustainable Development) (ed.) (2015) *Nature and the Wealth of Nations*, English Version, Department for the Economics, Assessment and Integration of Sustainable Development, Paris.

Chiabai, A. et al. (2011) "Economic Assessment of Forest Ecosystem Services Losses: Costs of Policy Inaction", *Environmental and Resource Economics*, Vol. 50, pp. 405-445, *http://dx.doi.org/10.1007/s10640-011-9478-6*.

Dasgupta, P.M. (2009), "The Welfare Economic Theory of Green National Accounts", *Environment and Resource Economics*, Vol. 42, pp. 3-38, *http://dx.doi.org/10.1007/s10640-008-9223-y*.

Dasgupta, P. and K.-G. Mäler (2000), "Net National Product, wealth and social well-being", *Environment and Development Economics*, Vol. 5, pp. 69-93, *www.cambridge.org/core/product/8819C6F796223EF600E7F5C339491944*.

Day, B. and D. Maddison (2015), *Improving Cost-Benefit Analysis Guidance*, Report to the Natural Capital Committee (NCC), NCC, London, *http://nebula.wsimg.com/ad8539d7216f5e6589bbe625c9750fff?AccessKeyId=68F83A8E994328D64D3D&disposition=0&alloworigin=1*.

Dietz, S. and N. Stern (2008), "Why Economic Analysis Supports Strong Action on Climate Change: A Response to the Stern Review's Critics", *Review of Environmental Economics and Policy*, Vol. 2(1), pp. 94-113, *https://doi.org/10.1093/reep/ren001*.

Fenichel, E.P. et al. (2016) "Measuring the Value of Groundwater and Other Forms of Natural Capital", *PNAS*, Vol. 113(9), pp. 2382-2387, *http://dx.doi.org/10.1073/pnas.1513779113.*

Fenichel, E.P. and J.K. Abbott (2014), "Natural capital: From Metaphor to measurement", *Journal of the Association of Environmental and Resource Economists*, Vol. 1(1), pp. 1-27, *http://dx.doi.org/10.1086/676034.*

Gerlagh, R. and B.C.C. van der Zwaan (2002), "Long-Term Substitutability between Environmental and Man-made Goods", *Journal of Environmental Economics and Management*, Vol. 44, pp. 329-345, *http://dx.doi.org/10.1006/jeem.2001.1205.*

Gowdy, J. et al. (2010), "Discounting, Ethics and Options for Maintaining Biodiversity and Ecosystem Integrity", in Kumar, P. (ed.), *The Economics of Ecosystems and Biodiversity: Ecological and Economic Foundations*, Earthscan, London.

Haines-Young, R. et al. (2009), *Towards a Common International Classification of Ecosystems (CICES) for Integrated Environmental and Economic Accounting*, Report to the European Environment Agency, Copenhagen.

Hamilton, K. and G. Atkinson (2006), *Wealth, Wellbeing and Sustainability*, Edward Elgar, Cheltenham.

Hamilton, K. and M. Clemens (1999), "Genuine savings rates in developing countries", *World Bank Economic Review*, Vol. 13(2), pp. 333-356, *https://doi.org/10.1093/wber/13.2.333.*

Hamilton, K. and J.M. Hartwick (2014), "Wealth and Sustainability", *Oxford Review of Economic Policy*, Vol. 30(1), pp. 170-187, *https://doi.org/10.1093/oxrep/gru006.*

Hamilton, K. and E. Ley (2013), "Sustainable Fiscal Policy for Mineral Based Economies", in Amadou, S., A. Rabah and B. Gylfason (eds.), *Beyond the Curse: Policies to Harness the Power of Natural Resources*, International Monetary Fund, Washington, DC.

Hartwick, J.M. (1992), "Deforestation and national accounting", *Environmental and Resource Economics*, Vol. 2, pp. 513-521, *http://dx.doi.org/10.1007/BF00376832.*

Hartwick, J.M. (1977), "Intergenerational equity and the investing of rents from exhaustible resources", *American Economic Review*, Vol. 67, pp. 972-4.

Hoel, M. and T. Sterner (2007), "Discounting and Relative Prices", *Climatic Change*, Vol. 84, pp. 265-280, *http://dx.doi.org/10.1007/s10584-007-9255-2.*

Kaveira, P. et al. (eds.) (2011), *Natural Capital: Theory and Practice of Mapping Ecosystem Services*, Oxford University Press, Oxford.

Krutilla J. and A.C. Fisher (1974), *The Economics of Natural Environments*, Johns Hopkins University Press, Baltimore.

Mace, G.M., K. Norris and A.H. Fitter (2012), "Biodiversity and ecosystem services: A multilayered relationship", *Trends in Ecology & Evolution*, Vol. 27(1), pp. 19-26, *http://dx.doi.org/10.1016/j.tree.2011.08.006.*

Mäler, K.-G., S. Aniyar and Å. Jansson (2009), "Accounting for Ecosystems", *Environmental and Resource Economics*, Vol. 42, pp. 39-51, *http://dx.doi.org/10.1007/s10640-008-9234-8.*

Mäler, K.-G. (2008), "Sustainable Development and Resilience in Ecosystems", *Environmental and Resource Economics*, Vol. 39(1), pp. 17-24, *http://dx.doi.org/10.1007/s10640-007-9175-7.*

Mäler, K.-G. (1991), "National Accounts and environmental resources", *Environmental and Resource Economics*, Vol. 1, pp. 1-16.

OECD (2016), *Biodiversity Offsets: Effective Design and Implementation*, OECD Publishing, Paris, *http://dx.doi.org/10.1787/9789264222519-en.*

OECD (2012), *OECD Environmental Outlook to 2050*, OECD Publishing, *http://dx.doi.org/10.1787/9789264122246-en.*

Pascual, U. et al. (2010), "Valuation of Ecosystems Services: Methodology and Challenges", in Kumar, P. (ed.) *The Economics of Ecosystems and Biodiversity: Ecological and Economic Foundations*, Earthscan, London.

Pearce, D.W. and G. Atkinson (1993), "Capital Theory and the Measurement of Sustainable Development: An Indicator of 'Weak' Sustainability", *Ecological Economics*, Vol. 8(2), pp. 103-108, *https://doi.org/10.1016/0921-8009(93)90039-9.*

Pezzey, J. (1989), "Economic Analysis of Sustainable Growth and Sustainable Development", *Environment Department Working Paper* No. 15, World Bank, Washington, DC.

van der Ploeg, R. (2014), "Guidelines for Exploiting Natural Resource Wealth", *Oxford Review of Economic Policy*, Vol. 30(1), pp. 145-169, *https://doi.org/10.1093/oxrep/gru008*.

Solow, R.M. (1986), "On the intergenerational allocation of natural resources", *Scandinavian Journal of Economics*, Vol. 88(1), pp. 141-49, *www.jstor.org/stable/3440280*.

Solow, R.M. (1974), "Intergenerational equity and exhaustible resources", *Review of Economic Studies*, Vol. 41, pp. 29-45, *www.jstor.org/stable/2296370*.

Sterner, T. and U.M. Persson (2008), "An Even Sterner Review: Introducing Relative Prices into the Discounting Debate", *Review of Environmental Economics and Policy*, Vol. 2(1), pp. 61-76, *https://doi.org/10.1093/reep/rem024*.

Vanoli, A. (2015), "National accounting and consideration of the Natural heritage", in *Nature and the Wealth of Nations – la Revue du CGDD*, décembre 2015, pp. 75-84, *http://temis.documentation.developpement-durable.gouv.fr/docs/Temis/0083/Temis-0083488/22322_ENG.pdf*.

Walker, B. et al. (2010) "Incorporating Resilience in the Assessment of Inclusive Wealth: An Example from South East Australia", *Environmental and Resource Economics*, Vol. 45(2), pp. 183-202, *http://dx.doi.org/10.1007/s10640-009-9311-7*.

WCED (World Commission on Environment and Development) (1987), *Our Common Future*, the Report of the World Commission on Environment and Development, Oxford University Press, Oxford, *www.un-documents.net/wced-ocf.htm*.

Weitzman, M.L. (1976), "On the welfare significance of national product in a dynamic economy", *Quarterly Journal of Economics*, Vol. 90, pp. 156-162, *www.jstor.org/stable/1886092*.

World Bank (2010), *The Changing Wealth of Nations*, The World Bank, Washington, DC, *https://openknowledge.worldbank.org/handle/10986/2252*.

PART III

Chapter 13

Ecosystem services and biodiversity

The valuation of ecosystem services has become a crucial element (perhaps the crucial element) in quantifying the contribution of ecosystems and biodiversity to human well-being. While the evidence base is broad and – at least for some ecosystem services – deep, reflections on this progress indicate a need for greater understanding of ecological production, especially as it relates to spatial variability and complexities in the way that services are produced. This is a truly interdisciplinary given the need for natural science to inform the stages of this analytical process. There is considerable debate remaining also about how to conduct decision analyses in those contexts where valuation and understanding of the natural world is likely to remain relatively uncertain. Such challenges need to be viewed in context. A growing number of large-scale ecosystem assessments has shown how the empirical record can be put to use in an informative and policy-relevant way. Such developments could be crucial in translating valuations into meaningful policy analysis.

13.1. Introduction

The valuation of biodiversity and ecosystem services is increasingly seen as a crucial element of robust decision making. An impetus for this has been large-scale "ecosystem assessments", which have helped clarify the way in which ecosystems contribute to human well-being. This is an antidote then to past practice which has all too often given cursory consideration, or even completely ignored, this link between nature and well-being in policy analyses.

The application of economic valuation techniques to the complexities of the natural environment raises a number of significant challenges. Perhaps most fundamental is the need to ensure that such applications are based upon a sound foundation of natural science.[1] This requirement for interdisciplinarity is given a conceptual framework within the so-called "ecosystem service" approach to decision making. While typically characterised as emanating from the natural sciences, the approach is highly compatible with economic analysis as it emphasises the role of ecosystems in providing services which, in turn, either support production or are direct contributors to well-being. Ecosystem services are therefore defined as contributors to anthropocentric values and while the natural sciences provide an understanding of the former, it is economics which is well placed to assess the latter. Economic valuation, in particular, becomes an essential element of the ecosystems service approach to decision analysis.

While the term "ecosystem services" is relatively recent, at least in the scheme of things having only being popularised in the wake of the Millennium Ecosystem Assessment (MA, 2005), environmental economists have been applying non-market valuation techniques to such services for many years (see, for example, Adamowicz et al., 1994; Ruitenbeek, 1989). Understanding the economic value of ecosystems is important for a number of reasons. One of these is undoubtedly the perceived persuasiveness of economic language. For example, Bateman et al. (2011b) estimate that, in the United Kingdom, ecosystem services help contribute to 3 billion outdoor recreational visits annually with the social value of the output created by these trips likely to be more than GBP 10 billion. Gallai et al. (2009) calculate the global value of the services provided by insect pollinators to be about USD 190 billion (in 2005) just in terms of the benefits arising from pollination of crops for (direct) human consumption. Thus, conveying what it is that the natural world provides us with in monetary terms is a powerful means of communicating the importance of conservation to a wider (and perhaps previously unreceptive) audience.

But beneath the rhetoric there is genuine substance in that these data can also be used to guide policy thinking and decisions. In the case, for example, of the recreational value of UK ecosystems, Bateman et al. (2011b) also show that how location (of these sites) matters. This is also pointed out in Wilson et al. (2014). A specific and moderate sized nature recreation site, for example, might generate values of between GBP 1 000 and GBP 65 000 per annum depending solely on where it is located. The critical determinant of this range is perhaps not surprisingly proximity to significant conurbations. Put another way, woodlands in the "wrong" place (i.e. relatively far from potential visiting populations) are unlikely to give rise to such high social values (other things being equal), an insight of particular importance if policy makers are contemplating new investments in these nature sites.

More generally, the key insight in explicitly placing a value on nature is that it redresses a fundamental imbalance whereby this value is – all too frequently – grossly misjudged or just plainly ignored in private and (much of) social decision-making. Demonstrating that nature has significant value for human livelihoods or human well-being more broadly is a crucial practical step in developing policy actions that address current and projected rates of ecosystem destruction and biodiversity loss. One much cited example, in this respect, is Barbier (2007). That study estimates the ecological value of mangroves in Thailand – in terms of providing fuelwood, a habitat that supplies fisheries and storm water attenuation (which reduces the risks of coastal flooding) – in order to compare those findings with the returns from the competing land use activity of shrimp farming. Thus, private profits under these two different uses are USD 584 and USD 1 220 per hectare respectively, giving, on the face of it, a clear (financial) case for mangrove conversion. However, social cost-benefit analysis reveals another story in that a representative hectare of mangrove is shown to generate a social value of USD 12 392.

Of course, the economic approach may not always provide the answer that ecosystems should be protected (and thus indicates the pitfall for those who see only the rhetorical worth in economic arguments). There is also a concern about the challenge of demonstrating the importance of ecological fundamentals – notably, "biodiversity" – in these assessments of the instrumental value of nature. And debates about the intrinsic value of nature remain relevant too. Nevertheless, and however the question is posed, determining how much of nature "ought to be" conserved is likely to require a significant effort to understand its value in economic terms as well as the (opportunity) costs of its conservation. The challenges are immense. While many of these are not insurmountable (as the growing evidence-base suggests), as is also discussed, in what follows, there is an inevitability to limits on valuing nature. How to do economic appraisal whenever these limits are reached is also an important question as illustrated in Chapter 12.

13.2. Ecosystem services

All life is embedded in various categories of *ecosystems*, where ecosystems are defined as life forms ("biota") and their abiotic environments. Thus, a forest or a wetland is an ecosystem, as are coral reefs, deserts, estuaries and rivers. All ecosystems generate *services* which are extensive and pervasive. Those services essentially maintain life on Earth so, in one sense, all ecosystem services are economic services – they have an economic value based on the benefits human beings receive from those ecosystems. An ecologist might select the following services as being of considerable importance, but would probably define them without necessarily having the focus on how humans benefit, which tends to be the economist's perspective. For example, the following indicates some services that have obvious human benefits. Ecosystems provide:

● Purification services: for example, wetlands filter water and forests filter air pollution.

● Ecological cycling: for example, growing vegetation takes in ("fixes" or "sequesters") carbon dioxide, and stores it in the biomass until the death of the vegetation, the carbon then being transferred to soil. Since carbon dioxide is a greenhouse gas, growing biomass reduces the concentration of those gases in the atmosphere.

- Regulation: natural systems have interacting species such that pests are controlled through natural processes, reducing the need for artificial controls. Ecosystems may regulate watershed and weather behaviour, reducing risk of floods.

- Habitat provision: habitats are stores of biological diversity which in turn may be linked to processes that reduce the risks of ecosystem collapse ("resilience"), even apart from providing sources of food, scientific information, recreational and aesthetic value.

- Regeneration and production: ecosystems "grow" biomass by converting light, energy and nutrients. This biomass provides food, raw materials and energy. Ecosystems ensure pollination and seed dispersal take place, ensuring that the systems are themselves renewed. It is estimated that some 30% of the world's food crops are dependent on natural pollination.

- Information and life support: Ecosystems are the products of evolution and hence embody millions of years of information. This information has scientific value but is also a source of wonder and life support.

One starting point for marrying notions of ecosystem service from the natural sciences to the requirements of economics is classification systems. There are a number of variations on these classifications. Common to almost all is a distinction between: provisioning services; cultural services; and regulating services. The former two services nicely capture some elements of the previous distinction between use and non-use (see Chapter 4). Provisioning services, for example, are typically physical products such as food and natural materials provided by nature. Cultural services, by contrast, describe the experiences that people enjoy as a result of interactions with nature (e.g. recreation), as well as more intangible pleasures arising from knowledge about the existence of nature or its spiritual value. Of course, while these services can be thought as being distinct for the purposes of classification, ecosystems might provide "goods" which fulfil both provisioning and cultural criteria (see, for a detailed discussion, Chan et al., 2011) as well as different types of cultural benefit: i.e. use and non-use. For example, a woodland might be valued both for its provision of recreational opportunities as well as for the knowledge that this natural area continues to be conserved or provided even if the person expressing the value does not observe directly this outcome. Table 13.1 provides an example of this classification, drawn from Markandya (2016) and based on ongoing work to classify ecosystem services for the purposes of ecosystem accounting.

Further classifications of ecosystem services do exist. Kumar (2010), for example, add habitat services in recognition of the role that ecosystems provide in protecting "gene pools" as well as crucial sets of interlinking habitats for migratory species. MA (2005) also emphasised the supporting services of ecosystems as the natural processes that underpin those services of provision, culture and regulation. These services, such as nutrient cycling, thus provide a further intermediate tier to ecological production and, indeed, it has since become more common to see these functions subsumed under the "regulating services" heading (e.g. Kumar, 2010). Other classifications, such as Heal et al. (2005) and de Groot et al. (2002), have focused more specifically on habitat services and regulating services.

While this emphasis is partial, it encapsulates a key distinctive element of the effort to understand the economics of ecosystems. This likens the enjoyment of (final) ecosystem services to a process of (natural) production whereby critical inputs are, for example, regulating services. As an illustration, it is these services – by e.g. regulating water flow (and the quality of that water) and the supply of insect pollinators – that

Table 13.1. Classification of ecosystem services

Section	Division	Group	Class
Provisioning	Nutrition	Biomass	Cultivated Crops
			Reared animals and their outputs
			Wild plants, algae and their outputs
			Wild animals and their outputs
			Plants and algae from in-situ aquaculture
			Animals from in-situ aquaculture
		Water	Surface water for drinking
			Groundwater for drinking
	Materials	Biomass	Fibres and other materials from plants
			Plants, algae, animals materials for agricultural
			Genetic materials from all biota
		Water	Surface water for non-drinking purposes
			Groundwater for non-drinking purposes
	Energy	Biomass based energy	Plant-based resources
			Animal-based resources
		Mechanical based	Animal-based energy
Regulation and Maintenance	Mediation of waste, toxics and other nuisances	Mediation by biota	Bioremediation by micro-organisms etc.,
			Filtration/sequestration/storage/accumulation by micro-organisms etc.,
		Mediation by ecosystems	Filtration/sequestration/storage/accumulation
			Dilution by atmosphere, freshwater, marine ecosystems
			Mediation of smell, noise, visual impacts
	Mediation of flows	Mass flows	Stabilisation and control of erosion rates
			Buffering and attenuation of mass flows
		Liquid flows	Hydrological cycle and water flow maintenance
			Flood protection
		Air Flows	Storm protection, ventilation and transpiration
		Habitat and gene pool protection	Pollination and seed dispersal
			Maintaining nursery populations and habitats
		Pest and disease control	Pest control
			Disease control
	Maintenance of physical, chemical, biological conditions	Soil formation and Composition	Weathering processes
			Decomposition and fixing processes
		Water conditions	Chemical condition of fresh and salt waters
		Atmosphere and Climate regulation	Global climate regulation by reducing GHGs
			Micro and region climate regulation
Cultural	Physical and intellectual interactions with biota/ecosystems	Physical and experiential	Experiential use of plants, animals landscapes
			Physical use of land/seascapes in different ways
		Intellectual and representative interactions	Scientific, educational, heritage/cultural, entertainment and aesthetic interactions
	Spiritual, symbolic interactions with biota/ecosystems	Spiritual and/or emblematic	Symbolic
			Sacred and/or religious
		Other cultural	Existence
			Bequest

Source: Markandya (2016).

contribute ultimately to the production of agricultural provisioning services (Goulder and Kennedy, 2011). Valuing ecosystem services has often focused on the end output, by asking what is the final service that ultimately benefits people. Clearly, knowledge of what ecosystems provide as final goods and services that is being consumed is important. Yet it is equally crucial to understand the way in which intermediate tiers of production contribute to this final output.

In many of these classifications, there appears to be no explicit place for the value of *biodiversity*. Indeed, a significant anxiety about recent ecosystem assessments is that the emphasis upon ecosystem services might ironically lead to the omission of the vital role which biodiversity plays in both the delivery of those services and as a source of value in itself. On the one hand, biodiversity can be thought itself of as a service. For example, pollinator biodiversity directly enhances agricultural production. Certain aspects of biodiversity, such as the continued existence of iconic species such as the polar bear, itself constitutes a good (i.e. a direct source of well-being). On the other hand, Mace et al. (2012) warn that exclusively focusing on that role risks missing something fundamental. As discussed in detail by Elmqvist et al. (2010), biodiversity acts as a supporting service underpinning the delivery of what Fisher et al. (2009) term final ecosystem services. So, for example, soil biodiversity enhances farmland fertility which in turn determines production of a good (here food). In fact, such functions provided by biodiversity have been likened by, for example, Pascual et al. (2010) to a form of insurance (following from earlier contributions such as Gren et al., 1994).

It is clear that ecosystems are "multi-functional" or "multi-product" – they generate an array of ecological-economic services. Unlike a multi-product firm, however, it was noted above that the "products" of ecosystems are usually not known with the level of certainty that would apply to a firm producing an array of market products. The products in question will also range from being purely private goods (e.g. fuelwood, clean water) through to being localised public goods (watershed protection) and finally to being global public goods (carbon sequestration and the non-use value of the ecosystem).

Initial clues in the search for practical ecosystem values can be found by reflecting on how ecosystem services ultimately provide benefits to people and businesses. This was discussed in Chapter 2 and is what Freeman et al. (2013) term: "The economic channel through which well-being is affected" (p. 13). These channels are manifold (e.g. Brown et al., 2007; Freeman et al., 2013) but can be summarised in three ways.

- First, there are those ecosystem services which are used as inputs to economic production. Examples include soil fertility which is an input to agricultural production. Water regulation and water purification services are inputs to those economic (producing) units which need a supply of clean water as an input, perhaps alongside e.g. other factors of production.

- Second, ecosystem services can act as joint inputs to household consumption. That is, there is use of ecosystem services in combination with expenditure on produced goods and services in providing a "product" for consumption. In such cases, an ecosystem services and the market goods or services are complementary inputs. Examples include nature services which in combination with travel expenditures are used to produce nature recreational experiences. However, an ecosystem service can be a substitute for a market good. An example is air purification services which can substitute for purchase of a produced good which filters air.

- Third, ecosystem services can be inputs which directly contribute to household well-being. That is, there is no existing economic production or household consumption where these services act as inputs. These services are consumed directly in generating benefits (which themselves are ultimately a source of well-being). Examples here are by their nature rather abstract, but include those services valued for reasons surrounding what is usually termed "non-use" or "passive-use", such as "true wilderness".

13.3. Valuing ecosystem services

Uncovering the true value of goods and using these data to ensure decisions contribute to improving human well-being is a defining rationale for economic analysis. A number of recent comprehensive reviews make clear the proliferation of methods – and applications of those methods – to assess the value of ecosystem services and biodiversity (see, for example, Pascual et al., 2011; US EPA, 2009; Bateman et al., 2011b; Kaveira et al., 2011; as well as Chapters 3 to 7 in this volume). These assessments have been important for revealing, on the one hand, what is known about ecosystem and biodiversity valuation and, on the other hand, in identifying what remains to be learnt. Table 13.2 provides a brief overview of the key approaches. What is important to note here is that *all* of these methods have been used in the ecosystems context. In large part, this breadth of methods reflects, in turn, the diversity of services that practitioners have sought to value rather than variety for its own sake.

The starting point for thinking about the valuation of ecosystem services is that such assessments rely upon standard economic theory but with an underpinning by the natural sciences (Daily, 1997; MA, 2005; Pagiola et al., 2004; Heal et al., 2005; Barbier, 2007; Sukhdev, 2008). Whether this valuation can be based on market prices or whether the analyst must look to evidence from non-market behaviour (be this actual or intended) depends on the characteristics of the ecosystem good or service in question. In some cases, valuation might begin with market prices. For example, provisioning services, such as food and fibre, are frequently market goods or near-market goods with close (market) substitutes. It follows, therefore, that market-based valuation has been prominent in such contexts, although perhaps these observed prices need to be adjusted for distortions (Table 13.2). However, the provisioning service is itself typically determined by some underlying service provided by an ecosystem process. Thus, while the valuation of this final output is relatively straightforward, the analytical heavy-lifting is often done through the specification and estimation of an ecological production function. In other words, ecosystem services frequently are valued as a productive input (see Barbier, 2007; Freeman, 2003; and Hanley and Barbier, 2009). In this approach, an attempt must be made to isolate and uncover the value of ecosystems services from the perspective of their effect on some observed level of output (Table 13.2). This approach can be applied to a range of market (consumption) goods but has also been used for valuing regulating and "protection" goods (where examples of the latter include flooding and extreme weather protection).

In other cases, however, the value that people place on ecosystem services is not adequately reflected in market prices, if at all. In such cases, non-market valuation techniques must be employed and applied to some ecological end-point which itself may have been estimated following some application of a production function. Revealed preference methods value non-market environmental goods by examining the consumption of related market-priced private goods. A number of variants of the revealed preference approach exist, depending on whether the environmental good and the related market good are complements, substitutes or one is an attribute of the other (Table 13.2).

Table 13.2. **Summary of economic valuation methods used in ecosystem service valuation**

Valuation method	Description	Typical applications to ecosystem services
Adjusted market prices	Using market prices adjusted for any distortions (e.g. taxes, subsidies, non-competitive practices)	Crops, livestock, woodland
Production function methods	Estimation of an ecological production function where the ecosystem service is modelled as an input to the production process and is valued through its effect on the output	Maintenance of beneficial species, maintenance of agricultural productivity, flood protection
Revealed preference methods	Examining actual expenditures made on market goods related to ecosystem services. When market goods are substitutes, avertive behaviour or mitigating expenditure approaches can be used (e.g. expenditures to avoid damage, such as buying bottled water or installing double glazing). Travel cost methods can be used when market goods are complements, (e.g. travel costs for recreation). When the ecosystem service is a characteristic of the market good hedonic price methods can be used (e.g. looking at the impact of noise or amount of green space on property prices)	Water quality, peace and quiet, recreation, amenity benefits
Stated preference methods	Using surveys to elicit willingness to pay for an environmental change (contingent valuation) or to ask individuals to make choices between different levels of environmental goods at different prices to reveal their willingness to pay (choice modelling)	Water quality, species conservation, air quality, non-use values
Subjective well-being (SWB) methods	Uses survey responses of measures of SWB, and investigate the extent to which ecosystem-related metrics are determinants of well-being. Valuation might entail looking at the income/ecosystem trade-off in reaching a given level of SWB	Water quality, species conservation, air quality depending on the availability of suitable metrics

In the first case, economists make use of the "weak complementarity" concept introduced by Mäler (1974) to examine how much individuals are prepared to spend on a private good in order to enjoy the environmental good, thereby revealing the value of the latter. For example, the travel cost method examines the expenditure and time that individuals are prepared to give up to visit natural areas for recreation. In cases of substitutability between goods, approaches such as avertive behaviour or mitigating expenditures to avoid damages can be used, such as buying bottled water to avoid drinking contaminated water. Finally, the hedonic property price method assumes that one can look at the housing market to infer the implicit value of the underlying characteristics of domestic properties be these structural, locational/accessibility, neighbourhood or environmental (Rosen, 1974). It can be used for example to examine the premium which people are prepared to pay in order to purchase houses in areas with greater proximity to green spaces or habitat types (Gibbons et al., 2011).

While revealed preference methods estimate original values by looking at *actual* behaviour, eliciting values by looking at *intended* behaviour is the province of stated preference (SP) methods. This is an umbrella term for a range of survey-based methods that use constructed or hypothetical markets to elicit preferences for specified changes in provision of environmental services (Table 13.2). By far the most widely applied SP technique is the contingent valuation method (see, for example, Alberini and Kahn, 2006).[2] However, in recent years, choice modelling has become increasingly popular. In this variant, respondents are required to choose their most preferred out of a (possibly relatively large) set of alternative policy or provision options offered at different prices and their willingness to pay is revealed indirectly through their choices (see, for example, Hanley et al., 2001; Kanninen, 2007).[3]

In theory, SP approaches should be applicable to a wide range of ecosystem services and can be used to measure future/predicted changes in those goods. Importantly, such methods are thought to be the only option available for estimating those services which are valued for "non-use" purposes. In practice, SP methods are mostly defensible in cases where respondents have clear prior preferences for the goods in question or can discover economically consistent preferences within the course of the survey exercise. Where this is not the case, then elicited values may not provide a sound basis for decision analysis. Such problems are most likely to occur for goods with which individuals have little experience and poor understanding of (Bateman et al., 2008a, 2008b and 2010). Therefore, while stated preferences may provide sound valuations for high-experience, use value goods, the further one moves to consider indirect use and pure non-use values, the more likely one is to encounter problems. Paradoxically then, where SP techniques are most useful is also where they have the potential to be less effective.

A number of solutions have been proposed for the problem of valuing low-experience goods. Christie et al. (2006) have proposed the use of intensive valuation workshops where participants learn about the environmental services being valued. However, the techniques involved are almost inevitably prone to reliance upon small unrepresentative samples which, after such intensive experiences, cannot be taken as reflecting general preferences. So while offering useful insights about overcoming the low-experience problem, it must be asked whether the cure is worse than the disease. Others have proposed and implemented extensions of conventional, individual based SP applications. Bateman et al. (2009), for example, use virtual reality software to convey images of landscape goods. This avoids the difficulties of conveying attributes of goods such as landscape in unfamiliar units, such as hectares. Results show a significant reduction in the rate of preference inconsistencies through the application of such techniques.

While significant strides can be made in filling out the ecosystem valuation matrix without recourse to what might be judged by some to be more "problematic methods", crucial gaps remain in the empirical record. This issue seems particularly acute in the case of many types of cultural ecosystem services. As stated by Chan et al. (2010, p. 206) "…few classes of value have been more difficult to identify and measure than those concerned with the cultural and non-use dimensions of ecosystems". Cultural ecosystem services include use-related values, such as leisure and recreation, aesthetic and inspirational benefits, spiritual and religious benefits, community benefits, education and ecological knowledge, physical and mental health. Difficulties arise as some of these cultural services may be bound up by non-use motivations such as altruistic, bequest and existence values (Krutilla, 1967).[4] Moreover, some of these benefits are also difficult to identify separately. As things stand there appears to be a generalised lack of knowledge and a specific dearth of monetary information about the contribution of cultural ecosystem services to well-being. The following sections therefore discuss some of the challenges with regards to the "health" and "non-use" values of ecosystems in particular.

Box 13.1. **Practical values for ecosystem services**

A range of these ecosystem services are presented in Table 13.3, from Markandya (2016), but based on an earlier synthesis of the empirical record by Groot et al. (2012). The table lists 22 ecosystem services in all classified by biome (very broad habitat types, both terrestrial and aquatic). The data there are presented in terms of the per hectare (ha) monetary value of an ecosystem service (expressed in terms of USD in 2007 prices).

A number of observations about the data are possible. First, the empirical record is incomplete most likely due to a combination of factors. It might be that in some cases a particular ecosystem service is insignificant for the particular biome. But it might be that data simply do not exist or the empirical record for that cell of the table is too thin to synthesise

---

Box 13.1. **Practical values for ecosystem services** (*cont.*)

in this way. Second, in other respects the table is remarkably full especially for certain biomes (notably for inland and coastal wetlands as well as tropical forests). This is perhaps striking given the novelty of this literature reflecting a lot of progress in a relatively short space of time. Third, the data in the table are suggestive of the importance of particular ecosystem services relative to one another and in the context of particular biome types. Moreover, in principle these per hectare values seem reasonably straightforward to apply to new policy questions. That is, if some amount of hectares of woodland are to be planted in some location what might be the expected change in ecosystem services that results? While not providing the exact answer (for reasons expanded on immediately below), the table gives a sense of how to think about answers to this question as well as indicating a summary of the evidence base that exists.

Just as important as these observations is a proper reflection on the issues that lay below the veneer of Table 12.3 and the subsequent "health warnings" that might be applied in interpreting these sort of data. For example, Markandya (2016) notes that these data are not necessarily always additive. Some regulatory ecosystem services are actually inputs to the generation of other provisioning ecosystem services. So the table while useful in a lot of a respects does not absolve the analyst from a fuller consideration of the stages of the natural and economic production processes whereby these ecosystem services enter. The details underlying these synthesis are important for other reasons too. Standardised per hectares values do not convey substantial spatial variation in ecosystem services especially where location really matters, as it does in this valuation context. There is no reason to believe that these data apply everywhere (and so may need adjustment) or are simply linear in the way that the table (implicitly) suggests. More generally, the table says nothing about the quality of the valuation studies that have been synthesised to arrive at this summary. Many of these issues are discussed in detail in a number of chapters elsewhere in this volume. For present purposes, it is important to note these considerations do not mean that Table 13.3 is of no practical use. Rather it makes clear that such values, while useful, need to be treated and used with care by analysts.

A final point relates once more to what the table misses. The challenge of missing ecosystem service value data has already been mentioned. Yet another issue is the emphasis on ecosystem services says little explicitly about the value of biodiversity, defined as by the Convention on Biodiversity as: "the variability among living organisms from all sources including, inter alia, terrestrial, marine and other aquatic ecosystems and the ecological complexities of which they are part; this includes diversity within species, between species and of ecosystems". What this means is that, in the context of Table 12.3, typical ecosystem services at best only implicitly reflect the contribution of this biodiversity (the contribution of the richness, complexity and resilience of species and the ecosystems that they inhabit) , if at all. For example, Mace et al. (2012) caution that ecosystem services and biodiversity should be viewed simply as synonymous terms. Nor is biodiversity just a particular type of (final) ecosystem service (e.g. the provision of the wild species). Biodiversity, as stressed by Mace et al., is also a regulatory of ecosystem processes and so a fundamental building block of the sorts of ecosystem service values summarised in the table.

Table 13.3. Summary of monetary values for each service by biome

International dollars per hectare per year, 2007 price level

	Marine	Coral reefs	Coastal systems	Coastal wetlands	Inland wetlands	Rivers and lakes	Tropical forests	Temperate forests	Woodlands	Grasslands
Provisioning services total	**102**	**55 724**	**2 396**	**2 998**	**1 659**	**1 914**	**1 828**	**671**	**253**	**1 305**
1 Food	93	667	2 384	1 111	614	106	200	299	52	1 192
2 Water				1 217	408	1 808	27	191		60
3 Raw materials	8	21 528	12	358	425		84	181	170	53
4 Genetic resources		33 048		10		1 504	13			
5 Medicinal resources					99					1
6 Ornamental resources		472		301	114				32	
Regulating services total	**65**	**171 478**	**25 847**	**171 515**	**17 364**	**187**	**2 529**	**491**	**51**	**159**
7 Air quality regulation							12			
8 Climate regulation	65	1 188	479	65	488		2 044	152	7	40
9 Disturbance moderation		16 991		5 351	2 986		66			
10 Water flow regulation					5 606		342			
11 Waste treatment		85		162 125	3 015	187	6	7		75
12 Erosion prevention		153 214	25 368	3 929	2 607		15	5	13	44
13 Nutrient recycling				45	1 713		3	93		
14 Pollination							30		31	
15 Biological control					948		11	235		
Habitat services total	**5**	**16 210**	**375**	**17 138**	**2 455**	**2 166**	**39**	**862**	**1 277**	**1 214**
16 Nursery services			194	10 648	1 287		16		1 273	
17 Genetic diversity	5	16 210	180	6 490	1 168	2 166	23	862	3	1 214
Cultural services total	**319**	**108 837**	**300**	**2 193**	**4 203**	**2 166**	**867**	**989**	**7**	**26**
18 Aesthetic information		11 390			1 292					167
19 Recreation	319	96 302	256	2 193	2 211	2 166	867	989	7	26
20 Inspiration					700					
21 Spiritual experience			21							
22 Cognitive development		1 145	22					1		
Total economic value	**491**	**352 249**	**28 918**	**193 844**	**25 681**	**4 267**	**5 263**	**3 014**	**1 588**	**2 871**

Note: Coastal systems include estuaries, continent shelf areas and sea grasses but exclude wetlands like tidal marshes, mangroves and salt water wetlands.

Source: Markandya (2016) – Adapted from De Groot et al., 2012.

13.3.1. Health values

Despite increased recognition that ecosystem services can have substantial effects on human health, both directly and indirectly, (e.g. Myers and Patz, 2009; Bird, 2007; de Vries, et al., 2003; Hartig et al., 2003; Mitchell and Popham, 2008; Osman, 2005; Takano et al., 2002; Ulrich, 1984) the knowledge on the complex relationships linking the biophysical attributes of ecosystems with the many aspects of human health remains limited (Daily et al., 2011)

Environmental quality and proximity to natural amenities is increasingly recognised as having substantial effects on physical and mental health, both directly and indirectly. Broadly this could arise in a number of ways. Ecosystems provide many services that sustain human health (such as nutrition, regulation of vector-borne disease or water purification). Also, natural settings could act as a catalyst for healthy behaviour, leading for example to increases in physical exercise, which affect both physical and mental health (Pretty et al., 2007; Barton and Pretty, 2010). Finally, simple exposure to the natural environment, such as having a view of a tree or grass from a window, can be beneficial, improving mental health status (Pretty et al., 2005) and physical health (Ulrich, 1984). Health outcomes in this respect can be disaggregated into two categories: reductions in mortality and reductions in morbidity (including physical and mental health).

While there is a large literature on health valuation, a crucial gap is in relation to the contribution of ecosystems to these improvements. Moreover, the statistical evidence for the health-ecosystem link is still to be established unequivocally. For example, on the link between physical exercise and availability of green spaces, the suspicion is that even if the physical health link can be more firmly established, the value is possibly likely to be small given the availability of substitutes for this physical exercise. Hence, it is likely to be the mental health benefit that is plausibly the more substantial of these two (bundled) health outcomes. Less is known with regards to valuation of these outcomes. However, it might be that subjective well-being approaches linked to monetary valuation are a promising path to explore further (see Chapter 7). A final but no less important challenge is to know what values are for *changes in* ecosystem provision whereas most work to date has examined the possible health benefits associated with *current* provision.

13.3.2. Non-use values

Environmental non-use values are often thought to be substantial (see, for example, Hanley et al., 1998). Critically, however, when and where these arise remains the subject of some discussion. Due to their intangible nature and disconnect from actual uses, the valuation of non-use benefits is complex. As a result, there appears to be no systematic body of evidence about non-use values and, importantly, little consensus about how the empirical record (such as it is) can be used for practical assessment in the context of project and policy appraisals or broader national-level ecosystem assessments. In the former, a particular concern might relate to whether a (change in a) non-use value relates to a specific and discrete proposal (or the provision of a service more generally). In the latter, a concern might be double-counting or erroneously assuming that the same (per household or individual) non-use value estimate applies to all of the parts rather than something more broadly resembling the whole. Put another way, the physical "unit" to which these non-use values can be applied is, on reflection, not at all obvious. Yet, given the possible importance of non-use value in certain ecosystem contexts, this issue surely merits further investigation.

One significant obstacle to addressing this challenge is that, as noted above, SP methods are often thought to be the only economic valuation techniques capable of measuring non-use values and so any doubts about the application of those methods or the accuracy of such valuations will loom especially large in this context. Challenges in the application of SP methods to non-use values are readily identified. Lack of experience and familiarity is likely to be important when respondents, for example, are asked about their preferences for conserving species which might well be located in distant lands. Related to this is the lack of adequate testing for preference consistency exhibited in many such studies (although, see for an exception, Morse-Jones et al., 2012, discussed in further detail below).

It may be, however, that other avenues for non-use valuation remain to be explored (although none appear to offer a general panacea for the challenges inherent in this endeavour). For example, legacies can be argued to represent a pure non-use value. That is, individuals leaving a charitable bequest to an environmental organisation in a will, for the purposes of supporting conservation activities, clearly will not experience the benefits of this work. Atkinson et al. (2009) estimate that while (in 2007) only 6% of all deaths in Britain resulted in a charitable bequest, their value remained substantial. And while legacies to environmental charities will be a relatively small proportion of this total, Mourato et al. (2010), for example, have estimated that this amounts to more than GBP 200 million in the financial year 2008/09.

Related to the notion of "non-use" is current interest in what has been termed "shared values" (see, for example, Fish et al., 2011). For some this appears to be unfinished business arising from earlier discussions about how people value environmental policy changes, more generally, as individuals or citizens (Sagoff, 1988). However, the concept has also been a way of conveying that there might also something extra to the value of an ecosystem over and above adding up different elements of its total economic value.[5] The emphasis on shared values traces this missing element of value to the way in which ecosystems have collective meaning and significance for communities of people related perhaps to "non-use" or perceptions about ecosystem aesthetics.

There is little obvious evidence to add empirical substance to these insights. However, the handful of studies that have sought to use deliberative monetary valuation approaches provide some practical understanding of the individual or collective value of certain proposed environmental changes in a group context. (e.g. Macmillan et al., 2002; Alvarez-Farizo et al., 2007). Investigating this notion of shared values for ecosystems through wider-scale testing than has been possible thus far is a possibly rich topic for further development. In such contexts, the "deliberative nature" of this valuation process (providing participants with information that they can reflect on) might also help mitigate problems of poorly informed consumers making valuation choices about possibly complex changes. There remains, however, an urgent need for a better understanding about the conceptual basis for "shared values" and, in particular, how it might be integrated within economic appraisal. For example, this might involve the recognition not only that i) the value of goods to an individual may differ radically from the value of the same good from a societal perspective, but also that ii) even these individual values are likely to be the product of social (and other) contexts.[6]

A readiness to understand "value" not just in terms of its economic interpretation can be seen in the work of the Intergovernmental Science-Policy Platform on Biodiversity and Ecosystems (IPBES). The IPBES was established in 2012 as an interface for science and policy for biodiversity and ecosystem services, and is administered by UNEP. While the work programme of the IPBES is wide ranging, its work on value is summarised in Pascual et al. (2017) and is firmly grounded in the "value plurality" discussed in Chapter 2. In other words, *instrumental value* – familiar in most economic applications, and the main focus of this chapter – is just one guiding principle that the IPBES considers as the value of nature's contribution to people.

This includes the notion of shared value, which Pascual et al. locate as a type of *relational value* defined as: "... values which do not emanate directly from nature but are derivative of our relationships with it and our responsibilities towards it" (p. 11) and envisaged as comprising cultural identity, social cohesion and shared moral responsibilities associated with ecosystems and biodiversity. The notion of *intrinsic value* is also explicit in this framework too: that is, values which are inherent in nature and independent of human experience and evaluation. In terms of the practical implications for appraisal of accommodating this mix of preferences and belief systems, this entails at the very least a strong degree of participative and deliberative approaches alongside "traditional" valuation techniques.

13.4. Valuation and policy appraisal

Much of the recent attention to the economics of ecosystems can be traced to the MA (2005) which made clear the scale of the challenge at hand in its identification of persistent and growing threats to ecosystems around the world. Importantly, the MA had the effect of broadening the focus of concern from biodiversity loss to cover, in addition, the loss of ecosystem services with the critical emphasis of the latter on "the benefits people obtain from ecosystems" (MA, 2005, p. 53). In addition, the focal valuation message in the Stern Review on Climate Change appears not to have been lost on decision-makers within the domain of conservation policy. Assessments including the G8/EU initiated "TEEB Review" (The Economics of Ecosystems and Biodiversity, TEEB, 2010) and the UK National Ecosystem Assessment (NEA, 2011)[7] can be viewed as attempts to generate a correspondingly increased awareness and strong policy response for biodiversity and ecosystem services as well as a concerted effort to build on the momentum and insights generated by the MA.

One of the largest ecosystem service valuation exercises conducted to date forms the core of the economic analysis underpinning the UK National Ecosystem Assessment (UK-NEA, 2011). This was based upon highly disaggregated, spatially sensitive, large observation databases, and provide decision makers with a rich and more holistic picture of the overall consequences of any given policy option. The advantages of such an approach were quickly realised by UK policy makers and the lessons of the UK-NEA were explicitly incorporated in the UK Natural Environment White Paper (Defra, 2011), published in the immediate aftermath of the former report. Such academic and policy developments suggest that the incorporation of value transfer techniques as tools for official policy formulation show promise. Notwithstanding this interim conclusion, there remains a need for tools capable of translating valuation information into policy action.

In the UK-NEA, value functions were estimated for multiple ecosystem services, including the provisioning value of agricultural food production, the regulating services of the environment as a store for greenhouse gases and the so-called cultural services of both rural and urban recreation (including urban greenspace benefits). Following Bateman et al. (2011a), the functions were simplified to focus upon the main – theoretically expected –

drivers of value, thereby avoiding the transfer of factors which only apply in a given context and are not general. The functions were also built in an integrated manner which linked the levels of each to the other. So, for example, if provisioning values are increased as a result of agricultural intensification, that same intensification feeds into an increase in greenhouse gas emissions and deterioration of rural recreation resources which result in a fall in both of these latter values.

An example of the output obtained from such analyses, Figure 6.5 in Chapter 6, illustrated findings from the UK-NEA analysis of rural recreation benefits arising from a change of land use from conventional farming towards multipurpose, open-access, woodland.[8] The distribution obtained by transferring a recreational value function across the entirety of Wales reflects various factors, including the distribution of population (this being highest in south western Wales and in the areas of England neighbouring the north-east) and the availability and quality of the road network. Such spatially disaggregated outputs allow decision makers to target resources in the most efficient manner; an ability that is clearly of great importance during times of austerity.

One further example of this challenge with respect to spatial variability can be illustrated with reference to those valuation studies that focus on the value of a representative unit (typically a km^2) of an ecosystem's area of extent. A naïve approach to aggregation might simply estimate total value as the product of this unit value and total ecosystem area. Barbier et al. (2008) illustrate the dangers of this where there is a non-linear relationship between ecosystem extent and the functions that it provides. Using the example of Thailand's mangroves in attenuating wave damage from more commonly experienced storm events, spatial heterogeneity arises because proximity (of mangroves) to shorelines is a critical determinant of the degree to which this function is provided: that is, it diminishes the further the ecosystem is (inland) from the shore. Taking explicit account of this heterogeneity is needed as a more defensible basis for aggregation. This is also required for more accurate policy analysis. Put another way, what Barbier et al. show is that the (estimated) marginal value of mangrove area in their study area in Thailand is declining. The total net benefits of protection of this ecosystem are at their maximum at around 8 km^2. Given that current mangrove area was 10 km^2, this means that while mangrove protection is frequently justified, some conversion might also be economically desirable.

While economics can contribute greatly to guiding the valuation of ecosystem services, it can also shape thinking about the implementation of policies aimed at delivering such values. Unfortunately, at present, many of the policies employed to deliver ecosystem services fail to heed either evidence regarding the way in which values can vary over different patches of ecosystems or the lessons of basic economic theory regarding incentives that actors possess to reveal truthfully their valuation of services that they enjoy. An example is provided by the UK Entry Level Stewardship (ELS) scheme (Natural England, 2010) which offers a flat rate payment to all farmers irrespective of their location. Such schemes fail to target payments to those areas which yield the highest values and provide no incentive for farmers to provide anything other than the basic level of land management consistent with the scheme. Similar approaches characterise much of the increasingly substantial payments made under Pillar Two of the EU Common Agricultural Policy.

Thus economic valuation of itself is insufficient to improve the efficient delivery of ecosystem services. A simple example illustrates the problem and how economic intuition can help. Suppose that policy makers seek to reduce diffuse water pollution from farms through a payment for ecosystem services (PES) scheme. A first requirement is to undertake a valuation exercise identifying those river catchments (and areas within those catchments) where reductions of pollution are likely to generate the largest net benefits. This might identify, for example, farms in locations above the inlet to water supply reservoirs as those most important to target. Now the focus ought to switch to the efficient implementation of such policies.

One rather naïve approach might be to simply ask farmers to state the levels of compensation they require to move towards modes of production which avoid diffuse pollution. Of course, farmers have an incentive to strategically overstate their compensation requirements. However, the economic theory of auctions suggests that even relatively simple approaches can significantly improve implementation efficiency (Vickrey, 1961; Clarke, 1971; Groves, 1973; Groves and Ledyard, 1977). For example, switching to a simple sealed bid contracting system might reduce the potential for strategic responses and improves incentive compatibility. This could be the case if farmers are told that contracts will be awarded according to the combination of pollution reduction and cost.

In certain circumstances even greater efficiency gains can be obtained. For example, where the delivery of ecosystem services can be readily measured (for example in policies seeking the protection of certain habitats) then land owners will be those best able to judge whether their land is particularly suitable for providing such goods (or faces the lowest opportunity costs). Such actors can outbid competitors by offering better outputs (or lower costs) than their rivals.[9] To date, practical examples of such agreements are generally confined to the experimental laboratory.

One further point is that valuing ecosystems and biodiversity valuation are complex endeavours and often at the frontier of valuation knowledge. This suggests good reason, in certain contexts, to be circumspect about the role that valuation might play in informing decisions about conservation. Decision-making in such situations where values are unknown – or where values cannot be established to any degree of validity – has generated much debate. In such cases, however, "caution" (given what might be lost) might be a sensible watchword. Possible responses include the adoption of ecological standards sometimes termed "safe minimum standards" to ensure the sustainability of resources which are not amenable to valuation (Farmer and Randall, 1998) or offsetting or compensatory projects validated for their ecological suitability (Federal Register, 1995). In such cases, valuation of benefits is downplayed perhaps for a greater emphasis on cost-effectiveness in meeting specified physical targets (see Chapter 12).

An illustration of this challenge in determining how exactly valuation could guide social decision-making is provided by the example of valuing biodiversity. Weitzman (1993) – using the example of the world's remaining species of cranes – defines biological importance of each species in terms of their taxonomic distinctiveness (e.g. of the whooping crane compared with other crane species)[10] and the likelihood of extinction (of a given species). Assuming that maximising (expected) diversity is the objective, species conservation becomes a problem of cost-effectively distributing the marginal (available) unit of money from conservation funds to where it achieves the highest pay-off. Typically, this will be where there is some combination of high diversity and low survival probabilities.

Ideally, it would be useful to extend such insights with reference to the preferences that people might have for diversity. Somewhat reassuringly, Morse-Jones et al. (2012), for example, find that stated preference responses reveal expected substitution patterns across ecologically similar species, e.g. different small amphibians. However, preferences need not always conform to what is ecologically feasible or sustainable. Thus, in the Morse-Jones et al. study, respondents had a massively stronger preference for iconic, "charismatic" animals which outweighs concerns regarding ecologically crucial issues such as extinction threat. So, for example, willingness to pay to conserve lions, even where these animals are not threatened by extinction, hugely outweighs stated values for say a species of frog, even when it is on the brink of extinction.

Another example is provided by Bateman et al. (2009). That study observes that while respondents had strongly positive preferences for enlarging an area of freshwater marshland suitable for visiting and viewing bird populations, they had negative values for an adjoining area of tidal mudflats, even though these were a major source of food attracting those birds to the area. In many respects, these findings are not surprising. However, what it does raise is a deeper question about whether the extent to which economic values can be a guide for decision-making or whether ecological constraints need to be considered. Clearly, the claim that human preferences are (almost always) "right" or "wrong" is overly simplistic at either extreme. However, where to draw the line is far from obvious and – given changing knowledge – is anyhow likely to be a shifting target. Nevertheless, while recognising the importance of economic values for thinking about the importance of ecosystems and guiding policy thinking, one needs to be mindful of the complexities and uncertainties involved.

13.5. Concluding remarks

The valuation of ecosystem services has become a crucial element (perhaps *the* crucial element) in quantifying the contribution of ecosystems and biodiversity to human well-being. A significant body of research has already begun to emerge and a number of recent national and international ecosystem assessments have helped provide further impetus to such efforts. Needless to say, significant challenges remain. Hence, while the evidence-base is broad and – at least for some ecosystem services – deep, reflections on this progress indicate a need for greater understanding of ecological production, especially as it relates to spatial variability and complexities in the way that services are produced. The size and significance of inevitable gaps in the empirical record as well as the ability to fill these gaps by judiciously transferring values; and, the scope and limits in using this evidence-base to inform practical decision-making both generally and, in relation, to concerns about whether the valuations that one can find in this literature genuinely tell much about the importance of ecosystem assets and biodiversity.

In this current chapter, the focus has been on valuation methods and particularly the challenges inherent in seeking to value non-market costs and benefits. Some of these challenges involve general considerations although other issues are specific to valuing ecosystems or at least seem particularly acute in that context. In some cases, for example, there might be good knowledge about the value of a particular (ecosystem) service endpoint. So, while valuing the benefits to physical and mental health (of proximity to greenspaces) might be feasible, establishing the causal link between experiences of nature and these health outcomes is the greater relative challenge. For other types of cultural value, particularly those related to "non-use", the suspicion is that these might be substantive in some contexts. Less is known in this instance to confirm systematically these suspicions. A natural response in the past might be to look to stated preference methods to provide this evidence. But there is increasing recognition that this method may not be well suited to eliciting values where those people asked to do the valuing lack familiarity with or experience of the (ecosystem) good. Ways of resolving this contradiction are in their infancy.

Such challenges need to be viewed in context. A growing number of large-scale ecosystem assessments has shown how the empirical record can be put to use in an informative and policy-relevant way. Such developments could be crucial in translating valuations into meaningful policy analysis. It may also offer some hope for shedding light on the value of what is lost when and if ecosystems and biodiversity are degraded and destroyed in more highly aggregated assessments. While such questions are commonplace elsewhere, in the ecosystem context these have only begun to be asked although related issues of valuing ecosystem complexity have a longer standing (see also the Annex to this Chapter). Progress on these matters, both in theory and practice, is surely only a matter of time. Nevertheless, it seems unavoidable that uncertainties will remain. That is, while one can conclude positively on the rapidly evolving scope for ecosystem and biodiversity valuation to contribute to a profound understanding of suitable policy responses, there remains room for debate about whether valuation is in itself enough to ensure effective policies. There is considerable debate remaining also about how to conduct decision analyses in those contexts where valuation and understanding of the natural world is likely to remain relatively uncertain.

Notes

1. Of course, such a comment does not apply only to this ecosystem context. A great many applications necessarily require interdisciplinary collaboration between, at a minimum, the natural sciences and economics (arguably extending to a much wider fusion of disciplines).

2. See, most for a summary, Carson's (2011) bibliography of published and unpublished CV studies from around the world.

3. A number of studies combine RP and SP approaches in order to enhance the respective strengths of these data and minimising limitations (see, for example, Adamowicz et al., 1994).

4. An existence value can be derived from the simple knowledge of the existence of the good or the service. In the context of the environment, individuals may place a value on the mere existence of species, natural environments and other ecosystem. If an individual derives well-being from the knowledge that other people are benefiting from a particular environmental good or service, this can be termed altruistic value. Such values accrue during an individual's lifetime, but vicarious valuation can also occur inter-generationally. The effect on well-being of knowing that one's offspring, or other future generations, may enjoy an environmental good or service into the future, such as a biodiversity-rich forest being conserved, is termed bequest value.

5. Arrow et al. (2000) have made an analogous point in the context of the physical processes that the value of some system as a whole may be more than the value of the sum of its parts perhaps because of complex ecological interactions.

6. In much in the same way, that is, as a move across locations, and consequent environments, will alter the value of any given resource: e.g. water in the desert has a much higher marginal value than in areas of high rainfall.

7. The UK NEA involved a team of over 160 natural scientists assembled to quantify the status of ecosystem processes and the final ecosystem services they generate across the UK, looking at individual habitats classifications (e.g. wetlands and woodlands) as well as ecosystems services across these classifications. In addition, an economics team complemented this work and its structure with the added emphasis on the value of habitats and ecosystem services under investigation.

8. This in turn builds on Bateman et al., 2003.

9. Such markets can also be designed to benefit private sector purchasers of ecosystem services. For example in countries where this institutional regime occurs, private water companies may be able to reduce their costs of providing potable water by avoiding costly treatment options by engaging

with land owners to reduce pollution inputs to rivers. Indeed, economic theory identifies the potential for multiple private sector bodies to combine to purchase such services provided that markets are created so as to avoid free-riding by ensuring that PES trades only go ahead if all parties contribute to their purchase (Guth et al., 2007; Potters et al., 2007; Ekel and Grossman, 2007; Bracht et al., 2008).

10. Genetic distinctiveness is defined, by Weitzman (1993), as the evolutionary distance each existing species is from a common ancestor species.

References

Adamowicz, W.J., J. Louviere and M. Williams (1994) "Combining Revealed and Stated Preference Methods for Valuing Environmental Amenities", *Journal of Environmental Economics and Management*, Vol. 26, pp. 271-92, *https://doi.org/10.1006/jeem.1994.1017*.

Alvarez-Farizo, B. et al. (2007), "Choice Modeling at the 'Market Stall': Individual Versus Collective Interest in Environmental Valuation", *Ecological Economics*, Vol. 60, pp 743-751, *http://dx.doi.org/10.1016/j.ecolecon.2006.01.009*.

Arrow, K. et al. (2000), "Managing Ecosystem Resources", *Environmental Science and Technology*, Vol. 34, pp. 1401-1406, *http://dx.doi.org/10.1021/es990672t*.

Barbier, E.B. (2012), "Progress and challenges in valuing coastal and marine ecosystem services", *Review of Environmental Economics and Policy*, Vol. 6(1), pp. 1-19, *https://doi.org/10.1093/reep/rer017*.

Barbier, E.B. (2009), "Ecosystems as Natural Assets", *Foundations and Trends in Microeconomics*, 4(8), pp. 611-681, *http://dx.doi.org/10.1561/0700000031*.

Barbier, E.B. (2007) "Valuing Ecosystem Services as Productive Inputs", *Economic Policy*, Vol. 22(49), pp. 177-229, *https://doi.org/10.1111/j.1468-0327.2007.00174.x*.

Barbier, E.B. et al. (2008) "Coastal Ecosystem-Based Management with Nonlinear Ecological Functions and Values", *Science*, Vol. 319, pp. 321-323, *http://dx.doi.org/10.1126/science.1150349*.

Barton, J. and J. Pretty (2010), "What is the Best Dose of Nature and Green Exercise for Mental Health? A Meta-study Analysis", *Environmental Science & Technology*, Vol. 44(10), pp. 3947-3955, *http://dx.doi.org/10.1021/es903183r*.

Bateman, I.J. et al. (2011a), "Economic Analysis for Ecosystems Assessments", *Environmental and Resource Economics*, Vol. 48, pp. 177-218, *https://doi.org/10.1007/s10640-010-9418-x*.

Bateman, I.J. et al. (2011b), "Economic Values from Ecosystems", in *The UK National Ecosystem Assessment Technical Report*, UK National Ecosystem Assessment, UNEP-WCMC, Cambridge, also available from *http://uknea.unep-wcmc.org/*.

Bateman I.J. et al. (2010), "Tigers, Markets and Palm Oil: Market Potential for Conservation", *Oryx*, Vol. 44(2), pp. 230-234, *https://doi.org/10.1017/S0030605309990901*.

Bateman I.J. et al. (2009), "Reducing Gains/Loss Asymmetry: A Virtual Reality Choice Experiment (VRCE) Valuing Land Use Change", *Journal of Environmental Economics and Management*, Vol. 58, pp. 106-118, *http://dx.doi.org/10.1016/j.jeem.2008.05.003*.

Bateman, I.J. et al. (2008a), "Contrasting NOAA Guidelines with Learning Design Contingent Valuation (LDCV): Preference Learning Versus Coherent Arbitrariness", *Journal of Environmental Economics and Management*, Vol. 55, pp. 127-141, *http://dx.doi.org/10.1016/j.jeem.2007.08.003*.

Bateman, I.J., A. Munro and G.L. Poe (2008b), "Asymmetric Dominance Effects in Choice Experiments and Contingent Valuation", *Land Economics*, Vol. 84, pp. 115-127, *http://dx.doi.org/10.3368/le.84.1.115*.

Bishop, R. (1978), "Endangered species and uncertainty: The economics of a safe minimum standard", *American Journal of Agricultural Economics*, Vol. 60, pp. 10-18.

Bockstael, N.E. et al. (2000), "On Measuring Economic Values for Nature", *Environmental Science & Technology*, Vol. 34, pp. 1384-1389, *http://dx.doi.org/10.1021/es9906731*.

Bracht, J., C. Figuières and M. Ratto (2008), "Relative performance of two simple incentive mechanisms in a public goods experiment", *Journal of Public Economics*, Vol. 92, pp. 54-90, *http://dx.doi.org/10.1016/j.jpubeco.2007.04.005*.

Brouwer, R. (2000), "Environmental Value Transfer: State of the Art and Future Prospects", *Ecological Economics*, Vol. 32, pp. 137-152, *https://doi.org/10.1016/S0921-8009(99)00070-1*.

Carson, R.T. (2011), *Contingent Valuation: A Comprehensive Bibliography and History*, Edward Elgar, Cheltenham.

Chan, K.M.A. (2011), "Cultural Services and Non-Use Values", in Kaveira, P. et al. (eds.) *Natural Capital: Theory and Practice of Mapping Ecosystem Services*, Oxford University Press, Oxford, *http://dx.doi.org/ 10.1093/acprof:oso/9780199588992.003.0012*.

Chiabai, A. et al. (2011) "Economic Assessment of Forest Ecosystem Services Losses: Costs of Policy Inaction", *Environmental and Resource Economics*, Vol. 50, pp. 405-445, *http://dx.doi.org/10.1007/s10640-011-9478-6*.

Christie, M. et al. (2006), "Valuing the Diversity of Biodiversity", *Ecological Economics*, Vol. 58, pp. 304-317, *http://dx.doi.org/10.1016/j.ecolecon.2005.07.034*.

Ciriacy-Wantrup, C.V. (1968), *Resource Conservation: Economics and Policies*, 3rd edition, University of California, Berkeley.

Clarke, E. (1971), "Multipart pricing of public goods", *Public Choice*, Vol. 11, pp. 17-33, *http://dx.doi.org/ 10.1007/BF01726210*.

Costanza, R. et al. (2017), "Twenty Years of Ecosystem Services: How Far Have We Come and How Far Do We Still Need to Go?", *Ecosystem Services*, Vol. 28, pp. 1-16.

Costanza, R. et al. (2014), "Changes in the Global Value of Ecosystem Services", *Global Environmental Change*, Vol. 26, pp. 152-158.

Costanza, R. et al. (1997), "The value of the world's ecosystem services and natural capital", *Nature*, Vol. 387, pp. 253-260.

Daily, G.C. (1997), *Nature's Services: Societal Dependence on Natural Ecosystems*, Island Press, Washington, DC.

Daily, G.C. et al. (2000), "The Value of Nature and the Nature of Value", *Science*, Vol. 289, pp. 395-396, *http://dx.doi.org/10.1126/science.289.5478.395*.

de Groot, R.S., M.A. Wilson and R.M.J. Boumans (2002), "A Typology for the Classification, Description and Valuation of Ecosystem Functions, Goods and Services", *Ecological Economics*, Vol. 41, pp. 393-408, *https://doi.org/10.1016/S0921-8009(02)00089-7*.

de Vries, S. et al. (2003), "Natural Environments – Healthy Environments? An Exploratory Analysis of the Relationship between Greenspace and Health", *Environment and Planning A*, Vol. 35, pp. 1717-1731, *http://dx.doi.org/10.1068/a35111*.

Eckel, C.C. and P.J. Grossman (2006), "Subsidizing Charitable Giving with Rebates or Matching: Further Laboratory Evidence", *Southern Economic Journal*, Vol. 72(4), pp. 794-807, *www.jstor.org/stable/20111853*.

Elmqvist, T. et al. (2010), "Biodiversity, Ecosystems and Ecosystem Services", in Kumar, P. (ed.), *The Economics of Ecosystems and Biodiversity: Ecological and Economic Foundations*, Earthscan, London.

Farmer, M.C. and A. Randall (1998), "The Rationality of a Safe Minimum Standard", *Land Economics*, Vol. 74, pp. 287-302.

Federal Register (1995), "Federal Guidance for the Establishment, Use and Operation of Mitigation Banks", *Federal Register*, Vol. 60(228), pp. 58605-58614.

Ferraro, P.J. et al. (2012), "Forest Figures: Ecosystem Services Valuation and Policy Evaluation in Developing Countries", *Review of Environmental Economics and Policy*, Vol. 6(1), pp. 20-44, *https:// doi.org/10.1093/reep/rer019*.

Fish, R. et al. (2011), "Shared Values for the Contributions Ecosystem Services Make to Human Wellbeing", UK National Ecosystems Assessment, *http://uknea.unep-wcmc.org/LinkClick.aspx?fileticket= OrzPtSfQ5ng%3D&tabid=82*.

Fisher, B., R.K. Turner and P. Morling (2009), "Defining and classifying ecosystem services for decision making", *Ecological Economics*, Vol. 68(3), pp. 643-653, *http://dx.doi.org/10.1016/j.ecolecon.2008.09.014*.

Freeman, A.M. III (2003), *The Measurement of Environmental and Resource Values: Theory and Methods*, 2nd Edition, Resources for the Future, Washington, DC.

Gibbons, S., S. Mourato and G. Resende (2011), "The Amenity Value of English Nature: A Hedonic Price Approach", Spatial Economics Research Centre, DP0074, London School of Economics.

Goulder, L. and D. Kennedy (2011), "Interpreting and Estimating the Value of Ecosystem Services", in Kaveira, P. et al. (eds.), *Natural Capital: Theory and Practice of Mapping Ecosystem Services*, Oxford University Press, Oxford.

Groves, T. (1973), "Incentives in teams", *Econometrica*, Vol. 41, pp. 617-631.

Groves, T. and J. Ledyard (1977), "Some limitations on demand revealing processes", *Public Choice*, Vol. 29(2), pp. 107-124, *http://dx.doi.org/10.1007/BF01718522*.

Güth, W.M. et al. (2007), "Leading by example with and without exclusion power in voluntary contribution experiments", *Journal of Public Economics*, Vol. 91, pp. 1023-1042, *http://dx.doi.org/10.1016/j.jpubeco.2006.10.007*.

Hanley, N.D. and E.B. Barbier (2009), *Pricing Nature: Cost-Benefit Analysis and Environmental Policy*, Edward Elgar Publishing, Cheltenham.

Hartig, T. et al. (2003) "Tracking Restoration in Natural and Urban Field Settings", *Journal of Environmental Psychology*, Vol. 23, pp. 109-123.

Heal G.M. et al. (2005), *Valuing Ecosystem Services: Toward Better Environmental Decision making*, The National Academies Press, Washington DC.

Kanninen, B.J. (ed.) (2007), *Valuing Environmental Amenities Using Stated Choice Studies*, Springer, Dordrecht.

Kaveira, P. et al. (eds.) (2011), *Natural Capital: Theory and Practice of Mapping Ecosystem Services*, Oxford University Press, Oxford.

Kumar, P. (ed.), *The Economics of Ecosystems and Biodiversity: Ecological and Economic Foundations*, Earthscan, London.

Mace, G.M., K. Norris and A.H. Fitter (2012), "Biodiversity and ecosystem services: A multilayered relationship", *Trends in Ecology & Evolution*, Vol. 27(1), pp. 19-26, *http://dx.doi.org/10.1016/j.tree.2011.08.006*.

Macmillan, D. et al. (2002), "Valuing the Non-market Benefits of Wild Goose Conservation: A Comparison of Interview and Group-Based Approaches", *Ecological Economics*, Vol. 43, pp. 49-59.

Mäler, K.-G. (1974), *Environmental Economics: A Theoretical Inquiry*, Resources for the Future, Baltimore.

Markandya, A. (2016), "Cost benefit analysis and the environment: How to best cover impacts on biodiversity and ecosystem services", *OECD Environment Working Papers*, No. 101, OECD Publishing, Paris, *http://dx.doi.org/10.1787/5jm2f6w8b25l-en*.

MA (Millennium Ecosystem Assessment) (2005), *Ecosystems and Human Well-being: A Framework for Assessment*, Island Press, Washington, DC.

Mitchell, R. and F. Popham (2008), "Effect of Exposure to Natural Environment on Health Inequalities: An Observational Population Study", *Lancet*, Vol. 372, pp. 1655-1660.

Moeltner, K., K.J. Boyle and R.W. Paterson (2007), "Meta-analysis and benefit transfer for resource valuation – Addressing classical challenges with Bayesian modelling", *Journal of Environmental Economics and Management*, Vol. 53, pp. 250-69, *http://dx.doi.org/10.1016/j.jeem.2006.08.004*.

Morse-Jones, S. et al. (2012), "Stated preferences for tropical wildlife conservation amongst distant beneficiaries: Charisma, endemism, scope and substitution effects", *Ecological Economics*, *http://dx.doi.org/10.1016/j.ecolecon.2011.11.002*.

Muthke, T. and K. Holm-Mueller (2004), "National and international benefit transfer testing with a rigorous test procedure", *Environmental and Resource Economics*, Vol. 29, pp. 323-336, *http://dx.doi.org/10.1007/s10640-004-5268-8*.

Natural England (2010), *Entry Level Stewardship: Environmental Stewardship Handbook*, Third Edition, Natural England.

Osman, L. (2005), "Chapter 2: Greenspace and its Benefits for Health" in CJC Consulting (ed.) *Economic Benefits of Accessible Green Spaces for Physical and Mental Health: Scoping Study*, Final Report for the Forestry Commission.

Pagiola, S., K. Ritter and J.T. Bishop (2004), *How much is an ecosystem worth? Assessing the economic value of conservation*, The World Bank, Washington, DC, *http://documents.worldbank.org/curated/en/376691468780627185/pdf/308930PAPER0Ecosytem0worth01public1.pdf*.

Pascual, U. et al. (2017) "Valuing Nature's Contribution to People: The IPBES Approach", *Current Opinion in Environmental Sustainability*, 26: 7-16.

Pascual, U. et al. (2010), "Valuation of Ecosystems Services: Methodology and Challenges", in Kumar, P. (ed.), *The Economics of Ecosystems and Biodiversity: Ecological and Economic Foundations*, Earthscan, London.

Pearce, D.W. (1998), "Auditing the Earth", *Environment*, Vol. 40(2), pp. 22-28, *http://dx.doi.org/10.1080/00139159809605092*.

Potters, J., M. Sefton and L. Vesterlund (2007), "Leading-by-example and signalling in voluntary contribution games: an experimental study", *Economic Theory*, Vol. 33, pp. 169-182, *http://dx.doi.org/10.1007/s00199-006-0186-3*.

Pretty, J. et al. (2007) "Green Exercise in the UK Countryside: Effects on Health and Psychological Well-being", *Journal of Environmental Planning and Management*, Vol. 50(2), pp. 211-231, *http://dx.doi.org/10.1080/09640560601156466*.

Ruitenbeek, J. (1989), *Social Cost-Benefit Analysis of the Korup Project, Cameroon*, Report for the World Wildlife Fund and Republic of Cameroon.

Sagoff, M. (1988), *The Economy of the Earth*, Cambridge University Press, Cambridge.

Sukhdev, P. (2008), *The Economics of Ecosystems & Biodiversity: An Interim Report*, European Communities, Brussels

Sutton, P. and R. Costanza (2002), "Global estimates of market and non-market values derived from nighttime satellite imagery, land cover, and ecosystem service valuation", *Ecological Economics*, Vol. 41, pp. 509-527, *https://doi.org/10.1016/S0921-8009(02)00097-6*.

Toman, M. (1998), "Why Not to Calculate the Global Value of the World's Ecosystems and Natural Capital", *Ecological Economics*, Vol. 25, pp. 57-60.

Turner, R.K. et al. (2003), "Valuing nature: lessons learned and future research directions", *Ecological Economics*, Vol. 46, pp. 493-510, *http://dx.doi.org/10.1016/S0921-8009(03)00189-7*.

UK-NEA (UK National Ecosystem Assessment) (2011), *The UK National Ecosystem Assessment: Technical Report*, UNEP-WCMC, Cambridge, UK, *http://uknea.unep-wcmc.org/*.

Ulrich, R.S. (1984), "View Through a Window may Influence Recovery from Surgery", *Science*, Vol. 224(4647), pp. 420-421, *http://dx.doi.org/10.1126/science.6143402*.

US EPA (2009), *Valuing the Protection of Ecological Systems and Services*, US EPA, Science Advisory Board, Washington, DC, *https://yosemite.epa.gov/sab%5Csabproduct.nsf/F3DB1F5C6EF90EE1852575C500589157/$File/EPA-SAB-09-012-unsigned.pdf*.

Vickrey, W. (1961), "Counterspeculation, auctions, and competitive sealed tenders", *Journal of Finance*, Vol. 16, pp. 8-37, *http://dx.doi.org/10.1111/j.1540-6261.1961.tb02789.x*.

Weitzman, M.L. (1993), "What to Preserve? An Application of Diversity Theory to Crane Conservation", *Quarterly Journal of Economics*, Vol. 108, pp. 157-183, *https://doi.org/10.2307/2118499*.

Wilson, L. et al. (2014), "The Role of National Ecosystem Assessments in Influencing Policy Making", *OECD Environment Working Papers*, No. 60, OECD Publishing, Paris, *http://dx.doi.org/10.1787/5jxvl3zsbhkk-en*.

ANNEX 13.A1

Marginal vs total valuation

Whether it is sensible to speak of the "total" value of a type of ecosystem and even more ambitiously the total value of *all* ecosystems has been the subject of considerable debate following a handful of studies that claims to do just this (e.g. Costanza et al., 1997; Sutton and Costanza, 2002). On the one hand, as Costanza et al. (2017) point, these studies have been highly effective both terms of raising the profile of the ecosystem service approach (judging from academic citations and beyond to public forums) and making the broad that ecosystems command considerable economic value. On the other, such highly aggregated studies are beset with challenges. To see some of the issues, consider Figure 13.A1. On the vertical axis is economic value in dollars. On the horizontal axis is a measure of the flow of ecosystem services (ES) which is assumed can be conflated into a single measure for purposes of exposition.

Figure 13.A1. **Stylised costs and benefits of ecosystem service provision**

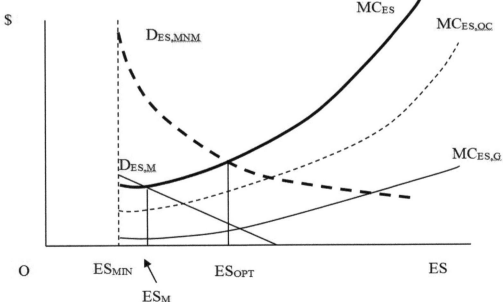

The first construct is a demand curve for ecosystem services, $D_{ES,M}$. This is a demand curve for the *commercial*, or *marketed*, services of ecosystems, i.e. those services that are associated with already established markets in which formal exchange takes place using the medium of money. Thus, if there is an ecosystem producing timber or fuelwood or wildmeat, and, say, tourism, and if these products have markets, then the demand for these products would be shown by $D_{ES,M}$. Another name for a demand curve is a "marginal willingness to pay" curve (mWTP) because the curve shows how much individuals are willing to pay for incremental amounts of the good in question, ES. While it is tempting to think of D_{ES} as a demand curve for *all* services of *all* ecosystems, this is a risky interpretation (see below). For the moment it is best to think of ES in Figure 13.A1 as covering a single ecosystem, say tropical forests.

The second construct is another demand curve but this time for all services from the given ecosystem, regardless of whether they currently have markets or not. This is $D_{ES,MNM}$ which is the demand curve for marketed (M) and non-marketed (NM) ecosystem services. As noted above, there are various non-market services such as watershed protection, carbon sequestration and storage, scientific knowledge, the aesthetics of natural ecosystems, and so on. It is known already that $D_{ES,MNM}$ lies above $D_{ES,M}$ everywhere. This is because, historically, ES have been abundant and hence there has been only a limited incentive for humans to establish property rights over them. As humans systematically expand their "appropriation" of ecosystems, however, there is an incentive to establish property rights because ES become scarce relative to human demands on them (Vitousek et al., 1987).

The two demand curves shown in Figure 13.A1 are downward sloping, as one would expect. The more ES there are the less humans are likely to value an *additional unit* of ES. There is no reason to suppose that ES are any different in this respect to other goods and services: they should obey the "law of demand". But notice what happens if there is a very low level of ES. Imagine a world with very few forests, very little unpolluted oceans, a much reduced stock of coral reefs, an atmosphere with a very much higher concentration of carbon dioxide and other greenhouse gases. In the limit, if there were no unpolluted oceans, no forests, extremely high concentrations of greenhouse gases, then the willingness to pay for one more unit of ES would be extremely high, perhaps on the way to infinity. For this reason, $D_{ES,MNM}$ bends sharply upwards as points closer to the origin on the horizontal axis are approached. Essentially, $D_{ES,MNM}$ is unbounded: there is some irreducible minimum ES below which marginal WTP would rise dramatically such that there is no meaning to the notion of economic value in this unbounded area.

Left alone, ecosystems might continue to provide the same ES year after year. But in order to maintain ES of value to humans it will be the case that certain costs are incurred. Figure 13.A1 shows the first category of these costs as $MC_{ES,G}$ – the marginal costs of managing ES. In the absence of any very strong evidence about the shape, $MC_{ES,G}$ is shown as a gently rising line. The second category of costs is of considerable importance and comprises the opportunity costs of providing ES. The assumption is that ES are best secured by conserving the ecosystems that generate them. This is not consistent with using the ecosystem for some other purpose, e.g. agriculture. Hence, a potentially significant cost of having ES is the forgone profits (more technically, the forgone social value) of the alternative use of the ecosystem. This is referred to in the figure as $MC_{ES,OC}$ – i.e. the marginal opportunity cost of ecosystem conservation. It is formally equivalent to the forgone net benefits of ecosystem conversion, i.e. "development". The sum of $MC_{ES,G}$ and $MC_{ES,OC} = MC_{ES}$ gives the overall marginal cost of conservation.

Figure 13.A1 is simplistic but it shows various points of interest. First, since the true *aggregate* costs of maintaining a given level of ES are given by the area under the overall MC_{ES} curve, and since the true global benefits of ES provision are given by the area under the $D_{ES,MNM}$ curve, the point ES_{OPT} shows the economically optimal level of ES provision. Second, any point to the left of ES_{OPT} has benefits of ES (area under $D_{ES,MNM}$) greater than the overall costs of their supply. But all such points also have an interesting feature. Unless attention is confined arbitrarily to points between ES_{MIN} and ES_{OPT}, all points to the left of ES_{OPT} have apparently *infinite* total benefits and this arises from the fact that the demand curve for ES is unbounded. As noted above, others may prefer to reformulate the issue and say that the idea of cost and benefit comparison for going below ES_{MIN} has no meaning. Third, while $D_{ES,MNM}$ reflects the true global benefits of ES provision, it is not an "operational" demand curve. This means that unless the WTP is captured by some form of market, or unless the evidence on WTP is used to formulate some quantitative restrictions on ecosystem conversion (bans, restrictions on type of conversion etc.), the demand curve that matters is $D_{ES,M}$. Figure 13.A1 shows the real possibility that failure to reflect true WTP in actual markets results in a serious under-provision of ES.

Figure 13.A1 can be used to explain why it is not possible to measure the *total* economic value of all ecosystems. This value would be the area under $D_{ES,MNM}$, but, as noted above, this area cannot be defined. If the view is taken that $D_{ES,MNM}$ becomes infinitely elastic at ES_{MIN}, then, the relevant area measuring total value would be unbounded. This explains, perhaps, why one economist referred to Costanza et al.'s (1997) estimate of the total value as "a serious underestimate of infinity" (Toman, 1998). Similar critiques of efforts to estimate the total value of all ecosystems, or even the value of a single global ecosystem, can be found in Pearce (1998) and Bockstael et al. (2000). Accounting for the value of (actual) changes in ecosystems may be a better focus as in Costanza et al. (2014). However, Chapter 12 noted that the empirical challenge of measuring such changes remains huge especially in the aggregate.

PART III

Chapter 14

The social cost of carbon

The social cost of carbon (SCC) is the central concept for the inclusion of climate change damages in the Cost-Benefit Analysis of public policy and public investments. It measures the present value in monetary terms of the damages incurred when an additional ton of carbon (or any other Greenhouse gas) is released into the atmosphere. The SCC can be added as a cost item for projects that induce carbon emissions, and as a benefit item for projects which induce a net reduction in carbon emissions. Most public projects have an impact on carbon emissions, but energy, transport and agriculture are key areas of concern where it will be important that the SCC is taken into account. In environmental policy, the SCC informs the optimal carbon price and the optimal level of emissions abatement. Implementation of carbon price (e.g. via a tax or permit system) will provide incentives for reduced carbon emissions across all sectors of the economy. Many countries now recognise the importance of the SCC and, as a result, have their own approaches to the estimation of the SCC. In this chapter the theoretical underpinnings of the SCC are explained, and the different approaches to the estimation of the SCC are elaborated upon. Since emissions of carbon have global impacts, which vary across time and space, and in many different sectors, calculation of the SCC is complex, requiring inputs from many different disciplines ranging from climate science, to agronomy, to social science, including economics. There are also considerable uncertainties at every stage of the process through which carbon causes damages. Three important questions which make the calculation of the SCC difficult are: What path will emissions take? How will emissions affect temperatures? How will temperatures cause damages? There are considerable uncertainties at each step of this calculation, which are compounded by the potential for 'threshold effects' and catastrophic outcomes. Yet the importance of climate change as a global problem, and the need to implement policies in line with commitments under international agreements means that many countries have already implemented carbon taxes or use the SCC routinely in their regulatory analysis. In this chapter the methods currently used to analyse and calculate the SCC are discussed. Some of the difficulties and disagreements on the issue are highlighted, and examples of current international practice on using the SCC in the CBA of public policy are explained.

14.1. Introduction

Anthropogenic climate change has been described as the "perfect storm" of environmental problems facing humanity. Part of this storm stems from the fact that the environmental and economic impacts of climate change are manifold and diffuse both across space and across time. Furthermore, despite the scientific consensus that temperatures are rising because of CO_2 emissions, climate scientists and economists recognise that there is a huge amount of uncertainty associated with several aspects of climate change. The question for public policy and for CBA is how to include the expected damages into the analysis of public projects and regulations, and what value should be placed on these damages.

The social cost of carbon (SCC) or social cost of CO_2 (SC-CO_2) is one of the most important concepts for informing the public policy response to climate change.[1] It represents the marginal damages of a unit of carbon or CO_2. The value of the SCC provides information for the valuation of carbon damages associated with climate mitigation public projects and policies, and should be used to set the Pigouvian pollution tax, or carbon price for emissions. Carbon emissions contribute to a stock of CO_2 (e.g. concentration) in the atmosphere and so the SCC reflects damages that are incurred as a result of the increasing stock over the lifetime of the emissions in the atmosphere. The SCC represents the present value of this stream of damages. With concentrations of CO_2 evolving over time, the SCC will vary depending upon the point in time that it is evaluated. For this reason, the optimal carbon tax will also vary.

Estimating the damages associated with the marginal carbon emission is a complex exercise. 4 key estimation steps are required: 1) Future emissions; 2) the impact of emissions on geophysical outcomes like temperature and precipitation; 3) the impact of geophysical outcomes on economic damages; and, 4) a welfare calculation of the present value of the damages using social discounting. At each step the analyst is presented with considerable uncertainty about the structural and parametric relationships between variables. There is *scientific uncertainty* in relation to key response parameters such as equilibrium climate sensitivity (the long run impact on global temperatures resulting from a doubling of CO_2) or transition sensitivity (the medium term response of temperatures to changes in CO_2 emissions). Some elements of this uncertainty are considered to be irreducible, even if it is expected that new information will arrive in the future. Beyond the scientific uncertainties, the correlation between temperature changes and economic damages is a huge additional source of uncertainty. There is a burgeoning literature on the nature of climate damages, but for the long-run the accuracy of the damage function still remains questionable, in part because there is often no historical precedent to work from.

The scientific uncertainty, and uncertainty surrounding climate damages, represent problems of uncertainty in the strictest, "Knightian" sense, cf. Chapter 8.[2] The tools of appraisal need to be mindful of the fact that effects of climate change are at best *ambiguous* and most likely are characterised by Knightian uncertainty. The estimation of the SCC needs to take into account these inherent risks and uncertainties, and reflect societal preferences concerning risks, uncertainty/ambiguity and the potential for catastrophic risks. Individual behaviour suggests that there is a preference for reducing risks, ambiguity and the probability of negative shocks. Many argue that the calculation of the SCC also should reflect such factors.

Climate change happens relatively slowly, with a long lead-time before damages occur, and significant inertia thereafter. Climate change is therefore an inter-generational issue whose impacts will affect future generations hundreds, possibly thousands, of years into the future. For this reason, any evaluation of the costs and benefits of climate change and associated mitigation strategies will be highly sensitive to the inter-temporal social welfare function used to evaluate societal well-being. As shown here and in Chapter 8, the SWF defines the social discount rate and hence the weight placed on future generations' well-being. As the aftermath of the Stern Review illustrated, disagreement on the social discount rate can determine the outcome of an evaluation of policies to mitigate climate change.

Second, climate change raises the spectre of catastrophic outcomes for future generations. As will be seen, economic analysis of climate change has typically looked at the average damages. Due to the long-term consequences of climate change, a low discount rate is required for many mitigation strategies to pass a cost-benefit test when the average effects are the main concern. However, if the probability distribution of damages has "fat tails", meaning that the likelihood of extremely bad outcomes is not vanishingly small, then these effects dominate any CBA, more or less irrespective of the discount rate. Reducing the likelihood of catastrophic events then becomes the main motivation for action on climate change.

This chapter discusses how, despite the apparent obstacles, the SCC has been estimated for use in CBA using a combination of the available climate science, climate models and economic models, evaluated using welfare economic approaches that underpin CBA. With a focus on the detailed procedures recommended in the US, the steps required to estimate the SCC will be explained and the values of the SCC that are in policy use described. In the main, estimates aimed at policy use have been derived from Integrated Assessment Models (IAM). The use of expert opinion and even simpler stylised models if climate and economy are also discussed.

Figure 14.1. **Global Carbon Emissions from Fossil Fuels and Growth of Carbon Emissions**

Million tonnes of carbon per year and per cent

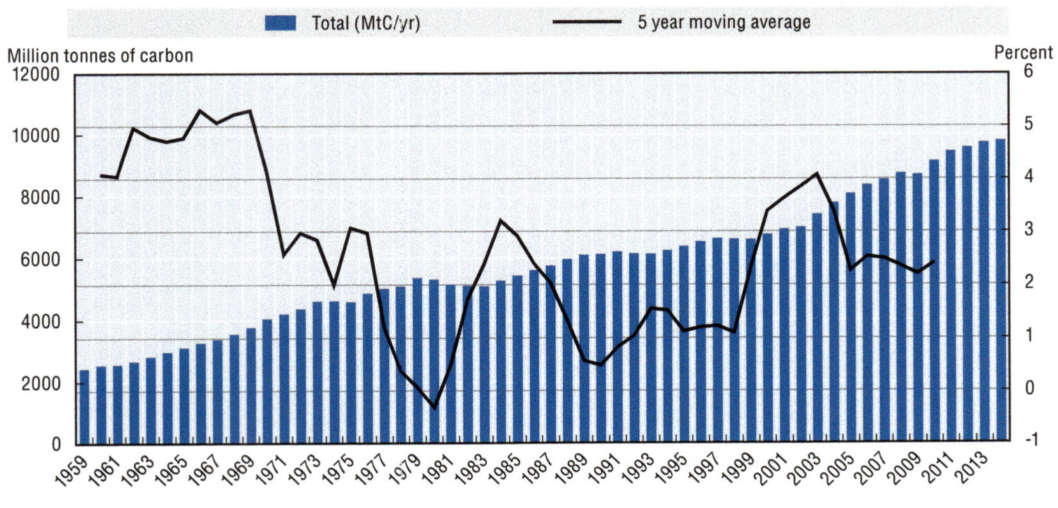

Source: *www.carbonbrief.org.*

14.2. The social cost of carbon and the optimal carbon price: Some theory

The purpose of this section is to provide a clear definition of the social cost of carbon (SCC) and illustrate the relationship between the SCC and the optimal carbon price. The SCC is typically defined as the present value of the damages caused by the emission of a marginal unit of carbon (or other greenhouse gas) into the atmosphere. Sometimes this is expressed in units of carbon dioxide (CO_2) as the social cost of carbon dioxide (SC-CO_2) (e.g. NAS 2017).[3] In the optimal first-best world of economic theory, the optimal carbon tax would be equated to the SCC. The SCC represents the optimal Pigouvian tax that should be applied to carbon emissions so that agents internalise the external cost of their decisions, and an optimal allocation is achieved in the economy. This section will show how in theory the optimal carbon tax and the SCC are linked in this optimal policy context. Subsequent sections will discuss the application of these principles and the different approaches that have been used to estimate the SCC. Once defined and estimated, the SCC can be used to inform the carbon price, or be used as the shadow price to value carbon in the evaluation via CBA of public policy (e.g. investment projects or regulatory change).

One important feature of carbon or carbon dioxide (CO_2) emissions is that it is a stock-pollutant: it contributes to a stock of CO_2 in atmosphere, which builds up and slowly dissipates over time. Climate change mitigation is therefore a dynamic problem, and the damages from CO_2 emissions today are likely to evolve over time and be persistent. Hence the SCC has two key features. First, it reflects the future damages that evolve over time after a marginal change in change in carbon/greenhouse gas emissions today, or at a particular point in time. Second, the SCC will change over time to reflect the evolution of the stock of greenhouse gas pollutants and the marginal damages that entails. The optimal carbon price must therefore also reflect the dynamic nature of the pollutant and evolve over time. A formal presentation of these points makes these ideas concrete.

14.2.1. A formal theoretical analysis of the SCC and the optimal carbon price. A simplified exposition of Hoel and Kverndokk (1996)

There is an expansive theoretical literature analysing the properties of the social cost of carbon, the optimal carbon price, and their dynamics over time. This literature provides insights on the optimal carbon tax and its path over time in optimal economies with different characteristics. The basic insight, however, stems from the fact that carbon is a stock pollutant, rather than a flow pollutant like street-level Nitrogen Oxide or effluent flows in rivers. The fact that CO_2 is a stock pollutant means that the social cost of carbon must reflect the damages over the entire planning horizon resulting from a marginal addition to the stock today.

In the framework of dynamic optimisation the social cost of carbon is represented by the negative shadow price on the CO_2 stock. Box 14.1 shows that this shadow *cost*, the social cost of CO_2 in this case, reflects the present value of the future damages of a marginal emission of CO_2 today. In a steady state this present value is simply given by equation [14.1], which is reproduced here:

$$SCCO2 = \frac{D'(S^*)}{r + \varphi} \qquad [14.1]$$

where S^* is the stock of CO_2 in the atmosphere, $D'(S^*)$ is the flow of marginal damages at each point in time, r is a discount rate, and ϕ is the decay rate of the stock of CO_2 in the atmosphere. Equation [14.1], shows that the SC-CO_2 is equivalent to the present value of an annuity of amount $D'(S^*)$. The $SC\text{-}CO_2$ increases in the marginal damages and decreases in the discount (r) and decay (ϕ) rates.

In an optimising framework, marginal benefits of emissions (from manufacturing, transport etc.) should be equal to the marginal damages associated with CO_2. This means that the optimal carbon tax should be equated to the $SC\text{-}CO_2$ or SCC depending on the units. [14.1] provides an expression for an optimal (steady state) carbon tax. Outside of the steady state in which the stock of CO_2 in constant over time, the optimal carbon tax should reflect the evolution of the carbon stock in the atmosphere, which in recent years has clearly been increasing (See Figure 14.1). Equation [14.3] in Box 14.1 represents the $SC\text{-}CO_2$ in this case.

Although it is possible to define the SCC and the carbon tax in optimal terms, often estimates of the SCC will often be estimated or approximated using a non-optimal "business-as-usual" baseline (e.g. Nordhaus 2017; Stern, 2007). The definition of the SCC as the present value of damages remains the same in these cases.

14.2.2. The optimal path of the carbon tax

The optimal path of the carbon tax has been the subject of a great deal of investigation in the theoretical world. The recommended paths of the tax differ depending on the specific model analysed. Modelling CO_2 emissions dynamically as a stock pollutant provides some important insights into the dynamic trade-offs that ought to be considered when thinking about the optimal path for the carbon tax. The details depend on the details of the specific modelling exercise. But there are some general findings which can inform the design of policy.

For instance, the model of Hoel and Kverndokk (1996) discussed in Box 14.1, a utility-maximising planner using a non-renewable resource which contributes to a stock pollutant, and which faces a backstop technology, would implement a carbon tax that would rise in the short run and fall in the long run. The associated stock of carbon emissions would follow a similar path, only with a delay, peaking later than the carbon tax would peak. These dynamics stem from their modelling assumptions, but the hump-shaped profile of taxes captures the trade-offs that are at stake when implementing policy. On the one hand, the static effect of a tax is to reduce resource extraction. On the other, the dynamic effect of a tax in the future is to reduce the present valuation of future extraction: the present value of the resource rent. Optimal extraction will adjust accordingly by increasing in the short run, and reducing in the future in order to satisfy the dynamics of the resource rent given by Hotelling's rule. The decrease in the optimal tax in the future counteracts this dynamic extraction effect, thereby reducing the level of emissions at each point in time (See Figure 14.2). The time profile of the SCC reflects these dynamic considerations, and indicates that optimal climate policy must take into account the likely dynamic response of profit maximising fossil fuel extractors to policy interventions.

Similar results are found in other studies. Ulph and Ulph (1996) also argue for a hump-shaped profile of carbon taxes. In their case, the result is that emissions are higher in the short run and in the long run, but the optimal policy removes the peak emissions that arise in the medium run. In the Hoel and Kverndokk (1996) model, extraction continues for longer than without the optimal tax. See Figure 14.2, in which the "business-as-usual", i.e. no carbon tax scenario has higher peak emissions but leads to a termination of the fossil fuel era at some point in finite time when the backstop technology becomes more economic.

Box 14.1. **The social cost of carbon and the optimal carbon tax**

A simplified exposition of Hoel and Kvernndok (1996)

Hoel and Kverndokk (1996) is among the most straightforward theoretical models which can be used to illustrate the theoretical meaning of the social cost of carbon and the relationship with the optimal carbon tax. The social cost of carbon is analysed in the context of an economy reliant on an exhaustible resource (e.g. fossil fuels) that produces a stock pollutant (e.g. CO_2). The problem is one of optimal depletion in the face of the stock pollutant that arises from the use of the non-renewable resource. This is a simplified representation of the problem of climate change being driven by fossil fuel use in the general economy. The following explanation provides some insights concerning the SCC and the optimal carbon tax.

The objective in Hoel and Kverndokk (1996) is to maximise present value of the sum of utility u(xt) over time (discounted at rate r) via the choice of the resource (pollutant) flow xt, given the fact that there is a finite stock of the non-renewable resource A0, the cumulative extraction of which induces a stock of atmospheric pollution, St which causes instantaneous damages $D(S_t)$. The stock pollutant evolves over time according to the dynamic equation:

$$\dot{S} = x_t - \phi S_t \qquad [14.2]$$

where xt is emissions of the pollutant, and ϕ reflects the rate of decay of the pollution stock via natural atmospheric and oceanic processes. The following Hamiltonian function captures the essential trade-off that is faced between the benefits consuming the resource xt (e.g. oil) which provides instantaneous utility, u(xt), and the build-up of the pollutant St. which causes damages D(St), and the dynamic effects of changes in the stock of pollution, $\dot{S} = x_t - \phi S_t$. The Hamiltonian is maximised via the choice of the control variable xt:

$$H^c\left(x_t, S_t, \mu\right) = u\left(x_t\right) - D\left(S_t\right) + \mu_t\left(x_t - \varphi S_t\right)$$

The solution to this problem balances instantaneous flow of benefits that the economy obtains from the use of non-renewable resources, u(xt), against the costs incurred in the future due to the increased stock of pollution, D(St), which accumulates over time according to (14.2).[4]

The shadow price of a stock of CO_2, μ, captures the marginal effect on inter-temporal well-being from a marginal increase in the pollution stock S_t. This will be negative, since pollution reduces welfare: it is a cost. This means that the social cost of carbon: SC-CO2 is equal to the θ = -μ. It is instructive to derive an expression for the SC-CO2. Using the Hamiltonian approach means that the shadow price μ evolves over time as follows:

$$\dot{\mu} - r\mu = -\frac{\partial H}{\partial S} = D'\left(S\right) + \phi\mu \qquad [14.3]$$

With SC-CO_2 defined as θ = -μ, the differential equation for θ implied by [14.2] yields the following expression for the SC-CO_2 (θ) at time t (Hoel and Kverndokk, 1996, p. 119):

$$\theta = \int_t^\infty D'\left(S_\tau\right)\exp\left(-\left(r+\varphi\right)\left(\tau-t\right)\right)d\tau \quad (=-\mu) \qquad [14.4]$$

[14.3] is an accounting identity which allows the SC-CO2 to be defined explicitly as (14.4). The relationship holds for non-optimal paths too. [14.4] shows explicitly that the SC-CO2 (θ) is the present value of the sum of future marginal damages D'(St) arising from a marginal unit of CO2, discounted at the composite discount rate, (r + ϕ), over the remaining planning horizon, $\tau \in (t, \infty)$.[5]

In an optimal solution, the marginal benefit of extraction today should be equated to the marginal cost in the future, θ. So the SC-CO2 equates to the optimal carbon tax. The SC-CO2 evolves over time according to the (14.3), and therefore so should the optimal carbon tax.

Box 14.1. **The social cost of carbon and the optimal carbon tax** (*cont.*)

In the simpler steady state, in which $S\tau = S^*$ for all time, the carbon tax becomes the present value of the annuity $D'(S^*)$:

$$SCCO2 = \theta = \frac{D'(S^*)}{r + \varphi}$$ [14.5]

Expressions (14.4) and (14.5) illustrate the general point that the SC-CO2 reflects the present value of all future marginal damages, discounted at the composite rate ($\phi + r$). The SC-CO2 decreases with a higher discount rate (r) and with more rapid decay of the pollutant (ϕ). The discount rate reduces value of future the damages, whereas the decay reduces the quantity of future damages.

Figure 14.2. **Optimal path of a carbon tax**

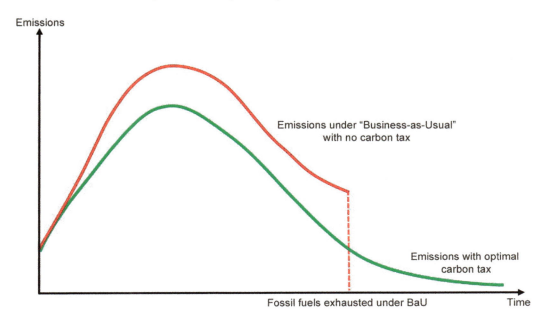

Source: Hoel and Kverndokk, 1996.

Alternatively, the "optimal carbon tax" scenario reduces emissions over in the medium term, but leads to an extended fossil era which overlaps with the use of the backstop technology. In each case, all economically viable resources are extracted. Many models of the optimal carbon tax lead to this essential point: optimal management of the stock pollutant involves smoothing out the time profile of emissions, possibly at the cost of longer fossil fuel eras.

14.2.3. *Carbon policy and the Green Paradox*

Analysis of the optimal path of the carbon tax illustrates the competing forces that policy must contend with, and the idea that, faced with a carbon tax, fossil fuel extractors have incentives to adjust their behaviour. The analyses suggest that naïve implementation of climate policies may induce unintended consequences. A literature related to the modelling of the social cost of carbon and the appropriate taxation policy concerns what is known as the Green Paradox. The Green Paradox states that certain policies that are aimed at reducing carbon emissions and abating climate change, may have the reverse effect of increasing emissions in the near-term, and potentially reducing welfare. The mechanism via which this can happen is that a steeply rising carbon tax, or rapidly falling cost of renewables (the backstop technology), has a similar effect as an expropriation risk: it makes fossil fuels worthless in the future and hence accelerates extraction by fossil fuel companies now (Sinn, 2008; van der Ploeg and Withagen, 2015). The Green Paradox concerns policies towards renewable resources and energy efficiency (Hoel, 2008), and even the enactment of successful international environmental agreements (Strand, 2007). In each case, the Green Paradox suggests that apparently helpful policies such as a carbon tax or renewable subsidies could have perverse effects on climate and welfare when mediated through existing markets and institutions.

A pivotal reference here is Sinn (2008) who analyses the impact of a carbon tax on a decentralised market economy. Sinn (2008) shows that in this context, a non-optimal tax on carbon, which rises at a constant rate over time, can increase the rate of extraction of non-renewable resources. The constant growth rate of the tax acts as an additional component of the discount rate, which quickens extraction. Underpinning this result is the idea that the property rights to subsoil assets are not perfect, so the tax essentially adds to the appropriation risk in the industry. The response to the tax moves the economy away from the optimal path of extraction. Sinn (2008) illustrates the potential for perverse outcomes of environmental policy, the importance of the existing institutions, and the insights from using dynamic frameworks. The rate of change of the tax is clearly an important consideration for taxation policy when it comes to carbon, as is the way in which taxes are internalised.

Starting from the perspective that not all fossil fuels can be used if the temperature targets of the Paris COP21 Accord are to be respected, Gerlagh (2011) shows that investment in alternative technologies is crucial to ensure that the era of fossil fuels ends, rather than being smoothed out over a longer horizon, as in other models. Ending the fossil fuel era might mean higher emissions in the short-term, but lower cumulative emissions overall. In such a context, the rate of reduction in the cost of the backstop technology determines how quickly non-renewables are "priced out'" of the market due to their increasing production costs and the rapidly falling backstop price. A similar result could be obtained when the deposits of non-renewables resources are of different qualities, and hence command different prices. In such cases it is likely that it will be inefficient to extract all reserves of fossil fuels, and the Green Paradox is no longer typically present (Gerlagh, 2011). Further analysis of the Green Paradox can be found in van der Ploeg and Withagen (2015).[6] The general conclusion is that a carbon price is the best way in which to regulate carbon emissions, and that if subsidies to renewable technology (or fossil fuels) are put in place instead of carbon pricing, a Green Paradox is likely in which emissions rise and accelerate global warming.

14.3. Estimating the SCC or SC-CO$_2$ using integrated assessment models (IAMs)

In order for climate damages to be considered in the analysis of public policy and public investments, or to inform the appropriate carbon price, an estimate of the SCC or SC-CO$_2$ (henceforth SCC) is required. The National Academy of Sciences (NAS 2017, Chapter 2) provides a framework for the estimation of the SCC which relies on the use of integrated assessment models (IAMs) of climate and economy.

IAMs vary in their precise purpose and their level of modelling detail. NAS (2017) refers to two distinct types of IAM: 1) Detailed-structure IAMs; and 2) Reduced-form IAMs. Detailed-structure IAMs provide detailed decompositions of specific aspects of climate and economy depending on the core research questions they attempt to address. Technological change in the energy sector (e.g. the WITCH model of Bosetti et al., 2006), adaptation in the agricultural and manufacturing sector, feedbacks between land and oceans (e.g. Reilly et al., 2012), and climate change risks, are just some of the specific themes that have been addressed by these detailed-structure IAMS (NAS 2017, p. 40). Another aspect of these detailed models is their finer-grained spatial focus, with analysis taking place at the regional level (e.g. the Asian-specific Integrated Model (AIM) of Matsuika et al., 1995).

The detailed-structure IAMs typically have not been used to estimate the global value of climate damages and the SCC since they are often not sufficiently developed to place an economic value of the damages, and then aggregate these damages to the global level. For this purpose, the typical approach has been to use more reduced-form IAMs. Reduced-form IAMs provide representations of the economy, climate and the carbon cycle that are highly aggregated. For instance, the complexity of global production is typically represented by one aggregate production function. This function transforms aggregate capital and labour into output, via exogenous technological change, and abstracts from the specifics of any particular sector or industry. Similarly on the climate side, the relationship between carbon emissions, temperature and economy are represented in simplified relational expressions. The advantage of these models is that they represent global aggregate measures of climate change and economic welfare, and therefore can be used to estimate the SCC.

A handful of reduced-form IAMs (henceforth simply IAMs) have been used to calculate the SCC. In each case there are four essential steps required to calculate the SCC (e.g. NAS 2017, p. 39):

1. *Emissions*: Projecting of the future path of output and CO_2 emissions;

2. *Climate Impact*: Projection of the impact of emissions on the physical world: including atmospheric and oceanic temperature change, changes in ecosystems and biomass productivity;

3. *Damages*: Calculation of the economic damages associated with the future path of emissions and the changes in the physical world that are projected to occur;

4. *Discounting*: Discount the stream of economic damages to obtain a present value (see Chapter 8)

The next section discusses how these steps can be undertaken in the context of a particular reduced form IAM, the DICE model (Nordhaus, 2017). Estimates from other IAMs are then presented followed by estimates that have been proposed for use in practice.

14.3.1. IAMs: 4 steps to estimate the SCC using the DICE model

The social cost of carbon: As discussed in the previous section, the social cost of carbon is the present value of the damages associated with an additional tonne of carbon or tonne of CO_2 emitted into the atmosphere.[7] The DICE model, and most reduced-form IAMs, uses the discounted utilitarian inter-temporal welfare function of the form: $W_\tau = \sum_{t=\tau}^{\infty} \exp(-\delta t) U(C_t)$, to evaluate the climate change damages, where δ is the utility discount rate and $U(C_t)$ is the instantaneous utility of a representative agent at time t. With emissions reflected by E_t and consumption represented by C_t, and inter-temporal welfare represented by W, the general expression for the SCC is:

$$SCC_t = -\frac{\partial W / \partial E_t}{\delta W / \partial C_t} \qquad [14.6]$$

The numerator of [14.6] is the impact of emissions on welfare (the present value of utility) and the denominator is the marginal utility of consumption, which means that the SCC is measured in terms of consumption, rather than utility. Typically the calculation is undertaken by perturbing the model with a non-marginal pulse of carbon emissions (or removal thereof) to a well-established baseline scenario, and then dividing by the magnitude of the pulse to obtain the per unit value of the SCC in monetary terms (Newell and Pizer, 2003; Nordhaus, 2014; 2017). The way in which emissions diffuse over time and affect the wider climate and economy varies from one modelling approach to another.

14.3.2. Step 1: Emissions: Projection of global output and emissions

The socio-economic module of the DICE model consists of the welfare function above and the productive sector which produces aggregate output and emissions of carbon. In its measure of global welfare, utility is multiplied by global population, $L(t)$ and a discount factor $R(t)$ at each point in time:

$$W = \sum_{t=1}^{T_{max}} U\big(C(t)\big)L(t)R(t) \qquad [14.7]$$

CO_2 Emissions come from aggregate output, $Y(t)$ and from exogenous land use emissions, $E_{land}(t)$:

$$E(t) = \sigma(t)\big(1-\mu(t)\big)Y(t) + E_{land}(t) \qquad [14.8]$$

where $\sigma(t)$ is the *carbon intensity* of output and $\mu(t)$ is the *emissions reduction rate*, reflecting technological and policy interventions. Output, $Y(t)$, is modelled as aggregate production function of technology, $A(t)$ and diminishing marginal product in capital, $K(t)$, and labour, $L(t)$:

$$Y(t) = A(t)f\big(K(t),L(t)\big) \qquad [14.9]$$

Aggregate output is either consumed, $C(t)$, or invested. Projections of output and emissions are governed by these relationships, with the essential parameters and functions ($\sigma(t)$, $\mu(t)$, $f(.)$) estimated using the best available knowledge, and growth of population, output and technological change projected using historical evidence or expert opinion (see Nordhaus, 2016). In the DICE model (DICE 2016R), growth in per capita output is assumed to be 2.1% per annum until 2050, and then 1.9% per annum until 2100. Population growth is assumed to follow the United Nations population predictions.

14.3.3. Step 2: Climate impact: the impact of emissions on the physical world

Each IAM defines an explicit relationship between emissions and the physical world based on information from climate science. One of the key aspects is the change in temperature that emissions will induce. In the DICE 2016R model, the relationship is characterised by several simple reduced-form expressions for the geophysical relationships. These expressions (which are omitted here for simplicity, see Nordhaus, 2017, p. 1519-1520) characterise: 1) the flow of CO_2 to and from atmosphere to upper ocean and biosphere, to deep ocean carbon *reservoirs*; 2) the radiative forcing (temperature effect) of CO_2 emissions in the atmosphere; and 3) the effect of radiative forcing on atmospheric and lower ocean temperatures.

The process of estimating parameters, calibrating the models and making projections is made difficult because there is a great deal of uncertainty surrounding the estimates. One particularly important parameter which is used to characterise the relationship between CO_2 emissions and atmospheric temperature change is the equilibrium climate sensitivity (ECS). ECS describes a long-run *equilibrium* relationship which indicates the change in temperature (positive or negative) as a result of the doubling of CO_2 concentrations in the atmosphere. This parameter is inherently uncertain (Roe and Baker, 2007), and there have been many different attempts to estimate its probability distribution using climate modelling, empirical estimates using historical data on temperature-CO_2 relationships, or interviews of expert opinion. Figure 14.3 shows the wide variety of estimates that are currently in circulation. The DICE 2016R model uses a mean value of 3.1°C based on Olsen et al. (2012). A related parameter is the transitory climate sensitivity (TCS). TCS describes shorter-run (50-100 years) relationships between CO_2 emissions and temperature change. The DICE model uses a value of 1.7°C for TCS.

Figure 14.3. Probability density function for equilibrium climate sensitivity

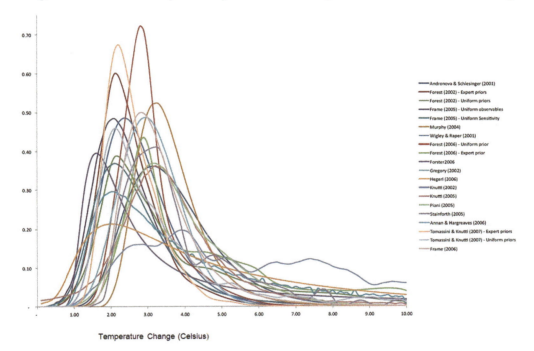

Source: Heal and Millner (2014).

The ECS of 3.1°C used in DICE 2016R lies within the range of 1.5°C-4.5°C that the IPCC's 5th assessment report (IPCC-AR5) considers with *medium confidence* to be *likely* (IPCC 2013, p. 16).[8] Reflecting the uncertainties surrounding this parameter, and based on numerous studies, the IPCC-AR5 continues to say that the ECS is "…very unlikely less than 1°C (*high confidence*), and very unlikely to be greater than 6°C (*medium confidence*)" (IPCC, 2013, p. 16). Furthermore, the IPCC-AR5 states that the TCS is *likely* in the range of 1°C and 2.5°C (*high confidence*). These statements are made based on a probability distribution which summarises many studies, including those in Figure 14.3, using Bayesian statistics.

The reduced-form IAMs model the complex geophysical relationships between emissions and the physical world in a very simplified and aggregated way, although the estimation of the parameters and relationships is informed by more detailed studies. For a more complete discussion of the issues surrounding the relationship between carbon emssions, the physical world and temperature, see the IPCC AR5 Working Group 1 report (IPCC, 2013).

14.3.4. *Step 3: Damages: Predicting and valuing climate damages*

The way in which expected temperature changes translate into economic damages, and how these damages are monetised, is another component of any economic analysis of climate change. Damages associated with climate change can take several possible forms (NAS 2017):

1. Damages to consumption: climate change affects the bundle of goods and services that are consumed;

2. Damages to capital stocks: damage to capital stocks can affect consumption indirectly e.g. via reductions in productivity. Applies to man-made, natural, human capital stocks.

3. Damage to non-marketed capital stocks: non-marketed benefits of human and natural capital stocks that affect welfare directly, not via consumption. Includes some amenity values, landscape values, cultural heritage, the onset of violence and disease, are good examples (NAS 2017, p. 152).

Climate damages may manifest themselves in changes in the level of consumption and GDP. However, climate damages to capital stocks (broadly defined) are likely to affect growth. Hence, these long-term consequences which need to be estimated in order to get a complete picture. Another element of the cost of climate change is the induced investment costs (e.g. flood defences), while an important mediating factor is the ability to adapt to climate change. The damage functions that are used in IAMs to estimate the SCC should take all of these factors into account. Of course, as the NAS (2017, p. 139) makes plain, IAMs are "constrained by the available literature and typically need to extrapolate beyond the relationships characterised in supporting evidence". Nevertheless, the IAMs damage functions do attempt to include many aspects of climate damages, reflecting micro-level, industry level, sectoral level studies aggregated to the economy, region and global level (Metcalf and Stock, 2017; Dell et al., 2014).

At the macro-economic level, several studies have attempted to estimate the costs of climate change either for the economy as a whole, by looking at the empirical relationship between GDP, as a supposed "catch-all" for climate damages, and climatic variables such as temperature (Metcalf and Stock, 2017). By looking at aggregated measures of economic performance such as country-level of region GDP, these studies overcome some of the difficulties in aggregating micro-level studies at the sector or industry level, which requires strong assumptions about the interactions between sectors. A recent example of this can be found in Dell et al. (2014) who estimate the relationship between country level GDP and temperature and precipitation fluctuations. They find that higher temperatures lead to large reductions in the level *and* growth rates of GDP, albeit only in poor countries. The impact on growth suggests that climate change may damage productive capital.

A number of studies have disaggregated the analysis to look at the impact of climate change (e.g. temperature and precipitation) on particular sectors of the economy. This is a natural line of enquiry since some sectors are likely to be more climate sensitive than others (e.g. agriculture and forestry). Dell et al. (2014) find that while a 1°C increase in temperature is associated with a short-run reduction of 2.7 percentage points in the growth rate, industrial productivity is similarly affected with a 2.0 percentage reduction in growth. This reduction in growth in industry is not among "downstream" agricultural industries, and accords with findings in other regions (e.g. Hsiang, 2010). Hence, the negative productivity effects of climate are not the exclusive reserve of what are traditionally thought of as climate-sensitive sectors, such as agriculture.

Another way in which macro-economic costs of climate change have been estimated is via structural economic models such as computable general equilibrium (CGE) models. Such models are IAMs in their own right, and include detailed structural relationships between environment and the economy. Since they capture general equilibrium effects between sectors, the CGE approach partially overcomes the aggregation problems associated with the sector level empirical approaches. For instance, Bosello et al. (2012) use a multi-country multi-sector CGE model to estimate the impacts for coastal regions (migration and land loss), tourism, agriculture (yield loss), energy (change in demand for oil and gas), floods (capital, land and labour productivity loss) and human health (productivity loss dues to heat humidity). The World Bank, using a similar CGE approach, estimated that the cost of adaptation alone to developing countries is at least USD 81 billion (World Bank, 2010).[9]

The structural relationships found in these CGE models are often informed by numerous empirical studies which take place at different levels of aggregation. There are macro-level studies, like Dell et al. (2014), which look at growth, possibly in some sub-sectors of the economy. Other studies use aggregated data for particular sectors, e.g. agriculture (Cline, 2007). Mendelsohn (2012) undertakes cross-sectional analysis in several regions of the developing world to estimate the impact of climate on the agricultural sector, by looking at the relationship between long-term climate variables and productivity levels (e.g. measured by land-rents) across different countries. Then there are micro-level studies within countries which have looked at the impact of climate change on adaptation on agriculture (Kurukulasuriya and Mendelsohn, 2008; Gorst et al., 2016; Di Falco and Veronesi, 2011; Deschenes and Greenstone, 2007; Schlenker and Roberts, 2009), on labour productivity (e.g. Zivin and Neidell, 2010) and on other socio-economic factors such as crime (Ranson, 2014; Hsiang et al., 2011) and mortality (Deschenes and Greenstone, 2011).[10] Adaptation in agriculture has been shown to increase yields in some cases (Di Falco and Veronesi, 2011; Gorst et al., 2016), and at the very least reduce the impact of climate change in others (e.g. Mendelsohn et al., 1994; Mendelsohn, 2012). Some have argued that in some regions, climate change is expected to increase agricultural productivity even without adaptation, and provide net benefits (e.g. Cline, 2007). Analogous adaptations are possible to avert productivity losses in industry also, such as the introduction of air conditioning.

One key distinction in the empirical literature concerns the empirical strategies used to estimate the relationships. Many studies use panel data approaches which rely on short-term fluctuations in temperature and precipitation to identify the effects. Longer term effects of *climate* change are at best captured by distinguishing between short-term and long-term effects in their dynamic analysis of these fluctuations. Some argue that short-term weather fluctuations (even if they reflect 5-10 year mean values) capture changes in weather but not climate. One chief weakness of the panel studies could therefore be that they fail to adequately capture adaptive responses which happen over longer periods of time (Burke and Emerick, 2016). These arguments have motivated the continued study of the relationship between longer-term average temperatures and economic aggregates in cross-sections of countries and regions (e.g. Mendelsohn et al.; 1994; Schlenker et al., 2005; Mendelsohn, 2012). The implication is that panel studies could over-estimate the cost of climate change because they ignore the full extent of adaptation. Yet cross-sectional studies suffer from the weakness in identification, since a third variable could be mediating the relationship between climate and, say, productivity such as institutional quality.

There are many other areas of research that have informed the damage functions used in IAMs. Sea-level rise is predicted to lead to loss of productive land, increased flooding, and possibly an increase in disease and migration (e.g. Stern, 2007). The nature of these damages, and the nature of the adaptive response, is often difficult to predict. There are many studies at the micro and macro-economic level which attempt to understand the likely economic damages in each case. NAS (2017, Chapter 5) and the IPCC-AR5 WGII report (IPCC, 2013b) provide excellent summaries of what is known so far about the damages and adaptation in different sectors of the economy.

Another important aspect of climate damages is *abrupt, non-gradual*, and possibly *catastrophic damages*. Such damages would occur if ecosystems cross a threshold, or reach a 'tipping point' beyond which they shift into another equilibrium. Examples of such potential tipping points include: i) the shifting of the Atlantic Gulf Stream; ii) the changing of the monsoonal circulation patterns; iii) the melting of the polar ice-sheets; iv) melting of the Arctic perma-frost and the associated carbon and methane emissions; and v) the collapse of the Amazon rainforest (e.g. Weitzman, 2009). A related aspect to climate damages is *feedback effects*. For instance, the melting of the Arctic perma-frost will lead to the release of large amounts of carbon currently stored in the frozen ground. This will cause a positive feedback which exacerbates climate change.[11] Beyond these geophysical tipping points, some have argued that even gradual climate change could lead to socio-economic tipping points, in which countries or regions slip into conflict traps, which could consequently stifle development (Hsiang et al., 2011; Hsiang et al., 2013).

Each of these events would cause abrupt damages and such catastrophic events, as well as the other sources of climate damage, need to be captured in the evaluation of the SCC and in the IAMs that attempt to estimate it. The problem for IAMs is that despite a growing literature and some robust estimates in some sectors, many aspects of the nature of climate damages, e.g. conflict and migration, are not known with a great degree of certainty. This is particularly so with regard to tipping points, catastrophic events and the probabilities associated with them (NAS 2017).[12]

Damages in the DICE model: The nature of climate related damages is a burgeoning area of research. Despite this on some key aspects there is a great deal of uncertainty: e.g. in relation to tipping points, and predictions over time. Nevertheless, the DICE model represents climate damages as an aggregation to the global level over regional level damage functions (NAS, 2017, Chapter 2) which attempts to capture the key features of what is known about the economic impact of climate change in a specific structural relationship.

The DICE model (Nordhaus, 2017) uses a highly aggregated damage function which translates atmospheric temperature change (T_{AT}) at time t into economic damages $D(T(t))$ of the following form:

$$D\big(T(t)\big) = \phi_1 T_{AT}(t) + \phi_2 \big[T_{AT}(t)\big]^2 \qquad\qquad [14.10]$$

Damages are assumed to be quadratic in temperature. The fraction of global output lost due to climate damages becomes is defined as:

$$1 - \Omega\big(T(t)\big) = D\big(T(t)\big) / \big[1 + D\big(T(t)\big)\big]. \qquad\qquad [14.11]$$

Consequently, global output, net of damages (and mitigation costs), is then equal to total production, Y(t), multiplied by Ω(T(t)) and $(1 - \Lambda(t))$:

$$Q(T) = \Omega\big(T(t)\big)\big(1 - \Lambda(t)\big) A(t) f\big(K(t)L(t)\big) \qquad\qquad [14.12]$$

where $(1 - \Lambda(t))$ reflects mitigation costs. The parameters of the damage function in Nordhaus (2017) were estimated based on an update of a survey of damage studies undertaken by Tol (2009, 2012), and updated to include non-marketed factors, omitted sectors and an estimate of catastrophic damages according to Nordhaus and Sztorc (2014).[13] The function leads to damages of 2.1% of global output at 3°C of warming, and 8.5% of output at 6°C of warming.

Given the complexity of estimating economic damages, the quadratic form used in the DICE model is the subject of debate, particularly in relation to catastrophic risks. One implication of (14.9) is that although the marginal damages of temperature change are increasing, the increase is quite modest within the expected range of temperature change.

In discussing this point, Weitzman (2010) proposes a greater emphasis on catastrophic damages and "tipping points", beyond which climate damages increase rapidly, and are possible irreversible. Weitzman (2010) argues that such damages could be better reflected by a damage function with a higher order polynomial form. Botzen and van den Bergh (2012) undertake a simulation of the sensitivity of the damages function to the changes in the functional form implied by Weitzman (2010). Their analysis uses the DICE model of Nordhaus and compares the damages found in Nordhaus (2008; 2017):[14]

$$\Omega\left(T(t)\right) = 1 / \left[1 + 0.0028 T_{AT}\left(t\right)^2\right] \tag{14.13}$$

to the higher order polynomial proposed by Weitzman (2010):

$$\Omega\left(T(t)\right) = 1 / \left[1 + \left(\frac{T_{AT}\left(t\right)}{20.46}\right)^2 + \left(\frac{T_{AT}\left(t\right)}{6.08}\right)^{6.754}\right] \tag{14.14}$$

These are but two possible characterisations of the damage function. The implications of each damage function are reproduced in Figure 14.4. For temperature changes in the region of 3°C, the two damage functions lead to similar predictions: a loss of around 2-2.5% of global income. For temperature change in the region of 6°C, the Nordhaus (2008) damage function leads to a 10% loss of output, whereas the Weitzman calibration leads to a 50% loss. The Weitzman calibration was based on expert opinion of the temperature changes required to exceed various climatic tipping points, such as the release of methane from the Arctic perma-frost (Tundra), and changes in the flow of Thermohaline Circulation (e.g. Gulf Stream) (Botzen and van den Bergh, 2012, p. 373; Weitzman, 2010).

Yet, as Pindyck (2013) points out, the extent of damages given a temperature rises in excess of 6°C are really unknown, and calibrating the damage function is an exercise involving guesswork and a certain amount of speculation. Differences between models arise as a result of the modelling assumptions that are used to resolve this issue and the generate projections. The FUND model, for instance, has detailed sector-specific damage functions, which in aggregate, using baseline parameters, lead to lower levels of damage at each temperature increase than the DICE model, and even leads to benefits over the range 0 to 3°C of temperature increase (Greenstone et al., 2013, p. 27). Alternatively, Howard and Sterner (2017) provide a meta-analysis of damage functions for climate change which concludes that damages are likely to be more severe than the DICE-2016R model.

14.3.5. Step 4: Discounting

Chapter 8 contains a detailed description of discounting issues. In the context of reduced-form IAMs, the issue of discounting reduces to how to calibrate the social welfare function in (14.7). The typical modelling assumption is to assume a constant utility discount rate, δ, and a utility function with a constant elasticity of marginal utility: $U\left(C(t)\right) = (1-\eta)^{-1} C_t^{1-\eta}$, where the parameters δ and η are components of the Ramsey Rule for the social discount rate: SDR $= \delta + \eta g_c$, where g_c, is the growth of consumption (see Chapter 8). Climate change is a non-marginal change to the economy. In the DICE model therefore, growth of consumption is an endogenous component that is an outcome of the optimisation procedure with and without climate policies. The only question remaining is how to choose the two welfare parameters δ and η? Disagreement on this issue alone has led to different policies on climate change being proposed (e.g. Stern 2007; Nordhaus 2008). In the DICE model Nordhaus proposes a positivist approach to the calibration which assumes that the social discount rate should reflect observed rates of return in the market place. This, it is argued, reflects the opportunity cost of investment in climate change mitigation, and the parameters of the social welfare function should be calibrated to ensure that the Ramsey Rule holds as follows: $r = \delta + \eta g_c$. This approach requires an empirical estimate of η and g. δ is estimated as a residual Nordhaus (2017, p. 1520). The SCC in the DICE model assumes that the global real rate of return on investment will be 4.25% until 2100, which is a global average of observed historical rates in the United States and the rest of the world.

Figure 14.4. The implications of temperature change for climate damages

Under different assumptions concerning the damage function

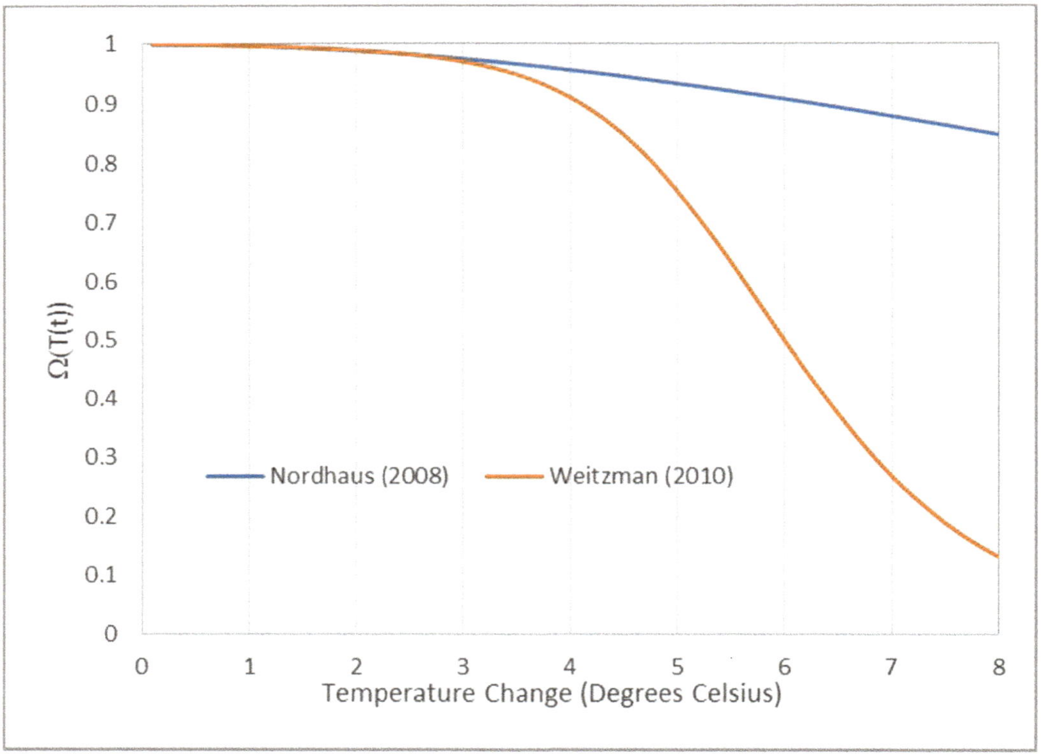

Source: Botzen and van den Bergh, 2012.

Other IAMs estimates of the SCC take alternative approaches to discounting. The Stern Review, which used the PAGE IAM, calibrated the social welfare function using a prescriptive or normative approach, which pointedly did not use market rates of interest to define the social discount rate (see Chapter 8 for more on this).

14.3.6. Summary

Each step of the process of calculating the SCC is subject to uncertainty in the relationships modelled, be they between economy and emissions, between emissions and climate or between climate and damages. Uncertainty surrounds climatic parameters such as ECS and TCS, as well as in relation to the spatial, temporal and probabilistic nature of climate damages. In addition to which, projections hundreds of years into the future are made on the basis of assumptions made today. The estimates of the SCC therefore need to be accompanied by a clear strategy for dealing with uncertainty, and be presented in a manner that makes it clear that uncertainty exists. Most estimates focus on central values yet provide summary statistics of the distribution of estimates based on consideration of different aspects of parameter uncertainty, e.g. the ECS parameter. Before discussing how uncertainty is dealt with in practice, SCC estimates from some important reduced form IAMs are presented. Above all, these estimates confirm the position of most researchers that the SCC is definitely not zero.

14.4. Uncertainty, catastrophic risk and Weitzman's dismal theorem

14.4.1. Uncertainty in the SCC and IAMs

There are many sources of uncertainty at each step of the calculation of the SCC. In step 1, the emissions that are likely in the future depend on unknown and uncertain future policies on climate and technology, for instance. In step 2, the parameters which map emissions into changes in the climate are not known with certainty, as discussed in relation to the Equilibrium Climate Sensitivity and Transitory Response Sensitivity described above (See Figure 14.3). In step 3, the translation of climatic changes into physical and economic damages is perhaps one of the largest sources of uncertainty. Finally in step 4, the components of the discount rate are either difficult to predict (interest rates, returns to capital and so forth) or the source of a great deal of disagreement (Drupp et al., 2017).

A key distinction when discussing uncertainty in the calculation of the SCC is between *structural uncertainty* and *parametric uncertainty*. Structural uncertainty refers to the uncertainty about which model, or indeed if any model, is the most suitable for capturing the relationships necessary to calculate the SCC. One key uncertainty here is in relation to the abrupt damages, thresholds and tipping points which may lead to potentially catastrophic outcomes. Parametric uncertainty relates to what goes on inside the models, for instance, Figure 14.3 illustrates the uncertainty surrounding the ECS parameter that is used to calibrate the relationship between emissions and temperature change in all IAMs. But parametric uncertainty extends to all parameters used, from economic relationships, e.g. technological change and growth, to aspects of the damage function, such as the elasticity of damages with respect to output and temperature particularly at higher temperatures, as seen in the damage functions shown in Figure 14.3 (NAS 2017).

From a policy perspective these uncertainties are important to understand and incorporate in the estimates of the SCC. The current practice in dealing with structural uncertainty is to use several models to estimate the SCC. In the US, as discussed below, the DICE, FUND and PAGE models are used and variation between them reflects the different modelling assumptions. In terms of parametric uncertainty, the standard approach is to assign probability distributions to parameters (as in Figure 14.3) and undertake Monte Carlo analysis. The US Interagency Working Group for the Social Cost of Carbon is estimated the SCC using 3 IAMs using 10000 draws from the distribution of the ECS proposed by Roe and Baker (2012) to build a distribution of estimates of the SCC (IWG 2016). The NAS (2017) report recommends undertaking this analysis at each of the 4 steps outlined above. Nordhaus (2017) undertakes Monte Carlo analysis for all the parameters in the model. Such approaches assume that probability distributions can be defined for all parameters. In many cases probabilities are at best ambiguous and often unknown, e.g. the likelihood of a catastrophic outcomes and tipping points. Such risks can dominate the welfare analysis of climate change since avoiding them can be highly valuable in welfare terms from an insurance perspective.

14.4.2. Catastrophic risk and Weitzman's dismal theorem

Weitzman's dismal theorem (Weitzman, 2009) is the proposal that the standard framework for CBA is not fit for purpose for evaluating the costs and benefits of climate change. The reason for this position stems from the uncertainty surrounding the damages associated with climate change. Weitzman argues that the probability distribution associated with uncertain factors such climate sensitivity are "fat-tailed". A normal distribution, for instance, is not fat-tailed since the probability of extreme events converges quickly to zero as one moves away from the central location of the distribution. Yet, by the best estimates, extreme values of climate sensitivity, e.g. values in excess of 6°C, do not have vanishingly small probabilities associated with them. Indeed, the IPCC fourth assessment report (IPCC AR4) concludes that the probability that climate sensitivity is in excess of 6°C is around 10%, with a fat-tailed distribution. With large climate sensitivity comes large potential economic damages, and potentially disastrous outcomes for humanity. It is these extreme events, Weitzman argues, that push standard CBA to the limits of its sensible use.

The argument contained in Weitzman (2009) is somewhat complex, but in a critique of the dismal theorem, Nordhaus (2011) provides a simple exposition of the basic principle. A more detailed analysis of the implications of the Dismal Theorem can be found in Millner (2013).

Suppose that social welfare is evaluated at each point in time using the standard expected utility framework:

$$E\left[U\left(\tilde{C}\right)\right] = \int U(C)f(C)dC \qquad\qquad\qquad [14.15]$$

In this framework, a catastrophic outcome would be captured by situations when consumption, C, is approximately zero. Weitzman's dismal theorem argues that the expected utility in such a situation will not converge because the expected marginal utility will become negative infinity. From a welfare perspective, what this means is that society would be willing to reallocate the entire wealth towards avoiding such catastrophic events. In the context of climate change, if future generations are subject to fat-tailed risks of catastrophic outcomes, the smooth trade-off between current and future generations disappears as the calculus of CBA would argue for an infinite investment in future well-beings.

The argument has caused great deal of interest in climate economics. Weitzman (2007) argued that arguments such as these could be used to justify the conclusions of the Stern Review: deep cuts in emissions are required now to avoid climate change, stating that the Stern Review might be right, but for the wrong reasons. It is extreme, and works only for particular utility functions and probability distribution functions. Nordhaus (2009) provides a simple explanation of these points.

Suppose that utility is iso-elastic in consumption, C, a typical assumption in applied work in economics and finance: $U(C) = -C^{1-\eta}$. This implies that marginal utility is given by: $U'(C) = -(1-\eta)C^{-\eta}$. If the probability distribution for C is a power law, then as C approaches zero, as it would in a catastrophic state, the probability density is given by the approximation: $f(C) = C^k$. In this case small values of k mean fatter tails, and large values of k, e.g. powers much greater than 1, mean thin tails. Figure 14.5 provides an illustration of how this might look in the vicinity of C = 0.

Figure 14.5. **The probability distribution of consumption**

Fat (k < 1) and Thin (k >> 1) Tailed distributions in the vicinity of C = 0

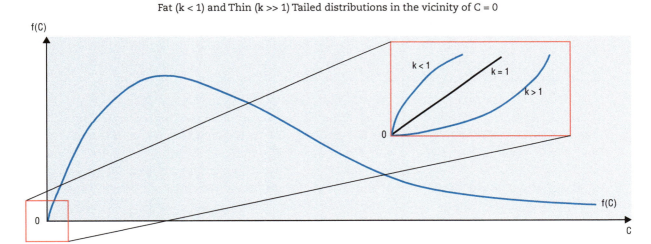

The upper graph shows the entire probability density function (pdf) for consumption. The lower graph magnifies the lower end of the pdf in the vicinity of C equal to zero, for alternative values of the parameter k. What Nordhaus calls the *conditional* marginal utility in the vicinity of zero is then given by:

$$U(C)f(C) = -C^{1-\eta}C^k = -C^{k+1-\eta} \qquad [14.16]$$

The expected utility in the vicinity of zero, between C = 0 and some (arbitrary) positive level of consumption, $C = \overline{C}$, is given by:

$$E\left[U(\tilde{C})\right] = \int_0^{\overline{C}} -C^{k+(1-\eta)}dC = \left[\frac{1}{\eta-2-k}C^{k+(2-\eta)}\right]_0^{\overline{C}} \qquad [14.17]$$

Finding the definite solution to this integral is only possible if $k + 2 - \eta > 0$. If $k + 2 - \eta < 0$, expected utility converges to minus infinity, since C to the power of a negative exponent is infinite when evaluated at C = 0. Both cases are possible with plausible parameter values for k and η, but the latter ($k + 2 - \eta < 0$) is a simple illustration of Weitzman's dismal theorem.

Weitzman's point is that when the tails of the distribution are fat, k is small in this example, then the welfare criterion fails to provide useable information, since it provides an infinitely negative valuation of catastrophic states of the world. Taken literally, a CBA along these lines would imply that all possible resources should be reallocated to averting the catastrophic risk. Yet, Nordhaus (2011) makes the point that the dismal theorem is not inevitable, even with fat-tailed distributions, since it depends on the preferences of the representative agent. Nevertheless, if $k + 2 - \eta < 0$, as it would be if society was very risk averse and η was very large, and the tails of the distribution are fat (k small) then the expected utility criterion fails to provide a useful measure of welfare. Under similar conditions, expected marginal utility becomes infinite, which becomes critical when evaluating marginal changes in consumption induced by public investment as would be the case in CBA. Expected marginal utility is infinite when $k + 1 < \eta$.

The basic intuition presented by Nordhaus (2011) was developed more comprehensively elsewhere and is discussed in detail by Millner (2013). Many authors have pointed out that non-convergence of the expected welfare criterion is not a general problem, but one that is more likely with iso-elastic utility functions. Yet, the problem remains a theoretical illustration of the frailties of particular frameworks when they are pushed to extremes. The consideration of fat tailed distributions and the welfare valuation of catastrophic risks is widely regarded to be the major concern in climate change economics, even if Weitzman's dismal theorem is an extreme case (e.g. Wagner and Weitzman 2013; Pindyck, 2013).

14.5. Estimates of SCC from integrated assessment models

The four steps for calculating the SCC have been outlined and the specific example of the DICE model has been used to illustrate the modelling assumptions used in each step, and the background studies that assist with the calibration of the model. There are many IAMs in use in the academic and policy world, and each differs in the assumptions it uses to undertake each of the 4 steps described above. Furthermore, while many IAMs exist for the purpose of analysing climate change policy, as Nordhaus (2014) points out, most of the estimates of the SCC that are in circulation in the policy literature have come from three of these models: Dynamic Integrated Climate and Economy model (DICE) written by William Nordhaus and colleagues at Yale, the Framework for Uncertainty, Negotiation and Distribution (FUND) model, by Richard Tol at the University of Sussex, and the Policy Analysis of Greenhouse gas Emissions (PAGE) model of Chris Hope of Cambridge University (Hope, 2007), which provided the basis for the results presented in the Stern Review (Stern, 2007). Comparing the SCC calculated from these different models highlights some of these fundamental differences.

Tol (2011) summarised estimates of the SCC from these and other IAMs and the results of this summary are shown in Table 14.1. Another recent summary of estimates can be found in Greenstone et al. (2013), in which similar models are compared under different scenarios.

Table 14.1. **Social cost of carbon from different IAMs**
USD per tonne of carbon (USD 1995)

Statistics	Integrated assessment models (Number of estimates, N)				
	All (211)	PAGE (42)	DICE (12)	FUND (112)	Other (73)
Mode	49	20	9	25	67
Mean	177	77	35	59	266
Standard deviation	293	119	51	75	403
Median	116	53	7	46	177
90% percentile	487	219	105	139	734
95% percentile	669	302	148	178	1 002
99% percentile	1 602	504	200	286	1 824
Probability SCC<0	25%	26%	23%	14%	25%

Source: Tol (2011, p. 431).

The summary statistics in Table 14.1 are raw and un-weighted statistics among the models selected. What these distributions illustrate is the wide variety of estimates of the SCC that exist in the literature. The variation stems from the different assumptions, both economic and in relation to the climate science, that are embodied in each of the models. The fact that many of the different estimates stem from the same models illustrates the different policy simulations that were undertaken, and the different parametric and other assumptions that have been deployed within each model, sometimes for sensitivity analysis. In short though, the weighted average estimate of the SCC across the three main models in 2011 was USD 62 per tonne of carbon, in 1995 dollars, or USD 92 per tonne of carbon in 2015 dollars.[15] The estimates vary tremendously and the distribution has a long tail extending to thousands of dollars. Two measures of the uncertainty in the estimates of the SCC in Table 14.1 are the standard deviation and the probability that the models report an SCC that is less than zero. As Tol (2011) shows, such is the uncertainty in the estimates, the standard deviations are large and there is a 25% chance that the models produce negative estimates of the SCC when summarising the models across all the assumptions that have been deployed in their many applications.

To illustrate the determinants of the variation, consider the estimates of the SCC obtained from Nordhaus (2014), which compares a variety of scenarios which differ in their policy target and parameters such as the discount rate in Table 14.2.

Table 14.2. **Social cost of carbon under certain assumptions**

USD per tonne CO_2, 2005

Scenarios	2015	2020	2025	2030	2050
Baseline	18.6	22.1	26.2	30.6	53.1
Optimal	17.7	21.2	25.0	29.3	51.5
2°C	47.6	60.1	75.5	94.4	216.4
Stern Review discounting	89.8	103.7	117.4	131.3	190.0
High discount	6.4	7.7	9.2	10.9	19.6

Source: Adapted from Nordhaus, 2014, p. 284.

The estimates in Table 14.2 are undertaken using the 2013 version of the DICE model: DICE-2013R. The basic economic and climatic assumptions remain constant across the scenarios. The differences between the scenarios are as follows. The baseline model assumes no additional climate policies are enacted henceforth. The optimal model optimises the response to climate change assuming that emissions reductions and international agreements are possible. The "Stern Review discounting" scenario uses the discounting parameters used in Stern Review (Stern, 2007) while the "High discount" scenario has a pure rate of time preference (δ) of 3.5%. The value of the SCC varies in fairly obvious ways in response to these scenarios.

First, in the DICE model, optimal emissions reductions do not manage to reach the 2°C target given the way in which damages are modelled. The 2°C scenario adjusts damages so that it is optimal to reduce emissions and meet this target. Inevitably, with damages increased, the SCC increases accordingly. This illustrates the importance of the damage function in determining the SCC, but also the view that the 2°C limit (let alone the 1.5°C agreed in the Paris Accord) is not necessarily what Nordhaus (2014) would recommend for climate policy: the costs are too high compared to the avoided damages.

The Stern Review used the PAGE model to evaluate the benefits and costs of climate change mitigation (Stern, 2007). The Review's analysis assumed that the rate of pure time preference (utility discount rate) ought to be equal to zero for reasons of intergenerational equity. This assumption places equal weight on utilities that accrue in the future as utilities that accrue today in the calculation of overall inter-temporal welfare. The normative calibration of the discount rate, which implies equal treatment of utilities, was debated both on normative and positive grounds (see e.g. Nordhaus, 2007; Weitzman, 2007; Dasgupta 2008). Practically speaking, the social cost of carbon is highly sensitive to the level of the discount rate, and its influence is plainly seen in Table 14.2, where the SCC of

USD 90 per tonne of CO2 in 2015 is nearly five times larger than the DICE-2013R optimal scenario. As a further illustration of the sensitivity of the SCC to the discount rate, the High discount scenario uses a pure rate of time preference of 3.5%, and the associated SCC is USD 6.4 per tonne of CO2 in 2015. Finally, the optimal path of the SCC is rising with the time horizon in the DICE model.

What these simulations illustrate is the sensitivity of the estimates of the SCC to some crucial assumptions concerning the IAM. The two sources of sensitivity here are the damage function (which is increased to make the 2C scenario optimal) and the pure rate of time preference. The former is the source of deep uncertainty (See e.g. Millner et al., 2013; Pindyck, 2013), and the latter is a source of disagreement (Drupp et al., 2017).

A more recent review of the SCC by Nordhaus (2017) illustrates some additional sensitivities of the estimates of the SCC by IAMs, and also how scientific advances can be incorporated into the IAMs in order to update the estimates to reflect the latest science. Table 14.3 shows how the estimates of the SCC have changed as a result of updates to 5 elements contained in in the DICE-2016R model which affect steps 1-4 above: 1) Damages; 2) Population growth; 3) Temperature sensitivity; 4) Decarbonisation assumptions; and, 5) The carbon cycle.

Table 14.3. **Social cost of carbon under different assumptions**

USD per tonne CO_2, 2010 international

Scenarios	2015	2020	2025	2030	2050
Baseline	31.2	37.3	44.0	51.6	102.5
Optimal	30.7	36.7	43.5	51.2	103.6
2.5°C	184.4	229.1	284.1	351.0	1 006.2
Stern Review discounting	197.4	266.5	324.6	376.2	629.2
Alternative discount rates					
2.5%	128.5	140.0	152.0	164.6	235.7
3%	79.1	87.3	95.9	104.9	156.6
4%	36.3	40.9	45.8	51.1	81.7
5%	19.7	22.6	25.7	29.1	49.2

Source: Adapted from Nordhaus, (2017, p.1520).

Table 14.3 shows the most recent estimates of the SCC and the path of SCC over time for similar scenarios as in Table 14.2. Nordhaus (2017) has the usual baseline and optimal scenarios, but the 2C scenario is replaced with a more realistic 2.5°C scenario. Nordhaus (2017) concludes that a maximum temperature increase of 2°C is unfeasible with the current level of technology, hence the 2.5°C scenario in the 2017 update (Nordhaus 2017, p. 1522). The 2.5°C scenario again adjusts damages so that it is optimal to reduce emissions and meet this target. This increases the SCC as before, from USD 31 per tonne of CO_2 to USD 184 per tonne of CO_2. This SCC is also sensitive to the discount rate, increasing over 6-fold in 2015 if a 2.5% discount rate is favoured over a 5% discount rate.

Tables 14.2 and 14.3 are not measured in the same units of the same base year. Yet Nordhaus (2017) shows that the updates to the DICE-2016R model affected the calculation of the SCC in the following way (% change in parentheses):

1. Damages (-14%);

2. Population growth (+6%);

3. Temperature sensitivity (+8%);

4. Economic assumptions on decarbonisation (+31);

5. The carbon cycle (+25%).

Ultimately, Nordhaus' preferred value of the SCC from the DICE model is USD 31 per tonne of CO_2 in 2015, rising to USD 102.5 in 2100. Yet there remains is a great deal of uncertainty surrounding these estimates. For instance, Howard and Sterner (2017) find an SCC almost 4 times this value after undertaking their meta-analysis of the damage function and showing that a higher damage function which better accounts for catastrophic risks and non-marketed damages is more appropriate.

14.6. The social cost of carbon: International experience

Several countries have enacted legislation or policies to ensure that carbon emissions are incorporated into the analysis of public projects and regulations (e.g. United States, United Kingdom and Canada). In some cases carbon emissions are regulated by carbon taxes (Finland, Sweden) or cap and trade instruments (e.g. European Emission Trading Scheme (ETS), California (ETS) in the United States, Alberta ETS Canada).[16] The United States uses the SCC in CBA of public projects and regulations while France recommends the abatement costs approach. In 2009, the United Kingdom moved away from SCC and focused on the abatement costs of meeting a specified emissions reduction under the *Climate Change Act* of 2008. Some of these cases are discussed below, starting with the United States.

14.6.1. Calculating the SCC in the United States: The Interagency Working Group

In the United States, a series of legal rulings have led to the Environmental Protection Agency having authority to regulate greenhouse gas emissions under the Clean Air Act (CAA), along with other air pollutants (Metcalf and Stock, 2017). In 2007, the case of Massachusetts vs EPA (549 U.S. 497) the Supreme Court ruled that the CAA gives the EPA authority to regulate tailpipe emissions of greenhouse gasses. In 2008, the U.S. 9th Circuit Court of Appeals ruled that the National Highway and Transport Safety Commission had acted "arbitrarily" when it refused to value carbon emissions due to the uncertainty surrounding the value of the SCC. Executive Order 12866 required agencies "to assess both the costs and the benefits of the intended evaluation and, recognising that some costs and benefits are difficult to quantify, propose or adopt a regulation on upon a reasoned determination that the benefits of the regulation justify its cost" (Section 1, part 6).[17] According to the Inter-Agency Working group Technical Support Document, the purpose of the SCC is to "allow agencies to incorporate the social benefits of reducing carbon dioxide (CO_2) emissions into cost benefit analyses of regulatory actions." (IWG 2016, p. 3).

The process by which the SCC is calculated is most developed in the United States. In 2010 an Interagency Working Group (IWG) was convened by the Council of Economic advisors (CEA) to develop estimates of the SCC that could be applied in accordance with Executive Order 12866. This resulted in a Technical Support Document (IWG 2010). In the interim the estimates were updated in 2013, as summarised by Greenstone et al. (2013), and in 2016 leading to an updated Technical Support Document (IWG 2016). These updates were in accordance with Executive Order 13563, which commits the agency to use the best available science in any regulatory decision making (IWG 2016, p. 6). Finally, a recent report by the National Academy of Sciences (NAS, 2017) responded to a request by the IWG for advice on how to approach future updates of the SCC to ensure that estimates are based on the best available science. Several important recommendations have been made which are discussed below.

The US Interagency Working Group (IWG, 2016) estimated the SCC using three IAM models: FUND, DICE and PAGE. The IWG used the most up-to-date versions of these models at that time and followed the procedure set out in Greenstone et al. (2013):[18]

1. The emissions trajectory EMF-22 from the Stanford Energy Modelling Forum was used to define the emissions scenarios;

2. 5 scenarios were defined: 4 business-as-usual scenarios resulting in high concentrations of CO_2 between 600 and 900 ppm, and a 5th scenario which involves mitigation and stabilisation of emissions at around 450 ppm;

3. The Equilibrium Climate Sensitivity (ECS) was drawn as a random parameter the distribution recommended by Roe and Baker (2007), calibrated to the IPCC-AR4 consensus statement. This resulted in a distribution with a "median of 3°C, a 2/3 probability of being between 2°C and 4.5°C and zero probability of being outside of the range zero to 10°C" (Greenstone et al., 2013).

4. Three discount rate scenarios were chosen by fixing the real rates of return in different emissions scenarios to 2.5%, 3% and 5%.[19]

5. Welfare effects were evaluated using a global welfare function (Equation [14.7]).

Following these steps the IWG (2016) estimated a schedule values for the SC-CO_2 which are presented in Table 14.4. This work led to a value of USD 40 per tonne of CO_2 being proposed for inclusion in cost-benefit analysis of public works and regulations, based on the 3% discount rate scenarios and year 2020. Once again, variation in the estimates across the 3 models stems from different modelling assumptions, but the estimates are clearly sensitive to the discount rate. Furthermore, as in the summary undertaken by Tol (2011), the values in Table 14.4 represent unweighted averages across models and scenarios.

Table 14.4. **Social Cost of carbon dioxide under different scenarios and discount rates**

%, SC-CO_2, 2007 USD per tonne of CO_2

Year	Average Impact 5%	Average Impact 3%	Average Impact 2.5%	High Impact (95th Pct) 3%
2010	10	31	50	86
2015	11	36	56	105
2020	12	42	62	123
2025	14	46	68	138
2030	16	50	73	152
2035	18	55	78	168
2040	21	60	84	183
2045	23	64	89	197
2050	26	69	95	212

Source: IWG (2016, p. 4).

Following these procedures and repeating 10 000 times, a range of estimates of the SCC were obtained reflecting the repeated sampling of the climate sensitivity parameter (IWG 2016; Greenstone et al., 2013). As shown in Chapter 9, Monte Carlo analysis: drawing parameters from a distribution and collating the estimates, is commonplace in CBA. It is also typical in the reduced form IAM models as a means of dealing with parameter uncertainty. While for 2020 the estimates had a 5%-95 percentile range of – USD 11 (FUND) per tonne of

CO_2 to + USD 370 (PAGE) per tonne of CO_2, using a 3% discount rate, the mean across all models was USD 42 per tonne of CO_2, in 2007 dollars. These estimates of the SCC are expected to increase over time as emissions become more damaging. For regulatory analysis, sensitivity of the SCC was recommended at USD 12 and USD 62 (in 2020, for discount rates 5% and 2.5% respectively). The 95th percentile value of USD 123 in 2020 reflects a damage function more akin to the Weitzman damage function in Figure 14.4. At the time these estimates represented the latest recommendations for the value of the SCC for regulatory analysis (IWG 2016).

Calculating the SCC in the United States: The NAS (2017) report responds to requests made by the IWG to provide advice on how to improve and update the calculation of the SCC in the future for regulatory analysis. It makes several recommendations for future updates of the SCC.

14.6.2. The SCC in the United States: Policy impact and future

Hahn and Ritz (2017) ask whether the use of the SCC in the US has had any effect on national policy, and undertake a systematic analysis of all federal regulations since 2008. Nordhaus (2017) notes that the SCC has been used in Federal Regulations with estimated benefits of up to USD 1 trillion, while Greenstone et al. (2013, p. 43) claims that three key policy areas in the United States have been influenced by the presence of SCC estimates: 1) US Department of Transport and the Environmental Protection Agency's standards for GHG emissions and fuel efficiency; 2) Colorado Public Utility Commission's hearing on retiring 900 MW of coal-fired power stations; 3) Declaration before the US Court of Appeals for the District of Columbia Circuit regarding EPA's GHG regulations.

Yet Hahn and Ritz (2017) find that the ranking of projects within the United States was unchanged by the presence of the SCC, despite making up approximately 15% of the benefits on average among the 53 regulatory policies that they analysed. Of course, there could be many internal reasons for such a finding, Hahn and Ritz (2017) argue this result could have many causes, ranging from non-maximising behaviour from regulatory agencies, to expectations that SCC will rise in the future. The lack of influence could have been deliberate, with the SCC chosen as a visible but ineffectual policy on carbon emissions, which allowed the administration to be seen to do something. Only 1 in 8 projects reviewed were significantly affected by the inclusion of the SCC (Hahn and Ritz 2017, p. 245).

The future of the SCC as part of the decision-making apparatus in the US became uncertain in March 2017 when Executive Order 13783 was signed by the incumbent president. Among other things, this Executive Order disbanded the Interagency Working Group on the Social Cost of Carbon, and nullified all of their Technical Support Documents (E.O. 13783, Section 5). Furthermore, the US administration is now looking more closely at an SCC that includes only domestic damages and includes the upper bound 7% discount rate for sensitivity (USEPA 2017, p. 1). With domestic benefits only, the SCC reduces to USD 7 per tonne of CO_2 (USD 1 per tonne of CO_2) for discount rates of 3% (7%), with 95th percentiles of USD 28 per tonne of CO_2 (USD 5 per tonne of CO_2), compared to the figures shown in Table 14.4. These figures represent reductions of between 80-95%.

14.6.3. The United Kingdom

In the United Kingdom, for instance, the use of the SCC in regulatory analysis was recommended in 2002, with values of between GBP 35 and GBP 140 per tonne of carbon proposed, with a central value of GBP 70 per tonne of carbon (approximately USD 250 per tonne of CO_2), to be used across government. In 2009, the way in which the UK government included carbon values in CBA changed from the SCC approach towards values based on the European Emissions Trading System (ETS) if the source was included in the ETS, or an abatement cost approach otherwise. All government projects and regulatory changes that have carbon impacts, which include those in transport, energy and energy efficiency, are advised to refer to the Government's short-term carbon values. These values are regularly updated with the most recent update taking place in 2016.[20] Table 14.5 shows the current estimates of traded and non-traded carbon emissions, and the predictions from 2010-30.

Table 14.5. **Traded and non-traded carbon costs**

United Kingdom, GBP per tonne of CO2eq, 2016 prices

Year	Traded			Non-traded		
	Low	Central	High	Low	Central	High
2010	13	13	13	29	57	86
2011	12	12	12	29	58	87
2012	6	6	6	29	59	88
2013	4	4	4	30	60	90
2014	4	4	4	30	61	91
2015	5	5	5	31	62	92
2016	0	4	4	31	63	94
2017	0	4	4	32	64	95
2018	0	4	5	32	64	97
2019	0	4	7	33	65	98
2020	0	5	9	33	66	100
2021	4	12	20	34	68	101
2022	8	19	31	34	69	103
2023	12	26	41	35	70	105
2024	15	34	52	35	71	106
2025	19	41	63	36	72	108
2026	23	48	73	37	73	110
2027	27	56	84	37	74	111
2028	31	63	95	38	75	113
2029	35	70	105	38	76	115
2030	39	77	116	39	77	116

Source: Data Tables supporting toolkit for valuation of carbon: *www.gov.uk/government/publications/valuation-of-energy-use-and-greenhouse-gas-emissions-for-appraisal*. The convergence of traded and non-traded values reflects the expectation that the ETS price will increase as the market matures and starts to encompass both stricter quantities and expands to include all sectors of the economy.

The switch from an SCC approach to the abatement cost approach stems from the passing of the 2008 *Climate Change Act* (Act of Parliament c 27) which makes it the duty of the secretary of state to ensure that net carbon emissions in the UK are 80% lower in 2050 than the baseline level in 1990, in line with the commitments under the Kyoto Protocol and subsequent agreements. The Climate Change Committee, made up of experts from relevant disciplines and civil servants, oversees the commitments under the Act and makes recommendations in the case that the targets are not being met.

14.6.4. *France*

In France the "carbon value", which is the estimate of the SC-CO_2, is now one of the "unit values" that appears in the CBA guidance alongside the value of statistical life and the discount rate. The values used start at approximately USD 27 (EUR 32) per tonne of CO_2 and rise at rate of 5.8% per year until 2030 and at the rate of discount (4.5%) thereafter. These increases over time reflect Hotelling's Rule for non-renewable resources which is an attempt to define the optimal time path of carbon values, as discussed in section 14.2, and reflect the increasing damages associated with carbon emissions (Quinet, 2013). The carbon value is used to inform the carbon tax which applies to ETS and non ETS industries alike.

14.7. Other approaches to calculating the SCC

14.7.1. Expert opinions on the SCC

In a series of critical articles, Pindyck (2012, 2013, 2016) discusses the weaknesses of integrated assessment models. The chief complaint is *not* that IAMs cannot be a useful tool for increasing the broad understanding of the likely impacts of climate change, and the efficacy of different policies on e.g. mitigation and technology. Rather, Pindyck criticises the use of these models as an input to actual policy measures, such as estimates of the SCC of the kind undertaken by the IWG (2016) for the US.

The reason for this criticism is that in some critical areas the models and their parameterisation is based on what Pindyck (2013) describes as "pure guesswork" on matters which are subject to a great deal of scientific uncertainty. The most crucial example of this is in the damage function for climate change emissions. As if equilibrium climate sensitivity (ECS: the long-run response to the climate of a doubling of CO_2 emissions) and the transitory climate response were not uncertain enough (e.g. see Figure 14.2), the way in which temperature change is translated into damages in the long-run is very difficult to define with any certainty, despite the burgeoning empirical literature on the estimation of climate damages. The problem is that projections of damages into the future are uncharted territory since they require temperature changes that have not been yet been witnessed. Particularly uncertain are the risks of catastrophic outcomes.

Pindyck (2013, 2016) also argues that in addition to these uncertainties and unknowable factors, should be coupled the general complexity and hence opacity of the models. Typically this means that the reason that policy or climate simulations lead to particular outcomes is often not easy to determine: one cannot tell what is driving what, and whether the outcomes are in a sense "real" or artefacts of some hidden-away assumption. In short, most IAMs can be thought of as black-boxes. Finally, there is a tendency for IAMs to analyse averages in temperature and hence average damages. The present value damages arising from changes in the central tendencies of climate typically do not amount to much more than 5-10% of GDP, equivalent to a moderately sized recession. This is because climate damages accrue only slowly when measured in this way, hence the sensitivity of these damage estimates to the social discount rate. For these reasons: i) parameter and model uncertainty; ii) opacity or lack of transparency; and, iii) focus on central tendencies of climate change, Pindyck is sceptical of the usefulness of IAMs.

As an alternative, Pindyck proposes simply asking experts for their opinion on the SCC, not by asking them directly, but by asking a range of simple questions about climate damages that allow a simplified model of climate to be calibrated and the SCC to be calculated based on the removal of catastrophic risks, rather than based upon average changes in temperature. The Annex provides some details of the approach and the questions that were asked. The key information required from the experts was: i) Emissions trajectories; ii) % reduction in GDP due to climate in 50 years; iii) the probability of X% reduction in GDP 50 and 150 years in the future; iv) the reduction in emissions required to reduce the risk of a 20% loss to zero; v) the discount rate. Together with some simple transparent modelling relationships between damages and emissions (See Annex 14.A1), the answers to these questions lead to an SCC based on expert opinions.

For instance, the answers to the probabilistic questions about reductions in GDP (iii above) allow the researcher to build a rudimentary probability distribution function for damages. Table 14.6 and Figure 14.6 provide an example of the probability distribution that could be drawn from an expert's responses to the Pindyck survey.[21]

Table 14.6. **Example of expert responses for the Pindyck (2016) survey**

Support of GDP loss	Cumulative distribution function	Survivor function
	P(GDP loss $\leq$ x)	P(GDP loss > x)
-7 **(min)**	0	1
2	0.2	0.8
5	0.4	0.6
10	0.7	0.3
20	0.8	0.2
50	0.95	0.05
100 (max)	1	0

Figure 14.6. **The cumulative probability, survivor and probability density functions**

For an example expert response to Pindyck's survey

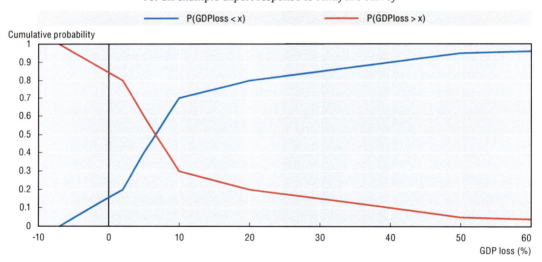

Note: Each point on the blue line graph represents a point at which the survey asked for the probability of GDP loss being larger than x%, except the furthest left point. The orange line is one minus this probability: the survivor function, which gives the probability of GDP loss being *greater* than x%.

The SCC can now be approximated by using the expert opinions. The estimate of the social cost of carbon proposed in Pindyck (2016) is composed of two parts. First, the expected benefits of the reduction in costs from eliminating damages greater than 20% of GDP. Second, the benefits are divided by the emissions reductions required to eliminate the prospect of extreme damages. It should be evident that this is an estimate of *average* SCC, rather than the typical SCC which values the damage from a marginal change in emissions.

The advantages of this estimate of the unit damages of carbon emissions are that it is transparent in the sense that it is parsimonious while capturing some of the most salient features of climate change and the evolution of damages. Furthermore, the focus is clearly on the most disastrous tail events that might be associated with climate change, rather than the gradual and moderate damages associated with changes in the central tendencies of temperature, e.g. the mean. With a few additional assumptions on the distribution of opinions it is easy to calculate the benefits of truncating disastrous outcomes.

The survey of experts in Pindyck (2016) calibrates the average SCC using responses from around 1 000 experts drawn from different disciplines, including economics and climate science. The SCC estimates were extremely heterogeneous but the average SCC was typically well in excess of USD 200 per tonne of carbon (USD 54.6 per tonne of CO_2) among all groups. The average across all groups was USD 290 per tonne of carbon (USD 79.1 per tonne of CO_2). Once outliers were removed, and those who claimed insufficient expertise, the average SCC was reduced to about USD 200 per tonne of carbon.

The simplified model of climate change and climate damages in Pindyck (2016) is in many ways a triumph of Occam's razor.[22] The transparency of the expression for the average SCC, and the assumptions that lie behind it, is obvious. Yet, the charge of there being a black-box behind these estimates arguably still remains, only in this case the black-box being deployed for each response is inside the head of the expert respondent. There may be offsetting errors in the aggregation process which make this survey approach more accurate, but there may be biases also. In the end it is not entirely clear that this approach is better in the sense of providing more sensible numbers, despite its obvious elegance and simplicity.

Perhaps the most important message that can be taken from the approach is that the social cost of carbon estimated from this approach is well in excess of the USD 42 per tonne of CO_2 that was the focus of regulatory guidance in the United States in the Obama presidency, and way above the USD 1 per tonne of CO_2 currently being proposed.

14.7.2. Simplified expressions for the SCC

Another approach to the estimation of the SCC is to develop a relatively simple closed-form expression for the SCC which depends on relatively few components and can be easily estimated for policy purposes. In some ways, Pindyck (2016) provides a simple understandable representation of the SCC (See Equation [14.A1.1] in Annex 14.A1) but this expression is not based on any clear distinct economic assumptions and a strong connection to climate science and economic theory is not its purpose. The research discussed in this section attempts to obtain parsimonious representations of the SCC than the IAMs, which are still strongly rooted in economic theory and climate science.

A number of papers have taken this approach using highly simplified/stylised models of climate and economy that capture the salient features of the climate change problem without deriving a closed form solution for the SCC (Golosov et al., 2014; Gerlagh and Liski, 2012). Van den Bijgaart et al. (2016) go further in providing a closed-form solution for the SCC in a deterministic framework, while showing that the approximation to more complicated (deterministic) IAMs is good.

The chief motivation for such expressions overlaps somewhat with Pindyck's critique of IAMs: the need for transparency and parsimony. One advantage of having simplified and transparent estimates of the SCC is that policy-makers and practitioners are more able to understand the principles behind it and generally engage with the concept, without the need for high level or technical knowledge about the model itself. Van den Bijgaart et al. (2016, p. 75-76) state that a major problem with IAMs is that they are "not accessible" to policy makers and members of the public. Inaccessibility is a major determinant of the SCC is often "accepted or not accepted on the basis of trust or mistrust" in its estimates and procedures.

The simple formula provided by van den Bijgaart et al. (2016) is as follows:

$$SCC = \frac{1.3\omega c^{\psi}}{m} \frac{1}{\varphi + \sigma} \frac{\varepsilon}{\varepsilon + \sigma} \left(\frac{Y}{L\bar{y}}\right)^{\xi - 1} Y \qquad [14.18]$$

where Y is income/output, L is population, and $\bar{y}$ is a reference consumption level. The other terms are all parameters relating to the 4 steps outlined above for estimating the SCC: 1) Output to emissions; 2) Emissions to temperatures; 3) Temperatures to damages; 4) Discounting. Table 14.7 provides details.

This representation of the SCC is extremely transparent and closely maps the SCC that emerges from many reduced form IAMs (See van den Bijgaart et al., 2016, p. 81-88), while remaining extremely transparent. Rather than being based on expert opinion it is based upon parsimonious functional relationships in the economic and geophysical domains, and well defined economic assumptions. Compared to an IAM, this expression for the SCC is relatively easy to explain to policy makers, while a publicly available excel spreadsheet allows practitioners to gain a sense of the relative sensitivity of the SCC to different parameter choices.[23]

Using typical parameter distribution assumptions for the DICE model, the SCC stemming from [14.18] turns out to be strongly right skewed, with a mean of approximately USD 40 per tonne of CO_2, a median of USD 17 per tonne of CO_2 and a 90th percentile of USD 84 per tonne of CO_2. These values closely map the estimates found in Table 14.3 and 14.4.

Table 14.7. **Parameters for the simple SCC expression in equation [14.18]**

Parameter	Meaning
ω	At reference consumption level $\bar{y}$ a 1°C rise in temperature leads to relative damages ω.
m	Pre-industrial emissions levels
ϕ	The decay parameter for the stock of CO_2 (as in Box 14.1)
ε	Temperatures adjust at rate ε to their long run equilibrium level.
σ	The climate discount rate: $\sigma = \rho + \eta g - \xi g - l$ Where l is population growth and ξ is described below.
ψ	The elasticity of damages with respect to temperature, T.
ξ	The elasticity of damages with respect to output, Y.

Source: van den Bijgaart et al. (2016).

14.8. SCC: Global or domestic values?

Another policy relevant issue when it comes to calculating the SCC is whether an individual country should use the *global* value of the SCC or whether it should focus solely on the present value of *domestic* damages of climate change (Fraas et al., 2016; Dudley and Mannix, 2014; Gayer and Viscusi, 2016). The convention has typically been to estimate the global SCC for use in public policy at the domestic level (IWG, 2016; NAS, 2017, Chapter 2). The argument for focussing on the global values is that CO_2 is a global pollutant, and so in order to internalise the global externality, all countries need to internalise that externality. It has also been argued that the international cooperation required to limit global warming is also more likely to be achieved if a global stance is taken (Revesz et al., 2017). In its discussion of the SCC, the Interagency Working Group (IWG 2010) estimated that the domestic SCC is between 7% and 23% of the global SCC for the US. Many caveats were placed on this measure, including the fact that many of the models used to estimate the SCC are not sufficiently spatially detailed to attribute damages at the country level. Furthermore, it was acknowledged that such estimates tend to ignore indirect damages to the US that occur via countries that are trading partners, for instance. The issue of domestic versus global damages is an active area of research (e.g. Kotchen, 2016).

Nevertheless, the idea of using domestic SCC has gained policy traction. In October 2017, the US EPA recalculated the SCC to be used for regulatory analysis on the basis of domestic damages only, coupled with a new sensitivity test to the highest discount in the range of discount rate recommended by the OMB (2003) guidelines: 7%. At a 7% discount rate, and using only domestic damages, the US SCC falls from USD 40 per tonne of CO_2 to USD 1 per tonne of CO_2 as a consequence (US EPA, 2017).[24]

14.9. Conclusions

For regulatory analysis and the evaluation of public projects, it is essential that the cost of carbon emissions is taken into account. An estimate of the SCC is required in order to include these damages in CBA and to inform the optimal carbon tax. Estimation is made difficult due to the complexity of the problem and the uncertainties that the future of climate change holds in relation to climate sensitivity, future economic growth and emissions paths, and the damages that can be expected as a consequence. Theory shows that care is needed in regulating carbon and setting the appropriate carbon tax over time, and that sub-optimal policies could lead to perverse outcomes like the Green Paradox, although such outcomes are not guaranteed.

On the estimation side, the United States has clear guidance on how to estimate the SCC for these purposes and up until recent policy changes, the SCC was routinely used in regulatory analysis and the analysis of policies, with a value of around USD 40 per tonne of CO_2 rising to over USD 100 per tonne of CO_2 in 2050. Many OECD countries use an estimate of the SCC in their appraisal of public projects and to inform their carbon taxes.

Integrated assessment models (IAM) are typically used to estimate the SCC, and these have been shown to be sensitive to the assumptions concerning climate sensitivity, climate damages and the welfare treatment of uncertainty and ambiguity. In particular the way in which catastrophic risks are treated in IAMs, both on the damages side and in the measurement of welfare side, is as strong determinant of the aggressiveness of the climate policy response. Greater uncertainty and ambiguity, coupled with fat-tailed probabilities of catastrophic events, leads to recommendations for more stringent climate policy, and larger estimates of the SCC.

In recent years the use of exert opinions on the SCC, and the development of simple transparent formulae for the SCC have been developed. Some argue that these approaches are better since they are more transparent and democratic, sometimes at no cost in terms of the range of values of the SCC that they produce. The calibration of IAMs for public policy advice is an area of active debate and further research due to the uncertainty associated with the science and economics of climate change, and disagreement concerning some of the crucial parameters that determine the SCC (e.g. the discount rate or ECS). The main success from the perspective of CBA is that estimates of SCC are currently appearing in the analysis of public policy, and are influencing decisions in ways that are likely to improve long-run social welfare.

The price of carbon is very unlikely to be zero. Evidence of the general agreement that the SCC is non-zero can be found in the widespread inclusion of monetary values of carbon in policy analysis across the OECD countries (Smith and Braathen 2015; ITF 2015).

Notes

1. Despite being called the SCC, it typically measures the damages associated with all greenhouse gases. This chapter assumes this throughout.

2. Knightian uncertainty describes a circumstance in which the risk associated with events cannot be represented by well-defined probability distributions. Events which are rare, or previously not experienced, are examples of Knightian uncertainties since the probability of these events occurring is not known. At best probabilities are ambiguous, and can be defined within some interval.

3. A tonne of CO_2 contains 0.273 tonnes of carbon, so the SC-CO_2 will be 0.273*SCC

4. Hoel and Kverndokk (1996, p. 118) also include the extraction costs which depend on the cumulated extraction of the resource. Abstraction from this feature simplifies the discussion here.

5. The composite discount rate reflects the fact that there are two reasons to value future damages less than today's damages. First, the opportunity cost, r. Second, the decay rate, ϕ. Both are reasons to put less weight on the pollution stock in the future.

6. van der Ploeg and Withagen (2015) is part of a symposium on the Green Paradox in the Review of Environmental Economics and Policy.

7. A tonne of CO_2 contains 0.273 tonnes of carbon.

8. In the IPCC (2013) a distinction is made between confidence and likelihood in relation to uncertainty. *Medium confidence* means a 5 out of 10 chance, high confidence mean an 8 out of 10 chance. Alternatively, *likely* means > 66% probability, and unlikely means < 33% probability, and very unlikely means < 10% confidence. For a full description see: *www.ipcc.ch/publications_and_data/ar4/wg1/en/ch1s1-6.html*.

9. See Perry and Ciscar (2014) for a summary of structural modelling approaches.

10. NAS (2017, Chapter 5) and Dell et al. (2014) have good summaries of damage-related studies. A symposium on adaptation in agriculture can be found in a symposium edition of the *Review of Environmental Economics and Policy*, July 2017.

11. For an analysis of cloud formation, see IPCC (2013), Chapter 7. For an analysis of feedback and irreversible impacts of climate change, see IPCC (2013), Chapter 12. See-level change is analysed in IPCC (2013), Chapter 13.

12. NAS (2017, p. 138) quotes the IWG (2010) report that highlighted the incomplete treatment of catastrophic damages as well as non-catastrophic damages in the current formulations of damages. Damage functions have been updated since 2010, e.g. Nordhaus (2017), but difficulties still remain in relation to the way reduced-form IAMs embody catastrophic risk and tipping points according to NAS (2017, p. 144).

13. Some arithmetic errors that appeared in Tol (2009; 2012) were corrected in recent DICE updates. See Tol (2014) and Nordhaus and Moffatt (2017).

14. Strictly speaking, for reasons of goodness of fit, the estimation uses a one parameter function, assuming $\varphi_1 = 0$, hence the formulation in (14.13).

15. At 2% inflation over 20 years.

16. Beyond this, a number of countries have implemented carbon taxes on different sectors of their economies. For example, Sweden and Finland have implemented carbon taxes, of USD 150 per tonne of CO_2 and USD 89 per tonne of C respectively.

17. See *www.epa.gov/laws-regulations/summary-executive-order-12866-regulatory-planning-and-review*.

18. Updates included changes to damages modules such as sea-level rise, regional scaling factors, adaptation, and carbon cycle parameters.

19. The lower 2.5% scenario is motivated by the literature on declining discount rates stemming from Newell and Pizer (2003), Groom et al. (2007) and more recently Freeman et al. (2015). See IWG (2010) and Chapter 8 of this book.

20. The list of traded and untraded short-term carbon values can be found here: *www.gov.uk/government/collections/carbon-valuation--2*.

21. To sketch the probability distributions, the minimum bound is the only additional information required beyond the questions in Pindyck (2016).

22. See *https://en.wikipedia.org/wiki/Occam's_razor*.

23. See: *http://dx.doi.org/10.1016/j.jeem.2016. 01.005.*

24. *www.federalregister.gov/documents/2017/03/31/2017-06576/promoting-energy-independence-and-economic-growth.*

References

van den Bijgaart, I., R. Gerlagh and M. Liski (2016), "A simple formula for the Social Cost of Carbon", *Journal of Environmental Economics and Management*, Vol. 77, pp. 75-94, *http://dx.doi.org/10.1016/j.jeem.2016.01.005.*

Bosello, F., F. Eboli and R. Pierfederici (2012), "Assessing the Economic Impacts of Climate Change. An Updated CGE Point of View", *FEEM Working Paper*, No. 2, *http://services.feem.it/userfiles/attach/201223111664NDL2012-002.pdf.*

Bosello, F., R. Roson and R.S.J. Tol (2006), "Economy wide estimates of the implications of climate change: Human health", *Ecological Economics*, Vol. 58, pp. 579-591, *https://doi.org/10.1007/s10640-006-9048-5.*

Bosello, F., R. Roson and R.S.J. Tol (2007), "Economy wide estimates of the implications of climate change: Sea level rise", *Environmental and Resource Economics*, Vol. 37, pp. 549-571, *https://doi.org/10.1007/s10640-006-9048-5.*

Botzen, W.J.W. and J.C.J.M. van den Bergh (2012), "How sensitive is Nordhaus to Weitzman? Climate policy in DICE with an alternative damage function", *Economics Letters*, Vol. 117, pp. 372-374, *http://dx.doi.org/10.1016/j.econlet.2012.05.032.*

Burke, M. and K. Emerick (2016), "Adaptation to Climate Change: Evidence from US Agriculture", *American Economic Journal: Economic Policy*, Vol. 8(3), pp. 106-140, *https://doi.org/10.1257/pol.20130025.*

Dell, M., B.F. Jones and B.A. Olken (2014), "What Do We Learn from the Weather? The New Climate-Economy Literature", *Journal of Economic Literature*, Vol. 52(3), pp. 740-98, *www.aeaweb.org/articles?id=10.1257/jel.52.3.740.*

Deschenes, O. and M. Greenstone (2007), "The economic impacts of climate change: Evidence from agricultural output and random fluctuations in weather", *American Economic Review*, Vol. 97(1), pp. 354-385, *https://doi.org/10.1257/aer.97.1.354.*

Deschenes, O. and M. Greenstone (2011), "Climate change, mortality, and adaptation: Evidence from annual fluctuations in weather in the US", *American Economic Journal: Applied Economics*, Vol. 3 (4), pp. 152-185, *www.aeaweb.org/articles?id=10.1257/app.3.4.152.*

Di Falco, S., M. Veronesi and M. Yesuf (2011), "Does adaptation to climate change provides food security?, a micro perspective from Ethiopia", *American Journal of Agricultural Economics*, Vol. 93(3), pp. 829-846, *https://doi.org/10.1093/ajae/aar006.*

Drupp, M. et al. (2017), "Discounting Disentangled: An Expert Survey on the Components of the Long Term Social Discount Rate", Forthcoming in the *American Economic Journal: Policy*, Working paper version: Drupp, M. et al. (2015). Grantham Research Institute on Climate Change and the Environment *Working Paper No. 172, www.lse.ac.uk/GranthamInstitute/wp-content/uploads/2015/06/Working-Paper-172-Drupp-et-al.pdf.*

Dudley, S. and B. Mannix (2014), "The social cost of carbon", *Engage, The Journal of the Federalist Society Practice Group*, Vol. 15, pp.14-18, *https://fedsoc.org/commentary/publications/the-social-cost-of-carbon.*

Fraas, A. et al. (2016), "Social cost of carbon: Domestic duty", *Science*, Vol. 351, Issue 6273, pp. 569, *https://doi.org/10.1126/science.351.6273.569-b.*

Freeman, M.C. et al. (2015), "Declining Discount Rates and the Fisher Effect: Inflated Past, Discounted Future", *Journal of Environmental Economics and Management*, Vol. 73, pp. 32-49, *http://dx.doi.org/10.1016/j.jeem.2015.06.003.*

Freeman, M.C., B. Groom and R.J. Zeckhauser (2015), "Better predictions, better allocations: Scientific advances and adaptation to climate change", *Philosophical Transactions of the Royal Society A: Mathematical, Physical and Engineering Sciences,* Vol. 373:2055, *http://dx.doi.org/10.1098/rsta.2015.0122.*

Gayer, T. and W.K. Viscusi (2016), "Determining the proper scope of climate change policy benefits in U.S. regulatory analyses: Domestic versus global approaches", *Review of Environmental Economics and Policy*, Vol. 10(2), pp. 245-63, *https://doi.org/10.1093/reep/rew002.*

Gerlagh, R. (2011), "Too much oil", *CESifo Economic Studies*, Vol. 57(1), pp. 79-102, *https://doi.org/10.1093/cesifo/ifq004.*

Gerlagh, R. and M. Liski (2012), "Carbon Prices for the Next Thousand Years", *CESifo Working Paper Series* 3855, CESifo Group Munich, *https://wwz.unibas.ch/fileadmin/wwz/redaktion/forschung/Matti_Liski_et_al_CarbonPrices_March25.pdf*.

Gorst, A., B. Groom and A. Dehlavi (2015), "Crop productivity and adaptation to climate change in Pakistan", Centre for Climate Change Economics and Policy Working Paper No. 214, *www.cccep.ac.uk/wp-content/uploads/2015/10/Working-Paper-189-Gorst-et-al.pdf*.

Greenstone, M., E. Kopits and A. Wolverton (2013), "Developing a social cost of carbon for US regulatory analysis: A methodology and interpretation", *Review of Environmental Economics and Policy*, Vol. 7(1), pp. 23-46, *https://doi.org/10.1093/reep/res015*.

Groom, B. et al. (2007), "Discounting the Distant Future: How much does model selection affect the certainty equivalent rate?", *Journal of Applied Econometrics*, Vol. 22, pp. 641-656, *http://dx.doi.org/10.1002/jae.937*.

Heal, G. and A. Millner (2014), "Uncertainty and decision-making in climate change", *Review of Environmental Economics and Policy*, Vol. 8(1), pp. 120-137, *https://doi.org/10.1093/reep/ret023*.

Hoel, M. (2008), "Bush meets Hotelling: Effects of improved renewable energy technology on greenhouse gas emissions", *Working Paper 2492*, CESifo, Munich, *www.cesifo-group.de/ifoHome/publications/working-papers/CESifoWP/CESifoWPdetails?wp_id=14556692*.

Hoel, M. and S. Kverndokk (1996), "Depletion of fossil fuels and the impacts of global warming", *Resource and Energy Economics*, Vol. 18, pp. 115-136, *https://doi.org/10.1016/0928-7655(96)00005-X*.

Howard, P.H. and T. Sterner (2017), "Few and Not So Far Between: A Meta-analysis of Climate Damage Estimates", *Environmental and Resource Economics*, Vol. 68, pp. 197, *https://doi.org/10.1007/s10640-017-0166-z*.

Hsiang, S.M. (2010), "Temperatures and Cyclones Strongly Associated with Economic Production in the Caribbean and Central America", *Proceedings of the National Academy of Sciences*, Vol. 107 (35), pp. 15367-72, *https://doi.org/10.1073/pnas.1009510107*.

Hsiang, S.M., K.C. Meng and M.A. Cane (2011), "Civil conflicts are associated with the global climate", *Nature*, Vol. 476, pp. 438-441, *https://doi.org/10.1038/nature10311*.

Interagency Working Group on Social Cost of Carbon (2010), *Technical Support Document: Social Cost of Carbon for Regulatory Impact Analysis under Executive Order 12866*, United States Government, Washington, DC, *www.epa.gov/sites/production/files/2016-12/documents/scc_tsd_2010.pdf*.

Interagency Working Group on Social Cost of Carbon (2016), *Technical Support Document: Social Cost of Carbon for Regulatory Impact Analysis under Executive Order 12866*, August 2016, United States Government, Washington, DC, *www.epa.gov/sites/production/files/2016-12/documents/sc_co2_tsd_august_2016.pdf*.

ITF (International Transport Forum) (2015), *Adapting Transport Policy to Climate Change: Carbon Valuation, Risk and Uncertainty*, OECD Publishing, Paris, *http://dx.doi.org/10.1787/9789282107928-en*.

IPCC (Intergovernmental Panel on Climate Change) (2013), *Climate Change 2013: The Physical Science Basis. Contribution of Working Group I to the Fifth Assessment Report of the Intergovernmental Panel on Climate Change*, Cambridge University Press, Cambridge and New York.

Kotchen, M.J. (2016), "Which Social Cost of Carbon? A Theoretical Perspective", *NBER Working Paper No. 22246*, National Bureau of Economic Research, Washington, DC.

Kurukulasuriya P. and R. Mendelsohn (2008), "Crop switching as a strategy for adapting to climate change", *African Journal of Agricultural and Resource Economics*, Vol. 2, pp.105-126, *www.eldis.org/document/A37588*.

Mendelsohn, R., W. Nordhaus and D. Shaw (1994), "The impact of global warming on agriculture: A ricardian analysis", *American Economic Review*, Vol. 84(4), pp.753-771, *http://dx.doi.org/10.1257/aer.89.4.1046*.

Mendlesohn, R. (2012), "The economics of adaptation to climate change in developing countries", *Climate Change Economics*, Vol. 3, No. 2, *http://dx.doi.org/10.1142/S2010007812500066*.

Millner, A. (2013), "On welfare frameworks and catastrophic climate risks", *Journal of Environmental Economics and Management*, Vol. 65(2), pp. 310-325, *http://dx.doi.org/10.1016/j.jeem.2012.09.006*.

Millner, A., S. Dietz and G. Heal (2013), "Scientific ambiguity and climate policy", *Environmental and Resource Economics*, Vol. 55, pp. 21-46, *http://dx.doi.org/10.1007/s10640-012-9612-0*.

NAS (National Academy of Sciences) (2017), *Valuing Climate Changes: Updating Estimation of the Social Cost of Carbon Dioxide*, National Academy of Sciences, *www.nap.edu/24651*.

Newell, R.G. and W.A. Pizer (2003), "Discounting the distant future: How much do uncertain rates increase valuations?, *Journal of Environmental Economics and Management*, Vol. 46, pp. 52-71, *http://dx.doi.org/10.1016/S0095-0696(02)0C031-1.*

Nordhaus, W.D. (2017), "Revisiting the Social Cost of Carbon", *Proceedings of the National Academy of Sciences*, Vol. 114, No.7, pp. 1518-1523, *http://dx.doi.org/10.1073/pnas.1609244114.*

Nordhaus, W.D. (2016), "Projections and uncertainties about climate change in an era of minimal climate policies", *Cowles Foundation discussion paper* No. 2057, *https://cowles.yale.edu/sites/default/files/files/pub/d20/d2057.pdf.*

Nordhaus, W.D. (2014), "Estimates of the Social Cost of Carbon: Concepts and Results from the DICE-2013R Model and Alternative Approaches", *Journal of the Association of Environmental and Resource Economists*, Vol. 1, pp. 273-312, *http://dx.doi.org/10.1086/676035.*

Nordhaus, W.D. (2011), "The Economics of Tail Events with an Application to Climate Change", *Review of Environmental Economics and Policy*, Vol. 5(2), pp. 240-257, *https://doi.org/10.1093/reep/rer004.*

Nordhaus, W.D. (2008), *A Question of Balance: Weighing the Options on Global Warming Policies*, Yale University Press, New Haven.

Nordhaus, W.D. (2007), "A Review of the Stern Review on the Economics of Climate Change", *Journal of Economic Literature*, Vol. 45(3), 686-702, *http://dx.doi.org/10.1257/jel.45.3.686.*

Nordhaus, W.D. and A. Moffat (2017), "A survey of the global impacts of climate change: Replicability, survey methods and a statistical analysis", *Cowles Foundation Discussion Paper* No. 2096, Cowles Foundation for Research in Economics, Yale University, New Haven. *https://cowles.yale.edu/sites/default/files/files/pub/d20/d2096.pdf.*

Nordhaus, W.D. and P. Sztorc (2013), *DICE 2013R: Introduction and User's Manual*, October 2013, available at: *www.econ.yale.edu/ nordhaus/homepage/documents/DICE_Manual_100413r1.pdf.*

Olson, R. et al. (2012), "A climate sensitivity estimate using Bayesian fusion of instrumental observations and an Earth system model", *Geophysical Resource Letters*, Vol. 117(D4), D04103, *http://dx.doi.org/10.1029/2011JD016620.*

Perry, M. and J.-C. Ciscar (2014), "Multisectoral perspective in modelling of climate impacts and adaptation", in Markandya, A., I. Galarraga and E. Sainz de Murieta (eds.) (2014), *Handbook of the Economics of Climate Change Adaptation*, Routledge Handbooks, Oxford.

Pindyck, R.S. (2013), "Climate Change Policy: What Do the Models Tell Us?", *Journal of Economic Literature*, Vol. 51(3), pp. 860-872, *http://dx.doi.org/10.1257/jel.51.3.860.*

Pindyck, R.S. (2016), "The Social Cost of Carbon Revisited", *NBER Working Paper* 22807, National Bureau of Economic Research, Washington, DC, *www.nber.org/papers/w22807.*

van der Ploeg, F. and C. Withagen (2015), "Global Warming and the Green paradox: A Review of the Adverse Effects of Climate Policies", *Review of Environmental Economics and Policy*, Vol. 9, pp. 285-303, *https://doi.org/10.1093/reep/rev008*

Quinet, E. (2013), *L'evaluation socio-economique en periode de transition*, Rapport du groupe de travail preside par Emile Quinet, Commissariat general a la strategie et a la prospective Tome I, Rapport final, Juin, *www.strategie.gouv.fr/sites/strategie.gouv.fr/files/archives/CGSP_Evaluation_socioeconomique_17092013.pdf.*

Ranson, M. (2014), "Crime, Weather and Climate Change", *Journal of Environmental Economics and Management*, Vol. 67, pp. 274-302, *http://dx.doi.org/10.1016/j.jeem.2013.11.008.*

Revesz, R.L. et al. (2017), "Letter – The Social Cost of Carbon: A Global Imperative", *Review of Environmental Economics and Policy*, Vol. 11, pp. 172-173, *https://doi.org/10.1093/reep/rew022.*

Roe, G.H. and M.B. Baker (2007), "Why is climate sensitivity so unpredictable?", *Science*, Vol. 318, Issue 5850, pp. 629-633, *http://dx.doi.org/10.1126/science.1144735.*

Schlenker, W. and M.J. Roberts (2009), "Nonlinear temperature effects indicate severe damages to US crop yields under climate change", *Proceedings of the National Academy of Sciences*, Vol. 106 (37), pp. 15594-98, *http://dx.doi.org/10.1073/pnas.0906865106.*

Schlenker, W., W.M. Hanemann and A.C. Fisher (2005), "Will U.S. Agriculture Really Benefit from Global Warming? Accounting for Irrigation in the Hedonic Approach", *American Economic Review*, Vol. 95 (1), pp. 395-406, *http://dx.doi.org/10.1257/0002828053828455.*

Sinn, H. W. (2012), *The Green Paradox*, MIT Press, Cambridge, Mass.

Smith, S. and N. Braathen (2015), "Monetary Carbon Values in Policy Appraisal: An Overview of Current Practice and Key Issues", *OECD Environment Working Papers*, No. 92, OECD Publishing, Paris, *http://dx.doi.org/10.1787/5jrs8st3ngvh-en*

Stern, N. (2007), *The Stern Review on the Economics of Climate Change*, Cambridge University Press, Cambridge, *www.cambridge.org/catalogue/catalogue.asp?isbn=9780521700801.*

Strand, J. (2007), "Technology treaties and fossil-fuels extraction", *Energy Journal*, Vol. 28(4), pp. 129-142, *http://dx.doi.org/10.5547/ISSN0195-6574-EJ-Vol28-No4-6*

Tol, R.S.J. (2014), "Correction and Update: The Economic Effects of Climate Change", *Journal of Economic Perspectives*, Vol. 28(2), pp. 221-26, *http://dx.doi.org/10.1257/jep.28.2.221.*

Tol, R.S.J. (2012), "On the Uncertainty about the Total Economic Impact of Climate Change", *Environmental and Resource Economics*, Vol. 53, pp. 97-116, *https://doi.org/10.1007/s10640-012-9549-3.*

Tol, R.S.J. (2011). "The Social Cost of Carbon", *Annual Review of Resource Economics*, Vol. 3, pp. 419-443, *https://doi.org/10.1146/annurev-resource-083110-120028.*

Tol, R.S.J. (2008), "The Social Cost of Carbon: Trends, Outliers and Catastrophes", *Economics: The Open-Access, Open-Assessment E-Journal*, Vol. 2 (25), *http://dx.doi.org/10.5018/economics-ejournal.ja.2008-25.*

Ulph, A. and D. Ulph (1997), "Global warming, irreversibility and learning", *Economic Journal*, Vol. 107, pp. 636-650, *http://dx.doi.org/10.1111/j.1468-0297.1997.tb00031.x.*

US EPA (2017), *Regulatory Impact Analysis for the Review for the Clean Power Plan*. US EPA, Washington, DC, *www.epa.gov/sites/production/files/2017-10/documents/ria_proposed-cpp-repeal_2017-10.pdf.*

Weitzman, M.L. (2010), "What is the "damages function" for global warming and what difference might it make?", *Climate Change Economics*, Vol. 1, pp. 57-69, *http://dx.doi.org/10.1142/S2010007810000042.*

Weitzman, M.L. (2009), "On Modeling and Interpreting the Economics of Catastrophic Climate Change", *Review of Economics and Statistics*, Vol. 91(1), pp. 1-19, *http://dx.doi.org/10.1016/10.1162/rest.91.1.1.*

Weitzman, M.L. (2007), "A Review of 'The Stern Review on the Economics of Climate Change'", *Journal of Economic Literature*, Vol. XLV, pp. 703-724, *http://dx.doi.org/10.1257/jel.45.3.703.*

ANNEX 14.A1

Pindyck (2016) survey and model

Pindyck's survey questions attempted to define the baseline emissions scenario and then the likelihood of particular damages occurring in terms of proportional losses in GDP. The questions were as follows:

1. What is the average GHG emissions growth rate under Business-as-Usual (BAU) over the next 50 years (i.e., no additional steps are taken to reduce emissions)?;

2. In the absence of any climate mitigation policy, what is the most likely climate-caused reduction (in %) in world GDP that will be witnessed in 50 years?

Then, the questions tried to get experts to specify the probability distribution associated with climate damages, in particular the likelihood of extreme tail events. The following questions were posed:

3. In the absence of climate mitigation, what is the probability that 50 years from now, climate change will cause a reduction in world GDP of at least 2, 5, 10, 20 and 50%?

The same questions were then asked in relation to the far-distant future, 150 years hence. Experts were further asked:

4. What reduction in the growth of emissions would be required to eliminate the tail of the distribution and push the probability of climate damages being greater than 20% of GDP to zero 50 and 150 years in the future?

The answers to question 3 implicitly specify a cumulative probability distribution function and survivor function for GDP damages in percentage terms like the one tabulated in Table 14.3, and plotted in Figure 14.6. Experts provided responses such as these for the two time horizons: 50 and 150 years. These are the kinds of inputs that would typically be produced by an Integrated Assessment Model, but in this case are produced from expert opinions.

The benefits of reducing extreme damages are calculated as follows (Pindyck, 2016):

$$B_0 = \frac{\beta Y_0 \left[E_1(z_1) - E_0(z_1) \right]}{(r-g)(r+\beta-g)(1-\exp(-\beta T))} \qquad \text{[14.A1.1]}$$

where the numerator is composed of two terms:

1. $[E_1(z_1)-E_0(z_1)]$: the change in the expected percentage reduction in GDP resulting from eliminating the tail risk. Expectation $E_0(z_1)$ is taken over the reduced range of values (probabilistic support) of damages, whereas $E_1(z_1)$ is the expectation over the entire support of damages;

and;

2. βY_0: the proportion in 1.) is multiplied by the initial level of GDP, Y_0, and the assumed growth rate of damages, β.

The numerator divided by the term $(1 - \exp(-\beta T))$ yields the instantaneous flow of benefits from reducing climate damages for the horizon T. The present value of this flow is given by dividing through by the effective discount rate, which is given composed of the discount rate on consumption, r, net of growth in GDP, g, and the growth of damages, β: $(r - g)$ $(r + \beta - g)$ (Pindyck, 2016, p. 11).

The emission reductions required to obtain this expected reduction in damages is calculated from the answers to question 4 above. The expert opinions on emission reductions imply a particular change in the growth rate of emissions: a reduction from m_0 to m_1. The differences between these trajectories in present value terms over an infinite horizon are given by (Pindyck, 2016, p. 11):

$$\Delta E = \frac{(m_0 - m_1)}{(r - m_0)(r - m_1)} E_0$$

where r is the discount rate and E_0 is the initial emissions level. Dividing through the experts' view of the gross benefits of the damage reduction by their opinion of the emissions reduction required provides an estimate of the average social cost of carbon. Combining the two equations yields the average social cost of carbon:

$$\frac{B_0}{\Delta E} = \frac{\beta Y_0 \left[E_1(z_1) - E_0(z_1) \right]}{(r - g)(r + \beta - g)(1 - \exp(-\beta T))} \frac{(r - m_0)(r - m_1)}{(m_0 - m_1)E_0} \qquad \text{[14.A1.2]}$$

PART III

Chapter 15

Health valuation

The valuation of health risks is a long standing area of both research and policy application. Even so, increasing evidence of the global burden of disease and especially the role of environmental pollution as a determinant of this burden has added a further urgency to this work. Considerable strides have been made in recent years in terms of clarifying both the meaning and size of the value of statistical life (VSL). One of the main issues has been how to "transfer" VSLs taken from e.g. from country-to-country or where life expectancy of those people who are the object of policy and investment project proposals differs. Needless to say, this still requires that applications are done with care and judgement. In some areas, the literature offers firmer guidance here than in others. Notably, age may or may not be relevant in valuing immediate risks – the literature is arguably ambiguous with regards to the empirical relationship. That said, in terms of practical guidelines, the empirical record has been important in translating findings in base or reference levels for health values for use of policy or project appraisal.

15.1. Introduction: the importance of health effects in CBA[1]

Environmental policy affects human health in a number of ways. First, by reducing environmental risks to lives, it may "save lives", i.e. reduce premature *mortality*. Second, it may improve the health of those living with a disease, e.g. a respiratory illness. This is a *morbidity* benefit, relating to physical health. Third, it may reduce the stresses and strains of living and thus improve *mental health*. By and large, environmental economics has focused on the first two types of benefit by evaluating how environmental policies improve provision of these benefits (such as actions to improve air quality in urban areas) or how projects diminish these benefits (such as energy or road transport investments). Less attention is paid to the third effect. That said, some would argue that these effects could be captured by individuals' willingness-to-pay to reduce stress – e.g. from excessive noise. The recent focus on subjective well-being (and its links to environmental quality as a determinant) has made more of this link to mental health (see Chapter 7).

A striking example of what is at stake is illustrated by the Global Burden of Disease project (see, for example, Murray et al., 2016). According to its most recent assessment, about 6.5 million deaths worldwide in 2015 were attributed to exposure to all air pollution.[2] In total, environmental risks (which also includes unsafe water and sanitation as well as household and occupational exposure to hazardous substances) is said to account for 29% of total mortality in that year. This Chapter begins by explaining how such physical magnitudes can be estimated. These are the bedrock of any subsequent economic assessment. The procedure here is to take an "objective" measure of risk arising from some change in an environmental variable, here a measure of air quality such as the concentration of particulate matter in the ambient environment. This is shown as a *dose-response function* or *exposure response function* and is used to estimate numbers of premature mortalities.

From an economic perspective, what really matters is the value that people place on these burdens. Section 15.3 sets out the relevant valuation concepts and identifies how practitioners have sought to empirically estimate these parameters. By and large, the procedure for valuing risks to life, i.e. *a mortality risk*, have involved an estimation of the willingness-to-pay (WTP) to secure a risk reduction arising from a policy or project, or the willingness-to-accept (WTA) compensation for tolerating higher than "normal" risks. The procedure involves taking the risk change in question and dividing this into the WTP (or WTA) for the risk reduction, to secure a "value of statistical life" (VSL).[3] However the VSL estimated, mortalities estimated using dose-response functions can be multiplied by that VSL to give an aggregate measure of the burden.

Of course, a proposal for a policy or a project entails *valuing changes* in such burdens. There is increasing evidence, however, that when a health benefit is present as an impact of a policy or investment project, it often appears to "dominate" cost-benefit studies. If so then it matters a great deal that the underlying theory and empirical procedures are correct. Much of the remainder of this Chapter then is concerned with a number of the debates surrounding the *validity* of VSL. Notable here is how estimates of WTP for risk reduction pass key tests such as "scope" which means that higher risk changes should be associated with higher WTP. Whether studies pass or fail such tests can be used to screen the quality of the empirical record, with OECD (2012) being one prominent example of this. This screening is often undertaken in order to establish a standard value for the VSL, which can be applied to mortality risks across countries; although perhaps adjusting for income differences. Others would take this further arguing that the VSL is heterogeneous, not just in income but in other policy relevant socio-demographic characteristics, notably such as age. The concern here is that a standard VSL "for all" might "overstate" health burdens given the (higher) average age of those primarily affected by environmental problems such as air pollution. Notwithstanding important questions about equity, whether this concern has a firm basis in empirical evidence has been the subject of some debate. And while the focus is primarily on mortality risk in this Chapter, valuing non-fatal health burdens – i.e. morbidity – is also relevant and discussed in the penultimate section.

15.2. The global burden of air pollution

The physical sources of health risk in urban and rural environments are both numerous and diverse. These include water-borne sources of illnesses and disease as well as health effects arising from changing temperature as a result of climate change. There is increasing interest also in the way in which the lack of access to green space might enhance human health (in both physical and mental health dimensions). It is fair to say, however, that particular attention has centred on the link between air pollution and health, notably particulate matter and especially tiny particles such as $PM_{2.5}$ (particulate matter of 2.5 microns or less in diameter).[4] These substances in ambient air across major cities, urban areas as well as rural locations are now seen as being implicated in large numbers of deaths around the world. The exact causes of mortality to which $PM_{2.5}$ contributes are varied but notably include heart disease and stroke as well as lung cancer, respiratory infection and chronic respiratory disorders.

This has far-reaching implications for environmental policy as well as investments in sectors such as transport and energy. For example, Hamilton et al. (2014) ties this to questions about the benefits of climate policy by looking at the possible size of the *health co-benefits* from mitigating greenhouse gases in energy projects. They estimate the value of air pollution mortality per tonne of CO_2 to be more than USD 100 for high income countries and USD 50 for middle income countries. Such numbers can be compared with the carbon prices in Chapter 14, for example.

The starting point for much of this economic analysis is the work of the Global Burden of Disease project (see Murray et al., 2016, Vos et al., 2016 and also GBD, 2013). This assesses ambient $PM_{2.5}$ by monitoring concentrations on the ground along with other approaches such as satellite observations. This complementary approach helps build a fuller picture of human exposure across e.g. urban areas in a more comprehensive way than has been possible in the past. The burdens are shifting too, as some regions experience decreasing exposure to $PM_{2.5}$ between 1990 and 2013 (much of Europe and the United States as well as parts of South East Asia) while other regions experience increasing exposure (sometimes substantially) such as South and Far East Asia, parts of Southern Africa and South America.

While concentrations of $PM_{2.5}$ measured by micrograms per cubic metre of air (μg per m^3) vary across locations (due to natural and human factors), the physical impact on premature or excess deaths is calculated in a number of steps for which, typically, the first is the calculation of the relative risk, RR, of death. This number compares the change in the risk of death from a given unit change in $PM_{2.5}$. For example, if the RR = 1.048 per 10 µg per m^3, this means that the risk of dying as a result of exposure to a 10 µg per m^3 change concentration of $PM_{2.5}$ is 1.048 times higher than previously.

RR therefore specifies the relationship between pollution concentrations (the dose) and the response (health effect). The results of existing statistical studies of the association between exposure to air pollution and human health effects (such as mortality risks) across populated areas allow estimation of RR as:

$$RR = e^{\beta(C_1 - C_0)}$$

where C_1 is the current level of pollution and C_0 is some reference level. The parameter β is a risk factor reflecting the severity of the health risk.

Critically this relative risk is used to calculate the "attributable factor" or AF: the proportion of fatalities (in a given year) which are attributable to exposure to pollutant levels above the reference level. This AF is calculated as follows:

$$AF = (RR - 1) / RR$$

So for example, for C_1 = 20 µg per m^3, C_0 = 10 µg per m^3 and β = 0.0047 then RR = 1.048. In this case, AF = 0.046. This means that 4.6% of total deaths are attributable to exposure to $PM_{2.5}$ at levels of 20 units rather than the reference level of 10.

For illustrative purposes, assume the geographical area of interest is a city with a population of 5 million people, all facing mortality risks due to air pollution. The death rate (all causes) is 9 per 1 000 people. So the total number of deaths in the city in any one year is expected to be B × POP = 0.009 × 1m = 45 000 deaths.

$$\Delta H = AF \times B \times POP$$

The AF estimated indicates how many of these total deaths are attributable to air pollution (strictly speaking, how many deaths because pollution concentrations 10 units above the reference level, in this example). Multiplying AF by 45 000 indicates that 2 070 deaths are caused by air pollution in this example.

These calculations assume that health impacts increase linearly with pollution concentrations (i.e. the broken line in the Figure 15.1. There is evidence, however, that the number of *extra* cases tails off as pollution concentrations increase, at least for certain types of cause of death, such as heart disease (i.e. the unbroken line in the same figure). The previous calculations do not capture this but the following expression does:

$$RR = \left(C_1 / C_0 \right)^{\gamma}$$

where Figure 15.1 illustrates this for the case where γ = 0.0073. The GBD study, as well as subsequent work by World Bank (2016) and Hamilton et al. (2014), also employ this latest evidence on this relationship. This allows a more realistic assessment of deaths which are likely to occur at higher levels of $PM_{2.5}$ concentration, such as those which prevail in many mega-cities in the developing world.

Table 15.1 reports some of the results of World Bank (2016) for 8 countries. It indicates ambient $PM_{2.5}$ concentrations and subsequent total deaths, estimated using a dose-response function along the lines just discussed. For each of these countries, the first row of reported numbers is the value for 2013. The second (italicised) row is the change between 1990 and 2013. The table indicates that ambient $PM_{2.5}$ declined over the period in 5 of these 8 countries. However, in The People's Republic of China and India in particular,

Figure 15.1. **The relationship between PM exposure and mortality risk**

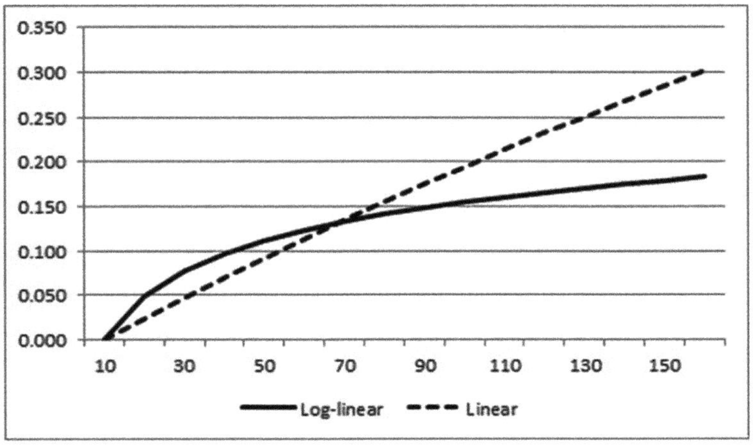

Source: Authors' calculation from assumed values and functional forms.

Table 15.1. **The health burden of ambient PM$_{2.5}$ by selected countries**
1990-2013

		Ambient PM$_{2.5}$ concentrations (g/m^3)	Total PM$_{2.5}$ deaths	Economic well-being losses (% of GDP)
Brazil	2013	16.5	62 246	3.0%
	Change 1990-2013	+6.8	+2 640	+0.00
The People's Republic of China	2013	54.4	1 625 164	10.0%
	Change 1990-2013	+15.1	+106 222	+3.00
India	2013	46.7	1 403 136	8.0%
	Change 1990-2013	+16.4	+359 954	+1.00
Russian Federation	2013	14.2	104 379	8.0%
	Change 1990-2013	-5.4	-9 365	-1.00
France	2013	14.0	21 138	3%
	Change 1990-2013	-8.7	-6 326	-2.00
Germany	2013	15.4	41 485	5%
	Change 1990-2013	-14.4	-29 651	-5.00
UK	2013	10.8	19 803	3.2%
	Change 1990-2013	-8.9	-25 650	-5.70
US	2013	10.8	91 045	2.8%
	Change 1990-2013	-5.7	-36 195	-2.50

Notes: Italicised values are changes. For ambient PM2.5 (column 3), this indicates how many points higher (or lower) concentrations were in 2013 compared with 1990. Column 4 indicates how the number of deaths has changed. Columns 5 and 6 relate economic damages to GDP. For example, in 2013, economic well-being losses are 10% of GDP. In 1990, this burden was 7%. The change is therefore described as +3.00 (3 percentage points higher).
Source: Adapted from World Bank (2016).

PM$_{2.5}$ concentrations increased, where in the latter this results in more than a 25% increase in annual mortality (in 2013 compared with 1990).

The contribution of studies such as World Bank (2016) is to work out what this means for PM$_{2.5}$ as an economic burden. This requires a link between health effects and human well-being, by estimating the monetary value of these health damages (D):

$$D = P \times \Delta H$$

For mortality risks, P typically is some measure of the value of statistical life (VSL), discussed in more detail in section 15.3. In World Bank (2016), a reference value of USD 3.8 million

(2011, prices) is assumed. This, in turn, is based on a study by OECD (2012), which sought to estimate (using the available empirical record) a reference value for VSL for high income countries. In the World Bank study, this value is then adjusted according to income differences across the countries. This is explained in more detail in Section 15.4 below.

Table 15.1 illustrates these monetary values in its final two columns. It is notable that even for those countries where $PM_{2.5}$ concentration declined over the study period, the economic burden in terms of well-being losses remained significant in 2013 as a percentage of country GDP. For Germany, this is 5% of GDP in 2013 (down from 10% of GDP in 1990). In Brazil, India and The People's Republic of China, ambient $PM_{2.5}$ increased over the period. This translates into a substantially higher mortality burden. For example, $PM_{2.5}$ mortality was over a third higher in 2013 in India than in 1990. The loss of economic well-being – defined in terms of how much those at risk would be willing to pay to eliminate these health risks – are consequently increasing too, reaching 8% and 10% of GDP in India and The People's Republic of China respectively.

Table 15.2 summarises the findings of this study for regions of the world for all air pollution, which includes ambient $PM_{2.5}$ exposure as well as ambient ozone exposure and indoor air pollution. It also describes this burden for ambient $PM_{2.5}$ only. In each case these values are reported as a percentage of regional GDP. As can be seen, the burdens are high, although not always almost all associated with ambient $PM_{2.5}$ as the cases of East Asia and Pacific, Latin America and Caribbean, South Asia and Sub-Saharan Africa indicate.

Table 15.2. **The economic burden of air pollution by region**
As a Percentage of GDP, 2013

	Based on VSL		Based on labour income	
	All air pollution	$PM_{2.5}$	All air pollution	$PM_{2.5}$
East Asia and Pacific	7.5	4.5	0.25	0.15
Europe and Central Asia	5.1	4.8	0.13	0.12
Latin America and Caribbean	2.4	1.5	0.13	0.09
Middle East and North Africa	2.2	2.0	0.14	0.13
North America	2.8	2.4	0.11	0.10
South Asia	7.4	3.1	0.83	0.39
Sub-Saharan Africa	3.8	1.4	0.61	0.23

Source: Adapted from World Bank (2016)

Basing this assessment on the VSL indicates the magnitude of the *loss of well-being* as a result of these health burdens. Relating these values to GDP is for comparative purposes: that is, to get a sense of the scale of these well-being losses rather than to claim that GDP straightforwardly could be higher were it not for the burden of air pollution. That said, it is highly likely that such burdens do impact negatively on the economy. To illustrate this, World Bank (2016) estimates the impact on income and productivity and so a more narrow emphasis of the burden on the economy. This is estimated as the loss in the (present value of) foregone earnings as a result of premature mortality. Not surprisingly, Table 15.2 notes that these magnitudes are far smaller than the corresponding well-being losses. Nevertheless, for South Asia and Sub-Saharan Africa in particular, this value is not trivial; nor is it attributable to ambient $PM_{2.5}$ only as indoor air pollution appears to contribute significantly to these economic losses too.

This "static" assessment may not reflect full impact of these health burdens on the economy. For example, this lost productivity translates into lost output, some of which in turn might have invested productivity and the returns on those actions consumed at a later date. Put another way, there is a dynamic impact of these mortality risks which may also need to be considered. For example, in the cases of both The People's Republic of China and Europe, (respective) contributions by Matus et al. (2012) and Nam et al. (2010) show that this matters empirically. As an illustration, the former study shows that the (dynamic) costs of air pollution were around 6% to 9% of GDP for The People's Republic of China over the period 1995 to 2005. This is at least one and half times greater than previous studies which looked only at these costs, over a comparable time period, from a "static" perspective.[5]

15.3. Valuing life risks: the VSL concept

The previous section ended with a discussion of the value of mortality risk, in the context of the global burden of air pollution. It is important to take a step back and consider the conceptual basis for this monetary valuation as well as the empirical issues which arise from the practical estimation of these values.

Starting with the conceptual details, the Annex to this chapter shows the standard derivation of the VSL expression for the simplest case. The final equation is:

$$VSL = \frac{dW}{dp} = \frac{u_a(W) - u_d(W)}{(1-p).u'_a(W) + p.u'_d(W)}$$

where W is wealth, p is the probability of dying in the current period (the "baseline risk"), (1-p) is the probability of surviving the current period, u is utility, "a" is survival, and "d" is death. The utility function u_d allows for bequests to others on death. The numerator thus shows the difference in utility between surviving and dying in the current period. The denominator shows the marginal utility of wealth (which is usually measured empirically as income) conditional on survival or death. The expected relationships between VSL, p, W and expected health status on survival are discussed in Annex 15.A1.

Figure 15.2 illustrates the link between WTP and risk levels. VSL is a *marginal* WTP and hence Figure 15.2 shows marginal WTP against the risk level. The status quo risk level is usually referred to as the initial or baseline risk level. Policy usually involves *reducing* risks so as the risk level declines so does marginal WTP, as shown in Figure 15.2, and as risk rises so marginal WTP is expected to rise.

Suppose the policy measure in question reduces risk levels from P_2 to P_1 in Figure 15.2. Then the WTP for that risk reduction is seen to be equal to the area under the marginal WTP curve between P_2 and P_1. Notice that marginal WTP may be fairly constant at low levels of risk (to the right of the diagram). Small differences in the initial (baseline) risk level are therefore usually assumed to have little effect in VSL studies.[6]

It tends to be assumed that the quality of the period survived affects WTP, i.e. WTP to reduce risks should be higher if the individual anticipates being in good health (apart from the risks in question), and lower if the individual expects to be in poor health. The equation implies that WTP rises with wealth since (a) it is assumed that the marginal utility of wealth is greater for survival than as a bequest when dead, and (b) there is aversion to financial risk. The former makes the numerator increasing in wealth.

As an example, suppose a policy promises to reduce risks from 5 in 10 000 to 3 in 10 000, a change of 2 in 10 000 (ΔRISK). Suppose that the mean WTP to secure this risk reduction is USD 750. Then the VSL is usually computed as: $\frac{WTP}{\Delta RISK} = \frac{750 \times 10\ 000}{2}$, and so the VSL would be around USD 3.8 million.

Figure 15.2. **Risk and willingness-to-pay**

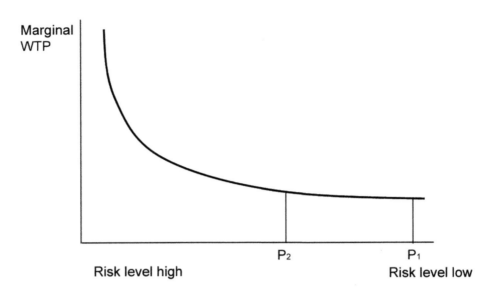

There are a variety of ways in which, as a practical matter, VSL might be estimated. Broadly speaking, these might be distinguished as to whether the underlying valuation concept is WTP to secure a risk reduction arising from a policy or project, or the WTA compensation for tolerating higher than "normal" risks. Studies of the former have involved use of stated preference techniques (see Chapters 4 and 5). But it also might involve looking at revealed behaviour such as avertive expenditures (see Chapter 3). The latter have involved hedonic wage risk studies (see Chapter 3).

One finding is that hedonic risk studies appear routinely to produce higher values than stated preference studies in context of public transport accidents. There are at least two reasons that might explain this. First, occupational risks tend to be higher than public risks. If valuations are reasonably proportional to risk levels, as the theory predicts, then one would expect higher values from occupational studies. Second, hedonic risk studies measure WTA, not WTP. While the relationship between WTP and WTA is still debated (see Chapter 4), a number of reasons have been advanced for supposing that WTA will exceed WTP, perhaps by significant ratios. One suggestion is that, whilst interesting, the hedonic wage studies do not "transfer" readily to the context of public transport accidents.

As an illustration of studies which have been applied to the transport accident context, Table 15.3 describes some VSL studies for Sweden drawing on a review by Hultkrantz and Svensson (2012). This reveals a range of estimates from EUR 0.9 million to EUR 6.2 million (2010 prices). In principle, estimates could be used to guide recommendations for an official VSL to be used in CBA. In this context, Hultkrantz and Svensson report that the official value for road traffic accidents in Sweden is just over EUR 2 million, which in the context of the table would put it towards the lower end of the range. Some of these studies, however, are estimating different things using different methods. For example, some estimate VSL for risks which are private goods while others estimate risks involving public goods. Some of these studies use revealed preference methods while others use stated preference. Asking what might be a defensible "consensus" value for a VSL, involves, in turn, asking further probing analytical questions of the empirical record.

Table 15.3. **Selected VSL Studies in Sweden from 2005 to 2010**

Publication	Study Year	Method	Type of good (and risk)	VSL, million euro (2010, prices)
Andersson	2005	RP	Road (private risk)	0.9
			Road (private risk)	1.6
Hultkrantz et al.	2006	SP	Road (private risk)	6.2
			Road (public risk)	2.4
Svensson	2009	RP	Seat belt (private risk)	2.3
			Cycle helmet (private risk)	4.0
		SP	Road (public risk)	2.3
			Road (public risk)	3.4

Source: Adapted from Hultkrantz and Svensson (2012).

This is essentially what OECD (2012) does in undertaking a meta-analysis of a large number of studies of mortality risk valuation drawn from around the world. Common to each is the use of stated preference (SP) surveys to estimate the VSL (specifically by eliciting respondent WTP for reductions in mortality risk). Broadly speaking, the intentions of this study are two-fold (but related). One is an analytical objective to understand better the sources of variation in VSL across original studies across countries. The other is to compute base values of VSL, which can be used within countries as well as used to transfer values across countries. Such base values can be adjusted in a number of ways to suit better the circumstances of the VSL context and country in which estimates are applied. But the point is that the prior meta-analytical probing of the empirical record provides a consistent basis for such adjustments.

Turning to results of OECD (2012), Table 15.4 illustrates that the mean VSL for the full sample of 856 VSL estimates was USD 7.4 million (2005 prices).[7] The Table also indicates that the median value was much lower, at about USD 2.4 million. As this publication explains, it is important to look beyond such headlines. One reason for this is that the range of mean VSL across these studies is large. To control for undue influence of the outer reaches of this range, the trimmed sample in Table 15.4 removes the highest and lowest outliers. Another reason is that some of the studies on which even this trimmed sample is based are likely to be of a higher quality than others. Here, "high quality" refers to satisfying criteria on what is broadly considered to be good practice. The OECD meta-study uses four such criteria for screening studies. First, is adequate information provided on the value of a risk change? Second, is there an adequate sample size (specifically, are main samples greater than 200 and sub-samples no smaller than 100)? Third, is the sample representative of a broader population? Fourth, did the authors of these various think their estimate was suitable for inclusion? These are reasonably generous criteria but when applied reduce the number of studies in this screened sample to 405.

Table 15.4 reports the mean VSL based on this screened sample to be about USD 3.1 million (in 2005 prices). For the subset of studies from OECD countries, the mean value is just under USD 4 million and about USD 4.9 million for EU27 country studies. As previously mentioned, these findings have a practical intent. OECD (2012) suggests a base-value of USD 3 million for use in OECD countries (2005 prices). This is based on the median VSL indicated in Table 14.4, thereby avoiding the extremes of the range within a sample. The report also suggests a lower and upper bound of -50% and +50%, reflecting likely sizes of transfer errors. So for these OECD countries, the range is USD 1.5 to USD 4.5 million (in 2005 USD). A slightly higher base value is recommended if the focus is the EU27 only: i.e. USD 3.6 million, again the median VSL for that sample in Table 15.4.

Table 15.4. **Mean VSL across studies**

USD million, 2005 prices, standard error in parentheses

	Full sample	Trimmed sample	Quality screened sample		
			All countries	OECD countries	EU27 sample
Mean VSL	7.42 (0.88)	6.31 (0.30)	3.12 (0.25)	3.98 (0.29)	4.89 (0.44)
Median VSL	2.38	2.38	1.68	3.01	3.61
Sample	856	814	405	261	163

Note: These values are weighted averages where each mean VSL estimate in each individual study is weighted by the inverse of the number of observations from each SP survey; Trimmed sample refers to removing the highest and lowest 2.5%.

Source: Adapted from OECD (2012).

15.4. VSL issues and debates

The previous section set the scene for VSL by briefly explaining the concept and moving swiftly through to discussing how base or reference values of VSL have been constructed from the empirical record. A critical question is: what explains these values? Clearly the answer to this question is important to practical matters such as what the magnitude of the VSL to use in CBA in a particular country in a particular risk context should be. But another reason why this question is so important is that it throws light on a number of conceptual and empirical puzzles that have also characterised debates about VSL. A number of these are discussed in turn, in what follows.

15.4.1. *The sensitivity of VSL to risk levels*

The theory of the VSL requires that WTP varies directly with the size of the policy-related risk: i.e. the risk change brought about by the policy or project in question, and for which the VSL is usually sought.[8] Indeed, it is widely considered that sensitivity to absolute risk is a basic test of the validity of any preference-based technique for measuring the VSL. Empirical investigation of whether what is expected in theory is actually borne out in practice has focused on a number of elements of this relationship.

An early review was Hammitt and Graham (1999) which looked at contingent valuation studies of WTP for risk reduction. In particular they tested for two predicted relationships: (a) that WTP should vary directly with the size of the risk reduction, and (b) for low probabilities (probability being their chosen measure of risk), WTP should be virtually proportional to the change in risk. Thus, if WTP for a change in risk ΔX (where X is small) is W, WTP for $\alpha\Delta X$, should be αW. They also look at "baseline risk", i.e. the level of risk from which ΔX deviates (the background risk as outlined above).

Of the 25 studies they reviewed (up to 1998), only 10 contain sufficient information to test scope sensitivity within sample (internal validity). And of those 10 studies, most confirm the first hypothesis that WTP varies with risk reduction, but not the second. Proportionality is not observed. Even in the former case, a significant minority of respondents report the same WTP regardless of the size of risk change, or ΔX. External validity (across sample scope tests) assessments showed a similar pattern, but with even the first hypothesis receiving only weak support.

OECD (2012) brings these findings further up-to-date, although notably the conclusions stay broadly the same. The size of the risk change is negatively correlated with VSL in the full sample, thus violating the expectation in theory that VSL should be invariant to whether respondents were offered a small or large risk reduction. Even screening, however, for those studies where there was clear scope insensitivity and excluding these from the analysis, this finding holds. Again what this indicates is that there is no proportionality and, as a result, VSL varies depending on the size of risk change "offered" to respondents.

That this problem appears to have persisted is an important finding, and naturally shifts attention to questions about why scope insensitivity may occur. For stated preference studies, the notable problems in communicating low risk levels to respondents, given that such low risks typically define environmental contexts.[9] Visual aids, and better communication more generally of these risk changes in surveys, might help although the persistence of the finding indicates that this is unlikely to resolve the issue. On the one hand, there is evidence that bad quality studies amplify the problem. On the other hand, even in high quality studies there is evidence that the problem persists to some degree, and so another issue might be "bad quality" human subjects (e.g. respondents in SP studies). That is, it may be that the nature of risk changes associated with environmental policy are simply too small for people to identify with in ways that might otherwise reasonably be expected. This echoes the behavioural debates playing out in SP research more generally (see Chapter 4).

The implications of the risk scope sensitivity analyses for environmental CBA are not easy to determine on the balance of such arguments, although perhaps suggest that caution and awareness of the issue in conducting sensitivity is needed at a minimum.

15.4.2. VSL and the income elasticity of willingness-to-pay

WTP should vary directly with income. Indeed, it is widely considered that sensitivity to income is the other basic test of the validity of any preference-based technique for measuring the VSL. Most studies find that this WTP does indeed vary with income. Apart from the requirement that WTP should vary with income as a theoretical validity test, the link between income and WTP is of interest for other more practical reasons. Often in valuation exercises there is the need to account for rising relative valuations of benefits and costs over time. This means ascertaining the likelihood that a given benefit or cost is likely to have a higher (or lower) real unit WTP in the future. For example, suppose that the willingness-to-pay to save a statistical life rises faster than the rate of inflation (which is always netted out in CBA). Then it would be correct to include that rising real valuation in the CBA formula over time.

Another reason is that studies such as OECD (2014) and World Bank (2016) make use of these findings for transfer exercises across space (e.g. country to country): that is, to "gap-fill" VSL estimates, from countries which have these data to those which do not and involves following the widely cited formula (see also Chapter 6):

$$VSL_i = VSL_{OECD} \times \left(\frac{Y_i}{Y_{OECD}} \right)$$

In this formula, VSL is an average of (quality scrutinised) studies from high income members of OECD. This VSL_{OECD} is simply adjusted downwards for use in countries where people have lower incomes (than the per capita average of these OECD countries) and, vice versa, for those with higher per capita incomes. Specifically, the World Bank study uses a more general form:[10]

$$VSL_i = VSL_{OECD} \times \left(\frac{Y_i}{Y_{OECD}} \right)^b,$$

where "b" is the income elasticity of VSL. This indicates how VSL (based on WTP to reduce health risks) varies with per capita income levels.

What value then should "b" take for this rudimentary value transfer?

The World Bank study uses a value for high-income to high-income country transfers b=0.8 (see also OECD, 2014). What this means is that if per capita income increases by 5% then VSL increases by 4% (i.e. 5% × 0.8). A finding in OECD (2012) supports this assumption as it estimates b to lies in the range 0.7 to 0.9, at least when considering the screened subset of what it considered to be higher quality studies.

For high-income to low-income transfers, World Bank (2016) assumed that b=1.2. What this means is that if per capita income increases by 5% then VSL increases by 6% (i.e. 5% × 1.2). This is a little bit different to the value of this parameter recommended in Hammitt and Robinson (2011). That review concludes that for transferring VSL estimates from high to low income countries a value of "b" of 1 is the most defensible assumption (see for example, Roy and Braathen, 2017).

Using sensitivity analysis in such circumstances is probably a sensible approach and World Bank (2016), for example, uses a range of 1.0 to 1.4 for assumed values of b for high- to low-income transfers, and a range of 0.6 to 1.0 for high- to high-income transfers.

15.4.3. The context of VSL

Assuming that VSL estimates are accepted for policy purposes, interesting issue arise about what its size is and whether a VSL estimated in one context, say road accidents, be applied to another context, say environmental pollution? Various countries adopt single values for the VSL and use them in policy appraisal. Usually, estimates are not varied by context but clearly there is a question about the extent to which the transferability of single values is valid.

Chilton et al. (2002, 2004) tested for the effect of risk context on valuations. These studies directly sought valuations of risks in rail and fire contexts and air pollution contexts relative to risks in road accidents. The general conclusion is that context makes little difference. Perhaps, at best, domestic fires are valued about 10% less than a road accident, probably reflecting the degree of control individuals feel they have over domestic fire. For air pollution values, the finding is that these are valued at 10% more than a road accident, so again, context appears not to have a significant effect on valuation. OECD (2012) appears to confirm those earlier findings for its larger pool of studies. There appears little evidence looking across the empirical record that context matters substantially.

One other specific aspect of these concerns about context is whether people value so-called "dread risks" differently. The idea here, for example, is the belief that there may be a higher WTP to avoid cancers than other diseases. This is because of the "dread" effect of such a serious illness. If so, there is a "cancer premium" to consider in estimating a risk context appropriate VSL. This is especially relevant in the case of air pollution, especially $PM_{2.5}$ which has been implicated in this particular health pathway.

Hammitt and Liu (2004) find evidence that there is a cancer premium which they estimate to be about one-third, i.e. VSL for avoiding a cancer risk is 1.3 times that of a VSL for some other disease. OECD (2012), however, does not find substantial support for this across the broader literature (although the sample size for this test remains small). However, inferences about this might be sought from the literature on WTP to avoid non-fatal cancers (NFCs). The indications here are that these values fractions of a VSL, but with values being proportional to some "dread" factor. If so, then it is not implausible to think that VSL might vary with type of disease causing death.

15.5. Heterogeneity and VSL: An age-related VSL?

Much debate in the VSL literature has focussed on its apparent heterogeneity. That is, the VSL appears empirically to differ across people depending on socioeconomic and demographic characteristics. By contrast, policy applications typically rely on "standard values": that is, estimates of the VSL which is invariant across different groups whose mortality risks are being affected by policy. One prominent venue in which this debate plays out is the way in which the age of individuals may (or may not) matter in relation to the VSL of people over their lifetime. While the typical practice is to apply standard values for the VSL regardless of age (or other individual characteristics), once the VSL discussion is placed in the context of environmental policy, such as air quality management, it is quite possible that age matters in a potentially significant way. This is because pollution control policy tends to "save" lives of older people, or, to put it another way, pollution has the effect of "harvesting" the older population.

Two risk contexts need to be distinguished in the CBA of health impacts arising from environmental policy: immediate and future risks. For *immediate risk*, the WTP to avoid that risk which could occur "tomorrow" or, at least, in the next few months or years, i.e. *acute risks*. But there are also *latent risks*, i.e. situations in which exposure now does not produce death until a much later period. Of course, the reality is that policy context is likely to be one of both immediate and future risks. In the air pollution example, the risk may well be immediate for older people since it is known that it is older people who tend to be most affected by air pollution, i.e. the risks they face are still acute. But for younger people, while immediate benefits are considerably less, the benefits of reducing pollution will accrue to this younger group when they are much older. This is not always the case of course and it is important to note as well a separate issue. Mortality risks may have a significant incidence among children – the issue of valuing children's (statistical) lives. Bringing the effects on children into the domain of CBA is potentially important, with a default position being to use the adult valuations of "own" life risks for the risks faced by children.

The question naturally arises as to whether someone aged, say, 70 years of age has the same WTP to avoid a mortality risk as someone of e.g. 35 years of age. More critically, environmental policies may save a disproportionate number of lives in the "very old" category, i.e. reducing mortality risks which imply extending (statistical) life months, weeks or even days later without the policy. The issue, then, is what weight should be attached to such risk reductions in a CBA.

Age is usually thought to have two potentially offsetting effects in relation to the VSL: (a) the older one gets, the fewer years are left so the benefit of any current reduction in mortality risk declines – that is, it would be expected for VSL to decline with age; (b) the opportunity cost of spending money on risk reduction declines as time goes by because savings accumulate, so WTP for risk reduction may actually rise with age. As Aldy and Viscusi put it: as an individual ages, life expectancy decreases (by definition) but economic resources that the individual has may vary as well. Given these possibly offsetting effects, the question is what reasonably might be expected with reference to either theoretical precepts, empirical evidence or some mixture of the both.

Theoretically, the literature suggests that WTP should vary non-linearly with age, with an upside-down "U" curve that probably peaks at some point around middle-age (Shepard and Zeckhauser, 1982; Arthur, 1981). A lot of debate understandably has surrounded whether this relationship is robust. Some of this debate has sought to probe further the theoretical grounds for this form of non-linearity (Johansson, 2002). While this understanding the nuances of the underpinning theory is important, it is accord between what is predicted in theory and the empirical evidence that has been the focus of more practical debate.

Not surprisingly this has entailed exploring the more prominent of those techniques which have been used to estimate the VSL; namely, revealed preference methods (specifically hedonic wage studies) and stated preference methods. With regards to the former, Aldy and Viscusi (2007) find that for labour market data there is the inverted U-shaped relationship between age and VSL. However, the decline (in VSL) later in life is less pronounced (i.e. flatter) than the corresponding increase in earlier life. Krupnick (2007) reviews some of the evidence from stated preference studies and concludes that: this "… offers a mixed and somewhat confusing picture of whether a senior discount exists across the preferences in the United States and abroad" (p. 274). What is driving this ambiguity is itself unclear and may boil down to different handling of these analytical issues across the empirical record rather than reflecting preferences. OECD (2012) finds at best weak evidence for an inverted U-shaped relationship between VSL and mean age in their meta-sample.

A somewhat different approach is provided by Aldy and Smyth (2014). This makes use of a "simulated" experiment which involves examining the economic choices across the life cycle of (identical) "virtual" individuals (from the age of 20 years old) along with their implied WTP for mortality risk reductions. Each year (up to very old age), individuals in this simulated sample make work and leisure choices as well as consumption versus saving decisions, in response to economic circumstances and mortality risks. Those simulated individuals surviving to the next period are also "asked" in this exercise how much they would be willing to pay to reduce mortality risks in the coming year by a small amount. The results indicate a VSL which clearly varies over the life cycle of these virtual people exhibiting the inverted U-shaped relationship that many suspect exists. Given the aforementioned impasse in the stated preference literature, it remains to be seen whether this relationship works also for "real" people (i.e. outside the setting of labour market choices). Nevertheless, this simulated study provides possibly important clues. This notwithstanding, the prospect of constructing a robust and broadly agreed schedule of age-related VSL estimates remains elusive. However, one proposal for a straightforward procedure that does this is explored in Box 15.1.

Box 15.1. **The value of a (statistical) life-year**

The belief that age matters in computing VSL has led some to focus on simpler approaches; notably a "value of a statistical life-year" (or VSLY). Typically, the procedure here is to divide the VSL of someone of a given age, say 40, by the remaining years of life expectancy, say 40. Each "life year" would then be valued at: $VSLY = \dfrac{VSL_A}{T-A}$, where T is age at the end of a normal life and A is current age. In keeping with the lifetime consumption model, however, it is usually argued that the remaining life-years should themselves be discounted (by discount rate, r), so that the calculation becomes

$$VSLY = \frac{VSL_A}{\sum_t \dfrac{1}{(1+r)^{T-A}}}$$

As an example, someone aged 40, with a life expectancy of 78 and VSL of USD 5 million would have a VSLY of USD 131 579 on the simple approach, and USD 296 419 on the discounted

---

Box 15.1. **The value of a (statistical) life-year** (*cont.*)

approach.[a] While attractive in principle (because of its simplicity), securing a VSLY in this way from a VSL rests on substantial assumptions. First, as noted, the lifetime consumption model may not itself be capturing the features relevant to valuing remaining life years. Second, the resulting VSLY is very sensitive to the assumption made about the discount rate. Note that discount rates are not directly observed in this approach but are superimposed by the analyst.

In essence, what the VSLY approach does is to replace the assumption (implicit in the way that VSL is typically applied) that age does not matter with an alternative assumption that age not only matters but it matters in a particular way: i.e. as specified by the assumed VSLY conversion calculation such as a constant value that is discounted.[b] Proponents of the approach would argue that this has an intuitive appeal. That is, someone with, say, 40 years of life remaining and facing an immediate risk would tend to value "remaining life" more than someone with, say, 5 years of remaining life. Needless to say, there are counterarguments. For example, perhaps there is a scarcity value of time itself, i.e. fewer years left results in a higher WTP for the remaining years. And, of course, a natural question is whether the VSYL is justified by the empirical evidence about how WTP varies with age.

The discussion elsewhere in this chapter has reflected the view that while there appears to be a basis for an age/VSL relationship in some respects, the relationship is far from agreed especially in the context of the mixed results from stated preference evidence. However, there appears greater agreement that the schedule of life-year estimates in the typical VSLY approach does not appear to find support in practically any of the evidence to date. It is important not to interpret this as saying no age relationship exists. Rather it requires a more detailed search and in all likelihood will involve a more nuanced relationship than "mechanistic" straightline approaches assume. One starting point here might be, for example, Desaigues et al. (2011) which estimates more directly the VSLY using a stated preference approach across 9 European countries.[c]

a) The issue arises of whether individuals have already discounted the future when providing their WTP response if the approach used is a stated preference study. If so, the simple approach is relevant. If not, the discounted approach is more relevant.

b) The VSLY approach also assumes that one would value an additional life year the same at different ages. Hence, it does not permit, by assumption, a situation where a 40 year old person might not care very much if he or she was told that life expectancy would be 82 years instead of 83, but for someone aged 75 that difference *could* matter much more.

c) However, Alberinin (2017) states that "The Desaigues et al. study was conducted in nine countries for a total of only 1 463 respondents. Individuals were presented with a graph that clearly mislabels the change in life expectancy and the econometric analysis of the responses is well below acceptable standards".

15.6. Valuing morbidity

The previous sections have been concerned with the valuation of premature mortality. The reason for this is straightforward. Overwhelmingly, the evidence points to mortality as being by far the largest economic cost of health burdens related to the environment (see, for example, OECD, 2014, World Bank, 2016, and Cropper et al., 2010). Nevertheless, in environmental contexts, costs arising from morbidity, i.e. non-fatal ill health should not be ignored and are likely to significantly support the evidence for policy action when incorporated in a CBA. This was recognised in early work on the health costs of air pollution, including notably the ExternE study by the European Commission.

Morbidity endpoints even for air pollution are manifold and whether these valuations need to be and indeed should be carried out on each and every relationship between say air pollution and illness depends on a number of considerations. Hunt et al. (2016), for example, identify five key relationships for which they judge to be most promising. "Promising" on their judgement accords to whether the relationship is robust and (largely) unbiased and can be applied, as a practical matter, across OECD countries as well as The People's Republic of China and India. The end-points they identify are the following:

- Hospital admissions for both respiratory and cardiovascular problems related to ambient ozone or particulate matter (PM);
- Restricted activity days (RADs) or lost work days related to ambient ozone or PM;
- Chronic bronchitis in adults related to PM;
- Acute[11] bronchitis in children (aged 6 to 18 years) related to PM;
- Acute Lower Respiratory Illness (ALRI) in very young children (under 5 years old) related to PM.

The point here is that these are relationships for which there is quantitative evidence, in e.g. medical and epidemiological studies such as the estimation of dose-response functions, about the relation between exposure to a pollutant in e.g. urban air and physical health impact. Moreover based on an extensive literature review, Hunt et al. make recommendations about the unit values to attach these physical cases. These are illustrated in Table 15.5 and are intended to be base case values which might be adjusted according to income differences as discussed in Section 15.4.2.

Table 15.5. **Proposed unit values in for selected morbidity end-points**

USD, 2010 prices

Morbidity end-point	Central value	Range
Chronic bronchitis (per case)	334 750	41 700 to 889 000
Hospital admission (per case)	2 000	600 to 3 300
Work loss (per day)	Country specific	
RAD (per day)	170	41 to 268
Minor RADS (per day)	62	53 to 70
Acute bronchitis in children (per case)	464	301 to 511
ALRI in very young children (per case)	464	301 to 511

Source: Hunt et al. (2016).

The study by Cropper et al. (2010) provides an illustration of how a range of morbidity costs (along with mortality costs) might be calculated using the example of PM_{10} in Chinese cities. The authors consider a range of evidence about the physical link between air pollution exposure and a number of health end-points and conclude the following:

- For chronic bronchitis, the evidence for The People's Republic of China is that incidents increase by 4.8% per 10 μg per m^3 of PM_{10}. Put in terms of the dose-response functions discussed earlier in this Chapter (Section 15.2), this implies a coefficient β of 0.0048.

- For hospital admissions, there is a 0.7% and 1.2% change in number of incidents for respiratory and cardiovascular cases respectively as a result of 10 μg per m^3 of PM_{10}. Workdays lost as a result of each case is then calculated as the duration of a stay in hospital.

Table 15.6 reports the physical cases (panel a) and monetary costs (panel b) of exposure to PM_{10} in The People's Republic of China for 2003 as estimated in Cropper et al. The table makes clear the finding that mortality costs are the critical category of impact in

Table 15.6. **Health impacts and ambient air pollution in The People's Republic of China in 2003**

a) Health cases and incidents ('000s)

	Premature mortality	Morbidity			
		Chronic bronchitis	RHA	CHA	Workdays lost to hospital stays
Mean	394.0	305.3	223.6	216.3	9 210
Range	134.6 to 628.3	265.6 to 341.9	156.5 to 286.0	99.2 to 324.3	6 108 to 12 970

b) Health costs in billion Yuan

	Costs of premature mortality	Costs of morbidity			Total costs
		Chronic bronchitis	Direct hospital costs	Indirect hospital costs	
Mean	394.0	122.1	3.4	0.47	519.9
Range	135.6 to 641.1	106.2 to 137.7	1.9 to 4.8	0.26 to 0.67	243.9 to 783.3

Source: Cropper et al. (2010).

terms of economic burden. However, the morbidity value of chronic bronchitis accounts for almost a quarter of the total health costs. This should not be a surprise given the severity of this illness and the large number of estimated incidents in the study year.

15.7. Conclusions

While this Chapter has focused exclusively on analytical matters, it is important to remember that there are often vociferous and compelling criticisms of economists' "value of (statistical) life" estimates. These debates are important. Whether those criticisms mean putting health impacts beyond the reach of the cost-benefit analyst is debatable, although broadly the implications for CBA are similar to those discussed in Chapter 12, in relation to constraints on a CBA recommendation.

But it is useful to bear in mind that all decisions involving tolerance, acceptance or rejection of risk changes imply such valuations. The reason is very simple: risk reductions usually involve expenditure of resources, so that not spending those resources implies a sum of VSLs less than the resource cost. Conversely, spending the resources implies a sum of VSLs greater than the resource cost. Morrall (2003) provides a good illustration of this. Covering 76 regulations, Morrall derives implied VSLs ranging from USD 100 000 for a regulation covering childproof lighters, through USD 500 million for sewage sludge disposal regulations, and up to USD 100 billion for solid waste disposal facility criteria.[12]

Knowing these implied VSLs serve several purposes. First, as mentioned, they are a reminder that there is no "escape" from the valuation of life risks. Second, they serve as a measure of consistency across public agencies: the implied VSL for, say, transport risks should not be significantly different to the implied VSL for pollution reduction, unless there is a reason to suppose that the risks should be valued differently. Third, even if there is no consensus on "the" VSL, such exercises show that some policy measures are not credible in terms of their stated goal of cost-effectively saving (statistical) lives.

While knowing implicit VSL is useful, the progress in estimating *explicit* VSL suggests that CBA can do a lot more. Considerable strides have been made in recent years in terms of clarifying both the meaning and size of the VSL. One of the main issues has been how to "transfer" VSLs taken from e.g. non-environmental contexts to environmental contexts and country-to-country. The former consideration has given rise to concerns about nature of the risks involved.

Needless to say, this still requires that applications are done with care and judgement. In some areas, the literature offers firmer guidance here than in others. Notably, age may or may not be relevant in valuing immediate risks – the literature is arguably ambiguous and there is still a choice to be made between VSL and a life year approach, or perhaps using both although simpler approaches for the latter appear to lack firm empirical support. That said, in terms of practical guidelines, the empirical record has been important in translating findings in base or reference levels. Studies such as OECD (2012) have been important in distilling this empirical record into something highly usable as illustrated for the recent World Bank (2016) estimates of the global economic burden of air pollution.

Notes

1. This chapter is necessarily selective in its coverage since the literature on valuing human health impacts is now extremely large indeed. As a result, the focus here is only on a selection of the issues that have occupied attention in the recent literature.

2. This includes ambient pollution (exposure to particulate matter and ground level ozone) as well as indoor air pollution.

3. Terminology varies: VSL is also known as a "value of a prevented fatality" and, despite the warnings of economists about this phrase, "value of life". Cameron (2010) provides a compelling argument about the problems of all this terminology in communicating this economic concept and, in doing so, makes a case for a re-labelling around the more literal, but wordier, term: willingness to swap alternative goods and services for a micro-risk reduction in chance of sudden death.

4. These particles are defined in other ways depending on the size: TSP (total suspended particulates); PM_{10} (particles of 10 microns or less in diameter). There exist rough rules of thumb for converting between these units e.g.: $PM_{10}/0.55 = TSP$; $PM_{10}/2 = PM_{2.5}$. So for example, a 90 µg per m^3 reduction in TSP equates to a 50 µg per m^3 reduction in PM_{10}. A 50 µg per m^3 reduction in $PM_{10} = 25$ µg per m^3 reduction in $PM_{2.5}$.

5. More generally, these substantial impacts might also be examined via a general equilibrium approach, given that these changes are non-marginal and economy wide. See, for example, Marten and Newbold (2017) for a recent discussion of this.

6. Terminology can be confusing. The initial or baseline risk level needs to be distinguished from the change in the risk level brought about by the policy in question.

7. This is a weighted average where each mean VSL estimate in each individual study is weighted by the inverse of the number of observations from each SP survey.

8. There is also a separate issue of background risk. The expectation is that a "competing risk", i.e. some other risk to life independent of the risk being addressed by the policy measure, will reduce the WTP for the policy-related risk because of the "why bother" effect. That is, the competing risk reduces the chance that the individual will benefit from a reduction in the policy-related risk. But, in general, the effect will be very small. Eeckhoudt and Hammitt (2001) cite the example of a male worker aged about 40 in the USA. The mortality risk for that age group is 0.003 and this translates directly into a reduction in VSL of just 0.3 of a percentage point. However, risks of death from air pollution are highest for the elderly whose background risks are very high, i.e. they are at high risk of death from other causes. The "why bother" effect comes into play in a significant fashion. If the effect is significant, this would be expected to show up in expressed WTP for those who have high competing risks, notably (a) those who are in poor health anyway, and (b) the aged. The extent to which the empirical literature picks up this effect is discussed below with respect to health states and age.

9. In wage-risk studies any lack of a WTP-risk relationship may be due to "self-selection", where higher risk tolerant workers may be selecting the more hazardous employment. Meta-analyses of wage-risk studies also produce somewhat more mixed results. As risk increases, one would expect WTA (since what is measured is the premium on wages to accept higher risks) to vary directly with risk levels. On the other hand, the self-selection effect may mean that less risk-averse workers gravitate to higher risk occupations. Mrozek and Taylor (2002) find both effects, i.e. a rising WTA at first followed

by a reduction thereafter. This "risk loving" effect has been noted in other occupational studies as well (for a summary, see Hammitt, 2002). On the other hand, Viscusi (2004) finds that wage premia vary directly with death risks and with injury risks in occupations, and Viscusi and Aldy's (2003) meta-analysis of wage risk studies for the USA finds VSL that vary directly with risk reduction but with only a minor effect of high risk on VSL (the implied VSL is USD 12-22 million for low risks and a tenfold increase in risks changes this to USD 10-18 million).

10. Roy and Braathen (2017) uses a slightly different formula:

$VSL\ C_{2015} = VSL\ OECD_{2010} \times (Y\ C_{2010}/Y\ OECD_{2010})^\beta \times (1 + \%\Delta P + \%\Delta Y)^\beta$, taking into account the changes in price and income levels since the baseyear used. One could argue for an additional modification: $VSL\ C_{2015} = VSL\ OECD_{2010} \times (Y\ C_{2010}/Y\ OECD_{2010})^\beta \times (1 + \%\Delta P) \times (1 + \%\Delta Y)^\beta$, thus not adjusting the change in the price level for the income elasticity.

11. Defined as an incident within the last 12 months.

12. Taking a USD 7 million "cut-off" point, Morrall finds that nearly all regulations aimed at safety pass a cost-benefit test, but less than 20% of regulations aimed at reducing cancers pass such a test. Finally, by employing "risk-risk" or "health-health" analysis (see Chapter 17), Morrall shows that USD 21 million of public expenditure gives rise to one statistical death. All policies cost money which ultimately comes from taxation, reducing the disposable income of taxpayers. Some of that forgone income could have been spent on life-saving measures. Hence, all government expenditure might cause life loss, at least to some extent. Any measure that implies a VSL of more than USD 21 million "does more harm than good", i.e. it generates more deaths than lives saved. 27 of the 76 regulations studies fail this test. Comparable studies exist for Sweden where the cut-off point is USD 6.8-9.8 million – see Gerdtham and Johannesson (2002) and the United Kingdom, where the cut-off is around USD 8 million (Whitehurst, 1999).

References

Alberini, A. et al. (1997), "Valuing health effects of air pollution in developing countries: The case of Taiwan", *Journal of Environmental Economics and Management*, Vol. 34(2), pp. 107-126.

Alberini, A. et al. (2004) "Does the value of statistical life vary with age and health status? Evidence from the US and Canada", *Journal of Environmental Economics and Management*, Vol. 48, pp. 769-792, http://dx.doi.org/10.1016/j.jeem.2003.10.005.

Alberini, A. (2017), "Measuring the economic value of the effects of chemicals on ecological systems and human health", *OECD Environment Working Papers*, No. 116, OECD Publishing, Paris, http://dx.doi.org/10.1787/9dc90f8d-en.

Andersson, H. (2005) "The Value of Safety as Revealed in the Swedish Car Market: An Application of the Hedonic Pricing Approach", *Journal of Risk and Uncertainty*, Vol. 30(3), pp. 211-239, http://dx.doi.org/10.1007/s11166-005-1154-1.

Cameron, T.-A. (2010), "Euthanizing the Value of a Statistical Life", *Review of Environmental Economics and Policy*, Vol. 4(2), pp. 161-178, https://doi.org/10.1093/reep/req010.

Carlsson, F., D. Daruvala and H. Jaldell (2010), "Value of Statistical Life and Cause of Accident: A Choice Experiment", *Risk Analysis*, Vol. 30(6), pp. 975-986, http://dx.doi.org/10.1111/j.1539-6924.2010.01399.x.

Chilton, S. et al. (2002), "Public perceptions of risk and preference-based values of safety", *Journal of Risk and Uncertainty*, Vol. 25 (3), 211-232, http://dx.doi.org/10.1023/A:1020962104810.

Chilton, S. et al. (2004), *Valuation of Health Benefits Associated with Reductions in Air Pollution: Final Report*, Department for Environment Food and Rural Affairs, London.

Cropper, M. et al. (2010), "What are the Health Effects of Air Pollution in China", in Heal, G. (ed.) *Is Economic Growth Sustainable?*, Palgrave Macmillan.

Desaignes, B. et al. (2011), "Economic Valuation of Air Pollution Mortality: A 9-Country Contingent Valuation Survey of Value of a Life Year", *Ecological Indicators*, Vol. 11, pp. 902-910, http://dx.doi.org/10.1016/j.ecolind.2010.12.006.

Eeckhoudt, L. and J. Hammitt (2001), "Background risks and the value of statistical life", *Journal of Risk and Uncertainty*, Vol. 23(3), 261-279, http://dx.doi.org/10.1023/A:1011825824296.

Hamilton, K. et al. (2014), *Multiple Benefits from Climate Mitigation: Assessing the Evidence*, Report to the New Climate Economy project.

Hammitt, J. and J. Graham (1999), "Willingness to pay for health protection: Inadequate sensitivity to probability?", *Journal of Risk and Uncertainty*, Vol. 18, 33-62, *http://dx.doi.org/10.1023/A:1007760327375*.

Hammitt, J. and J.-T. Liu (2004), "Effects of disease type and latency on the value of mortality risk", *Journal of Risk and Uncertainty*, Vol. 28(1), 73-95, *http://dx.doi.org/10.1023/B:RISK.0000009437.24783.e1*.

Hultkrantz, L., G. Lindberg and C. Andersson (2006), "The Value of Improved Road Safety", *Journal of Risk and Uncertainty*, Vol. 32(2), pp. 151-170, *http://dx.doi.org/10.1007/s11166-006-8291-z*.

Hultkrantz, L. and M. Svensson (2012), "The Value of a Statistical Life in Sweden: A Review of the Empirical Evidence", *Health Policy*, Vol. 108, pp. 302-310, *http://dx.doi.org/10.1016/j.healthpol.2012.09.007*.

Hunt, A. et al. (2016), "Social Costs of Morbidity Impacts of Air Pollution", *OECD Environment Working Papers*, No. 99, OECD Publishing, Paris, *http://dx.doi.org/10.1787/5jm55j7cq0lv-en*.

Johannesson, M. and P.-O. Johansson (1996), "To be or not be, that is the question: An empirical study on the WTP for an increased life expectancy at an advanced age", *Journal of Risk and Uncertainty*, Vol. 13, pp. 163-174, *http://dx.doi.org/10.1007/BF00057866*.

Markandya, A. et al. (2004), *EC NewExt Research Project: Mortality Risk Valuation – Final Report – UK*, European Commission, Brussels.

Morrall, J. (2003), "Saving lives: Reviewing the record", *Journal of Risk and Uncertainty*, Vol. 27(3), pp. 221-237, *http://dx.doi.org/10.1023/A:1025841209892*.

Mrozek, J.R. and L.O. Taylor (2002), "What determines the value of life? A meta-analysis", *Journal of Policy Analysis and Management*, Vol. 21(2), pp. 253-270, *http://dx.doi.org/10.1002/pam.10026*.

Murray et al. (2016) "Global, regional and national comparative risk assessment of 79 behavioural, environmental and occupational and metabolic risks or clusters of risks, 1990-2015: A systematic analysis for the Global Burden of Disease Study 2015", *The Lancet*, Vol. 388(8), pp. 1659-1724.

OECD (2014), *The Cost of Air Pollution: Health Impacts of Road Transport*, OECD Publishing, Paris, *http://dx.doi.org/10.1787/9789264210448-en*.

OECD (2012), Mortality Risk Valuation in Environment, Health and Transport Policies, OECD Publishing, Paris, *http://dx.doi.org/10.1787/9789264130807-en*.

Roy, R. and N.A. Braathen (2017), "The Rising Cost of Ambient Air Pollution thus far in the 21st Century: Results from the BRIICS and the OECD Countries", *OECD Environment Working Papers*, No. 124, OECD Publishing, Paris, *http://dx.doi.org/10.1787/d1b2b844-en*.

Svensson, M. (2009) "The Value of a Statistical Life in Sweden: Estimates from Two Studies Using the Certainty Approach Calibration", *Accident Analysis and Prevention*, Vol. 41, pp. 430-437, *http://dx.doi.org/10.1016/j.aap.2009.01.005*.

Viscusi, W.K. (2004), "The value of life: Estimates with risks by occupation and industry", *Economic Inquiry*, Vol. 42(1), pp. 29-48, *http://dx.doi.org/10.1093/ei/cbh042*.

Viscusi, W.K. and J. Aldy (2003) "The value of statistical life: A critical review of market estimates throughout the world", *Journal of Risk and Uncertainty*, Vol. 27(1): 5-76, *http://dx.doi.org/10.1023/A:1025598106257*.

Vos, T. et al. (2016) "Global, regional and national incidence, prevalence and years lived with disability for 310 diseases and injuries, 1990-2015: A systematic analysis for the Global Burden of Disease Study 2015", *The Lancet*, Vol. 388(8), pp. 1545-1602.

World Bank and IHME (Institute for Health Metrics and Evaluation) (2016), *The Cost of Air Pollution: Strengthening the Economic Case for Action*, The World Bank, Washington, DC, *http://documents.worldbank.org/curated/en/781521473177013155/pdf/108141-REVISED-Cost-of-PollutionWebCORRECTED file.pdf*.

ANNEX 15.A1

Deriving the value of a statistical life

The standard approach to the VSL is to assume that an individual's utility function for wealth (W) and mortality risk (p) is expressed in the utility function:

$$U(p, W) = (1 - p) . u_a(W) + p . u_d(W) \qquad [15.A1.1]$$

where U is (expected) utility, $u_a(W)$ is the utility conditional on surviving – i.e. the utility of being alive – and $u_d(W)$ is the utility conditional on dying. It is assumed that $u'_a > 0$ and $u''_a < 0$. The former assumption says that marginal utility of wealth is increasing in wealth, and the second says that the individual is averse to gambles with expected value of zero, i.e. individuals are averse to financial risk.

This is a one-period model, and for the sake of simplicity, $u_d(W)$ can be interpreted as including bequests etc. so that it is not necessarily equal to zero, i.e. $u'_d \geq 0$. It is further assumed that:

$$u_a(W) > u_d(W) \quad \text{and}$$
$$u'_a(W) > u'_d(W) \qquad [15.A1.2]$$

The second condition simply means that more wealth provides more utility if the individual survives than if he/she dies. Put another way, additional wealth yields more utility in life than as a bequest.

The corresponding indifference curve is:

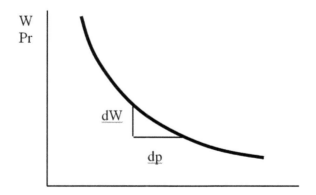

Differentiating [15.A1.1] whilst holding utility constant gives:

$$\frac{dU(.)}{dp} = (1-p)\cdot u_a'(W) - u_a(W) + p\cdot u_d'(W) + u_d(W) = 0 \qquad [15.A1.3]$$

so that

$$VSL = \frac{dW}{dp}\Big|_{EU=\,constant} = \frac{u_a(W)-u_d(W)}{(1-p).u_a'(W)+p.u_d'(W)} \qquad [15.A1.4]$$

The numerator shows the difference between utility if the individual survives or dies in the current period. The denominator is the expected marginal utility of wealth, conditional on survival and dying, each event being weighted by the relevant probabilities. The denominator is often called the "expected utility cost of funds" or the "expected utility cost of spending".

Baseline risk

Given the inequalities [15.A1.2], VSL > 0. VSL also increases with baseline risk, p, the so-called "dead anyway" effect (Pratt and Zeckhauser, 1996). Hammitt (2000) points out that this effect cannot be large for small risk changes because survival probabilities for any year are much higher than mortality probabilities ((1-p) is large, p is small). As p increases, the numerator in [15.A1.4] is unchanged because p does not affect it. But the denominator changes since the first expression declines and the second increases. Given the likely probabilities, the decline outweighs the increase and the denominator thus decreases. VSL rises with baseline risk, but not by much.

Wealth

The effect of wealth changes on VSL depends on financial risk aversion in the two states – survival and death. Risk neutrality and risk aversion are sufficient to ensure that VSL rises with W. Since $u_a'(W) > u_d'(W)$ the numerator increases in wealth. Since $u_a''(W) < 0, u_d''(W) < 0$, the denominator declines with wealth. Hence VSL rises with wealth.

Health status

The relationship between VSL and health status on survival is strictly indeterminate, although many studies assume that VSL will be higher for survival in good health than for survival in poor health, which seems intuitively correct. Hammitt (2000) points out that survival in bad health may limit the individual's ability to increase utility by spending money – the marginal utility of wealth may be lower for survival in bad health than in good health. The denominator in [15.A1.4] is smaller if survival means bad health. But the numerator is also smaller, so the relationship between VSL and health state is dependent on exact values and could be positive or negative.

Latency

Equation [15.A1.4] says nothing about latency, i.e. exposure to risks now may result in death much later (e.g. arsenicosis, asbestosis etc.). The relevant VSL (call it VSL_{lat}) is:

$$VSL_{lat} = \frac{VSL_T}{(1+s)^T} \cdot P_T \qquad [15.A1.5]$$

where VSL_{lat} is the VSL now for an exposure risk occurring now, T is the latency period after which the individual dies, s is the discount rate (technically, the individual's discount rate) and P_T is the probability that the individual will survive the latency period, i.e. the probability that he/she does not die from other causes in the interim period. Essentially, then, the relevant VSL is the discounted value of the future VSL at the time the risk effect occurs, adjusted for the probability of surviving during the latency period. If WTP varies with income and income increases with time, then, rather than discounting future WTP at the relevant discount rate, a *net* discount rate may be used. If s is the discount rate and WTP grows as n % per annum, the net discount rate will be (s-n) % per annum. A convenient case occurs where s = n since this reduces the problem to one of using undiscounted values.

Hammitt and Liu (2004) present a somewhat more sophisticated version of [15.A1.5] for a latent effect where the risk change occurs as a "blip', i.e. a temporary risk reduction as opposed to a permanent reduction of risk. (For a permanent risk reduction, WTP needs to be summed for each of the future periods). Their equation is:

$$WTP_0 = \frac{WTP_T}{\left(1/(1+s)\right)^T . a_T . (1+g)^{T\eta}}$$

[15.A1.6]

where WTP_0 is willingness to pay for a risk reduction now, WTP_T is willingness to pay for a risk reduction in T years' time, s is the personal discount rate, a is a factor linking age to WTP (a = 1 if age has no effect on willingness to pay, with a < 1 being the usual expectation), g is the growth rate of income and η is the income elasticity of willingness to pay for risk reduction. Equation [15.A1.6] thus makes an explicit attempt to modify the VSL equation for (a) age and (b) interim income growth during a latency period.

Age

Equation [15.A1.4] does not tell us if WTP (and hence VSL) varies with age. Age is usually thought to have two potentially offsetting effects: (a) the older one gets, the fewer years are left so the benefit of any current reduction in risk declines – we would expect VSL to decline with age; (b) the opportunity cost of spending money on risk reduction declines as time goes by because savings accumulate, so WTP for risk reduction may actually rise with age. Technically, therefore, VSL may vary with age in an indeterminate manner.

Cost-benefit analysis in practice

PART IV

Chapter 16

Current use of cost-benefit analysis

It is important to take stock of the extent to developments in environmental CBA have found their way into actual assessment. This chapter looks at this from the perspective of a number of OECD countries across policy sectors such as energy, transport and environmental policy, via questionnaire responses. What this finds is that there are large variations in the extent to which CBA is being carried out, and the extent to which various environmental impacts are being taken into account in these analyses, across economic sectors and across analytical contexts. For example, energy sector investments and policy proposals are relatively well covered in CBAs, but there is far narrower coverage of non-climate environmental impacts in those assessments. Cataloguing such use is important. Of course, it does not of itself provide answers to inevitable questions about why CBA is used in one context but not another. Nor did the responses provide a clear picture of the influence of CBAs on the final decisions. It must also be recognised that use and influence are moving targets in the sense that both are probably evolving reasonably rapidly given developments in environmental CBA.

While the preceding chapters have discussed the theory of cost-benefit analysis, the present chapter describes the current *use* of cost-benefit analyses (CBA) in assessments of public investment projects in selected sectors; transport and energy in particular. It also describes the use of CBA in *ex ante* assessments of a range of public policies, and in *ex post* assessments of both investment projects and public policies. The chapter is primarily based on responses to an OECD questionnaire developed for the preparation of this chapter, with responses provided by Delegates to the Working Party on Integrating Environment and Economic Policies, under OECD's Environment Policy Committee, supplemented by information provided by various other contacts in member countries.[1] The chapter also draws upon responses to a similar 2014 questionnaire, used in the preparation of Smith and Braathen (2015).[2]

Out of the responding countries, 24 indicated that general guidelines on the preparation of CBAs, across different sectors and types of assessments have been prepared. 19 respondents indicated that these guidelines had a compulsory status at the national level, while 5 said they were more advisory. 6 respondents said that these guidelines also had a compulsory status vis-à-vis lower levels of government; 7 said their status in such a context was advisory, while 6 respondents indicated that the national guidelines had no status vis-à-vis lower levels of government. 9 OECD member countries have not responded to either of the two questionnaires. The reasons for not responding can vary from country to country, but one can assume that on average, the use of CBA is less developed in the countries that have not replied.

16.1. Current use of cost-benefit analysis in ex ante assessments of public investment projects[3]

The questionnaire addressed *ex ante* cost-benefit analyses of public investment projects in two sectors with potentially large environmental impacts: the transport sector and the energy sector. The replies received indicate that CBAs in general play a more important role in assessments of investment projects in the former than in the latter of these sectors, and that environmental impacts are given more attention in the transport sector assessments than in the CBAs carried out regarding public investments in the energy sector.

In both sectors, there are commonly clear criteria for how to do CBAs;[4] in 88% of the replies regarding the transport sector and in 76% of the replies regarding the energy sector, cf. Figure 16.1.[5]

In many cases it is indicated that the level of detail required in the CBA varies, e.g. with the size of the project. For example, in relation to transport sector projects, Denmark indicated that "the level of detail depends on the stage of planning in which the CBA is included. In general, the level of detail shall be proportional with the size of the project in terms of cost and the level of information needed to take a decision". France indicated that the required level of detail "depends on the size of the potential investment. All state projects are supposed to be subject to ex-ante socio-economic assessment but the

Figure 16.1. **Are there clear criteria for how to do CBAs of investment projects?**

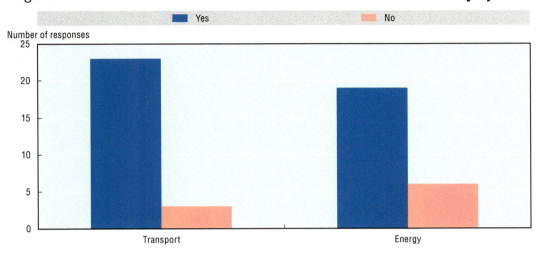

requirements depend on their size". Israel indicated that "small-scale projects which are safety related or local projects based on social-economic criteria are also exempted from a full economic evaluation". Ireland's "Common Appraisal Framework for Transport Projects and Programmes" sets out expenditure thresholds, which determine what level of analysis is required. New Zealand stated that CBA is required for all improvement projects larger than NZD 300 000, and that evidence of value-for-money is required for all other projects.

All or *most* of the transport sector investment projects had been subject to a CBA during the last 3-5 years in around 88% of the countries responding. The similar share regarding energy sector investments was 50%. Three countries replied that no energy sector investment project had been subject to a cost-benefit analysis during this period, cf. Figure 16.2.

Figure 16.2. **What is the share of cases in the last 3-5 years that have been CB-analysed?**

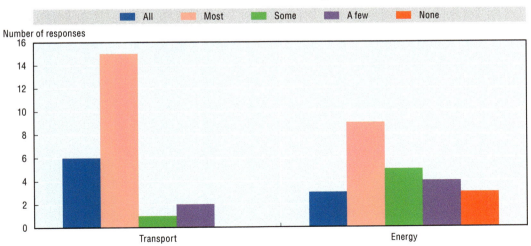

> ### Box 16.1. **Project assessments in a federal state**
>
> The vast majority of investments in the transportation sector in Canada are administered by provincial and municipal governments. A great part of these investments are infrastructure investments, which are supported under the New Building Canada Fund announced in 2014 and the Investing in Canada Plan announced in federal Budget 2016 and Budget 2017. While transportation projects, as well as other eligible categories of projects, are required to meet federal programme criteria under these programmes, including benefits and outcomes, there are no specific federal requirements for a cost-benefit analysis. Although it is possible that similar considerations are taken into account in provincial and territorial infrastructure projects, the limited information provided by the provinces does not suggest a formal requirement or consistent application of a standardised approach at the provincial level.

Environmental impacts in CBAs

Looking at the way environmental impacts are addressed in the CBAs, the differences between the two sectors are quite noticeable. For example, a large majority of the CBA guides that cover public transport sector investment project include clear rules for how to assess changes in greenhouse gas emissions; in the energy sector, this share is slightly above 50%, cf. Figure 16.3.

Figure 16.3. **Are there clear criteria for how to include GHGs in CBAs?**

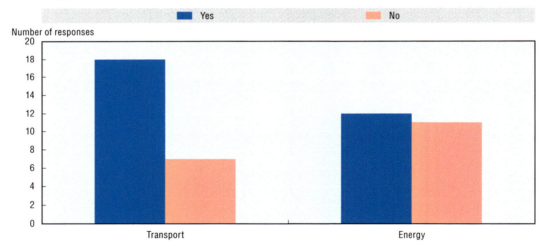

Among country examples, Switzerland indicated that GHG emissions amongst other environmental impacts are considered where relevant based on current scientific knowledge. In the energy sector, the United Kingdom indicated that estimated impacts on GHG emissions should be included where it has a significant impact on costs or benefits. Several European countries indicate that they are required to follow guidelines of the European Union in relation to the assessment of transport sector investment projects.[6] For example, Hungary indicated that GHG emission must be calculated according to the size of project and according to the mode of transport. For all EU-funded projects costing more than EUR 1 million and for income-generating projects, impacts must be calculated. If a CBA is not required, then a GHG calculation is not needed either. Similarly, Estonia indicated that "CBAs are carried out according to the relevant guidelines issued by the European Commission". Italy indicated that for most transport investments financed with EU funds, a CBA analysis has been performed.[7]

Similarly, *all* or *most* of the transport sector investment assessments during the last 3-5 years had covered GHG emission changes in 68% of the responding countries. Regarding assessments of public energy sector investments, in only around 30% of the countries had *all* or *most* of the CBAs included impacts on GHG emissions, cf. Figure 16.4. The reported values per tonne of CO_2 emissions are much higher in the transport sector assessments than in the – fewer, cf. Figure 16.5 – energy sector assessments. The full distribution of the carbon values in use in the two sectors are shown in Figures 16.6 and 16.7. Figure 16.8 illustrates the unweighted average of the carbon values.[8] Part of the explanation of why the averages differ is that different countries have provided information regarding carbon values they apply as regards the two sectors; in other words, the averages for the two sectors include information regarding the values applied in different countries. But *if* impacts on GHG emissions represent a larger share of the total impacts of an energy investment project than of a transport sector investment, it is also possible that ministries responsible for the energy sector investments could have an incentive to use lower carbon values than their transport sector counterparts.[9]

Figure 16.4. **Which share of CBAs in the last 3-5 years has included impacts on GHG emissions?**

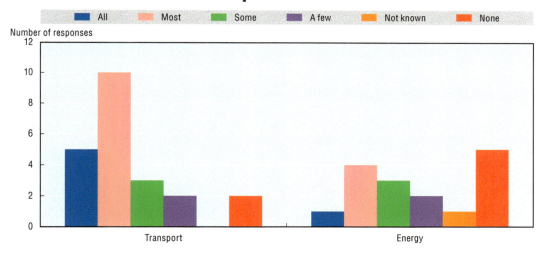

As is clear from Figures 16.6-16.8, in both the transport and the energy sectors, the carbon values that are applied in CBAs depend on *when* emission changes are estimated to occur, with higher values being applied for changes expected to occur in the distant future, in some cases very much higher values. This is in line with the fact that the damages caused by GHG emissions will be increasing over time, cf. further discussion in Chapter 14 and Smith and Braathen (2015).

Another important difference between CBAs in the two sectors presented in Figure 16.9 is that more non-climate environmental impacts are being considered regarding transport sector investments than in CBAs of energy sector investments. More

Figure 16.5. **For how many countries have monetary carbon values been reported?**

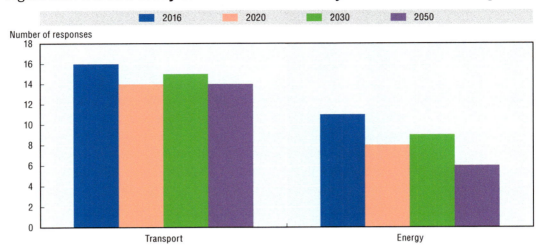

Figure 16.6. **Monetary carbon values used in the transport sector**

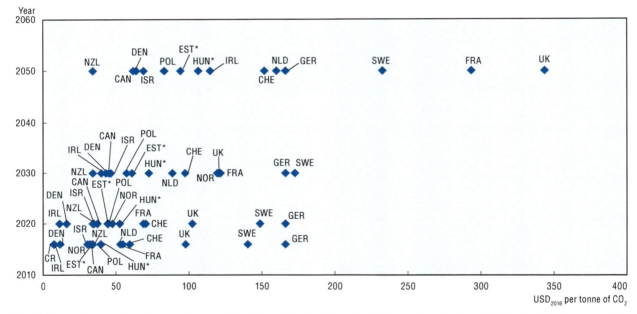

Note: Information regarding the countries marked with an * is taken from the 2014 questionnaire. For the Netherlands, values according to their "high" scenario are shown. Values in a "low" scenario are one quarter of the values shown here. Following the publication of CPB/PBL (2016) in November 2016, assessments should also include "efficient CO_2 prices according to a 2°C scenario". Those values are from 25% to more than 6 times higher than the values from the "high" scenario, cf. Table 2 in CPB/PBL (2016).

than half of the countries that responded to the questionnaire as regards transport sector investments indicated that their CBAs address emissions of PM and NO_x as well as noise, and a third or more of them also address emissions of SO_2 and CO, as well as water pollution and impacts on biodiversity.[10] In relation to energy sector investments, only for NO_x did more than 30% of the replies indicate that this impact was included in the CBAs.

Some countries have defined common values to be used in CBAs for a number of non-climate environmental impacts, but in many cases, these impacts are included in the assessments without commonly defined economic values – if they are included at all. To the

Figure 16.7. **Monetary carbon values used in the energy sector**

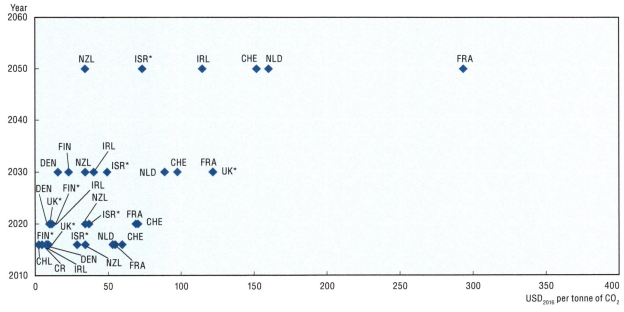

Note: Information regarding the countries marked with an * is taken from the 2014 questionnaire. For the Netherlands, values according to their "high" scenario are shown. Values in a "low" scenario are one quarter of the values shown here. Following the publication of CPB/PBL (2016) in November 2016, assessments should also include "efficient CO_2 prices according to a 2°C scenario". Those values are from 25% to more than 6 times higher than the values from the "high" scenario, cf. Table 2 in CPB/PBL (2016).

Figure 16.8. **Unweighted average of reported monetary carbon values**

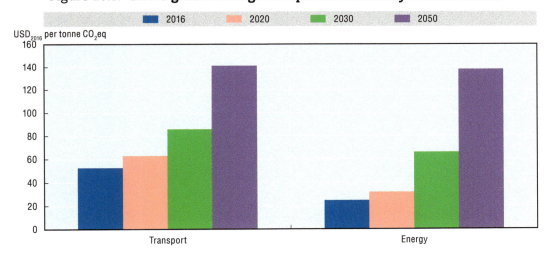

extent that this means that the value of these impacts are not quantified in the CBA, this would be very unfortunate, as in several cases where such impacts *have* been quantified, some of them are very large, e.g. compared with quantified estimates of the economic value of climate change impacts. Non-climate impacts that directly affect human health and mortality can especially have large importance for the outcome of a CBA.

A related issue is the treatment of non-priced impacts in CBAs. In CBA guidelines in for example Norway, considerable emphasis is put on this issue. Methods have been developed to characterise and aggregate non-priced impacts, most of them linked to the environment, and

Figure 16.9. **Which other environmental impacts are typically included in the assessments?**

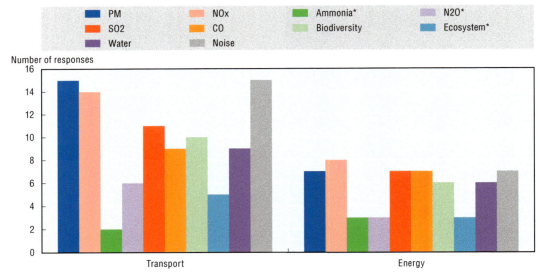

Note: *These impact alternatives were not listed in the 2014 questionnaire.

Box 16.2. **Relative magnitudes of different environmental problems**

The values reported by Israel can be used to illustrate the magnitude of different environmental problems. According to OECD (2015), in 2012, Israel emitted 78 million tonnes of CO_2 equivalents, 182 000 tonnes of NO_x and 174 000 tonnes of SO_2. In the questionnaire used in the preparation of this chapter, the country indicated a value of USD 30.6 per tonne for CO_2 emissions taking place in 2016; USD 22 760 per tonne of NO_x and USD 22 640 per tonne of SO_2. This means that the *total* GHG emissions in the country are valued at around USD 2.4 billion, while the *total* NO_x and SO_2 emissions are valued at USD 4.1 billion and USD 3.9 billion, respectively.

For the outcome of a cost-benefit analysis it is, however, the *change* in the emissions of the different pollutants caused by a project or policy – not the level of total emissions – that are of relevance.

---

guidance is provided on how to integrate these impacts in a CBA. The rule in the Norwegian guidelines is that non-priced impacts should count on par with monetised impacts.

The fact that more non-climate impacts are included in assessments of transport sector investments than in energy sector assessments is probably to a large extent explained by transport activities causing a wider range of impacts than most energy investments; for example, few energy projects will cause high levels of noise affecting many people. However, many energy projects will – directly or indirectly[11] – affect emissions of PM, NO_x and SO_2, but also such impacts are only included in the CBAs in a about 30% of the countries responding to the questionnaire.

Discounting

Regarding both sectors, the large majority of the responding countries indicate that future costs and benefits should be discounted (cf. Figure 16.10), and most of the countries have fixed common discount rates to be used. The reported average discount rate applied

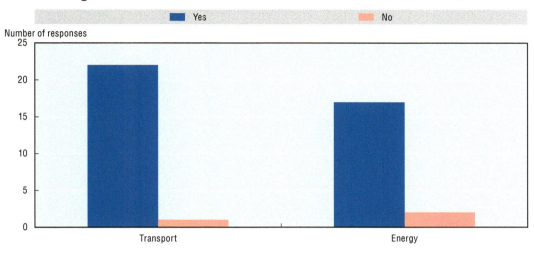

Figure 16.10. **Are future costs and benefits to be discounted?**

in energy sector projects is slightly higher than the average reported for the transport sector – 4.78 vs. 4.64% for impacts occurring in the first 30 years – but this difference is influenced by the fact that it is not exactly the same countries that have provided information about the discount rates to be applied in the two sectors.

A few countries apply lower discount rates for impacts that are expected to occur further out in the future. For example, Denmark apply a 4% real discount rate for impacts occurring in the first 30 years, 3% for impacts occurring after between 30 to 50 years and 2% for even later impacts. Norway does the same. The United Kingdom uses real discount rates of 3.5%, 3% and 2.5%, respectively.[12]

Figure 16.11 illustrates the different discount rates applied to impacts at different times in the transport sector. The average rate referred to above clearly masks a very high degree of variability in the rates applied, with a range stretching from 1.7% to 8.3% being applied to impacts that occur in the first 30 years. This definitively has a very strong impact on the present value of impacts occurring in future years.

For example, if discounted over a 30 year period, an impact worth EUR 20 thirty years from now will have a present value of EUR 12.06 if a discount rate of 1.7% is applied. This is more than a third more than the present value of an impact worth EUR 100 thirty years from now, if a discount rate of 8.31% is applied to the latter, yielding a present value of EUR 9.12. If discounted over a 100 years period, the present value of a future impact of EUR 20 is EUR 3.71 if the discount rate is set to 1.7% – relatively similar to the present value of an impact worth EUR 100 if a discount rate of 3.5% is applied, namely EUR 3.21.

The reported timespans of CBAs in the transport sector are somewhat longer than the reported timespans of energy sector investment assessments. Whereas 60-70% of the assessments of transport sector investment projects take into account impacts occurring for at least 40 years, few, if any, energy sector CBAs include impacts occurring so late. The difference *might* be explained by a stronger "commercial" focus of the energy sector assessments, concentrating much on relatively near-term revenues that the projects might generate. However, e.g. in relation to climate change, many energy projects can have impacts that last much longer than 40 years.

Figure 16.11.   **Real discount rates applied in the transport sector**

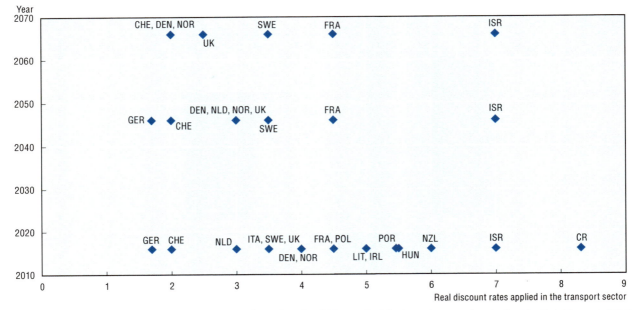

Note: The discount rates shown for 2016 represent those that should be applied for impacts occurring during the first 30 years. Rates shown for 2046 represent those that are to be applied to impacts occurring after between 30 and 50 years, and those shown for 2066 are those that are to be applied to even more distant impacts.

Concerns about distributive impacts are not addressed enough[13]

The two sectors are relatively similar with respect to a question on whether or not CBAs are supposed to address the distributive impacts of the investment projects. Only around a third of the countries responded that addressing such impacts is *compulsory* or done *often*, cf. Figure 16.12. In the energy sector, this was done at least *sometimes* in almost 90% of the responding countries, while one third of the countries responded that this was *rarely* or *never* done in respect to transport sector investments.

Figure 16.12.   **Do the CBAs normally include estimates of the distribution of costs and benefits?**

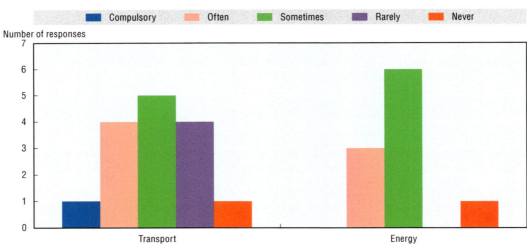

A relatively good independent quality control

The CBAs are normally carried out internally within the respective ministries, by external experts working under contract for these ministries, internally in government transport or energy agencies, or by external experts working for these agencies. The ministries of finance do, for example, generally not seem to be directly involved in the preparation of these investment assessments.

It is, however, relatively common that CBAs of investment projects in these two sectors need to be subject to some form of independent quality control. 55-65% of the respondents in both sectors indicated that this is *compulsory or* done *often*, while most of the remaining respondents said that this was sometimes done regarding transport sector investments. More countries indicated that this was rarely done in connection with energy sector investments, and one country responded that it was never done in this connection. In around 60% of the responses, independent scrutiny of the CBAs was introduced sometime after 2010.[14]

The public is not systematically invited to provide comments on CBAs

It is also relatively common practice to make *ex ante* CBAs of investment projects in these two sectors publicly available (cf. Figure 16.13), but slightly less common invite the public to provide comments on these CBAs (cf. Figure 16.14). In 60-80% of the replies regarding the two sectors it as indicated that it is *compulsory* or *often* done to make the CBAs publicly available, but 15-20% of the responses regarding the transport sector and 6% regarding the energy sector indicated that this is *rarely* or *never* done.

Figure 16.13. **Are the CBAs generally made publicly available?**

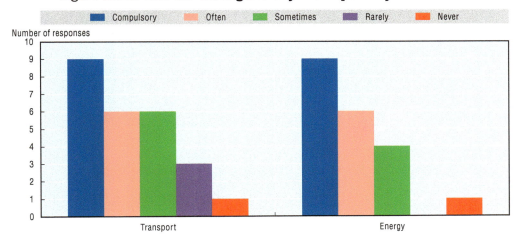

50-60% of the replies said that it was *compulsory* or *often* done to invite public comments, but about 25% of the responses regarding both sectors indicated that public comments were *rarely* or *never* invited. In about 75% of the replies regarding both sectors, it was indicated that it was *compulsory* or *often* done to make the CBAs available to the parliament.[15, 16]

In all the responses regarding both sectors, it was indicated that the influence of the CBAs on the final decisions were as a minimum *moderate*; in some cases it was said to be *large*, or even *very large*, cf. Figure 16.15.[17] In most cases, it was indicated that there has been *no clear trend* regarding the influence of the CBAs over the last 10-15 years,[18] but about 30% of the replies regarding the transport sector suggested that the influence had increased over this time period, cf. Figure 16.16.

Figure 16.14. **Is the public invited to provide comments on CBAs?**

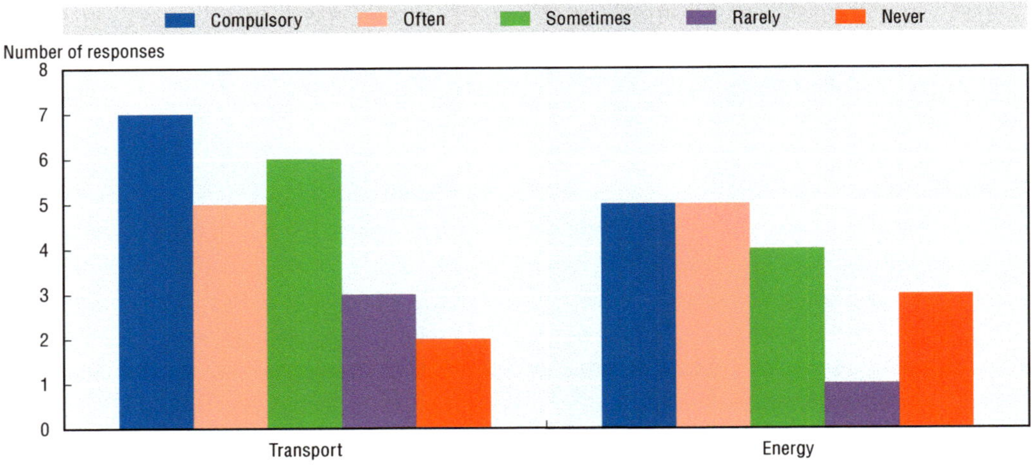

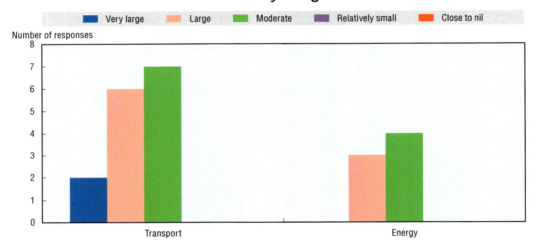

Figure 16.15. **What is typically the impact of CBAs on the political decisions finally being made?**

Figure 16.16. **Have there been any changes in the impacts of CBAs over the last 10-15 years?**

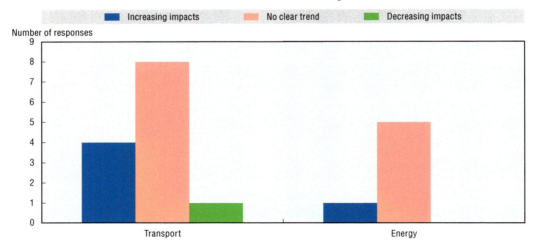

16.2. Current use of cost-benefit analysis in assessments of public policies

This section describes and compares the replies received regarding *ex ante* and *ex post* CBAs of various public policies; this could for example be regulations regarding fuel efficiency standards, proposals regarding stricter vehicle emission standards, the introduction of an environmentally related tax or a cap-and-trade system, etc.[19] Approximately the same number of countries have responded to these parts of the questionnaires as for the public investment projects discussed above, but there are some differences as regards exactly which countries responded.[20]

No *exact* definition of what represents a separate "policy" was provided, so the basis for the responses will vary somewhat – but the responses are thought to represent the treatment of at least "major" policies, for example policies with significant economic impacts.[21]

Criteria for ex ante assessments are more developed than for ex post assessments

The responses received make it clear that the routines for doing *ex ante* policy assessments are much better developed than routines for doing *ex post* assessments – there are clear criteria for how to do CBAs in 75% of the countries in relation to *ex ante* analyses, but only in less than 50% of the countries as concerns *ex post* analyses, cf. Figure 16.17. About two thirds of the countries responded that CBAs had been done regarding *all* or *most* of new (major) policy initiatives whereas *ex post* CBAs have only rarely been carried out in most countries, cf. Figure 16.18.

Figure 16.17. Are there clear criteria for how to do *ex ante* **or** *ex post* **CBAs of public policies?**

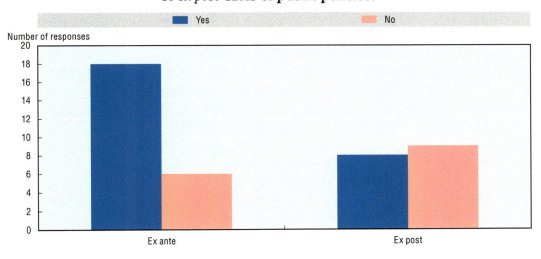

More could be done to take into account environmental impacts in CBAs

In a majority of the responding countries (60-75%) there are not clear rules in place for how to include greenhouse gas emissions in the assessments, neither in relation to *ex ante* nor for *ex post* analyses of public policies, cf. Figure 16.19. However, in relation to policies where changes in GHG emissions can be expected to be of the more important impacts, the situation might be better: In some 40-80% of the cases, countries reply that changes in GHG emissions had been taken into account in *all* or *most* cases, cf. Figure 16.20.[22] It is, however, remarkable that four out of 20 countries that have responded to this question regarding

Figure 16.18. **What is the share of policies in the last 3-5 years that have been CB-analysed?**

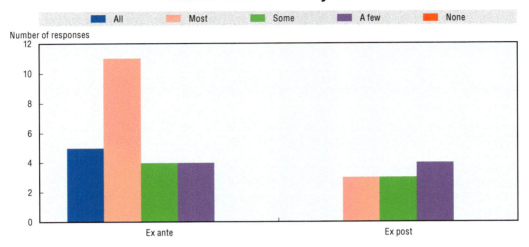

Figure 16.19. **Are there clear criteria for how to include GHGs in CBAs of public policies?**

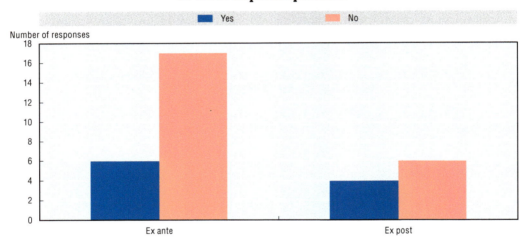

Figure 16.20. **Which share of CBAs in the last 3-5 years has included impacts on GHG?**

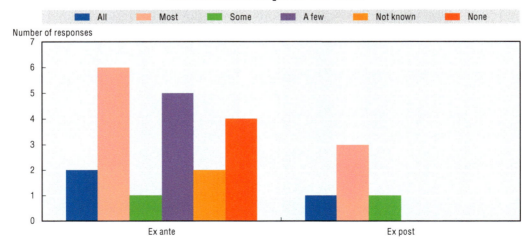

ex ante policy assessments indicate that in no cases have impacts of these policies on GHG emissions been taken into account.

Figure 16.21 illustrates the number of respondents that have provided monetary carbon values to be used in policy assessments for different years; between five and ten have done so with respect to *ex ante* assessments, but only three countries have provided such values in relation to *ex post* policy assessments. Figures 16.22 and 16.23 display the full range of the reported carbon values (using the same scale on the horizontal axis as was used regarding the transport and energy sectors above), and Figure 16.24 shows the unweighted average of the reported values.

Figure 16.21. How many countries have reported monetary carbon values for policy assessments?

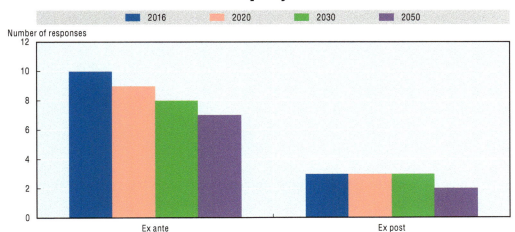

Figure 16.22. Monetary carbon values used in *ex ante* policy assessments

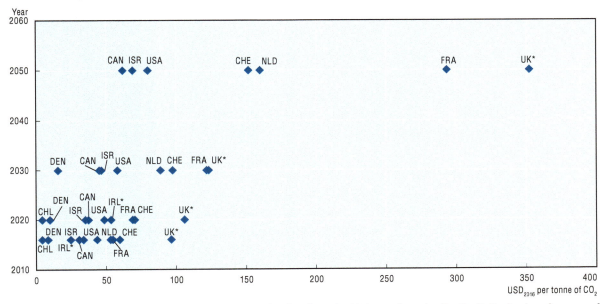

Note: Information regarding the countries marked with an * is taken from the 2014 questionnaire. For the Netherlands, values according to their "high" scenario are shown. Values in a "low" scenario are one quarter of the values shown here. Following the publication of CPB/PBL (2016) in November 2016, assessments should also include "efficient CO_2 prices according to a 2°C scenario" for climate-related policies. Those values are from 25% to more than 6 times higher than the values from the "high" scenario, cf. Table 2 in CPB/PBL (2016).

Figure 16.23. **Monetary carbon values used in** *ex post* **policy and project assessments**

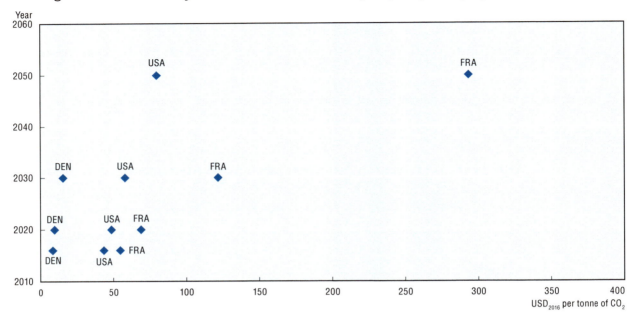

Note: The graph only presents the "central" values used in the United States to date (although agencies were guided to present results using a range of 4 values in *ex ante* regulatory analysis). The guidance in the United States is currently undergoing revision.

Figure 16.24. **Unweighted average of reported monetary carbon values**

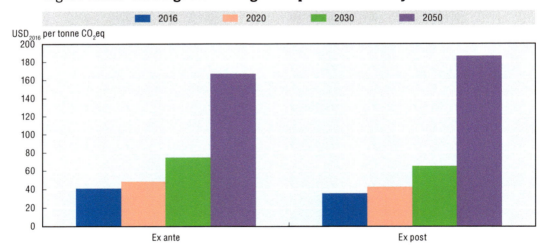

Figure 16.25 illustrates the extent to which environmental impacts other than GHG emissions are being taken into account in *ex ante* and *ex post* policy assessments. While such impacts seem to be relatively well covered in *ex ante* analyses, it is remarkable that only two replies indicate that such impacts are included in *ex post* analyses. As mentioned above, the evidence from studies where a wide range of environmental impacts have been included in policy assessments indicate that impacts on human health – e.g. from PM and NO_x – can be very large compared with quantified estimates of the costs of climate change.[23]

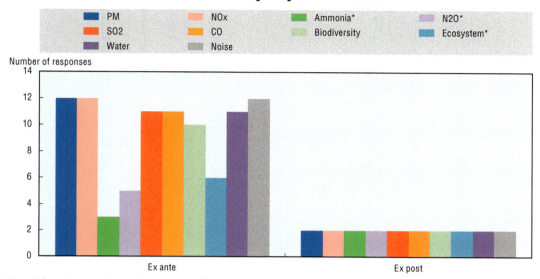

Figure 16.25. **Which other environmental impacts are typically included in the policy assessments?**

Note: *These impact alternatives were not listed in the 2014 questionnaire.

Discounting

Figure 16.26 illustrates the use of discounting in *ex ante* and *ex post* policy assessments. While a number of countries have indicated that discounting is to take place, it is remarkable that four out of the 23 countries that responded to this question said that future costs and benefits in *ex ante* analyses are *not* to be discounted. The robustness of such policy assessments seems very limited.

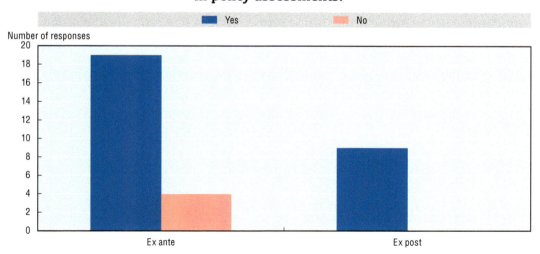

Figure 16.26. **Are future costs and benefits to be discounted in policy assessments?**

The unweighted average of the reported real discount rates are somewhat higher regarding *ex ante* analyses than for *ex post* analyses – 4.46 vs. 4.42% for impacts occurring in the first 30 years.[24] Figure 16.27 spells out the full distribution of the reported discount

Figure 16.27. **Real discount rates applied in** *ex ante* **policy assessments**

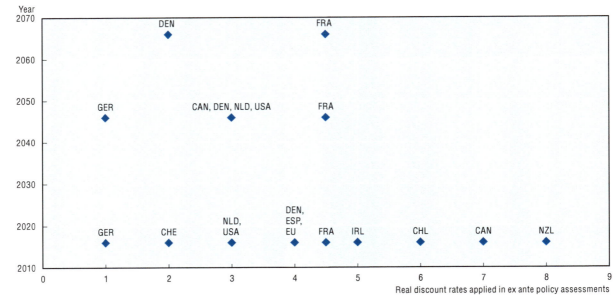

Note: The discount rates shown for 2016 represent those that should be applied for impacts occurring during the first 30 year. Rates shown for 2046 represent those that are to be applied to impacts occurring after between 30 and 50 years, and those shown for 2066 are those that are to be applied to even more distant impacts. In the United States, assessments using a higher discount rate of 7% are also carried out.

rates regarding *ex ante* analyses. As for the sectors discussed in Section 16.1, the range is very wide – which, as mentioned above, can have a very strong impact on the outcome of the policy assessments.

Distributive impacts[25]

Figure 16.28 indicates that it is relatively common for both *ex ante* and *ex post* CBAs of public policies to include estimates of the distribution of costs and benefits. Comparing with Figure 16.12, it also looks as if it is somewhat more common to address such impacts in policy assessments than in assessments of investment projects in the transport and energy sectors.

Figure 16.28. **Do the CBAs normally include estimates of the distribution of costs and benefits?**

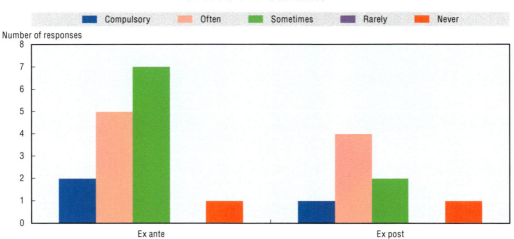

The institutional setting of CBAs

It is typically the respective ministries that carry out the CBAs internally, sometimes also with the help of external experts. However, compared with what was mentioned regarding the transport and energy sectors, the role of the ministries of finance is clearly more important regarding CBAs of public policies.

Figure 16.29 indicates that it is very common to make CBAs of public policies publicly available – and more so than what is the case regarding investment projects in the transport and energy sectors. Figure 16.30 demonstrates that it is also quite common to invite public comments on CBAs of public policies.

Figure 16.29. **Are the CBAs of public policies generally made publicly available?**

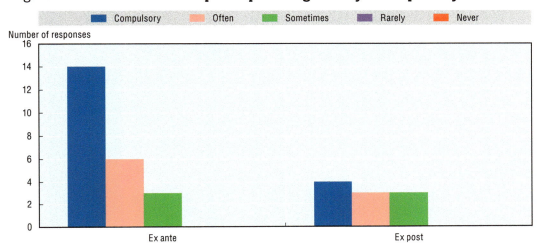

Figure 16.30. **Is the public invited to provide comments on CBAs of public policies?**

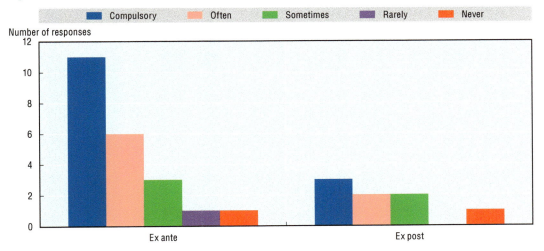

Given the low number of replies, one should be careful in drawing any conclusions, but Figure 16.31 indicates that the CBAs do have some impacts on the current or future policy decisions. Figure 16.32 indicates that there hardly have been any clear trends as regards these impacts over the last 10-15 years.

Figure 16.31. **What is typically the impact of CBAs on current or future political decisions?**

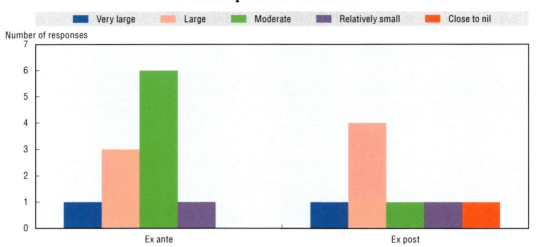

Figure 16.32. **Have there been any changes in the impacts of CBAs over the last 10-15 years?**

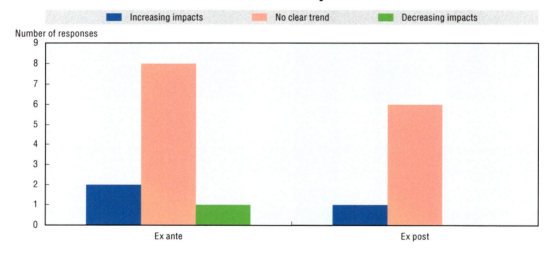

16.3. Cross-cutting comments

This chapter has documented that there are large variations in the extent to which cost-benefit analyses are being carried out, and the extent to which various environmental impacts are being taken into account in these analyses, across economic sectors and across analytical contexts.

Ex ante assessments of public transport sector investments are generally best covered by CBAs, as regards the environmental impacts that are being addressed and the values that are attached to the different impacts. The use of CBAs in this sector dates back many decades, and it is not so surprising that more and more environmental impacts are being taken into account, reflecting increased scientific knowledge and public awareness of the many consequences for the environment and human health that transport activities can entail.

Also energy sector investments and policy *proposals* are relatively well covered in CBAs, but with narrower coverage of non-climate environmental impacts.

The questionnaire responses do not provide much information about the reasons for these differences. However, if the CBA rules largely were developed at a time when a new energy project typically would trigger *additional emissions* of greenhouse gases and other pollutants, could it be that political pressure from often large firms in the energy sector has had a significant impact on the formulation of these rules? Today, an increasing share of energy sector investment projects is likely to have small impacts on such emissions, and some projects can even cause a net reduction of them. Is it possible that these developments will contribute to more focus on the environmental impacts in the projects' assessments, and higher values attached to the different impacts, in the future?

Neither in relation to investment projects nor regarding public policies are *ex post* costs-benefit analyses so well developed.[26] Such analyses could, if they were well executed, provide very useful input for the design and implementation of future investment projects or new public policies, but there is certainly a risk that they primarily are executed in order to attract "praise" for recent projects or policies, or to discredit projects or policies implemented by an earlier government. This indicates that there could be major benefits from institutionalising the implementation of such analyses after a certain amount of time – at least for major projects and policies – and from making some independent, well-respected institution responsible for carrying out the analyses.

The responses received regarding the influence of CBAs on the final decisions did not give a very clear picture. It can therefore be useful to also draw on additional information – which seems to be available mostly regarding the transport sector.

Eliasson et al. (2015) assessed the impact of CBAs on decisions regarding transport sector infrastructure investments in Norway and Sweden. In Norway, they found no evidence that appraisal results affect project selection. Taking voting patterns into account, they could not find any measure of benefits, cost, or efficiency with a significant correlation with project selection, neither in relation to the government's proposals in the National Transport Investment plans, nor as regards the Road Administration's selection of projects. In Sweden, on the other hand, appraisal results seem to affect decisions. Eliasson et al. found that the Swedish Transport Administration's selection was strongly linked to CBA results. The selection made by the politicians in the government, by contrast, was only weakly linked to CBA results, and only for small projects.[27]

However, the situation in Norway might have changed somewhat. In a joint report from the transport agencies and Avinor,[28] prepared as input to the National Transport Plan 2018-2029, it is stated in the foreword that "Socio-economic cost-effectiveness, as well as civil protection and consistent standards and development, have been decisive factors for the investment portfolios", see Avinor et al. (2016).

The replies to the questionnaires discussed above were (naturally) provided by civil servants – not by the people making the final decisions – generally the responsible ministers and the members of parliament, and similar. Civil servants and policy makers can use CBAs in different ways, with different motivations. Mouter (2016) indicates that in relation to the transport sector in the Netherlands, the CBAs of investment projects are mostly disclosed to Parliament at the stage when they serve as background documentation to the minister's decision about "the preferred alternative". Only in exceptional cases is the CBA sent to members of Parliament at an earlier stage.[29] In contrast to members of Parliament, the ministers and the high-level civil servants can receive a draft of a CBA report well in advance. The civil servants will sometimes use CBA in an early stage of the planning practice to assess and optimise project initiatives.

Notes

1. Australia, Austria, Canada, Chile, the Czech Republic, Denmark, France, Germany, Ireland, Israel, Italy, Mexico, Netherlands, New Zealand, Norway, Poland, Sweden, Switzerland, the United Kingdom and the United States have responded to all of or parts of the questionnaire – i.a. depending on the relevance of particular parts of the questionnaire in their institutional setting. In addition, the European Commission and the accession countries Costa Rica and Lithuania responded to that questionnaire. When the term "countries" is being used in the text below, it is referred to the replies from all the respondents.

2. Information regarding Estonia, Hungary, Japan, Spain and Turkey from that questionnaire has been used. In addition, information from this 2014 questionnaire has been used to supplement answers to the more recent questionnaire for some of the countries listed above.

3. When the following text refers explicitly to reply options used in the questionnaire, the terms are placed in *italics*.

4. Examples of guidance documents include Treasury Board of Canada Secretariat (2007), HM Treasury (2011), CPB/PBL (2013), Direction générale des Infrastructures, des Transports et de la Mer (2014), European Commission (2015), New Zealand Treasury (2015), Department for Transport, Tourism and Sport (2016), and Interagency Working Group on Social Cost of Greenhouse Gases (2016). Official Norwegian Reports (2012) also discusses a number of issues in relation to CBAs.

5. In some of the responding countries, almost all investments in the energy sector are carried out by private or public companies operating on a commercial basis. The questionnaire did not address the project assessments carried out by such companies.

6. Cf. Regulation 1303/2013 of the European Parliament and of the Council. The European Commission prepared a new guide to CBA in December 2014. The most important requirements are part of Commission Implementing Regulation no. 207/2015 of 20 January 2015. The guide builds on experience gained in the appraisal of major projects in the previous programming period, from 2007 to 2013, and aims to provide practical recommendations and case studies for the authorities and consultants involved in preparing project documentation, cf. *http://ec.europa.eu/regional_policy/ sources/docgener/studies/pdf/cba_guide.pdf.*

7. Some years ago, a structural reform was introduced in Italy that requires CBA of infrastructural investment projects in the framework of a wider public investments planning reform. Each central ministry was to submit to an *Interministerial Committee for Economic Planning* a master plan which should make consistent all plans for public works under its competence and develop guidelines for the assessment of these projects. However, no ministry has yet developed such guidelines.

8. For the respondents for which only information from the 2014 questionnaire is available, the 2014 carbon values have been assumed to be still valid in 2016, but the numbers for each of the years have been adjusted for changes in the GDP deflator between 2014 and 2016.

9. The validity of this point will depend on whether the given energy project will tend to increase or decrease GHG emissions – i.e. whether the assessment concerns e.g. a coal-fired power plant or a wind turbine park. When assessing the GHG impacts of a given project, it is also important to consider interactions with pre-existing policy instruments. For example, in jurisdictions covered by a binding "cap" on emissions related to electricity generation, new investment projects (in coal-fired generation or in renewables) will not have an impact on total emissions, as long as the "cap" remains unchanged.

10. Impacts on emissions of ammonia and on ecosystem services where not listed as possibilities in the 2014 questionnaire.

11. Indirect impacts can e.g. occur when a renewable power plant replaces a fossil-fuel-based power plant, thus reducing emissions of (also) local air pollutants.

12. Groom and Hepburn (Forthcoming) discusses the introduction of declining discount rates in a few selected countries – and the choice of not introducing such rates in the United States and the Netherlands.

13. This issue was not addressed in the 2014 questionnaire. The comments in this section were based on 13 replies regarding the transport sector and 8 responses concerning energy sector investments.

14. This issue was not addressed in the 2014 questionnaire. The comments in this section were based on 17 replies regarding the transport sector and 11 responses concerning energy sector investments.

15. This issue was covered also in the 2014 questionnaire. The comments here are based on 25 responses regarding the transport sector and 20 regarding the energy sector.

16. It is also important at what point in time a CBA is presented to the parliament. This issue was not addressed in the questionnaire, but is e.g. discussed in Mouter (2016). The author indicates that in the Dutch practice, it happens regularly that CBAs are published very close to the debate which allocates funds to different transport infrastructure projects. For example, "for the two major infrastructure projects which were decided upon in 2014 (...) the CBAs were published one working day and three working days, respectively, before the debate". One can hardly expect the CBAs to have much impact in such cases.

17. However, regarding the energy sector, there were only seven replies to this question, which was not addressed in the 2014 questionnaire. Regarding the transport sector, 15 replies were received.

18. The question asked referred to CBAs "and similar quantified analyses". This does i.a. mean that any shift from the use of CBAs to the use of multi-criteria analyses would not be reflected in the responses.

19. In the questionnaire used, it was indicated that in the part concerning *ex post* analyses, any rules in this regard for both public investment projects and public policies would be of interest. For presentation purposes, the replies received are compared to the part that only addressed *ex ante* policy assessments. However, there is little reason to assume that there are any clear differences in rules pertaining to *ex post* assessments of public investment projects and public policies.

20. For example, whereas the parts on transport and energy sector investment projects were of limited relevance for Federal authorities in the United States, the country provided detailed replies regarding *ex ante* and *ex post* policy assessments.

21. For example, the CBA requirements under the Executive Order 12866 in the United States are more rigorous for "economically significant" regulations with benefits or costs greater than USD 100 million in any given year or which will adversely affect, in a material way, the economy, a sector of the economy, productivity, competition, jobs, the environment, public health or safety, or state, local, or tribal governments or communities.

22. For example, Sweden indicated that while there were no clear criteria for the inclusion of GHG emissions in the analyses, effects that are of large socio-economic significance, such as changes in CO_2 emissions, should routinely be addressed.

23. See for example the assessments prepared by the U.S. Environment Protection Agency of the benefits and costs of the 1990 *Clean Air Act Amendments*, available at *www.epa.gov/clean-air-act-overview/benefits-and-costs-clean-air-act-1990-2020-second-prospective-study*.

24. In addition, Mexico reported a *nominal* discount rate of 12% in both cases.

25. This issue was not addressed in the 2014 questionnaire. The comments in this section were based on 15 replies regarding *ex ante* assessments and 8 responses concerning *ex post* assessments.

26. Dudley (2017) discusses possible reasons for this, with a focus on regulations in the chemicals sector.

27. The Swedish plan was decided in 2010 and covered the period 2010-21. The Norwegian plan was decided in 2012 and covered the years 2014 to 2023.

28. The transport agencies comprise the Norwegian National Rail Administration, the Norwegian Coastal Administration and the Norwegian Public Roads Administration. Avinor is a state-owned limited company running 46 airports and Air Traffic Management services.

29. Eliasson et al. did not discuss the role of the Members of Parliament, but in both Sweden and Norway, information about the cost-benefit ratios of different projects is available to them at an early stage.

References

Avinor et al. (2016), *National Transport Plan 2018-2029*, Avinor, Jernbaneverket, Kystverket, Statens Vegvesen, Oslo, *www.ntp.dep.no/Forside/_attachment/1525049/binary/1132766?_ts=1571e02a3c0*.

CPB/PBL (2013), (Netherlands Bureau for Economic Policy Analysis/Netherlands Environmental Assessment Agency), General Guidance for Cost-Benefit Analysis, CPB/PBL, The Hague, *www.cpb.nl/en/publication/general-guidance-for-cost-benefit-analysis*.

Department for Transport, Tourism and Sport (2016), Common appraisal framework for transport projects and programmes, Department for Transport, Tourism and Sport, Dublin, *www.dttas.ie/sites/default/files/publications/corporate/english/common-appraisal-framework-2016/common-appraisal-framework2016_1.pdf*.

Direction générale des Infrastructures, des Transports et de la Mer (2014), Note technique du 27 juin 2014 relative à l'"évaluation des projets de transport, Ministère de l'"Écologie, du Développement durable et de l'"Énergie, Paris, *www.developpement-durable.gouv.fr/IMG/pdf/Note_technique_ completesignatureok.pdf.*

Dudley, S. (2017), "Retrospective evaluation of chemical regulations", *OECD Environment Working Papers*, No. 118, OECD Publishing, Paris, *http://dx.doi.org/10.1787/368e41d7-en.*

Eliasson, J. et al. (2015), "Does Benefit-Cost Efficiency Influence Transport Investment Decisions?", *Journal of Transport Economics and Policy*, Vol. 49, pp. 377-396.

European Commission (2015), *Better Regulation Guidelines*, Commission Staff Working Document, European Commission, Brussels, *http://ec.europa.eu/smart-regulation/guidelines/docs/swd_br_ guidelines_en.pdf.*

Groom, B. and C. Hepburn (2017), "Looking Back at Social Discount Rates: The Influence of Papers, Presentations, Political Preconditions and Personalities on Policy", *Review of Environmental Economics and Policy*, Volume 11, Issue 2, 1 July 2017, pp. 336-356, *https://doi.org/10.1093/reep/rex015.*

HM Treasury (2011), *The Green Book: Appraisal and Evaluation in Central Government*, HM Treasury, London, *www.gov.uk/government/uploads/system/uploads/attachment_data/file/220541/green_book_complete.pdf.*

Interagency Working Group on Social Cost of Carbon (2016), *Technical Support Document: Social Cost of Carbon for Regulatory Impact Analysis under Executive Order 12866*, August 2016, United States Government, Washington, DC, *www.epa.gov/sites/production/files/2016-12/documents/sc_co2_tsd_ august_2016.pdf.*

New Zealand Treasury (2015), *Guide to Social Cost Benefit Analysis*, New Zealand Treasury, Wellington, *www.treasury.govt.nz/publications/guidance/planning/costbenefitanalysis/guide/.*

OECD (2015), *Environment at a Glance 2015: OECD Indicators*, OECD Publishing, Paris, *http://dx.doi.org/ 10.1787/9789264235199-en.*

Official Norwegian Reports (2012), *Cost-Benefit Analysis, Official Norwegian Reports NOU 2012: 16*, *www.regjeringen.no/contentassets/5fce956d51364811b8547eebdbcde52c/en-gb/pdfs/nou2012201200 16000en_pdfs.pdf.*

Smith, S. and N.A. Braathen (2015), "Monetary Carbon Values in Policy Appraisal: An Overview of Current Practice and Key Issues", *OECD Environment Working Papers*, No. 92, OECD Publishing, Paris, *http://dx.doi.org/10.1787/5jrs8st3nguh-en.*

Treasury Board of Canada Secretariat (2007), *Canadian Cost-Benefit Analysis Guide -- Regulatory Proposals*, Treasury Board of Canada, Ottawa, *www.tbs-sct.gc.ca/hgw-cgf/finances/rgs-erdg/wwad-cqnf/col/ analys/analys-eng.pdf.*

PART IV

Chapter 17

Political economy of cost-benefit analysis

Questions about why patterns of use and influence are how they are bound up with political economy, necessitating a richer understanding of the policy formulation process. If, in the extreme, all decisions were to be made on the basis of CBA, decision makers would have no flexibility to respond to the various influences that are at work demanding one form of policy rather than another. In short, CBA, or, for that matter, any prescriptive calculus, compromises the flexibility that decision makers need in order to "act politically" or meet other policy objectives. Unsurprisingly, this constrains use or shapes the nature of use in particular ways. Political economy then seeks to explain why the economics of the textbook is rarely embodied in actual decision-making and related to this, policy-formulation processes. But explaining the gap between actual and theoretical design is not to justify the gap. So while it is important to have a far better understanding of the pressures that affect actual decisions, the role of CBA remains one of explaining how a decision should look if the economic approach is adopted.

Footnote by Turkey:

The information in this document with reference to "Cyprus" relates to the southern part of the Island. There is no single authority representing both Turkish and Greek Cypriot people on the Island. Turkey recognises the Turkish Republic of Northern Cyprus (TRNC). Until a lasting and equitable solution is found within the context of United Nations, Turkey shall preserve its position concerning the "Cyprus issue".

Footnote by all the European Union Member States of the OECD and the European Union:

The Republic of Cyprus is recognised by all members of the United Nations with the exception of Turkey. The information in this document relates to the area under the effective control of the Government of the Republic of Cyprus.

17.1. Introduction

The methodology of cost-benefit analysis (CBA) has been developed over a long period of time. It has also been subjected to many criticisms, as has its theoretical basis – welfare economics. Nonetheless, most (though certainly not all) economists continue to recommend the use of CBA as a "decision-informing" procedure. Chapter 16, furthermore, indicated findings about substantial use of CBA across OECD countries, at least insofar as certain environment-related policy sectors were concerned. Yet, such evidence on *actual* policy and investment decisions also reveal another story: appraisal processes often downplay the role CBA, despite it commanding consensus among economists, and actual decisions (based perhaps on that appraisal) often are made in a manner that seems to be inconsistent with CBA. One reason for this disparity between theory and practice is fairly obvious: other factors which are important to making a decision often require other tools to be used additionally in impact assessment more generally (see Chapter 18). In some cases these other factors may be deemed more important than information about monetary costs and benefits, and when this further evidence implies a different recommendation to CBA, it will be the latter that "loses out". Nor can governments simply design policy measures without taking account of political and institutional realities. This, in turn, highlights a number of important considerations.

First, what economists may regard as an "optimal" instrument design tends to serve one overriding goal – *economic efficiency*. This demands that other goals are considered also in making actual decisions. Such goals are not necessarily consistent with each other, but play a part in shaping practical policy formulation as well as how specific tools such as CBA are actually used.

Second, government is not simply a guardian of social well-being in the manner usually assumed in CBA textbooks. In fact, while "government" is a convenient umbrella term, this is comprised of a variety of different actors who are internal to the policy formulation process who, in turn, are joined by others who are external to the process but who also have a stake in the outcome. This includes pressure groups and lobbies which, in turn, can represent sets of conflicting interests and objectives.

Third, the above considerations indicate that the political and institutional context in which CBA takes place is complex. And so too is the ability of appraisal actors to negotiate this reality. That is, instead of decision makers being all-knowing and all powerful, those involved in appraisal are better thought of as, to paraphrase Cairney (2016), limited in their ability to generate, as well as process, all of the necessary information ideally needed to make "optimal" decisions. Put another way, these actors are rational (given their objectives) but this rationality is bounded, in interesting ways.

What all of this amounts to is that the "social welfare function" that underlies CBA is not the same as the social welfare function (or functions) that those involved in policy and investment formulation adopt. As a result, actual policy and "optimal" policy need not coincide. Evaluating exactly why this "gap" exists is very much a *political economy* approach to policy analysis and the policy process. This is the subject of this chapter, the remainder of which is structured as follows. It begins by continuing the discussion in Chapter 16 of use and influence of CBA in investment and policy decisions, although some of this relates more generally to its role in impact assessment processes rather than CBA per se. This discussion then moves on to examine possible explanations of such patterns of usage, including the political motives for using (or downplaying or not using at all) CBA. A more realistic view of the "how" and "why" of CBA use should not absolve decision makers from trying to do better, however. Indeed, a number of innovations that move practice in this direction of travel are also discussed.

17.2. CBA in reality: Use and influence revisited

Chapter 16 provided a range of responses by policy actors, in OECD countries, about their use and influence of (environmental) CBA in policy formulation. This revealed a double-edged interpretation. On the one hand, CBA is used (sometimes extensively) and, on the face of it, those involved in this process perceive that it is influential, and so these practical efforts are not in vain. On the other hand, this uptake is not as widespread as it might be, given progress both at the CBA frontier and in translating this progress into practical applications. Such findings broadly accord with those elsewhere in an emerging empirical literature, based on quantitative and qualitative data, which seeks to assess the extent of use of CBA.

For example, evidence on the use of CBA in the World Bank was revealed in an assessment by the Independent Evaluation Group (IEG) (2011). The proportion of World Bank projects using CBA dropped significantly from 1970 to 2000. According to IEG (2011), one (proximate) explanation for this trend was a shift in investment portfolio from policy sectors with a tradition of using CBA (e.g. energy, transport and urban development) to sectors which do not have such a tradition (e.g. education, environment and health). Nonetheless, the IEG report still found a significant reduction in the use of CBA in traditional sectors which the World Bank remains heavily committed towards investing in (e.g. physical infrastructure). Moreover, given the strides made in extending CBA thinking and practice to novel project contexts, a question inevitably arises as to why this progress has not been translated into actual appraisal in these new sectors.

In the United States, a review of 74 impact assessments issued by the US EPA from 1982 to 1999 found that while all of these regulations monetised at least some costs, only about half monetised some benefits (Hahn and Dudley, 2007). Fewer still (about a quarter on average), provided a full monetised range of estimates of benefits although the number doing increased notably over the sample period. This raises important points. Clearly, there is more to do to increase the use of CBA, not least to bring actual practice in line with official guidelines. However, nor is it the case that use of economic appraisal is entirely lacking; it is usually present but often partially implemented.

A logical further question then is whether, when applied, CBA applications were any good in terms of their quality. Some of the indicators assembled by Hahn and Dudley (2007), for the United States, identify a number of relevant issues. For example, even for those (U.S. EPA) applications which estimated costs and/or benefits, it was relatively uncommon for these estimates to be complete (rather than monetising a small sub-set of impacts) and for point estimates to be accompanied by a range (that is, low and high estimates of the value of a given impact).

Moreover, the consideration of different options or alternatives, in cost-benefit terms, was also infrequent. More commonly, practice involved simply comparing some (presumably) favoured single option for a policy change with the status quo. A similar finding emerged from another recent study of EU studies of environmental projects for which financing was requested under regional assistance schemes (COWI, 2011). In other words, the question of what various options (Chapter 2) are under consideration may have been asked at the outset of the appraisal process. However, there is apparently less tangible evidence that CBA was brought to bear on that question at that stage.

There is also valuable information to be gleaned from studies, more broadly, of the impact assessment process. Turnpenny et al. (2015) present evidence of this use – for EU member states as well as the Commission itself – of impact assessments generally rather than more narrowly focusing at CBA. However, as the table indicates some form of CBA is one element of this via use of "monetary assessment". Specifically, the authors look at 325 policy cases involving impact appraisals across 8 political jurisdictions. (These are the Cyprus, Denmark, European Commission, Finland, Greece, Ireland, Poland and the United Kingdom.) In some cases, these assessments appear to be substantial documents, particularly in the case of the European Commission. In other words, either extremely concise writing or rudimentary analysis appears to be the case, at least at face value given average length of each assessment report. Use of monetary assessment is similarly diverse. It ranges from 0% in Cyprus to 92% in the United Kingdom as Table 17.1 indicates. Of course, this does not tell how comprehensive that assessment was in terms of a full CBA. But it likely gives a first impression of the extent to which cost-benefit thinking is developed more formally in the appraisal process.

Table 17.1. **Policy appraisal across selected European jurisdictions**

Country/Organisation (period covered)	Stated motivation for appraisal	No. of impact appraisals	Ave. length of report (pages)	Monetary assessment (%)
Cyprus (2009-11)	Better legislation, reduce administrative burden	20	14	0
Denmark	Better regulation; evidence-based policy-making;	50	2.5	56
European Commission	Better and more efficient regulation; consultation and communication	50	84	44
Finland (2009)	Better regulation; participation and transparency; evidence-based policy-making	50	2.5	18
Greece (2010-11)	Better regulation; consultation, deliberation and participation and transparency; reduce administrative burden	36	17	14
Ireland (2004-10)	Reduce administrative burden; better regulation; evidence-based policy-making; consultation	49	13	45
Poland (2008-10)	Better regulation; evidence-based policy-making; reducing regulatory costs; transparency and consultation	20	7	40
United Kingdom (2007-10)	Reduce administrative burden; transparency and accountability; assess costs and benefits	50	38	92

Source: Adapted from Turnpenny et al. (2015)

CBA was extensively used in 2014 in a Canadian assessment of its air quality management options (Canadian Department of the Environment and Department of Health, 2014).[1] The values estimated included those associated with health improvements as well as a range of environmental values, such as impacts on agricultural productivity (through reductions of ground-level ozone exposure), reduced soiling of residential and commercial buildings (through reductions in ambient air pollution) and improved visibility. This appears to give very high benefit-cost ratios – in the range of 15 to more than 30 – for regulations which increase the environmental standards that (non-transportation) engines, boilers and heaters as well cement production meet. Assuming these values are roughly accurate, this indicates some clear economic merits to tightening these standards. An interesting feature of this analysis is that it is the culmination of a collaborative institutional process involving, amongst others, federal, provincial and territorial governments across Canada.[2]

Howlett et al. (2015) conducts a survey of nearly 3 000 decision-makers in prominent policy departments in Canada at both the Federal and the Provincial levels. This includes those working in sectors in addition to environment: education, finance, health, transport and welfare, among others. Their results indicate that technical analysis including CBA (but also risk analysis and financial impact analysis) is used as extensively in environment as in (most) other departments and that expertise and capacity for making decisions was comparable in that sector with that in other departments. However, environment is more of an outlier in terms of respondents judging that evidence actually informs decision-making in this sector and adequate support and resources to undertake evidence informed work. That is, respondents working in this policy sector were relatively dubious on these criteria compared with those working in other prominent policy sectors.

Further interesting insights emerge where studies have also tried to pinpoint influence of CBA on decisions. For example, IEG (2011) find *relatively* higher returns for World Bank projects for which *ex ante* CBA had been undertaken. Yet, disentangling the influence of appraisal on project outcomes from other confounding factors is a challenge as the IEG report acknowledges. Hahn and Tetlock (2008) review evidence of influence of economic appraisal on a number of health and safety regulations in the United States. This appears to indicate little effect in weeding out regulations which protect life and limb at inexplicably high cost. Moreover, where influence can be identified, CBA has tended to be used to formulate the specific details of an already chosen option. That is, it is more difficult to find examples where CBA has been used to help guide thinking about appropriate policy responses from the outset of the decision process. Therefore, it appears at least in this context, actual applications have not taken advantage of the strength of CBA (and similar technical methods) identified by Turnpenny et al. (2015) which is the possibility to assess options at the design stage of the policy formulation process. By contrast, at least some of the more prominent evidence that exists instead suggest that CBA has been used for fine-tuning design once a policy decision has been made.

That the quality of many CBA applications could fall short, and possibly far short, of good practice might lead to scepticism about whether there is a serious commitment to using economic appraisal to guide policy formulation. There is, however, a risk of concluding too gloomily. So while the point immediately above indicated an absence in some jurisdictions of use of CBA at the outset of policy formulation, there appears significant use of CBA even earlier in the policy cycle in playing an agenda-setting role too. In the United Kingdom, the Stern Review on the Economics of Climate Change (Stern, 2007) and the UK National Ecosystems Assessment (NEA, 2011) are examples of this. Other large-scale ecosystem assessments – such as the TEEB Review (TEEB, 2010) – use benefit assessment to provide important evidence and arguments about what has been lost when ecosystems are depleted and degraded. While not a substitute for policy (which will then require evaluation), this sort of knowledge is important for framing policy thinking and subsequent formulation.

In addition, studies of use and influence are taking stock of what is a moving target given that practice – and its extent – is evolving (more-or-less) continually. There is certainly much more evidence and nuance to unearth as well. Companies in the water industry in England and Wales, for example, make use of social CBA as one element of the investment case that they put forward to the water services regulation authority OfWAT under the periodic pricing reviews that this sector is subject to. This has resulted in a huge grey literature on the practical implementation of stated preference methods – notably approaches based on choice modelling – within the water sector. Lessons about use undoubtedly can be found too in these studies; however, as these data are both proprietary and unpublished (in large part), the extent to which these lessons can be learned easily is more questionable.

17.3. The politics of CBA

The fact that decisions are often inconsistent with, or downplay, CBA can be squared with the reality that, in practice, CBA is only one input to the decision and, in some circumstances, other considerations (as well as analytical tools) trump the thinking that is codified in that economic appraisal. What this means, in practice, needs exploring further and at best a "marker" indicating an urgent need for a more detailed and nuanced understanding of actual policy formulation and how CBA fits into these processes.

Indeed, this policy-making model is, in the words of Adelle et al. (2012, p. 402): "...a far more chaotic model of policy making, in which many actors pursue multiple goals" than is commonly assumed in CBA texts.

For example, the "many actors" referred to might consist of those who are "internal" (to the appraisal process such as serving officials and ministers) or those who are "external" actors (perhaps members of the legislature or external consultants, and so on) (Turnpenny et al., 2015). The "multiple goals" might reflect the various motives these actors have for utilising CBA (or, conversely, downplaying its role). For Dunlop et al. (2010) this helps explain their observations about what they term an "incomplete contract": the mismatch between the codification of assessment requirements in official guidelines and the discretion that appears possible in practice. Much of the debate here in the literature is usually conducted in terms of assessment tools and impact assessment more generally. However, this remains highly relevant for thinking about the issues that pertain to CBA, and thus use of CBA can understood in this context.

As such, Dunlop et al. (2010) identify four motives underlying the usage of assessment tools.

- The first is the one which will arguably be most familiar for cost-benefit practitioners. This is an "instrumental usage", characterised notably by an objective to inform evidence-based policy-making. This fits a more rationalistic approach to using analytical tools for policy formulation.

- Second, there is "political usage". This could refer to situations where appraisal is used by some political entity to exercise control over the policy formulation process. This can take a variety of forms depending on political and institutional context (Turnpenny et al., 2015). But in the U.S. context, Posner (2001) argues that an interpretation of CBA use is that it has been a way in which politicians (e.g. elected political representatives) exercise power over the agencies that formulate policy. This, in turn, might simply be based on wanting to delay decisive (and possibly irreversible) action by the latter until sufficiently satisfied that these actions are consistent with political objectives (Radaelli, 2008).

- Third, there is a "communicative usage" which refers to using an appraisal tool for consultation. Again, this can take a variety of forms from long-standing formal consultation processes to more substantive interactions between some authority and stakeholders, perhaps even involving deliberation. Tools within the policy formulation process, as well as the process itself provide a medium for these interactions, presumably to a greater or lesser extent depending on the characteristics of that tool.[3]

- Lastly, there is a "perfunctory usage" which encapsulates pragmatism, where appraisal is required but not implemented by institutional actors with any conviction. In this sense, appraisal in the policy formulation process exists but reflects perhaps what Radaelli (2008) calls political symbolism: that is, is the use of a particular policy formulation tool "merely" (or perhaps mostly) a "ritual" or simply a "box to tick"?

Table 17.2. **Examples of motives underlying the usage of assessment tools**

	Political	Instrumental	Communicative	Perfunctory
Climate change I – assessment of options for addressing climate change in Europe post-2012 (EC)	X			
Groundwater protection – directive to improve protection of groundwater from pollution (EC)	X			
Air pollution – strategy on air pollution (EC)		X	X	
Landfill – policy for implementation EU Landfill Directive (UK)		X		X
Climate change II – policy on linking Kyoto Protocol project credits to the European Emission Trading Scheme (ETS) (UK)				X
Environment / health – plan for preventative action of environmental sources of health impacts (EC)	X			X

Source: Adapted from Dunlop et al. (2010).

A key point here is that appraisal of a particular proposed action does not need to trace its genesis to one of these motives for usage only. In this respect, Table 17.2 describes the findings of Dunlop et al. (2010) in the context of impact assessment, in the European Commission or within the United Kingdom, more generally (rather than CBA specifically). The table includes those assessments relating to environmental proposals and summarises the motives for usage that the authors were able to ascribe, based on the four types of usage previously defined, and is based on judgements made from a detailed inspection of relevant policy documents and so on. The findings indicate that actual appraisal may reflect more than one of these possible usages, even for the handful of environmental proposals discussed here. Moreover, instrumental usage is not necessarily a motive for appraisal; indeed, on the basis of the table, it is a motive in 2 of the 6 cases illustrated and it is never the sole motive according to Dunlop et al.

While these results relate to impact assessment more generally, the findings possibly do throw light on discussions about the quality of CBA considered in Chapter 16 and the previous section of the current chapter. That is, recognising a broader set of motives underlying the usage of analytical tools such as CBA provide an interpretation of findings about shortcomings in CBA uptake or its quality which have typically been identified in the handful of studies that have posed this question. It also might explain why in practice policy-makers resort to a range of analytical tools for appraisal, that are themselves either incomplete or just as problematic as CBA (if not more so) (see Chapter 18).

As an illustration, recall that for Posner (2001), political usage of CBA might be motivated by a desire for control by politicians of the bureaucracy. In this case, politicians value CBA for reasons other than wishing for actual decisions to be literally bound by its recommendations. Indeed, Posner uses the example of the 1999 Senate Bill in the United States as an example of this flexibility. This mandates that while CBA is undertaken, the proposed action for which the appraisal is done – itself need not be guided by it. Alternatively, political usage might shape the character of a CBA. For example, political agendas about public management, however, may influence the implementation of CBA by perhaps being content with a focus mostly on cost burdens, or benefits from the narrow standpoint of a particular sector of society (e.g. small or medium enterprises, etc.) (Radaelli, 2008).

Put another way, advocacy of CBA – in policy processes, based on non-instrumental usages – does not necessarily require politicians to view its worth as a way of achieving the social goal exemplified in the standard cost-benefit criterion: economic efficiency. In turn, this may also provide an explanation of shortcomings in CBA quality, such as apparently inadequate quantification and valuation of impacts. Adelle et al. (2012) thus ask "quality for whom?" in relation to such judgements about shortcomings. In other words, while the evaluation of actual CBA by economists has been (logically enough), based on their own criteria, what is "good enough" from the perspective of those within the policy process, juggling an array of motives and priorities, might be quite different.

All this has a practical importance too for making recommendations about how the appraisal process can do better. Typically, these proposals have focused on improving guidance and building capacity (i.e. investing in technical expertise). For example, in 2015, the Third Report of the UK Natural Capital Committee (NCC) in advocating better treatment of natural capital in UK public policy recommends that: "The Government should revise its economic appraisal (Green Book), implementing our advice, and as a matter of urgency, apply the revised guidance to new projects." (NCC, 2015, p. 6). Quinet et al. (2013) (for France) also makes substantial recommendations about French guidelines in order to address new appraisal challenges. Such guidance are focal documents and so are important starting points. Yet, the argument in Adelle et al. (2012) is that there are higher level considerations that may ultimately constrain better practice (or simply constrain it living up to what is currently intended to do). Relieving these constraints – which might otherwise lead to watered down forms of CBA – is likely to be a considerable challenge, however, raising questions about political leadership, institutional context and bureaucratic culture.

Similarly, capacity and expertise may also constrain both acceptance and use of CBA given that it requires an input of time and effort in order to understand the underlying rationale and some of the technical details. Hertin et al. (2009) note a trend in countries such as the United Kingdom and Germany, for internal actors (e.g. serving officials) in appraisal processes to deal less frequently with policy matters in the substantive areas in which they had trained or had very little training in formal policy analysis. One distinguished economic advisor in the United Kingdom remarked, for example, on the distinction between:

> "the theorists who seek to trap the inner secrets of the economy in their models and the practitioners who live in a world of action where time is precious, understanding is limited, nothing is certain and non-economic considerations are always important and often decisive" (Cairncross, 1985).

CBA, with its elaborate theoretical underpinnings and reasonably well-defined but extensive rules for valid implementation, may therefore be too complex for the busy civil servant wrestling with a complex array of policy motives. The situation will be worse where economic advice or expertise is regarded as an "appendage" to higher-level decision-making. There are two views of such situations: (a) that they reflect a poor understanding of the relevance of CBA, and economic techniques in general, or (b) that the decision-making structure itself reflects the distrust that is felt about economic evaluation techniques. The former view seems easier to fix than the latter, although the political literature on CBA (and impact assessment, more generally) appears to suggest that it is these trickier issues that really matter insofar as these constrain use.

Howlett et al. (2015) emphasise an important grouping of external actors involved in the appraisal process that must have had some role in easing this constrain. These are analysts, including consultants on the outside but working for governments on its policy analysis. In the context of environmental CBA, this might include undertaking environmental valuation (whether estimating primary or secondary monetary values) and preceding stages (such as estimation of physical parameters to be valued) or subsequent steps in the CBA process. As Howlett et al. note, this work undertaken by well-trained external personnel might even supplant internal analysis. In this way, capacity and technical expertise are being outsourced, on the one hand relieving capacity constraints, on the other hand presumably raising interesting issues about the governance of this outsourcing process.

It is important to acknowledge that situating CBA in these wider considerations about the policy formulation process does not inevitably mean that it will fall short in the core mission that cost-benefit practitioners envisage for it. Adelle et al. (2012), for example, wonder whether political controversy can be lessened, and so more easily resolved, by transferring a contested issue into a technocratic context such as CBA. On the fact of it, use of CBA might be a means to reduce the influence of special interest groups in the formulation process. Assuming those interest groups are not purely "honest brokers" in that process, this might be viewed as no bad thing (see, for example, Posner, 2001). Alternatively, CBA could be an avenue for interested parties, outside of Government, to monitor an agency and its proposals, offering some additional tier of scrutiny (Radaelli, 2008).

A possible example of this in the United Kingdom is the appraisal of HM Government proposals for a proposed investment linking London with the Midlands and North of England by high speed rail network (HS2). CBA formed part of the official case for government financial support and significant scrutiny of the official CBA of HS2 by those opposed to the scheme. Discussion focussed on costs which were left out of the appraisal; particularly the landscape changes and biodiversity losses that the new infrastructure may cause. Debate has also surrounded the estimation of time savings for business travellers that a faster train service provides. What is interesting here is the way in which cost-benefit arguments have contributed to shaping this debate and, moreover, the economic content of this debate has not been the sole preserve of technical experts.

17.4. Incentives, behaviour and CBA

Another way in which CBA quality might be assessed is by asking: "how accurate is it?". Testing this might involve first of all a mechanical exercise to compare the results of *ex ante* and *ex post* CBA studies of the same intervention. An *ex ante* CBA is essentially a forecast of the future: estimating likely net benefits in order to inform a decision to be made. *Ex post* CBA – i.e. conducting further analysis of costs and benefits of a project at a later stage – can be viewed therefore as a "test" of that forecast. That is, what can be learned – e.g. for future, similar applications or the accuracy with which CBA is undertaken generally – with the benefit of this hindsight? Actual use of CBA is less common than use of economic appraisal ex ante. But there are some important exceptions. For example, Meunier (2010) documents extensive official use of *ex post* CBA for transport infrastructure investments in France going back a number of years.

Such assessments can provide useful and additional insights which could improve the way the *ex ante* CBA is done (and its findings interpreted) (Meunier, 2010, Quinet et al., 2013). Flyvbjerg et al. (2003) provide a meta-study of the *ex ante* and *ex post* costs of transport infrastructure investment in Europe, USA and other countries (from 1920s to 1990s). The results are revealing: *ex post* cost escalation affected 90% of the projects that they examined. Nor are cost escalations a thing of the past according to these data. HM Treasury (2018) for example provides guidance for incorporating such findings into actual appraisal through official premia on investment costs (and timetables to completions) in the case of physical infrastructure projects. However, the direction of bias is not uniform across policy contexts. The opposite can be found in the case of environmental policy regulations. For example, MacLeod et al. (2009) find evidence across the EU for lower regulatory costs *ex post* (than predicted ex ante), a finding they attribute to firms affected by these burdens finding more cost-effective ways of complying with policy. For the United States, however, Hahn and Tetlock (2008) find no systematic evidence of such bias for environmental regulations.

Addressing cost optimism in public investment projects (or more generally appraisal optimism) might start from at least two points. One is to "live with it". This is the UK procedure in that it is recommended in official guidance to build in a "premium" to estimated capital and operating costs of e.g. public projects involving investment in infrastructure. A second response is to "overcome it". That is, to see it as a technical result of poor analysis, and seek to do better through more training for practitioners and so on. However, discussions about such matters clearly also need to consider the "political economy of CBA" and behavioural incentives that actors in this process face. This is a point made by De Rus (2011) in the context of rail projects: demand forecasts always seem too high and cost forecasts always seem to be too low, all viewed from an *ex post* perspective. Forecasting is undoubtedly challenging and so may result in these technical errors being made. However, strategy and incentives possibly plays its part as well.

For example, Florio and Santori (2010) look at the issue of appraisal optimism in the context of the EU appraisal of the Cohesion and Structural Funds disbursed as part of its regional policy.[4] An issue arises here because in making its decision to approve financing for projects, the EU is reliant on the information (about costs and benefits) that it receives from those in eligible regions proposing investments (such as in transport or environmental infrastructure). This might be a regional or national authority which in turn could be using information provided by private agents (e.g. a contractor of some description).

A member country or regional jurisdiction (that is eligible for EU funds) proposes a project. To substantiate this request for assistance, the jurisdiction must firstly determine the net present value (NPV) of the project on social CBA terms. If the social NPV>0, then it is required to do a financial analysis of the cash flows associated with the project. If the financial NPV>0, the EU will not (co)finance the project, on the grounds that the project pays its own way. Only if the financial NPV<0, will the EU consider financing part of the funding gap that exists.

COWI (2011) illustrates the incentive problem starkly here in the following quotation from a EU Member State representative that appraisal is: "… a matter of making the financial analysis look as bad as possible in order to increase the funding need, and to make the economic analysis to look as positive as possible in order to justify the public funding" (p. x). There is an increasing suspicion that such incentives could explain a lot of what might have been previously thought to be simply an analytical shortcoming.

How is the suggested appraisal bias possibly an issue of the incentives that policy actors that CBA process face? One problem is that inevitably the EU, as "principal" in this appraisal process, has limited ability to assess the veracity of the social and financial CBA presented as part of the case put by the jurisdiction as the "agent". For example, imposing this sort of scrutiny is costly and, anyhow, assessors inevitably have bounded rationality (limited time and ability, given other pressing priorities). To the extent that there is scope for (and willingness to) exaggerate financial costs and social benefits, then this institutional context could provide the ingredients for this to happen.

Addressing this has to involve altering these incentives. Some of this has been introduced into the process already with "co-financing". For example, some of the burden of cost inefficiency falls on those jurisdictions now sharing the burden of paying for the project along with the EU. Florio and Sartori (2010) propose *ex post* accountability as an additional instrument. That is, if a jurisdiction knows there is a good prospect that its appraisal process will be scrutinised *ex post* and that this scrutiny will be highly likely to result in any shortcomings being exposed and possibly "punished" in some way, then incentives to do the *ex ante* assessment properly, in the first place, are heightened.

Of course, these are important "ifs" and "ands". While punishment or reputational risk presumably will be a concern for the agent, whether the principal is really prepared to play the role of accuser, to this extent, is another matter. Put another way, this may be either unfair (because inaccuracy arose for unknown reasons beyond the agent's control) or politically difficult. More generally, whether *ex post* studies can be routinely undertaken is an open question. There may be little appetite amongst politicians for adding costly *ex post* studies to look at decisions which are literally history and a potential source of political embarrassment (Hahn and Tetlock, 2008). That said, serious consideration of the political economy of CBA, in this way, is to be welcomed as a way of improving the CBA process.

17.5. Improving the process of appraisal

Of course, explaining shortcomings in actual CBA, relative to the ideal, while important does not justify them and the role of CBA remains one of explaining how a decision should look if the economist's conception of this approach is adopted. The question then is what implications these explanations have to shape actual CBA more in the mould of the latter. An important notion here is the institutional infrastructure that might help this process. This must include ground-rules for practical CBA applications – i.e. mandated use, guidelines, manuals, etc. – as well as technical capacity. But, as the discussion in previous sections indicated, this is unlikely to be enough in itself.

Equally, if not more, crucial then is strengthening other aspects of the process by which CBA is done. This might include formal institutions to scrutinise (and rate) the quality of appraisals. For example, impact assessment in the EU is one prominent area of this and itself reflects an ongoing process with the most recent guidelines strengthening the potential role for CBA (European Commission, 2009a, b). This now requires that the executive summaries of Impact Assessment (IA) reports "… provide a clear presentation of the benefits and costs (including appropriate quantification) of the various options …" (p1). This is supplemented for more prominent CBAs in the EU IAs by more detailed guidance on assessing and valuing non-market impacts. But an interesting innovation to all of this architecture of economic appraisal is the addition of independent scrutiny of IA conclusions and appraisal via an independent Regulatory Scrutiny Board (RSB), formerly the Impact Assessment Board.

The RSB, in its original form, was established in 2007 to have a role in evaluating formal impact assessment of policies (rather than projects). This is a substantive role, as a positive decision by this body is needed for a proposal which is the subject of the impact assessment to be presented to the European Commission. The RSB is able to demand improvements in the assessment evidence as well as require a resubmission of the evidence, in the light of these revisions. A recent example of an IA subject to this scrutiny is European Commission (2013a) which sets out options for institutional rules to develop unconventional energy resources (e.g. shale gas) in Member States (including a potential new Directive if current legislation, particularly on environmental protection, is deemed insufficient). Important aspects of this appraisal that the RSB opinion document (European Commission, 2013b) focuses on asking for clearer identification of economic benefits (both in terms of assessing impacts on economic activity and fiscal revenues) and a greater consideration of costs and benefits of options more generally (as well as specific queries about how compliance cost estimates were calculated for those data which were presented in the original IA).

Table 17.3 summarises the percentage of assessments which the RSB required to be resubmitted. Notably, the number of required resubmissions initially increased since its establishment and has not appeared to have exhibited any noticeable decline in subsequent years, although clearly the series here is limited given the novelty of this institution. The number of IA submitted is, however, noticeably less in 2014 and 2015. Interestingly, the problems raised do not appear to have changed much in recent evaluations of these IAs (e.g. 2012-15) compared with earlier verdicts. Banable (2013) summarises some of the key issues which emerged from the scrutiny work that this body undertook in the period 2009 to 2012. Amongst the most prominent and frequent conclusions on the quality of IAs generally have been issues identified with the analysis of impacts, definitions of project objectives, baselines and options, as well as the assessment of economic impacts.

Table 17.3. **Percentage of assessments which had to be resubmitted**

	2007	2008	2009	2010	2011	2012	2013	2014	2015
% Re-submission requested	9%	33%	37%	42%	36%	47%	41%	40%	48%
No. of IA initially submitted	102	135	79	66	104	97	97	25	29

Source: Regulatory Scrutiny Board (2015).

In the United Kingdom, the Regulatory Policy Committee (RPC) is a roughly analogous institution to the RSB. All its information and reports are online publicly available, which provides some transparency for "outsiders" to view the committee's work. A key element of this work, however, is that its remit focuses on the evidence for the business case as well as the impact of a proposal for business interests (and charitable or voluntary bodies). Obviously, this is different from scrutinising the evidence for the social case, perhaps one based on standard CBA. Nevertheless, its recommendations are based on detailed scrutiny. For example, in its evaluation of the UK plastic bag tax (RPC, 2014), which would require retailers to charge for use of (disposable) plastic bags by their customers, the RPC questioned the assumption in the cost-benefit analysis conducted by Defra that revenues from the tax would be passed on to charities (rather than boost business profits) and that cost savings would be passed on to consumers.

On the face of it, the verdicts of the RPC have teeth. Ultimately it confirms or rejects the evidence put before it, given its terms of reference (judgements about the costs and benefits to business, the quality of the evidence, and so on). The RPC assessment of a Defra proposal on biodiversity offsetting (RPC, 2013) goes further in its criticisms, giving it a "red rating" as not fit for purpose. In particular, this verdict picked up on an apparent lack of provision for enforcement and monitoring, as well as the increased costs the proposal would impose on developers (given the policy was partly targeted on requiring property developers to offset the loss of greenspace and biodiversity resulting from their construction projects).

The UK and EC RSB cases are not unique; other examples exist for other countries too, such as France (see, for example, Quinet et al., 2013). Indeed, a large number of OECD countries have some form of similar institutional structures some of which are at arm's length from Government (see OECD, 2015). Further evidence of scrutiny at the EU level can also be seen in the institutions of the Chemicals Directive (i.e. REACH, see for example, European Commission, 2007). Under this regime, the use of (new and existing) chemicals by industry is licenced with these permissions only approved if an applicant can show that the net social benefits are positive.

The creation of these institutions might be viewed as a positive development. At the very least, it allows routine evidence to be collected about the quality of appraisals and in both the cases above made available to a potentially wide audience. And while the RSB's reports make for sobering reading about recent IA quality, the existence of this institution provides a platform as well as the incentives for doing better in the future. All of these measures could have an important influence on the quality of CBA from the outset (e.g. if poor quality or inadequately detailed appraisals become more likely to rejected).

It is important to ask critical questions as well. The membership of the RSB, while independent and full-time, appears to be former high-level officials in economic, social and environmental decision-making in the EU. A natural question to ask is to what extent members should be representative of the diverse actors in the appraisal process and what the composition should be between "internal" and "external" actors in that respect. One other issue is that any such body is reliant on information provided and proper scrutiny, as EU cohesion funds example indicates, is both costly and difficult (see Florio and Sartori, 2010).

Another interesting question surrounds the underlying motive for these institutions: that is, is it simply better practice for "instrumental usage" reasons or is it something else, such as to exercise political control and perhaps limit proposals. Hence, while this is pure speculation currently, one question might be whether a fall in the number of IA being submitted (such as that in Table 17.3) is due to a possibly "chilling effect" of this scrutiny and, moreover, whether that effect is an anticipated (deliberate) consequence of its design. In the case of the RPC, the terms of reference more overtly point (at least in some respect) to "political usage" given its emphasis within an apparent deregulation agenda. The RPC itself appears aware of this, as well as the dynamic effect this might have on the evidence it sees. An example of this recognition is a report on the RPC's work by the (Parliamentary) Public Accounts Committee (PAC, 2016). This notes both a RPC finding that, in 2014, only one third of cases it examined had satisfactory assessment of social costs and social benefits and the fact that this body has no power to influence this by rejecting these assessments, for example (given its remit to focus on regulatory (net) costs to business). Put this way, given these weak incentives it is not surprising that policy proposers provide incomplete or sub-par evidence on social benefits (despite this being a requirement and the subject of numerous guideline documents, starting with HM Treasury, 2018, and so on). Of course, RPC's reach – or some other organisational body – could be broadened in this way to correct that imbalance.

Greater uptake of CBA, of course, could depend also on how practical and accessible the tool is to routine use. Renda et al. (2013) provide an assessment of the role and use of IA methods amongst EU Member States and beyond and discuss critically how different approaches might be routinely used. That judgement is based on a range of criteria, including burdens imposed by data requirements and whether applications can be done by generalists or only those with access to specialist skills (of using economic models, and so on). Responding to policy needs in a timely way is an important attribute for appraisal processes to be judged against. In this respect, the growing breadth and depth of environmental valuation databases is a notable development. This includes the pioneering EVRI database (Environmental Valuation Reference Inventory) maintained by authorities in Canada (*www.evri.ca*) (see Chapter 6).

In the United Kingdom, the Environment Agency is using CBA to consider options for compliance with the EU's Water Framework Directive. An interesting feature of these appraisals is that much of the detailed appraisal work is undertaken by dozens of environment officers – with little previous training in economic approaches – working in relatively local river management catchments. In this case, local knowledge of ecological conditions is combined with valuation data which has been collated more centrally. What this means is that if the data provision challenge can be surmounted, transforming this into meaningful appraisal need not be the preserve of the economic specialist.

17.6. Conclusions

CBA works with a very precise notion of *economic efficiency*. A policy is efficient if it makes at least some people better off and no-one worse off, or, far more realistically, if it generates gains in well-being for some people in excess of the losses suffered by other people. In turn, well-being is defined by people's preferences: well-being is increased by a policy if gainers prefer the policy more than losers "disprefer" it. Finally, preferences are measured by willingness-to-pay (accept) and this facilitates aggregation across the relevant population: the numeraire is money. The underlying social welfare function consists of the aggregate of individuals' changes in well-being and would typically take a form such as the following:

$$\Delta SW = \sum_{i,t} \Delta W_{i,t}$$ where Δ signifies "change in", W is well-being and ΔW can be positive for

some individuals and negative for others, i is the ith individual and t is time (discounting is ignored, for convenience). For a policy to pass a CBA test, ΔSW must be positive.

Political economy suggests that actual decisions are not made on the basis of this social welfare function. While simplistic as it stands, this immediately explains why CBA may be rejected or its use (and character) falls short at the political level: it simply fails to capture the various pressures and motives for usage amongst governments in making decisions. The essential point is that the textbook recommendation is formulated in a context that is wholly different from the political context. CBA is, quite explicitly, a normative procedure. It is designed to prescribe what is good or bad in policy-making. But politics can be thought of as the art of compromise, of balancing the various public and specialised interests embodied in what might be termed as a "political welfare function".

If, in the extreme, all decisions were to be made on the basis of CBA, decision makers would have no flexibility to respond to the various influences that are at work demanding one form of policy rather than another. In short, CBA, or, for that matter, *any* prescriptive calculus, can compromise the flexibility that decision makers need in order to "act politically".[5] Unsurprisingly, this constrains use or shapes the nature of use in particular ways, as discussed in this Chapter. Political economy then seeks to explain why the economics of the textbook is rarely embodied in actual decision-making and related to this, policy-formulation processes. But explaining the gap between actual and theoretical design is not to justify the gap. So while it is important to have a far better understanding of the pressures that affect actual decisions, the role of CBA remains one of explaining how a decision should look if the economist's social welfare function approach is adopted.

Notes

1. See: *www.gazette.gc.ca/rp-pr/p1/2014/2014-06-07/html/reg2-eng.html* (accessed December 2017).

2. See: *www.ccme.ca/en/resources/air/aqms.html* (accessed December 2017).

3. The discussion in Chapter 16 of countries' current practices regarding the publication of CBAs in different contexts is of relevance here.

4. The EU Structural & Cohesion Funds (SCF) disbursed more than EUR 300 billion over the period 2007-13. How parties applying to the SCF should carry out CBA is illustrated in a guidance document (European Commission, 2008).

5. European Parliament (2018) includes the following statement in a draft opinion on the interpretation and implementation of the interinstitutional agreement on Better Law-Making:

   "The Committee on the Environment, Public Health and Food Safety calls on the Committee on Legal Affairs and the Committee on Constitutional Affairs, as the committees responsible, to incorporate the following suggestions into its motion for a resolution:

   …

   Impact assessments

   8. Reiterates its call for the compulsory inclusion in all impact assessments of a balanced analysis of the medium- to long-term economic, social, environmental and health impacts;

   9. Stresses that impact assessments should only serve as a guide for better law-making, and as an aid for making political decisions, and should in no event replace political decisions within the democratic decision-making process, nor should they hinder the role of politically accountable decision-makers;

   10. Considers that impact assessments should not cause undue delays to legislative procedures, nor should they be utilised as procedural obstacles in an attempt to delay unwanted legislation;

   …".

References

Adelle, C., A. Jordan and J. Turnpenny (2012), "Proceeding in Parallel or Drifting Apart? A Systematic Review of Policy Appraisal Research Practices", *Environment and Planning C: Government and Policy*, Vol. 30, pp. 401-415, *http://dx.doi.org/10.1068/c11104*.

Banable, S. (2013), "The European Commission Impact Assessment System", Paper presented to the Conference on Theory and Practice of Regulatory Impact Assessments in Europe", Paris, June 2013.

Cairncross, A. (1985), "Economics in theory and practice", *American Economic Review*, Vol. 75, pp. 1-14, *www.jstor.org/stable/1805562*.

Cairney, P. (2016), *The Politics of Evidence-based Policy Making*, Palgrave Macmillan, London.

COWI (2011), *Report on Ex-post evaluation of Environmental Cohesion Fund Projects 2003-2008*, European Commission, Directorate-General Regional Policy, Brussels.

de Rus, G. (2011), *Introduction to Cost-Benefit Analysis, Looking for Reasonable Shortcuts*, Edward Elgar, Cheltenham.

Dunlop, C.A. et al. (2012), "The Many Uses of Regulatory Impact Assessment: A Meta-Analysis of EU and UK Cases", *Regulation and Governance*, Vol. 6, pp. 23-45, *http://dx.doi.org/10.1111/j.1748-5991.2011.01123.x*.

European Commission/DG ENV (2013a), *An Initiative on an Environment, Climate and Energy Assessment Framework to Enable Safe and Secure Unconventional Hydrocarbon Extraction*, European Commission, Brussels.

European Commission/Impact Assessment Board (2013b), *Opinion on 'DG ENV – An Initiative on an Environment, Climate and Energy Assessment Framework to Enable Safe and Secure Unconventional Hydrocarbon Extraction'*, European Commission, Brussels.

European Commission (2009a), *Impact Assessment Guidelines*, SEC(2009)92, European Commission, Brussels, *http://ec.europa.eu/smart-regulation/impact/commission_guidelines/docs/iag_2009_en.pdf*.

European Commission (2009b), *Memo: Main Changes in the 2009 Impact Assessment Guidelines Compared with 2005 Guidelines*, European Commission, Brussels, *http://abrio.mee.government.bg/upload/docs/revised_ia_guidelines_memo_en.pdf*.

European Commission (2007), *Reach In Brief*, European Commission, Brussels, *http://ec.europa.eu/environment/chemicals/reach/pdf/publications/2007_02_reach_in_brief.pdf*.

European Parliament (2018), *Draft opinion of the Committee on the Environment, Public Health and Food Safety for the Committee on Legal Affairs and the Committee on Constitutional Affairs on the interpretation and implementation of the interinstitutional agreement on Better Law-Making*, European Parliament, Brussels, *www.europarl.europa.eu/sides/getDoc.do?type=COMPARL&reference=PE-615.308&format=PDF&language=EN&secondRef=01*.

Florio, M. and D. Sartori (2010), "Getting incentives right, do we need ex post CBA?", *Working Paper No. 01/2010*, Centre for Industrial Studies, Milan.

Flyvbjerg, B., M.K. Skamris Holm and S.L. Buhl (2003), "How common and how large are cost overruns in transport infrastructure projects?", *Transport Reviews*, Vol. 23(1), pp. 71-88, *http://dx.doi.org/10.1080/01441640309904*.

Hahn, R.W. and P.M. Dudley (2007), "How well does the U.S. Government do benefit-cost analysis?", *Review of Environmental Economics and Policy*, Vol. 1(2), pp. 192-211, *https://doi.org/10.1093/reep/rem012*.

Hahn, R.W. and R.C. Tetlock (2008), "Has economic analysis improved regulatory decisions?", *Journal of Economic Perspectives*, Vol. 22(1), pp. 67-84, *http://dx.doi.org/10.1257/jep.22.1.67*.

Hertin, J. et al. (2009), "Rationalising the Policy Mess? Ex Ante Policy Assessment and the Utilisation of Knowledge in the Policy Process", *Environment and Planning A*, Vol. 41, pp. 1185-1200, *http://dx.doi.org/10.1068/a40266*.

HM Treasury (2018), *The Green Book: Central Government Guidance on Appraisal and Evaluation*, HM Treasury, London, *www.gov.uk/government/uploads/system/uploads/attachment_data/file/220541/green_book_complete.pdf*.

Howlett, M. et al. (2015), "Policy Formulation, Policy Advice and Policy Appraisal: The Distribution of Analytical Tools", in Jordan, A. and J. Turnpenny (eds.), *The Tools of Policy Formulation: Actors, Capacities, Venues and Effects*, Edward Elgar, Cheltenham.

Independent Evaluation Group (IEG), (2011), *Cost-Benefit Analysis in World Bank Projects*, World Bank, Washington, DC, *https://ieg.worldbankgroup.org/Data/Evaluation/files/cba_full_report1.pdf*.

Macleod, M. et al. (2009), *Understanding the Costs of Environmental Regulation in Europe*, Edward Elgar, Cheltenham.

Meunier, D. (2010), *Ex post evaluation of transport infrastructure projects in France: Old and new concerns about assessment quality*, Laboratoire Ville Mobilité Transports, Université Paris-Est, *www.civil.ist.utl.pt/ContentPages/694954807.pdf*.

NCC (Natural Capital Committee) (2015), *State of Natural Capital*, Natural Capital Committee, London.

OECD (2015), *OECD Regulatory Policy Outlook 2015*, OECD Publishing, Paris, *http://dx.doi.org/10.1787/9789264238770-en*.

PAC (House of Commons Committee of Public Accounts) (2016), *Better Regulation: Eighteenth Report of Session 2016-17*, House of Commons, London, *www.publications.parliament.uk/pa/cm201617/cmselect/cmpubacc/487/487.pdf*.

Posner, E.A. (2001), "Controlling Agencies with Cost-Benefit Analysis: A Positive Political Theory Perspective, *The University of Chicago Law Review*, Vol. 68(4), pp. 1137-1199.

Quinet, É. et al. (2013), *Cost-Benefit Analysis of Public Investments: Summary and Recommendations*, Report of the Mission Chaired by Émile Quinet, Commissariat Général à la Stratégie et à la Prospective, *www.strategie.gouv.fr/sites/strategie.gouv.fr/files/atoms/files/cgsp-calcul_socioeconomique_english4.pdf*.

Radaelli, C.M. (2009), "Rationality, Power, Management and Symbols: Four Images of Regulatory Impact Assessment", *Scandinavian Political Studies*, Vol. 33(2), pp. 164-188, *http://dx.doi.org/10.1111/j.1467-9477.2009.00245.x*.

RPC (Regulatory Policy Committee) (2014), "Impact Assessment Opinion: Plastic Carrier Bags Charge", Regulatory Policy Committee , London, *www.gov.uk/government/uploads/system/uploads/attachment_data/file/499221/2014-9-4-RPC14-DEFRA-2124_2_-Plastic_Carrier_Bags_Charge.pdf* (Accessed 10/03/2017).

RPC (2013), "Impact Assessment Opinion: Biodiversity Offsetting", Regulatory Policy Committee , London, *www.gov.uk/government/uploads/system/uploads/attachment_data/file/260635/2013-10-03-RPC13-DEFRA-1840-Biodiversity-Offsetting.pdf* (Accessed 10/03/2017).

Stern, N. (2007), *The Stern Review on the Economics of Climate Change*, Cambridge University Press, Cambridge, *www.cambridge.org/catalogue/catalogue.asp?isbn=9780521700801*.

TEEB (2010), *The Economics of Ecosystems and Biodiversity, Mainstreaming the Economics of Nature. A Synthesis of the Approach, Conclusions and Recommendations of TEEB*, Routledge, Oxford.

Turnpenny, J. et al. (2015), "The Use of Policy Formulation Tools in the Venue of Policy Appraisal: Patterns and Underlying Motivations", in Jordan, A. and Turnpenny, J. (eds) *The Tools of Policy Formulation: Actors, Capacities, Venues and Effects*, Edward Elgar, Cheltenham.

UK National Ecosystem Assessment (2011), *The UK National Ecosystem Assessment: Synthesis of the Key Findings*, UNEP-WCMC, Cambridge.

PART IV

Chapter 18

CBA and other decision-making approaches

A significant array of decision-guiding procedures is available. This chapter shows that they vary in the degree of comprehensiveness where this is defined as the extent to which all costs and benefits are incorporated. In general, only multicriteria assessment (MCA) is as comprehensive as CBA and may be more comprehensive once goals beyond efficiency and distributional incidence are considered. All the remaining procedures either deliberately narrow the focus on benefits, e.g. to health or environment, or ignore cost. Procedures also vary in the way they treat time. Environmental impact assessment and life-cycle analysis are essential inputs into a CBA, although the way these impacts are dealt with in "physical terms" may not be the same in a CBA. Risk assessments, of which health-health analysis and risk-risk analysis are also variants, tend to be focused on human health only. The essential message is that the procedures are not substitutes for each other.

18.1. Introduction

This volume is concerned with recent developments in environmental cost-benefit analysis (CBA). Chapters 16 and 17 also identified that one of these developments is extensive use of CBA to assist actual policy formulation and actual decision-making, whether this be in choosing between policies or investment options for projects. A point made in Chapter 17 is that understanding this use needs to be based on a realistic understanding of the policy process, and the political economy of CBA. One manifestation of how CBA is actually used is that it is seldom, if ever, the only input to a decision. This will not be news to anybody, and most – including most economists – will view this as a perfectly healthy situation. Where different actors in this analytical process reasonably might disagree, however, is over the weight which evidence from a CBA should receive in making recommendations relative to the other tools which jostle for attention in policy and project formulation.

There are many reasons for emphasising a range of tools, rather than one in particular, including (not restricted to) the following:

- A desire for procedures which address different facets of evidence relevant to the decision-making process. This might reflect a recognition that no single policy formulation tool alone is adequate for such a task and that an array of tools might mitigate against the perceived shortcomings on any one. For example, some tools may be more suited for considering the minutiae of options available, while others are better suited for helping strategic choices about the future from which these more detailed options might follow.

- A need to fill information and evidence gaps left by an incomplete implementation of a particular procedure such as CBA. For example, Dudley et al. (2017) identify a number of points on a "checklist" as to whether consideration of costs and benefits in policy formulation[1] follows commonly accepted guidelines about best practice. Actual implementation might fall short in one or several of these points either by accident (e.g. the difficulty of valuing certain impacts) or design (e.g. a policy culture that takes a different standpoint on the merits of valuing certain impacts or the proportional information needs of the decision at hand). In at least some of these cases, other procedures may play an important part too.[2]

- A (related) desire to ensure that the tools used in policy formulation reflect a plurality of understandings (and perhaps "belief systems") about the world in which policy decisions are being made. So, for example, if a particular tool rests on conceptual foundations which some find unpalatable, then other approaches can provide a "voice" for different perspectives. Of course, it is a challenge for the policy process to consider all these perspectives side-by-side but considering a range of tools acknowledges explicitly the complexity of reality, rather than seeking to circumscribe evidence gathering to one approach.

- A desire to have procedures that can be widely understood and which are not reliant on experts, and so which are perhaps more participatory or deliberative. Given the need for decision-makers to be accountable and for decisions often needing to command broad support this deliberation provides an important function.

- A (pragmatic) desire to have decision-aiding procedures that are not so demanding in informational terms. This might, in turn, derive from a desire to have "rapid" procedures given that political decisions cannot always wait for the results of more informationally demanding approaches.

Over the years, various techniques of appraisal have emerged in the environmental field in addition to CBA. A (non-exhaustive) list includes:

- Cost-effectiveness analysis (CEA)
- Risk assessment
    - ❖ Comparative risk assessment
    - ❖ Risk-benefit analysis
    - ❖ Risk-risk analysis
    - ❖ Health-health analysis
- Environmental assessment
    1. Environmental impact assessment
    2. Strategic environmental assessment
    3. Life-cycle analysis
- Multi-criteria analysis
- Participatory approaches
- Scenario analysis.

In this chapter, each of these procedures is looked at. Space forbids a detailed assessment (see the edited volume by Jordan and Turnpenny, 2015, for such detail). But – given the focus of this volume – the main idea in what follows below is simply to "locate" CBA in this range of procedures. It is important to understand that the procedures vary significantly in their comprehensiveness and that it cannot be assumed that each is a substitute for the other. Indeed, as set out above, it is important not to succumb to the temptation of viewing these approaches simply as a menu of alternatives for one another. That is, some of these tools and procedures may be essential inputs for another on this list. Some procedures may involve a combination of approaches (for example, using participative procedures to shape "scenarios" or "cost-benefit" assessments). Different procedures may "come into their own" at different points in the policy cycle. And, as previously mentioned, the practical counterpart of the frequently made general (but reasonable-minded) statement – that any single policy formulation tool is only one input to making recommendations about decisions – is surely that these procedures usually need to be considered side-by-side.

18.2. A (select) gallery of additional procedures

18.2.1. Cost-effectiveness analysis

The easiest way to think about cost-effectiveness analysis (CEA) is to assume that there is a single indicator of effectiveness, E, and this is to be compared with a cost of C. Suppose there is now just a single project or policy to be appraised. CEA would require that E be compared with C. The usual procedure is to produce a cost-effectiveness ratio (CER):

$$CER = \frac{E}{C} \qquad [18.1]$$

Notice that E is in some environmental unit and C is in money units. The fact that they are in different units has an important implication which is, unfortunately, widely disregarded in the literature. A moment's inspection of [18.1] shows that the ratio is perfectly meaningful – e.g. it might be read as dollars per hectare of land conserved. But the ratio says nothing at all as to whether the conservation policy in question is worth undertaking. In other words, CEA cannot help with the issue of whether or not to undertake any conservation. It should be immediately obvious that this question cannot be answered unless E and C are in the same units.

CEA can only offer guidance on which of several alternative policies (or projects) to select, given that one has to select one. By extension, CEA can *rank* any set of policies, all of which could be undertaken, but given that at least some of them must be undertaken. To see the limitation of CEA, equation [18.1] should be sufficient to show that an entire list of policies, ranked by their cost-effectiveness, could be adopted without any assurance that any one of them is actually worth doing. The notion of "worth doing" only has meaning if one can compare costs and benefits in a manner that enables one to say costs are greater (smaller) than benefits. In turn, that requires that costs and benefits have a common *numeraire* which, in principle, could be anything. In CBA, the numeraire is money.

If it is supposed that there are $i = 1....n$ potential policies, with corresponding costs C_i and effectiveness E_i then CEA requires that the policies are being ranked according to

$$CER_i = \frac{E_i}{C_i} \qquad\qquad [18.2]$$

This ranking can be used to select as many projects as fit the available budget $\bar{C}$, i.e.:

$$Rank \quad by \quad CER_i \quad s.t \quad \sum_i C_i = \bar{C} \qquad\qquad [18.3]$$

A further issue with CEA is the process of selecting the effectiveness measure. In CBA the principle is that benefits are measured by individuals' preferences as revealed by their willingness-to-pay for them. The underlying value judgement in CBA is "consumer" or "citizen sovereignty". This amounts to saying that individuals are the best judges of their own well-being. Technically, the same value judgement could be used in CEA, i.e. the measure of effectiveness could be based on some attitude survey of a random sample of individuals. In practice, CEA tends to proceed with indicators of effectiveness chosen by experts. Rationales for using expert choices are (a) that experts are better informed than individuals, especially on issues such as habitat conservation, landscape protection, etc. and (b) that securing indicators from experts is quicker and cheaper than eliciting individuals' attitudes.

18.2.2. Risk assessment

As discussed below, there are a number of variants on this approach. Common to all is placing the "riskiness" of policy actions or new projects at the front and centre of appraisal (relative to the risks of not acting). And while a cost-benefit practitioner might argue that CBA has a variety of ways in order to reflect risk and uncertainty in making recommendations about options for policy and investments project, a virtue of this risk-based approaches is that these consider such matters in a more straightforward and transparent way. As such, these approaches merit consideration alongside more general tools for policy formulation such as CBA.

A general approach to this problem is summarised under the heading of risk assessment (RA). This involves assessing either the health or environmental risks (or both) attached to a product, process, policy or project. A RA may be expressed in various ways:

● As the probability of some defined health or ecosystem effect occurring, e.g. a 1 in 100 000 chance of mortality within a certain timeframe from continued exposure to some chemical;

- As a number of incidences across a defined population, e.g. 10 000 premature deaths per annum out of some population;
- As a defined incidence per unit of exposure, e.g. X% increase in premature mortality per unit air pollution;
- As a "no effect" level of exposure, e.g. below one microgram per cubic metre there may be no health effect.

RAs may not translate into decision-rules very easily. One way they may do this is if the actual or estimated risk level is compared with an "acceptable" level which in turn may be the result of some expert judgement or the result of a public survey. A common threshold is to look at unavoidable "everyday" risks and to judge whether people "live with" such a risk. This may make it acceptable. Other procedures tend to be more common and may define the acceptable level as a no-risk level, or even a non-risk level with a sizeable margin of error. Procedures establishing "no effect" levels, e.g. of chemicals, define the origin of what the economist would call a "damage function" but cannot inform decision-making unless the goal is in fact to secure that level of risk. Put another way, "no effect" points contain no information about the "damage function".

Comparative risk assessment (CRA) involves analysing risks but the distinction in this approach is to look at this for several alternative projects or policies. The issue is then which option should be chosen and the answer offered by CRA is that the option with the lowest risk should be chosen. Efforts are made to "normalise" the analysis so that like is compared with like. For example, one might want to choose between nuclear energy and coal-fired electricity. One approach would be to normalise the risks of one kilowatt hour of electricity and compute, say, the expected number of deaths per kWh. The option with the lowest "death rate" would then be chosen. However, in this case, the normalisation process does not extend to cost, so that CRA may want to add a further dimension, the money cost of generating one kWh. Once this is done, the focus tends to shift to cost-effectiveness analysis – see above. An issue here concerns the nature of risk. "One fatality" appears to be a homogenous unit, but if people are not indifferent to the manner of death or whether it is voluntarily or involuntarily borne, then, in effect, the normalisation does not adequately reflect this. Of course, this assumes that context (in this case, of mortality risk) matters and Chapter 15 indicates that there is ambiguous evidence for this, although the existence of "dread risks" cannot be ruled out entirely.

Risk-benefit analysis (RBA) tends to take two forms, each of which is reducible to another form of decision-rule. In other words, RBA is not a separate procedure. The first meaning relates to benefits, costs and risks, where risks are treated as costs and valued in money terms. In that case, the formula for accepting a project or policy would be:

[Benefits – Costs – Risks] > 0

This is little different therefore to a CBA rule.

In the second case, the RBA rule reduces to CRA. Benefits might be standardised, e.g. to "passenger kilometres" and the risk element might be fatalities. "Fatalities per passenger kilometre" might then be the thing that should be minimised. As with CRA, cost may or may not enter the picture. If it does, then RBA tends to result in CBA or cost-effectiveness analysis.

Two further variants of these risk-centred approaches look more closely as health risks. For example, risk-risk analysis (RRA) asks what would happen to health risks if some policy was adopted and what would happen if it was not adopted. The "with/without focus" is familiar in CBA. The novelty tends to be the fact that not undertaking a policy may itself impose costs in terms of lives or morbidity. For example, a policy of banning or lowering consumption of saccharin might have a justification in reducing health risks from its consumption. But the with-policy option may result in consumers switching to sugar in place of the banned saccharin, thus increasing morbidity by that route. The advantage of RRA is that it forces decision makers to look at the behavioural responses to regulations. Once again, however, all other components in a CBA equation are ignored, so the procedure is not comprehensive.

In this respect, health-health analysis (HHA) is similar to RRA but instead of comparing the risks with and without the behavioural reaction to a policy, it compares the change in risks from a policy with the risks associated with the *expenditure* on the policy. As such, it offers a subtle focus on policy that is easily overlooked. Since policies costs money, the money has to come from somewhere and, ultimately, the source is the taxpayer. But if taxpayers pay part of their taxes for life-saving policies, their incomes are reduced. Some of that reduced income would have been spent on life-saving or health-enhancing activities. Hence the taxation actually increases life risks. HHA compares the anticipated saving in lives from a policy with the lives lost because of the cost of the policy. In principle, policies costing more lives than they save are not desirable. HHA proceeds by estimating the costs of a life-saving policy and the number of lives saved. It then allocates the policy costs to households. Life risks are related to household incomes through regression analysis, so that it is possible to estimate lives lost due to income reductions. Once again, the procedure is not comprehensive: policies could fail an HHA test but pass a CBA test, and vice versa.

18.2.3. Environmental assessment

Just as in the case of risk assessments, there are a number of variants of approaches that focus on environmental impacts of policies and projects under the broad heading of "environmental assessment". As discussed below, one of these approaches fulfils the task of quantifying these environmental impacts in physical terms (or where this is not possible perhaps the analysis is in qualitative terms). As such, this is critically important basic information without which subsequent approaches – such as CBA – simply could not be conducted. Just as importantly, this environmentally focused assessment might turn up invaluable information about the criticality of environmental changes arising from policy or project proposals. In doing so, this provides information crucial for the sort of sustainability concerns set out in Chapter 12. Other environmental assessment tools add to this picture by perhaps considering how proposals contribute to cumulative pressures on the physical environment or the way in which environmental impacts have a life-cycle (and so a range of indirect impacts become relevant to quantify).

A starting point for thinking about these environmental tools are systematic procedures for collecting information about the environmental impacts of a project or policy, and for measuring those impacts. This is usually known as environmental impact assessment (EIA). Of course, given its focus, EIA is not a comprehensive evaluation procedure given that it does not consider non-environmental impacts or policy and project costs. Less obvious, but also important, is whether environmental impacts are recorded in a way that signals the ways in which impacts vary with time. Nonetheless, EIA is an essential part of any evaluative procedure. If CBA is used as a benchmark, then EIA is an essential input to CBA.

CBA covers the other impacts of projects and policies, and it goes one stage further than EIA by attempting to put money values on the environmental impacts. Most EIAs do make an effort, however, to assess the significance of environmental impacts. Some may go further and give the impacts a score (the extent of the impact) and a weight (its importance). Weights might be derived from public surveys but more usually are determined by the analyst in question. Unlike CBA, EIA has no formal decision-rule attached to it (e.g. benefits must exceed costs), but analysts would typically argue that its purpose is to look at alternative means of minimising the environmental impacts without altering significantly the benefits of the project or policy.

In general, then:

- EIA is an essential input to any decision-making procedure;
- Impacts may be scored and weighted, or they become inputs into a CBA;
- EIA would generally look for ways to minimise environmental impacts without changing (significantly, anyway) the benefits or costs of the project or policy.

Strategic environmental assessment (SEA) is similar to EIA but tends to operate at a "higher" level of decision-making. Instead of single projects or policies, SEA would consider entire programmes of investments or policies. The goal is to look for the synergies between individual policies and projects and to evaluate alternatives in a more comprehensive manner. An SEA is more likely than an EIA to consider issues like: is the policy or project needed at all; and, if it is, what are the alternative options available? In this sense, SEA is seen to be more pro-active than EIA, which tends to be reactive. Proactive here means that more opportunity exists for programmes to be better designed (from an environmental perspective) rather than accepting that a specific option is chosen and the task is to minimise environmental impacts from that option. Again, while it encompasses more issues of concern, SEA remains non-comprehensive as a decision-guiding procedure. Issues of time, cost and non-environmental costs and benefits may not figure prominently. Relative to the benchmark of CBA, SEA goes some way to considering the kinds of issues that would be relevant in a CBA – e.g. the "with/without" principle and consideration of alternatives. A crucial point that SEA might pick up on is the degree to which an apparently marginal policy or project has a cumulative impact on the physical environment generally or some natural capital asset specifically.

Life-cycle analysis (LCA) offers a further perspective in that it does not only look at the impacts *directly* arising from a project or policy, but also at the whole "life-cycle" of impacts. For example, suppose the policy problem is one of choosing between the "best" forms of packaging for a product, say fruit juice. The alternatives might be cartons, bottles and cans. LCA would look at the environmental impacts of each option but going right back to the materials needed for manufacturing of the container (e.g. timber and plastics, glass, metals) and the ways in which they will be disposed of once consumers have drunk the juice. Included in the analysis would be the environmental impacts of primary resource extraction and the impacts from landfill, incineration, and so on.

LCAs proceed by establishing an inventory of impacts and then the impacts are subjected to an assessment to establish the extent of impact and the weight to be attached to it. Relative to the benchmark of CBA, LCA is essentially the physical counterpart to the kind of environmental impact analysis that is required by a CBA. In itself LCA offers no obvious decision-rule for policies or projects. Though sometimes advocated as comprehensive decision-guidance, LCA does not (usually) consider non-environmental costs and benefits. However, if the choice context is one where one of several options has to be chosen (we must have cans or bottles or cartons, but not none of these), then, provided other things are equal, LCA operates like a cost-effectiveness criterion (see above).

18.2.4. *Multi-criteria approaches*

Multi-criteria approaches look at manifold and diverse dimensions of policies and investment projects. A virtue of these approaches is that these are considered within the same analytical framework. So, for example, if metrics reflecting various decision relevant parameters relating to "efficiency", "effectiveness", "equity" as well as "administrative simplicity and governance" need to be considered under the one umbrella then multi-criteria techniques provide a useful framework for doing this in a coherent way. As such, this goes further than CBA which can only consider such parameters to the extent these can be reflected in robust monetary valuation. But as with CBA, this comprehensiveness might come at a cost in that manifold impacts are not easy to disentangle and important debates about the "parts" relating to the options relating to decisions become lost in what is happening to the "whole".

One such approach – multi-criteria analysis (MCA) – is similar in many respects to CEA but involves multiple indicators of effectiveness. Technically, CEA also works with multiple indicators but increasingly resembles simple models of MCA since different effectiveness indicators, measured in different units, have to be normalised by converting them to scores and then aggregated via a weighting procedure. Like CEA, policy or scheme cost in an MCA is always (or should always be) one of the indicators chosen. The steps in an MCA are as follows:

- The goals or objectives of the policy or investment are stated.

- These objectives are not pre-ordained, nor are they singular (as they are in CBA, which adopts increases in economic efficiency as the primary objective) and are selected by "decision-makers".

- Generally, decision-makers will be civil servants whose choices can be argued to reflect political concerns.

- MCA then tends to work with experts' preferences. Public preferences may or may not be involved.

- "Criteria" or, sometimes, "attributes" which help achieve the objectives are then selected. Sometimes, objectives and criteria tend to be fused, making the distinction difficult to observe. However, criteria will generally be those features of a good that achieve the objective.

- Such criteria may or may not be measured in monetary terms, but MCA differs from CBA in that not all criteria will be monetised.

- Each option (alternative means of securing the objective) is then given a score and a weight. Pursuing the above example, a policy might score 6 out of 10 for one effect, 2 out of 10 for another effect, and 7 out of 10 for yet another. In turn, experts may regard the first effect as being twice as important as the second, but only half as important as the third. The weights would then be 2, 1 and 4 respectively.

- In the simplest of MCAs, the final outcome is a weighted average of the scores, with the option providing the highest weighted score being the one that is "best". More sophisticated techniques might be used for more complex decisions.

- To overcome issues relating to the need for criteria to be independent of each other (i.e. experts' preferences based on one criterion should be independent of their preferences for that option based on another criterion), more sophisticated techniques might be used, notably "multi-attribute utility theory" (MAUT). MAUT tends to be over-sophisticated for most practical decision making.

The formula for the final score for an investment project or policy using the simplest form of MCA is:

$$S_i = \sum_j m_j . S_{ij} \qquad\qquad [18.4]$$

where i is the ith option, j is the jth criterion for selection, m is the weight, and S is the score.

MCA offers a broader interpretation of CEA since it openly countenances the existence of multiple objectives. Issues relating to MCA and which are the subject of debate are as follows:

- As with CEA, when effectiveness is compared with cost in ratio form, MCA cannot say anything about whether or not it is worth adopting any investment project or policy at all. Its domain is restricted to choices between alternatives in a portfolio of options, some of which must be undertaken. Both MCA and CEA are therefore "efficient" in the sense of seeking to secure maximum effectiveness for a given unit of cost, but may be "inefficient" in the sense of economic efficiency. Annex 18.A1 illustrates the problem further and shows that MCA produces the same result as a CBA only when (a) the scores on the attributes are the same, (b) the weights in the MCA correspond to shadow prices in the CBA, and (c), which follows from (b), the weight on cost is unity.

- MCA generally proceeds by adopting scores and weights chosen by experts. To this extent MCA is not as "accountable" as CBA where the money units reflect individuals' preferences rather than expert preferences. Put another way, the raw material of CBA is a set of individuals' votes, albeit votes weighted by income, whereas experts are unelected and may not be accountable to individual voters.

- MCA tends to be more "transparent" than CBA since objectives and criteria are usually clearly stated, rather than assumed. Because of its adoption of multiple objectives, however, MCA tends to be less transparent than CEA with a single objective.

- It is often unclear how far MCA deals with issues of time discounting and changing relative valuations.

- Distributional implications are usually chosen as one of the objectives in an MCA and hence distributional impacts can be clearly accommodated in an MCA.

18.2.5. Participatory approaches

Where the political system is sensitive to the public interest there is likely to be emphasis on consultation and participation, perhaps based on more deliberative approaches to policy formulation. This is something that should concern cost-benefit practitioners too. The reason for this is that lack of participation can easily engender opposition to a project or policy, making it difficult to implement and costly to reverse. Participation may also produce better policy and project design since those most affected are closer to the issue than analysts and decision makers.

While there is a case for saying that some of the valuation techniques used in environmental CBA – notably, stated preference approaches – involve consulting people directly as well as eliciting their preferences about policy changes and new projects, this is not the same thing as a truly participative or deliberative approach. For example, the elicitation approach in stated preference studies tends to be between (independent) interviewer and a single respondent or increasingly via cost-effective but impersonal on-line platforms). Nevertheless, Chapter 4 does indicate a handful of studies which show the potential to adapt these approaches to incorporate more deliberative aspects.

In order to assess whether particular tools are sufficiently participative, it is useful to take a step back and define what this means. At least three versions of the term seem relevant here: (a) participation as consultation, i.e. taking account of the preferences of affected parties; (b) participation as influence, i.e. ensuring that affected parties influence the direction and form of the project or policy; and (c) participation as benefit-sharing, i.e. ensuring that affected parties receive a share of the resulting benefits. Frequently what is meant by participation is not the recording of public preferences, but the need to consult with pressure groups who would otherwise stand in the way of policy. It is senses (b) and (c) above that matter in political decision-making rather than sense (a). Yet (a) is what underlies CBA whereas (b) and (c) are not accorded status in CBA. Again, there is a rationale to secure that participation by seeking out additional tools for policy formulation.

As Hisschemöller and Cuppen (2015) identify there is not necessarily a formal characterisation of participatory tools. However, what links approaches that are participative according to these authors, are efforts to meaningfully build in dialogue – in some forum – rather than rely on expert (and political) judgement alone. On this view, a number of familiar policy formulation tools are participative if implemented in ways fitting this emphasis on dialogue. This could include MCA where participants (e.g. stakeholders in a decision) enter into an interchange with analysts perhaps over the dimensions of the policy or project choice as well as the weights with which to attach to these dimensions. It might also include CBA depending on how it is conducted with stakeholders (such as making use of deliberative approaches based on focus groups and citizens' juries, for example).

As an illustration, the Environment Agency in England uses CBA extensively to guide its decisions on options for meeting policy objectives especially on water catchment management. A notable element of these applications is the EA's use of participation, with the aim of boosting transparency and engagement regarding the CBA that it conducts, the benefit valuation toolkit that it uses for valuing changes in water quality and the way in which this evidence will be used.[3] Specifically, stakeholders (which include environmental and conservation charities, water companies and other affected groups) are invited to deliberate on how this analysis is undertaken, including being invited to recommend inputs to toolkits such as the appropriate environmental values being used. Of course, as in any such deliberation, here is a risk of stakeholders suggesting evidence that suits their own interests. However, combined with suitable scrutiny of recommendations, what this deliberation can do is take advantage of new information about policy or project options as well as legitimating decisions.

18.2.6. Scenario analysis

Tools such as CBA provide a forecast of the future. This might involve forecasting the costs and benefits involved when specific options involving some policy change or investment project are implemented. But, in principle, this forecast also could look at these impacts at an earlier stage of the policy cycle. That is, perhaps when the policy problem (and suitable responses) is still being defined. Forecasting is a relatively precise exercise for this purpose given the degree of quantification that this modelling entails. And it may be that the policy formulation process would also benefit from tools which have a greater degree of an exploratory or even abstract nature, especially if policy responses (and their consequences) are not yet well-defined.

Scenario analysis (SA) is one such tool is this respect, defined by Pérez-Soba and Maas (2015) as lying somewhere between speculation and forecasting. That is, the latter is suited for those problems where both complexity and uncertainty are relatively low (or presumably where uncertainty is analytically tractable – see Chapter 9 in particular) whereas the latter is characterised by the converse (i.e. a high degree of complexity and genuine uncertainty). Hence, according to Pérez-Soba and Maas, SA suits those policy problems where these characteristics are present at intermediate levels. The explorative nature of SA provides a means of probing the implications of possible futures that are plausible (in that they may happen) but diverse involving novelty such as surprises and shocks. Getting a sense of credible strategy and narrative (rather than detailed plans) might be a strong feature of such exercises, although the broad implications of chosen scenarios on socioeconomic or environmental outcomes are clearly of significant interest too. Looking forwards in this way is not the only of conceptualising scenarios. It may also involve "backcasting" or starting from a specified future scenario (perhaps one which is judged to sustainable or desirable) and working backwards to how that outcome might be achieved.

One example of the use of SA is the UK National Ecosystem Assessment (NEA) (2011). This defined six scenarios in all – described as "story-lines" – with each of these exploring a different path for deliberate management of ecosystem services. Some of these scenarios, for example, privileged economic growth (narrowly defined as GDP growth) or national security. In doing so, the role of ecosystem services in development is downplayed perhaps at the expense of agricultural expansion and intensification. In other scenarios, enhancing ecosystem services is at the front and centre of these futures. However, the ways in which those storylines are developed are several. For example, one scenario stressed making these services work better for the whole economy (as direct or indirect inputs to economic activity) while another compartmentalised ecosystem services as largely the domain of a protected countryside supplying amenity (as well as perhaps intrinsic beauty) rather than asking what ecosystems "can do" for the economy.

In turn, each of these scenarios implies particular paths for policies, plans and human behaviour. Understanding the differences and similarities across scenarios then is an important part of this SA. For cost-benefit practitioners it may be that this approach lacks the precision of a CBA. Of course, this is the point; the SA is arguably all the more useful because this precision is not attainable given the characteristics of the problem. However, it may be that it is possible to be precise about components of the problem. To use the above illustration once more, a further chapter in UK NEA (2011) explored how elements of the scenarios could be turned into forecasts. Given that each scenario implied a different path for ecosystem services and if some of these could be quantified and valued then the size of ecosystem benefits – arising in a particular scenario – could be ascertained in this way. Specifically, this valuation was applied to carbon storage, nature recreation and compared to the value of agricultural food production under these different scenarios, thereby further helping to shape policy thinking about these possible futures.

18.3. Conclusions

A significant array of decision-guiding procedures is available. This chapter shows that they vary in the degree of comprehensiveness where this is defined as the extent to which all costs and benefits are incorporated. In general, only MCA is as comprehensive as CBA and may be more comprehensive once goals beyond efficiency and distributional incidence are considered. All the remaining procedures either deliberately narrow the focus on particular impact categories, e.g. to health risks or environment, or ignore cost. Procedures also vary in the way they treat time. Some approaches such as EIA are essential inputs into a CBA, although the way these impacts are dealt with in "physical terms" may not be the same in a CBA.

The message here is that these various procedures are not substitutes for each other. And in a very real sense, this is the key point. Cost-benefit practitioners are comfortable with the idea that CBA is only one input to making recommendations about decisions on policies and investment projects. These additional approaches represent other candidate tools to provide those further inputs. In fact, it may be that these can help not hinder the usefulness of CBA, for example, by legitimating its recommendations by greater use of deliberation in its practical execution in policy formulation.

Nevertheless, this conciliatory conclusion should not be interpreted as a case of "anything goes". Much of the debate about CBA in relation to other procedures starts with critical reflections on the limitations of the former. That is, what is it that the CBA approach misses and so how other complementary approaches might address these apparent shortcomings? Of course, just as it is crucial to consider critically CBA, any recommended other approaches also should be subjected to similar critical analysis as well as practical applications being evaluated against relevant benchmarks such as official guidelines.

Notes

1. Specifically, the context in that paper is (US) regulatory impact analysis.

2. For example, with reference to some of the procedures discussed late on in this chapter, perhaps this might involve identifying policy targets in physical terms, using some form of environmental or risk-based assessment, and formulating policy with reference to options which provide the most cost-effective ways of achieving those outcomes.

3. Steve Arnold, UK Environment Agency, personal communication.

References

Dudley, S. et al. (2017), "Consumer's guide to regulatory impact analysis: Ten tips for being an informed policymaker", *Journal of Benefit-Cost Analysis*, Vol. 8/2, pp. 187-204, https://doi.org/10.1017/bca.2017.11.

Hisschemöller, M. and E. Cuppen (2015), "Participatory assessment: Tools for empowering, learning and legimating", in Jordan, A. and J.R. Turnpenny (eds.), *The Tools of Policy Formulation: Actors, Capacities, Venues and Effects*, Edward Elgar, Cheltenham.

Jordan, A. and J.R. Turnpenny (eds.), *The Tools of Policy Formulation: Actors, Capacities, Venues and Effects*, Edward Elgar, Cheltenham.

Pérez-Soba, M. and R. Maas (2015), "Scenarios: Tools for coping with complexity and future uncertainty?", in Jordan, A. and J.R. Turnpenny (eds.), *The Tools of Policy Formulation: Actors, Capacities, Venues and Effects*, Edward Elgar, Cheltenham.

UK NEA (2011), *National Ecosystem Assessment: Technical Report*, UNEP-WCMC, Cambridge.

ANNEX 18.A1

Multi-criteria analysis and the "do nothing" option

For the "do nothing" option to be included correctly in an evaluation it is necessary for costs and benefits to be measured in the same units. When MCA adopts the form of cost-effectiveness, with the multiple criteria of effectiveness being compared *in ratio form* to cost, then MCA cannot evaluate the "do nothing" option. This is because the units of effectiveness are weighted scores whilst the measure of cost is money. Numerator and denominator are not in the same units. The "escape" from this problem is for costs to be given a score (usually the absolute level of money cost) and a weight. If we think of the weighted scores as "utils" (or any other unit of account) then MCA can handle the "do nothing" option. If the ratio of benefits to costs is less than unity, the "do nothing" option is rejected. Similarly, if utils of benefits minus utils of costs is negative, the do something option would also be rejected.

In this way, MCA can be modified to handle the do nothing option. However, it can easily be shown that MCA will give the same result as CBA under very limited conditions.

Table 18.A1 shows the procedure adopted in a simple MCA. Let the score for E1 be 10, E2 = 5 and E3 = 30. The scores are multiplied by chosen weights, assumed to be W1 = 4, W2 = 6, W3 = 10. Cost is weighted at unity. The sum of the weighted scores shows that "do something" is a "correct" choice. If the weights W1…W3 are prices, then Table 18.A1 would appear as a CBA, i.e. MCA and CBA would produce formally identical results.

Table 18.A1. **Weighted input data for an MCA: cost weighted at unity**

	Do something: raw scores	Do something: weighted scores
Cost	- 50	- 50
E1	+10	+ 40
E2	+ 5	+ 30
E3	+30	+300
Sum of (weighted) scores	- 5	+320

Table 18.A1 shows that the selection of weights is important. An "unweighted" approach (which means raw scores are weighted at unity) would reject the policy but the weighted approach would accept it. As long as the weights in Table 18.A1 correspond to the prices in a CBA, however, then CBA and MCA would generate the same result.

Finally, if it is assumed that shadow prices and MCA weights are the same, but that the weight applied to cost in the MCA is, say, 8, then weighted cost would appear as -400 in Table 18.A1 and weighted MCA would reject the do something option.

The conditions for CBA and MCA to generate the same result can be summarised in this way:

1. Attribute scores must be the same;

2. MCA weights must correspond to shadow prices and, in particular:

3. Costs must be weighted at unity.

ORGANISATION FOR ECONOMIC CO-OPERATION AND DEVELOPMENT

The OECD is a unique forum where governments work together to address the economic, social and environmental challenges of globalisation. The OECD is also at the forefront of efforts to understand and to help governments respond to new developments and concerns, such as corporate governance, the information economy and the challenges of an ageing population. The Organisation provides a setting where governments can compare policy experiences, seek answers to common problems, identify good practice and work to co-ordinate domestic and international policies.

The OECD member countries are: Australia, Austria, Belgium, Canada, Chile, the Czech Republic, Denmark, Estonia, Finland, France, Germany, Greece, Hungary, Iceland, Ireland, Israel, Italy, Japan, Korea, Latvia, Luxembourg, Mexico, the Netherlands, New Zealand, Norway, Poland, Portugal, the Slovak Republic, Slovenia, Spain, Sweden, Switzerland, Turkey, the United Kingdom and the United States. The European Union takes part in the work of the OECD.

OECD Publishing disseminates widely the results of the Organisation's statistics gathering and research on economic, social and environmental issues, as well as the conventions, guidelines and standards agreed by its members.

OECD PUBLISHING, 2, rue André-Pascal, 75775 PARIS CEDEX 16
(97 2018 04 1 P) ISBN 978-92-64-08515-2 – 2018